Selected works of Jawaharlal Nehru

AT THE WASEDA UNIVERSITY AFTER RECEIVING AN HONORARY
DEGREE OF DOCTOR OF SCIENCE, 7 OCTOBER 1957

Selected works of Jawaharlal Nehru

Second Series

Volume Thirty Nine

(1 August – 31 October 1957)

A Project of the
Jawaharlal Nehru
Memorial Fund

Enquiries regarding copyright
to be addressed to the publishers

PUBLISHED BY
Jawaharlal Nehru Memorial Fund
Teen Murti House, New Delhi 110 011

ISBN 019 569150 4
ISBN 978 019 569150 4

DISTRIBUTED BY
Oxford University Press
YMCA Library Building, Jai Singh Road, New Delhi 110 001
Mumbai Kolkata Chennai
Oxford New York Toronto
Melbourne Tokyo Hong Kong

TYPESET BY
Digigrafics
D-69, Gulmohar Park
New Delhi 110 049

PRINTED AT
Lordson Publishers Pvt Ltd
C 5/19, Rana Pratap Bagh
Delhi 110 007

Editor

Mushirul Hasan

FOREWORD

Jawaharlal Nehru is one of the key figures of the twentieth century. He symbolised some of the major forces which have transformed our age.

When Jawaharlal Nehru was young, history was still the privilege of the West; the rest of the world lay in deliberate darkness. The impression given was that the vast continents of Asia and Africa existed merely to sustain their masters in Europe and North America. Jawaharlal Nehru's own education in Britain could be interpreted, in a sense, as an attempt to secure for him a place within the pale. His letters of the time are evidence of his sensitivity, his interest in science and international affairs as well as of his pride in India and Asia. But his personality was veiled by his shyness and a facade of nonchalance, and perhaps outwardly there was not much to distinguish him from the ordinary run of men. Gradually there emerged the warm and universal being who became intensely involved with the problems of the poor and the oppressed in all lands. In doing so, Jawaharlal Nehru gave articulation and leadership to millions of people in his own country and in Asia and Africa.

That imperialism was a curse which should be lifted from the brows of men, that poverty was incompatible with civilisation, that nationalism should be poised on a sense of international community and that it was not sufficient to brood on these things when action was urgent and compelling—these were the principles which inspired and gave vitality to Jawaharlal Nehru's activities in the years of India's struggle for freedom and made him not only an intense nationalist but one of the leaders of humanism.

No particular ideological doctrine could claim Jawaharlal Nehru for its own. Long days in jail were spent in reading widely. He drew much from the thought of the East and West and from the philosophies of the past and the present. Never religious in the formal sense, yet he had a deep love for the culture and tradition of his own land. Never a rigid Marxist, yet he was deeply influenced by that theory and was particularly impressed by what he saw in the Soviet Union on his first visit in 1927. However, he realised that the world was too complex, and man had too many facets, to be encompassed by any single or total explanation. He himself was a socialist with an abhorrence of regimentation and a democrat who was anxious to reconcile his faith in civil liberty with the necessity of mitigating economic and social wretchedness. His struggles, both within himself and with the outside world, to adjust such seeming contradictions are what make his life and work significant and fascinating.

As a leader of free India, Jawaharlal Nehru recognised that his country could neither stay out of the world nor divest itself of its own interests in world affairs. But to the extent that it was possible, Jawaharlal Nehru sought to speak objectively and to be a voice of sanity in the shrill phases of the 'cold war'. Whether his influence helped on certain occasions to maintain peace is for the future historian to assess. What we do know is that for a long stretch of time he commanded an international audience reaching far beyond governments, that he spoke for ordinary, sensitive, thinking men and women around the globe and that his was a constituency which extended far beyond India.

So the story of Jawaharlal Nehru is that of a man who evolved, who grew in storm and stress till he became the representative of much that was noble in his time. It is the story of a generous and gracious human being who summed up in himself the resurgence of the 'third world' as well as the humanism which transcends dogmas and is adapted to the contemporary context. His achievement, by its very nature and setting, was much greater than that of a Prime Minister. And it is with the conviction that the life of this man is of importance not only to scholars but to all, in India and elsewhere, who are interested in the valour and compassion of the human spirit that the Jawaharlal Nehru Memorial Fund has decided to publish a series of volumes consisting of all that is significant in what Jawaharlal Nehru spoke and wrote. There is, as is to be expected in the speeches and writings of a man so engrossed in affairs and gifted with expression, much that is ephemeral; this will be omitted. The official letters and memoranda will also not find place here. But it is planned to include everything else and the whole corpus should help to remind us of the quality and endeavour of one who was not only a leader of men and a lover of mankind, but a completely integrated human being.

New Delhi
18 January 1972

Chairman
Jawaharlal Nehru Memorial Fund

EDITORIAL NOTE

Is tarah taye kee hai hamnain manzilen
Gir paray, gir kar uthay, uth kar chaley

(We have reached our goals where we stumbled,
fell down and rose; and marched again)

Jawaharlal Nehru, the Prime Minister, recited this verse from the ramparts of the Red Fort on 15 August 1957. It summed up the pace of India's fortuitous journey towards change and progress. It alludes to heartbreaking reverses, as also to the changing pace of India, the growth of science and technology, and the success of the economic plans. The challenge before the nation was: to root out completely the weeds of parochialism, secularism and such narrow prejudices and re-establish the spirit of nationalism (p. 45).

The nation's economy and its growth were central to the Prime Minister's concern. At the same time, he was deeply concerned that rapid changes should not entail difficulties to the common man. This sentiment was reflected in his letter to T.T. Krishnamachari:

> The first thing we have to do is to create, as far as possible, a healthy, brotherly and comradely climate and show our goodwill to all concerned, so that every section should feel that our measures are meant for its good also as well as others. Even if it hurts somebody, or some section, he or that section should be made to feel that we aim at their good, though the overall interests of the country necessitate our taking some steps. Thus, even when we hurt, we are trying to soothe (pp. 49-50).

In the section "National Progress", we have a series of important documents relating to industry, community development schemes, planning and foreign exchange difficulties. Of special interest are the speeches at the Congress Parliamentary Party meetings on taxation, and the letter to the Chief Minister (p. 95) on the continuing ejectment of tenants in various States. This concern for the poor remained a dominant strain in Nehru's thinking.

A number of rare speeches and letters reflect on a variety of themes. They range from access to historical records (p. 183) to the status of women (p. 189), from the All India Sikh Educational Conference to a concert for children's fund.

To the students of Lucknow University, he admonished: "You should shun fanaticism, narrow-mindedness and rigidity of thought and keep your minds open and free to receive fresh ideas. The shackles of caste, community or region that fetter the minds are great impediments to the progress of the country." In the same speech he opposed the intrusion of the party politics in university affairs (pp. 199-200). A thoughtful speech is on the responsibility of writers (p. 195).

The promotion of Urdu was one of Nehru's passions. But he found, much to his dismay, that Urdu was being neglected in Delhi and Uttar Pradesh, his home state. He observed that there were seldom arrangements for teaching Urdu in the Delhi schools. He was, moreover, distressed by the removal of Urdu signboards: "even now most people, like *tongawalas*, taxi drivers, etc., know Urdu much more than any other language and they are rather lost when the signboards are not in Urdu" (p.203).

The Prime Minister's grip on administrative matters is truly amazing. For a man who was preoccupied with intricate policy matters – domestic and foreign – he still found time to, for example, go into the details of the construction of the All India Medical Institute. He was unhappy to discover that the original estimate of Rs 172 lakhs had gone up to Rs 625 lakhs (p. 244). The exchanges on the Prime Minister's New House are, likewise, quite instructive.

This volume incorporates rich documentation on the States and Union Territories, especially Save Hindi agitation in Punjab and formation of Naga Hills Tuensang Area under MEA, on defence, on the Indian National Congress, and the uncertainties in Kashmir. Readers will also discover a wealth of information on 'External Affairs'. The documents cover the speeches of the Prime Minister delivered during his visit overseas—in Tokyo, for example.

The letter to Norodom Sihanouk is instructive:

I am writing to you on the eve of India completing ten years of Independence. We are celebrating this occasion, which also happens to be a hundred years after the great struggle for independence which took place in 1857-58. That was a violent struggle which was suppressed with great cruelty. Later other methods were adopted and, generation after generation, our people carried on this struggle for freedom till they attained it on the 15th August, 1947.

We achieved Independence and started on a new pilgrimage to a welfare state so as to raise the standards of our people and remove the curse of poverty. We have struggled hard during these years, while we have solved many problems, many more afflict us. Indeed the more we progress, the harder becomes the struggle and the greater the problems we have to face we realize that a price has to be paid for everything good.

Let me conclude with a reference Nehru makes to a letter written by Wajid Ali Shah to Canning, the Viceroy. Apparently, Wajid Ali, the deposed King of Awadh, had asked for exemption from income tax. The Viceroy refused, pointing out that nobody was exempted, including himself. At that time the exemption limit in India was Rs 200 per annum.

We thank various individuals and institutions for their help in publishing this volume. Shrimati Sonia Gandhi granted permission to consult and publish the papers in her possession. They are referred to as the JN Collection. We have also had access to important collections at the Nehru Memorial Museum and Library, the Secretariats of the Prime Minister and the Cabinet, and the Ministries of External and Home Affairs, Planning Commission, National Archives of India, and the Press Information Bureau. The All India Radio allowed us to use the tapes of Jawaharlal Nehru's speeches.

For their scholarly assistance in the collection of archival material and its subsequent organization, I am indebted to Ms Geeta Kudaisya, Ms Shantisri Banerji, Dr Jawaid Alam, Mr Sailen Dutta Das and Mr Syed Ali Kazim. Equally my thanks to Ms Malini Rajani and Ms Kulwant Kaur for their editorial assistance.

11 April 2007   MUSHIRUL HASAN

CONTENTS

1. General Perspectives

2. National Progress

I. Economy

II. Food and Agriculture

(i) Foodgrain Prices

(ii) Agricultural Production

IV. Language Issue

V. Tribal Affairs

(i) The Nagas

(ii) NEFA and Other Matters

VI. Science and Technology

3. Administrative Matters

I. General

9. External Affairs

•

I. Foreign Policy

II. The Asian Tour

(i) Japan

IV. General

II. Rahat Ara's Case

ILLUSTRATIONS

ABBREVIATIONS

AFP	Agence France Presse
AICC	All India Congress Committee
AIR	All India Radio
BA	Bachelor of Arts
BRCS	British Red Cross Society
C&I Ministry	Commerce & Industry Ministry
CID	Criminal Investigation Department
COAS	Chief of the Army Staff
CPI	Communist Party of India
CPSU	Communist Party of Soviet Union
CPWD	Central Public Works Department
CS	Commonwealth Secretary
CSIR	Council of Scientific and Industrial Research
CWC	Congress Working Committee
DDPA	Delhi Development Provisional Authority
DG	Director General
DSP	Deputy Superintendent of Police
DVC	Damodar Valley Corporation
FAO	Food & Agriculture Organization
FM	Finance Minister
FRI	Forest Research Institute
FS	Foreign Secretary
GATT	General Agreement on Tariffs and Trade
HAL	Hindustan Aircraft Limited

I&B Ministry	Information and Broadcasting Ministry
IAF	Indian Air Force
IAS	Indian Administrative Service
ICS	Indian Civil Service
INCWUS	Indian National Committee of the World University Service
INTUC	Indian National Trade Union Congress
LCC	London County Council
LIC	Life Insurance Corporation
MA	Master of Arts
MEA	Ministry of External Affairs
MHA	Ministry of Home Affairs
MLA	Member of Legislative Assembly
MLC	Member of Legislative Council
MP	Member of Parliament
NATO	North Atlantic Treaty Organization
NEFA	North East Frontier Agency
NES	National Extension Service
NMML	Nehru Memorial Museum and Library
NWFP	North West Frontier Province
P&T	Posts & Telegraph
PAC	Public Affairs Committee
PCC	Pradesh Congress Committee
PEN	International Association of Poets, Playwrights, Editors, Essayists and Novelists
PEPSU	Patiala & East Punjab States Union
Ph D	Doctor of Philosophy
PIB	Press Information Bureau
PM	Prime Minister
PMS	Prime Minister's Secretariat

PoK	Pakistan occupied Kashmir
PPS	Principal Private Secretary
PSP	Praja Socialist Party
PTI	Press Trust of India
PWD	Public Works Department
RPI	Republican Party of India
SCF	Scheduled Castes Federation
SEATO	South East Asia Treaty Organization
SG	Secretary General
SGPC	Shiromani Gurdwara Prabandhak Committee
SP	Superintendent of Police
SS	Special Secretary
UK	United Kingdom
UN/UNO	United Nations Organization
UNCIP	United Nations Commission for India and Pakistan
UNESCO	United Nations Educational, Scientific, and Cultural Organization
UNRRA	United Nations Relief and Rehabilitation Administration
UP	Uttar Pradesh
UPCC	Uttar Pradesh Congress Committee
UPI	United Press of India
US/USA	United States of America
USSR	Union of Soviet Socialist Republics

1
GENERAL PERSPECTIVES

1. Economic Freedom is the Next Step[1]

Brothers, sisters and children,

I am happy that this rain has come. It might have worried some of you whose clothes are slightly drenched. But in this rain I see a symbol of our country's prosperity, of its becoming green and fertile and our hearts also being refreshed. Children, my greetings to you on this auspicious day, it is you who will build the future of this country. You have to prepare yourselves with firm determination and stout hearts to embark on the journey of wiping out poverty from the country in the same united way in which we wiped out slavery. We have completed one journey of consolidating our freedom, the foundations of which were laid a hundred years ago by our people with their blood, sweat and tears. We have before us now another journey of emancipating our people economically. But any nation that undertakes the mighty task of wiping out unemployment and poverty is bound to meet with reverses. We often stumbled and fell in our struggle for freedom. We faced heartbreaking reverses, but we did not give up. We again rose and marched on. In the same way today we have to face the challenges of these economic and other difficulties in a united and firm manner and rebuild a new India.

How many among you here remember the face of India before freedom? If you do not remember it, you cannot compare the conditions in those days in the cities and villages with the present times? It was a tremendous task, requiring hard work to change those conditions. It could not be done by magic. It was hard and persistent work, which brought India freedom. We require this capacity for hard work and unity to rebuild a new India. Whenever a country wants to go forward rapidly, it has to face the challenge of many odds. We have to understand that we may stumble and fall. Only those people do not stumble, who are always sitting at ease or just reclining. When people march forward, they are bound to stumble. We have gone forward in this way:

Is tarah taye kee hain hamnain manzilen
Gir paray, gir kar uthay, uth kar chaley[2]

Many people when faced with difficulties tend to lose heart and turn their

---

1. Speech from the ramparts of the Red Fort after unfurling the National Flag on the Tenth Anniversary of Independence, Delhi, 15 August 1957. From *The Hindu* and *The Hindustan Times*, 16 August 1957.
2. We have reached our goals in a manner where we stumbled, fell down and rose, and marched again.

backs and slink away. They are frightened by these difficulties which appear to them like a big mountain. But big things are only achieved by facing difficulties of every kind. One can see the progress India has achieved by looking around at the conditions in the neighbouring countries. We are not so much worried about the world as we are about our own duty to our country. We have taken a big job on our hands. We are doing it. And we will do it.

On this historic day, memories of a hundred years of glorious struggle and achievements beckon us to greater effort. The torch of freedom, lit by the freedom fighters a hundred years ago like Tatya Tope,[3] Nana Sahib,[4] Kunwar Singh,[5] Liaquat Ali Khan[6] and above all the Rani of Jhansi,[7] was kept aloft and burning by those who succeeded them. Dadabhai Naoroji,[8] Lokmanya Tilak[9] and Mahatma Gandhi in their turn carried the torch and faced the might of British

3. Alias Ramchandra Pandurang (1813-1859); born at Gola, Maharashtra; one of the most important figures of 1857 Revolt; became general in Nana Sahib's army and organized the strategy of war against the British at several places in UP and MP; was captured in sleep and executed on 18 April 1859.

4. Nana Govind Dhondu Pant (1820-1859); adopted son of Peshwa Baji Rao II; was denied the family title and estates by the British; defeated the British forces and assumed the control of revolutionary government at Kanpur; facing heavy odds, he was forced to retreat to Nepal and believed to have died there of fever on 24 September 1859.

5. (circa 1782-1858); born at Jagdishpur, Shahabad, Bihar; joined the revolutionary forces at Arrah in July 1857 and proclaimed himself the ruler of Shahabad; defeated the British at Arrah but failed to stop their advance and was dislodged from Jagdishpur; died of severe wounds received during a battle at Shahabad.

6. Known as Maulvi Liaquat Ali; he was a teacher in his early life and organized the revolt in Allahabad Division in June 1857; he could not succeed and left for Kanpur with his followers; Government records show that he was later arrested in Bombay; found guilty in a trial in July 1857.

7. Lakshmi Bai (1835-1858); became regent of Jhansi State after the death of her husband Gangadhar Rao in 1853; took up arms against the British as they refused to recognize her adopted son and seized her State; attacked the British forces and drove them out of Jhansi in June 1857; fought against the British with great courage but was mortally wounded in the battle at Katah-Ki-Sarai in Gwalior.

8. (1825-1917); known in the pre-Gandhian era as the Grand Old Man of India; devoted his life and wealth to the national movement in India; through his articles and speeches hammered the point that India was economically backward precisely because the British were ruling it in the interests of their trade, industry and capital; and poverty and backwardness were the inevitable consequences of colonial rule.

9. Bal Gangadhar Tilak (1856-1920); India's most influential and important proponent of militant nationalism; strong advocate of *Swadeshi* leading to Swaraj as a birthright to be demanded; imprisoned in Mandalay Jail in Myanmar from 1908 to 1914; founder of Deccan Education Society and two weekly papers *Kesari* (Marathi) and *Mahratta* (English); author of *Orion, Arctic Home in the Vedas* and *Gita Rahasya*.

imperialism. We have today to remember the lessons of unity, religious tolerance and fellow feeling taught by Mahatma Gandhi and other great sons of India and go forward in a united and determined manner.

India is celebrating today the Tenth Anniversary of her Independence and the First Centenary of the 1857 Struggle. Some historians have tried to belittle the importance of the "War of Independence" of a hundred years ago. But the basic fact is that the India of those times did rise gloriously against the foreign yoke and a large majority of common people joined the struggle. And people of all religions, Hindus, Muslims and others, together rose and bore every suffering to attain freedom. There is no doubt that it was a War of Independence in which the foundations of freedom were laid with the blood of the people. The most lovable name of the freedom fighters of those times is of Rani Lakshmi Bai of Jhansi. These names are in our hearts and will remain in our hearts always. Their memory will remain fresh for centuries.

Now, our neighbour Pakistan is a part of our heart and body. How can we ever think of fighting against Pakistan? This would only be tantamount to harming ourselves. If Pakistan through its foolishness entertained enmity towards us, it would be only harming itself. No doubt our relationship with Pakistan is strange because even if there is bitterness against each other, even if there is some anger, it is a very close relationship of thousands of years which mere laws cannot obliterate. If some harm comes to India, it is bound to harm Pakistan also. Similarly, if Pakistan is harmed, it will affect India too.

So, we want that we remain in peace and friendship with Pakistan and our relations grow in such a manner that they remain happy in their freedom and we remain happy in our freedom. This does not imply that India can be cowed down by threats and made to abandon her rights. It will be neither doing justice to ourselves, nor to Pakistan nor to others. It would not be a good example too. So, we will remain firm on our rights and defend them with all our strength and with cool minds and go forward. We will be friends of all.

Coming to the international situation, India does not like the cold war which is raging in the world. We think this cold war engenders jealousy in the heart. It is a wrong thing. It makes the heart narrow. No country can grow in this manner. India's hand of friendship is stretched out towards all countries. We want to shake hands with all countries.

But in the ultimate analysis, India's position in the world will depend on her own internal achievements. If India is respected today in the world, it is because of our achievements during the last ten years. The world has taken note of a strong nation having entered the world arena, a nation which is making progress rapidly. So, it is only after seeing our ten years' work, that the world has begun to respect us.

5

There may be passing difficulties but they have to be overcome with determined effort. We will overcome them and step by step our nation will go forward. There will be more work and we will be able to eliminate unemployment and especially the suffering of our people, living in villages or cities today, who for centuries have borne the burdens of poverty. We have completed one journey of freedom. The second journey has just begun. It is before us. We will reach its end also by remaining united.

We have gathered here in hundreds and thousands to celebrate this day. This day is the Tenth Anniversary of our Free India and the Centenary of the big War of Independence, which took place here a hundred years ago. You are here in your big numbers, but more than that, other people were gathered here too. The memories of those caravans which came here, caravans of people who showed courage, served India, served our nation, and went away after doing their duty. They may be here or they may be in our minds or they may be seeing what India's position today is after a hundred years. It is ultimately the efforts made by these people through their blood, sweat and tears, who gave their lives for the country, that have brought the results which we see today. It is this story of ups and downs of a hundred years that we see today in this city of Delhi and especially in this Red Fort, whose every stone relates this story.

Before me is Chandni Chowk, the famous bazar of Delhi for centuries. This Chandni Chowk has seen mighty processions of kings and emperors, it has seen the country taking a turn in its history, it has seen the fall of a mighty empire and the birth of a new State. Here processions went by of old India, of Moghul emperors, of British rulers, on big elephants. Those times came and went and now Free India's time has come. We are today seeing the truths of a hundred years of struggle. We have now to see that we preserve the fruits of this struggle.

In these ten years the face of India has changed to some extent and our voice has reached the ears of other people in the world. This is a voice which is a little different from the voices they have been hearing. We did not growl, we did not shout because we learnt our lessons under the leadership of Mahatma Gandhi, who worked silently. But behind this silent work of ours there is determination and strength. India entered the world arena as one of the wrestlers. But it is not to fight anyone, but to serve ourselves and to some extent serve the world also. During the last ten years, the path has been cleared to some extent for the people of India to go forward. Many thorns in this path have been cleared and brushed aside. But still some more thorns remain. In the political field, the path has been very much cleared. India has now to clear the economic path and go forward.

Now, the world is facing a strange situation. The atomic and hydrogen bombs are hanging on the head of the world menacingly and no one knows when they explode. Yet, this same atomic power can be used for the good of humanity.

6

India today is facing many problems. The one relating to foodgrains is especially important. The prices of foodgrains are rising, affecting everyone. But the burden on those whose income is low is more than on others. That is a matter which certainly cause worry. But it is a worldwide phenomenon. India, however, will get over that and other problems. The trouble is that big projects like steel plants and river valley schemes take some time to complete. The results that flowed from them will come only after some time. But all those are definite signs of the people going forward. The whole of India today is like a big workshop where the *kisan*, the mill worker and the engineer or anybody else are immersed in their daily tasks. The day is coming nearer when the entire nation will reap the fruits of these big projects. We must remember that we have to stand on our own legs. Nobody will come from outside to take us forward. We have to depend on our own efforts. India is both an old country and a new one. It has its past of 5,000 years. Yet, it is a young country which is only ten years old. We have to see where we are going today. Our War of Independence was started 100 years ago with blood. It was suppressed. Even though it was put down for the time being, the battle was not over. It was continued by others in later years who consolidated the unity of the people, and brought them together.

The Buddha Jayanti celebrations took place last year and the 2,500th birth anniversary of the great son of India had refreshed the minds of the people and the impact that his teachings made on vast masses of humanity is tremendous. It is that message of peace and love taught by the Buddha and Mahatma Gandhi that has given strength and unity to the people of India. We can go forward only when we continue to follow these principles and work in a cooperative and united manner. *Jai Hind!*

2. Pledge of Loyalty to the Nation[1]

Brothers and sisters,
The biggest question that was before our people in 1857 and which is there today in 1957 and which will ever remain so in the future also is: What is your

1. Speech at a public meeting held at Ramlila Grounds to commemorate the Centenary of 1857 War of Independence, Delhi, 16 August 1957. From *The Hindu* and *The Hindustan Times*, 17 August 1957. President Rajendra Prasad presided over the meeting, and Vice-President S. Radhakrishnan also spoke on the occasion.

first and foremost loyalty? Is your loyalty to your family, your ward, your city, your caste, your religion, your province, your language or is it first and foremost to your country—India? There should not be any clash between these different loyalties. But in the event of a clash, the first and foremost loyalty of every Indian should be to India. All other loyalties are secondary and puerile as compared to the loyalty to India. All these second rate loyalties must be shoved into the background. The time has come when every Indian has to search his heart consciously and make up his mind determinedly about his first loyalty to India which must have precedence over every other loyalty—to family, community, caste, language, village and province. Any man who today raises his hand against his neighbour in the name of language or province, raises his hand against India. This man has not understood what freedom of India is. He is himself fully not a free person.

We must also remember that our entire future depends on the answer our people give to this question of our loyalty to India. We are living in dangerous times when weak and disunited nations cannot stand and must go down. We have to fulfil a pledge to the heroes of the War of Independence and to those who gave their life during the last hundred years for the freedom of the country. We also have to fulfil a pledge to the voice of the future which beckons us to greater endeavour. This pledge was of loyalty to the country.

I want to hear your answer to this real and vital question of your first and foremost loyalty. Is your first and primary loyalty to India or to a thousand other small petty parochial things? I want you to take this pledge: Our first and foremost loyalty is to India. We will serve India and we accept without reservation unity of India as paramount and all other things as secondary. If you accept this pledge then please raise your hands and your voice in approval.[2]

We suffer from this old disease of quickly disintegrating into groups, quarrelling over small, petty, parochial things and forgetting national issues. India was enslaved primarily because of this internal weakness. We are all in one boat, we have to go forward together. If some people begin to jump about in it, then the boat will not go forward but it will surely capsize.

You and I remember with pride some names which have become famous in our history. They are loveable names that we remember, these names of 1857. But you must remember this also that there were some of our own people who committed utter treachery against our own country and people. It was some of our own people who sided with the British and helped in suppressing the sentiment of freedom and establishing British rule.

2. Nearly half a million hands went up spontaneously amidst thunderous shouts of "our foremost loyalty is to India" and "we will serve India."

So, in India today there is a big responsibility on us. We have a pledge to fulfil to the events of these hundred years from 1857 till 1957 so that we will successfully complete this task of consolidating India. One thing we have completed. We became free. But in the present times, mere political freedom is not considered enough until it is followed by economic freedom and poverty is eliminated and there is all around progress. Even if we leave aside, for the time being, this question of economic freedom, we have to consider how far political freedom can remain if the nation has not got internal strength. This strength does not come by making speeches in the Ramlila Maidan which we often do. There is need for something else than mere speeches to make the country strong. One real and vital thing is the firm resolve in our hearts of our unity and our first loyalty to India before which all other loyalties have to bend and succumb. Have we come out of our old ruts of thinking? Have we come out of our old mind whether it is in social life or matters of caste or community or religion or province or language?

Our real work is in India. We have to increase the country's wealth and eradicate poverty. We cannot do it by fighting amongst ourselves or by going on strikes. I accept that sometimes people are so frustrated, whether Government servants or others, that they think of going on a strike. Sometimes their grievances are not looked into promptly which was not a good thing. These grievances should be gone into immediately but it will be a folly to harm themselves or India by hampering the work. If we have to increase the wealth of our country, we should not adopt methods like strikes which stop our work and retard production. We can certainly find ways and means to ensure that workers' grievances are speedily looked into and redressed. But all these questions have to be viewed against the overall good of the country and the progress of the country.

India today is in the midst of the story of these hundred years and the challenge of the future. You and I are on the sharp edge of the blade of a sword. We must profit from the lessons of this past epoch. The year 1857 was a strange year in some ways. It was a hundred years earlier, in 1757, that the British had slowly started to entrench themselves in the country. Our habit of being complacent prevented many people in those times from realizing that a big imperialism was growing up in the country. Some people were just praying with their beads and did not understand the new power that was growing. They thought that they knew everything in the world and did not have to learn anything from anyone. In this complacency, they ignored the new knowledge, new weapons, new trade and new science that had been growing in the world. The result was India was occupied by a foreign power which came from 6,000 miles away.

Foreign imperialism was established in India with a lot of fraud. But along with it there was treason on the part of the Indian people themselves. There

9

were internecine quarrels and Indians themselves invited the enemy to subdue their neighbour with whom they had a quarrel. The India of those times was the India of the Rajas. These Rajas took pride in fighting each other. The British helped one Raja against the other and ultimately subdued them all. India in those times was a fallen nation. But still some sparks were left in some bosoms which wanted India to be free. These sparks started the conflagration of 1857. In later years, there were sporadic risings in nearly all parts of India. But none was of the magnitude of 1857. A big War of Independence was fought in 1857 which was suppressed with lot of *zulum*. This movement had to fizzle out. The circumstances of the times were such that it could not succeed. But it was inevitable. In fact, nations grew only by undergoing these very struggles.

We remember the 1857 War of Independence today. The brightest side of it was that hearts which had been suppressed were aflame again and courage which had been crushed again reasserted itself. The nation, which appeared to have become lifeless and accepted slavery, rose again and made an unsuccessful effort to overthrow the foreign yoke.

History had other examples of nations facing utter defeat. The cases of Germany and Japan were there. They had been completely defeated in the last War. But ultimately the question that arose was how people faced the circumstances imposed by a defeat. In 1857, we saw valiant signs of people facing up to the might of an imperial power. People perhaps do not know how many events took place after that. There were risings in Malabar, now Kerala, in Andhra, in Maharashtra and in the Punjab and other places. Those events showed us that whatever weaknesses we might have had, we had still life in us. There were sparks in our hearts which came out repeatedly.

Indian revolutionaries who, in their impatience and exasperation at foreign rule took to bomb-throwing to destroy that rule. It was clear that by throwing bombs, an imperial power could not be destroyed. But violent activity became a symbol of the same spark of freedom which was in the hearts of the people. Their acts might have been called foolish, but the entire nation had great respect and regard for those people who paid the price of their lives for the country's freedom.

Mahatma Gandhi forged a new weapon and gave it to the people. The fact was that before Gandhiji the people had no weapon, even though Lokmanya Tilak did rouse them and became, in his time, the voice of India. What was this weapon? It was not a weapon of violence. It was a non-violent weapon but weapon it was all the same. Mahatma Gandhi's voice was very soft and feeble but behind this voice there was the strength of steel and the strength of determination. Gandhiji breathed new life into the nation which had been frustrated with hopelessness. In this way, India ultimately attained her freedom and became independent to undertake new responsibilities.

In the present day world of atom and hydrogen bombs, a world conflagration can start only between powers possessing these weapons. No nation can fight atomic weapons with conventional weapons. These atomic weapons are possessed by a few today. But they may be possessed by many more in the course of the next ten years if a ban was not put on their production. India has neither the wherewithal to have these weapons nor the desire to possess them. But the danger of this menace is ever present. A wrong step by an atomic power can set into motion a chain of events that can poison the entire atmosphere of the world bringing untold destruction. We have to face all this not by having the atomic weapons. We have to do it in our own way just as we faced British imperialism. I do not mean that we should not have an army. No man with any sense of responsibility will say that. But our real strength lies in our getting over our narrow-mindedness and ideas of high and low.

India must keep pace with scientific development and the people must broaden their minds. We are passing through a period of grim tests. We have to stand on our own legs. We must persevere hard and remember the biggest lesson of the 1857 War of Independence that it was because of divided loyalties, of giving precedence to local issues of language and caste over national affairs that India lost her freedom. We have to guard against this disease and go forward with courage and determination. *Jai Hind!*

3. National Unity is of Utmost Importance[1]

Friends and comrades,

I have been asked to speak to you in English because unfortunately I cannot speak in Kannada. It is always a great delight to me to come to this beautiful city of Mysore. It is beautiful not only because of its gardens and buildings, but, if I may say so, because of its people. Coming from other turbulent parts of India, it is a soothing experience to come to Mysore. I have come here today, or

1. Speech at a public meeting, Town Hall Maidan, Mysore, 21 September 1957. AIR tapes, NMML.

rather yesterday, and many others have come from various parts of India to meet Acharya Vinoba and to participate in a conference which has been convened here, the *Gramdan Parishad*, to consider this question of *Gramdan* and how we can help it and how we can spread it all over India.[2]

What is this *Gramdan*? I am not going into any great detail. But *Gramdan* is connected intimately with the villages of India; with the agriculture of India; with the peasants of India; and, because of that it is connected with something that is most important in India. What is the most important thing in India? Many things are important. There are many things that are very important today and it is difficult to pick and choose. The Independence of India or the Freedom of India, is important. We have achieved it; but it is important that we secure it and maintain it and not allow it to be tarnished or weakened in any way. I say that because some people may think that having achieved Independence, nothing more need to be done. But a great man said once that 'Eternal vigilance is the price of liberty".[3] The moment we become careless and complacent, the moment we become lazy, we imperil the freedom of our country. At any time that is important but today it is more important than ever. You see and you read about great changes in the world: great blocs of military nations, atom bombs and hydrogen bombs and ballistic weapons, how are we to meet these great perils? Not by having the atomic bomb which we have not got and which we do not want. We can only meet these perils by our unity, by stoutness of heart, by working hard and by making our nation prosperous and strong. That is why we have been planning—the First Five Year Plan and now the Second Five Year Plan, because we are anxious and eager quickly to build up this great country, make it prosperous because strength comes from a prosperous people, not from a poverty-stricken people.

So, we have this Second Five Year Plan. And you hear now and you read about it that we are in difficulties about the Second Plan. You read about foreign exchange difficulties and other difficulties. Of course, there are those difficulties. Difficulties come to those people who want to do great things. There are no difficulties for people who do nothing at all. There are no dangers or risks for people, who lie in bed all the time, except the risk of, well, slowly dying in bed. It is only when country moves forward fast that it encounters difficulties. Those

2. The two-day all-party conference on *Gramdan* movement began on 21 September at Yelwal, a tiny village about ten miles from Mysore city. Vinoba Bhave presided over the conference and Rajendra Prasad, Jayaprakash Narayan, U.N. Dhebar, Ganga Saran Sinha, Sankaran Namboodiripad and Dhirendra Mazumdar attended the conference which was organized by Akhil Bharat Sarva Seva Sangh.
3. Thomas Jefferson (1743-1826), the third President of USA.

difficulties are a sign of its progress, of its vitality and we need not be frightened of them. The strength that makes us go forward will also make us overcome these difficulties. But they are difficulties, and we must recognize them. And perhaps, it is a good thing that we have to face these difficulties because they make us realize that the path we have to pursue, and the way we have to go is not an easy way. How can it be easy to raise up this great country with 370 million people? It is a tremendous task. All these millions and millions of people from Kashmir and the Himalayas in the North right down to the South to Kanyakumari have to be raised, it is a tremendous job; one-sixth of the human race to be raised. So, we have undertaken a great task, a proud task, a task worthy of you and me and of the people of India. And we should not be afraid of these difficulties. But we should also realize that it requires hard work from us, it requires unity from us, it requires cooperation amongst all of us whether we live in the North or the South or the East or the West. It requires peaceful effort, and all that. If we do all that, then the difficulties will vanish away like the mists and clouds that come and go.

You will be knowing that just at present, our Finance Minister has gone to attend some meetings in America and there is a good deal of effort on his part to raise some credits or loans to meet some of our present difficulties.[4] If he succeeds in raising those credits and loans, well and good, and we shall be grateful to those who give them and it will make our task a little easier at present. But if he does not succeed in getting much help, then also well and good. We shall not get frightened because our difficulties are greater. We shall only realize that we have to work harder. Maybe, we shall change our pace a little here and there, we shall change our Plan here and there, but we are determined to go ahead whether we get help from abroad or not. And we are determined to maintain our Independence, our freedom of action and not to be bound down by anything and made to go in a direction in which we do not want to go. So, today in the 10th year or rather the 11th year of our Independence, we are facing these big problems which come to great nations that are on the move. Not only we but many countries in the world are facing these problems and sometimes their problems are more difficult than ours.

And now, as I told you at the beginning, we have come here to attend a *Gramdan* Conference convened on behalf of Acharya Vinobaji. Now what is

---

4. India's foreign exchange needs had risen to about $ 2,000 million during the Second Five Year Plan period and the Indian Government was planning to meet that gap by drawing on sterling resources, by imports of foreign capital and by getting external assistance from friendly countries and the International Bank. T.T. Krishnamachari visited West Germany, USA, Canada and UK from 17 September to 25 October 1957 for this purpose.

this *Gramdan* about? It is about the future of our agriculture and our peasantry. In India a vast number of people live in our villages far more than in the cities— I do not know, maybe 75% or thereabouts live in villages. Therefore, if India is going to march ahead, it is the villages of India that have to go ahead. It is not enough to have beautiful cities like Mysore and Bangalore. We have to make our villages also beautiful, we have to make the people who live in our villages also to have the benefits of good food, good clothing and other amenities of life. That is a big task. Unfortunately, there are more people in this country than there is land for them. What are we to do? And, more unfortunately still, our population is going on increasing fast. What are we to do about it? We talk a great deal about more production in the country, more wealth, more production of food, more production of cloth, and more production of everything. That is wealth—true. But we want a little less production of one thing and that is— babies. Now, here is this great population in our villages attached to the land and many of them are very poor. They have very little land. The first thing to remember is that we shall have to give many of those people in the villages other work than land, so that the burden on the land is less. They should have other occupations. Do you remember—you should remember if you know India's history—that when about 150 or 200 years ago when, the British people came to this country there were a large number of handicrafts and artisans and many people engaged in other occupations rather than depending on land. But many of our cottage industries and other industries and manufactures were crushed by the British. And many of those people who had other occupations had no occupation left and they went to the land. Therefore, the burden on the land in India increased. And one of the big causes of the poverty of India is this great burden on our land, or if I may put it differently, is our people not having enough occupations—variety of occupations. Now, in the last few years, more and-more occupations are coming in. Industry is growing. Many things are growing. That is true. But, for a hundred years and more, people were thrown on the land by the policy pursued by the Foreign Government of the day. And that is the principal cause of the poverty of India. Now, in order to get rid of that, we have to draw people away from land—some of them—and give them other work, other occupations. Of course, even then a vast number will remain on the land. That is right. But not so many as today. Therefore, we have to find work for many people who are dependent on the land and work in some kind of industry, whether it is big industry or small industry or cottage industry or village industry. That is the first thing to remember. Even then a very large number of people will remain on the land. And many of them will have very small bits of land—one acre, two acres, three acres. How are they going to better themselves? Well, they can better themselves a little by organized efforts, better seeds, better manure, better

14

techniques, new implements and all that. In other countries agriculture yields much more than in India. The yield per acre for anything—for wheat, for rice, for anything—is much more in other countries than in India. Why should that be so? Because they employ new techniques which we do not do here. It is difficult to employ new techniques if our farm holdings are just one or two acres. The poor peasant has not got enough resources. He cannot do anything nor the Government can do anything. Therefore, the only proper way for him to better himself is through cooperatives. You have heard of cooperatives and perhaps you think that cooperatives mean credit cooperatives, banking cooperatives giving some money, lending some money to the peasant. That is useful. But that is not enough. We should have cooperatives for every kind of agricultural activity. These cooperatives are called Service Cooperatives so that the peasants together in a village or in two or three villages, can function jointly, can get good seeds, can get good manure, can get good fertilizers, can get good implements, can get good advice and then can sell their produce well, by marketing it well. If they do it through cooperatives, they will produce more and they will get good prices for it—by using new techniques and through the cooperative method. Therefore, cooperatives are essential and when I talk about cooperatives, I mean not very big cooperatives but a cooperative for one village, two villages, three villages, so that people may know each other and trust each other and cooperate with each other. That has become quite essential for our agriculture. You know that we have put an end to the big landlords, to the big zamindars and all that. Our ideal is that the land should be owned by the tiller, by the man who works there and not by some absentee person. And many laws have been framed to give effect to that in many States. Much remains still to be done. That will be done. But even after doing that, unless we have cooperatives, the poor peasant with the small patch of land can never make much progress. Therefore, cooperatives are necessary. I have talked to you about service cooperatives—various services done together. But there is another type of cooperative which goes a step further. That is the cooperative where joint farming is done. That is, the peasants join together to till their fields together and then they share the produce according to their share. I think that this joint farming is not only good, but we should try to do it. Because that has many advantages. It will produce more, undoubtedly—it will do away with the boundaries between innumerable thousands of holdings. You get much more land. The peasant gets more and the community gets more. So, I think that joint farming is good. But I do not want joint farming—or I do not want anything—without the agreement and the goodwill of the peasants. Because if we do anything against their approval, that is against our practice, against our methods and it will not succeed, because we want people to do something willingly, by understanding it. Therefore, we are not going to push down, force down this joint farming on our peasants unless they agree to it. First of all, we want to have service cooperatives and when they like the idea of joint farming, then they can have joint farming cooperative also. That is the procedure. Now, what I have said to you applies generally to all our country. Our peasants have very small holdings. If they had big holdings then it would not have mattered. They could work separately. But a person having one acre or two acres cannot make much progress unless he cooperates with others. Of course, cooperation is good anyhow.

Apart from service cooperatives and farming cooperatives, it is the temper of cooperation we want, the temper of helping each other, the temper of helping our neighbour, and the temper of thinking ultimately that all this great population of India is a great family, of which all of us are members. You live in Mysore and you are proud of Mysore City and Mysore State. And I do not live in Mysore City but I am also proud of Mysore city. It is as much mine as yours. You have no right to think it is only yours. So also, if I come from Delhi or North. Delhi is not my property—it is yours, it is everybody's. Or, see the great Himalayas in the North. Whose property are they? Nobody's. But they are all our inheritance, yours and mine and everybody's. So, we have to get out of this narrow thinking: we belong to this city, this village, this State. We belong to this great country of India. And this great country is the inheritance of every single Indian—man, woman, boy and girl. Our country belongs to us. And all the people who live in it are our neighbours, our colleagues, our comrades and we have to work together for the advancement of the country. After all what is India? India is a big country on the map. India has many mountains, India has many rivers, India has many States, India has deserts, India has forests, India has cities, India has villages. It is true. But still what is India? Many things. Thousands of years of history, that is also India. Thousands of years of culture, that is also India. See, what a proud inheritance we have—these thousands of years of culture that has come down to us! All that is India. But in the final analysis, what is India today? India is you—you and I. India is not outside us. I am a little, little tiny bit of India; each one of you is a small bit of India. We are all bits of India. India is not something outside us and so, when we think of India we must think of all these little bits of India—we and you and all the millions and consider them as one whole, forming this great body of India. So, I was talking to you about this cooperative method which is not only good for agriculture, it is good for everything. We should like our whole lives to become more and more cooperative for the benefit of everyone of us and for the country.

Do you know how the Congress describes what it says its creed, its objective. Article (1) of Constitution of the National Congress says: "The objective of the National Congress is the attainment of"—I am sorry I do not remember the exact words—"of a cooperative commonwealth of a socialist pattern". So, we think of whole of India as a cooperative commonwealth. So, you see how cooperation comes in our entire picture of India. Because we want to think of India and the hundreds of millions of people here as belonging to one vast family and we want that to be of the socialist pattern.

Now, socialism is a big word and many people mean different things of it. It does not matter. Let people think differently. We do not want to confine the meaning of a word in a particular way. We do not want to limit it. But something that socialism means certainly is this: that while on the one hand the individual counts—each one of you is an individual different from another—each one of us is a citizen of India, each one of us as a citizen has rights, has freedom which are guaranteed by the Constitution and we attach great value not only to our national freedom but to our individual freedom. That is so. But at the same time, the society, the great community of India also is important. And as I told you, if India progresses all of us progress. If India does not, we don't either. Therefore, socialism means the progress of all—not of a few persons going ahead—but the progress of all in a cooperative way. Socialism means not some people rich and many people poor, but the whole nation profiting by the wealth of the nation. It is difficult to make everybody equal because people are different. Some people physically are tall and some are short. There is a great deal of difference between Pantji and myself. So people differ. Some people may be cleverer, some people may be more foolish than others. You cannot make everybody a wise man. But we must give opportunity to all. Everybody must have equal opportunity. Now, having equal opportunity those who are stronger, those who are cleverer, well, go further ahead. Certainly. But others should also have that opportunity. Today, unfortunately, most people in our country, many of them do not have any opportunity. All these people in our villages, their children, do not have too much opportunity. They do not even go to school. They may not have good clothing, they may not have good food, they may not have good houses. All this means lack of opportunity. We must give opportunity to all. Therefore, we want all the 370 million people of India to advance. It is not easy. But we shall do it. Not quickly, but as time goes on.

Now to come back again to *Gramdan*—I told you that we should like to aim at cooperative farming but not without the consent of the people—not suddenly, but train them up to it and get their consent. Meanwhile we want to have other forms of cooperatives. Not cooperative farming but service-cooperatives. But in the case of *Gramdan* where a whole village has been donated by those who own it, there it is easier to start with cooperative farming because they have themselves agreed to give the village. So, it may be that in that event we can start with various cooperative farms in the *Gramdan* villages. Now agriculture produces many things. It produces food and many other articles, it produces cotton from which clothing is made, it produces hundreds and thousands of things as you know. In fact, most of the things that go into industry—in big industries and the mills—the raw material comes from agriculture. So, agriculture is very important. Most important of all, of course, is food. If a country does not have enough food then what is the country going to do? Either it will have to get food from other countries or starve. Now, it is not good for us to get our food from other countries. That means we have to pay heavily for it and a poor country paying its money for food to other countries is very bad. We become poorer still. Therefore, it has become important that we must have enough food in this country and, more than enough food. We can stock it and we can even export it. Therefore, the most important thing in our Five Year Plan or in anything that we do today is more food production. If we do not succeed in that, then the rest of the Five Year Plan becomes very very difficult. If we succeed in our food production, as we will, then the rest of the Plan becomes much easier. We should keep the food prices down. And life is easier for everybody and we can devote our attention to other things. Therefore, you must remember that food production is the first thing in India today. In this connection I may tell you, perhaps you know, that here in Mysore there is an Institute—the Central Food Technological Research Institute. Nine years ago, I came here to Mysore and I gave it a little push.[5] It started then.[6] I came in between too to see it. I saw it yesterday and I was very happy to see what great progress it has made and how many things it is making. I hope that soon these articles of food will be available to everybody who wants them in India—all kinds of good things. Now, food is the most important thing. Remember that.

Now, one other thing that I want to tell you, especially, the young men and young women here and everybody, is that many of us in India have got into very bad habits. We think that doing some manual labour is bad. Only low class people do work with their hands. All the clever people sit on a desk and do brain work or become clerks. This is, if I may tell you, silly nonsense. Anybody who believes that doing manual labour is bad, does not know anything about the modern world. He is a relic of some past feudal age. We do not want such people in India. We want everybody in India to realize that doing work with your hands is a fine thing. We want everyone to realize the dignity of labour, the

5. During his visit to Mysore on 29 December 1948, Nehru formally accepted on behalf of the Central Government the Cheluramba Mansion, situated on 160 acres of land, as the location for the Institute.
6. The Institute was inaugurated on 21 October 1950. For Nehru's message on the occasion see *Selected Works* (second series), Vol. 15 Pt. I, p. 65.

importance of labour. As a matter of fact labour is not only with your hands, your head has to work too. A good peasant has to think also. A good carpenter works with his head and his hands. Therefore, I should like—and I should really like—every person, even those whose work is of an intellectual kind, even professors and others, even lawyers and others, to do some work with their hands too. Of course, some doctors do it when they cut you up with their instruments—surgeons and others. I think that is important—that all of us, especially our young men, and boys and girls realize that it is a good thing for everyone to do some work with hands. I should like every school and college to have some manual work in its curriculum. That teaches you a great many things and at the same time it gives you health.

Now, I have talked to you about odd things. But the big thing for us is to build up this India of ours which after many hundreds of years has become independent and now it has got to solve the other great problem of becoming a prosperous country. And for that we are working today through the Second Five Year Plan and all that. But we can only work successfully if we work in unity, and when we forget our small quarrels—quarrel between State and State, quarrel between the peoples speaking one language and another, quarrel between one caste and another caste—it is terrible, how many quarrels we have! Now, in Madras State, somewhere near Madurai—I think Ramanathapuram—people of different castes are quarrelling, hitting each other on the head, and sometimes even killing each other.[7] Now, that is a bad thing. How can we make progress if we are so primitive and foolish and so caste-ridden and all that. I think that in the last many hundreds of years, India has suffered greatly due to caste. Because caste has separated us into different compartments. It has prevented the growth of national unity and even now it comes in our way. So, we have to get over this caste business, we have to get over provincialism, statism and linguism and all that. You should be proud of your language—that is good. But that does not mean that you should quarrel with people who speak another language or live in another State. Therefore, unity is of the utmost importance and you should realize that India is more important than your State or my State or any State or town or city. And, if India progresses, all of us progress. Otherwise we do not.

Another thing you know, we achieved our freedom under the leadership of Mahatma Gandhi. Mahatma Gandhi told us many things and I am afraid we sometimes forget them. We carried on this great struggle of freedom peacefully against a great empire and we won. And now I see people forgetting peaceful methods and indulging in violence. That is against all our principles and if we

---

7. As a result of clashes between Maravars and Harijans for eleven days from 14 September 1957, about 40 persons were killed in Ramanathapuram District.

indulge in it, India will split up, India will go to pieces. All our strength will be wasted and all our Five Year Plans, etc., may not be successful. So, you must remember these basic things. After all a country goes ahead not because it is big by number. We have 370 million people of India, but only 10 years ago these 370 million or 360 million people were under British rule. Numbers do not make any difference. It is quality that makes a difference, the quality of the people, the training of the people, the character of the people, and the standards of the people. England, a small island in Europe, built up a great empire all over the world. They had a very small population in England. When the British people came to India 250 years ago, I think their population was 20 million—two crores only. Those two crores spread out all over the world. Why? You may criticize them, you may call them imperialists and all that. But remember that two crores of people in England had some virtues. Otherwise they would not have done all that they have done. They were united, they worked together, they worked hard, they were adventurous, they were not afraid, they crossed thousands and thousands of miles of sea to come to India, to go to America, and to go to all kinds of countries. And they studied science and science gave them strength because science releases the forces of nature—and puts them at your disposal. Science released these great forces which brought about the Industrial Revolution—the steam engine and the steamship and the railway and the aeroplane and electricity—all that—these are the children of science. And now the terrible child of science is the atom bomb. So, the British people, because of their unity, because of their adventurousness, of their fearlessness and because they studied science, made them so strong that, although they were small in numbers, they became the strongest nation in the world for 100 years.

If we are to progress we shall not progress because we are 370 million people. But we shall progress if we are a united people, if we hold together, if we work hard, if we do not quarrel amongst ourselves, if we give up everything that separates us and if we train ourselves in science and engineering. That is why I want our schools and colleges to train students in engineering, and in other technical subjects. It is no good taking an Arts degree today, a BA or an MA, it is some little good, but not much good. Today what counts is training in technical subjects. Every engineer today will find work. Every MA may not find work. He may have to wait, sometimes. So, here are these big problems. Think sometimes of this country which is your patrimony, your inheritance. Think of the snow-covered Himalayas right in the North, think of them as something of yours which nobody can take away from you. And think also of this broad land of India and your own state and down below Kanyakumari, think of our past history, what we have achieved, think also of our failures, think of our disunity, think of how we used to quarrel and take a pledge that we will not commit the same errors again, that we will not allow ourselves to be fooled again by anyone who tries to separate us or tries to weaken us. And then think of the future that we are building—the future of India. Think of that. Is that not a tremendous task which fills you with pride that you and I and all of us are building brick by brick, step by step this magnificent future of India. I am afraid I have done my share of building. I have a little time left and I hope to do something more during that time. But you, who are young men and young women, you have got your whole life before you—what a wonderful life it is going to be—building this magnificent India and in the process raising not only yourselves up but this enormous country and the 370 or 380 million people of India. That is the tremendous prospect for the future.

Of course, you will have difficulties. No big thing is done without any difficulty. Anything that you get easily, you will lose easily. It is only when you have paid the price through tears and sweat and sometimes blood and toil, the things that you achieved that way are worth having. And if you do not do that, the big things will escape you. Well, you have got a big enough task, and you have got plenty of opportunities for sweat and hard work, I hope there will be no blood, but there will be toil and there may be tears. But you will always, I hope, have the thought that you are working for this greatest of all causes, the cause of advancing India and taking forward these 370 million people and making them happy and contented and prosperous. And then all of us working for peaceful ends not only in our country but in the world. *Jai Hind!*

Will you say *Jai Hind* three times with me. *Jai Hind, Jai Hind, Jai Hind!*

4. Work Hard for Higher Production[1]

Your Highness,[2] Friends and Comrades,

It is over 26 years ago, I first came to Mercara and that was the last occasion also. Many of you present here probably, were not born then. Many of you may have been little boys and girls then. Some of you may have been grown-up people. So, you see how old I am. I came here 26 years ago and spent a brief few hours here, but the picture I got of Mercara and Coorg[3] remained in my mind all this time. It was a beautiful and lasting picture and I wanted to come back here, but fate willed it otherwise. And though I wandered about India a good deal— and of course since that day, 26 years ago, I spent many years also in prison— so, I could not come here. And I must, therefore, apologize to you for the seeming negligence on my part. But really it was I who paid the penalty for it, and not so much you. This time, during these many years, friends from Coorg have often invited me, pressed me to come to Mercara. And I always said to them that I wanted very much to come here and I would do so. But various kinds of work came in my way. In this occasion, if I may say so, the chief cause of my visit here is General Cariappa,[4] who met me a little while, some weeks ago—in Delhi and pressed me once more, as he had done so many times, to come here and told me, reminded me, that I was coming to Mysore City for a conference, the *Gramdam* Conference. And, I thought that this might be possible and I am glad that at last this has taken place. And I am very happy to be here in your lovely hills.

Coming from Mysore today, I was told, that it was about two hours' drive from Mysore, fast drive but about two hours and that it was a good road. Well, it took me four hours. The road was not bad, but my friend, who was accompanying me, Mr Poonacha[5] decided to take me all over Coorg before he brought me to Mercara. So, we wandered about through lovely hills and valleys and through

1. Speech at a public meeting, Police Parade Grounds, Mercara, 22 September 1957. AIR tapes, NMML.
2. Jaya Chamaraja Wodiyar, former Maharaja and Governor of Mysore State at this time.
3. After Independence, Coorg became Part C State of India with Mercara as its capital. According to the States Reorganization Act of August 1956, Coorg became a part of the bigger Mysore State that came into being on 1 November 1957.
4. Former Commander-in-Chief of Indian Army and High Commissioner in Australia and New Zealand.
5. C.M. Poonacha, who was the Chief Minister of Coorg, joined as the Minister for Home Affairs and Industries in S. Nijalingappa Government of Mysore State.

your villages and little towns, and I am glad we did so because that gave me an even better impression of Coorg than a straight drive might have done.

Now, what is so special about Coorg? Small place, relatively. Till a year ago or so, it was a little State of India. Now it is a part of the larger and famous State of Mysore.[6] And, of course, both before and now, it is an intimate part of the still larger country of India. That continues. But whether it was a separate little State or whether it is a part of Mysore State—it makes little difference. Because in either event, we are all together in India. And, in either event, the individuality, that Coorg and the people of Coorg possess, remains and will remain. There is no question of your losing that individual stamp of being Coorgis, because a political rearrangement, administrative rearrangement has been made.

I wander about all over India and I love to see the great variety of this country—the tremendous richness of this country from the Northern snowy peaks of the Himalayas down South to Kanyakumari. And I love to see both the variety and the unity of India because both are important. Of course, unity is important and variety gives richness. For, if everybody was alike, life would be a dull place. So, it is good that various parts of India have their own individuality in this great unity of India. It is true that in the past while India certainly was there and was one, there were many parts of it politically, although India's ancient culture was stamped on the whole of India, in a sense, a cultural unity was there with all its diversity. But politically, they had different histories and sometimes, to some extent, different traditions. In the modern world, it is not possible for small entities to exist satisfactorily. There is a tendency all over the world for larger entities. It was inevitable, therefore, that India should be a great united nation. This reorganization of States, that took place later, was also inevitable.[7] I am not talking to you about minor changes here and there, but the basic urge to reorganize was inevitable. That really should make no great difference if we remember the basic fact that counts today and that is India. And that is, that you and I and all of us, who live in this great land, are citizens of India—not of Coorg or Mysore or any particular State or part of the country. If you go outside India to any foreign country, you are recognized there. How? By the fact that you are a

6. The new Mysore State was twice as big as the old one because vast Kannada-speaking areas from Bombay, Hyderabad and Madras were added to it. The Part C State Coorg had now become a district of the new Mysore State.
7. The States Reorganization Act of August 1956 provided the new structure of the Indian Union with fourteen States and six Union Territories that came into being on 1 November 1956. The new structure included (1) six new States—Kerala, Mysore, Bombay, Madhya Pradesh, Rajasthan and Punjab, (2) Andhra Pradesh, constituted by the merger of Telengana area of Hyderabad State with the existing Andhra State, and (3) Madras, Bihar and West Bengal with restructured boundaries.

citizen of the Republic of India, you have the passport of the Union of India. That is your sign manual. That is what makes people in other countries treat you with respect. They do not know our different States in India—most of them— but they know India. Therefore, we must always remember this basic fact of India and not get lost in the numerous divisions of this country. Divisions are there and they are good in their own way, divisions—geographical divisions, political, administrative divisions, linguistic divisions—so many others. They are good provided always, we see them for what they are and not allow them to interfere with this conception of India and our citizenship of India. It is quite clear that if we are going to progress in India, it is India that will progress. Not one part of India. If India goes down, all of us go down. We are, in a sense, in one big boat. The boat must sail on, further and further—the boat of India. So, this fact you must always remember. Now, I ask, what is the particular, well, individuality of Coorg? It has been a small State of India—yet, it is very well-known. People know that it is rather a beautiful State with its hills and other beautiful features. But I suppose, in the rest of India, it is known for two things specially. One is, that it seems to produce quite a considerable number of Generals for the Indian Army. Our first Commander-in-Chief, the Indian Commander-in-Chief after Independence was a Coorgi, General K.M. Cariappa, a fine General and a fine gentleman. Our present Commander-in-Chief, rather I should be more correct, our Chief of the Army Staff, is General K.S. Thimayya. And there are many others, I believe, in the Indian Army. So, that is the first thing about Coorg that is known—that it produces fine soldiers. The second thing that is known about Coorg is, that it produces good coffee. And the third thing I should like to say is that it produces rather fine women. So, these are three important elements in Coorg's life, all important. And may you continue to possess all the three.

If Coorg was a separate entity, cut off from the rest of India, the talents of the people would be confined to Coorg itself. Now, they have a great field to play upon, the field of this great country of India. Now, we talk, as you know, nowadays, a great deal about the Five Year Plan. There was the First Five Year Plan and now there is the Second Five Year Plan. What is all this talk about Five Year Plan? Well, before we became independent we talked about one thing specially. What was that? That was Independence. We had many problems then, but the over-riding problem, the most important thing for us all over India was the Independence of our country. We talked about it, we worked and laboured for it and vast numbers in India suffered for it. Many laid down their lives for it. Because for a country that is not independent, the most important thing is independence. Ultimately, under the leadership of Mahatma Gandhi we became independent. Having become independent, our job was not finished. We arrived at one big stage of our journey. But as soon as we arrived there, we realized that the journey was a very long one still and there was no resting time or resting place for us. So, if I may use military language—I hope I am correct in using it in this way—we have to pack up our knapsacks, whatever they are, and get ready to march again.

The coming of Independence meant a great thing for us—politically, psychologically, culturally and all that. But in the main, it meant that we were free to choose our path then. No outside authority could direct us or coerce us. But even when the Independence came—the fact remained that our country was a poor country. And many hundreds and millions of our people lived a very hard life. Many of them just subsisting, working hard and just getting enough to eat and sometimes not even that. So, the next biggest problem for us was to attack this poverty of India. We were a peaceful country even in our struggle with the British Empire. Mahatmaji taught us to use peaceful methods, not to have hatred against anyone with whom we fight. So, when we became independent also, we wanted to remain peaceful with all the world. We did not want any kind of trouble or war against any other country or people. But there was another type of war that we had to fight. What was that type of war? That was the war against poverty, against so many things in India which are bad—poverty, disease and many other things. This was a very big thing. Because it was not a question of finding some posts or jobs for a few people—few hundred people or a few thousand people. It was a question of 370 million or 37 crores of people. You cannot find jobs for 37 crores of people. You have to raise their standards in some other way. And this search for the way, how to raise them, resulted in the Five Year Plan. Now, you cannot do this quickly, you cannot do this by magic. You can only raise a country by working hard, and by producing wealth for the country, producing goods for the country—wealth is goods, the things you want; wealth is your food, wealth is your clothing, wealth is the many things that you want. Money, gold and silver are really not real wealth. They are media of exchange. The shopkeeper wants them, the moneylender may want them. You do not eat gold and silver, nor do you otherwise use it except—you might use it, some women might use it as jewellery here and there. One can do without gold and silver but one cannot do without food. So, real wealth is what one produces for use. The first important thing is food. Second clothing. Third, well, if you like, the house you live in. Fourth, education. Fifth, health. Sixth, work and so on. These are important things. Your work is important, whether you work in your fields or in a factory or anywhere else; your work produces goods that people require. It produces the wealth of the country. The countries that are very rich today like America or England—are rich because they produce great many things in their fields and factories. So, we have to produce much more in our fields and factories—big factories, small factories, household factories, cottage industries—we have to do that. And we have to do that quickly. Because the longer we delay the more difficult this problem becomes for us. Our population becomes bigger and bigger. It needs more food to eat, more clothing to wear, more houses to live in, more jobs and so on and so forth. Now, that is a very intricate problem and we cannot get it by shouting slogans or by passing resolutions. Therefore, Five Year Plans were adopted and the first Five Year Plan was a modest one and a good one and we were successful. Then we started a much bigger Plan because we have to go ahead fast. And we are putting up big things, huge steel factories and other things which cost us a lot of money. But we also have realized that the most important thing still is food. We have to produce more food—more rice, more wheat and more other agricultural things. That is essential. Because if we do not have food how can we survive? So, in this Second Five Year Plan, the first and most important thing is food production and, other agricultural production. The second very important thing is development of industry. Now industry is of many kinds—big industry, very big plants, we must have them, like iron and steel plants—then medium industry and then small industry, cottage industry, and village industry. Now, we are having the big industry but at the same time it is very important and essential for us to have cottage industry and small industry. Otherwise we will not get work for all our people, and we will not produce so many things that we can produce by this cottage industry.

Now, I am not going to tell you all about the Five Year Plan. Because that is a very big thing. But you must realize that this Five Year Plan is not some kind of a book of charts and pictures and statistics. When you think of the Five Year Plan, think of it, try. It may be in a book or on a paper. Try to think of it as a structure on which you have got to put flesh and blood, because the Five Year Plan represents the 370 million people of India marching ahead. Now, when you think of the Five Year Plan—as a great march of 370 million people of India, then it becomes something vastly important, something much more than an odd factory or an odd something, but something much more than a book of statistics. It is a people on the march. It is a historic event. It is the changing face of India. It is removing from India the curse of poverty, which has been with our people for ages past. It is one of the great things not only in India but in world history.

The moment India became independent, something big happened in the world. It was not merely a political change. But the energies of a great people, which had been suppressed largely, which were restricted and tied up—those restrictions were removed, those bonds were taken away and the energies of this great and mighty nation became released. And when the energies of the nation are released, of a great country like this, then big things happen. It may be that some things that happened are bad or good. Many things that happened since Independence have distressed us very much. But, the main thing to remember is that the energies of this country which had been kept back and tied up for generations were released and we began to bring about all kinds of changes, some good and some bad. Now, it should be our endeavour that the bad changes should not take place, that the bad trends should be stopped and good ones encouraged. Now, when we are at present living at this tremendous period of history, of India's history, when the whole people are on the march, when they have to cross great mountains of difficulties, it requires hard work, of course. Do not imagine that it is easy. It is a very difficult task. But it requires, above all, a sense of unity, a sense of cooperation, and a sense of discipline. We may not have worn uniforms and march about like soldiers keeping in step. But try to think of the people of India as a kind of army on the march, through all kinds of difficult territories, deserts and wastelands, swamps and all that. We have got to go through that, before we arrive at the promised land, that we aim at. So, all this requires a sense of unity, a sense of discipline, and a sense of cooperation. When we aim at big things, we have to be big people, not to be frightened, not to get tired, and not to get disheartened. Big things can only come after big efforts. If anything comes to you easily, it will be taken away easily from you—you will loose it. Therefore, I want you and specially the young amongst you, our young men and young women, to realize what a tremendously important and exciting time this is when we are living. I know the great difficulties that many of our people suffer from. If there are no difficulties, there will be no problems. It is to solve those difficulties, that all our efforts are directed. But remember this that we are on the way to solving them, we may not completely solve them quickly, not in the Second Five Year Plan, not in the Third Five Year Plan. But, of course, progressively, we shall solve them. At the end of the Second Five Year Plan we shall be in a stronger position and our people will be a little better. At the end of the Third Five Year Plan, I hope, our people will be much better. But still the march and the journey will go on. Remember this. You know what world we are living in. It is a tremendous world, a difficult world with the atom bomb and all that. Well, we are not going to meet the atom bomb with an atom bomb. But we ought to meet it with our unity, our faith in our country and our discipline. And I am quite sure that we do that. And, no power or no strength that anyone else could have, would be able to coerce us, or to suppress us. Now, that is so.

But remember another thing. We, in India, have lagged behind other countries in many ways—in science, and in technology. We got left behind. We are catching up to them. Our science is growing, our technology is growing. We have tens of thousands of engineers coming out of our technical schools and all that. We shall no doubt catch up. We have to learn much from other countries, we shall

27

learn it. But at the same time we cannot become copies of other countries. No country, that merely imitates another country, has any strength. An ancient great country like India with tremendously powerful cultural roots in the soil of India, roots which go far down to thousands of years should not imitate other countries blindly. So, we have both to learn from others and to be ourselves, to be true to the soil of India. Not in the sense of putting ourselves or closing ourselves in. It was bad for India, when it closed herself in. It was bad for India when it developed into a thousand ramifications due to the caste system, which separated us into different compartments. We lost the sense of unity. We thought only of our little group, our caste or whatever it is. As now people sometimes think of their language groups. Everything that separates is bad, everything that joins is good. Therefore, we are, while learning from every part of the world and opening out our doors and windows to all the thoughts, that come from the rest of the world, are yet to be true to our country. Remember also that in this great age of science and technology and the atom bomb, the bigger weapon destroys the smaller weapon. The atom bomb destroys every other weapon that exists. How are we to meet the evil? We have not got the atom bomb nor do we want it. But there is something, which even the atom bomb cannot destroy and that is the spirit of man—that is the character of a people which gives them strength. And, so, in this age of science and technology, in this age of rapidly changing things, it is as important as ever and much more important that we should develop the strength of character, high standards of behaviour, discipline, and social organization of cooperation. There is too great a tendency nowadays among our young people sometimes to forget this, to go in for indiscipline, to go in for petty shouting and this and that and demonstrations and all that. I do not mind shouting, I do not mind demonstrations, I do not mind even misbehaviour, but I want the strength of character behind it, not just simple folly and excitement. Because, men like me, as I told you, I am getting old in years. But, I am still pretty fit and I can still run about a good bit and do a hard day's work. But, after all, tomorrow is for the youth of this country, not for people like me. We have done our job. We do a little more before we pass on. But the real responsibility for running this country is going to fall on the youth of the country, the men and the women. The young people who are out of college or in college, they will have to face these great responsibilities and they have to train themselves for it. Because you cannot do anything worthwhile without training. You cannot do the simplest thing. If you want to make a chair you have to be a carpenter, and have a carpenter's training. You cannot make a chair, simply because you want to make it. You have to become a carpenter. And if you want to make a bridge, you do not stand at the side of the river and shout slogans like "Let there be a bridge". There will be no bridge, however loud you shout. You have to be an engineer to build a bridge, and only then will the bridge come. If you and I and all of us have got to build this great and noble mansion of India, you won't get it by slogans and shouting. We shall only get it by training ourselves, by hardening ourselves, by disciplining ourselves and by cooperating with each other. That is why it is so important for those who are young today specially to train themselves, to train their character, to train their abilities and know-how to work properly.

What does working mean? Our people in the last many years, some generations maybe, got it into their head that manual labour was something for menials and lowdown people, for people of low castes. The higher castes were too superior for manual labour and they did intellectual work or they went and fought. That was a noble work. Well, intellectual work is good and fighting for a good cause is good. But if a country or any people think that manual labour is bad, that country is doomed because it is manual labour that carries on the world. Not only manual labour—manual, intellectual—all mixed up. Therefore, it is important that we develop respect for the dignity of manual labour. If you go to huge, rich countries like the United States, they respect manual labour. You go to a communist country like Russia, they respect manual labour. Every country that gets on in the world, respects manual labour, whether it is socialist or capitalist or communist. It is only the backward countries that do not respect it. It is a bad thing. It is my opinion that every child—boy and girl—in school and college—should devote part of his or her time in some kind of manual labour and manual work. It will be good for them.

So, now, I have sat here surrounded by these pleasant, green hills and looking at all the faces of this friendly crowd around me and the evening shadows are falling and it has been a pleasant experience and an experience that I shall remember long. And I am very grateful to you for having given it to me, and for the welcome and the affection that you have shown me. Soon I shall go back to Mysore and, tomorrow morning, I shall fly to Delhi. I shall carry back with me the memory of this pleasant visit and all of us, friends and comrades in Mercara and in Coorg. Thank you.

Now you say *Jai Hind* with me three times. *Jai Hind, Jai Hind, Jai Hind!*

5. Greatest is the Spirit of Man[1]

Mr Chairman,[2] Vice Chancellors, friends,
I did not, as you have just heard, quickly and gladly welcome the idea of coming here. I resisted it. I tried to avoid having to come here on this occasion for a variety of reasons. It is not particularly easy for me to come and I did not like the idea of coming here just for a few minutes. Also, I am very sorry to confess, that I do not know much about the World University Service and I did not want to plunge in when I did not know what it is all about. But I must say that the visit of the representative of this service,[3] who was just speaking, has rather swept me off my feet and his enthusiasm and earnestness found some echo in my mind, and so here I am. Not knowing quite what I am supposed to do and having arrived here to inaugurate the discussion on 'University in a Welfare State', it is all much the same, and really does not matter what title you give to it. It just struck me that it is almost exactly 50 years ago, it will be, I think, in about 10 days time, when I first went to the University myself. It is a long time—half a century. In 1907, in the beginning of October, I joined the University of Cambridge and here we are in 1957, approaching October, so, long time. Anyhow, and from the point of view of the university generations, many generations passed through this period and because of this lapse of time, I often doubt, how far I can understand the university mind of today or the students' mind or the teachers' mind, because normally each generation has a mind of its own, more specially when great changes are taking place, as they have, after all. Since I was at the University, two World Wars have come over. Great revolutions have taken place, empires have fallen and even in our own little way, we managed to push away the British Empire from India. So, all these things have happened, no doubt producing enormous impressions on the mind of the people and the mind of the young.

Take it the other way. My own generation was very powerfully influenced by Gandhiji and the great movement that convulsed India for a couple of generations

1. Speech while inaugurating the five-day national seminar on the role of a university in a welfare state organized by the Indian National Committee of the World University Service, Address Hall of the Osmania University, Hyderabad, 23 September 1957. AIR tapes, NMML.
2. O.P. Bhatnagar, Vice-Chairman of the INCWUS, presided over the meeting.
3. Parimal Mookerjee, General Secretary of the INCWUS, explained the nature and scope of WUS.

and which led to our Independence. I wonder, often, how many of you—or how many of the students and the younger generation of India today—think in that close and intense way about Gandhiji, as we used to do. Obviously, you do not and you cannot think in that particular way. You know his name, you shout his name, you read about him perhaps, but you cannot have the same emotional experience which changed the lives of hundreds of thousands of people of my generation and convulsed India. I cannot convey that to you—that powerful impression we had. Gradually, Gandhiji's name is becoming a story book name about which you have heard, as one of the great heroes and sages of India who no doubt influenced you and the country and will continue to influence us for generations and for hundreds of years and maybe thousands of years, but in a rather distant and impersonal way.

So, these tremendous changes are taking place and between myself as a student and you as students, there are gulfs of world convulsions, national convulsions, and to some extent personal emotions and personal convulsions. How then am I to put myself in touch with your mind. It is not a question of words. It is an odd thing, but if I speak, let us say to the present audience, perhaps I find it easier to put myself in touch with their minds although I am very very different from the present. Obviously, there is no point in my speaking to them or to you or to anybody and just blending words with you or throwing about some elegant phrases unless I can find some entry into your mind and something behind the mind, the emotional stuff that you are made of. If I have any influence with the people of India it is because, I suppose, I touch some deeper chord in their mind. I touch their hearts a bit. They are receptive while well, partly because I am receptive to them. It is always the two-way traffic, you cannot have this one way. And even when I speak to an audience, I want to be receptive to them in so far as I can and not merely feel off something I have thought of previously which may have no fitness, which may not suit the audience I am addressing. And so, you will be surprised to learn, I approach my audiences, even learned audiences, often with a deliberately cultivated blank mind. That is to say that it is not a mind in a rigid mould, it is not a mind which is determined to say that something, whether the other fellow wants it or not, and so I approach you with a blank mind, not knowing or having forgotten even the subject of the seminar. That has its advantages and disadvantages.

Well, how do you feel, the young men of today in the universities with so many pulls, with a certain lack of, shall I say, overpowering call which some of us felt; the call, let us say, to free India, and to attain the Independence of India. That is achieved. Now, have you got any single call like that? You can, of course, have it. The mere call of building up India, it is a tremendous thing. Then, it is not such a simple issue and you are pulled in different directions partly this, that and another. The world is also pulled in different directions. You see this amazing thing in the world today, what is called the cold war which inspite of every effort, I have yet failed to understand how any reasonable person can talk about it, much less indulge in it. It does not matter what your views are. The cold war is not a method to advance your views. It is the reverse method, because, you see, I have been bred up, however unworthy I might be, to some extent, in the Gandhian tradition and we are the children of the Gandhian age, and we can never get rid of that, not that we want to indeed. And, I suppose, of the 101 lessons that Gandhiji taught us perhaps the most important was that means are important, means are even more important than ends or at least as important. Means govern ends. You cannot merely talk about ends and do what you like to achieve because in the process of achievement, if the means to it are bad or twisted or distorted, well, you will not reach the end at all, you will reach somewhere else. Now, if our aim in life is a good life how can we reach the good life by unworthy means, by evil methods? It seems to me a bad stuff. If it is as an individual question it certainly is so, as a national question, it is certainly to be so or also as an international one.

If our aim in international politics is peace, how can we achieve it by constantly talking about war and preparing for war? How can we get rid of hot war by always indulging in cold war? It seems to me illogical and unreasonable and lacking in sense, this kind of proposition. I know, of course, that life is not terribly logical neither for the individual nor much less for the nation. All kinds of illogical things come up and when we have to face them often enough, we have to follow the path of the lesser evil because the alternative is worse. That is true and I am not, therefore, dogmatizing about anything. But I do say that one should at any rate yield at a certain way, one should at least accept this fact that following an evil method will not lead to good. Whether it is internationally, nationally or in our individual lives, we are pulled in different directions. Young men were attracted, in my time and I hope they always will be, to intellectual pulls. We wanted people to think and we did not want to produce people of set moulds. Certainly, a university will, probably, set some kind of a principle not to inhibit or restrict your thinking but rather to encourage you to think correctly, scientifically, logically and to get rather traits of character etc., which may be called cultural, civilized and spiritual, call them what you will, and they make you tolerant to others, to other opinions, to other views and yet if you are firm on your views, well and good, which does not make you break the head of a man if you disagree with him. And yet oddly enough, nations try to do so all the time. It is curious how uncivilized nations are compared to any normal individual standard of civilization. So, it is a good thing if you argue, if you talk, if you discuss passionately because the world is full of tremendous problems and your minds should be awakened to them, should think of them. It is bad to have a complacent mind and not to have an inquisitive and inquiring mind, and it is good to some extent to have a vagrant mind. At any rate whatever virtues or failings I have possessed, I have been in mind, a little wayward and vagrant. But the waywardness and vagrancy should be controlled somewhat, disciplined somewhat, otherwise it will be difficult. But, you have to have those two, otherwise too much discipline makes Jack a dull boy. But too much waywardness may ultimately make him go to pieces. You should strike a balance. Obviously any organized community must have discipline, discipline of body, discipline of thought, and of action. Otherwise it will come into conflict. All life is discipline in a sense. And, yet, nobody wants the discipline of the robot, because then that discipline kills creativeness. We have to have both creativeness and discipline and we have to balance the two. In a war, probably war being an extreme and unhappy state of human society, discipline becomes dominant and creativeness, except in a very narrow field, dies or is crushed. Untruth comes up in war, and intolerance comes up too. You do not tolerate anything. That admittedly is bad. Therefore, we should try to cultivate the opposite of this, at least at the time of peace. If we convert our peaceful living into a kind of shadow of war-living, then we are lost and doomed indeed as a generation and that is the odd thing that after its tremendous and terrible experiences of wars and the like in the course of a generation or two, still we, when I say we I do not mean my country or myself or you but broadly the world, pursue—do not seem to have learnt any good lesson from them—the same evil way which unless checked lead to the same evil consequences.

Well, I am not going to talk to you about the world as a whole, it is too big a subject. I want you to think of it as a background of your generation. I do not know how you see it. I cannot enter into your minds. It may seem to you normal because you have grown up in it. It is quite possible that just after four or five years of World War II, many people began to think that it was a normal state of affairs for war to continue and peace was odd. But surely, it is not normal for humanity to live in this way—either real war or this kind of pseudo war which is sometimes even worse than real war—because it perverts our sense of values, standards and everything. Well, we cannot take the burden of the world upon us. It is a heavy enough burden—the burden of India that we have to carry and remember this—that those of us, people of my generation, well, have largely had their day, they may have a few more years and all that, and we may function effectively, no doubt, we will certainly. I have every intention of doing so as far as I can, but the fact remains that the burden of this country must necessarily fall on those of this present generation, not a passing generation like mine, will fall on the young people, will fall, if not tomorrow but a little later, on those

33

who are in universities today inevitably. And if you seek to understand India of tomorrow, there are many ways of doing that, of course, of trying to do that— peeping into the future politically, economically, culturally, this, that and other, in many ways—we plan for it and we call it perspective planning, distant planning and all that , but in the final analysis I look for that future in the faces of the young men and young women of today, and even in the children of today. Because basically they are the future, they are going not only to shape the future of India but they are the future of India. What is India? Not an entity apart from the humanity in it. I once asked, I was in the Punjab—I stopped at a little village. A lot of stout Jats were sitting there and they shouted *Bharat Mata Ki Jai*. I stopped, and I asked them who is this *Bharat Mata* you were shouting about? So, they looked at each other not knowing what to say. I said is it some old lady, long haired lady you see in pictures etc., or sitting somewhere in a cave and they said no. I asked, what is it? Well, they were sons of the soil, a Jat is wedded to his soil, more to the mother earth, than his son or daughter or wife. So, he said, *Bharat Mata* is *dharti*, mother earth. I said, yes *dharti* but of what place, *dharti* of your village, or your district or your State? Then again they were confused. So, I put them question after question and their confusion grew. They said you tell us about it. Why ask us questions? So, I said, well *Bharat Mata*, first of all, is not an old or young woman sitting anywhere, inspite of the pictures you may see. *Bharat Mata* is many things, many things I have tried to look for and discover *Bharat Mata* or India or Hindustan in many ways—I have read books and seen statues and monuments and so on and so forth. *Bharat Mata* has mountains, that is *Bharat* too, of course, and rivers and deserts and cities and villages and all that and much more. *Bharat Mata* ultimately is you and me and each one of you is a bit of *Bharat Mata*. Now, this amazed them that they were *Bharat Mata*. We are *Bharat Mata*? I said yes. You are *Bharat Mata* and not only you 360 million people are also *Bharat Mata* in India. Every man, woman, boy, girl, child in India is a tiny bit of *Bharat Mata*. And, so, when you shout *Bharat Mata Ki Jai*, well, you are shouting your own *jai*. So, I tell you that I look for the future of India not so much in the economists' statistical tables or the Planning Commission's plans, they are all important, of course, but rather into the faces and eyes of the young men and women and children that I see. Trying to judge, it is difficult, trying to judge of what calibre they were, what thoughts came into their minds, what urges, what passions, what character there was, what strength of mind, what ideas moulded them and all that. It was all these mixed things that move us and various impressions of them come to me, sometimes good, sometimes bad. I do not attach too much importance to them because I know even bad things are fleeting. I need not get worried. I may sometimes say rather strong things, oh! young men at our universities are misbehaving, and are indisciplined. Of course, they are misbehaving, of course, they are indisciplined and one feels rather sad about it. Not that one dislikes the spirit in young people, certainly not, but one objects to evil. Well, some forms of misbehaviour are much better but there are some things which, if I may say so, are more inexcusable than murder. A murder is bad. If you commit murder you will probably be hung by the neck till you are dead as a punishment. A person may commit murder in a stress or excitement, in anger, in passion. It is bad. He suffers for it but one can understand the murderer's viewpoint, at any rate I can understand it very well. And I have seen people, lived with them in prison, persons sentenced to life imprisonment, very decent people and if I may say so, rather higher than the average in India we meet outside. So, I can excuse a murderer, although that depends, of course, on the type of murder, although he must suffer the penalty of the law and should not escape. But there are some things worse than murder because they involve a degradation of the spirit, and they involve vulgarity of the deeper kind. They show that the man doing it is a mean person and out of that man nothing good can be expected unless by some strange sea change he goes through a conversion or what not and brings himself up. What can you do with a person who has, well no background of, if I may use the word—nobility— in him or her. We are all imperfect. Nobody is perfect. We have our failings, we have this, that, another. But unless you have something worthwhile in you, you cannot do very much in life. You may carry on. You may shout, do what you like and it is this that I deeply regret when some evidences of this kind of thing come up. It is not that violence is evil though violence is bad. But the meanness, the vulgarity, the degradation of the spirit that comes out in acts of indiscipline and the rest is also bad. Because no nation is going to grow unless there is some foundation of spirit and character.

I am coming to you today from Mysore.[4] I went there three days ago to attend a conference on *Gramdan*. You know, *Gramdan* and *Bhoodan* were started by Vinoba Bhave and I have been with him seeing him again for the last two days. I went this morning to say goodbye to him as I was coming away here and it struck me how, as it struck me very much of course, during my youth, in earlier days, when I worked with Gandhiji, how great was the spirit of man, how much more powerful than anything else devised, even as Gandhiji with his spirit who was more powerful than any atom bomb or any other kind of armament. And that struck me often when I saw Vinoba Bhave, this shadow of a man, ill, weak, almost hardly substantial you might say, airy, going on his *padyatra*, foot pilgrimage from village to village. Our big people may laugh at him and our economists may say what does this mean and what does this amount to and here

4. Nehru was in Mysore from 20 to 23 September 1957.

was this man of spirit working through the Indian masses and no doubt bringing about all kinds of sea changes in them imperceptibly but powerfully. And then I wondered if at this present juncture in history any other country can produce such people.

Previously, I suppose other countries have them too. Whether this is a sign of our primitiveness or our goodness, I do not know, both perhaps. Anyhow, it is a good thing in so far as I am concerned, and it struck me that a lot of progress is taking place in the world and undoubtedly magnificent civilizations have been built up in the last two hundred years or so in Europe. Europe built up a resplendent civilization and culture. We should recognize that whether it is language, literature, music, science, technology and all that, they are brilliant, the products of Europe. And, in fact, in our lives, in our external lives, we also are more or less reflections of this technological civilization. We are trying to build it up ourselves in our industry and our technology. That is probably true. And I hope we shall succeed in it. Nevertheless, the idea that went on striking me is something this man of spirit represents, something the spirit, whatever it may be which I do not know; I do not know in the sense that I cannot describe it to you. I cannot seize it or get a grip of it but I feel, it is something in its own way much bigger than these external features of civilization that we see. I do not say that it is necessarily in conflict with it but I do say that all the civilization in the world, minus some kind of spirit or spiritual background, may well be rather empty, and may well lead to wrong ends. It has led us to great wars, destructive wars, and it may lead us to even worse disaster unless checked by something of the spirit because logic and reason somehow cannot stand up before fear and apprehension and hatred and all that. It is only things of the spirit that can stand up to fear, that can stand up to hatred, that can stand up to violence and nothing can suppress the things of spirit because they are unafraid. How can you suppress a man who is unafraid? There is nothing to suppress. So, all these thoughts occurred to me these days when I was sitting with Vinoba Bhave and when we were looking at this India of ours, this peculiar amalgam of every century, from the earliest to the 20th Century. You see the latest techniques here or almost the latest techniques here and you also see the most primitive ways of living here. You see the highest forms of thinking, the highest flights of philosophy and the lowest and most degraded forms of practice. Everything you find, everything good, everything evil in this country and we have inherited both the good and the evil. How are we to keep to the good and nourish it and nourish ourselves with it and fight the evil? That is the problem before us and if we build up India we should only build it up as a worthwhile country, by nourishing the good, increasing it and taking nourishment from it for ourselves and suppressing the evil. What is evil? I do not know! How am I to define the good and evil? These are some things above definition but you feel it. Hatred is evil, violence is evil, anything that separates is evil; anything that joins is good. Well, you may accept that. You may have better definitions. So, in India everything that separates is evil, everything that joins is good; and we have enough separatist tendencies in India today, whether they are provincialism, statism, linguism, casteism and communalism. Even religion which is supposed to join us becomes a separating factor which is used and exploited.

So, everything that separates is bad. I think, that one of the basic failings of India in the last few years or maybe 1000 years or more I don't know, has been the caste system because it separated, because while doing some good in its own way, I do not deny that, but basically from the larger point of view, it encouraged narrowness of living. So, we have to get rid of all these barriers. Of course, ultimately we shall have to get rid even of the national barriers and begin to think more and more internationally and make friends with the world. Maybe, that is too big for us for the present although the choice is some kind of internationalism between nations. There is no other way and we should develop that, but some people when talking about internationalism become exceedingly woolly in their thinking and forget even nationalism. That is not internationalism, just as nationalism is not some kind of vague repetition of slogans and phrases. It should be something active, positive and not negative. So, internationalism, when it comes, should also be something active and not flabby nonsense as many people imagine it to be; they have no strong passions, therefore they are cosmopolitans. They have no feelings for this country or that therefore they say we are cosmopolitan, we are universal. Well, I have no great attachment or great regard for this kind of woolliness and flabbiness in thinking or living but nevertheless, I do believe in internationalism and I do believe we have to go that way.

When I wandered about the various parts of the world, it surprises me and it surprises me even more than ever, how good people are everywhere, how friendly they are, and how full of generosity and hospitality they are. Unless you touch them on some raw spot, unless you evoke some national hatred in them or more specially unless you touch some chord of fear in them. Then they lose all the basic hospitality, generosity, friendliness, because they are afraid—and nothing is more unreasonable than an animal that is afraid, he misbehaves, bites, and he shouts like a mad dog. I see all over the world, countries of all kinds, great and powerful countries like the United States of America which is supposed to be a capitalist country or a communist country like the Soviet Union, I find people there extraordinarily likeable, very friendly, very hospitable and just oozing the milk of human kindness. And yet the American or the Russian if he suddenly thinks, and mind you they are friendly to each other too, not that, but suddenly if you touch some chord of fear in them, then they are terribly afraid of each other. Oh! America is an imperialist power which will crush, which is always trying to intrigue against Russia. Then the Americans will say that these communists are scheming to put an end to us. And then all their fears and their passions are roused and there is no logic or reason. How can we get out of this business? Nobody in the world, I am sure some mad individuals apart, wants war. Everybody wants peace in every country and yet we go on preparing for war and wasting our substance in war because of fear. Well, there it is. Anyhow, when a person is young at the university or college, etc., one presumes, I hope my presumption is correct, that he is less liable to the fear-complex than grown-ups are. Take it as rigidity. When you get rigid in anything then it is difficult to change. Well, young people are not supposed to be rigid, although I must say sometimes in India people are born old and rigid. I cannot help that. But normally speaking, young people are not rigid, ought not to be rigid in mind. Just as they should be flexible in body, they should be flexible in mind and not tied down to fears and dogmas. I hope, the students in our universities will remain flexible but again flexibility does not mean flabbiness of body or mind. You have to train your minds just as you train your body. Make your minds, well, sharp and keen enough to be able to cut knots of many problems we may have to consider. But remember that the sign of civilization is tolerance, and the restraint you show. I suppose it might well be said that the measure of civilization is the restraint that the individual shows. That does not mean that he is passionless or that he does not feel strongly. Restraint is when you feel strongly and restrain yourself. A wooden horse may be a horse to look at but not much of a horse. It is the real fiery horse which, if you can restrain, shows that you are a horseman, because you are not sitting on a wooden thing and restraining it, there is no restraint about it. It is better if the horse runs away with you than your riding a wooden horse. So, we have to develop these basic qualities.

Now, coming to our Five Year Plans, we will produce and we should produce engineers by hundreds and thousands and they are absolutely essential, far more necessary than lawyers and the like, meaning no ill-will to the lawyers but merely pointing out that they are becoming less of the salt of the earth than they were. So, we shall produce all the engineers and of various types of technicians and technologists and the like and the scientists above all, but the fact remains that behind that there has to be certain basis, well, I hate to use the word 'spiritual basis' and I am not using it in any narrow sense at all, but certain standards, which one holds on to, certain culture, certain civilization, certain restraints and above all a certain living substance—life, because ultimately, if a community has life, then it does something. If it is just a semi-dead community without life, then nothing comes out of it, for a dead community there is no virtue or vice. It is life which is very important and I will tell you that the thing Gandhiji did in this country was to put life in it. So, we have to realize that the burden of building India is going to be carried by us and by nobody else. It is a dangerous thing and a fatal fallacy to imagine that others are going to pull us out and solve our problems. The moment a country begins to rely on others to solve its problems and to carry its burdens, that country is decadent and loses its vibrant life that a people should possess.

There is talk today that our Second Five Year Plan is in great difficulties. Of course, it is. We will be having difficulties and every person who wants to go ahead at a rapid pace, every community and every nation will constantly have difficulties. It is the measure of the effort that we are taking. It is the thing we should be proud of and it should enable us to gird up our loins all the more to face them and conquer. Of course, in the normal ways and dealings between nations, we welcome help. We are glad of it, we are grateful for it, we ask for it and if it comes we are grateful naturally. That is happening in the normal way. But the moment we begin to think that our future and even the future of the Plan depends on somebody else's generosity, then you have lost foot. You have slipped and it does not matter how much money you get you will not build yourselves up because the builders of India must be the people of India and nobody else. We can get ideas from abroad, we can get help from abroad, we can get cooperation from abroad, a hundred and one things but we must remember that it is we and we only, who can build up India and we can build it up by remembering two things and the two are slightly contradictory. One is that in the past, some hundreds of years ago, India became very isolated, cut itself off from the rest of the world almost, by thinking no end of itself. India became self-righteous by saying we are highly spiritual and we are very advanced. And we thought, there is no need to look to any other country. The others are *mlechas* or barbarians or whatever they may be and we are the advanced people. Any individual or nation which begins to think this way is already on the verge of stupidity and it will become more and more lost in itself because it has lost the art of growing. It has stopped. It is just trying to hold on to something and if you stop growing you become smaller, you fade off.

We had all kinds of strange customs, touch me not, do not eat with this man, do not marry that man, do not do this, do not do that. And if you go across the seas which is *Kala Pani*, you are kicked out of your caste, most amazing! Narrow-mindedness grew up in a nation which had been known for its adventurousness of thought, action and body. Our people had gone out to the whole of Asia and outside Asia too, a thousand and two thousand years ago as signs of India's cultures are present there. Here, we got confined in the cell of narrow-mindedness. So, we must not be narrow-minded. We must not be isolationist. We must keep our minds open and imbibe the knowledge, the learning and the wisdom of everybody. That is one sign of it. The other is doing all this, we should never allow ourselves to be uprooted from our soil. If you uproot yourself then you become rootless. You may be clever, you may be an able individual, perhaps with difficulty may find another root though it is difficult. But a nation does not do that, cannot do it, the whole community cannot do it, that is to say, essentially, you have to grow on the soil of India and the moment you discard it, disclaim it and deny it, then you are rootless. You can, as has been the genius of India, grow in any direction but maintaining your roots is important. If you merely imitate others, you cannot grow. You can learn from others and you have to learn a great deal from others but you cannot grow by imitativeness. Of course, today's world becomes more and more, shall I say, well, universal, and ideas and ways of living becoming more and more common. That is true. That is a natural process. We shall also adopt that and be affected by it and the people should also be affected by us. So, it is much late than I thought and I have got to rush, rush back to my aircraft and go off to Delhi. I might tell you I have to preside over an important meeting in Delhi at 5.00 p.m. today. Otherwise, I might have stayed on. Well, I do not know what you think of what I have said, but I have enjoyed talking to you. Thank you.

6. Stand by the Ideals of the UN[1]

Brothers and sisters,

The Syrian crisis has posed a serious threat to peace because the two major Powers, the United States and the Soviet Union, have come out in the open to back Turkey and Syria respectively.[2] Any new war would only lead to the

1. Speech at a mass meeting organized by the United Nations Association of the Delhi Pradesh Congress Committee on the occasion of the twelfth anniversary of the founding of the United Nations, Ramlila Grounds, Delhi, 24 October 1957. From *The Hindu* and *The Statesman*, 25 October 1957. Sushila Nayar, President of the Association, presided over the meeting.

2. From mid-September 1957 onwards, the situation in the Middle East deteriorated as a result of Soviet and Syrian allegations of Turkish troop concentrations on the Syrian border aimed at invading Syria and overthrowing the existing regime with the help of the United States. These were denied by the Turkish and US Governments and both of which stressed that the tension arose primarily from Soviet attempts to convert Syria into a Communist "satellite" by supplying arms to her.

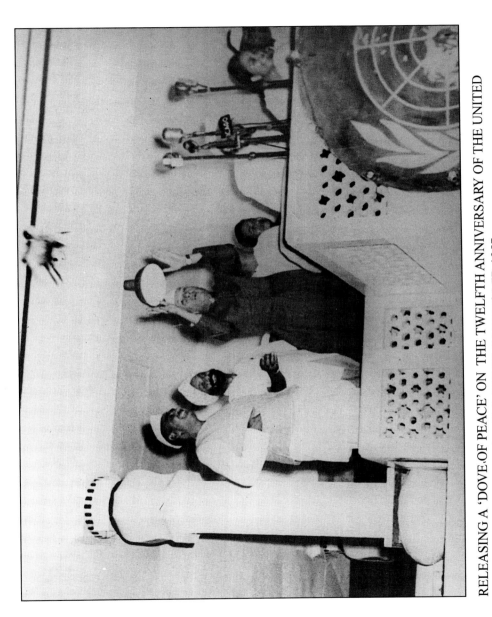

RELEASING A 'DOVE OF PEACE' ON THE TWELFTH ANNIVERSARY OF THE UNITED
NATIONS, RAMLILA GROUNDS, DELHI, 24 OCTOBER 1957

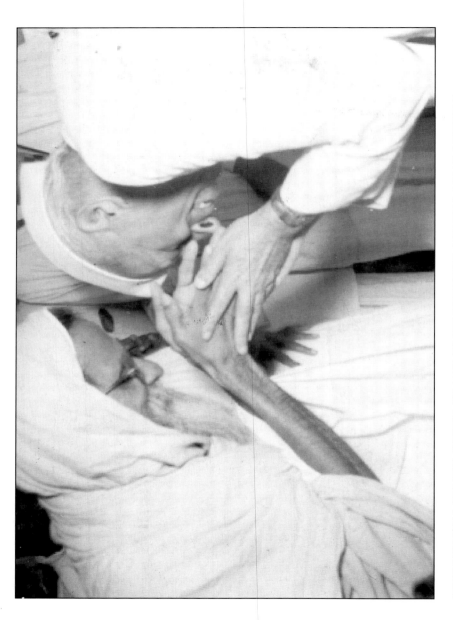

WITH VINOBA BHAVE AT THE *GRAMDAN* CONFERENCE, YELWAL NEAR MYSORE,
21 SEPTEMBER 1957

(Courtesy: HT Photo Library)

destruction of the world because of the new weapons forged by the big Powers which would make the last War look like child's play.

We live nowadays in danger of annihilation and destruction. We stand on a precipice from where we might have already tumbled down but for the UN. I can only hope that as far as Syria is concerned the present discussions at the UN would prove fruitful and that a peaceful solution of the problem would be found.

The UN Day is being celebrated everywhere today and it is but appropriate that on this occasion the people of India should take a look at its achievements and shortcomings. Representatives of the free nations of the world are now meeting in New York to thrash out various questions of international concern. There are endless arguments, and many questions remained unsolved. The UN had not been able to solve several problems. The question of Kashmir, with which India is concerned, is there and so is the question of apartheid in South Africa. The sufferings of the Algerian people in their struggle for freedom has not evoked a solution yet. Lately, the question of Syria has assumed significance. When such big questions are not solved, it is natural to ask what the UN has achieved. But one should also look at the other side of the picture and ask what would have been the fate of the world if there had been no United Nations. In its 12 years of existence the UN has averted one or two big wars. There is no doubt about it. I am sure that if the UN had not been there, the problems of the world would have been much worse.

Any criticism of the UN should not overlook the fact that it represented independent nations of the world governed by their own policies and approaches. There is an atmosphere of tension, hatred and hostility in the world and it is no fault of the UN if it reflected this atmosphere to some extent. I, however, hope that the UN would become a very effective instrument for achieving world peace. Asia is not well represented at present in the world body. Nevertheless, it is the duty of everyone to stand by the ideals of the UN and to strengthen the cause of peace.

I visited Japan recently[3] and prior to that the Scandinavian countries[4] and wherever I went, I was warmly received with love and affection. This demonstration of love and affection by the people of various countries I have visited is not for me as an individual or the country that I represent but the ideals and principles that India has been advocating. India's voice of peace is being heard everywhere with respect and whether in Japan, China, Russia or the United States, it has won the hearts, of course, of peace-loving peoples.

3. From 4 to 13 October 1957.
4. Nehru was on a goodwill tour of Denmark, Finland, Norway and Sweden from 15 to 25 June 1957.

41

I go to these countries to make friends, not to make enemies. There I lay emphasis on things on which we have common views. Although Japan and China do not share with India views on several matters, they have also much in common with India. On many issues on which they had different views, they held friendly discussions.

I have no doubt that the policy of non-alignment and pursuit of peace that India has been following is the right and logical policy for this country. It is derived from the great principles laid down by Emperor Asoka several centuries ago. We may make mistakes here and there but the basic policy will remain. It is a sound policy and has had its impact on the peace-loving nations of the world. Ultimately, a true and right policy will always succeed, and I have no doubt that our policy provides the right approach to the problems confronting the world. It takes note of the passionate desire for peace on the part of the peoples of the world whatever may be the line adopted by Governments or various countries.

Wherever I went I emphasized the points of agreement between India and those countries. This way India is able to strengthen her friendship with various countries and promote greater cooperation. This does not mean that I had not faced the differences with other nations squarely. But a right approach always helped to clear misunderstandings and lead to a large measure of agreement on various issues.

India stands against military alliances and blocs because she values her independence and freedom of action. We do not want to fight any one, we want the friendship of all. But where would we be if we barter away our freedom. As far as I can see, I do not see how any Government in India in the next ten or one hundred or one thousand years can basically change the policy that we are pursuing. The country would become strong only through this policy and any deviation from the path would make India untrue to herself.

Mahatma Gandhi's teaching that means are as important as the ends held good not only for individuals but also for nations. Nations which followed that principle may suffer temporary setbacks but they will never be defeated. Mahatma Gandhi had preached to the world the Gospel of Ahimsa. We take pride in what Gandhiji had taught us. But we tend to forget the core of his teachings. We go on wrong channels indulging in petty quarrels and overlooking national interests.

The recent riots in Ramanathapuram district in Madras between two castes do not do credit to India abroad. In Punjab, in the name of saving Hindi, a strange performance has been going on for six months.[5] I am not going into its details now but I only mention it to show that however good the ends might be,

---

5. A Save Hindi agitation was started on 27 September 1957 to protest against the language policy of the Punjab Government.

a wrong approach cannot yield the desired results. The Hindi agitation is ruining Punjab and I feel very sad about it. I cannot understand what the agitators want to achieve. Even if it is supposed that Government has made some mistakes, is that the way to correct things? It is a strange thing that young men go to jail in the name of satyagraha when the ways adopted by them are a negation of satyagraha. Some people have taken the name of President Rajendra Prasad in connection with the language agitation in Punjab. The President expressed to me his pain at his name being dragged into the controversy.

In these days of tremendous advance of science when attempts are being made to conquer space, it is rather odd that some people here shall be indulging in petty things. The world is changing a great deal. We in India have to change our mental outlook. The Ramanathapuram riots and the Punjab language agitation have demonstrated how far we are left behind. I wonder how the young men of today can build up the country if they cannot fit into the new rhythm of life that has opened before us.

While Indians had spread the message and culture of this country to countries like Japan, China, Mongolia, Cambodia and Indonesia several hundred years ago, today we prefer to be frogs in the well. We are still bound down by caste distinctions and outmoded customs. We fight over small things. It is time that the country get rid of such things and seize the opportunities to go ahead.

There is a movement in the South that Hindi should not be forced down on the people there. This is a reaction produced by the Hindi agitation in Punjab. The Language Commission has submitted its report and its recommendations have to be viewed in the right perspective.[6]

I know that people in the South, in Andhra and Tamil Nad and other parts, are learning Hindi with enthusiasm. At the same time, any attempt to force Hindi on them will not succeed. Coercion will only produce opposite results. The decisions on the Language Commission report should, therefore, be based on understanding and not coercion. Only with cooperation and understanding from the people that any decision be peacefully implemented.

The country's difficulties in implementing the Second Plan are the inevitable outcome of our efforts to make rapid progress. These difficulties must be faced with courage and determination. Our Finance Minister has visited several countries and tried to make arrangements for loans and he is due in a day or two. He will tell us what he has been able to achieve. It is possible that some

---

6. The Official Language Commission, constituted on 7 June 1955, submitted its report on 6 August 1956 to the President. It was presented in the Parliament on 12 August. For details see *post*, p. 204.

arrangements might be made for meeting our requirements. But there is no need to be frightened or alarmed in the event of our not getting substantial foreign assistance. One thing that we have to remember is that whatever be the assistance that we may get, ultimately we can march ahead only through our own efforts. We must willingly bear any burdens in the process of building up our country.

The other difficulty that the country is experiencing is the failure of rains in some parts of the country such as Bihar, Uttar Pradesh, Orissa, Chattisgarh and Maharashtra. A good harvest had been hoped for but the rains failed and the crops suffered damage. Fate has cheated us. We must prepare to meet the situation calmly. In the last three or four days, however, a few showers have been reported in some of the areas. Perhaps they may do some good. *Jai Hind!*

7. Stop Indulging in Petty Squabbles[1]

The most important problem facing us is to ensure the speedy realization of the economic changes envisaged in the country's Five Year Plans. We must pay concerted attention to this aspect of national life. We cannot afford to fritter away our energies in petty quarrels like linguistic issues and caste differences. If we indulge in linguistic and provincial squabbles in this atomic age, when international boundaries tend to appear more notional than real, then it is doubtful whether we can bestir ourselves to the task of building the economic edifice of free India.

In the modern world, we are face to face with the progress of science, the atom and its uses, both destructive and possibly beneficial uses for mankind. Man has come in possession of a vital force through the discovery of atomic energy. And technology, the child of science, has changed the fundamentals of world thought and the relations between nations. We have to understand the implications of such tremendous progress in the scientific field in relation to India's role both for the progress and promotion of her own economic and social interests and her relationship with the nations of the world.

---

1. Speech at a public meeting, Vadodara, 26 October 1957. From *The Hindu* and *The Hindustan Times*, 27 October 1957.

At home also, things are changing fast and many changes are taking place in the spheres of industry, production and expansion of economy. Those changes may not appear fast enough to some people who talk of revolution and revolutionary changes. But the changes of which they talk meant violent changes, bomb-cult and such other violent acts. Such an approach to the economic problems of an underdeveloped country like India can only serve a spectacular or demonstrative purpose but will not bring about the desired change in the standard of life of the common man.

Thus a great responsibility rested on our shoulders. We must look back and assess the contributions we have made for the welfare of the millions in the past and look ahead to plan out what we can do for promoting the welfare of the millions of our countrymen. This can be successfully accomplished only if we understand the problems before us in the context of world affairs.

Instead of encouraging noble missions and keeping up the traditions of the past, a section of the people raised social barriers some decades ago against travel overseas and imposed several hardships on those who dared. The result was that various types of social disabilities came into existence and today we suffer from most humiliating caste distinctions and in some cases, as in Ramanathapuram, from caste conflicts.

One of the basic problems before free India is how to root out completely the weeds of parochialism, sectarianism and such narrow prejudices and re-establish the spirit of nationalism. It is true that the people of a particular state or religion love their language but it is very difficult to understand how any sensible people can carry on an agitation for or against such issues. That betrays complete ignorance or inability to understand the lessons of history of this country.

We have to remember the task of ensuring the success of economic plans before the nation. Talking big will not solve problems of national reconstruction. To talk of socialism or any other ism without real national effort on a planned basis is unrealistic and will not take the country ahead. Therefore, the Government has prepared plans for the coordinated and orderly development of the nation's economic life.

It is true that we are confronted with the problem of foreign exchange when we are entering an important stage of the Second Plan. Such a difficulty is bound to crop up in an underdeveloped economy and the remedy lay not in holding out one's hand in despair but in trying to overcome the difficulty by constructive efforts. That is why our Finance Minister has gone on a mission with the object of finding out if foreign assistance of loan can be obtained for the complete execution of our Plan.

We have to remember that our responsibility and burden, of fulfilling the Plan will not be lessened even if the needed foreign aid is available. We have to bear the brunt of planned development by a greater resolve and accelerated effort for increased production, so that the burden on the shoulders of the common man can be minimized.

The Community Development Schemes are really revolutionary in concept. They have produced remarkable results in nearly two and half lakh villages of the country in the last five years. But the tempo of this success has to be kept up, and production potential of those developed village units shall be maintained. Otherwise all the plans of development will fail and thereby increase our dependence on imported foodgrains.

This objective of increasing the production to a certain extent can be achieved through village cooperatives and village panchayats. The former can encourage cooperative farming so that small holders who cannot adopt modernized methods of production will also be benefited. And the village panchayats will concentrate on increasing the production of village and small-scale industries. This will open fresh avenues of employment and encourage production of indigenous goods.

During my recent visit to Japan and Europe,[2] what has impressed me the most in war-ravaged Japan and Western Germany is the enormous rebuilding the people of those countries had accomplished within a period of twelve years. Another thing which impressed me is the fact that the people of those countries have a high respect for India and her people. That is because the pioneers from India had crossed the high seas carrying the message of peace to distant lands.

2. After visiting the Scandinavian countries from 15 to 25 June 1957, he attended the Commonwealth Prime Ministers' Conference in London from 26 June to 5 July. Subsequently, he was in the Netherlands on 8 and 9 July. For his Japan tour, see *post*, pp. 550-626.

2
NATIONAL PROGRESS

I. ECONOMY

1. To T.T. Krishnamachari[1]

New Delhi
August 2, 1957

My dear TT,[2]

A friend, whose integrity and earnestness I value, has written to me in some distress.[3] I do not agree with his views about some matters, but I am glad that he has written to me, as, I take it, he represents a viewpoint which is perhaps widely held.

As you and I should know these currents of opinion, I am giving below some kind of a summary of what he has written. It is our business to carry every shade of public opinion with us without sacrificing any principle. In fact, even when we oppose any person, we try to put our position in a way so as to hurt him as little as possible, that is, to put it at the lowest in a politician's way.

The friend, to whom I have referred, lays stress on the difficulties of our tasks, more particularly in a democratic set-up, to which we must, of course, adhere. The first thing we have to do is to create, as far as possible, a healthy, brotherly and comradely climate and show our goodwill to all concerned, so that every section should feel that our measures are meant for its good also as well as others. Even if it hurts somebody, or some section, he or that section should be made to feel that we aim at their good, though the overall interests of the country necessitate our taking some steps. Thus, even when we hurt, we are trying to soothe.

The main point stressed is that our approach should be friendly to every section and individual and nothing should be said which might irritate or frighten. At present, according to him, a wave of fear, founded or unfounded, has gripped many people because of our taxation measures and what has been said in regard to them. There is a crisis of confidence when confidence is so necessary for us.

This argument is not concerned with the actual measures, but rather with the effect produced by the way they have been put forward.

1. JN Collection.
2. Union Minister of Finance.
3. Manubhai Shah, Union Minister of State for Industry, had sent a note to Nehru through U.N. Dhebar.

Reference is then made by him to the scheme for compulsory deposits which, according to him, has created a depressing climate; also to the publicity given to the buying of shares by Insurance Companies and Corporations in India. He does not object to this being done, but to the manner of doing it and to the publicity given to it which destroys the faith not only of the industrialists, but of the middle class people by making them think that this is a device to expropriate and acquire the enterprises.

He goes on to say that the running down of our propertied classes, though justified often, ends in demoralizing not only them, but the large middle class and even the lower middle class.

Reference is made to the taxing of Joint Stock Companies in the Wealth Tax. This, according to him, will result in a tendency of formation of private limited and partnership companies which will be unhealthy and a reversal of a social process.

Further, he refers to the inevitable harassment and irritation which would be caused to the people in the collection of Expenditure Tax and Wealth Tax,[4] which again will create a great deal of public antagonism and wealth will go underground.

I have given you, in brief, what he has written to me in some pain and anguish. I do not agree with some of his analysis of the measures. But, if it is true that there is some kind of a fear and demoralization setting in in large sections of the public, then we should try to check this tendency and soothe the people. We have to deal not only with our Party in Parliament, but the people generally and have to carry them with us, more especially in these times of crisis.

As you know, I am entirely with you in the taxation measures that you have suggested. The only thing that has worried me and to which I have given utterance, is my fear of harassment and intrusion of the tax collector, in private lives.

I am writing to you because I thought you should be informed of what many people think and do not always say. I myself was a little surprised to get this letter.

Yours sincerely,
Jawaharlal Nehru

4. The Wealth Tax Act, passed by the Lok Sabha on 29 August and the Rajya Sabha on 5 September 1957, provided for an annual tax on the net wealth of individuals and Hindu undivided families. It also formulated rules to determine the value of assets and tax rates. The Expenditure Tax Act, passed by the Lok Sabha on 4 September and Rajya Sabha on 11 September 1957, provided for an annual tax on personal expenditure above a prescribed limit by individuals and Hindu undivided families.

2. To N.C. Thimma Reddy[1]

New Delhi
August 4, 1957

Dear Thimma Reddy,

Thank you for your letter of the 3rd August, which I have just received and read with interest.[2]

It is not clear to me how the loan you mention, can be obtained. If it is obtainable, we would welcome it. The Finance Minister is obviously most interested in this matter, and we have sent some of our senior officers connected with the Finance Ministry to foreign countries for this purpose. The Finance Minister is himself going to the United States for a meeting of the World Bank next month.[3] I have no doubt he will explore all feasible avenues. I am forwarding your letter to him.

Yours sincerely,
Jawaharlal Nehru

1. JN Collection.
2. Reddy wrote about the possibility of securing a loan of 2000 million Dollars from the Export and Import Bank of Washington, channelled through England or Germany. Since the rules of the Bank did not permit loans except on exports or services from America, such loans could be arranged or advanced through the exports from America into Germany or England. This would mean that India's creditor countries would be Germany and England from whom India could get credit on the same terms as they got from the US.
3. T.T. Krishnamachari left on 17 September 1957.

3. Wealth and Expenditure Taxes[1]

The Minister of Finance gave a brief account of the representations received against the imposition of Wealth and Expenditure Taxes and gave details of the

1. Minutes of the Cabinet Meeting, New Delhi, 7 August 1957. JN Collection.

concessions he had in mind to reduce hardship in certain cases. A general discussion followed in the course of which it was suggested that companies might be altogether exempted from Wealth Tax. No final decisions were taken, but there was general agreement that harassment should be reduced to the minimum in the levy and collection of the taxes.

2. The Prime Minister reminded the Cabinet that these taxation measures etc., had to be considered not merely with regard to their immediate efforts but also to the extent to which they would help or hinder production in the country and the success of the Five Year Plan. In spite of the foreign exchange gap and other difficulties, production had to be increased and the taxation policy of Government should be geared up to secure this objective.

4. Expenditure on Foreign Dignitaries[1]

Questions similar to the one attached have been sent to me and I have ventured to point out to Mr Speaker[2] that any comparisons of expenditure in regard to foreign dignitaries is likely to prove embarrassing to them as well as to us. Further that, it is difficult for us to have full figures of the State Governments' expenditure on such occasions.

2. I would respectfully suggest to Mr Speaker that part (b) of this question may not be allowed for the reasons stated above. If it is desired that we should give a list of foreign dignitaries who came here from 1955 to 1957 or those who are expected to come in the current year, we shall endeavour to give this information. But I would prefer not to give comparative figures of expenditure.[3]

1. Note to Lok Sabha Secretariat, New Delhi, 9 August 1957. JN Collection.
2. M. Ananthasayanam Ayyangar.
3. However, in response to a question in the Lok Sabha on 5 August, Nehru gave the following figures of expenditure incurred on the visits of foreign dignitaries during the previous three financial years: 1954-55—Rs 7,57,156; 1955-56—Rs 22,21,535; and 1956-57—Rs 21,50,000.

5. Economy Measures[1]

Radha Raman[2] and eighteen others: Will the Prime Minister be pleased to state:

(a) whether Government have decided to take suitable economy measures to cut down its expenditure in certain respects;

(b) if so, the steps taken in this direction;

(c) whether it has been decided to set up economy units in all Ministries;

(d) if so, with what specific instructions; and

(e) the amount of money that would be saved as a result of economy drive?

Jawaharlal Nehru: (a) to (d). With a view to ensure that the Government's financial and other resources are utilized to the best possible advantage, it was recently decided that each Minister and Secretary should give urgent and continuous attention to the maintenance of efficiency, integrity and economy in the administration. To this end, they have been called upon to review the nature, volume and quality of the work at all levels and to take practical steps to remove deficiencies and to effect economies. In this task, they will be advised and assisted by the Economy Unit of the Ministry of Finance and Organization and Methods Division of the Cabinet Secretariat.

In pursuance of this decision, all the Ministries and Departments have set up internal machinery in the form of Economy Committees. These Committees are engaged in the scrutiny of the present and projected activities to see whether some of them can be reduced, postponed or abandoned. The Committees are also reviewing the levels of expenditure on staff and contingencies, so that revised and more austere standards may be adopted and enforced.

Orders have already been issued in all Ministries, directing that no new posts should be created and no existing vacancies filled without the personal approval of the Secretary, and calling upon all concerned to observe the utmost economy in the expenditure on travelling allowances and on items such as furniture, stationery, electricity, telegrams, telephones and the like.

(e) It is not possible, at this stage to give a full estimate of the savings which may be effected as a result of these measures, which are still in progress. A

1. Reply to a question in the Lok Sabha, 9 August 1957. *Lok Sabha Debates* (second series), Vol. V, col. 7693-7699. Extracts.
2. Congress Member from Chandni Chowk, Delhi.

statement is, however, placed on the Table of the House to indicate the decisions which have so far been taken in the different Ministries and Departments, and the approximate savings expected ....

Tarkeshwari Sinha:[3] Is it a fact that in the debates on the budget, it has been pointed out by so many Members that over-budgeting is taking place, that is, an amount that is allotted in a particular budget is not spent and again the same amount is brought forward for the next year's budget? May I know what action the Government has taken or proposes to take to see that this over-budgeting does not take place and suitable ways and means are found to see that an amount that has not been spent is not brought forward in the next year's budget in toto?

JN: It is a question with which the Finance Minister could deal with more profitably. But, I will say this about what is called over-budgeting. Let us take the External Affairs Ministry. We want a number of new Missions opened. They agree and they are provided for. Yet, we do not open them under pressure of circumstances. Or, on the other hand, take defence. We just cannot get the things which we want to get. They are not available. We want them the next year. It is not that we do not want them. We just cannot get because of difficulties. That kind of over-budgeting is inevitable. That type of over-budgeting, to put in more money than is really necessary, is of a different type which should, of course, be avoided. That is a matter of finance.

So far as this question of economy is concerned, under stress of circumstances, we do not get something which we want. A great measure of economy has been achieved by abandoning projects, big economy by abandoning a project or postponing it till better days. For instance, the Ministry of Mines and Fuel and the Department of Iron and Steel have abandoned some projects and thereby, for the moment, saved about Rs 2 crores, and Rs 1,87,00,000. This is a kind of economy in the sense that we do not do what we intended to do, because we thought we could postpone.

Hem Barua:[4] Is it drilling operation?

JN: I believe it includes some drilling somewhere.

The other type of economy, the normal type, of course, is seeing that there is no waste, etc. That is right approach to this question. I do not suppose the House or anybody wants economy to be achieved at the cost of efficiency. That is no economy at all. That is wasteful. Inefficient working is the most wasteful of all. Nowadays, there are what might be called scientific methods of computing work, and work-study methods which, I believe, started originally in the United States

3. Congress Member from Barh, Bihar.
4. PSP Member from Guwahati, Assam.

in industrial concerns. Gradually, they were applied to administrative offices. Most countries have adopted them and thereby effected considerable savings with increase of efficiency, just seeing how a particular job can be done more efficiently and with the least energy, if I might say so. You can see that in industrial establishments. You can see that in higher techniques and all that. But it is not so easily visible in administration. But it can be done, and it has been done. Considerable changes have been made.

Even in England, last year, I noticed this in various Departments. I was surprised at the good results of this work-study. The work-study method is being adopted by our Methods and Organization Department. It takes time, that is, studying the methods of work and little things such as where a file goes to or not and so on. You save time thereby. You save waste.

So, these are the various methods which are being adopted.

Parvathi Krishnan:[5] The statement laid on the Table refers to economy measures that are being instituted with regard to administration, that is, decrease in the number of posts and so on. But, apart from that, I would like to know what measures are being taken to check the large amount that is being spent on travelling allowances of various officers and officials and committees both inside the country and when they go outside.

JN: There can be no precise rule about travelling allowance, except that only unavoidable travelling should be indulged in. Those instructions have been issued. As to the results of this, possibly, it may be estimated partly, but on the whole, it cannot be estimated. For instance, for people going abroad, we apply a much stricter rule now; in the case of people going abroad, unless it is absolutely necessary, we do not encourage them to go abroad.

Internally, each Ministry has to deal with the matters. We have told them that they should avoid travelling unless it is really necessary.

Mahanty:[6] May I know whether about 40 peons or attendants have been retrenched as a result of the economy measures of the Government of India, in the Central Secretariat?

JN: I could not give the number, but of course, a number have been. But, as a matter of fact, so far as I know—I speak subject to correction—we do not want normally to retrench people. Certainly, we do not retrench any permanent employees even if they are unwanted; we try to find some other place for them. So, when we talk about retrenchment, that means that one Ministry is giving them up for the moment, and we have to provide for them elsewhere...

---

5. CPI Member from Coimbatore, Tamil Nadu.
6. Surendra Mahanty, Ganatantra Parishad Member from Dhenkanal, Orissa.

Surendranath Dwivedy:[7] My question was this. The Taxation Enquiry Commission had suggested that a high-powered body should be appointed to go into the question of expenditure on non-developmental schemes, in order to bring about economy in those schemes. May I know why Government have not appointed such a body and this matter of economy is being examined Ministry by Ministry?

JN: The honourable Member did not listen carefully to what I said. We have got, first of all, a department of the Cabinet Secretariat, called the Methods and Organization Department, whose chief function is to be continuously doing this, and doing it, if I may use the word, rather scientifically, to measure the output of work and see how efficiently and how economically it can be done and also otherwise trying to economize.

Apart from that, what the honourable Member said has actually been done, that is, each Ministry is dealing with this. I do not remember what the Taxation Enquiry Commission said about a commission. But personally, I do not see how a commission, unless the commission itself is a permanent one sitting year after year, looking into the work, and coming and sitting in an office—can give any useful advice....

7. PSP Member from Kendrapara, Orissa.

6. To T.T. Krishnamachari[1]

New Delhi
August 11, 1957

My dear T.T.,

Have you given thought to an attempt being made to get foreign exchange from Indians abroad.[2] I think I mentioned this matter to you briefly the other day. The Chinese Communist Government has made many such appeals and, I believe, has met with some success in getting money from Chinese overseas.

1. T.T. Krishnamachari Papers, NMML. Also available in File No. 37(35)/56-59-PMS and JN Collection.
2. India was facing foreign exchange problems due to, according to a Reserve Bank study, excess expenditure on imports of (i) food, (ii) raw materials, (iii) machinery, iron & steel and other metals, and (iv) a number of manufactured items.

FINDING THE WAY OUT

THE ECONOMIC SITUATION

Besides Nehru, Cabinet colleagues Morarji Desai, Gulzari Lal Nanda, Govind Ballabh Pant and T.T. Krishnamachari.

"FINDING THE WAY OUT", A CARTOON FROM *SHANKAR'S WEEKLY*, 18 AUGUST 1957

The Prime Minister has defended Mr T.T. Krishnamachari's recent statements.

Leftist leaders Renu Chakravarti, Ajoy Ghosh and A.K. Gopalan complain to Nehru of Finance Minister Krishnamachari's utterances, which, they think, are incompatible with a Socialistic pattern of society.

"THE KID", A CARTOON FROM *SHANKAR'S WEEKLY*, 27 OCTOBER 1957

Even if we cannot get any very large sum from Indians in other countries, I do not see why we should not make this attempt. We shall certainly get some money and, apart from the sum involved, this is psychologically a good thing to do for them and for us. It makes them interested in India's problems and India's development.

At present, there are, I believe, some restrictions in the way of Indians abroad sending money to India. I do not quite know what they are, but surely they can be relaxed so as to encourage them to send money. We would probably get a fair sum from East Africa, Hong Kong, Singapore and maybe other places.

You know that I shall be passing through Hong Kong on my way back from Japan in October. If previously an appeal is made not only to Hong Kong but to other places, perhaps my visit could give a fillip to it. I would not like to make that appeal myself when I am there, though I can refer to it privately.

The other day I was told that the sugar factories in Maharashtra (several of them are cooperatives) could begin functioning from October and thus produce much more sugar and give much more money in the shape of taxes both to the Government of India and the State Government. But they are unable to start work soon because of some rather petty difficulties. I am not quite sure what these difficulties are. It has something to do with some loan being given to them at this stage or perhaps it is some part of a machine which they must have. The Bombay Government, it is said, insists on their buying these machines in India and they cannot get it in time. Could this matter not be looked into?

There is another small matter which has been mentioned to me. At Santa Cruz Airport near Bombay, there is a bookstall. Large numbers of foreigners come and they want to buy not only books but the other articles displayed. They want to pay in foreign exchange but that particular bookstall is not allowed to deal with foreign exchange, the reason being that some other bookstall in some other distant part of the Airport has got the license for the foreign exchange. I suggest that wherever foreigners congregate, these facilities should be given to them to buy things in foreign exchange.[3]

Yours sincerely,
Jawaharlal Nehru

---

3. Nehru also wrote to Y.B. Chavan, the Chief Minister of Bombay, on the same day regarding the sugar factories and the bookstall at the Santa Cruz Airport.

7. Stout Hearts and Cool Minds to face Stormy Weather[1]

Comrades,

When I asked just now what was on the agenda, Algurai[2] could not tell me. We are holding this meeting because the Rajya Sabha has been convened from today and our Party should be in full strength. There are many things to discuss. You know that in the last fortnight or so, there has been a great deal of talk of strike, by the Posts & Telegraph Department and some others too.[3] It is obvious that such a strike would cause a lot of inconvenience to everyone and does not benefit anyone. Some people feel that their demands are justified and so they have a right to strike. Others feel that it is rather irresponsible of them to keep threatening to go on strike and there ought to be a confrontation. I feel that both these views are wrong. Whatever our differences of opinion, we should remember that we have to think of a joint line of action, not by attacking or pushing one another around. That is not the right way. So, we have to form a plan of action by understanding the problem and by compromise. There will be difficulties, but they ought to be overcome. After all, in times of war, there are innumerable difficulties, losses etc., that cause much sorrow; by comparison, these are nothing.

There are many facets to these strikes, many problems. You will see that in the terms of reference of the Commission which is being set up[4] these problems are mentioned because we want them to be enquired into. On the one hand, it is obvious that the burden on the Postal authorities and others has increased. That is a fact. On the other hand, it can be argued that compared to the others, their condition is much better. This also cannot be doubted. Both these things are

---

1. Speech at a meeting of the Congress Parliamentary Party, New Delhi, 12 August 1957. Tape No. M 26/c (i), NMML. Nehru first spoke in Hindi.
2. Algurai Shastri was Secretary, Congress Party in Parliament and Rajya Sabha Member from Uttar Pradesh.
3. The Posts and Telegraph Employees' Federation and the National Council of the Confederation of Central Government Employees' Unions gave a call for a nationwide strike from the midnight of 8 and 9 August 1957, if their demands for appointment of a pay commission and merger of dearness allowance with pay were not met.
4. The reference is to the Second Pay Commission, appointed by the Central Government on 3 August 1957 under the chairmanship of Justice B. Jagannatha Das.

right. It is also true that the economic condition prevailing in India today is by no means good. It is a difficult situation. And it is not feasible for us to take any step which may add to those difficulties. Suppose we concede their demands and as a result prices shoot up, they will remain where they were and the country would suffer. So, these are the problems. There is no question of our party or Government or Parliament wanting to suppress anyone's genuine demands. They are our own people. There is no question of suppressing them. We have to solve the problem by trying to make them understand. I feel very disturbed by the fact that in any situation we deteriorate rapidly to threats etc. It is not easy to consider matters coolly under such circumstances. So, I am keen to find a way to prevent the situation from deteriorating. As far as possible, let us take up the problems as they arise and try to solve them and if we cannot solve them, let us explain why they cannot be solved.

Moreover, there is a good deal of difference between the conditions of Government servants and industrial labour in big factories. It can be said of any sector that their employees should be paid in proportion to what they produce. You can imagine as to how much wealth is being produced in the factories, so industrial labour must get more. Now, the government machinery does not produce much, it is merely bureaucratic work. In the third category fall services like the Posts & Telegraph, the Railways, Municipality etc. etc., who are intimately connected with the day-to-day lives of people. So, we are trying to find ways and means to settle this matter in a just manner.

Now, I want to talk of the Government departments. To some extent, there is provision for interdepartmental consultations, but it is not enough. In two ways it is not good enough. One, these staff committee meetings etc., take place only when matters reach a crisis point. Secondly, only the demands of the moment are taken note of and examined. This is not right. The staff committees should meet and consider things like staff efficiency, possible improvements in the working of an office etc., and it is wrong to think that only a minister or a secretary or high-ranking officials can express their opinion in these matters. Obviously, their views are very important but I feel that everyone can help to throw some light on common problems. There should be an atmosphere in the offices in which people can come together to examine how to improve the working of the office, how complaints can be dealt with and not meet only when there is a dispute. It is not easy to change the atmosphere at once. In other countries, there are certain arrangements for this kind of thing – in England, in the government offices, you may have heard of the Whitley Councils etc.

etc.[5] In the beginning they had a lot of difficulties. There was no mutual trust. Those who occupied higher posts were rather puffed up. But gradually things changed and officers began to understand how to deal with their subordinates. The latter also began to be aware that all of them were working towards a common goal, for the good of all. So, the atmosphere changed, work improved and matters began to be dealt with as and when they arose. I think, they have an Arbitration Board to deal with service matters. It is not a tribunal composed of outsiders but of service members themselves. And I have heard that disputes seldom go higher up for settlement, they are dealt with within the service. This shows that an atmosphere of mutual trust and cooperation exists. We must try to bring about this in our country also. We are seeking recourse, more and more often, to strikes etc., wherever a dispute arises. The country is strangely disturbed, and common sense seldom prevails. Well, I suppose, this is not peculiar to India alone, but is true of other countries too. Perhaps it is the spirit of the times. But we have to deal with it with understanding and not in a momentary passion. Otherwise there would be total disruption.

So, whether it concerns government employees or bigger issues are involved, it has become imperative that we should think about these things coolly and dispassionately keeping in mind the basic principles. Otherwise, there can be a lot of damage. You see the picture that our country presents at the moment. Student unrest and other disturbances, in Punjab, in Assam and elsewhere, I won't go into all that. I am merely pointing out the lay of the land. There is total want of trust. Backbiting, petty bickerings and attempts to solve problems with force, pressure, slogan-mongering, etc. etc. This is not a good sign for a nation. No one is going to benefit. But this is what is happening. So, at least we in Parliament, in the Congress, should consider these matters calmly and not get carried away. We should not indulge in loose talk, in Parliament or outside which may lead to an increase in tensions. This responsibility rests with all of us. The Budget session is ahead.

5. In Britain, a good deal of procedure was evolved for the solution of staff problems in the Civil Service. There were "recognized" Civil Service Associations with rights to be consulted on issues concerning its members. The Whitley Councils, set up in 1919 in various departments with a Civil Service National Whitley Council, sought to secure the greatest measure of cooperation between the administration and the general body of staff with a view to increase efficiency combined with the well-being of the employees. There were local Whitley Councils in a city, regional ones for particular regions and country-wide councils to deal with points which were of interest to the members throughout the country. Apart from these, there were in each ministry, one or more Welfare Officers whose full-time duty was to look after the welfare of the staff. In 1957, there were 28 Chief Welfare Officers in Whitehall.

Now, I think, I have spoken for a long time in Hindi, I shall say a few words in English.

I have just been referring to the recent facts of strikes etc., which happily are over.[6] We had to issue an Ordinance only a few days ago.[7] You may have heard both in the Lok Sabha and in the Rajya Sabha today that it was stated that the Government have advised and requested the President to revoke that Ordinance because it is not considered necessary.[8] The Ordinance would not have been passed if the need for it had not been thought to be urgent and immediate, otherwise normally we would have waited for the normal course of events. If we want to pass any legislation, we go to both the Houses. But the Rajya Sabha was not meeting then and fortunately as that particular emergency has passed, there was no need for the Ordinance left, and as I said the Government have advised the President and requested him to revoke it. Neither the Ordinance was there, nor did we bring in that Bill to threaten people, to frighten them. We were compelled by circumstances to take steps to protect essential services. Now that the threat to them no longer is there, there is no need for the Ordinance.

We all know that people have to face difficulties owing to rise in prices[9], cost of living etc. No doubt the Posts and Telegraph people as well as other Government employees have to face these difficulties but also you know very well that there are others in State Governments who are probably and unfortunately worse off than the Posts and Telegraph people. Thus there are the States' employees, who are certainly worse off. There are others like teachers and others who are worse off still, so that the problem is not confined to one group of employees. We must have sympathy for them, at the same time we have to view the picture as a whole. That is why in the terms of reference to the proposed Commission of Enquiry, we have laid stress on the context in which we function, the economic position, the Five Year Plan etc., and we have even asked them to keep in view the condition of State employees and all that, we have to keep all this in view. We recognize that Government employees or indeed others should be a contented people, should be paid enough so that they may lead a relatively contented life. It is true that we are passing through difficult times economically and we cannot do what we want to do. We hope to do it later. What we can do, we will do soon. I do not look upon this period as a long

---

6. The call for strike was withdrawn on 8 August 1957.
7. The Essential Services (Maintenance) Ordinance, promulgated on 7 August 1957, empowered the Government to declare any strike illegal in the services regarded as essential for the community.
8. It was revoked on 12 August as the call for strike was withdrawn.
9. The index of wholesale prices (1952–53= 100) rose to 112 in July-August 1957.

period. I have often talked about building up our economy, our industry and our working for tomorrow, but even though we may work for tomorrow we can never forget today. People have to live today and eat today and carry on their other occupations today, and we cannot wait for a distant tomorrow. So, both today and tomorrow have to be taken into consideration, but considering the demands specially from Government employees what has worried me most in recent weeks is that there is no adequate machinery to deal with them and so they mount up till at least they come up in this form of threat, etc.

Now, there is some thing wrong about that, and we are all responsible for it. I think, there should be a machinery not only to consider demands as such when they arise but really to promote a cooperative atmosphere between people working in a ministry or department, whatever it is. Whatever their grade of work might be, that they must feel that they are parts of a cooperative organization and that their profit and benefit lies in a cooperative approach to problems. Of course, we have had in the past several committees and all that, sometimes they have functioned, sometimes they have not. But, even when they have functioned, they have functioned too much as committees to discuss complaints, I do not like that approach. Naturally, complaints have to be considered, the approach is how to function better and more cooperatively and everyone even those who may be employed in relatively subordinate capacities, should be made to feel that they are partners in a big concern and their advice, their suggestions should be invited and welcomed—that is quite possible that some suggestions coming from them may be very helpful. You see, once you introduce that atmosphere then this tug of war business does not go completely but it is lessened. You try to understand their viewpoints. There is no 'you' and 'they', in fact we try to understand our viewpoints, respective viewpoints. And really these committees, service associations and committees should not function in the sense of a Minister or a senior officer sitting there and listening to people at the bar who give their complaints, that is not the way to do it. It is a mutual concern in which we discuss matters, frequently not only complaints but general work—how it can be improved, greater efficiency, less waste all that, that is the approach. I mentioned the Whitley Councils, of course, they are well known, they are pretty old about 30, 40 years or more. When they were first introduced in England, they were looked upon with rather some apprehension by the parties concerned, but now, I believe, there is a great deal of confidence in them, they meet on equal terms, discuss matters frequently. They generally come to agreements, if there is no agreement, there is a kind of a service, inter service I mean, some arbitration council not a tribunal and all that. I am told that seldom any matter goes up there, because they settle it amongst themselves usually. So, I think, more attention should be given to that, indeed we are giving it. The Home Ministry is particularly concerned so are all our Ministries. I have referred to this because it is a subject very much in our minds but this is only a very small part of the headaches that we have now. It is quite astonishing how many headaches a head can have at one time. Winston Churchill said recently, I remember, that in old days each Parliamentary session dealt with one major subject, which occupied the whole session. He said now each Cabinet meeting deals with more than one major subject which previously would have occupied the whole session of Parliament. That is our position too. We have to do that in Cabinet meetings or anywhere. The subjects we deal with normally take a whole session of Parliament, but we have to compress them one over the other. Well, we cannot escape the pace of events and the pace of attempted progress and all that is happening in the world. The fact is our little heads have to bear many many headaches at the same time. There is the broad economic situation, there is the food situation, intimately connected with each other and as I have said previously to you—it seems to me more and more clear that almost every thing depends in the measure we hold food prices, keep them at reasonable levels, not allow them to go up, it is of vital consequence. That is to say apart from more food production which we must have and which is the basis of food prices really, other measures have to be taken. But we must be clear in our minds that we will take any measure that may be necessary to keep food prices at reasonable levels, even though the measure we take is not to our liking, we have to take it; otherwise the consequences will be still less to our liking. The whole of our Five Year Plan depends on food prices. Food prices go up, other things follow, the estimates of the Plan go up and it is completely outside our control. Why is this agitation and demands from various classes of Government employees and others—in the final analysis because food prices have gone up. You see, it is all tied up. So, you see that is the most vital thing. We laid stress on industrial development in the Second Five Year Plan, rightly, because then there is no progress for India without industrial development, but there is no industrial development unless you have agricultural development. So, we come back to agriculture and more production of food etc. There it is.

Now, in this session we are dealing with certain taxation measures, which as you know are rather novel, novel for India certainly, and therefore, they have elicited a good deal of comment both in their favour and against, which is right and natural. We should have plenty of discussion etc. At the present moment the Select Committee is sitting, considering them[10] and perhaps some of you know

10. The Select Committee Report on the Wealth Tax Bill was presented in the Lok Sabha on 17 August 1957 by A.K. Sen, the Union Law Minister. Report on the Expenditure Tax Bill was submitted on 26 August 1957.

that our Congress Executive Party met to consider some matters. Then the Executive decided that it would be a good thing for them to meet the Congress Members of the Select Committee. So, on two occasions the Congress Executive and the Congress Members of Select Committee met jointly and informally, that is about 50 of us met informally, and discussed at some length, some aspects of these measures. They are very good meetings with a frank talk and we had met not merely to pass resolutions, because that after all, is either the function, on the one hand, of this Party or of Government, on the other hand, the Government have to decide or the Party has to decide or the Party Executive has to decide. Anyhow, that did lead to a great deal of understanding and clarifications. I do not say that every matter has been cleared up. The Select Committee is still sitting and arguing and all that. And I said during the last session also that so far as the broad principles involved in these taxation measures are concerned, which Parliament has approved, they are on the right lines. I am no expert, I have no knowledge enough to give very definite opinions about details but broadly, I think, they are on the right lines for the future. At the same time, you see, these taxation measures affect, on the one hand, because of excise duties and the rest, everybody and specially the common people. It is impossible to do otherwise because of the stress and strain of circumstances. On the other hand, these particular measures called the Wealth Tax and the Expenditure Tax, affect, well, the more prosperous people in the country, not very many compared to the population, the top fringe, prosperous fringe and no doubt to some extent they are an additional burden to them. Well, in any event, I think, they should not complain. More especially, when a great part of the burden is spread out over others who can even less afford to bear it. Nobody likes heavy taxation but one likes still less to allow the economy of the country to deteriorate which brings unhappiness and misery to all the people. We have to face these crises.

Now, coming to these Bills some people talk, criticise them that, oh! these Bills do not bring socialism in our country. Others may say, no they are socialistic and all that. Well, it seems to me that to expect any such taxation measure to bring socialism shows a misunderstanding of socialism. Socialism is not brought about by merely taxing people. Socialism is a method of production, a method of distribution, a method of many things; it grows, it cannot be brought about by a magic, and it is a strange notion that socialism comes by simply removing the rich people from a country. Well, there is not much logic behind it or understanding. One wants equality, one aims at it, that is a distant result of the society you build, you cannot impose it, you may, of course, in theory, and yet you may be terribly far from socialism or socialistic production or distribution or anything, or you may even stop the wheels of progress to go ahead. Our first objective must necessarily remain production and production even at the cost of equality, let that be quite clear. You cannot have equality in poverty, that is not socialism, that does no good. We want gradually to go in one direction, of course, more for psychological reasons, because it is vulgar for wealth to be flaunted, it is bad, but the main thing is production. It is only countries that are producing wealth are building up their future, there is no other way, and of course, added to that, equitable distribution. Now, these Bills do not bring about socialism but they are a step in the right direction. There are many difficult problems in these Bills, they are new, we have no past experience of them. Even in other countries there is not much experience. It is a venture in a new field and however wisely we may decide, we shall discover later on that they are capable of improvement naturally, and however wisely we may decide some people will disagree with them, some may agree, it is bound to happen. Whenever you take a new step, that happens. Now, there are two aspects of this matter that have to be kept in mind, one is that we have not introduced these Bills merely to, what shall I say, to punish people—that is absurd, we want the various processes that are working in India all to be encouraged, if we have various sectors working, public or private, we want all of them to work, we do not want to suppress one, if we did, we do so directly. There is no point in doing so indirectly. We want the private sector to function, we want the public sector, of course, to function and we want the cooperation of everybody but necessarily step by step this has to move in a certain direction, and it is in that direction that these taxation measures point. I hope that in the course of the few months, a year or 18 months, some of our present difficulties will go less, they will not disappear, naturally. It is not so easy but the immediate difficulties may lessen somewhat, of course, by the end of next year, let us say, but the difficulties will remain throughout the Second Five Year Plan till we get some of our new things, like the iron and steel plants functioning, then they bring about a better balance.

Well, these Taxation Bills will come out of the Select Committee soon, come up before Parliament, and I do not know but if it is the wish of the House to consider, I mean this House, our Party, we can meet to consider any aspect of them on which there is any particular doubt. Because even among Congress Members there is sometimes doubt, they should go the Executive Committee which will no doubt meet whenever necessary to give them its advice. We are in fact meeting tomorrow morning for this purpose. Now we are on the eve of our Independence Day, 15th August, and we are celebrating not only our Independence Day but 10 years of Independence and a hundred years since the struggle of 1857. And we are celebrating them on August 15th and 16th, all over the country. Some people criticised us for choosing these dates and not May 10th, when the first shot was fired or whatever it was, in the struggle of 1857. Well, there are a number of reasons for us to choose this. First of all, we are not celebrating a particular event only or what happened in Meerut on the 10th of May. We are celebrating the whole two years 1857 and 1858 of that struggle. Secondly, we are celebrating it as the precursor of the other struggles in other forms that that took place for 90 years afterwards. Thirdly, we are celebrating the end of the struggle by achieving Independence. So, we are trying to put this composite picture before the country and not merely one part of it. Well, ten years of Independence, I think, there is a good deal to show for which we can take credit for these ten years. At the same time what concerns us more is not what has been done in ten years' time but what we are doing today and what we will do tomorrow. And as I just said in my Hindi speech, there are so many headaches that sometime one is surprised that a little head can contain so many headaches at one and the same time, but there they are. And we have to face these situations calmly, coolly with unity and solidarity and not be swept away as many people are unfortunately, our young friends, students get excited. I do not mind anybody getting excited, I do not even mind anybody occasionally misbehaving. But I do mind wrong types of misbehaviour and people thinking that it is courageous to go about breaking things and committing violence and throwing stones, that passes my understanding, more specially when it is called satyagraha. It is a pity. I am not blaming anybody, but it shows that there is a spirit of irresponsibility, to some extent even of a disintegrating spirit in the air. People rush off and get excited about relatively small matters and immediately they indulge in this kind of satyagraha. In the case of Punjab or Assam, I am not going to the merits of these questions, or the student satyagraha in Rajasthan,[11] and of course, there are many other things in the many other States of India, the most powerful factor is having this unity and a great responsibility comes upon all of us, on these matters. I have ventured to mention it, lest we forget or we celebrate our ten years' Independence and hundred years since the first great struggle for Independence. We are passing through rather stormy weather and we shall require stout hearts and cool minds for it. Thank you.

11. The students were protesting against enhancement of fees. Their agitation turned violent between 29 July to 6 August and was called off on 19 August after the announcement of the fee concessions by the State Government.

8. To H.V.R. Iengar[1]

New Delhi
August 13, 1957

My dear H.V.R.,[2]

Thank you for your letter of the 9th August.[3]

I am not an expert in the cooperative movement, that is to say, I have no personal experience of it, although I have read about this movement in India and elsewhere. For a long time past my impression has been that a cooperative movement should essentially be non-official, though some official help may be given. The essense of cooperation was a development of self-reliance, fellow-feeling and a capacity to work together for common purposes. Past experience in India indicated that it had been too much officialized and there was no real life in it except in some places where some earnest people devoted themselves to it.

In the new circumstances it seemed to me that this element of self-reliance should be developed and further that the members of cooperatives should have some intimate knowledge of each other. That is, it should not be something impressive with a big boss sitting somewhere and the members of the cooperatives having no sensation of real ownership or management. For this reason, I was inclined to think that too big a cooperative was not usually desirable, though, of course, a number of smaller cooperatives should be linked together in a big one. Also, that a cooperative which mainly revolves round credit, while it could do good, would not take roots in the people. It would be more like a bank.

This was my broad approach to this question. I have not analyzed it in any detail. But as the Community Development Schemes progressed and began to cover more and more the activities of the rural areas, it seemed to me essential

---

1. File No. 37(51)/57-PMS. Also available in JN Collection.
2. Governor of Reserve Bank.
3. Iengar wrote about the beginnings of a peaceful revolution in some areas through integrated cooperative development in the field of agricultural cooperation. The essence of the scheme was share capital or borrowing power and it covered marketing, processing, credit and storage of foodgrains. He pointed out that the integrated scheme was discussed at various levels since 1955 and was incorporated in the Second Five Year Plan. Iengar expressed concern at the suggestion of suspending financial assistance to large-scale societies pending consideration of the whole basic issue at a meeting of the Cooperative Development and Warehousing Board.

that the cooperatives should be an integrated part of these schemes. I have often said so.

I confess that when these matters came up before the Cabinet, I did not consider them in any detail and we agreed to the general propositions put before us. I was anxious to push the cooperative movement. Later, however, some aspects struck me. One was that the approach of the Rural Credit Committee appeared to be based on the assumption that our village folk were not competent enough to do anything worthwhile in this respect and therefore, the State should interfere much more actively. That did not fit in with my approach, because, if this is so, then there is not much hope for the development of rural India. I know of the feelings of our village people, but nevertheless I believe that the only way to train them is to make them responsible.

V.T. Krishnamachari[4] spoke to me after my return from Europe and took a strong view. I was rather impressed by his argument, more especially as he was a very old cooperator with a great deal of experience. Among other things he said that some well-established small cooperatives which had lasted for several decades have now been wound up or absorbed in larger ones. I could not understand why this should be done. Anyhow, I told him that I would consider this matter further and discuss it with my colleagues and especially with the Food Minister who is responsible for these.

As I have told you above, I cannot speak from experience and my views are based on theory and a strong bias towards a non-official movement. I am getting a little tired of officializing everything. In the conditions as they exist in India, this does not lead to efficiency generally nor to enthusiasm, though, of course, individuals make a difference anywhere. I do not say that the present scheme being worked with the help of the Reserve Bank is necessarily opposed to what I have been thinking. But I do want to understand it better and see how far we may be drifting perhaps in a wrong direction. Perhaps it would be as well to experiment both with the small cooperatives and the large ones, though a very large one, I think, would definitely be something impersonal and therefore will not have that spirit of cooperation which we should like to develop. In any event I feel sure that this should be integrated with the Community Development movement.

Some figures I saw of the development of small cooperatives in connection with the Community Development movement during the last two or three years were rather impressive.

It is difficult perhaps to generalize more especially in a large country like India. It is possible that different varieties of cooperatives may suit different

4. Deputy Chairman, Planning Commission.

places in different conditions. Your experience of Gujarat and other places is, of course, very important. So far as I know, cooperatives generally in other countries, as in Scandinavia, are almost all relatively small. Why should not small cooperatives link up for some purposes with a bigger organization which would have the advantage of bigness and at the same time the intimacy of a small cooperative?

The other day my attention was drawn to the fact that in spite of clear directions issued by the Government of India, a number of Banks had advanced large sums of money to rice millers and others. This had encouraged hoarding. I mentioned this to the Finance Minister and he said he would write to you about it and enquire how these Banks had been allowed to do this. The Finance Minister told me that apart from this, large sums of money given by the Reserve Bank for these cooperatives, might also have helped in this hoarding business which is so harmful at the present juncture especially.[5]

Yours sincerely,
Jawaharlal Nehru

5. See also Food and Agriculture.

9. To B.V. Keskar[1]

New Delhi
August 15, 1957

My dear Balakrishna,[2]
Your letter of August 15th about publicity on the AIR of the Five Year Plan. In the course of this note it is said that the matter supplied by Departments of the Government for this kind of publicity usually are dull. I entirely agree. Therefore, some steps should be taken to present this matter in a more lively and interesting form.

I do not know if even a specialized staff as you suggest will be able to do this much better. That depends entirely on the individuals in the specialized staff. I

1. File No. 43(38)/56-64-PMS. Also available in JN Collection.
2. Union Minister of Information and Broadcasting.

imagine that it will probably be more worthwhile to get non-officials to give special talks on this. Such non-officials can be chosen with care. There may be sometimes University people or Members of Parliament or journalists, to speak of one aspect of the Plan or of a particular project or undertaking which they had visited. Anyhow, the purely official approach is not good enough.

Yours sincerely,
Jawaharlal Nehru

10. To V.T. Krishnamachari[1]

New Delhi
August 15, 1957

My dear V.T.,

I am sending you a letter from a Dutch Professor in Amsterdam and a book that he has forwarded to me. This book contains a thesis by an Indian scholar on *Some Economic Problems of Public Enterprises in India.[2]*

The subject, as you know, is of great interest to us. I have not read this book, as I have no time at present. Perhaps some of your people in the Planning

---

1. File No. 37(62)/57-PMS. Also available in JN Collection.
2. Professor Abram Mey had sent Parmanand Prasad's book on public sector which dealt with the problems of management. According to Prasad if some specific conditions were fulfilled, a rapid change in economic conditions could be achieved. These were: (i) temporization and harmonization of evolution in different branches of long and short term plans; (ii) normative working of managerial economies; and (iii) prevention of loss of acquired new wealth by inefficiency or by application of wrong managerial methods. Mey wrote that normative costing and normative value problem were specifically treated in the Amsterdam University's Economics Faculty. Moreover, they were put in practice in public administration after the Second World War, when Mey was Director of State Budget in special charge of reorganization and the country's rehabilitation.

Commission might read it and send me a little note about it. I do not expect any long note. Just a brief one to indicate what the line of thought is in this book.[3]

Yours sincerely,
Jawaharlal Nehru

3. V.T. Krishnamachari replied on 10 September that the author recognized the Government's role in developing large-scale industries in an underdeveloped economy. The Government, simultaneously, must ensure efficiency of operation and freedom from political enterprise combined with accountability to Parliament.

11. To Morarji Desai[1]

New Delhi
August 15, 1957

My dear Morarji,[2]

I have been reading the Annual Report for 1956-57 of the Hindustan Machine Tools Ltd., at Jalahalli. I remember much criticism being levelled at this factory during the past years. Reading the new report, therefore, has been a pleasing surprise, for it shows marked progress and, indeed, a profit after making all other payments for interest, depreciation, reserve fund, etc. I think this is very satisfactory.

I should like your Ministry to convey to the Managing Director, M.K. Mathulla,[3] our appreciation of the successful working of this undertaking and ask him to convey this to the staff and workers.

Yours sincerely,
Jawaharlal Nehru

1. File No. 17(21)/56-58-PMS. Also available in JN Collection.
2. Union Minister of Commerce and Industry.
3. Mathew K. Mathulla (b. 1907); Assistant Deputy Controller of Accounts, Tata Iron & Steel Company, 1934-48; Chief Executive Officer, Air India, 1948-51; Controller of Accounts & Managing Director, Sindri Fertilizers & Chemicals Ltd., 1951-54; Joint Secretary, Ministry of Production, Government of India, 1954-56; Managing Director, HMT Ltd., 1956-64; Chairman, HMT Ltd., 1964.

12. To Morarji Desai[1]

New Delhi
August 16, 1957

My dear Morarji,

I was informed recently that we were importing a large quantity of bolts and nuts. We make some of these ourselves, but, apparently, not enough and production is very slow. Recently our Naval people made some, presumably for their own use, and they did it much more efficiently. Perhaps this might be looked into.

Also, I think that we can make quite enough pins, girders and ball-bearings. I do not know if we import them. There is also the question of electric batteries.

There is a considerable demand for black pepper abroad. Do we export it in any quantity? Is there a ban on various kinds of oil—mustard, linseed, groundnut; oil-cakes and oil-seeds? All these are commodities which can be exported for good foreign exchange.

Yours sincerely,
Jawaharlal Nehru

1. JN Collection.

13. To Lal Bahadur Shastri[1]

New Delhi
August 16, 1957

My dear Lal Bahadur,[2]

Somebody was telling me that the average rate of movement of goods trains in India was very slow. This average is apparently worked out on a twenty-four

1. JN Collection.
2. Union Minister of Transport and Communications.

72

hour basis, including steps etc. Could you find out what this is and ask your people to try to raise this average and bring it nearer the average of other countries? Obviously, if this could be done, movement of goods would be faster. It is in these matters that improvement pays good dividend. The same wagons can be used again and again much sooner.

Yours sincerely,
Jawaharlal Nehru

14. To Manubhai M. Shah[1]

New Delhi
18th August 1957

My dear Manubhai,[2]
Your letter of August 16 about the drug industry.[3]

In the talks you have had or are having with German or American firms, does the question of price come in? I mean that will we be tied up in any way with German or American prices or can we produce the goods at our own and at a cheaper price? The price factor is important because we want to give these medicines and drugs at cheap prices. At present these prices are prohibitive. Also, will we have to pay royalties to these firms? Will these royalties be fairly heavy and continuous?

1. File No. 17(48)/56-66-PMS. Also available in JN Collection.
2. Manubhai Mansukhlal Shah (1915-2000); Minister of Finance, Government of Saurashtra, 1948-56; Minister of State for Industry, Government of India, 1956-62; Union Minister, Industrial Trade, 1962-64, Commerce, 1964-67; Chairman, Gujarat Industrial Development Corporation and Gujarat Industrial Investment Corporation, 1967-70.
3. Manubhai Shah wrote about his discussion with General Sokhey on the Government's approach to drug manufacture in India. He elaborated four principles: (i) desirability of State drug industry; (ii) collaboration with such firms as would implement the project in the shortest time; (iii) give favourable financial terms; and (iv) provide facilities for exchange of research.

Since writing the above, I have seen a letter from General Sokhey to me.[4] I enclose a copy of this. I think that we should be clear about some of the points that he has raised.

You might show this to Morarjibhai.

Yours sincerely,
Jawaharlal Nehru

4. S.S. Sokhey, a nominated Member of the Rajya Sabha at this time, warned about the consequences of collaboration with powerful monopolies like Bayer, Merck, and Sharpe & Dohme International on a share-capital basis. He favoured the offer of the Soviet Union of all technical and financial aid, who had no commercial interests in the matter.

15. To T.T. Krishnamachari[1]

New Delhi
19th August 1957

My dear T.T.,

In reading through some old papers dealing with the King of Oudh, I came across a letter from the then Governor-General (Canning, I think) to the ex-King, Wajid Ali Shah who was still addressed as "His Majesty". Apparently, Wajid Ali Shah had asked for exemption from income tax. The Governor-General in his reply which is dated 1860 regrets his inability to exempt him because he says that nobody is exempt, including himself. In the course of the letter, it is mentioned that the exemption limit at that time in India was Rs 200/- per annum.

This may interest you.

Yours sincerely,
Jawaharlal Nehru

1. File No. 37(60)/57-58-PMS. Also available in JN Collection.

16. To Lilavati Munshi[1]

New Delhi
August 20, 1957

My dear Lilavatibehn,[2]

Thank you for your letter of August 20th with which you have sent what you call some notes in the form of a speech. I have read these notes with some surprise. I doubt if any Opposition member could have attacked our policy so vigorously as you have done. This speech or the notes are a broad-sided attack on almost everything that the Government is doing. The taxation proposals or any other policies of the Government are not the private monopoly of the Finance Minister or any one Minister, but represent the considered views of the Government. They are meant to meet conditions as they are. No country, to my knowledge, has progressed without having to go through the pains of progress. If we could advance happily without any particular effort, then there will be no difficulty at all.

Yours sincerely,
Jawaharlal Nehru

1. File No. 37(60)/57-58-PMS. Also available in JN Collection.
2. (1899-1976); eminent Gujarati writer and social activist; wife of K.M. Munshi; imprisoned during freedom movement; Member, All India Congress Committee, 1931-34, Bombay Legislative Assembly, 1936-52; President, Bombay Women's Association, 1947-48, Bharatiya Stree Seva Sangh, 1948-66 and of the Bombay branch of the All India Women's Conference, 1948-49; Member, Rajya Sabha, 1952-58.

17. No Element of Defeatism[1]

...H.N. Mukerjee:[2] Will the honourable Minister please tell us if there was any truth in the report made in a section of the press regarding an alleged confidential document of a rather defeatist nature from the Economic Division of the Planning Commission to the Prime Minister in early June, and whether the Government intend having intensive consultations with Members of Parliament as was done in early 1956, to be followed up by a debate in the House to prevent a pruning of the Plan of the sort which the private sector is crying for?

Jawaharlal Nehru: The honourable Member has referred to some document which is supposed to have come to me. I do not quite know which one he is referring to. Both as Chairman of the Planning Commission and as Prime Minister, I receive numerous appreciations and documents. Naturally, since we have been greatly concerned about it, I am in constant touch. I have no recollection of what may be called a defeatist document. I have been analysing the situation and pointing out various aspects of it, some good, some bad. Anyhow, so far as the Government are concerned, there is basically no element of defeatism in their outlook. They are facing the position. I should like to make it perfectly clear. Obviously, there are difficulties. Those difficulties are not hidden. Everybody knows them. I have no doubt that basically the economy of India is a very sound economy, and we shall, as always in such matters, one has to, face the difficulties that come in the way. As for consultations with Members of Parliament, we are always very happy to have such consultation. I do not know, I shall try to evolve a method during this session so that we may have talks on the situation.

---

1. Reply to a question in the Lok Sabha, 21 August 1957. *Lok Sabha Debates*, (second series), Vol. V, cols. 9041-9042. Extracts.
2. CPI Member from Calcutta Central, West Bengal.

18. Discussion on Taxation Proposals—I[1]

It is often said that the Congress Party, even though it has well stated objectives, nevertheless is rather an amorphous body. That is so and that is not only so, but to some extent, it is inevitably so, because the Congress by virtue of its origin and history, is still, by and large, a nationalist organization with a strong bent and direction towards certain economic goals. It is not what might be called a sectarian organization in the economic sphere or any other, that is, its doors are open to people who may not subscribe to even a particular defined objective apart from the creed. But gradually to begin with, it was purely a nationalist organization. Inevitably, as it became a mass organization, it developed an economic content as it had to, because it became principally an organization spread out in the rural areas, it developed an agrarian outlook, a pro-peasant outlook, that is a natural growth. And gradually, it developed broadly a socialistic outlook, then it started more and more thinking on those lines and that outlook became more defined and relatively more precise. Even so, its outlook has been rather pragmatic, not a doctrinaire outlook like, for instance, let us say anyone who is a socialist or a communist or who calls himself Marxist—when you know exactly or more or less what Marxian is or Marxism is, when you agree with it or not—that is what I call a doctrinaire outlook with fixed dogmatic interpretations of economic and historical phenomena and fixed methods of approaching them. There may be the difference between the socialist and the communist, that the socialist broadly speaking as a group does not encourage or does not want to encourage violent methods, individuals may and do, I mean to say broadly speaking, while the communist has no hesitation and in fact perhaps the basic thing is that communists somewhere at the back of their minds believe in seizure of power by some kind of violence, but leave that out, the methods, the broad outlook of theirs is Marxist. Now, that is a precise outlook. It is what is called a scientific outlook, the science may be right or wrong, I think, it is about 50 per cent right and 50 per cent wrong, or whatever the percentage may be, I think that interpretation today is rather out of date, I think that even accepting the basis of it, it has to be applied with all kinds of variations in different conditions, different countries and different conditions of growth. Obviously, if you go to Central Africa and try to apply Marxism, it cannot be the Marxism that would apply to industrialized countries. It is obvious. The approach in an

1. Speech at the Congress Parliamentary Party meeting, New Delhi, 26 August 1957. Tape No. M-26/c (ii) & M-27/c (i), NMML.

industrialized community is one approach of Marxism, the approach in a non-industrialized or under-developed community is another. The whole of Marxism developed with the background of Western Europe which was rapidly being industrialized, you must remember that Marxism, at least right or wrong, is a carefully thought out system. I think, it has no application today, it is out of date mostly, and of course, even Marxism has changed so much in the application—in the Soviet Union, in China it is different, in other countries, it is different. I was reading only yesterday a brilliant criticism of what happened in the Soviet Union, a criticism by Trostsky, many years ago he wrote it, he was brilliant.

Now, what I wonder is your theory, those members who spoke of socialism, what is Mr Agnibhoj's[2] theory, what is Mr Mool Chand Jain's[3] theory, because we are all the time being told about this socialist pattern of society, but I have not had a word yet of how things should come off except presumably by heavier and heavier taxation or otherwise trying to equalize people by getting money from one and giving it to the other. Now that is a very noble ideal but it has absolutely nothing to do with socialistic pattern of society. Let us not be confused. Our emotional reactions are that we should remove these anomalies, remove this rich man and the poor man that is perfectly right, we should do that obviously, but it has nothing to do with socialism, I say, let us be clear about it, I do not want this socialist pattern to be thrown at me without the least thought as to what it is and how it can be realized, that is point number one.

The whole question of socialism arose out of the growth of industrialization. The word socialism is unknown, before industrialization came in Europe. It grew first, a kind of great socialism, a humanitarianism, socialism that grew, that is the kind of socialism which many of us feel, that is, we do not want these inequalities, it grew in the beginning of the 19th century. Later in the 19th century came, what is called, scientific socialism, Marxism etc. Anyhow, it was a product of the Industrial Revolution, it was a product of the new machine coming in, it was a product of a society which was producing much more. Previous to that society was rigid, the social structure whether it was feudal, whether it was something else, it was rigid and production was more or less limited, poverty was there and there was no means of combating it. When the new machines

---

2. Rameshwar Umaro Agnibhoj (1911-1987); Congressman from Madhya Pradesh; imprisoned during freedom movement; Member, Legislative Assembly, Central Provinces, 1936; Minister in Madhya Pradesh Government, 1946-52; Member, Rajya Sabha, 1952-58.

3. Mool Chand Jain (b.1915); Congressman from Punjab; imprisoned during the Quit India Movement; President, DCC, Karnal, 1955-56; Member, Punjab Legislative Assembly, 1952-57; Member, Lok Sabha, 1957-1962.

came then new wealth were being produced. Even though it was being badly distributed and questions arose as to why this new wealth should not to be evenly distributed, why should it make people richer, those questions had hardly arisen previously, in the feudal age when the land produced something, the landlord took a great part of it, the poor peasant got very little, they starved. There was no hope for the future except some peasant risings, when they suffered too much, they knocked down and burnt the landlord's house. So, the whole conception of socialism is the use of higher techniques for producing wealth otherwise there is no socialism, otherwise there is poverty, and you cannot remove poverty by measures which may be good of course, by measures of taking some money, existing money and just distributing it. That may be good or bad, discuss it on the merits, but it does not remove the real poverty of the country because the real poverty is ultimately an equation, an equation of what you produce in the country year by year. Of course, if you like, it is a very small matter or what you have got in the country already in the shape of wealth, that is a very small matter, the real thing is what you produce year by year. The Nizam may have, I do not know, a hundred crore, two hundred crores or 300 crores. I have no idea of what he has or what he has not. You may take the 300 crores from the Nizam, you may do good works from it, you may build hospitals, you may distribute it to the poor people but it makes no difference to the poverty of India, that is, to the productive capacity of India, unless that is used for productive purposes and to increase wealth. In a sense the Nizam's wealth or such like persons' wealth is, what shall I say, some kind of accumulations which are not bad for the country. That is to say, in times of crisis they are there. Whatever the accumulation, after all what is all this, you talk about capital accumulations, all these princes and Nizams what they have got, are capital accumulations through generations from their peasantry and from their subjects. Well, it was a bad way of doing it but it was an old way. If they are in the country, that is, they do not go out of the country, they may be, what the Finance Minister has called, something like a reserve fund, like the sterling balances, but nevertheless, anything in the country is a certain reserve which the country can use in times of need. You may gradually get it by taxation or in times of emergency. But leave out the Nizam. The point is the whole question whether it is socialism or growth, consists in greater production through higher techniques, that is the basic thing. When Lenin talked about communism in the early days, he said communism formula is Soviets plus electricity. You see they were thinking of higher techniques—electric power, machines, and all that, that was communism. Lenin did not hesitate after a few years of the Revolution to go back and introduce a modified form of capitalism called the New Economic Policy because he felt that his country, that is, Soviet Union was not quite prepared—it was going to pieces economically—for the step he wanted to take and he gave it a breathing spell and then Lenin died, Stalin went ahead. Whether Stalin did right or wrong is no concern of mine. I am saying that these are not things which you can do out of the air. In China, which is a communist state, they are not following the same path as the Soviet Union. They are moderating themselves sometimes, sometimes not, they are, as a matter of fact today, in possibly greater difficulties, the same type of difficulties that we are having here. Did you see the other day in a newspaper, that they rationed cloth there, and they reduced the ration to six yards per capita. Think of six yards, our per capita consumption today is 17 to 18 yards, about three times and it is increasing. Now that itself shows how economic circumstances are influencing them, and they are a communist state, they have no ups and down, and they have no riches and all that, as far as one can see. In regard to food too, rationing system is becoming stricter and stricter. I am not blaming their system, I am merely telling you facts. Here is a communist society which has no inhibitions but economic laws and economic circumstances compel them to do something. They are in great difficulties whether they may not have foreign exchange problem as we have, but they have a slightly different foreign exchange problem. After all, they have to pay, whether it is even to Russia, they have to pay. They do not get free things, they may get credits more easily than we do but they have to face the difficulties. They lay the greater stress on heavy industry because that is the basis for industrialization. Having done so, they realized that after all agriculture is the most important thing of all. As we, naturally realize.

We want heavy industry in our country, we must have it, there is no socialism in this country, it does not matter what you do unless you have heavy industry, it is a basic preposition I would say, you cannot have industry unless you have heavy industry. The use of the word socialism without that has no meaning. It simply means, if you succeed in doing it, some kind of spread out of poverty all over, equalize poverty, that means your productive apparatus is not functioning properly. That is a thing which none of us wants. We want, apart from socialism, a Welfare State. That is, to begin with, everybody having a certain degree of welfare, opportunities etc., food, clothing, housing, education, health and work and opportunity to grow, that is not socialism, that is part of socialism, socialism is something more. Socialism is where ultimately the productive apparatus should be basically controlled by the community, the big productive apparatus. Socialism need not necessarily do away, so far as I am concerned, with the petty farmer, may or may not be, it is immaterial. It does not necessarily follow that socialism must be collectivization of land, though I do believe in cooperatives. There are many ways. But the point is, there should be no accumulation of economic power and wealth. The ultimate goal can only be reached when production is so tremendous that you can pick up anything you like, everybody can pick up what he likes. When there is so much food, you can have what you like, leave out the luxury foods, but the normal foods should be quite enough. When there is so much cloth, well, you can have as much cloth as you like cheaply. When every essential need of a human being is provided for cheaply that is the ultimate state of communism and which is next stage, when there is abundance of goods you can pick them up, you will hardly sell them, you just pick them up and store, they are lying about, everybody picks up what he likes. Practically there is something distant about communist state but leave that out. The point is the whole thing, socialism or communism depends upon wealth production, not on the restricting wealth production. Wealth production can only come, well, from the land, from industry, etc. From the land it comes by higher techniques, from industry also it comes from higher techniques, both come by higher techniques. Higher techniques in industry specially are very costly, you have to put up the Iron & Steel plant and spend 400 crores of Rupees or 500 on it, as a basis to provide steel for the rest of the industry. Now, you see, if we want a socialist structure of society, we must concentrate on higher production and higher techniques, in land and in industry, that becomes essential. And every step that we take whether it is taxation or any other, we must keep in mind to increase production and higher techniques. If by any thing that we do that suffers, then we may make a little gain today but tomorrow it slips away from our hands.

Remember also, we talk about a socialist structure, that is true, but the fact of the matter is that today we are living under a capitalist structure in India. A modified and a controlled capitalist structure but nevertheless a capitalist structure, it is a modified and controlled socialist sector, it is there and it is growing. But by the whole structure I mean buying and selling and all this. We have a public sector and a private sector, true. But taking both together the normal apparatus of our life is capitalist—the market for this or that. The socialist structure grows and when it is powerful enough, it will begin to affect the texture of our lives later, it does today only in a very little sense. Even the public sector, however big it becomes, does not mean socialism, it means a part of socialism. We want public sector to grow. Now, we have adopted a policy of both public sector and private sector. We have not done that as a kind of appeasement of somebody like the capitalists but we have deliberately done it as the only policy which in present circumstances yields the biggest results. Added to that, we want to increase the public sector as an important and strategic industry. I am quite certain that if we want it today, let us take an extreme example, as say in China, they have taken hold of all retail shops, make them state, let us suppose leave out the big things, but if we took hold of all the retail shops, what would happen—utter confusion and collapse. Would the State run all the retail shops in India? You see, you talked about socialism but the major thing is that when anybody talks about control, you say no. What is socialism but all control, hundred per cent control, to the right, to the left, above and below. You do not realize that. You see, you must be logical about it. If there is socialism when production is so tremendous that everything is there, pick it up. But if production is not enough in socialism, controls become necessary. But you do not want them, and rightly so, I think, I do not want controls either, as far as possible, here and there we may have to have them, but not generally speaking. Because not that controls are bad, but we are not trained enough to have a proper system of controls with integrity and there is a great danger of corruption and all that is happening all over the country, that is the real reason not the theory of it, the theory is perfect. So, I said it would be confusion and collapse if we decided that all the retail shops in India should become State-owned. We cannot do it, it is an impossibility because we have not got the trained men. On the one hand, we without any gain might simply stop the machinery of all these things and then, we go wrong, prices and everything, yet that would be a step in a sense, a very socialistic step; we cannot do it, we are not prepared for it. Whether we will ever be prepared I do not know, whether it is necessary or not I do not know. In my socialism it is not necessary that everybody should be a State employee. In my socialism it is not necessary, as I said, that the land should be collectivized. I do believe, however, in cooperative farming, that too gradually, step by step, when the farmers agree to it, by democratic process. Generally speaking, I believe in the small farmer, but my difficulty is that he cannot take advantage of the modern techniques because he is too small. Therefore, I believe in cooperatives that he should cooperate remaining himself as a small farmer, cooperate with other small farmers to take advantage of cooperatives to increase his yield and other things, profit himself and the State profits. Therefore, please remember that when we have to consider any kind of advance, you may call it socialism or you may just call it higher standards for our people, call it what you like, first step is that we have to produce more. We can only produce more ultimately by higher techniques, you can only have higher techniques by considerable and large-scale investments in those techniques, whether it is land or elsewhere, whether it is fertilizer for the land, and you have to build a fertilizer factory or buy fertilizers from abroad, both ways you have to spend money. You want investment for that. How do you get the money for investment? Well, taxation, yes, certainly by taxation, but all the taxation that any Finance Minister can put on in India—it does not matter what tax it is—is not enough for us, realize that, because I am talking about the immediate future not for ever and ever, because we want to advance rapidly. We have three Iron and Steel plants, we are spending

Rs 500 crores on these plants. I am just giving one example, there are many others. Can any taxation cover all the expenditure that we are incurring or that we want to incur in our Second Five Year Plan? You have to borrow money. I am not quite sure what the Soviet Union did, it may be an exception, but it is an exception which we cannot follow, because the Soviet Union went through a period of extreme agony for the people. We dare not, no democratic government can do it or wants to do it. We cannot. But leave the Soviet Union out. Every country which has developed, industrialized itself, has been helped by loans, investments from other countries, apart from its own work. America is the richest country today in the world. America was developed by money from England, or from other countries and South America was developed by other countries. Therefore, whether it is loans from our own people because loans from our own people are important, or loans from abroad or credits, without that all your taxation will not carry you through. Of course, you can reduce your tempo of progress and do something in 20 years that you want to do in five years, that is a different matter. But then tempo becomes smaller and meanwhile social problems come in and overwhelm us. We have to go fast, we have no escape from it. Apart from everything else, an increase of, I do not know how many millions, population every year, who want to eat, who want to dress, who want work, that itself is a social problem. But that is to keep just at the level, but we want to go ahead. Therefore, we want much more money, even more than the taxation can supply us. Taxation should be used, as much as possible, certainly, always keeping in view that it helps the productive apparatus in the country and not injure it. One of our friends, I think, Mr Mool Chand Jain, said about the bad atmosphere created in the country by certain people, capitalists or others, call them what you like, by running down this legislation and saying that the country is going to the dogs and so on and so forth. I think that is a very wrong thing and it is highly objectionable thing. It is my conviction, my basic conviction, that the economy of India is a sound economy. We may have difficulties. India has the strength to do things, it has even the wealth and potential to do things, more than people think but we cannot suddenly use it up. Here in Assam we find oil. Now oil is probably the most easily convertible form of wealth. You can just throw it in the market when people pick it up and pay you in gold for it, here we are. It is there and we cannot use it immediately. We cannot use it until we put up plants and this and that and refineries and all that, it takes years. We cannot even put up the refineries because an argument is going on about the refineries. You see the things that come in the way.

So, although wealth is there, we cannot immediately use it. So, there are many types of wealth in India, potential wealth which are there but it will take us time and further investment to use that wealth, so, I think, it is very wrong for people to go about shouting and creating an atmosphere of depression and defeatism. There is no question of defeatism, but at the same time it is equally bad for people to have to be complacent—all is well nothing is to be done. That is equally bad if not worse. Because undoubtedly, we have taken on a big job, and the big job requires hard work. Now I give you an example. Take France, it is brilliant in science and literature, in many things, even in technique, their machines are very good but they are not hard working in that sense, they like holidays, they like this, they want six hours a day of work or seven hours whatever it is and the result is often, their governments do not seem to last long. And the result is they are having a boom in industry and yet economically, they are on the verge of collapse, it is a very odd situation. Ultimately, it is hard work that is important, whatever steps we may take. I was talking about some people who create an impression of defeatism, but now in a country which wants to go ahead, it is essential to have, to create a belief and an impression of growth, of going ahead, of optimism, of progress which is the reverse of the defeatist thing, that is quite essential, it helps obviously, nothing succeeds like success. So, that it is tremendous injury, people to go on running things down and all this, they are doing it wherever they might be. But I do not think there is any reason for us to be defeatists but as I said we dare not be complacent and we must realize that hard work is necessary, and we must realize that the problem that we have to face is not a new problem for us; every country is facing it. China is facing an even more difficult problem and there, as I said, they have no inhibitions about rich men and others, they take their property but the problem remains because the problem is not solved by money going from one pocket to another, the problem is basically of production, of creation of new things. Finally, the man, as something said long ago, who makes two blades of grass grow where there is one blade, is a benefactor to humanity. Whether that is in the field or the factory or somewhere else. Judged from this point of view, this succession, we have to create, we have to encourage all the incentives for production, we have to create a feeling of confidence in the country that we are going ahead and producing more and more. These are basic things. We have to create confidence even in the rest of the world. Because frankly, we want the rest of the world to help us too by loans, we do not want any gifts, only loans and other things. All these factors have to be kept in mind which will increase wealth which then leads us step by step towards better living conditions, a welfare state and gradually to the socialist state. Meanwhile, of course, we should proceed on the other side, if you might call gradual levelling—gradual, because if the levelling process is such as to stop or to slow down the productive apparatus then it is doing harm. The taxation is supposed to level gradually, that has to be borne in mind. Of course opinions may differ as to where the balance lies between the two but you cannot simply talk about this levelling process, this man is a rich man, knock off his head. Now, a man who is not productively rich like the prince, broadly speaking, he is not creative or productive, and does not matter much what he does or does not do. But the productive elements in the community whether they are technical people, whether he is the engineer of any kind, or the doctor or technician, these are the people we have to encourage, we have to train, and among the productive elements is also the capitalists, very much so. Forget some big people, who exploit the situation and make money, deal with them in other ways if you like, but today if we want to go ahead,we must not only have the public sector functioning but the private sector producing as much as they can and if the private sector or some individual makes some money thereby, I do not like it, but I allow him to make the money because I am keen on wealth being produced. I try to tax him in other ways but I do not want to do something which is going to imperil my productive apparatus at a moment when we want it above all things to produce. We have many ways of dealing with the individual who misbehaves, let us perfect them, let us get as much out from him by taxes but the apparatus must not suffer. Secondly, the individuals, I am not talking of the capitalists now, but the individuals who are the most important individuals in the community—the technicians, the scientists and others, they must be encouraged. The other day, I was reading an article about science in Soviet Union, by a very eminent British scientist, who had gone there recently. He said that the Soviet Union was spending more on science than all the rest of the world put together, including a rich country like America, because they attach value to science. A scientist there is the highest paid of all. In America, which is a highly capitalist society, the differences in the pay of scientists were one to five, in England the differences were one to seven, in the Soviet Union the differences were one to twenty-five, so much more they pay, twenty-five times they pay because they want to encourage science. I remember, I asked them when I was there, about payment, 'Oh!' they said, Mr Khrushchev told me, "we gave up the idea of equal pay long ago, we want incentives, we want the man to do his best and we pay for good work if he is a brilliant man, we pay him anything he demands, because we want that brilliance out of him". See, that is the way, they are practical people, they want results and they are doing it. We have to face this question daily. Now that we are going into high class industry, technical men, it is our misfortune that some hundred-two hundred of our brilliant men are working abroad, in America, in Germany and all over the place, and it is not that they are very avaricious, not that but still we want some kind of inducements to do creative work. So, keep all these things in mind.

Now two or three matters we have referred to. Our friend Mr Mool Chand Jain was laying great stress on the fact that these taxes affect 36,000 families only. That is probably true, whether it is 30,000 or 40,000, that is immaterial obviously. Only a handful of people in our country pay income tax, absurdly small number. In England with a population of, I forget, about 7 crores, 3½ crores pay income tax, think of that, more than half the population of England pays income tax, terrific number. It shows the standards, how high they have risen. And it is a fact that it is a sign of a poverty-stricken country that most people are below any level of taxation, they may pay a little rent or something whatever it is. We have to raise it, but the fact that 36,000 people are affected only shows that we are such a terribly poor country, we want more people to be affected, we want more people to come up to that level. Suppose I put it to you, suppose that by an equalization of all of the moneys that are at our disposal in India, if we could equalize everybody's income, at its present level, what would the Finance Minister do afterwards, he will have nobody to tax at all. He simply sits tight, there will be no income tax left of any type, there will be no wealth tax, no tax, except maybe this indirect taxation, we will rely upon that, you see it is an odd position. You can't jump from one structure of society to another, you can go to it gradually but only through the process of wealth production, then you can go, if you stop the process of wealth production, then you are hampered, you just remain in the ditch where you are, you do not get out of it. Ah! but this process of wealth production should be such that the community benefits by it, that is a different matter. As we are today, situated as we are circumstanced, we want to encourage every possibility and every individual that produces wealth in India, private sector, public sector, whatever it is, because we want the wealth in India, then by taxation we can deal with that. Now as I said the princes do not come in the category of wealth producing individuals, they are only wealth consuming and if we deal with them in another way as suggested, it is because of a number of factors and frankly, the principal factor is that we, as a Government in our Constitution and otherwise, gave them some guarantees and we gave them those guarantees not because of the love of them, but because to have a peaceful transfer of power in India in 1947. It was a price, and if you like, a heavy price that we paid for them. It was not a heavy price for peace, because if it had not been peace the price will be much heavier, terribly heavier, that is why we paid the price. Now, I do not like, as I said the other day, that I did not like this at all at that time, but there it was, it was a price and we paid it, and I do think that to some extent our honour is involved in it. I do not mean to say this condition should remain for ever there, we are changing it, they are being changed, but I do not wish to break a pledged word which this very Government gave to people, for me, the four or five or six or seven crores that we might get out of them in this way is nothing compared to the value of our word which was much more important. As a matter of fact, I want you to appreciate that this is the best way that we have suggested. Now, in the amendments, I think, there is a reference to the possibility of compounding with them. I hope this will be acted upon because that will ease my conscience because compounding means their agreement and my agreement, it does not mean that we have broken our pledged word, but of course, under the pressures that exist today they will compound, they are bound to compound. In fact they have made offers which are on the whole very favourable to us. In fact, I cannot say whether the capitalists or princes go to the Supreme Court no doubt, I have no doubt that people will go to Supreme Court, nobody wanted to prevent them from going to Supreme Court, there are enough lawyers to force them to go to it, so they will go. But that apart, by this process of compounding, we get rid of this problems and we get the money quickly and without difficulty, it may be a little less. But we get it quickly and without difficulty.

Now, two things have been mentioned specially about the house that has been exempted, one house or one palace and jewellery. Stress has been laid on the house that has been exempted. I think, stress might have also been laid on many houses and palaces that are not exempted. Surely, that is very important because most of them have far more than one house, many more, and it is other houses that are not exempted that count. Now, if you think of it, it is all very well for you to say that take possession of the house or whatever it is, but our Government will be put in an impossible position as these houses and palaces are unsaleable, nobody wants them. Old-styled houses which cannot be used for modern purpose, which costs a lot in maintenance, in repair and all that, nobody wants them very much, and I know quite a number of these princes have come to me and said, "for God sake relieve us of these houses because they add burden to us. We have to keep hundreds of people to look after them or thousands of people". So, they are welcome in the sense they are big houses but really they are not wealth producing, we get nothing out of them. Nevertheless, they have not been excluded. It may be of course, that when our man goes to compute the value of this palace, he may put it down to no value or big value, it depends because it is no good putting it at a value which nobody in the world is going to pay for it. The last is sale value or take the zamindars' houses, not in cities but in the districts. Here is a big house, nobody is going to buy it, if you like, of course, if you can use it, you can take it, but my knowledge of the zamindars' houses is nowadays that you cannot make use of those houses for any decent purpose. They are so badly made and crumbling and all that, you cannot use it, unless you spend large sums of money on repairs. So that, so far as exempting one house is concerned, that is no great thing and it is, you see, we do not want to create social upsets. The Nizam has, I forget, about 10,000 persons who were employed in *Sarf-e-Khas*. I am not talking about his private men in his palace that is a different thing, but 10 or 12 thousand persons were employed in

Sarf-e-Khas. *Sarf-e-Khas* had been taken over by Government. He is still paying those 10,000 or 12,000 persons, not very much, I suppose, but still he is paying them. Now suddenly, suppose these 12,000 persons are some day thrown into the street, well, it is a great nuisance whether for Hyderabad, for Andhra Government, or any government. Social problems arise everywhere and we want to ease this period of transition, obviously they cannot be supported forever all these thousands and thousands of persons, but gradually this process is going on, it has gone on in the last five to six or to ten years, it is going on. This Wealth Tax will push this process, more so we are going in that direction without creating major social upsets and you can take it from me that you cannot get much more from the princes, that is to say short of expropriation and telling them to stop everything, you can't, because it would mean far greater upsets and difficulties which you have to face. Then again this is a matter you begin, this talk for the first time. We can consider how it progresses, what the results are, we can see. Then about the suggested amendment about jewellery is an extraordinarily good one. What is the amendment? The amendment is that such of the jewellery as is considered a heirloom and is looked upon as the property of the State is exempted. Now, somebody said there are no lists of this, it does not matter. We say either the rule says that this is my personal property or it is State property which he can use, but which he cannot sell, which he cannot dispose of; there is a wealth which remains with the State of India, that wealth. So, he is to choose, he has to make a difficult choice, because if he says it is a personal property then tax comes in, if he says that it belongs to State although he can use it, then it becomes the property of the State definitely and a part of the wealth of the nation. So, I think, it is a very good alternative to place before him. Let him choose, we are not going to press him to choose this way or that way, whichever way he chooses we accept. So, I should like you to consider this broad approach to this Bill and may be to the next Bill, expand the tax from this point of view that we are going along, we must have some philosophy. It is not merely a question of knocking somebody on the head. It is true, it is quite easy for me or for you to go to the Ramlila Ground and deliver a speech of how we are going to knock all the capitalists on the head or all princes on the head, but that is not very helpful. We have to utilize them to the best advantage and think always of the productive apparatus increasing, becoming more and more powerful.

19. To Jagjivan Ram[1]

New Delhi
27th August, 1957

My dear Jagjivan Ram,[2]

Yesterday there were some questions in the Lok Sabha about the price of locomotives made in Chittaranjan and in Telco. There were so many questions that the Speaker has, I believe, fixed some day for a discussion.[3]

I should like to have some particulars about these prices. I understand that the price of the Telco locomotive (small size) is about the same as the Chittaranjan (big size). The price of the imported small size locomotive is much less than Telco's price. Further that Chittaranjan can make the smaller locomotives at a much lesser price than Telcos are doing.

All this is very confusing and I shall be grateful if you will have some figures sent to me.

Yours sincerely,
Jawaharlal Nehru

---

1. JN Collection.
2. Union Minister of Railways.
3. On 5 September, Feroze Gandhi raised the question of higher prices being paid by the Government of India to Telco for manufacturing boilers and locomotives under the agreement signed on 20 August 1947, which took effect from 1945.

20. Discussion on Taxation Proposals—II[1]

Before we consider the Expenditure Tax, there are two matters which I should like to refer to. One is a letter received from Dr Sushila Nayar.[2] This relates to the Wealth Tax which has already been passed. Now, for your information, I might tell you that when the Executive of the Party met and considered this matter, they decided three things. The question raised was about the equipment, etc., which medical practitioners use whether that equipment should come within the purview of the Wealth Tax or not. In the original draft it was said that there was a ceiling for tools and instruments for everybody up to Rs 10,000. Now, when we were discussing this, it was pointed out by the Finance Minister that to make a special exception in law for one profession might be considered as almost unconstitutional perhaps because it was discrimination and therefore it is difficult to make a special exception for medical practitioners although they may be more concerned with it than others. In a sense, every profession, every technical profession has tools, all kinds of tools. Ultimately, the Executive Committee came to three decisions. First was to raise the ceiling for tools and instruments for everybody from Rs 10,000 to Rs 20,000. The second was to exclude instruments of scientific research from the levy of Wealth Tax. Now, this is not discrimination for a profession, it was a general thing that instruments used for scientific research by anybody should be excluded, that is all right and these two have been passed in the Act. The third because we found considerable difficulties in dealing with a profession, the Executive Committee said, and the Finance Minister agreed with this, that some rules should be framed so as to exclude or deal in a special way with tools, equipments etc., which are used for

---

1. Speech at the Congress Parliamentary Party meeting, New Delhi, 2 September 1957. Tape No. M-27/c (i), NMML. Extracts.
2. (1914-2001); medical attendant to Mahatma Gandhi and his Ashram; participated in freedom movement; imprisoned with Gandhiji and Kasturba, 1942-44; Secretary, Advisory Leprosy Board, Gandhi Smarak Nidhi, 1950-52; Chief Medical Officer, Badshah Khan Hospital, Faridabad, 1950-52; MLA, Delhi, 1952-56; Minister of Health, Rehabilitation, Transport and Cheritable Endowments, Delhi Government, 1952-55; Speaker, Delhi Assembly, 1955-56; India's Representative to the Social Commission of UN, 1955-58; Member, Lok Sabha, 1957-1971 and 1977-79; Union Minister of Health, Local-Self Government, Town Planning and Family Planning, 1962-67; President, AIIMS, New Delhi, 1964-67; Director of Mahatma Gandhi Institute of Medical Sciences, and President of Kasturba Health Society, 1964-2001; President, Academic Committee of AIIMS, 1977-1979.

the purpose of relieving pain. But it would apply mostly to medical instruments. A rule should be framed to that effect, that was the decision of the Executive Committee accepted by all of us and by the Finance Minister. There the matter stands and the Bill has been passed.

Now, Dr Sushila Nayar subsequently said that she rather doubted whether these rules could be legitimately framed by the Finance Ministry. Therefore, she wanted some kind of authority to do so in the Act itself, when the Act is passed. I should personally think that if a thing is agreed to by the Finance Minister, he will see to it that suitable rules are framed. I do not think any suitable rules will not be for a profession but rather for instruments to relieve pain etc., etc., that type of thing, treatment of pain, I think that this should be adequate and we should leave it at that and see what happens.

Another point is, a Member, Shri Dasappa[3] came to me and went to the Finance Minister also in connection with the Life Insurance Corporation Bill. I shall read out a letter which I have received, that the object of above Bill etc., written in the statement itself is that the knowledge and experience of the business acquired by the companies and firms who were working as principal agents should not be lost to the general insurance industry. As the Insurance Act stands now, the firms carrying on as principal agents could not carry on as such after 31st August 1957. This was done evidently to eliminate intermediaries between the insurer and the ordinary agents. The present Bill is to enable such firms if they so desire to continue as ordinary agents. My amendments, that is Mr Dasappa's amendment, is to apply the same principle to the firms who used to function as chief agents or special agents in the life insurance business and enable them, if they so desire to continue as ordinary agents. It is merely an enabling position and costs no extra or abnormal obligation on the Corporation. This is only fair to the firms who have been in the life insurance business and what is more will materially help in increased business for the Life Insurance Corporation with no additional obligations whatever. I request you to have the matter considered at the meeting of the Executive Council of the Party, etc. The Finance Minister has written a small note to the Secretary of our Party: "Please refer to your letter of given date regarding Dasappa's suggestion to hold a meeting. He has written to the PM. What he suggests is not an amendment to the present Bill, it is a major change in the policy of the Life Insurance Corporation. The present Bill contemplates continuing companies who are principal agents in the field of general insurance as ordinary agents. He wants to take advantage of this amendment to include a provision in the law that companies could be agents of the Life Insurance Corporation as well." You see the difference, one is general

3. H.C. Dasappa was Lok Sabha Member from Bangalore.

insurance, the other is making them agents of the Life Insurance Corporation as well. This is not a matter which I could decide, even assuming I want to, without the question being considered by the Life Insurance Corporation Board and by the Cabinet. In any event, I am not in favour of the amendment. So, that is the position. I confess, I am not expert enough in life insurance matters to have any opinion about this. But the Finance Minister, as he has written, thought this was extending the scope of the Bill which was dealing in the particular matter of general insurance to include in this the life insurance too. I thought I should inform you of this.[4]

...It has no bearing on this Bill. You cannot start discussing anything you like, for example, the Jallianwala Bagh or Mutiny, etc. After all, there should be some relevance. There is no point in becoming emotional and passionate. This is the city of Delhi, not the Punjab. What is this *tamasha* you are creating here. You are making reckless allegations as if everyone present here is dishonest, corrupt, etc. You and your colleagues seem to be the only ones upholding the flag of Independence. Is it proper for you to say such things? It is really amazing. Do use your brains a little. Talk some sense. You are out with a knife for everyone. Have you said anything from beginning to end which is to the point except that the moneyed classes want to protect their wealth? There should be some logical argument, after all, you cannot achieve *Swaraj* or socialism by merely abusing others.

> Mool Chand Jain: My concrete proposal is that there should be no concessions and the original Bill should be passed. Only then we can justify all our other taxation proposals before the country.

JN: I said his emotions, what Mool Chandji said, well, do honour to his emotions and feelings, and it is right that we should have these emotions and feelings. But we have to have something more than emotions and feelings when we are considering rather complicated questions, economic and other questions. And I am quite sure that Mr Mool Chand Jain would perform a very great service if he used those feelings and emotions for constructive thinking on these very complicated questions. Yesterday, I ventured to speak in the AICC, and here also last time I spoke— we are apt to confuse a number of things. If you look at the picture of the world today we see something that is very alarming and that is, that certain rich countries are becoming richer and richer and richer, and the fact is that they have got the wealth producing apparatus functioning with such efficiency that they go on producing more and more wealth, the more you have the more you get, now that applies everywhere. It applies to the underdeveloped

4. Nehru spoke in Hindi after this.

countries, the real difficulty is, you have to make an underdeveloped country a wealth producing country, and by wealth I mean, of course, production whether it is from land, whether it is from industry, whether it is from anything. Now, it is a difficult thing to do that, to get that machine. Ultimately, all this depends why are the wealthy countries today wealthy in the world, because in the last hundred years or more they have built up certain scientific methods of production, taking advantage of technology and the rest. And because this is most important of all, they have built up trained people, trained in technology, trained in other things, trained in bodily fitness, bodily health, mental health, it is the individual that counts ultimately. The two processes go together, that is, the individual improving and thereby doing better work, producing more wealth and so on, it is tied up. If you leave things to pure change as presumably in a society based on orthodox principles of laissez-faire, then there is not a shadow of a doubt that divergences increase, that the fleet of foot and the strong run, go ahead and knock down the others and leave the others behind, there is no doubt about it. I have not a shadow of doubt that India of today, if we did not take particular care to protect the scheduled castes and the scheduled tribes, will go to the dogs, go to the war, not that they are not competent but they have not the chance and if you give them more chance you have to come in the way of laissez-faire and all that. So that we have to remember always these broad principles, how are we to cross this barrier of poverty because poverty itself unfortunately encourages poverty, it drags down a man, just as riches increase more riches, it is an unfortunate fact. In ten years we have worked hard, we made some progress, I think, but fact of the matter is that in these very ten years the distance that separated us from the citizens of the United States and the citizens of India ten years ago, is far greater today than it was then. It is getting richer and richer and richer because of the productive apparatus. There it is. And this process will go on and here we are gasping for breath. Population increases, our production increases but not so much as to give enough of the good things of life to it because our apparatus of production is not functioning well. Now the Second Five Year Plan is to make that apparatus function. The only test of future progress is, how will you make that apparatus successful and function to produce more and more and a part of that inevitably, apart from social problems, is improving the individual in India by better education, better health because of better technical education and the like. Now, you have to see these problems constructively as a whole, merely giving way to righteous indignation, which is quite justified and legitimate if you see the poverty around you. Now, we as members, know all very well. Expressing our indignation on occasions, but as Members of Parliament, we have to take a more painfully constructive view. It is painful, these appraisals—what we can do, what we cannot do, how we can do it, and only then we can really achieve results in constructive thinking, that is why I interrupted. I am sorry, I interrupted my colleague Mool Chandji because I liked his enthusiasm and all that he has got so much energy in him but I would like him to think on these problems in this constructive way because they are terribly difficult problems and we really fight for survival as a country, as everything here, this wretched population is increasing by five million or how much per year I do not know. The thing we produce most is babies in this country, not food, not clothing, babies of course, unlimited babies, other things are all limited.

21. Soviet Assistance for Manufacture of Drugs[1]

Some time back, the Planning Commission considered the utilization of the five hundred million Roubles credit offered to us by the Soviet Government. They made some suggestions, and I understand that a Soviet team is here now to discuss this.

2. There is one matter, however, which has not been fully decided upon yet. This is about the Drug Industry. Some decisions were made by the Commerce & Industry Ministry, and the Planning Commission also, I think, considered them and approved of them. Subsequently, suggestions were made that the Soviet offer for this as a whole might again be considered. We were also told that the Soviet were prepared to advance us an additional credit for a hundred million Roubles.

3. I think that it would be desirable for this question of the Drug Industry to be considered by the Economic Committee of the Cabinet. They would consider not only this particular question, but the context in which all this has arisen.

I suggest that you might get in touch with the Commerce & Industry Ministry and request them to prepare a paper for the Economic Committee of the Cabinet. I have written to Shri Morarji Desai on this subject also.

---

1. Note to M.K. Vellodi, Cabinet Secretary, New Delhi, 2 September 1957. File No. 17(48)/56-66-PMS. Also available in JN Collection.

22. To Chief Ministers[1]

New Delhi
September 5, 1957

My dear Chief Minister,

Recently at the meeting of the AICC,[2] there were long discussions on the land problem. Many of you must have participated in them. I am not for the present referring to various aspects of this problem, important as they are. But it seems to me that something of the most important significance and importance is to prevent ejectment of tenants. Information comes to me from time to time about this ejectment continuing in various states and sometimes this is on a fairly large scale. In fact, the very measures of land reform that are initiated sometimes lead to this type of ejectment.

I think that each state must deal with this matter urgently and effectively. If the law is lacking, then something should be done forthwith to rectify it. But apart from the law, it is the administrative set-up that can deal with this matter effectively if it chooses to do so. My own impression is that District Magistrates and others are lax in this respect. I am sure they could do a great deal if they were told of the vital importance of preventing ejectments.

The Congress President[3] has drawn my particular attention to this matter. I feel as strongly as he does on this subject. I earnestly hope that you will take measures to stop all kinds of ejectment of tenants immediately.

Yours sincerely,
Jawaharlal Nehru

---

1. JN Collection. Also available in G. Parthasarathi (ed.), *Jawaharlal Nehru: Letters to Chief Ministers 1947-1964,* Vol. 4 (New Delhi, 1988), pp. 554-555.
2. Held in Delhi from 31 August to 2 September 1957. See *post*, pp. 455-456.
3. U.N. Dhebar.

23. *Khadi Gramodyog*[1]

Khadi Gramodyog is an unpretentious journal which serves a useful purpose.[2] To all the workers of Khadi Gramodyog and those interested in these subjects, it brings the experience of others and reports of progress being made.

It must be remembered that in our Second Five Year Plan, for all the stress on heavy industry, the role of cottage industries is duly emphasized. So far as our Community Development Schemes are concerned, the promotion of cottage industries is one of their most important tasks, next only to increasing food production.

I am convinced of the importance of the growth of village industries in India, but I am equally convinced that they can only grow if they use the highest techniques available to them. I hope, therefore, that the attempt to utilize higher techniques by our cottage industries will always continue to be made.

1. Message sent to Pranlal S. Kapadia, Secretary, Khadi and Village Industries Commission, New Delhi, 7 September 1957. JN Collection.
2. It is a monthly journal published from Bombay by Khadi and Village Industries Commission and deals with the issues of rural economy.

24. To D.P. Karmarkar[1]

New Delhi
7th September, 1957

My dear Karmarkar,[2]

In a report I have received about the Community Development Schemes, the following passage occurs:

"In regard to Panchayat, as PM knows, this subject at the Centre, is vested in the Ministry of Health. Ministry of Health as it is, is more oriented towards its primary function, namely, health than of local self-government. In local self-government they are for obvious reasons more oriented towards

1. File No. 17(28)/57-PMS. Also available in JN Collection.
2. Union Minister of State for Health.

institutions in urban areas than those which relate to the villages. Panchayats and even the District Boards, therefore, suffer in default."

Panchayats is, of course, a very much State subject and the Centre, I suppose, has done very little in regard to them. I do not know what the Health Ministry does so far as Panchayats are concerned. It seems to me that there is a close connection between the Panchayats and the Community Development Schemes. Indeed, the Panchayats are supposed to be an integral part of these Schemes. Therefore, it would be more appropriate and useful if this subject of Panchayats, in so far as the Centre deals with it, is put under the Ministry of Community Development.[3]

I hope that you will agree with this suggestion.

Yours sincerely,
Jawaharlal Nehru

3. Nehru also wrote to S.K. Dey on 17 October 1957 (not printed) that this would require some change in List II of the Seventh Schedule.

25. To T.T. Krishnamachari[1]

New Delhi
September 9, 1957

My dear TT,

Your letter of September 9th.[2] I have not quite understood it. As I understand it, the total foreign exchange cost for the Bhilai Plant having gone up by Rs 23-50

1. File No. 17(214)/56-66-PMS.
2. T.T. Krishnamachari had written that the negotiations between the Indian and Soviet representatives had started for utilization of the Russian aid of about Rs 60 crores. The directive was to negotiate the aid for five projects namely, (i) Heavy Machine Building Plant, (ii) Coal Machinery Plant, (iii) Development of Korba Coal fields, establishment of a washery and a Central Workshop, (iv) Optical Glass Factory, and (v) Thermal Power Station at Neyvelli based on lignite. Krishnamachari wrote that in view of difficult foreign exchange situation, it might be desirable to suggest that a part of this credit should be utilized for Bhilai Steel Plant, for which foreign exchange to the tune of Rs 23.50 crores more was required.

crores, this money has to be found either from the credit of 500 million Roubles (Rs 60 crores) or by an additional credit of about Rs 25 crores from the Soviet Union. If we can obtain the additional credit, then the question of substitution does not arise, that is, the five projects already agreed to are not interfered with. I have no objection to the Soviet team being asked for an additional credit of Rs 25 crores as suggested.

I do not like the idea of the five projects which we decided upon after long discussion, to be interfered with or partly given up. This for two reasons: firstly, because, having arrived at a certain decision after a very long consultation and discussion, it would not be fair for us to bypass that decision; secondly, and this is more important, this kind of shifting about must necessarily create a bad impression on the Russians. As I told you, in another connection the other day, I have a feeling that we have not dealt with the Russians in a forthright manner about various matters. They have offered help to us in many ways and on many occasions. We have encouraged them to do so and then allowed the matter to drop. I know that they feel this and think naturally that we have done this for political reasons. I should not like any such impression to remain with them, far less to be strengthened.

If we try to go back on those five projects, this is bound to create some surprise and misunderstanding in their minds. They are suspicious people. Also, it would mean that we cannot make up our minds.

If, however, we hold to those five and point out to the Russians that owing to various reasons or developments, the foreign exchange cost of the Bhilai Plant has gone up and this has created difficulties for us. Either the Bhilai Plant will have to be delayed, which we would not like to happen, and I am sure the Russians would not like it either, or some additional arrangement in the shape of credit has to be made. I imagine that if this is put to them this way, they are likely to agree to this additional credit.

It is not clear to me how the foreign exchange component of the Bhilai Plant has gone up by Rs 23.50 crores. I was under the impression that the Russians had agreed to take charge of this foreign exchange component of that Plant.

Yours sincerely,
Jawaharlal Nehru

26. Exemptions from Wealth Tax[1]

Please write to the Honorary Secretary of the Indian Merchants' Chamber, Kampala (Uganda) as follows:-

Dear Sir,
The Prime Minister has received your letter of the 27th August regarding the Wealth Tax. He has also received your cable.
I am desired to inform you that according to the law relating to Wealth Tax, as finally passed, the request of your Chamber has been fully met, that is, the foreign wealth of Indians not resident or not ordinarily resident in India is totally exempt from this tax.

1. Note to K. Ram, Principal Private Secretary, New Delhi, 9 September 1957. JN Collection.

27. Message for *Kurukshetra*[1]

Every year I am asked to send a message to *Kurukshetra*[2] for the Community Development Programme. I have gladly done so because of my great interest in this programme and the importance I have attached to it.

This programme now covers more than half of rural India and is advancing rapidly with the intention of covering all our villages.

But it is not the extent of its coverage or the number of villages that are included in this scheme that is of primary interest to me. What I am deeply interested in is the quality of the work done and the extent to which this programme is vitalizing our rural people and producing better human beings.

Nothing can be more important than this vital work of building Indian humanity. It is the peasant who has borne the burden of India for ages past. It is

1. Message to the fifth anniversary issue of *Kurukshetra*, New Delhi, 9 September 1957. JN Collection.
2. A fortnightly journal published by the Ministry of Rural Development in Hindi and English.

on the growth and betterment of our peasantry that the future of India must necessarily depend.

Today, we are laying the greatest stress on two lines of advance—greater food production and more cottage and small-scale industries. Food has become the corner-stone of our planning and this means more intensive growth. We have made many appeals in the past for this purpose and they have brought results. The time has now come not merely for general appeals but for a specific and planned approach to each village and almost to each family, so that targets may be laid down and we may work up to them.

What is the future of our peasantry? The great number of them have barely one or two acres of land to cultivate. It is possible and necessary to increase the yield of this little patch of land and thus to better somewhat the condition of the peasant. But there is a limit to this, the limit laid down by the smallness of that holding.

There are too many people in India subsisting on land. This means that many people must take to other activities and occupations. Some of these can be whole time activities and some part time allied to agriculture. Herein is the importance of our cottage and small industries programme. No doubt, as large industries grow up, many people from the rural areas will be attracted to them. But however speedy the growth of large industries, the major problem of unemployment and other occupations will not be solved by them. It can only be progressively solved by the development of cottage and small-scale industries.

Even so, how will the peasant function with his small patch of land? It is not possible for him to take advantage of modern techniques or the facilities offered by new methods unless he works in cooperation with others of his kind. Cooperation is the key to his future growth and the cooperative movement thus must spread all over the country and comprise all the villages and peasants of this vast land.

What kind of cooperation? There are the so-called service cooperatives, there are those which deal with credit. We have in the past laid stress mostly on credit cooperatives and they are no doubt helpful, but they are not enough. We must cover a much larger field through our cooperative movement. Indeed, the cooperative movement should enter into the life of the peasant in as many ways as possible and, together with the Panchayat, must be the main bulwark of our rural structure.

The next stage of cooperation is joint farming and there has been some argument about this. I have no doubt that joint farming, wherever possible and agreed to, will be good, but it must be clearly understood that there can be no imposition and this can only be brought in by the agreement of the parties. To begin with, there must be the service cooperatives and as these succeed, the next step may well be some joint farms. Where new land is brought into cultivation, it may be possible to have this joint cultivation to begin with.

I would prefer relatively small cooperatives comprising one or two or three villages. It seems essential to me that a cooperative should not be controlled from above, not too officialized, but should represent the spirit of self-reliance and self-growth of the people. Also there should be an intimacy about its members, otherwise it becomes impersonal and difficult for the villagers to consider as something their own.

This whole movement, as our entire political and economic structure in India, must be conditioned by the democratic process.

The Community Development Programmes have undertaken a mighty task and they are gradually building up a trained and peaceful army of young men and young women. If they are trained properly and work well, they will be the salt of the Indian earth.

28. To S.N. Mishra[1]

New Delhi
September 10, 1957

My dear Shyam Nandan,[2]

Your letter of the 31st August. I am sorry for the delay in answering it. I thought that there was no need to answer it as I had decided to attend the celebration of the National Plan Day on the 13th September by the Planning Forums in the Universities and constituent colleges all over India.[3]

I am happy to learn of the great progress made by these University Planning Forums. It was only a little over a year ago that I inaugurated the first conference of these Planning Forums. The account you give in your letter of this progress is most encouraging and heartening. I must congratulate you and, of course, the Vice Chancellors and the teachers and students of the Universities on the success that has been achieved.

I think, this movement is of great importance. After all, it is the large student body in India that will have to shoulder the burden of building up our country in

1. JN Collection.
2. Union Deputy Minister for Planning.
3. See the next item.

101

the future and to participate in the great schemes of development which are so outstanding a feature of our country today.

I send you and all others who are participating in these Planning Forums all my good wishes.

Yours sincerely,
Jawaharlal Nehru

29. University Planning Forums[1]

Please do not cheer impetuously. Try to understand the issue before forming an opinion. I was about to say that it is obvious that today's agenda will be conducted mostly in Hindi. I may say a few words in English too. But I wanted to give the proceedings a different complexion at least at the beginning. It would seem that you have come here determined to be pleased and to laugh. It is a very good idea provided it does not cloud the other issues. The argument that arose just now between the Vice Chancellor[2] and myself was who should invite whom, whether I should invite him to speak or he should invite me to sit down. One difficulty in that was I was already seated. It was not possible for me to get up and then take a seat at his invitation.

Anyhow, he has discharged a difficult duty by seating me when I was already seated. Now it remains for me to invite him to outline the proceedings of this function. I would like to mention that when Dr Rao came to me a few days ago to invite me, I was not quite sure when I would be able to get away, today being the last day of the Lok Sabha session. But when I heard about this Planning Forum being held in the Delhi University and the enthusiasm it has generated, I felt a strong urge to come here. I do not remember the exact date. But, I think, the idea of Planning Forums in Universities was first mooted by, I think, Shyam Nandan Mishra. At least he had talked to me about it. It seemed a very good idea to me. It has now spread to many colleges and Universities in India. I was

1. Speech at the Delhi University Planning Forum, New Delhi, 13 September 1957. AIR tapes, NMML. Original in Hindi.
2. V.K.R.V. Rao.

102

reassured to hear about the number of places where the idea has been taken up and good work is being done. It is obvious that the decisions that we take in Parliament are of great significance. But what is in a sense even more important is how the minds of youth in India work and how they are preparing themselves to shoulder the burden of this country in the future.

Everybody talks about planning today. But mere talking is of no help. There must be serious thinking and debate around these issues. It provides stimulation to the mind. So, I am happy to see the progress made by the Planning Forums in India. It is a very welcome and essential move. I have felt reassured by the attitude and outlook of our youth and the load seems to have lightened. Times change, people come and go. Soon a time will come when big responsibilities will fall upon your shoulders. India's progress depends on the extent to which you the boys and girls in Universities all over India prepare themselves, physically and mentally, rise above personal consideration and foster unity and cooperation.

What is India after all? It has many aspects to it. Long time ago I wrote a book called *The Discovery of India* and the quest is still on. I catch glimpses of the myriad faces of India and the more I see of it, the more remains to be understood. There can be many answers to the question as to what India stands for. You can look at it from the historical viewpoint or geographical. Its population, rivers, lakes, mountains and cities all go to make up India. But ultimately it is you and I who are India. It is not the mountains and rivers but human beings who are important because we constitute India. We are not apart from India. It is the 37 crores of human beings who make India. Therefore, India will progress only to the extent that we realize this and work together to build a new India bursting with health and vitality. It is in your hands now. Our time is almost up.

It is up to you to think about larger national issues coolly and objectively. Enthusiasm is one thing. But making a noise will get you nowhere. The world is full of complex problems which we have to understand and overcome with courage and fearlessness, without moaning about adversity as some people do.

It is obvious that we are facing grave problems. In some people's perception, India is trying to get out of the deep mire of poverty in which we had been stagnating for centuries. Obviously, there are bound to be difficulties. But we cannot tolerate continuing in that mire any longer.

So, you must think about these issues and argue and debate in order to find some answers. It is obvious that you must listen carefully to what the great pundits like your Vice Chancellor Dr Rao, has to say about these matters. He has given considerable thought to them. Even I seek his advice when I am in a quandary. We are gathered together to hear Dr Rao and I request him to address the gathering now.

30. Foreign Assistance for Development Schemes[1]

In his opening remarks the Chairman, Shri Jawaharlal Nehru, observed that the Standing Committee was meeting soon after the meeting of the National Development Council to consider certain difficult situations affecting the development schemes of the Centre and the States. Referring to the items of the agenda the Chairman suggested that items 1 and 4 could be considered together and similarly items 2 and 3. Item 5 was connected with 2 and 3 but might be taken up separately. The general position was fairly clear but the Finance Minister would give some latest figures about the foreign exchange position. It was perfectly clear that they had to exercise the greatest restraint and cut down imports to the barest minimum. It would be pretty hard to give up many things considered to be important but on the other hand it was essential that the whole structure should not suffer.

2. The Chairman observed that the main purpose of the Finance Minister's tour abroad was to attend the meeting of the World Bank but he would also see how far substantial credits could be obtained abroad. It was clear, however, that whatever credits could be obtained, they had to live a hard life. In the First Five Year Plan they did not have to stretch themselves and no particular effort was needed. Planning necessarily meant stretching and it was good that they had to face suddenly the realities of the situation and the facts of life....

11. The Chief Minister, West Bengal[2] mentioned that propaganda should be done among the people against overeating. His own personal experience was that a large proportion of the people who were sick got their illness as a result of eating too much. Dr Roy said that it was perhaps not necessary for every person to have 3000 calories. He saw in Japan that even men working for more than 13 hours a day were taking only food with a calories value of 2200. The problem was really one of balancing the diet. Dr Roy said that it would be desirable to draw the attention of the States to do propaganda in this regard.

The Chairman observed that there was ill-health in India mainly because of the unbalanced and unhealthy food, excess of rice, wheat etc....

---

1. Summary record of the fifth meeting of the Standing Committee of the National Development Council, New Delhi, 14th September 1957. File No. PC/ CDN/29/15/57, Coordination Branch, Planning Commission. Only extracts are available. For the next meeting see *post*, pp. 153-155.
2. B.C. Roy.

19. Dr Sinha[3] then referred to the particular difficulty which was experienced by Bihar State with regard to the first year of the Second Five Year Plan. He said after the discussion with the Centre, the Plan target for the year 1956-57 was fixed at Rs 22 crores, out of which the State was expected to find Rs 8 crores and there was a gap of Rs 14 crores. Actually from the State's own resources, they spent Rs 8 crores during 1956-57. Out of the additional Rs 14 crores which was spent, the State had not got loans and grants from the Centre amounting to Rs 12 crores. In spite of the fact that the Planning Commission had agreed that the State should get the additional Rs 2 crores which they had not got the amount so far. With regard to the year 1957-58 also, a Plan of Rs 30 crores has been settled after due consultation between the Centre and the State. The State's own contribution would be Rs 12 crores. Out of the remaining 18 crores, so far as the information at the State's disposal went, they would get Rs 11 crores. The remaining 7 crores, referred specially to irrigation and power projects, and certain other projects which were of vital interest to the States. The Chief Minister, Bihar, said that because of the paucity of domestic and foreign exchange resources some rephasing of the Plan would be necessary, but once a Plan has been settled, there should be no uncertainty regarding any portion of the amount.

The Chairman suggested that matters of this sort should be discussed by the Chief Minister and his officers with the Finance Ministry and the Planning Commission.

20. The Finance Minister, Madras (Shri C. Subramaniam) said that the main point for discussion was the question of increasing the total national resources available. The division of such resources as between the States and the Centre was a matter of secondary importance. It is gratifying to note that the Central Government has led the way in the matter of raising revenue resources. If an effort was made, it would certainly be possible to raise further resources. At the same time it has to be borne in mind that taxation by the Central Government and the State Government had to be borne by the same people. Moreover, before the State Government could levy taxes they had to take into account the extent of Central taxation. Apart from this, Shri Subramaniam felt that the existing resources were not being utilized to the maximum advantage. He referred to the decision taken about 18 months ago regarding the replacement of the Sales-Tax on sugar, tobacco and cloth by Excise Duty but the matter was still hanging fire. Evasion of Sales-Tax could be stopped only by the levy of duty at the production point. Some of the States which were industrially advanced were afraid of losing revenue as a result of the proposed replacement of Sales-Tax by the levy of Excise Duty. Just as in dealing with the food Shri Subramaniam said that the

3. Sri Krishna Sinha, Chief Minister of Bihar.

problem of taxation should be looked at from the national point of view and there should be no insistence on obtaining advantages to individual States. Shri Subramaniam said that the proposal made was the simplest and would not hit the consumer to any great extent. Shri Subramaniam said that if they all sat down and discussed the question, it would be possible to select many more articles to be taxed at the source and the formula for distribution could be evolved by the Finance Commission. Unless the problem of raising taxation resources was approached in this manner, it was doubtful whether the States would be able to reach the targets laid down in the Plan. Shri Subramaniam suggested that all existing Sales-Tax legislation should be reviewed and wherever possible alternative methods of collecting taxes at source should be adopted, at least for the Second Plan period.

21. The Chairman observed that it was surprising that no action has been taken on a firm and unanimous decision taken by the National Development Council regarding the replacement of Sales-Tax by Excise Duty on certain articles. The Finance Minister said that the Finance Commission was likely to suggest a formula for the distribution of the realizations from Excise Duty for three categories separately, cloth, sugar and tobacco. The Finance Minister added that on the rates which they were proposing the Excise Duty collections would have been about Rs 15 crores. The total collections indicated by the States, however, came to Rs 26 crores. Shri Subramaniam said that if they were all prepared to accept the Finance Commissions' recommendations, it was possible to proceed straightaway. The Chairman observed that the recommendations of Finance Commission would be available soon and suggested that the matter could be considered at the Conference of the Finance Ministers which was being convened in November....

35. The Chief Minister, Mysore (Shri S. Nijalingappa) said that he agreed with the remarks of the Finance Minister regarding the difficulties but they must realize that a lot of hope has been raised among the people that a large number of industries and power projects were being started. Large number of applications for starting new industries were also being received and there was disappointment that some of the schemes were not going through. There were also requests that machinery should be imported on deferred payments system. He suggested that after reviewing the present position regarding foreign exchange they might encourage the system of getting machinery on deferred payments. Regarding resources, Shri Nijalingappa said that the State has been able to increase resources to a large extent. About two or three crores of Rupees were expected from agricultural taxation and they hoped to get encouraging response to the open market loan. Efforts were being made regarding small savings and they expected to get about 8 crores of Rupees. He said that so far as resources

were concerned, Mysore was in a poor state as they had a number of liabilities immediately as they became a separate State. Even so they were optimistic and every effort would be made to fill up the gap.

36. The Chairman observed that while talking about deferred payments people seemed to think that they were getting things free. By accepting deferred payments future liabilities were added to and great difficulties would have to be faced later. A time has come when they had to think of cutting out even essential things. Even food production would suffer because it was not possible to provide all that was required. The Chairman observed that it was a question of cutting off arms and legs and required a lot of effort....

49. The Chairman enquired how far Community Development movement was being utilized for increasing agricultural production. The Minister for Food and Agriculture,[4] said that at present there was greater coordination between the activities of the Community Development Department and the Agriculture Department. But it could not be said that there was complete coordination in Community Project areas. During 1956-57, agricultural production has increased by 6% as against 5.4% for the whole country. Shri S.K. Dey, the Minister for Community Development, said that the National Sample Survey Organization had undertaken crop cutting experiments both for the *Kharif* and the *Rabi* crops. Three studies have been conducted so far and the tentative results showed that in the NES and CD areas, a 20% increase has been achieved in the *Kharif* crop as compared to the average production in the country.

50. During the discussion which followed it was pointed out that information regarding percentage increase over average production in the country was not significant. What was significant was the progressive increase achieved in the Community Development and National Extension Service areas from year to year. The Minister for Community Development said that it was extremely difficult to measure the progressive increases in the same plot of plant. He added that it was the verdict of the statistical people that an increase has been achieved in the NES and Community Development areas as compared to the other areas. This conclusion was based on three tests over a period of three years of *Kharif* and one year of *Rabi*. In response to a suggestion from the Chairman that a note on the subject should be furnished, the Minister for Community Development said that a note on the subject was being prepared by the National Sample Survey Organization and would be available immediately.

51. The Minister for Community Development, said that instructions had been issued to the States that all agricultural facilities should be concentrated in the Community Project areas and National Extension Service blocks. If the

4. Ajit Prasad Jain.

Agricultural Departments in the States acted on these instructions and paid attention to two or three essential points, there could be substantial increase in food production. One of the essential needs was improved seeds. Secondly, there was the question of supply of fertilizers and good manures. It was clear that there could be 8 to 10% increase in production without any difficulty if fertilizers and good manures could be supplied. The Japanese method of cultivation could not be adopted unless commercial fertilizers were available. Shri Dey said that there was enormous room for increase in agricultural production particularly in the field of rice in the States of Orissa, Bihar, Assam, Bengal, Madhya Pradesh and Andhra Pradesh. An administrative organization was required to push forward the improved methods but all the States have not yet been properly geared for it. If this could be done with the organization which has been set up in the Community Projects and the National Extension blocks, tangible and quick results could be shown.

52. The Minister for Food and Agriculture, said that the question of fertilizers should also be looked upon from the point of view of earning foreign exchange. about 50% of the foreign exchange was earned by exports of cash agricultural crops. If cotton and jute manufactures were added the percentage would be 60.

53. The Chairman observed that wherever necessary the agriculturists should be given sufficient time, to appreciate the advantages of fertilizers which was linked with the provision of irrigation water. Dr B.C. Roy, the Chief Minister of West Bengal, referred in this connection to the fact that an area which was next to the canal got a larger quantity of water because of the absence of a proper canal system. The Chairman suggested that the possibility of spraying water might be considered.

54. The Chairman enquired whether steps were being taken to introduce improved tools. The Minister for Community Development said that improved ploughs were being introduced. For the Japanese method of paddy cultivation everyone was required to resort to line sowing for which weeders were required. Special drills were also being introduced. Shri Dey added that these were all cheap tools. In answer to a query by the Chief Minister of West Bengal, Shri Dey said that the average cultivator, apart from the cultivator in the Community Development area, was also taking advantage of the improved tools. Farmers came 15 to 20 miles to see these improved tools in operation.

31. Marketing of Village Industries' Products[1]

The progress made in pilot project was reviewed. Marketing was felt to be the chief problem. Prime Minister suggested that intensive efforts should be made to create local markets for the products of village industries in the block areas. This could be accomplished to a large extent if cooperative stores were opened in the villages. The societies should have both producers and consumers as members and should do everything possible to enlarge the consumers' demand. A suggestion was made that, possibly, a system of exchange of products (as was introduced in West Bengal sometime ago) might also be considered in this connection. Such exchange of goods produced by artisans in villages could be more effectively brought about if Panchayats were closely associated with marketing, as in certain areas in Bihar.

1. Summary record of the meeting of the Central Committee of the Ministry of Community Development, New Delhi, 17 September 1957. File No. 180/CF/56, Cabinet Secretariat Papers.

32. To Vijaya Lakshmi Pandit[1]

New Delhi
September 17, 1957

Nan dear,[2]
Our Finance Minister, T.T. Krishnamachari, left Delhi this afternoon on his way to Washington. From there he will go to Canada and then to London for a few days and then probably to Germany.[3] Although he is going there to attend the World Bank meetings in Washington, importance is attached to his visit from another point of view, that is, how much credit he can get there. We are in very

1. JN Collection.
2. India's High Commissioner in UK.
3. Krishnamachari returned on 25 October 1957.

grave difficulties which will pursue us for the next few years. The next eighteen months or so are peculiarly difficult.

I do not think there is any hope or chance of our getting substantial help from the United Kingdom. The United States is the only country, apart perhaps from Western Germany, which can help us substantially. We have now to think in terms of hundreds of crores.

Because of this foreign exchange difficulty we have been cutting our plans and projects down to the bone, and sometimes a bit of the bone is taken off too. Only this morning we considered this matter in the Cabinet and we laid down a figure for foreign exchange expenditure during the next six months. This took into consideration such credits abroad as had been promised or were likely to come. It did not include the additional help that we may get in the shape of credits from the United States or other countries as a result of TTK's visit. Taking this figure, we had to cut down very rigorously almost all our plans so much so that even some of our production units have to be stopped or suspended for the time being because we just cannot afford the foreign exchange for the machinery involved. Our past commitments are so heavy that we cannot add to them.

This is a very painful process because it comes in the way actually of the very plans for production that are so necessary for us in order to gain foreign exchange. But there it is, and for the moment, we do not propose to expand at all, so long as further avenues of credit are not visible.

The External Affairs Ministry is not concerned with these plans and projects, but in view of the very difficult situation we have to face, it seems to me that we should do our utmost to save foreign exchange wherever possible. Our biggest expenditure in foreign exchange, in so far as the External Affairs Ministry is concerned, is in London. You are considering this matter, and, I believe, have received our own proposals for economy. I wonder if you could pay particular attention to any cuts that can be made in the immediate future. Every little saving will help us. The general question of reorganization might be considered at some greater leisure, though even that should not be delayed much.

One of our women MPs, namely Maya Chettry[4], whom you probably know, came to see me this afternoon. She is a Nepali and rather a nice woman, quiet and decent. I was much surprised to learn from her that she had been selected by some Gurkha organization to attend "the World Veterans' Federation" meeting in Berlin which, I believe, is due to begin on October 25 and last about a week or so. To think of this frail and gentle-looking woman sitting with the War Veterans is rather odd.

---

4. Maya Devi Chettry (1921-1993); Member, Rajya Sabha from West Bengal, 1952–64; author of many books in Nepalese.

However, I am writing to you because after her visit to Berlin, she wants to go to Paris and later to London for a few days. I hope you will give her every help and look after her. This is her first visit abroad and she will be by herself.

Yours,
Jawahar

33. To Morarji Desai[1]

New Delhi
September 18, 1957

My dear Morarji,

Thank you for your letter of the 17th September, which I received today.[2] I am very glad to read the account you have sent me of the developments in various fields of industry and trade. I have found it very interesting and informative. I shall refer to just a few matters below.

I agree with you that labour should be given incentives and it is not possible to pay labour in the State enterprises at a less rate then that prevailing in private enterprises. You refer to bonuses. Perhaps, these may be thought of. But, it seems to me that it would be advantageous to us to adopt the piece rate system. This is an incentive to higher production and also yields higher wages. In the Soviet Union, this, I believe, is practised.

1. JN Collection.
2. Desai gave an overview of developments in the field of industry and trade. Regarding labour, he wrote that the public sector would have to follow the convention of profit-sharing bonus, as in the private industrial undertakings, or find some equally acceptable alternative. The proposals for Nangal Fertilizer Project were under scrutiny. Negotiations had started with the Russians on various projects for implementation against their 500 million Rouble credit. Desai was anxious to cover the entire foreign exchange, required for completion of these projects, by this credit. Desai mentioned several difficulties in fulfilling the target of 16 million tons annual production of cement such as availability of foreign exchange, transportation, and coal supplies. This required setting up of cement plants in suitable locations in consultations with the Ministries of Railways, and Steel Mines and Fuel. The current annual production of cement at 6.2 million tons from 28 factories was on the increase. He informed that the production of cotton textiles during the first half of this year had gone up by 126 million yards and was expected to increase further. From shortage of cloth in mid-1956, surplus stock was available now. Production of handloom sector had also increased.

111

About cement plants, I entirely agree that they should be decentralized. In fact, we should pay far more attention to this dispersal of plants of various kinds, wherever this is possible, in order to lessen the load on railways. From the strategic point of view also, this is desirable.

I am glad to note that the production of the cotton textile mills has gone up considerably and there is, in fact, an accumulation of stocks. You do not say anything about the export of these cotton textiles. I know that the competition abroad is pretty severe, but it is worth investigating how far we can export them, even if we have to subsidize this a little in some way. This will enable us not only to get foreign exchange, but also to establish ourselves in foreign markets.

I entirely agree with you that it would be tragic to do anything which starts a reverse trend in our production. I do hope that whatever cuts may be necessary, they will not be such as to affect our production.

Yours sincerely,
Jawaharlal Nehru

34. Mundhra Group of Companies[1]

So far as I know, the reputation of this gentleman is not good. Normally both the suggestions made should be given effect to, that is, an investigation into the affairs of the group of companies and appropriate action against the management of the companies concerned for contravention of the provisions of the Companies Act.[2]

---

1. Note to D.L. Mazumdar, Secretary, Company Law Administration, Ministry of Finance, New Delhi, 19 September 1957. JN Collection. This was produced as Exhibit No. 24 before the Chagla Commission.
2. D.L. Mazumdar had forwarded a letter from the Regional Director, Company Law Administration, in Calcutta regarding the affairs of the Mundhra Group of Companies. Mazumdar wrote: "At the end of June this year, the Life Insurance Corporation had to come to the rescue of Shri H.D. Mundhra in circumstances which are probably known to F.M." However, the shares of the Mundhra Group of Companies had been backsliding. The Regional Director suggested an investigation into their affairs under sections 237 to 239 of the Companies Act, and appropriate action against their management for contraventions of the specific provisions of the Companies Act. Mazumdar had forwarded a copy of the Regional Director's letter to the Chairman of the LIC.

2. In view of the consequences of an investigation, I cannot say anything definite at this stage. But some time or other this action will have to be taken. I presume we should wait for the response of the Life Insurance Corporation.

3. Meanwhile the action against defaulting companies need not be delayed.

35. Why Foreign Exchange Difficulties?[1]

During the past few months, there has been much discussion in regard to foreign exchange and a number of steps have been taken to reduce imports as well as various other measures in order to meet the situation.

2. In the course of the various discussions which have taken place, reference has been made to a number of factors which have led to the position that has been created. Some of these factors were outside our control; some were within our control.

3. I think that it is necessary and important that a full note should be prepared by the Planning Commission analyzing all the reasons and factors which have led to our present situation in regard to foreign exchange. There should be a scientific appraisal so that we may know exactly what happened and where we went wrong, and to serve as a warning for us in the future. It is, I take it, the function of the Planning Commission to keep itself and the Government informed of various trends so that, when necessary, steps may be taken to prevent any untoward occurrence. The whole purpose of planning is to know, as far as we can, what is likely to happen so that we can adjust ourselves accordingly. A plan has to be based on reality and to be in constant touch with reality. Otherwise there can be no planning.

4. We have talked about perspective planning. That surely includes a consideration of these factors. As I have said above, we cannot be certain of international developments, though we can keep them in view and to some extent allow for them. But even when some unforeseen occurrence takes place, we should immediately consider the consequences of it and take such steps as may be necessary to meet these consequences.

5. It is apparent that some things have happened, internally and externally,

---

1. Note to the Deputy Chairman, Planning Commission, Lokaranjan Mahal, Mysore, 20 September 1957. File No. 37(35)/56-66-PMS. Also available in File No. PC/CDN/6/4/57, Coordination Branch, Planning Commission and JN Collection.

which we had not planned for, and now we are facing the consequences of these. I am not interested in finding fault with anyone and I suppose that all of us have to shoulder the responsibility. What I am interested in is to understand as clearly as possible what has happened and why it has happened.

6. In this matter some Ministries will necessarily have to be consulted by the Planning Commission and their cooperation sought. Presumably, the Finance Ministry and the Ministry of Commerce & Industry are chiefly concerned. There may be others.

7. An obvious question that arises is why our import policy was on such a big scale so as to produce this big hiatus now. Is it the public sector which is chiefly responsible for this or the private sector? So far as the public sector is concerned, we should know exactly, at every stage, where we are. In regard to the private sector, I am given to understand that it has done very well and exceeded anticipations. That is good in so far as it goes. But if this excess, whether in the private or in the public sector, goes beyond what was laid down in the Plan, then all our planning is affected.

8. I am concerned more about the future than the past, but we have to learn from the past in order not to err in the future. Therefore, I would request you to have a full note prepared in the Planning Commission on the subject and to take the cooperation of the Ministries concerned in it.

9. I am sending a copy of this note to the Ministry of Finance, the Ministry of Commerce & Industry and the Cabinet Secretary.

36. Talk with Vinoba Bhave[1]

It was again in September 1957 that Nehru met Vinoba at Yelwal after the completion of the *Gramdan* Conference. It may be recalled that at this historic conference, different political parties had decided to lend their unqualified support to the *Gramdan* movement. It was also resolved to forge close coordination between *Gramdan* and Community Development in various parts of the country. Pandit Nehru repeated his expectation that *Bhoodan* and *Gramdan*

1. Note on Nehru's talk with Vinoba Bhave at Yelwal, near Mysore on 21 September 1957, as recorded by Shriman Narayan in *Vinoba—His Life and Work* (Bombay, 1970), pp. 309-310. Gulzarilal Nanda, Union Minister of Labour and Employment and Planning, and Shriman Narayan, General Secretary, AICC, were also present during the talk.

campaigns would help in promoting cooperative spirit among the people so that, wherever possible, smaller plots of land could be pooled into bigger ones for better cultivation. Vinoba agreed that this would be desirable, although he did not wish to put any undue pressure on the donees: "The small cultivator should be educated in the advantages of cooperation. But the formation of cooperative societies should be entirely voluntary."

Since the Second General Elections were now over, Vinoba raised the question of electoral reforms once again. This time I could notice a sense of embarrassment on the face of Pandit Nehru. After these elections, the Congress had come out with flying colours at the Centre and in all the States. But Nehru confessed: "Frankly, I am not sure whether a system of indirect elections at the higher levels would really work. It may raise, in turn, a crop of new difficulties and complications. A smaller number of electors in the indirect system of elections may succumb to monetary temptations and vitiate the whole system. There is a definite advantage in appealing to a bigger electorate which could rise above caste and money considerations." He further admitted: "I do not really know how to set about this reform. Other political parties may react quite adversely. Perhaps, I myself lack the courage of conviction. I, therefore, feel rather helpless in the matter."

Before he left for Mysore by road en route to Delhi, Nehru held Vinoba's hands in his, gently bowed in reverence and repeated his decision to ask S.K. Dey, Union Minister in charge of Community Development, to establish close contacts with *Sarvodaya* workers for enabling the *Gramdan* movement to make a visible impact on land reforms in India.

37. Cable to T.T. Krishnamachari[1]

I have just returned from Mysore where I attended *Gramdan* Conference. Also visited Coorg.

There has been some little sensation here about report of some interview you are said to have given to *New York Times* Correspondent in Delhi before your departure. I have not seen *New York Times*, but report here has been given much publicity and given rise to all kinds of questions. I suppose report in *New York*

1. New Delhi, 23 September 1957. JN Collection.

Times is distorted and exaggerated account of what you may have said rather casually.

You are reported to have said that India will collapse and go over to communism if substantial aid is not given and in fact that our Five Year Plan is a Plan to fight communism. Reference is made to Kerala and Dange[2], and Russia and China by name as if both these countries were potentially hostile to us and might help Dange to bring about communist revolution in India.

This has rather boosted Dange and Communist Party in India. But real questions that are asked are whether we have changed our policy of non-alignment and have practically joined anti-communist bloc of countries. Also whether India has no future unless large-scale help comes from America.

Reference to friendly countries as potentially hostile may lead to embarrassing situation for us.

All this is producing rather unhealthy reactions here. I feel sure you could not have meant all you are reported to have said. Perhaps you might clear up these misunderstandings when occasion arises during your tour abroad.

You must be having a very heavy time. We send you all our good wishes.

2. S.A. Dange, General Secretary, AITUC; Member, Central Executive Committee of CPI; elected to Lok Sabha in 1957.

38. To Manubhai M. Shah[1]

New Delhi
September 24, 1957

My dear Manubhai,

Your letter of September 22nd came here when I was away in Mysore.[2]

1. File No. 17(48)/56-66-PMS. Also available in JN Collection.
2. Manubhai Shah discussed the possibilities of collaboration with the American and German firms for drug manufacture. He suggested that discussions with the USSR should go ahead for Sulpha drugs, anti-tubercular drugs, analgesics and anti-pyretics, but vitamins and synthetic harmones could be considered with the USSR only if the Finance Minister's negotiations with the American firm did not fructify. He argued that in these vital industries, technological superiority should take precedence over financial credits.

I think this matter will have to be considered in its entirety by the Economic Committee of the Cabinet. The sooner this is done, the better. It will not be right to take piecemeal decisions. The fact that the Finance Minister is in the United States, does not make much difference to this. Apart from the fact that he is exceedingly busy there, it will not be proper for him to deal directly with firms.

The financial aspect, though, of course, important, is, as you say, not the only consideration. Technological superiority is at least as important. There are other aspects too, such as the question of royalties, tie-up in regard to prices and future developments and also the integration of these various aspects of the drug industry.

Yours sincerely,
Jawaharlal Nehru

39. On European Common Market[1]

I have seen telegram No. 796 dated September 23rd sent by H.M. Patel[2] about the Common Market.

2. In regard to this matter we have made our position quite clear and we cannot resile from that position. It is not necessary for us to go about doing propaganda against it. On the other hand, for us to remain silent on vital matters of policy is not correct. I do not know in what form the treaty is coming up in GATT and how voting is likely to take place. There is no question of total opposition, but the question of overseas territories is an important one and we cannot allow that to pass without making our position perfectly clear. There are some other factors too about this Common Market proposition which we view with some apprehension.[3] Will you please let me know in what form this matter is coming up and how voting is likely to take place.

1. Note to Finance Ministry, New Delhi, 24 September 1957. JN Collection.
2. Principal Secretary, Finance Ministry, Government of India.
3. See also *Selected Works* (second series), Vol. 38, pp. 557-558 and 669.

40. Maithon Dam[1]

Maithon Dam[2] and other DVC projects will not only benefit the people of West Bengal and Bihar but the whole of India. As a matter of fact, the benefits of the various development projects completed so far and under way will be enjoyed by generations of Indians even two hundred years hence. Actually, it is not enough to build dams, reservoirs and generate electricity. These will not be done fully until the DVC authorities make people utilize the stored water and electric power to improve the look of the countryside of the valley.

The contiguous areas of West Bengal, Bihar and Orissa are fast becoming the "Ruhr" of India. About one thousand crores of Rupees have been spent or are in the process of being spent in three States. Many dams have been built; steel mills are also built with the intention of developing the country.

The DVC projects are being undertaken with three ends in view— flood control, irrigation and power generation. There is increasing demand for power in the country and it should be supplied not only to big industry but also to villages and small-scale industries. It is my earnest hope that in this area the concerted efforts of the Indian people will enable us to forge ahead and be free of dependence on foreign aid. Foreign assistance may or may not come in quantity. We will, therefore, have to rely on our own efforts.

I congratulate those who have worked here, those big and small engineers, who have joined this undertaking. We are fortunate in having cooperation in this work even from outside our country. Eminent engineers from America, Germany and France have put in their endeavour in making it a success, and in this sense, this Dam is an international cooperative endeavour. The more such cooperation we have, the better for the country and the whole world.

A suitable memorial should be built to perpetuate the memory of those who died accidentally while working on the Dam. The success of the Second Five Year Plan depends on more agricultural production. If we do not intensify production in the fields, the Plan will fail. Our whole economy is linked with more and intensive agricultural production. The cultivators in India should follow the example of the Chinese peasants and undertake extensive and intensive cultivation. It is a matter of regret that the people have not developed their land

1. Speech at the opening of the Maithon Dam, 27 September 1957. From *The Hindu, Amrita Bazar Patrika* and *National Herald*, 28 September 1957.
2. Two and a half mile long and 162 feet high Maithon Dam, the third DVC project, was built on the confluence of the rivers Barakar and Damodar at a cost of about Rs 17 crores.

to the required extent. In China where productivity from land is low, people have made up the deficiency by extensive and intensive cultivation. There the cultivated land area is less than in India, but the production is four to five times more, also due to intensive cultivation.

I cannot understand why people in Bihar where there is great wealth in land have not taken to intensive cultivation. We should remember that the future of India depends on greater production from land.

Our food production is now below expectations. I am surprised that in Bihar, where the land potential is very great, why they should lag behind the all India average in food production. Ultimately, India's riches will come from the land and not from factories. Great dams and power stations are built to benefit the people. It is important that while building them we have to concert measures on their utilization as well and not wait till their completion. If there is delay in utilizing these works for irrigation and beneficial purposes, crores of Rupees will be lost. We have many cases of such wastes in this land of ours.

The Damodar Valley Corporation is not there merely to construct dams but also to foster industrial activity. Otherwise the country will be wasting precious years. There are many kinds of wastage in our country but nothing is so expensive as delay in the utilization of water and power flowing from dams.

India is "power hungry". There has been a time when it was asked what India would do with all the power she was going to produce. Now, a few years later, I can see that the demand for power is so great that if power stations are built even in the remote corners of India, demand will overcome supply.

I do not wish that the electricity produced by these projects should be given only to the big factories. The DVC should find out ways by which electric power can reach every home in every village for cottage and small industries.

I have been told about the sufferings of the local Santhals, who had been displaced by the construction of the Dam. A considerable period of time have been taken for proper planning of their housing and other needs. This is very bad. In these days, the success of a project is to be judged not only by how much benefit it gives to the people but also by how much suffering of the people it relieves.

I am happy that a settlement has been reached on Naga problem. I hope peace and normality will soon return to the area. Other tribal people in autonomous districts of Assam also have some complaints. I think they should remain with Assam, but the Government is willing to consider the question of giving them more autonomy. I am shortly leaving for Japan, I have requested the Home Minister, Pandit Pant to visit the area and to discuss the matter with the tribal leaders.

41. To Mohanlal Saksena[1]

New Delhi
September 28, 1957

My dear Mohanlal,[2]
Your letter of September 27th.[3]

So far as the Second Five Year Plan is concerned, it is being continuously revised from the point of view of what is called the hard core of the Plan. As a matter of fact, it is this hard core that is the biggest part of the Plan, as it includes the Iron and Steel Plants and some other very big undertakings.

I am sorry to learn about your wife's ill health.

You suggest various schemes. They are all attractive, but it is difficult to say much about them till they are worked out. Cooperative societies, especially in rural areas, must necessarily be intimately connected with the Community Development Schemes. I suggest that you might discuss them with or write to S.K. Dey. He will be interested and will, I am sure, like to cooperate with you.

As per your milk schemes, I suppose these have been postponed because they required some expensive machinery from abroad. But, if anything can be done without this machinery, it should be attempted.

So far as the fruit industry is concerned, especially the mango, I believe a good deal of thought is being given to this. Essentially, these are State matters.

Your affectionately,
Jawaharlal Nehru

1. File No. 17(5)/57-PMS. Also available in JN Collection.
2. A Congressman from UP and former Union Minister for Rehabilitation.
3. To solve the problem of foreign exchange and inflationary prices, Saksena suggested division of the Second Plan into two parts—a basic plan catering to basic needs of the people and capable of implementation with indigenous resources; and the other providing for other needs and depending on foreign assistance. He wrote about starting (i) labour and workers' cooperatives which would guarantee employment, provide full quota of labour needed for cultivable land and consequently increase agricultural yield per acre; (ii) a milk cooperative; and (iii) development of fruit industry for export purposes like export of mango from Malihabad and neighbouring areas. He cited the examples of California and Palestine, where orchards and fruit industry played a very important role in their economy.

42. Working of Government Corporations[1]

I should like to have some information about the matters mentioned below:

1. *The Insurance Corporations:* It appears that ever since the State took over the Insurance, the business has been going down. I should like to have some figures. What steps have been taken to activise this? Insurance, more than anything else, requires active field workers. The best of our officers cannot do much. Have we paid any special attention to these field workers or do we expect, in a Governmental way, for work to flow in by itself?

2. *Industrial Finance Corporation:* From all accounts this has done very well and has been of great help in encouraging industry. I am told that this is unable to function adequately now for lack of money. Is this so? It would be unfortunate that this good and productive work should be stopped or slowed down for lack of funds.

3. *Small Savings:* Has this been pursued actively and energetically? What are the recent figures?

4. My attention has been drawn to the fact that the executive and appellate authority in the Central Board of Revenue is vested in the same person. That person happens to be good and efficient. But it is pointed out that it is not a good practice for the same person to deal with these two separate activities and that a bifurcation of the two would be desirable. I should like to have a note about this.

---

1. Note to Finance Ministry, New Delhi, 29 September 1957. JN Collection.

43. To Govind Ballabh Pant[1]

New Delhi
October 2, 1957

My dear Pantji,

Namboodiripad[2] and Ajoy Ghosh[3] came to see me this morning. The talking was done by Ajoy Ghosh. He discussed two specific matters. One was our financial difficulties, and the other was the Official Language Report.

As for the financial difficulties, Ajoy Ghosh said that we should nationalize the banks and various other undertakings to get the money. I told him that this seemed to me very unwise, apart from any theory. In order to get control of a little money for investment we would upset the whole structure of our economy and put a barrier to our getting much larger help which was so essential. As it was, we had effective control of the commercial banks. A little more control would make little difference to us, but would create an atmosphere of great difficulty for our industry and future growth. We were not starting from scratch. We had to take things as they were and build on them, making such changes from time to time as were desirable and feasible. Any vital change, such as he suggested, would, for some time at least, completely upset our economy and injure our productive apparatus....

Gulzarilal Nanda[4] has sent me a note about his impressions of his tour in Kerala. I do not know if you have seen this. I am enclosing it.

Yours affectionately,
Jawaharlal Nehru

1. File No. 37(35)/56-66-PMS. Also available in JN Collection. Extracts. For the remaining paragraphs of this letter see *post*, pp. 204-205.
2. E.M.S. Namboodiripad, Communist leader and Chief Minister of Kerala.
3. General Secretary, CPI.
4. Union Minister of Labour and Employment and Planning.

44. To K.D. Malaviya[1]

New Delhi
October 2, 1957

My dear Keshava,[2]

Some days ago, you sent me a note in which you mentioned some talk you had with Mr Smelov[3] of the Soviet delegation which is here at present. In this, you mentioned of an informal and personal proposal from him to the effect that if a formal request is made by the Government of India, the USSR could send a party for detailed project study of transport, pipeline and refinery. You asked me whether such a formal request should be made to the USSR.

I think that in this matter we have to be very cautious, and every step taken should be after full consultation and consideration. We are at present, as you know, in a very difficult financial position, both external and internal, and I do not want to add to these difficulties by getting entangled in any way internationally. As it is, remarks have been made from time to time by many of our colleagues, which sometimes raise difficult problems about our broad policies as well as our present intentions.

On the one side, there is the very great need of large-scale foreign aid to get through the core of our Second Five Year Plan. On the other side, it is clear that we are not going to sacrifice our basic policies in order to get aid. That would lead us nowhere. To balance between these two is not an easy matter. So far as large-scale aid is concerned, as far as one can see, only the United States can give it in any quantity. We may get some aid from Western Germany and we may probably get some aid in the shape of machinery etc., and credits from the Soviet Union. The latter will be helpful generally but not directly in regard to foreign exchange. We have for the present to wait for T.T. Krishnamachari's return. I am also going away for a fortnight. Later, we shall have to discuss these matters in their broad aspects and come to important decisions. Till then, it is better not to take any step which might add to our difficulties, or raise complications in our international relations.

So far as the Soviet Union is concerned, we are considering quite a number of matters in relation to them. There is the five hundred million Roubles loan and

1. File No. 17 (47)/56-65-PMS. Also available in JN Collection.
2. He was Union Minister of State for Mines and Oil.
3. N.A. Smelov was the leader of the nine-member Soviet delegation, which was in India to discuss utilization of 500 million Roubles aid to India.

a suggestion that another one hundred million might be added to it. There is the machine building industry and the drug industry, both of which are being considered in connection with Russian or other help.

I suggest, therefore, that we should be very cautious at present, and no step should be taken without the fullest consultation. In particular, of course, Swaran Singh[4] should be kept in intimate touch with developments.

Yours affectionately,
Jawaharlal Nehru

4. Union Minister of Steel, Mines and Fuel.

45. Repatriation of Money from Overseas Indians[1]

During my recent stay at Hong Kong, I appealed to the Indian community there to invest money in our Government of India Bonds, Savings Certificates, etc.[2] There was a general desire to do so, but I could not answer a number of questions that were put to me.

I was asked to increase the maximum limit of Savings Certificates. It seemed to me that if a person wanted to invest a larger sum, there were other ways of doing so. Anyhow, there are likely to be investments of two types from Hong Kong, one of relatively small sums which might come in monthly or quarterly, and the other larger sums from time to time.

As I was leaving Hong Kong, I received two letters which I am sending you. I suggest that you send the necessary information to our Commissioner in Hong Kong, Shri Adarkar,[3] who will convey it to the persons who have written the letters as well as to others.

This is not merely a question of getting some money from our countrymen abroad for investment here, but also of associating them with our development plans.

1. Note to Ministry of Finance, New Delhi, 17 October 1957. JN Collection.
2. Nehru made this appeal informally and did not mention this issue in his address to the Indian community on 14 October 1957.
3. B.P. Adarkar.

124

46. To Atulya Ghosh[1]

New Delhi
20th October 1957

My dear Atulya Babu,[2]

Thank you for your letter of 15th October with which you have sent a copy of a letter addressing to Sardar Swaran Singh.[3] I have read the letter with interest. The points you have raised certainly deserve consideration, and I have no doubt that Swaran Singh will reply to you and tell you as to what is being done.

You refer to planning for a whole district when a steel plant is located there. Planning for a township is, of course, done and this percolates to the district. But to ask for the planning of a whole district in connection with a particular plant would probably be too much of a burden. Of course, to some extent this larger planning has to be done. That is the State Government's task. We cannot expect the Central Government to plan for a whole district because it is putting up a plant there.

Yours sincerely,
Jawaharlal Nehru

---

1. File No. 17(37)/57-66-PMS. Also available in JN Collection.
2. Member, Lok Sabha at this time.
3. Atulya Ghosh wrote about the frustrations and resentment of young enthusiastic engineers in Bhilai and Rourkela, who had returned after training in USSR and Germany. They found no real work in the steel plants and their confirmation in the regular scale after one-year probation was refused because plants were not ready yet. Ghosh suggested development of villages within 20-mile radius of the plant simultaneously with the building of the steel plants. He cited the example of Jamshedpur city which had a very high standard of living but a few yards away from it existed a primitive rural district. He feared the same fate for Durgapur.

47. To Swaran Singh[1]

New Delhi
October 21, 1957

My dear Swaran Singh,

The Soviet Ambassador[2] came to see me today. This was in regard to various matters. Also partly because he would be leaving us finally next month.

In the course of our talks he mentioned the Bhilai Plant and said that the machines for it were being rapidly got ready and would soon begin to be sent. According to the agreement arrived at, 515 or so Indian specialists were to be sent to the USSR for training to work these machines. Out of these only 55 had been sent thus far. This will delay matters greatly as the stage had been reached when without these specially trained experts it would not be possible to install or work the machines.

Therefore, he said that at least 500 should be sent to the Soviet Union even for a short time to understand these machines as they are being made and to learn how to install them. Otherwise Russians will have to be sent for to install the machines. It was surely better for Indians to learn this and do it themselves and then work the machines.

The Ambassador said that someone in his Embassy had had a talk with Bhoothalingam[3] who pointed out that the main difficulty had been that of the expenditure involved. The Ambassador told me that the Soviet Government would be prepared to consider this question favourably and make some arrangement so as to reduce the expenditure involved.

He then asked me if he could see you and discuss these matters relating to the Bhilai Plant. I agreed with him and said that it would be a good thing if you could meet him and discuss these matters.

Yours sincerely,
Jawaharlal Nehru

1. File No. 17(37)/57-66-PMS. Also available in JN Collection.
2. Mikhail A. Menshikov.
3. Subramanya Bhoothalingam (b. 1909); joined ICS in 1931, served in the Ministry of Industry, 1940-55; Chairman, Hindustan Steel, 1955-58; Secretary, Ministry of Steel, Mines and Fuel, 1955-61; Secretary, Department of Expenditure, Ministry of Finance, 1961-62; Ministry of Economic and Defence Coordination, 1962-63, Ministry of Finance, 1963-66; Director General, National Council of Applied Economic Research, 1967.

48. Transfer of Panchayats to Community Development Ministry[1]

The Minister for Community Development suggested to me some time ago, that as Panchayats were intimately connected with Community Development work, it will be desirable to transfer Panchayats to his Ministry from the Health Ministry. I have had some correspondence on this subject with the Health Minister who pointed out that Panchayat was a part of local self-government, etc., and, in any event, corporations, municipalities, local boards, etc., should remain with Health. In case Panchayats by themselves were transferred, this would require, he said, a change in List II of the Seventh Schedule.

2. I am inclined to think that it would probably be desirable to put Panchayats with the Community Development Ministry. I should like you to find out, after reference to the Law Ministry if necessary, if this can be easily done, without much fuss. There is no hurry about it. We shall take this matter up, as suggested by the Minister for Community Development, after the report of the Committee on Planned Projects, that is, some time in November. Meanwhile, however, this matter might be looked into.

3. I am sending you the correspondence on this subject.[2]

1. Note to Cabinet Secretary, New Delhi, 23 October 1957. JN Collection.
2. See also *ante*, pp. 96-97.

49. Coordination between Planning Commission and Various Ministries[1]

On the 8th of June 1957 I sent you a letter in which I specially drew your attention to the importance of coordinating the activities of various Ministries *inter se* and with the Planning Commission. The question of priorities has always been

1. Note to the Members of the Cabinet and the Planning Commission, New Delhi, 24 October 1957. File No. 17(245)/57-59-PMS. Also available in File No. PC/CDN/6/4/57, Coordination Branch, Planning Commission and JN Collection.

an important one, but it has become still more important because of the financial difficulties that we have to face. No single Ministry can consider this question by itself. Only the Cabinet and the Planning Commission can see the picture as a whole.

2. I suggested, therefore, that such matters should come up to the Cabinet, but before this was done, the Planning Commission should be seized of them and should send their recommendations. I further pointed out that a Ministry sometimes spends time and labour over some proposal and practically finalizes it and only then sends it to the Planning Commission or the Cabinet. I suggested that this was not a correct approach. Before any decisions were taken and indeed before the proposal had been worked out in any detail, the Planning Commission should be consulted at an early stage of formulation. This would save much time and labour and it might also help the Ministry concerned in formulating the proposal in a manner which might fit in with our broad policy.

3. I shall not repeat what I wrote in my letter of the 8th June 1957,[2] but I would like you to refer to it again.

4. On the 20th September 1957 I addressed a note to the Deputy Chairman of the Planning Commission.[3] Copies of this note were also sent to the Ministries of Finance and Commerce & Industry. I mentioned this matter also in the Cabinet. I am sending you a copy of this note.

5. We have to make vital decisions in the course of the next few days or weeks. Many matters have been kept pending till the return of the Finance Minister. He will be returning tomorrow and we shall immediately confer with him about the general situation. This does not mean that we shall be in a position to come to immediate decisions. But these decisions cannot wait for long and they will have to be made in the course of the next few weeks at the most. I am anxious that our approach to these problems should strictly comply with the procedure I have suggested in my letter of the 8th June. We cannot afford to function in separate compartments any more, and every major proposal should go through the normal procedure of consultation with the Planning Commission and then presentation before the Cabinet.

6. I think that at least part of our difficulties in the past have arisen because we have by-passed this procedure. We have to learn from our past mistakes. That is the reason why I have asked the Planning Commission specially to prepare a paper to indicate how and why the difficult foreign exchange situation has arisen. Much happened beyond our control, but much may also have happened which was in our control if we had only exercised it. At any rate the matter

2. See *Selected Works* (second series), Vol. 38, pp. 60-62.
3. See *ante*, pp. 103-114.

requires very careful consideration so that we can avoid any lapse in the future.

7. Meanwhile, I would repeat that we have to take particular care not to take any major step without consultation with the Planning Commission and later consideration by the Cabinet.

50. Encourage Handicrafts Production[1]

I am glad to learn of the celebration of Handicrafts Week early in November.[2] From every point of view, it is necessary to encourage the production of our handicrafts and their sale not only in this country, but also abroad. Our handicrafts are things of beauty, and they have made a name for themselves in various parts of the world. It would be a tragedy if we could not maintain and encourage this tradition of a beautiful craft which also helps us in gaining foreign exchange.

I hope, therefore, that everything will be done to encourage handicrafts in this country.

1. Message for the Handicrafts Week, New Delhi, 29 October 1957. JN Collection.
2. The Handicrafts Week was celebrated all over the country in the first week of November 1957.

51. Shortage of Foreign Exchange[1]

Item 1:- Note analyzing the causes of the Foreign Exchange Shortage.

The Planning Commission considered the note on the above subject prepared in the Planning Commission and the note received from the Ministry of Finance.

The Chairman[2] enquired how such large commitments of foreign exchange expenditure came to be built up before the fact was fully appreciated. He had

1. Summary record of the meeting of the Planning Commission, New Delhi, 30 October 1957. File No. PC/CDN/29/15/57, Coordination Branch, Planning Commission.
2. Nehru was the Chairman of the Planning Commission.

asked for reasons behind recent developments in regard to foreign exchange to be reviewed carefully so that for the future proper procedures could be established. Finance Minister explained that the Second Five Year Plan began with a gap on account of foreign exchange. Some remedial action in regard to the private sector could have been taken earlier if the significance of the foreign exchange gap in the Plan had been fully recognized. For instance, the Open General License should have been abolished when the Second Plan commenced. The import of capital equipment came largely under Open General License. The requests for foreign exchange which now came from the private sector were for fairly small amounts required for completing or balancing plants for which imports had been arranged earlier. If earlier action had been taken, however, commitments of foreign exchange might have been less to the extent of, say, Rs 100 crores.

2. Referring to the figures of increased imports in 1956-57 given in para 4 of the Planning Commission note, the Chairman suggested that a fuller break up might be furnished.

3. The Chairman enquired to what extent the break up of outstanding commitments on account of the private sector, which aggregated to about Rs 400 crores, was available. It was pointed out that there had been considerable difficulty in ascertaining outstanding commitments for the private sector because, imports of machinery came largely under Open General License; and the commitments of the order of about Rs 200 crores might be outstanding at any time in the normal course. Such information as was at present available had been obtained through a test check carried out at the ports through customs authorities.

4. With reference to the terms used in trade returns, e.g., provisions and oilman stores, cutlery and hardware etc., the scope of items covered by such descriptions was briefly explained. It was stated that the classification had now been changed in accordance with the international classification.

5. Professor Mahalanobis suggested that it would be desirable to consider from the point of view of planning requirements and details of information provided by applicants for import licenses and the character of information, made available to the Planning Commission by the Ministry of Commerce and Industry. It was agreed that a committee consisting of officers from the Ministry of Commerce & Industry and Finance and the Planning Commission should examine and make recommendations regarding information furnished in applications from import licenses, sanctions issued by Chief Controller of Imports and information furnished by the Ministry of Commerce and Industry to the Planning Commission and others concerned.

6. Reference was also made during the discussion to certain questions of

procedure connected with import licenses, e.g., the period during which they were valid and other aspects.

7. The suggestions made in para 9 of the Planning Commission paper regarding the future procedure for ensuring that the Planning Commission was fully in touch with matters pertaining to foreign exchange allotments were generally approved.

Item 2: <u>Note on the programme of work to be undertaken by the Planning Commission in relation to the review of the Plan.</u>

The suggestions contained in this paper were approved. In the course of discussion, it was pointed out that during the review of the programme, the coal production programme would need attention and that there might be some scope for re-examining the details of the programmes for railways and ports. The question was raised whether it was open to the Planning Commission to consider the possibility of staggering one of the steel plants. It was pointed out that it was open to the Planning Commission to consider all aspects of the subject, including those bearing on the immediate foreign exchange requirements as well as those relating to the needs of development during the Third Five Year Plan. It was pointed out that the scope for review in connection with steel plants might be limited because of contracts which had already been entered into.

Paper for the Cabinet: The Chairman suggested that the Planning Commission might circulate the note on item 1 for analyzing the causes of foreign exchange shortage with a suitable covering note which might include also the substance of the Planning Commission note on the programme of work relating to the review of the Plan and other conclusions which had been reached.

Meetings of the Planning Commission: It was agreed that from the following week, regular meetings of the Planning Commission might be held on Tuesdays and Fridays. The Chairman agreed that he would endeavour to attend the meetings of the Planning Commission on Tuesdays. These would be held at 9 a.m.

52. To V.T. Krishnamachari[1]

New Delhi
October 30, 1957

My dear V.T.,

Late at night, I have seen some papers which are apparently going to be considered at a meeting of the Planning Commission tomorrow morning, October 31st. These papers relate to (1) the utilization of Russian aid and the development of the drugs and intermediates industries and (2) the Foundry-Forge Project and the Czechoslovak proposal.[2]

I am greatly interested in both these matters and would have liked to attend the meetings of the Planning Commission when it considers them. But, I am afraid I cannot come tomorrow morning.

I have rather hurriedly glanced through these bulky papers. It is difficult for me to grasp the full import of what they contain in the short time and, anyhow, I am no expert. There are, however, some points which I am bringing to your notice.

There are many references in these papers to the offer of the Soviet Government of an additional one hundred million Roubles aid for the drugs industry. It is further stated that this "Russian aid is specifically limited to the development of the drugs industry and cannot be used for other projects already included in the Plan". I should like to make it clear what the position is in regard to this one hundred million Roubles. No official offer has been made about this to us and we have not discussed it at any time with the Russians. General Sokhey reported to us, after a talk he had had with the Russians in Moscow, that they were prepared to give an additional one hundred million Roubles for the drugs industry. We did not like this approach of General Sokhey directly to the Russians, and have not pursued this matter since then because we wanted to be clear in our own minds before we approached the Russians. The Russians are a little annoyed at the fact that they make offers which are either not accepted by us or are kept pending for a long time without any decision. So, we did not wish to approach them in any way till we had decided as to what to do ourselves. I think, however, that they will probably be prepared to give this one hundred million Roubles, but it cannot be said definitely that this aid would be specifically limited for a

1. JN Collection.
2. Krishnamachari replied on 31 October that this meeting was for preliminary consideration of these subjects.

particular purpose. Anyhow, as we are considering this matter, we might presume for the present that this money might be forthcoming, though the details of it are lacking.

Utilization of Russian aid for the drugs and intermediates industries: When this matter came up before the Economic Committee of the Cabinet, the Commerce & Industry Ministry made a number of proposals about the utilization of the Russian aid of five hundred million Roubles. The only question that was discussed at the time, was about intermediates. In regard to these, the C&I Ministry had recommended that Bayer's offer should be considered favourably. It was pointed out then that we had no details or comparative estimates about the various offers. There can be no doubt that Bayer's was a first-class firm, but that did not necessarily mean that others in the USSR or elsewhere were not good. The report of our own experts seemed to be very largely based on what they considered the technological superiority of the Bayer group. While admitting the acknowledged quality of Bayer's, it did not necessarily follow that others were inferior. From all accounts, the Soviets had made very rapid progress in the drugs industries as in some other important branches of science and technology. Anyhow, the question could not be disposed of without further consideration.

Our object was to decide after a fuller consideration of all the aspects– cost factor was important, foreign exchange, deferred payment etc. Also, the quality.

Whether we are in a position now to decide about intermediates, on the data before us, I do not know. It is suggested that further enquiries should be made from Bayer's. It appears that, after the Russian report on the drugs industry, no further enquiries were made from them on the line suggested for Bayer's. The normal course might well have been to have full enquiries from both of these, so that we might be able to compare the two. As this might involve some time and, in any event, some enquiries have to be made, it might be worthwhile to come to some decisions about the other proposals of the Commerce Ministry regarding the utilization of the Russian aid. That is to say, we may decide about those items and not delay that decision while we are enquiring about intermediates. This would enable us to go ahead with the schemes agreed to. In the note sent now, it is stated that "Bayer's estimate is still only a rough projection" and inevitably this will require much further examination, just as any proposal of the Russians about intermediates would require more enquiries. It might thus be possible and desirable to separate the question of intermediates from the others.

I am naturally anxious that the best offer in regard to intermediates, taking every aspect into consideration, should be accepted, whether this is German or Russian. I am quite unable to judge of comparative costs, but from the note, it

133

appears that the engineering and royalty fees demanded by the Germans as well as the Italians are high. This is partly justified on the ground that the industry is a secretive one. This is just a point which, I think, inclines one the other way. To get tied up with secret processes, may well hinder our development. This question was considered repeatedly and fully when we first put up our Penicillin plant. The same argument was raised then in favour of some American firms. We decided, however, to start the plant ourselves in collaboration with some UN subsidiary organizations. The result has been successful, and we are free to do what we like. To be tied up with secret processes of private firms, must inevitably restrict our freedom of movement, and to some extent, control prices.

There is the question of international patents. I rather doubt if this comes in the way. We are, in fact, going to change our Patents Law, and, I think, there are many ways of dealing with this matter.

Inevitably, if we go to a private firm, we have to pay heavy and continuous royalties. I see also that interest demanded by the Bayer's group is seven and a half per cent, which is rather heavy. As far as I can remember, the Soviet interest was two and a half per cent. Then, again, Bayer's want ten per cent to be paid at the time of signing agreements. If this cannot be avoided, then it will mean a fairly substantial payment in foreign exchange right at the beginning. It is suggested in the note that it might be possible to get some deferred credit for this. There is also some kind of credit insurance cost referred to in the note.

It is suggested that the German group will take ordinary shares up to the full value of the fees and know-how payments, which are considerable. I have an idea that in another connection, it was thought rather unwise to get tied up in this way, as this was likely to lead to difficulties.

I have just written some odd points that struck me above, because my mind was not clear on this subject. But, as I have suggested, we might well go ahead with the other part of the Commerce & Industry Ministry's recommendations regarding the utilization of Russian aid and deal with the question of intermediates separately and more fully after we have much more information both from the German group and the Soviets.

The Foundry-Forge Project: From the note, it appears that there is general agreement on two points: (1) that heavy castings and forgings are fundamental to the development of heavy engineering, and, therefore, should be regarded as a project of very high priority, and (2) that the Czech terms are the best obtainable and, therefore, should be accepted.

The only difficulty, and it is a substantial one, is the question of making some payments amounting probably to about 2.5 crores, by 1960. The Cabinet has laid down that we must not make any fresh commitments about foreign exchange. We have, therefore, to examine any such project with the greatest care. This question of payment also appears to arise in the case of Bayer's proposal, as I have mentioned above.

I have no doubt that the Foundry-Forge project is of great importance and high priority. About the terms offered, I am no judge. But, presumably, they are good as the C&I Ministry and their experts say. I rather doubt if it is worthwhile or desirable to start fresh and entirely different negotiations now about this matter with other firms.

Apart from these two projects, there is one matter which has been much in my mind since my visit to Japan. In discussing industrial progress with the Japanese, it struck me that they were much more in favour of relatively small plants spread out over various parts of the country, than to have very big plants. More particularly, they said this about iron and steel. This is a matter for expert advice. But, I have a feeling that we have rather got into the habit of thinking of big and bigger plants. That is, of course, both the American and the Russian way and, in some cases, it has, no doubt, advantages. But, I think, it is worth considering carefully whether we should not concentrate more on smaller projects which are spread out all over the country. These are less costly, they save transport to some extent, and they give satisfaction to different parts of the country. Naturally, their location is limited by various factors such as availability of raw materials etc. But, in regard to some other industries, these limiting factors might not be there.

I am not suggesting this in connection with the particular questions you are now considering about Russian aid or the drugs industries or the Foundry-Forge Project. It is only a general observation I am making for the consideration of the Planning Commission.[3]

Yours sincerely,
Jawaharlal Nehru

3. Krishnamachari supported Nehru's observation about the Japanese idea of small plants. He reminded Nehru of his mentioning about the Chinese projects for setting up small iron and steel plants and the Australian projects for small cement plants. He wrote that this pattern was much more suitable for India than the heavy industry pattern of USA and Russia.

II. FOOD AND AGRICULTURE

(i) Foodgrain Prices

1. To N. Sanjiva Reddy[1]

New Delhi
August 1, 1957

My dear Sanjiva Reddy,[2]

You must be aware of and must appreciate the grave financial crisis through which we are passing. This is both in regard to foreign exchange[3] as well as internal resources.[4] While many factors have contributed to it, there can be no doubt that one of the principal reasons relates to foodgrains production[5] and prices.[6]

It might be said with a good deal of truth that our economy depends upon the proper production and distribution of foodstuffs. Certainly, our Five Year Plan depends upon it. Food prices are dependent on what we grow and how this is distributed, apart from subsidies and import of foodgrains from abroad.

1. File No. 31 (25)/56-64-PMS. Also available in JN Collection.
2. Chief Minister of Andhra Pradesh.
3. In the nine months from January to September 1957, the foreign exchange reserves declined by Rs 252 crores. The pressure on balance of payment, noticed since April 1956 continued through 1957. The current account deficit for 1956-57 was Rs 293 crores and grew to Rs 298 crores in the first half of 1957-58.
4. The strain on resources, both internal and external, became evident soon after the Second Five Year Plan commenced. As against the ceiling outlay of Rs 4800 crores over the five-year period, outlay for the first two years was estimated to be Rs 1515 crores. Financing of this outlay was estimated to have involved deficit financing by the Centre and the States aggregating to about Rs 600 crores.
5. The major factor for balance of payment deficit was the sharp increase in the import of foodgrains. The food production was not adequate to meet the increasing demand and the country had to import large quantities of foodgrains worth Rs 101.6 crores in 1956-57 and Rs 88.1 crores between April to September 1957.
6. The foodgrain prices were also on the rise aggravating the deficit. The index of wholesale prices was 106 in March 1957 and rose to 112 by July-August 1957. Rice prices rose by nearly 10% during this period.

136

If internal food prices go up, this causes distress to innumerable people and, at the same time, it undermines our Plan. If we have to import food from abroad, this means a heavy drain on foreign exchange.

If there is, unfortunately, a real scarcity in the country, then we have to import foodgrains from abroad, whatever the burden that might involve. At the present moment, food and especially rice prices have risen and are causing considerable distress. A bad feature has been that even during a season when prices go down normally, these prices did not go down.

And yet, it appears to be true that there is enough food and enough rice in the country to go round, if only it was properly distributed. There are surpluses in some areas and hoarding with a view, no doubt, to getting ever higher prices. Surely, there is something wrong about this, and it is a wrong which is causing, and will continue to cause, great upsets in our economic structure.

Among the rice surplus States are Orissa, Madhya Pradesh and more especially Andhra Pradesh. If we are to get enough rice to build up a stock, apart from supplying present needs, we have to get it from these three States, and get it at a reasonable price. We have been getting some rice from Orissa, but we are having enormous difficulties in getting it from Andhra, which has the greatest surplus of all and where there appears to be a great deal of hoarding.

It was with a view to get this rice from the hoarders that Parliament passed some legislation about two or three months ago.[7] That was a moderate piece of legislation, fair to all concerned. I am told, however, that you have not been agreeable at all to any kind of compulsory procurement of rice in Andhra. And so we have got stuck there.

I should like you to consider the consequences of all this. If the situation deteriorates much more, we shall have to think of controls on a fairly wide scale. We want to avoid this. But, if we drift, then we shall become helpless. The only possible course open to us is to buy rice compulsorily at a reasonable price from the hoarders and thus build up an adequate stock. We cannot allow the price of rice to remain at a high level. We want to be fair to the cultivator and to give him an adequate price. But it would be utterly wrong to allow the retail or wholesale hoarders to profit by their anti-social activities at the cost of the nation and our Five Year Plan.

As it is, we have arrived at a stage when we are likely to be compelled to reduce many of the important projects in our Plan. The States will suffer, and so will the Central Government. The only way to hold these inflationary tendencies is to hold the price of rice and the only way to do this is to have large stocks of

---

7. To requisition foodstocks at prevailing average market price, the Government passed the Essential Commodities (Amendment) Bill on 1 June 1957.

rice. These stocks can be obtained from the surplus States I have mentioned above and, more especially, Andhra. If your Government does not cooperate in this, then the result will be bad for India, and equally bad for Andhra Pradesh. We shall have to give up some of our major projects.

This is a logical conclusion from which there is no escape. I want you, therefore, to think about this, and I hope that you will facilitate our Food & Agriculture Ministry to secure this rice from the people who are hoarding it in Andhra.[8]

Yours sincerely,
Jawaharlal Nehru

8. Sanjiva Reddy assured Nehru on 8 August 1957 of procuring rice at reasonable rates using this legislation, if the Central Food Ministry gave the State Government such a directive after studying the food problem of South Zone.

2. To Jagjivan Ram[1]

New Delhi
August 1, 1957

My dear Jagjivan Ram,

Thank you for your letter of the 1st August about food movements from ports.[2] I agree to your setting up a special committee at Secretaries' level to make a coordinated plan for food movements.

I agree also that you should set up the mechanical handling plant at Bombay.

Yours sincerely,
Jawaharlal Nehru

1. File No. 31 (46)/57-58-PMS.
2. Jagjivan Ram had enclosed a note about food movement from ports, which showed average daily loading from Bombay 167 wagons and from Calcutta 51 wagons in July 1957.

3. To Harekrushna Mahtab[1]

New Delhi
August 1, 1957

My dear Mahtab,[2]

In my fortnightly letter which I am sending today, you will see that I have discussed the question of food prices at some length.[3] In looking at our economy and our Five Year Plan etc., we arrive inevitably at the conclusion that agricultural production and especially food production is the only foundation on which we can go ahead. With this is allied food prices and, more especially, rice prices. In a sense, therefore, rice prices at present control not only the future of our Five Year Plan, but the future of India.

Food prices can only be controlled by having large stocks, and stocks can only be built up by large-scale procurement from surplus areas. Large-scale procurement cannot be voluntary, as this itself sends up prices. It has, therefore, to be compulsory, though of course, at reasonable prices. There is no escape from this argument.

If so, then the surplus rice States, of which Orissa is one, have to play their full part. I am afraid that the surplus States have not been very cooperative in the past, and they seem to have had a soft corner for their middlemen and hoarders. I am glad that now Orissa is helping in the procurement of rice, and I understand that forty thousand tons have been procured. But, this is not enough.[4]

The crisis is a grave one, and we have to think in the broadest terms in regard to it. Some apparent local or State advantage may accrue if prices go up, but in the result the State itself will suffer, apart from India.

We have, unfortunately, arrived at a stage when we are likely to be compelled to cut down many of the projects in Five Year Plan.

Yours sincerely,
Jawaharlal Nehru

1. File No. 31 (25)/56-64-PMS. Also available in JN Collection.
2. Chief Minister of Orissa.
3. See *post*, pp. 793-794.
4. In his reply of 27 August 1957, Mahtab wrote that he was continuously striving for maximum production of foodgrains, a safe supply system for internal distribution in scarcity and deficit areas, and maximum procurement for export to the Centre to meet the requirements of other States. He cited his differences with the Central Food Ministry and requested that necessary powers be delegated to the State Government to deal with local and regional problems.

4. To T.T. Krishnamachari[1]

New Delhi
August 10, 1957

My dear T.T.,

Ajit Prasad Jain has often complained that various banks were advancing money very generously on paddy and rice. This had helped the hoarders to hold on to their stocks and this was against the policy laid down by us. He has now sent me a copy of a letter he has addressed to you on this subject today.[2]

I do not understand why our directions have been disregarded and in fact violated. More so that even the State Bank is supposed to have done so.[3]

Yours sincerely,
Jawaharlal Nehru

1. File No. 31 (25)/56-64-PMS.
2. A.P. Jain wrote to T.T. Krishnamachari on 10 August 1957 that actual advances by banks were about 50% more than the advances permitted under the directive issued by the Reserve Bank of India on 7 June 1957 to the Scheduled banks restricting the amount of advances for purchase of paddy and rice.
3. Krishnamachari wrote to Nehru that he was writing to the Reserve Bank about this. He also said that apart from these credits, a sum of about three crores of Rupees, given to new cooperatives, had also helped in this process.

5. To Ajit Prasad Jain[1]

New Delhi
August 11, 1957

My dear Ajit,

I have noticed in *The Hindu* of August 10 that the Madras Government have promulgated an Order[2] under the Essential Commodities Act empowering their

1. File No. 31 (25)/56-64-PMS. Also available in JN Collection.
2. The Rice and Paddy Requisitioning Order was issued by the Madras Government on 7 August 1957.

officials to requisition rice or paddy stocks from holders in the State, etc. In the article in *The Hindu* it is stated that corresponding action must be taken in Andhra. What is the position now in Andhra? Also in Orissa and Madhya Pradesh in regard to requisition of rice and paddy? You wrote to me the other day that you intended taking some steps. Have these been taken?[3]

Yours sincerely,
Jawaharlal Nehru

3. A.P. Jain replied on 12 August 1957 that the acquisition staff in Andhra Pradesh was ready with the necessary legal authority for acquisition of rice and paddy. He wrote that if the purchase operations in Orissa did not proceed as planned, action under the law would have to be taken. He wrote that the stocks in Madhya Pradesh were not heavy and the situation there might not warrant any action.

6. To Satya Narain Sinha[1]

New Delhi
August 18, 1957

My dear Satya Narain,[2]

I enclose a letter from Asoka Mehta,[3] Chairman of the Foodgrains Enquiry Committee.[4] You will see that he wants to have the names of such persons from our Party as might have discussions with them in regard to the subject under enquiry. Will you please make a list of such people in the Congress Party.

1. File No. 31 (48)/57-58-PMS. Also available in JN Collection.
2. Union Minister of State for Parliamentary Affairs.
3. Mehta had enclosed a questionnaire on behalf of the Foodgrains Enquiry Committee.
4. The Committee was set up by the Government of India on 24 June 1957 to investigate the causes of rise in prices despite higher production and suggest remedial measures which would prevent speculative hoarding and arrest undue rise in prices. The Committee, which submitted its report in 1957 itself, emphasized the need for price stabilization, control over trade of foodgrains and its progressive socialization. It also suggested all out efforts to step up production and checking at the same time the high rate of increase of population. The Committee felt that the gravity of the food situation demanded national efforts transcending regional and party considerations.

Ministers, of course, should not be included. Any Ministers who wish to meet Asoka Mehta will do so separately. Indeed, some have met him already.[5]

Yours sincerely,
Jawaharlal Nehru

5. Satya Narain Sinha replied on 4 September that Members of the Congress Party Standing Committee on Food and Agriculture and Congress Members of the Informal Consultative Committee of his department discussed the questionnaire of the Foodgrains Enquiry Committee and had appointed a Sub-Committee to study it in detail. About 30 Congress Members were going to meet the members of Foodgrains Enquiry Committee on 9 September.

7. To K.M. Munshi [1]

New Delhi
August 21, 1957

My dear Munshi,[2]

Thank you for your letter of August 19th. We have at present no intention of introducing food controls as existed previously.[3] The idea is to procure an adequate quantity of foodgrains from the surplus States, chiefly Orissa and Andhra.

I am drawing the attention of the Food Minister to your previous letter.

Yours sincerely,
Jawaharlal Nehru

1. File No. 31 (25)/56-64-PMS. Also available in JN Collection.
2. Munshi was Union Minister of Food and Agriculture during 1950-52 and at present President, Bharatiya Vidya Bhavan, Mumbai.
3. Procurement and distribution of food by the State began in India in 1943 when Bombay introduced food rationing, and the practice was followed later in other parts of the country. Towards the end of 1947, food was decontrolled resulting in the escalation of food prices and this necessitated reintroduction of controls in September 1948. Due to the increase in total food production in 1953-54, controls were relaxed in 1953 and a policy of complete decontrol was adopted in 1954.

8. To Ajit Prasad Jain[1]

New Delhi
August 24, 1957

My dear Ajit,

A person writes to me from Bombay complaining that while the price of rice in the fair price shops in Calcutta is Rs 16/- per *maund*, the same rice in a fair price shop in Bombay is sold at Rs 20/- a *maund*. He demands an explanation.

Is this statement correct and, if so, what is the reason?[2]

Yours sincerely,
Jawaharlal Nehru

1. File No. 31 (25)/56-64-PMS.
2. Jain confirmed on 25 August 1957 that it was correct but there was nothing wrong with the prices in Bombay and Calcutta as they related to different varieties. Jain explained that about 80,000 tons of superior long fine variety of rice was imported from the USA which could easily sell in the market at Rs 25 per *maund* and more. After consultations it was decided to issue that rice at Rs 20 per *maund*. He wrote that the fine rice at Rs 20 per *maund* would shortly be issued in Calcutta and also in some other places. He pointed out that this was cheaper than the coarse rice in the market.

9. To Harekrushna Mahtab[1]

New Delhi
August 25, 1957

My dear Mahtab,

Please refer to your d.o. letter no. 1362-CM dated the 5th August, 1957, regarding the draft Rice Mills Industry (Regulation) Bill on which comments have been invited from the Orissa Government along with the other State Governments

1. File No. 31 (51)/57-PMS. Also available in JN Collection.

before its introduction in the Parliament.[2] I referred your letter to our Food and Agriculture Minister because he is dealing with this matter. It is, therefore, in consultation with him that I am writing to you.

This Bill is designed to put a stop to indiscriminate establishment of new rice mills or expansion of the existing mills to the detriment of the hand-pounding industry. It would not affect the provisions of the Essential Commodities Act under which the Centre will continue to have various powers even in regard to rice mills. As in the case of the Essential Commodities Act, provision has been made in the draft Rice Mills Industry (Regulation) Bill that powers can be delegated to the State Governments.

I feel that your apprehensions that the present Bill, if enacted, would mean that the Government of India would be taking over the rice mills or that the rice mills would become foreign bodies to the State or that the Government of India would use the provisions of this Bill to utilize them solely for exporting foodgrains from inside the State without caring for the pressing local needs, are not justified. As I have stated, the purpose and the scope of the Bill are entirely different.

I think, I ought to mention that while it is important that local requirements should be met, it is essential in the present food situation in the country that the Centre should have the authority to arrange for equitable distribution and for maintaining a control over the prices. To take away this authority from the Centre would not be to the interest of the country as a whole.

Yours sincerely,
Jawaharlal Nehru

2. The Bill was passed by Lok Sabha on 2 May 1958 and by Rajya Sabha on 7 May, and received President's assent on 18 May 1958.

10. To N. Sanjiva Reddy[1]

New Delhi
6 September, 1957

My dear Sanjiva Reddy,

I have written to you previously on the question of rice procurement and you have been good enough to reply.[2] I am afraid, however, that the situation in Andhra continues to be very far from satisfactory and there have been great difficulties in procurement of rice in spite of the decisions we have taken and the orders that have been issued.

This is a very vital matter and I want to draw your special attention to this because on this depends our future policy, and, indeed, Andhra's future is involved in it too in many ways. I have been discussing this with our Food & Agriculture Minister and he is much perturbed. He is, in fact, thinking of visiting Andhra later in the month. I do hope you will take every step to expedite this procurement.

Yours sincerely,
Jawaharlal Nehru

1. File No. 31 (25)/56-64-PMS. Also available in JN Collection.
2. For Sanjiva Reddy's reply of 8 August 1957 to Nehru see *ante*, p. 138.

11. To Ajit Prasad Jain[1]

New Delhi
September 18, 1957

My dear Ajit,

In one of your reports some time ago, I read that a large quantity of foodgrains had been sent from Bombay to Kashmir. This odd fact has stuck in my mind. It has seemed to me that there is something very wrong about our system of

1. File No. 31 (46)/57-58-PMS. Also available in JN Collection.

allotments or supplies when we have to move foodgrains these huge distances by Railways. It is not only wasteful but is a strain on the Railways.

It seems to me, therefore, some very careful thinking and planning is necessary to avoid this kind of long transportation. Sometime, I am told, that foodgrains goes backwards and forwards between same places. This is eminently a case where what is called work study is needed. Careful planning and arrangements would reduce cost as well as strain on Railways and time, of course.

In an emergency one has to do whatever is possible. But such an emergency should not be allowed to arise as far as possible. I imagine that some thought is, no doubt, given in your Ministry to this matter, but perhaps not too much thought and there is not much looking ahead. I wish that this question should be considered with great care. Efficiency as well as economy consist in looking after such matters and not merely in trying hard to reduce odd bits of expenditure.[2]

Yours sincerely,
Jawaharlal Nehru

2. A.P. Jain replied on 25 September 1957 that mostly imported rice was being supplied to States. As only small quantities were procured from Orissa and Andhra, the requirements of Jammu and Kashmir would have to be met out of imports and had to be transported there from ports. He informed that out of 23,500 tons of rice supplied so far, 22,000 tons had to go from Kolkata and 1,500 tons from Mumbai. Jain wrote that all avoidable cross movement had ceased as a result of creation of zones. He also wrote that a close liaison was maintained by a senior railway officer posted in the Food Department as Chief Director of Movement. A Standing Committee consisting of Chairman, Railway Board, Member (Transportation), Railway Board, Transport Secretary, and Food Secretary frequently reviewed the situation.

12. To Ajit Prasad Jain[1]

New Delhi
19 September, 1957

My dear Ajit,
Someone told me that your Ministry has given permission for *maida*, *suji*, etc., to be sent from the UP to South India without any permission being necessary and without any limit as to quantity. If this is so, will this not rather come in the way of your various other measures? The point is that if there is no limit as to quantity, consequences might be produced which may be unfortunate.[2]

Yours sincerely,
Jawaharlal Nehru

1. A.P. Jain Papers, NMML. Also available in JN Collection.
2. Jain replied on 24 September 1957 that out of about 10,000 tons consumption of fine products of wheat such as *suji*, *maida* etc., per month in South India, a little less than 50 per cent was produced locally. The balance of about 5000 tons was imported from the North, which was a small quantity. This was being done to encourage the consumption of wheat and wheat products in South India, where wheat prices had gone up as a result of creation of wheat zones.

13. To Ajit Prasad Jain[1]

New Delhi
24 September 1957

My dear Ajit,
Kasturbhai Lalbhai[2] came to see me today. As you know, he has been intimately connected with the development of Kandla Port, right from the days of the original project till now. He told me that this port had been completed in all respects

1. File No. 27 (32)/57-PMS. Also available in JN Collection.
2. A well known industrialist and banker from Gujarat.

with modern machinery for loading and unloading large store houses and in fact, all the usual equipment. In spite of all this, it was not being used properly or enough.

The whole object of having the Kandla Port was to replace Karachi and to supply the north of India. But even when it is ready, it is Bombay and Calcutta that continue to be used even at the cost of paying large sums of money as demurrage. He said that probably Rupees sixty lakhs have been paid in demurrage on ships in Calcutta and Bombay. That is a considerable sum of money. Many of these ships could easily have been moved to Kandla. Kandla is also considerably nearer various places in the north than Bombay is. He said that the gain would be about 240 miles.

Why then do we not use Kandla Port when it is simply waiting to be used? Perhaps it might be said that the Railway authorities have not got enough metre gauge wagons and locomotives. If so, it is up to the Railways to provide these.

It is true that for the present we have got over the big hump in Bombay and Calcutta and in other ports and there are not many ships waiting in port. That is good in so far it goes. But the fact remains that Kandla should be used much more and Bombay and Calcutta much less. Our imports and exports will increase in future and we have to build up other ports.

Kandla apart from other advantages, has apparently far better storage facilities than you will get anywhere else. Thus, everything points to Kandla being made use of in a big way and ships not being sent to Calcutta or Bombay unless there is some very special reason.[3] Will you please look into this matter for the future? It is painful to think that we have paid sixty lakhs in demurrage when a modern port with all new equipment stands by and is not used adequately.[4]

Yours sincerely,
Jawaharlal Nehru

3. Nehru also wrote to Lal Bahadur Shastri, Minister of Transport and Communications, and Jagjivan Ram, Minister of Railways, as to why Kandla Port was not being fully used.
4. On 26 September, A.P. Jain replied that in fact in June 1957 the Railway Board made special arrangements for the movement of foodgrains from Kandla at the rate of 900 tons per day. Accordingly, three ships were diverted to Kandla in July and four in August making a total of about 70,000 tons of wheat. There was no doubt that Kandla should be made use of as much as possible, but so far as foodgrain imports were concerned, the requirement of the area which could be served by the metre gauge lines emanating from Kandla was rather limited, Jain added.

14. To Ajit Prasad Jain[1]

New Delhi
September 29, 1957

My dear Ajit,

Bakhshi Ghulam Mohammed[2] came to see me this afternoon. He had just reached Delhi. Among other subjects, he spoke naturally about food and the food requirements of his State. I told him, as I had told him previously in Srinagar, about our own grave difficulties, etc. He said that he realized and because of it had taken some steps in recent months which were by no means easy. He has both reduced the quantity of the ration and increased the price. It was true that, even so, this price was much lower than the rest of India. But it was impossible for him to go beyond this now.

He added that there was a great lack of food almost all over the State, especially in distant rural areas and the position was becoming an exceedingly difficult one. There was food scarcity all over the place and naturally the Opposition was taking full advantage of this. As you know, there is a probability of Shaikh Abdullah being released in the future.[3] The prospect of this food situation continuing and worsening and Shaikh Abdullah finding it so was a serious matter for consideration.

There is no doubt that owing to the recent floods,[4] etc., considerable loss has been caused and that at present there is lack of food or very grave scarcity in many places. I suppose we have to help them to the best of our ability.

I asked Bakhshi Sahib to see you. He seemed to be somewhat reluctant. He said that the reception you had given him when he had seen you or even when he had telephoned to you did not encourage him to seek an interview with you.

This, of course, does not help at all. I hope you will invite him to see you and discuss this matter with him, because something has got to be done. He is thinking of leaving Delhi day after tomorrow, 1st October.

He gave me a note on the food situation, which I am enclosing.

Yours sincerely,
Jawaharlal Nehru

1. JN Collection.
2. Prime Minister of Jammu and Kashmir.
3. Shaikh Abdullah was released on 8 January 1958 but rearrested on 30 April.
4. The flood situation in Jammu worsened on 19 September and as a result 59 people died in Doda district alone and 9 in other parts of the Province, 2000 houses collapsed and 7000 acres of land badly affected. In Srinagar, the Srinagar-Awantipur-Anantnag Road was breached and grain stocks damaged. See also *post*, Kashmir, p. 488.

(ii) Agricultural Production

1. To Panjabrao S. Deshmukh[1]

New Delhi
12 August 1957

My dear Panjabrao,[2]

You wrote to me some time ago about the success of Sea Island Cotton fibre in India. I was talking to Shiva Rao[3] today and he said that about five years ago attention had been drawn to this matter by, I think, Poona College of Agriculture. Is that so? If so, it seems to have taken a long time to get this going.

Shiva Rao further told me that in Japan they had produced a new kind of fibre called the Ramie fibre which is far better than jute and very strong indeed. The Poona College of Agriculture has been experimenting with this with some success. They want to carry on their experiments but cannot do so for lack of money. Do you know anything about this matter?

Yours sincerely,
Jawaharlal Nehru

1. JN Collection.
2. Union Minister of State for Cooperation in the Ministry of Food and Agriculture.
3. Congress Member of Lok Sabha.

2. To Panjabrao S. Deshmukh[1]

New Delhi
August 15, 1957

My dear Panjabrao,

Thank you for your letter of August 14. I have read the attached letter which I am returning.

There is one matter which has troubled me. Some two years ago or more there was a great deal of propaganda about the Japanese method of rice growing[2] and the great results that were coming from it.[3] Lately I have not heard anything about this and in fact, as you know, the rice position has been very difficult. What has happened to the great progress we were making? Is it confined only to a few places and has not spread?

Yours sincerely,
Jawaharlal Nehru

1. JN Collection.
2. The Japanese method is the 'raised bed seeding method' which protects the seedlings from being washed away in case of excessive rains and gives scope for watering them during periods of drought by a limited supply of water through cans. The seedling can be prepared in a compact area and transplantation later is not difficult. This method can be adopted by agriculturists without any additional cost or labour.
3. For example, this method had been adapted in Bombay State in 1952 and the increase in production was approximately 6000 pounds of paddy per acre as compared to 800 pounds per acre previously. The amount of paddy required for seeding purposes did not exceed 8 to 10 pounds per acre, while previously it was 60 pounds per acre.

3. To Ram Shankar Lal[1]

New Delhi
September 6, 1957

Dear Ram Shankar Lalji,[2]

Your letter of the 4th September.[3]

When I spoke in the AICC I referred not to the FAO but to the World Bank.[4] The World Bank had sent a mission here about a year or two ago and it was in their report that they had said that foodgrain production in India was very low.[5] It should be possible to increase it three-fold or four-fold.

That did not mean a sudden increase to that extent. If any Community Project can increase it by 50 per cent that is a very good increase. The World Bank figures were for the whole of India, the average of which is very low indeed. This does not mean that in any selected area where the production is higher than average, the same increase can be made. But, taking all the factors, this can be done. Thus there is plenty of *usar* land. There is no doubt that this *usar* land can be cultivated after a little treatment. In Uttar Pradesh alone there are three million acres of *usar* land. The National Botanical Gardens in Lucknow have already shown how it is possible to bring back this *usar* land under cultivation.

There are many demonstration farms in our country and we are adding to them. In fact, we want such farms in every Community Project area.

Yours sincerely,
Jawaharlal Nehru

1. File No. 31 (30)/56-PMS. Also available in JN Collection.
2. (1902-1991); lawyer and Congressman; imprisoned during the freedom struggle; President, District Congress Committee, Basti, 1937-39; Member, AICC; Member, Uttar Pradesh Legislative Assembly, 1946-51; Member, Joint Select Committee of UP Legislature on Zamindari Abolition; Member, Lok Sabha, 1957-62; publisher, *Panch Mukh* (Hindi).
3. Ram Shankar Lal reminded Nehru of his speech at the AICC referring to the possibility of three or four-fold increase in production of grain in India as indicated by the FAO experts. However, in the most progressive Community Project areas also, the increase was not more than 50% inspite of better seed, manure and irrigation facilities. He suggested inviting a FAO expert to undertake a demonstration farm in India.
4. See *post*, pp. 455-456.
5. The World Bank Mission, headed by Thomas H. McKittrick, visited India in early 1956 to study the economic programmes and policies of India, and sent a copy of its report on 30 June 1956 which was released to the Press on 14 August in the same year.

152

4. Cooperative Farming Societies[1]

...78. 4) As regards ceilings on existing agricultural holdings, it was agreed that States which had enacted the necessary legislation should ensure that the programme was administratively implemented within a given period, say, three years. Other States which had not yet enacted legislation for ceilings should complete the legislative measures needed by the end of 1958-59. Adequate safeguards should be provided for preventing evasion.

79. In opening the discussion on cooperation, the Chairman observed that there were different varieties of cooperation. Broadly speaking, there was no dispute that there should be as much cooperation as possible, that is to say of service cooperatives. Further it was not good enough to have cooperation mainly for supplying credit. It must be on a wider basis and the wider the basis the better. The only question for argument came in regard to the final form of joint farming.

80. The Chairman observed that regarding service cooperatives two points arose for considerations. The first point related to the size of the cooperatives namely, whether they should be relatively small societies in which people knew each other or larger ones covering a number of villages. The second point was whether and if so to what extent the official element should be brought into the cooperative movement.

The Finance Minister, Madras,[2] said that the question whether the cooperative society should be a small one or a big one would depend on local and various other factors and it should be left to be decided by each State Government. In some cases if the members knew each other intimately that would be conducive to the proper working of the society and better management. In some other places there might not be sufficient resources if the society was small and it would be necessary to link two or three villages.

The Deputy Chairman observed that they had now worked out certain bases for taking a decision on this question, and circular letters were being issued to the State Governments regarding the lines on which the cooperative societies should be formed and what should be the ceiling for membership etc.

81. The Chairman observed that the aim should be to promote the spirit of cooperation and if the cooperative movement was too much officialized the

1. Summary record of the fifth meeting of the Standing Committee of National Development Council, New Delhi, 15 September 1957. File No. PC/CDN/29/15/57, Coordination Branch, Planning Commission. Only extracts are available.
2. C. Subramaniam.

self-help element would go away. The cooperatives should not have big bosses and suitable provision should be included in the rules of the cooperative society.

The Chief Minister of West Bengal remarked that at the same time the cooperative societies needed a little guidance from somewhere.

82. The Chairman observed that it was inevitable that the cooperatives must be intimately tied up with the Community Projects Development Schemes and this factor to some extent would determine the size of the society.

In the last two years two kinds of progress has been made; on the one hand in the Community Development Project areas, quite satisfactory progress has been made in regard to small cooperatives. The other type of progress has been made recently in some areas with credits from the Reserve Bank of India. What impressed him more was the progress made in the Community areas with little effort and the money coming from the peasants themselves.

83. Shri Subramaniam, Finance Minister, Madras said that in the NES and Community Development areas in Madras, they had fixed a target, October 1958, by which time every village should be covered by a Panchayat and a multi-purpose cooperative society. In new areas taken up for NES and Community Development blocks it has been stipulated that within one year all the villages in that area should be covered by Panchayats and cooperative societies. Shri Subramaniam suggested that if some target like this was fixed it would be easy to work.

84. The Deputy Chairman observed that in the letter which is now issued to the States, targets have been fixed for all States. In the progress report on the First Five Year Plan certain figures regarding the cooperative development have been given. Progress has been good in the NES and Community Development areas. At the end of 1952-53 there were 5 million members and about 2 ½ million members were added in three years and about 1 ½ million in the last year.

85. The Chairman observed that regarding joint farming his proposition was that in the conditions which existed in India joint farming was likely to yield results, in so far as it would be possible to pool resources and utilize modern techniques. In a wheat area joint farming was immediately worthwhile; in a rice area it might be less worthwhile. The Chairman suggested that the idea of joint farming should be propagated but any concrete steps towards this should be based on the consent of the people. A start on cooperative joint farming might be made where fresh land was reclaimed and with *gramdan* lands.

86. The Deputy Chairman observed that there were already more than 2,000 cooperative farming societies in different States. Many of them were not working quite satisfactorily. The first step was to see that they all worked satisfactorily; thereafter experiments could be tried in favourable areas.

87. The Chairman observed that a peasant having an acre or two acres of land

might with a little help produce more foodgrains but it would not be possible for him to get out of the circle of poverty. He will ultimately have to sell out. Eventually it would be necessary to take people away from the land and give them some other employment but it should not happen that a man was forced to sell on account of poverty....

5. Step up Food Production[1]

Food is the most important thing for human beings. Everything comes only after that. There is great scope for increasing food production in the country and we are going to do it.

I congratulate you on the good work you are doing and wish you success. I do not believe in scientific researches for research sake. The results of the research should be judged not from laboratory results or by pilot plant results but by larger practical results for which, of course, this Institute[2] is not responsible.

The Food Institute is aimed at achieving something not on paper but to give good, nutritive and cheap food for the people. Food production is everything to them today. Government is determined to increase the country's food production by thirty to forty per cent and we are confident that we can do so within a very short period. The works carried out at the various Community Project areas have demonstrated that it is possible for them to reach the target and even exceed it in shorter time. In a country like India much depended on rainfall. Lack of rain will certainly create disaster, but the fact remained that we have to increase food production very greatly in this country.

Some foreign banking experts some years ago remarked that food production in India should be stepped up by three to four hundred times than at present for improving the country's economy. I feel that it is possible to increase the country's food production by improved methods of agriculture and intelligent cooperation of the cultivators.

1. Address to the staff of the Central Food Technological Research Institute, Mysore, 20 September 1957. From *The Hindu*, 21 September 1957 and *The Hindustan Times*, 22 September 1957.
2. The Institute was inaugurated on 21 October 1950. For Nehru's message on the occasion see *Selected Works* (second series), Vol. 15 Pt. I, p. 65.

6. To Morarji Desai[1]

New Delhi
September 26, 1957

My dear Morarji,

You will remember that we had some correspondence about the fertilizer projects some time ago. Normally, of course, all the fertilizer projects should be in your Ministry. But it was felt that the fertilizer projects that are connected with the Rourkela and Neyveli projects should, for the present, continue with the Ministry of Steel, Mines & Fuel, that is, this should be so in the initial stage. As soon as they are constructed and begin to function, they should be transferred to the Ministry of Commerce & Industry.

This matter was discussed at one of our afternoon informal meetings of Cabinet Ministers, which was held at Gulzarilal Nanda's house. Unfortunately, you were then unwell in Madras.

We felt then that it would be desirable for the present to leave these two projects which are so intimately connected with Rourkela and Neyveli, with the Ministry of Steel, Mines & Fuel. Of course, there should be intimate cooperation even at this early stage between that Ministry and your Ministry.

Yours sincerely,
Jawaharlal Nehru

---

1. JN Collection. A copy of this letter was sent to M.K. Vellodi, Cabinet Secretary.

7. To Ajit Prasad Jain[1]

Maithon
September 27, 1957

My dear Ajit,

You mentioned to me yesterday that the per acre production in Bihar was one of the lowest in India. This matter had been revolving in my mind since then and I should like you to send me some figures about the rate of per acre production of foodgrains as well as, if possible, of other agricultural produce, in the different States in India. This comparison will be helpful in getting a picture of the present position in various parts of India.

The more I think of this matter, the more I feel that our approach to this question of intensive production has been superficial. We issue ardent appeals for it and no doubt we do something also, in the sense of better seeds, fertilizers, etc. I have no doubt that the Community Development blocks will be able to take this matter in hand more effectively, partly because their approach is likely to be a little more practical.

I still feel, however, that something should be done by us to get out of the office and the layman's approach to the problem. The more we go in for specialized and technical work, the more it is necessary to have technical personnel to deal with this. We are far too much in the habit of using our administrative personnel for specialized work. This administrative personnel is good in its own way. But it is too much to expect them to put themselves in the place of an actual farmer. I know that I find it difficult to do so because of lack of practical experience.

In other countries, whether communist or capitalist, the practice of having specialized personnel has grown greatly and has yielded results. We shall inevitably have to do this, whether in agriculture or in industry and not rely on the administrative side to look after effectively the technical approach.

Agricultural production and, more especially, food production, is the most important problem for us today. I think, therefore, we must tackle it in the specialized way and gradually introduce practical and technically trained people into our work.

When I wrote to you about the unloading of ships carrying foodgrains and the movement of these foodgrains by train, you replied to me and said that this was carefully looked into by various parties concerned. I still think that this

1. File No. 31 (30)/56-PMS. Also available in JN Collection.

might require a little more re-thinking and that Kandla port should be used much more.[2] From every point of view, this seems to me advantageous. It is so far the most efficient port we have from the point of view of equipment. Also, the political and labour problems that confront us at the ports like Bombay and Calcutta will not face us there. Further, the storage capacity at Kandla is not only big, but also efficient. I was told during the rainy season that there was difficulty in unloading ships in Bombay because there was no place to keep the foodgrains and they might be washed away by the rains. This cannot happen at Kandla where storage facilities are excellent and on a very big scale.

The only question that arises is that of the distance for the Railways to carry the foodgrains. That is important, but, even so, it is less important than many other factors to be borne in mind. Even from the distance point of view, the whole of North India is nearer Kandla and the distance of haulage is less. I should like you to have your experts look into this matter more thoroughly.

Yours sincerely,
Jawaharlal Nehru

2. Nehru wrote to A.P. Jain earlier on 24 September on this aspect., See *ante*, pp. 147-148.

8. To M.S. Thacker[1]

New Delhi
28 September 1957

My dear Thacker,[2]

You will remember the argument that arose about the administrative control of the Forest Research Institute, i.e., which Ministry should deal with it, I have just been reading a report of the Expert Committee of which you were also a member.[3]

1. JN Collection.
2. Maneklal S. Thacker was Director, CSIR.
3. The Government of India appointed an Expert Committee on the Forest Research Institute and Colleges, Dehradun, on 31 January 1956 with H.G. Champion as Chairman (i) to review the progress of research done during the past five years, (ii) to study the organization of the Institute and suggest improvement, and (iii) to advise on steps to be taken to secure publicity and quick application of the result of research.

158

As a result of this reading, I have written a note which I am sending to the Minister of Food & Agriculture.[4] I enclose a copy.

Recommendation is made that the Inspector-General of Forests should be appointed a member of the CSIR. Has this been done? What else is being done by the CSIR to encourage cooperation of the FRI with our other work?

Yours sincerely,
Jawaharlal Nehru

4. See the next item.

9. Functioning of the Forest Research Institute[1]

The Food & Agriculture Minister was good enough to send me a copy of this report in June last, on the eve of my departure for Europe. Unfortunately, I have had no time to read it. Now at last I have done so and I am noting down some of the points that have struck me.

2. The first thing I should like to know is what action has been taken in regard to the various suggestions made in this report.

3. It was a good idea to have this Expert Committee and to get a well known scientist from abroad to be the Chairman of it. The scientist is the Professor of Forestry at Oxford and no doubt he is a high-class expert. It has struck me, however, that it would be desirable for our Forestry Department and Institute to keep in touch with the countries whose chief business is forestry such as Finland or some of the other Scandinavian countries.

4. It appears from this report that the inner working of the Institute was not notable for harmony and indeed that there has been often a pull in different directions. The report refers to this in moderate language, but the meaning is clear. What exactly has been done about this matter because it is clearly absurd for an Institute to be run without harmonious working?

5. It also appears from the report that there have not been adequate contacts with other institutes and organizations which deal with matters of common

1. Note on the Report of the Expert Committee on the Forest Research Institute, Dehra Dun, 28 September 1957. JN Collection.

interest. Thus, the FRI should have the closest contact with the National Chemical Laboratory, the Drug Research Institute at Lucknow, the National Botanical Gardens at Lucknow and possibly some other institutes. Complaint is made in the report that even contacts with the State Forest Department are not good. This is very unfortunate. Then there are the Universities. An institute of this kind should have this living contact with the teachers as well as the growing generation in the Universities. I think that the facilities should be given to University teachers and senior students interested in forestry to visit the Institute. At the same time, senior teachers at the Institute should sometime visit the Universities and speak about forestry. This should be a two-way traffic.

6. It may be possible also to devise some simple courses, say, for four weeks or six weeks for the students of forestry in the Universities. They could come to the Institute for a month or so and get into intimate touch with the realities of forest work and the problems that arise. They need not be people who intend joining the forest service. The point is that this Institute, as others, should be in living touch with research and educational institutes and with the younger generation who could imbibe something of forestry from the Institute and realize the importance of it.

7. In the course of the report it is stated that Wood Research workers should not be retired at the age of 55. It seems to me quite absurd for technically and scientifically qualified persons to be made to retire at a fixed age, even though they are fit and healthy. This should apply not only to the Wood Research workers, but to others also.

8. It is stated somewhere that Hindi should not be introduced for the present. I do not quite understand what this means. I suppose no one suggests that the work of the Institute should be done in Hindi. But it would be helpful if gradually Hindi was introduced so that ultimately the changeover might not be too sudden. But this should not be done at the expense of the work.

9. There is reference to films being made. I think that there should be a fairly comprehensive film on forests. This will lead up to the work of the FRI. The film can be made a fascinating one. It must necessarily be in colour if it has to show forest. I do not quite know whether this Institute can make it, but the Films Division of the I & B Ministry might undertake this with the help of the Institute.

10. Whenever I have visited the Institute, I have been much impressed by the quality of the work being done there. But at the same time I have complained that this work does not lead to substantial practical results. It remains on the laboratory stage or at the most primary stage. What is being done to bring it into this practical range? It is suggested in the report to have some kind of a person who will boost this work and get in touch with industrialists and the like. I do not think this is at all feasible or worthwhile. There is now an organization

specially meant to bring the results of our research work to industry. I forget the name of it. But it started, I think, recently. Also, the whole object of the Council of Scientific and Industrial Research is to do this and the FRI should, therefore, keep into most intimate touch with this Council. They should naturally be in direct touch with the Hindustan Aircraft and the Railways.

11. Reference is made to the fact that there are big gaps in the work being done and that little attention is paid to some aspects. A list of these aspects is given. Also, it is stated that there is overlapping and the same work is being done by two separate sections. In other words, there is no proper integration of the work. One department seems to have the cameras and the other the photographer. A criticism has also been made about getting expensive apparatus, even though it is seldom used, such as electronic microscope.

12. This separatist and isolationist approach not only of the Institute itself but all its separate sections is obviously undesirable. There must be harmonious working within the Institute and no overlapping in equipment or work. In the same way the Institute should not try to do work which is being done by other institutes or laboratories. They should rely on the National Physical Laboratory for the work which is being done there and the National Chemical Laboratory for their variety of work.

13. There is some reference somewhere in the report to new buildings being put up and also a chemical laboratory. At the present moment we cannot afford to have new buildings and there is far too much a tendency to spend money for brick and mortar. Apart from this, why should not be chemical work be largely done by the National Chemical Laboratory?

14. I have jotted down some notes about matters which have occurred to me on a rapid reading of this report. I should like to know what is being done in the FRI in regard to these matters as well as the various recommendations of the report.

10. To Morarji Desai[1]

New Delhi
September 29, 1957

My dear Morarji,

I suppose you know a fruit called *Mirabolum*. I believe this is what is called *ritha* in Hindi in this part of the world. It is used especially for washing. I understand that it occurs in large quantities in the Jabalpur area in Madhya Pradesh. Some of it is exported and then processed outside India. It has been suggested to me that it should be easy to process it here and then export it. This will obviously be much more advantageous to us. Perhaps you might have this enquired into.

Yours sincerely,
Jawaharlal Nehru

1. File No. 44(33)/57-PMS. Also available in JN Collection.

11. Practical Knowledge of Agriculture Needed[1]

It seems to me rather odd that a man of the experience and competence in agriculture like Shri Santokh Singh should be at a loose end without his services being utilized. Agricultural production has been, and is even more so now, our most important activity. I have no doubt in my mind that this cannot be tackled adequately by theorists, but by practical farmers who also know theory.

2. Anyhow, if the Planning Commission does not think that it can utilize Shri Santokh Singh's services, there the matter ends so far as the Planning Commission is concerned. I spoke to the Minister of Food & Agriculture some two or three weeks ago on this subject. I think that we must somehow try to get out of the rut in which we have been working in regard to agriculture with people sitting in offices who know little precious about it.

1. Note to Cabinet Secretary, New Delhi, 20 October 1957. JN Collection.

III. EDUCATION & CULTURE

1. Need for Affordable Books[1]

The whole object of the National Book Trust is to help the writers and also the publishers, to create an atmosphere in which they can flourish. I remember when we first considered this question of formation of a Book Trust it was pointed out that we have got into a vicious circle. The book reading public in India is extraordinarily small compared to any comparative standard. Books are expensive, and the writers do not get much out of the books. Publishers, except those who produce educational textbooks, also do not prosper much. It is not merely because many people in India cannot afford to buy books. There is a vast number who can buy books. If people who go to cinema, give one-tenth of the money they spend on cinema to books, you would have enormous number of books sold in India. We feel that one of the ways to break this vicious circle is to produce good books cheaply. If they are able to do this, people will buy books and read them and this habit will grow.

Steps are being taken in countries like the UK and the United States to bring out cheap editions of classics and other good literature. What the Government has done here by establishing this Trust will undoubtedly help the public and the authors. To begin with, we are not dealing with the modern books with which the publishers are concerned. Though the Trust is not prohibited from bringing out such books, it will concentrate on translations from the classics and translations from foreign languages and from one to the other of our own languages, and of books which are recognized to be good.

Occasionally, new books may be published by the Trust, but normally speaking, it does not invade the domain of private publishers. It will rather help in creating a climate for book reading and book buying which must inevitably profit the reader and the publisher and will certainly not bring about a conflict with the publishers.

1. Speech at the inauguration of the National Book Trust, New Delhi, 1 August 1957. From *National Herald* and *The Hindu*, 2 August 1957. S. Radhakrishnan inaugurated the Trust.

There must have been some misunderstanding in the minds of writers and publishers when they passed a resolution disapproving the formation of the National Book Trust. In order to bring out cheaper books, fancy paper and binding can be dispensed with both by Government and private publishers, otherwise the price of the book goes high and people are discouraged from buying it. Instead of binding, paper covers can be used as was the practice in France.

I hope that, apart from carrying out the objects laid down at the time it was established, the Trust will also be a kind of 'book hospital', generally to understand what comes in the way of books being purchased and read. In America, there are book hospitals to find out why a book has failed and what is wrong with it. Often the publishers find some reasons for failure—maybe the title was not attractive enough or they do something which I shudder to think. They may change the title of the same book and curiously enough, they get away with the book and people buy it.

Side by side, I would like a large number of small libraries to grow up everywhere. If that happens, it will help not only the reader but the writer and the publisher also because certain books which are approved by the libraries will have a large sale.

2. Value of Physical Education[1]

I am sorry I am unable to be present at the inauguration of the Lakshmi Bai College of Physical Education.[2] I am happy that this college has come into existence and has been appropriately named after one who has immortalized herself in India's long story. The date chosen for the opening ceremony is also appropriate.

We have to grow in many ways in this country, in fact we have to make good in every way. Sometimes, in our desire to advance in every direction, we spread ourselves out too much. It is better to concentrate on what comes first and then deal with other aspects of our plan of progress. Here, as elsewhere, we have to have a system of priorities.

1. Message to Lakshmi Bai College of Physical Education , Gwalior, 1 August 1957. JN Collection.
2. The College was inaugurated on 17 August.

But, so far as physical culture is concerned, surely it should be given a high priority, so that we might build up a healthy nation and thereby contribute to the physical well-being of our people. India is a vast country and we have people who, given the chance, can shine in the field of athletics and games. Considering our size, we are backward in this matter. Recently, I visited the little country of Finland which has a relatively small population. But it is a country of athletes who have won quite a considerable number of gold medals in the Olympic Games.

It is good to shine in athletics as in other departments of human activity. But what we aim at is to raise the general standard and give our boys and girls the opportunity to build their bodies up as well as their minds and character.

I send my good wishes to the Lakshmi Bai College of Physical Education and express the hope that it will live up to the name which they have adopted.

3. To B.C. Roy[1]

New Delhi
August 3, 1957

My dear Bidhan,[2]

Our Defence Minister, Krishna Menon, tells me that some kind of a request has come from your Government to our Defence Ministry for a plot of land in Barrackpore, which belongs to the Defence Ministry. It is proposed, I am told, to put up some kind of a memorial column or something like it there in honour of Mangal Pandey, the sepoy who fired the first shot in 1857.[3]

I rather doubt if it will be proper or advisable to use a piece of land belonging to our Defence establishments for this purpose. Whatever we may think of Mangal Pandey's act, it is not a good example to set to the men in our Army, and to have

---

1. JN Collection.
2. Chief Minister of West Bengal.
3. (d. 1857); a resident of Ballia, UP; soldier in 34th Native Infantry in the East India Company; objected to the use of animal fat for greasing the cartridges of the new Enfield Rifles; influenced by refusal of his compatriots at Behrampore to use the greased cartridges, he broke into open mutiny on 29 March 1857 at Barrackpore near Calcutta; court-martialled on 6 April and hanged at Barrackpore on 8 April 1857.

this memorial in land appertaining to the Army would be to draw very particular attention to this.

Personally, I do not think any ornate memorial is necessary for this purpose. Perhaps, a plaque somewhere will be enough. But, if you want some kind of a memorial, I would suggest that it should be put up somewhere else, and not on land belonging to our military.

Yours,
Jawahar

4. To Abul Kalam Azad[1]

New Delhi
August 3, 1957

My dear Maulana,[2]

Dr S.N. Bose,[3] Vice Chancellor of Visva Bharati, came to see me today and spoke to me about the reorganization and development of the Tagore Museum at Santiniketan. Long ago we decided that there should be such a Museum. In a few years' time, there is going to be the Centenary of Tagore's birthday. It would be fitting if this Museum etc., was part of this celebration.

The estimate for this Museum etc., is a capital sum of Rs 6 lakhs and an annual grant of Rs 52,000. This will be something more than a Museum—a cultural centre.

I think that we should certainly have this Museum and the amount asked for, considering the purpose, is not very great. It is true that we cannot add to our

---

1. File No. 40(9)/56-59-PMS. Also available in JN Collection.
2. Union Minister of Education and Scientific Research.
3. Satyendra Nath Bose (1894-1974); eminent scientist; taught Physics at Dhaka University and Calcutta University; worked with Albert Einstein in Germany, 1925-26; Chairman, National Institute of Science, New Delhi, 1948-50; Vice Chancellor, Visva Bharati University, 1956-58; Nominated Member, Rajya Sabha, 1952-59; Member, Governing Body, CSIR; awarded Padma Vibhushan, 1954.

liabilities at present. But I do not suppose we shall have to find the money for some time. If, however, an assurance is given, they can go ahead with this scheme.

I enclose Dr Bose's letter.

Yours sincerely,
Jawaharlal Nehru

5. To A.K. Gopalan[1]

New Delhi
August 3, 1957

Dear Gopalan[2],

Your letter of August 1st. I agree with you that the circus in Kerala is certainly worth preserving and encouraging. But I am afraid many of the suggestions which you have made are beyond our capacity, even though they are considered desirable. At present more especially, we cannot undertake any special expenditure. If the Kerala Government can do anything for it, I shall be glad.

Thus, we cannot think of having an institution for training circus personnel. Useful as that might be, obviously it cannot be given priority over the many other more important things that we have to do. Nor do I think that a special train can be fitted out for this purpose.

So far as wild animals are concerned, they are normally looked after in the many preserves that we have all over the country. I do not know anything about having a scientific breeding centre for wild animals.

I suppose the Entertainment Tax in the States is a State subject and it is not for the Government of India to deal with it.

In regard to one thing, that is, concessions by railway authorities, this is a Government of India matter. I am referring this to the Railway Minister.

Yours sincerely,
Jawaharlal Nehru

1. JN Collection.
2. CPI Member of Lok Sabha.

6. To Y.B. Chavan[1]

New Delhi
August 6, 1957

My dear Chavan,

You will remember that I wrote to you once suggesting that it was desirable to give some encouragement to European music in India, and more especially in Bombay, where there is considerable field for it. I think that this encouragement will help Indian music also indirectly.

I have now received a note from Miss Khurshed Naoroji[2] about a Children's Concert Society. It seems to me worthy of support. I do not suppose that much support is necessary, but a little push would be very helpful. Perhaps you could find out more about it from Khurshedbehn Naoroji, 78 Napean Sea Road, Bombay-6.

Yours sincerely,
Jawaharlal Nehru

---

1. JN Collection.
2. (1917-1968); granddaughter of Dadabhai Naoroji; arrested for violating ban on entry while working with Abdul Ghaffar Khan for unity of various tribes in NWFP in 1940; arrested for intervening on behalf of workers of Tata Steel, Jamshedpur, during a strike in 1942; had keen interest in western music.

7. To D.P. Karmarkar[1]

New Delhi
August 7, 1957

My dear Karmarkar,

Your letter of August 3rd about Dr Hem Chandra Govel.[2] I do not know this man and, therefore, can offer no opinion about him. But, it seems to me that your Ministry is taking a very narrow view.

We discussed in Cabinet the larger question of Indian students abroad, more especially those taking scientific and technical subjects, and we came to the conclusion that we should give them an assurance of employment, that is, if they were good enough. That employment will not be to any particular post. Indeed, they might simply join a pool of employment, and we could use them temporarily for any purpose till they could be properly absorbed. It seemed to the Cabinet that the present practice was very unsatisfactory. On the one hand, we shout loudly for more and more trained personnel, for more doctors etc. On the other hand, when a trained person appears, we have no job for him, and he knocks about from pillar to post.

There is obviously something very wrong about this. This is not a question of making an exception in the case of Dr Govel, but rather of getting hold of a person or persons because we are bound to need them in future. We must not think too much in terms of a few odd appointments. Honestly, I do not understand this peculiar policy that we have adopted. I have been writing repeatedly to the Planning Commission, to the Home Ministry and others on this subject, and I am told that they have accepted the suggestion I made and are trying to work it out.

Does the Health Ministry think that there is no need for additional doctors in India, why then do we have more and more medical colleges being set up?

Of course, we cannot guarantee any particular post to anybody. But, what we should be able to guarantee to a person, provided he has the requisite qualifications, is to engage him and keep him on our rolls and give him any

---

1. JN Collection.
2. The Rockefeller Foundation, New York, had agreed to award a fellowship to Hem Chandra Govel for studying Public Health at Columbia University. But they had laid down a condition that a post should be available to Govel on his return to India. Govel wrote to Nehru on 11 July 1957 in this regard.

work that may be available. It may be that we do not find for him a very suitable work to begin with. He may have to wait for it. But, we shall have him with us.

Presumably, a person who has been selected by the Rockefeller Foundation, has some competence.

Sukthankar was dealing with this whole question of employing people in a pool or otherwise, even if we have not got immediate posts for them. He has now gone,[3] but, possibly, the Cabinet Secretariat might know about it, or the Home Ministry. You might enquire, I shall await your reply before I write to Govel.

Yours sincerely,
Jawaharlal Nehru

3. Y.N. Sukthankar, the Cabinet Secretary, was sworn in as Governor of Orissa on 31 July 1957.

8. To B.C. Roy[1]

New Delhi
August 12, 1957

My dear Bidhan,

I am writing to you about the proposed memorial to Mangal Pandey. You told me on the telephone today that you wanted to put up some rather inconspicuous memorial almost by the roadside.

I have had a talk with Pantji also and previously I had discussed this matter with the Defence Minister. Our difficulty is that any memorial like this in a place where our soldiers frequently visit might well be a bad example for them. They are bound to see it daily when they go to the temple nearby or to the playing field.

It may be separated from the military ground, but that does not get over the difficulty of its attracting attention of soldiers constantly many of whom will,

1. JN Collection.

no doubt, visit it. We would very much prefer such a memorial to be in a place where our soldiers would not normally go to.

This is not a question of a little land being surrendered or not, but rather of the effect it would produce on our Army men. I should like you to consider this.

Yours sincerely,
Jawaharlal Nehru

9. A Memorial for Mangal Pandey[1]

I sent you a copy of a letter I had written to Dr Roy about the proposal to put up some small memorial to Mangal Pandey.[2] I had another letter from him last night, which I enclose. You will see that he is very anxious to put up something or other, which will be outside the military area. I do not quite know where it is. I have just telephoned him and he said that the Military Commandant, Barrackpore, had visited this place with one of the civil officials and agreed that a small area might be used for this purpose. It is not quite clear to me where this is, but the Military Commandant seems to think that it did not matter. I have, therefore, told Dr Roy on the telephone that if the Commandant agrees, he can go ahead with this matter in that particular spot.

Perhaps you might issue orders accordingly to the Commandant that if he agrees, this might be done.[3]

1. Note to V.K. Krishna Menon, Defence Minister, New Delhi, 15 August 1957. JN Collection.
2. See *ante*, pp. 165-166.
3. Defence Minister responded that a formal request by the West Bengal Government would enable the Government of India to issue order for giving up the military land to be walled off for a memorial for Mangal Pandey, as suggested by Nehru.

10. To J.C. de Graft-Johnson[1]

New Delhi
August 18, 1957

Dear Dr de Graft-Johnson,[2]

Thank you for your letter of the 16th August.[3]

As you know, I have been greatly interested in the Department of African Studies of the Delhi University. I have been interested in it for a variety of reasons, the chief among these being my conviction that India and the countries of Africa should know each other much better so that they might be able to cooperate in the future to the advantage of both. I have long attached great importance to Africa and I am sure the countries of Africa will play an ever greater part not only in that great continent but in the world.

I am sorry to learn from you that you have not been satisfied with the working of this Department. In spite of my great interest in it, it has not been possible for me to be closely associated with it. I am, therefore, rather ignorant of recent developments there. But one thing you can be sure, that is, our desire to keep this Department functioning and growing. If it was important to start this Department some years ago, it is much more important today to continue it.

I do not know who is on the Advisory Committee of African Studies. Your Membership of that Committee appears to me to be obviously desirable.

I suggest that you discuss the future of your Department with the Vice Chancellor, Dr V.K.R.V. Rao. I am sending him your letter. I am also communicating with the Ministry of Education on this subject.

Yours sincerely,
Jawaharlal Nehru

1. JN Collection.
2. Professor from Ghana, came on Indian Government's invitation to teach in the Department of African Studies, University of Delhi.
3. Graft-Johnson raised several points regarding the Department of African Studies of Delhi University. He felt he was unable to make a full contribution to its affairs other than assisting initially with the drawing up of syllabus and teaching as he was excluded from the Advisory Committee. Regarding employment of the students of this Department, Graft-Johnson suggested that the invitations for the posts in Africa, received by Ministry of Education through Ministry of External Affairs, be publicized in such a way as to attract students in these studies. He also pointed out that there was no provision for the African Studies to be included in the IAS examinations.

11. To B.C. Roy[1]

New Delhi
20th August 1957

My dear Bidhan

You know that some of the descendants of the old King of Oudh, Wajid Ali Shah,[2] have been living in Calcutta. Wajid Ali Shah was deposed by the British in 1856, i.e., a year before the 1857 rising. He migrated to Matiaburj, Calcutta, with his various wives and children. One of his wives, Hazrat Mahal,[3] and one son, Birjis Quder, however, did not approve of the King's submission to the British and remained behind in Lucknow. In 1857 they joined the rising and played quite a notable part in it. In the recent book by Dr S.N. Sen[4] entitled *Eighteen Fifty-Seven*, Hazrat Mahal is referred to as "the Queen mother herself never lost heart and moved among her men with a spirit that deserved better success".

Even on the collapse of the rising, Hazrat Mahal refused to submit to the British and she went to Nepal. The British are said to have offered her many inducements to return, but she refused all these offers to become a British pensioner. She had taken large sums of money with her to Nepal out of the King's treasury. She spent all this in meeting the expenses of the thousands of refugees who had gone from India to Nepal after the rising had been crushed by the British. She is said to have died in poverty in Nepal in 1874. Dr S.N. Sen says "She was a better man than her husband".

1. JN Collection.
2. (1823-1887); last ruler of Oudh; ascended the throne in 1847; was patron of classical Hindustani music, *thumri*, dance, drama, poetry; was himself a gifted composer and Kathak dancer; composed many new ragas; considered as the first playwright of the Hindustani theatre; was deposed by the British in 1856; exiled to Matiaburj near Kolkata where he died on 1 September 1887.
3. (d. 1879); wife of Wajid Ali Shah and last Begum of Oudh; one of the leaders of the Revolt of 1857; as Regent, she seized control of Lucknow in association with revolutionary forces and set up her son Birjis Quder as the King of Oudh; intensified war efforts in association with Nana Saheb; died in Nepal in April 1879.
4. Surendra Nath Sen (1890-1962); Director, National Archives of India, 1947-49; Vice Chancellor, Delhi University, 1950-53.

Her son, Birjis Quder, married Emperor Bahadur Shah's[5] granddaughter, Mahtab Ara Begum, who was also a refugee in asylum in Nepal. Birjis Quder had also continued to live in Nepal. In 1893 he returned to India, apparently with the intention of organizing some trouble against the British. A few months after, he was assassinated in Calcutta together with a daughter, his son and some others. He lies buried with his father in Wajid Ali Shah's tomb in Matiaburj. Birjis Quder's son was Meher Quder who is still living in Calcutta.

You have known Prince Yusuf Mirza, a grandson of Wajid Ali Shah, who lived in Calcutta. Yusuf Mirza belonged to the loyal section of the family and, therefore, got fairly good treatment from the British.

On the coming of Independence on the 15th August 1947, Yusuf Mirza went to Lucknow and actually had himself crowned in some way as King of Oudh. This was rather ridiculous and, I think, the local government asked him to quit Lucknow. Meher Quder, the son of Birjis Quder, considered himself the rightful descendant of Wajid Ali Shah and a successor to his interests. In August 1947, learning of what Yusuf Mirza was going to do, Meher Quder made it clear that Yusuf Mirza had no authority to do this and that if there were any legal rights anywhere, they belonged to him, Meher Quder. Anyhow, Meher Quder wrote to the Governor of UP abdicating and giving up such legal rights as he might possess.

All this is rather silly, but I am writing about it just to give you the background.

The loyal section of Wajid Ali Shah's family was treated on the whole well by the British Government; not so this other section. Anyhow, Meher Quder has been getting a pension of Rs 500/- per month. This continues even today. I think his children get some small sum too, probably Rs 75/- each. One of his youngest sons is a very bright boy who has done well at the Aligarh University, getting first. He has taken his M.A. and is now studying for Ph.D. He intends appearing for the IAS examination. He is only 22 now.

Meher Quder and his sons have presented a memorial to the President asking for various reliefs – higher pensions, restoration of some old jagir, refund of some old confiscated Government Promissory notes, etc. It is absurd to think of restoration of any jagir or of any refund of Government Promissory Notes confiscated in the last century. But we are inclined to feel that his pension might be raised. Obviously, Rs 500/- per month in Calcutta is not much. He is an old man now and is said to be heavily in debt.

5. Bahadur Shah Zafar (1775-1862); last Mughal Emperor; ascended the throne in 1837; calligrapher and Urdu poet known as Zafar; also wrote commentary on Sheikh Saadi's *Gulistan*; assumed leadership of revolutionary forces against the British in 1857; was imprisoned on 21 September 1857 and kept in Red Fort, Delhi; later banished to Rangoon where he died in December 1862.

I have written to you this long story, although it was not necessary to do so. What I would like to know from you is if you could kindly find out about Meher Quder (his full name is Prince Meher Quder Zahid Ali Mirza). What is his state now, what does he do, is there anything objectionable about him, etc.? His address is 11, Marsden Street, Calcutta-16. The memorial he has presented is on his own behalf as well as his three sons Anjum Quder Roushan Ali Mirza, Kaukub Quder Sajjad Ali Mirza and Nayyer Quder Wasif Ali Mirza. If you could give us any information about the sons also, I shall be grateful.

I do not want you to make any kind of an elaborate inquiry. I just want to know what the general report is about them or what their reputation is. Also, if possible, what their debts are.

Yours sincerely,
Jawaharlal Nehru

12. To B.V. Keskar[1]

New Delhi
August 23, 1957

My dear Balkrishna,
What I slightly feared is happening. Your film on 1857 etc., is being criticized by people from the South. They say that the South has been ignored as if there was no freedom fighter there during these hundred years.[2] I think, there is some truth in this and your people should have been more careful. Even now, is it not possible for you to put in some episodes from the South?

---

1. File No. 43(102)/57-PMS. Also available in JN Collection.
2. Members of Parliament from the Southern States were much upset over the documentaries "1857" and "100 Years of Freedom," which did not show the participation of South India. Questions were raised about leaving out such freedom fighters as Veerapandya Kattaboman and his brother Veera Maruthu of the pre-1857 era and great revolutionaries like V.O. Chidambaram Pillai, V.V.S. Iyer, Vanchinathan, Subramanya Siva and the national poet Subramanya Bharathi of the years 1907-08. Similarly, many names of the Gandhian era could also be mentioned.

2. Dr V.K.R.V. Rao, Vice Chancellor of Delhi University, came to see me today and suggested that there might be a committee on propaganda etc., more especially about the Five Year Plan. He said he had many ideas on this subject and he would gladly serve on such a committee. I think, this is a good idea. Why not have a small committee to discuss not only the Plan, but other forms of domestic propaganda to pull people up?

Yours sincerely,
Jawaharlal Nehru

13. Restricting Passports for Studies Abroad[1]

Please reply to the letter from Maulvi Hifzur Rahman.[2] Also, separately, to M.F. Shaikh of Ahmedabad. You can give them briefly the reasons why we have been compelled to refuse a passport and our policy governing this. This policy is a general policy of not giving passports to persons who are not properly qualified to pursue studies in foreign countries and there is the special policy now of restricting passports because of the difficulty of foreign exchange.

It is clear that Shaikh has no qualifications to be admitted to a technical institute in India or in the UK. We are sure that no technical institute in the United States can admit a person with his qualifications. In fact, scholars from India, who have graduated here, have not been admitted there because they did not get a first-class in their BA examination. It is difficult, therefore, for us to understand how he can be admitted to a proper institute without any previous training whatever.

Also, in regard to dollar exchange, the Registrar of the Institute in the US himself says that at least 500 dollars are needed. Unless we are quite sure that not only this money, but further monies required for his stay in the United States, and these are likely to be considerable, are available, we cannot think of issuing a passport.

1. Note to K. Ram, Principal Private Secretary, New Delhi, 24 August 1957. JN Collection.
2. Member, Lok Sabha at this time.

You might further add that brilliant Government of India scholars, who have been admitted into institutes abroad, have been kept back from going because of this foreign exchange difficulty.

14. To Govind Ballabh Pant[1]

New Delhi
August 24, 1957

My dear Pantji,

I mentioned to you today about two letters from Laxmi Bai, Rani of Jhansi, which were shown to me in original. I have had these letters sent to the Director of Archives for being repaired and for taking photostat copies. I cannot, of course, say positively that these letters are genuine, but I am definitely inclined to think that they are. Both their appearance and the fact that they come from the normal custody, go to indicate this. The two men who brought these, stated that they were descendents of Maharaja Mardan Singh,[2] Ruler of Banpur State, to whom Rani Laxmi Bai wrote the letters. A note attached gives their account of what they have been getting from Government.

I am sending you this note as well as other papers including copies of Rani Laxmi Bai's letters, also a pamphlet entitled *Vidrohi Banpur*. Perhaps, you might have this matter examined.

If we are satisfied about the authenticity of these letters as well as of the men who brought them, then the question arises what we should do about it. We should certainly keep these letters in our Archives. I do not think it will be desirable to make a lump sum payment for them. These people will probably waste it. A monthly payment would be much more suitable, although this ultimately amounts to much more. They seem to have large families and they

---

1. JN Collection.
2. (d. 1879); Ruler of Banpur jagir in the Chanderi State of Madhya Pradesh; organized a strong force of Bundela patriots and captured many strongholds of the British during the revolt of 1857; had to withdraw from Chanderi, Banpur and other places in the face of superior British might; tried to reach Jhansi in order to form a joint front with Rani Laxmi Bai but had to surrender to the British on 5 July 1858; was imprisoned at Meerut and Mathura where he died on 22 July 1879.

live in very straitened circumstances. After you have seen these papers, perhaps we can have a talk about this matter.

Yours sincerely,
Jawaharlal Nehru

15. To Zohra Husaini[1]

New Delhi
August 24, 1957

My dear Zohra,[2]

I received your letter of the 20th August two days ago. Of course, you can come and see me if you so like, but I do not think I shall be able to help you in this matter at this stage.[3]

The question of scholars going abroad came up before us some days ago. We did not like any person going at this stage unless this visit was connected with the technical training required for our developmental schemes. We said so and asked the list to be examined again. Strictly speaking, the rule already laid down did not apply to you. I have no doubt that you are a more brilliant student than most others who are going. But it would not be right for us to frame a rule and then not to follow it. You may be able to go abroad sometime later, say next year. For the present, however, we must stick to our rule and decision.

This does not mean that I consider philosophy a subject of less importance than other subjects. Indeed I consider it very important and I wish there was

---

1. JN Collection.
2. Daughter of K.G. Saiydain, Secretary, Ministry of Education, Government of India.
3. Zohra Husaini, a philosophy student, was one of the twenty scholars who had been chosen to go abroad and had now been dropped out. T.T. Krishnamachari had earlier mentioned to Nehru that there was no point in encouraging any person to go out for post-graduate work in philosophy. In a letter to Krishnamachari on 22 August 1957 (not printed), Nehru commented that she was an outstanding person and had won the highest prizes available in India. Encouraged by the Vice-President, she had carried on her studies at his instance and was to go abroad. Nehru asked Krishnamachari to reconsider the matter and wrote that out of twenty scholars "to keep back a Muslim girl would be unfortunate."

much more philosophy in the world than there is. But philosophy does not put out a fire when we have a fire raging. We have to find out other ways of dealing with a critical situation.

There is no reason why this should come in the way of the career for which you have been training yourself and for which you will, no doubt, be very well suited.

Yours sincerely,
Jawaharlal Nehru

16. To Harekrushna Mahtab[1]

New Delhi
August 25, 1957

My dear Mahtab,

Please refer to your letter of the 9th August, with which you forwarded an application from the Kala Vikash Kendra.[2] From the note attached to the letter of the Kala Vikash Kendra, it appears that a sum of Rs 39,000/- is asked for all kinds of activities. The impression conveyed upon me is that many things are attempted to be done without any proper preparation for them, and just the sums involved are totalled up and a request for a grant made.

I understand that a request for a grant was made to the Sangeet Natak Akademi in 1955-56. They received grant-in-aid as follows:

(i) From the Sangeet Natak Akademi - Rs 3,000/-
(ii) From the Orissa State Academi - Rs 1,750/-

The next year, the Kendra asked the Sangeet Natak Akademi for a grant-in-aid of Rs 10,020/- for 1956-57. In forwarding this application, the Orissa State Academi observed that the Kala Vikash Kendra had not been able to utilize the entire grant sanctioned for 1955-56. Partly because of this and partly for other reasons, the Sangeet Natak Akademi decided not to make any grant that year. It is obvious that if the previous grant has not been spent, the justification for subsequent grants is not great. It is not money that usually comes in the way, but

1. JN Collection.
2. Situated at Gangamandir, Cuttack, this institute was recognized by Sangeet Natak Akademi.

a trained and experienced organization which can utilize it to the best advantage. The various types of activities which are given in the application of the Kendra, are so diverse that it is difficult to understand how they will be able to carry them on without a very great deal of experience.

Further, the Sangeet Natak Akademi has pointed out to me that the Orissa State Academi has already undertaken a project for survey and preservation of folk dances and songs of Orissa. It is much better equipped to undertake this work than the Kendra, and it has received a grant of Rs 5,000/- from the Sangeet Natak Akademi. Duplication of this activity is obviously not desirable.

I take it that the Orissa State Academi should be considered the primary body responsible for the study and preservation of Orissa folk dances and songs. Orissa is rich in folk art, and we should like to encourage this study in every way. But, dispersal of energies and overlapping of work will not be good.

I should like you to consider these matters and avoid this type of dispersal, overlapping and possible conflict. I am sending you a cheque for Rs 10,000/-. I leave it to you to utilize it to the best advantage for the development of folk art, dance and song, etc. You may, if you like, give this sum entirely or partly to the Kala Vikash Kendra. But, in any event, you should make sure that they have the capacity to use it to proper advantage, and they should not overlap with the work of the Orissa State Academi with which they should have close and cooperative relations.

Yours sincerely,
Jawaharlal Nehru

17. To Abul Kalam Azad[1]

New Delhi
August 25, 1957

My dear Maulana,
Some time ago, I wrote to you about some charges of vandalism in regard to our protected monuments and, more especially, about Sanchi. My letter was forwarded to the Director-General of Archaeology who sent a note in reply. That note, so far as I can remember, did not quite meet the charges made and generally did not satisfy.

1. File No. 40(133)/57-PMS. Also available in JN Collection.

2. This matter has again been brought up before me by Rukmini Devi, MP.[2] Her brother, N.Y. Sastry was a Grade 1 Officer of the Department of Archaeology and thus had practical knowledge of what was happening. He made serious charges of vandalism and incompetence. He has, I believe, written fully to the Archaeological Department in the course of the last two years drawing attention to these various matters.

3. I now enclose a letter I have received from N.Y. Sastry. In this reference is made to the irreparable damage done to the great Stupa at Sanchi. Sastry says that he wrote about this fully to the Education Department on the 6th May 1954. According to him, although his charges were found to be true, nothing much was done about them. What is still worse, the same persons continue to function in spite of their proved incompetence. Another case is mentioned at Nalanda where it is said the remains of the old brick pavements were destroyed and a new pavement of modern bricks was constructed in connection with the Buddha Jayanti celebrations.

4. I am much concerned at these charges and, I think, they require careful looking into by the men at the top. If it is found that some people are not competent for their task, they should be removed.[3]

Yours affectionately,
Jawaharlal Nehru

2. Rukmini Devi Arundale was a noted theosophist and Bharat Natyam dancer; nominated Member of Rajya Sabha.

3. Azad replied on 4 September that the Director-General of Archeology told him that defects in conservation work on the monuments were largely due to the inexperience of the subordinate staff. Whenever reported, the defects had been removed with the help of the experienced staff. Regarding the Stupa at Sanchi, the DG said that the technical defects had been rectified at the cost of the contractor and the monument was receiving constant attention of his Department. Regarding Nalanda, the DG said that the decayed brick pavement had been recently replaced by new bricks of the same size, in conformity with the practice prevailing in the Department, of replacing worn out material of the monument with the new one of the same type. This was followed very extensively over the last fifty years at most of the monuments including Mohenjodaro, Harappa, Sarnath, Sanchi etc. Without such replacements it could not have been possible to preserve the excavated structures.

18. To Govind Ballabh Pant[1]

New Delhi
26 August 1957

My dear Pantji,

Dr Bidhan Roy has replied to the letter I sent him about Prince Meher Quder of the House of Oudh. I enclose his letter and note.

The position, therefore, is fairly clear. Nothing is reported against Meher Quder or his family and in fact all the reports are in his favour. The house he lives in belongs to him. The family lives on the first floor in a state of destitution. The lower floor has been let out on a rent of Rs 225/-.

Meher Quder gets a pension of Rs 500/-. He has his wife, a widowed daughter and three sons and apparently a large number of other dependents. His debts amount to Rupees fifty thousand. Apparently, much of this money has been borrowed from his own uncle.

In a telegram I received from Meher Quder there is some reference to his sons getting Rs 75/- per month pension after his death. At present I suppose the sons do not get anything separately for their education or otherwise.

I suppose there is no further information that we have to gather. Or perhaps the Home Ministry has some information about these pensions.

We have now to decide what to do about this matter. As I said previously, there is no question of restoration of old property or Promissory Notes etc. The only question is what increased pension to give him and whether we should give him any lump sum also.

Yours affectionately,
Jawaharlal Nehru

---

1. JN Collection.

19. Consultation of Historical Records[1]

From the papers on this file I see that you wrote to the Home Secretary on August 2nd. Presumably no reply has come from him yet.[2]

2. I am not at all satisfied with the noting on this file by Intelligence or by the Director of Archives. The papers required are very old, probably over thirty years old. No question of secrecy should apply to such papers, unless there is some very extraordinary reason in regard to a particular document. In fact, they should be considered, more or less, public papers. To say that they can only be seen by research scholars is not very helpful. Any person can become a research student for a time. The mere fact that he is investigating some matter may make it necessary for him to look at some old papers. Also the fact that a Communist wants to see them is irrelevant.

3. I do not particularly fancy this hush hush policy about old public documents. Nor do I understand how our relations with the British Government might be affected by these as PPS has somewhere stated.

4. As I said previously I could understand some particular paper being kept secret.

5. If the Director of Archives has any doubt about the desirability of any papers being shown or not, he should send me a list of them and I shall examine them.

6. Normally speaking, the only understanding that is necessary is that nothing will be published without Government's permission.[3]

1. Note to Principal Private Secretary, New Delhi, 27 August 1957, JN Collection.
2. This was regarding withdrawal of permission to Sohan Singh Bhakna, Gurmukh Singh and Karam Singh Cheema of Desh Bhagat Yadgar Committee to consult papers in the National Archives for writing a history of the Ghadar movement. They met Nehru on 4 May to seek his help in the matter but got a reply later from his PPS conveying that these were secret papers. They argued that material pertaining to Independence movement was sacred national heritage and belonged to all patriots. At Nehru's instance, K. Ram enquired on 2 August if the Home Secretary, A.V. Pai would allow at least some of the records to be made available to the Committee, and whether the publication of a revised history of the Ghadar movement would in any way adversely affect the happy relations between India and the UK.
3. However, the Home Minister, G.B. Pant noted on 1 September 1957: "I am not as a rule in favour of giving undue prominence to surreptitious or violent activities. I have a feeling that their effect on the whole cannot be wholesome. Such material when placed at the disposal of persons who believe in subversive and violent methods can be used by them in an insidious, if not open, manner for encouraging violence. It would be difficult to prevent anyone from making use of the material that is made over to a private individual in any manner he likes." In view of Pant's opinion, Nehru directed on 6 September that the matter should be allowed to rest.

20. To Sri Prakasa[1]

New Delhi
August 30, 1957

My dear Prakasa,[2]

I have had some surprising news from Vijaya Lakshmi. You know the picture you sent to the Duke of Wellington. (Did you send one picture or two? Vijaya Lakshmi talks about two pictures).[3]

Vijaya Lakshmi writes to me that the two pictures are fakes. The Duke of Wellington met her somewhere and was quite upset about it. He did not accuse us of trickery. Apparently, long ago, about sixty years ago, somebody repainted them. The original picture has thus disappeared.[4]

I am just letting you know about this. I have written to Vijaya Lakshmi that we have another picture and a better one, but I do not see why I should make a present of it to the Duke unless he is prepared to give us some treasures in exchange.

Yours affectionately,
Jawaharlal Nehru

1. File No. 40(89)/56-58-PMS. Also available in JN Collection.
2. Governor of Bombay.
3. These portraits were sent to the seventh Duke of Wellington, Gerald Wellesley, from Raj Bhawan, Madras in exchange of some portraits and sketches of Tipu Sultan. See also *Selected Works* (second series), Vol. 34, p. 83; Vol. 36, pp. 195-196; Vol. 37, p. 564.
4. Sri Prakasa replied on 23 September that he must take full responsibility for the last restoration in 1955 of these portraits which were in bad condition and even torn in parts. He met Mrs Margarete Scheidemann, mother-in-law of K.L. Mehta, ICS. She was an expert at restoring old paintings and had done some good work at the National Museum, Delhi and other places. At Sri Prakasa's request, she undertook the work, and the portraits were fully restored and the damages repaired. He wrote that he was very anxious that the Duke of Wellington should be assured that both the portraits of the Duke of Wellington and the Marquis Wellesley that had been supplied to him from Madras were genuine.

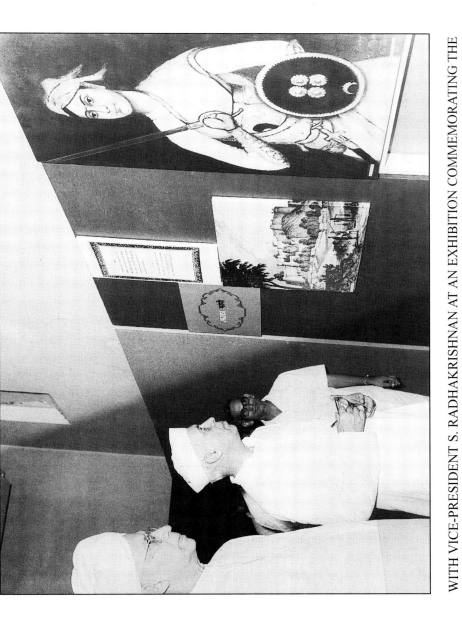

WITH VICE-PRESIDENT S. RADHAKRISHNAN AT AN EXHIBITION COMMEMORATING THE CENTENARY OF 1857 STRUGGLE, NEW DELHI, 14 AUGUST 1957

WITH THE NAGA DELEGATION, NEW DELHI, 25 SEPTEMBER 1957

21. *Russian-Hindi Dictionary*[1]

I welcome the publication in India of this *Russian-Hindi Dictionary* and I congratulate the compiler of it. This has been a pioneer venture on his part and, like all pioneering undertakings, has entailed a great deal of hard work. It has also been, I believe, for him a labour of love.

In the world of today, it is essential for nations to have ever greater understanding of each other. That understanding comes more from a study of each other's languages than from any other source. It is only a knowledge of the language that opens out the real thought and heart of a people. We in India have had considerable knowledge of the English language and this has enabled us to develop many contacts with the literature and thinking of the English speaking world. We have also got, to some extent, knowledge of other foreign languages. But Russian, which is not only a great and rich language in itself but is also today the vehicle of scientific, technological and other avenues of human thought, is not yet adequately known in India. I hope that the knowledge of the Russian language will increase here and this will bring about in India closer understanding of the Russian people and their great achievements. I hope also that Hindi, our national language, will be more widely known in Russia. The process of understanding between two nations and peoples is always a two-way traffic. A Dictionary is a symbol of that two-way traffic. I hope that this Dictionary will help in this process.[2]

1. Foreword to the *Russian-Hindi Dictionary*, edited by W.R. Rishi for Sahitya Akademi, New Delhi, 18 September 1957. JN Collection. Also available in File No. S.A. 63E, Russian-Hindi Dictionary 1957-58, Sahitya Akademi Records.
2. The Foreword was translated into Hindi under the supervision of Harivansh Rai Bachchan and into Russian by the Cultural Attache of the Soviet Embassy in Delhi.

22. University of Jabalpur[1]

The inauguration of the University of Jabalpur is an event of significance not only to Jabalpur but the whole of Madhya Pradesh. The University starts in a big way with seventeen colleges and ten Faculties and eight thousand students on its rolls. I welcome this and send my greetings to the teachers and students of this University.

And yet, while I welcome this, I am a little anxious nowadays whenever new colleges or universities are started. I am convinced more than ever that it is not numbers or quantity that count but quality. The University of Jabalpur will not justify itself by its number of colleges or Faculties or students but by the quality of its work and the kind of training it gives and the type of persons that come out of it.

There is frequent criticism now that the standards in our Universities had gone down, that there is indiscipline and usually a complete absence of the academic atmosphere which should be the special privilege of a University. I hope that the University of Jabalpur will belie these fears and maintain a high standard.

1. Message on the inauguration of the University of Jabalpur, New Delhi, 19 September 1957. JN Collection.

23. Tourist Week[1]

I am not much of a tourist myself, and I do not like to be hustled and pushed about from place to place. My idea of visiting a country is to see the places I like and not necessarily those that have a star mark in the guide book. I like to linger where I feel in the mood to do so and to try to absorb the spirit of the place, to think of the past age which gave birth to that architectural wonder, or

1. Message for the 'Tourist Week' to M.V. Dhonde, Mayor of Bombay, Corporation Hall, Bombay, 19 September 1957. JN Collection.

the modern age which builds great plants and giants of industry. If I go to the mountains, as I love to do when rarely I have the chance, I feel exhilarated with some kind of a communion with nature, more especially, if I am on the glaciers or snowy peaks which pierce the heavens.

All this is not the way of the tourist, and I fear it is seldom my way too. I cannot find the time to live the life of my choice. The world today limits and restricts and conditions our activities, and drives us in many directions without consulting our wishes in the matter. So, we suffer the fate of becoming tourists whether we wish it or not.

Long years ago, I started on my discovery of India and tried to find out what this ancient and yet very young country was. I even wrote a book about it. But all my efforts and my thinking only led me to see some glimpses of this wonderful country. There is always more to see, more aspects of India to be discovered. I fear that I would be a very bad guide for tourists, for I would probably sit down in some place and upset their programme. Anyhow, they will have better guides than I am and, therefore, they will not suffer from my waywardness.

24. To R.K. Sidhwa[1]

New Delhi
September 23, 1957

My dear Sidhwa,

I have your letter in which you ask me about astrology. I am not particularly interested in this subject, but since you ask me a question, I shall endeavour to reply to you.[2]

Science is something which can be studied by pursuing the scientific methods, that is, observation of facts and conclusions drawn from them and checked again by further observations. There should be no pre-conceptions. I do not think this method has been followed or can be followed in regard to the stars.

1. JN Collection.
2. R.K. Sidhwa, former Union Minister of State for Home Affairs, enquired about Nehru's reasons for stating that astrology was not "science". Sidhwa quoted the dictionary meaning of meteorology as the science of weather and of astrology as the science of the stars. He argued that despite the inaccurate forecasts, "meteorology governs weather, the air transport and sea movements in the whole world."

The stars, as is well known, are very very far away, and the light that we see coming from them, may have started on its journey hundreds of years ago. Therefore, any observation that we make, might be relevant to when the light started hundreds of years ago and not now. The stars may not be there now for what we know.

Apart from all this, I am not interested in anyone telling me my future.

Yours sincerely,
Jawaharlal Nehru

25. To D.M. Bose[1]

New Delhi
October 1, 1957

My dear Bose,[2]

Thank you for your letter of the 29th September. I am glad to learn that arrangements are being made for a suitable celebration of the Birthday Centenary of Acharya Jagadish Chandra Bose. I hope that it will be possible for the Government of India through the Education Ministry to help in this celebration. Unfortunately, the time is being propitious for any adequate help, because of the financial stringency and the strict rules we have framed about every kind of new expenditure which is avoidable. I see also that the time is very limited as the Centenary is on November 30th.

It is good of you to ask me to be President of the Committee and I appreciate the honour. But I have tried successfully to avoid any such association with committees. I am overburdened with work and merely my association, for the show of it, is not proper.

Of course, you will have all my good wishes for it.

Yours sincerely,
Jawaharlal Nehru

1. JN Collection.
2. Debendra Mohan Bose (1885-1975); scientist and J.C. Bose's cousin; Professor of Physics, Calcutta University, 1914-38; Director, Bose Institute, 1938-75; Fellow, National Institute of Sciences of India; Member, Indian Science Congress Association and its President in 1953; Member, Asiatic Society of Bengal and its President, 1955-57.

26. *Women of India*[1]

I have not yet read this book as a whole, but I have looked through many of the pages in proof, and I have noted with pleasure and surprise, the comprehensive manner in which this subject has been treated. It is never easy, and seldom successful, for a number of authors to combine to produce a book. In the present case, however, I think that these difficulties have been overcome and something has been produced, which is worthwhile, instructive and a pleasure to read.

This book had to be written. It may be the forerunner of other and fuller treatments of this subject. But, even as it is, it gives us a broad survey which, I think, is of great importance. There are two views, among others, about Indian women. One is the typical old Indian viewpoint of the Indian woman being a symbol of purity, faithfulness, submission and devotion to her husband. The great symbols are Sita and Savitri. The other view is, mostly to be found in some Western countries, that the Indian woman is backward, suppressed and treated almost as a chattel. Both these views are far from the truth, and deal with some imaginary conceptions, little related to life, for life is much more complicated, and these simple definitions do not give us much insight into its working. I suppose that none of us can be truly objective in discussing a subject of this kind. In a country like India, with its enormous variety, it is easy to pick up some one aspect here and there and generalize from it. So, we can indulge in praise of the women of India and find many examples to justify our praise. We can also condemn their position in Indian life and also find examples to justify this. For my part, I am partial to the women of India, and the more I have wandered about this great country, the more I have felt a certain pride in our womenfolk.

Women in India, as these pages will show, have played a very important part in our social life and in our history. They have played this part in every branch of national activity, from high learning to valour in the battlefield. But, it is their unobtrusive work in the household, in the village or in the larger community, that has moulded the nation.

They are essentially faminine, and that is as it should be. But, then, I have always felt that India, for all her manly qualities, is especially noted for the feminine virtues – gentleness, tenderness, a certain patient resignation, and a

---

1. Foreword to *Women of India*, edited by Tara Ali Baig, New Delhi, 2 October 1957. JN Collection. The book was published by the Publications Division, Government of India, in January 1958.

quiet and, sometimes, amazing courage of a somewhat passive kind. I say this realizing that I am generalizing when I should not do so, because there are all kinds of men as well as all kinds of women in this country. But, I suppose it is true that the idea of women in India is chiefly connected with these feminine virtues as well as, perhaps, with some feminine failings. Long ago, our ancient law-giver, Manu, descending from the high level of the law, advised as to what the names of women should be. He said: "Let the names of women be good to pronounce – sweet, simple, pleasant and appropriate; let them terminate in long vowels and resemble words of benediction". Thousands of years have moulded and conditioned our race. Today, we pass rapidly through various phases of transition. That is inevitable and not to be regretted. But, I doubt if all these coming changes, big as they are, will uproot us from our old foundations. Someone said about another country words which might be applied to India: "She lives in her own time, in the rhythm of her own history, which does not quite keep time with the clocks of the twentieth century".

Yet, the twentieth century is upon us with all its destruction of the old, and hopes and fears of the future. We live in India simultaneously in almost all the ages and centuries that have preceded this middle of the twentieth century. We are busy coordinating them and trying to fit them into each other, to keep the old roots and to have fresh branches and fruit and flower in this present day world of ours. The rhythm of our time is an ever-changing one. The clock ticks on often leaving our thinking and our policies behind.

We talk of revolutions, political and economic. And yet, the greatest revolution in a country is the one that affects the status and living conditions of its women. It is in so far as our revolution has affected our women, that it is basic. I believe, it has done so, not perhaps in a dramatic and aggressive way, but rather after the old Indian fashion of combining change with continuity. And yet, there have been many dramatic phases of this change even in our time. It was Gandhiji, that wonderful man and great revolutionary, who brought a dramatic change among our women, when at his bidding they came out in large numbers from the shelter of their homes to take their part in the struggle for India's freedom. Once the old shackles were removed, it was no longer possible to replace them in the same way. Attempts were no doubt made to go back, but they were bound to fail.

Now, the full impact of modern life is being felt by our womenfolk in the cities chiefly and in our schools and colleges. I do no know what the final outcome will be, except that it will be different from the past, though perhaps not so different as to affect the essential characteristics of India's women. This book shows how women are playing their part in a multitude of activities and doing well. There is no doubt in my mind about their capacity, and now that opportunities are coming their way, an increasing number of them will make good.

A Frenchman once wrote that the best way to judge of the position of a nation was to find out the status of its women. I think, this is correct. In spite of many brilliant examples in the past, I think, it would be true to say that the position and status of women in India for many hundreds of years has not been a good one, in law or in public or social life. In recent years, they have made good politically and in other departments of human activity. And now, I am happy that some of the recent legislation that we have passed in our Parliament has rid them of many legal shackles and thus helped to raise their status. They have many hurdles yet to overcome. But, they have been given the opportunity to develop according to their own ability and genius. I have no doubt that many of them will take advantage of these new opportunities and thus demonstrate afresh their inner worth.

To those who live in India and, therefore, come in contact with Indian women, this book will bring much information which will enlighten their minds and give them more correct information of what our women have done and are doing. To those chiefly abroad, this book will be even more useful as presenting a picture not only of the past but of the changing present in India.

27. To B.C. Roy[1]

New Delhi
October 18, 1957

My dear Bidhan,

Keskar, our Minister for Information & Broadcasting, has sent me a copy of the Calcutta Gazette of September 20th, in which a notification of the Government of West Bengal is printed in regard to the exhibition of films.[2] Keskar has already written to you on this subject. I do hope that this order of the Government of West Bengal does not come in the way of the exhibition of films made and licensed by the Central Government. We are concentrating on films for Five

---

1. File no. 43(105)/57-58-PMS. Also available in JN Collection.
2. This was regarding exhibition of documentaries and newsreels in cinema houses in West Bengal.

Year Plan publicity etc. If each Government has its own rules which come in the way of exhibition of the Central documentaries, then it will be difficult to have any large-scale publicity.

A similar question arose some time ago in Madras, but the Madras Government agreed to our request.[3] I hope you will kindly look into this matter.

Yours,
Jawahar

3. For details, see *Selected Works* (second series), Vol. 31, pp. 275-278.

28. All India Sikh Educational Conference[1]

I am sorry I am unable to attend the All India Sikh Educational Conference to be held at Jullundur. I should like, however, to send my good wishes on this occasion.

Education, more than any other subject, should be considered from the broad point of view of cultural and national development. Unfortunately, these broad aspects are often forgotten and people get excited over trivial affairs. If India is to grow and develop, as she must, it will have to be as a whole and not in bits and patches. In this age of tremendous scientific and technological advance, it is only the country which can take the broad view and look at things in long perspective, that can make good. We have to get out of our narrow communal outlook, or else we shall remain stunted.

The Punjab is one of our States with the greatest vitality and capacity for progress. Unfortunately, this vitality is sometimes turned in the wrong direction, as it has been recently, and its vital energy is wasted in futile conflict. I earnestly trust that this is a passing phase and that the people of the Punjab will pull themselves out of this rut and act as men of culture with a broad and national outlook.

1. Message to 40th Session of All India Sikh Educational Conference, New Delhi, 19 October 1957. JN Collection. The Conference was held in Jalandhar from 26 October to 28 October 1957.

29. Association of Medical Women[1]

All my good wishes to the Association of Medical Women in India on the occasion of its celebrating fifty years since it was founded. We want more and more doctors, men as well as women, and we want them particularly to go out to our villages and rural areas where their need is the greatest. I think that every graduate doctor should serve an apprenticeship for a period of at least two years in a rural area before he or she works in an urban area.

The profession of medicine, more than almost any other type of work, requires a spirit of understanding and service. I hope that our doctors will have this spirit of service and will carry their message of healing wherever they go.

1. Message to the Association of Medical Women, New Delhi, 20 October 1957. JN Collection.

30. To B.V. Keskar[1]

New Delhi
October 24, 1957

My dear Balakrishna,

The Japanese Delegation to the Red Cross Conference has brought a movie film dealing with tests of nuclear weapons. They want to show this to the delegates to the Red Cross Conference.[2] They want permission for this.

They are under the impression that they cannot show it unless they get the permission of the Indian Government. I do not myself see why this permission should be necessary for a film to be shown privately to the delegates in the Conference Hall. Anyhow, we should give the permission. Will you please, therefore, write to Red Cross Conference people about it and tell them that

1. File No. 28(31)/56-57-PMS. Also available in JN Collection.
2. International Red Cross Conference was inaugurated by Rajendra Prasad on 28 October 1957 in New Delhi. For Nehru's address on the occasion see *post,* pp. 743-746.

there will be no difficulty about this film being shown to the delegates? You might also write to the Chief of Japanese Delegation whose letter I enclose.

Yours sincerely,
Jawaharlal Nehru

31. Concert for Children's Fund[1]

I am happy to know that Miss Marian Anderson[2] has consented to give a concert in aid of the Prime Minister's Children's Fund. Those who will have the privilege to be present at this concert will themselves listen to this great artiste. In addition to this, the proceeds of this concert will be utilized for a purpose which, I think, is very important and is dear to me. This is the welfare of the children of India. Out of this Fund, various children's organizations are helped, and we are trying to build up Bal Bhavans or places where children can play and learn. The children of India have innumerable needs and, unfortunately, we fulfil very few of them at this stage. But, we realize that it is our first duty to look after this rising generation who will form the India of tomorrow.

I am grateful to Miss Anderson for helping us in this task.

---

1. Note, New Delhi, 25 October 1957. JN Collection.
2. (1902-1993); US contralto concert and opera singer; toured Europe in 1930; was barred from singing at the Constitution Hall, Washington D.C. in 1939 because she was black; became the first black singer to appear at the New York Metropolitan Opera in 1955; was appointed as an alternate delegate to the UN in 1958.

32. Responsibility of Writers[1]

Mr President[2] and comrades,

As I have just said, I have hardly any great claim to be here as a writer although I have been honoured by the Vice-President of the PEN organization of India. Because many years ago, I wrote some books and some people found some virtue in them. I have not become a writer and for many years I have had no occasion, opportunity or time to write in that way. And such creativeness as I have possessed has flown in other directions. But whether I am a writer or not, I am an admirer of writers and, I think, they perform not only a useful but an essential function at any time, more specially now. Now, what a writer is, is more than I can define. And I do not know if it is easy to define what a writer is. In a sense everybody is a writer now. Every person who may occasionally write something in a newspaper or anywhere calls himself a writer and there is no way to say he is not a writer. People sometimes ask and, I believe, I think, you have got in your subjects for discussions, something about the writer's responsibility in a rapidly changing society. As if the tribe of writers is a peculiar caste kind of thing or group, separate from the rest of mankind, which has to discharge its responsibility to mankind from the peculiar or particular point. Well, it may be true to some extent in the distant past where writing or reading, for that matter, was limited to a few persons. It ceased to be there when reading and writing has become so common that almost everybody can indulge in them to some extent. In the olden days, I believe, our ablest and greatest men in any country probably had a library of twenty, thirty, forty books. That is a great library. But they were very solid books which they had and they wrote and they wrote some solid stuff too. And in the manner of writing and the manner of copying and preservation, one used to take enormous labour. Nobody could write rather casually for a casual reader. Well, now things have changed and millions of people read and write and obviously that is a good thing. But also obviously this tends to submerge the good in the bad. There is a danger, obviously. But everybody does something—and just like plenty of bad coins coming in and the good coins be rather hidden by the bad. There is that danger. However, I suppose ultimately what is good, survives. So, what is a writer, it is difficult to

1. Speech at the inauguration of the fourth session of the PEN (International Association of Poets, Playwrights, Editors, Essayists and Novelists) Conference, Baroda, 26 October 1957. AIR tapes, NMML.
2. S. Radhakrishnan.

say now and it will become more and more difficult in India and we hope, every people, everybody in India becomes literate and capable of writing. Now what exactly do you expect? Let us say what the State to do about this matter. The State or Parliament cannot produce good writers. It can produce conditions in which good writing may flourish or may be encouraged. That is the most the State can do. It may produce conditions where vast numbers of people, will get to know how to write, fairly competently and then it is upto them to become good writers or not. The State cannot do it. That is, it can spread good education in so far as it can and out of this mass of people who are supposed to be educated, more and more people will rise higher. Just like in this era of science and technology, the State should aim at producing vast numbers of engineers of all grades and large numbers of scientists, of all grades. That does not mean that the State can produce the top most kinds of scientists. The State cannot.

But out of this vast reservoir of scientists, there is much greater chance of scientific progress being made and sometime even very top ranking men coming out of it. So, what the State can do is, well, prepare this big reservoir of writers etc., or of people out of whom writers can come by giving other facilities and, encouraging them. Then again of course, it is very important—the question of the individual freedom of the writers. As you know, in our country, our Constitution lays down not only for writers but for everybody the importance of the individual freedom. And that applies to every individual and much more to the writer. That is as soon as writing is put in a straight jacket, it may be competent, but it is bound to lose its inner flavour and creativeness is bound to suffer. On the other hand, it may cause a great deal of licence in your writing. By licence, I mean, loose writing and all that and unfortunately, you have to face that, more especially, when you hear this widespread education and everybody wants to do something without the real discipline. Well, it's a race, I suppose, between the indisciplined crowd who might submerge the disciplined writers and the good writers, and bad writers managing to keep their heads up and influencing the others. Again, I don't think the State can do very much. It can, of course, create conditions to encourage good writers, to see that they go ahead. By encouragement I do not mean a kind of State favour or a court favour which encourages those people whom the State approves of, not because of their competence, but because perhaps of their views. That will be unfortunate. Therefore, it is better for academies, literary and other authorities to be independent rather than just purely controlled by the State, although the State should help them. Anyhow, there is no doubt about it, that enormous responsibility rests on everyone of us whether we are writing or not, on those of us who feel, those of us who are sensitive, and writers presumably are supposed to be sensitive, in these changing times and periods today.

So, many of the old standards are gone and are going and so many of us are in search of something old or new. Obviously, we cannot float about all the time, one has to find some roots. Either stick to the old roots or the new roots or a mixture of the two. You have to change your view of life when everything round about you changes. We live today, whatever we like to call it, in industrial age. We cannot go on imagining that we are living as people used to live 2000 years ago in India, in the forests. It is not done. It may be an ideal existence but it is not there. Those are gone. You have to live in the modern age, you have to live in an age on the threshold of the atomic age. We have to live in kind of an age in which interplanetary travel itself begins to be foreseeable, all these are tremendously revolutionary conceptions, far more revolutionary than the ordinary jargon of revolution or the ordinary slogan of revolution which some people may shout. Now, how far do we grasp that and at the same time not allow ourselves to be swept away by the wings of heaven of our labour—keep our roots—keep ourselves firmly planted on the soil if we stand and yet keep our heads high enough to understand these changing things or try to understand them, try to adapt ourselves to them. Unless we can somehow adapt one to the other or try to go on adapting them, our future becomes one of, as I said, floating about and that is not good enough. So, these are the tremendous problems that we face and like all others, whatever our job in life may be, we have to think about them. It becomes particularly so for the writers, both directly to think about them or even more so, perhaps indirectly, because the direct form is seldom appreciated. It is the indirect way of these which usually sinks into the readers' mind.

I ventured just to put a few ideas before you but here we have come to listen to our President and we are fortunate in having as the President of this PEN organization, a person who has the amazing, ability to keep his feet on the ground and head in the clouds and join them together. This is a tremendous thing. Never to lose grip of reality, never to lose grip of the fundamentals of life that has made life great in the past in our country and elsewhere, and at the same time, he is an ancient sage and a very modern philosopher which is really a remarkable achievement. In these troubled times when we go through disturbing times when peoples' minds are tormented, it is our President who can help us more than, perhaps, any of our politicians or others. And so whenever he speaks, he speaks not only to the audiences' requirements but to vast audience all over the country and sometimes beyond the country too; because his words are words of national importance and also of international importance because they carry with them something, that spirit of universality which affects everybody wherever he maybe. Therefore, whether he goes to China or the United States of America, he has his words counted for the people there, even though they might be looking in different directions. His words and wisdom brings them nearer to each other and joins them. So, we are fortunate enough in having him here to deliver this Presidential address and try to bring more light to our puzzled minds. Thank you.

33. Children's Museum[1]

Children and adults,
Guptaji[2] spoke before me. There were some speeches before that. But I could not hear properly because all of you were making a great deal of noise which is not right. Now you must remain quiet. Many things have been said about the Museum. But the one thing that has stuck in my mind is that children are given hot sweet milk in the evenings. I do not know how many children get it. I want that not only the children of Lucknow but of the whole of India should get hot sweet milk everyday so that they can become strong and healthy.

Well, I have been invited to inaugurate this Museum. I do not know what there is inside because I have not seen them. But usually museums grow with time. People donate things. But a better way of enlarging the museum is to make things yourselves. Nothing has been said about that so far. Normally children's museums display mostly things made by children. It encourages children to be creative. So, it is a good thing to start even if the Museum is not very large to begin with. You can build up the collection gradually.

I am happy to be here. There is a park here and different kinds of toys. Now a Museum has come up and I hear there is a hospital too. But why should you fall ill? You must be healthy. Anyhow, it is a good thing for you to have so many facilities. But I wonder how many children are able to avail of them in such a vast city like Lucknow. Actually, there ought to be small Bal Bhavans in practically every area and every village. Children can be taken to visit the big museum or Bal Bhavan on special occasions. This is a good Museum. But there must be more of them.

---

1. Speech at the inauguration of the Children's Health and Educational Museum in the Motilal Nehru Park, Lucknow, 27 October 1957. AIR tapes, NMML.
2. C.B. Gupta, former Minister for Health and Planning, UP.

I have not come here to make speeches. I am happy to have had the opportunity of meeting all of you. You must be in schools. You must study well and learn to play as well. Book learning alone is not a good thing. Some parents do not understand this. You must study as well as play a lot. In fact, you should learn while you play. My love and blessings to you.

34. Students should Keep an Open Mind[1]

You should shun fanaticism, narrow-mindedness and rigidity of thought and keep your minds open and free to receive fresh ideas. The shackles of caste, community or region that fetter the minds are great impediments to the progress of the country. Do not hold rigid opinions and keep an open mind. Time will come for you to hold opinions, or to change them, but even then you should avoid becoming fanatics.

The intrusion of party politics in University affairs can bring no benefit. Political parties have their good and bad points, but when the students adopt them fanatically without any responsibility except that of tendering advice to this man or that, it becomes a foolish thing. It often happens that University unions or students' unions pass pompous resolutions and not only advise the Government on national problems but also on international problems. If you are such capable men, why you continue to be in the Universities? You can very well go and run the administration of the world.

A poster was handed to me containing some questions about the Hindi agitation in Punjab. The first question asked in the poster was why was Gurmukhi being imposed on the Hindus there? My answer to that question is that why do you ask such silly questions which have no bearing on the reality of the situation which you do not understand. The way questions have been put show nothing but stupidity, foolishness, narrow-mindedness, ignorance and parochialism. I do not remember more epithets to condemn such attitude of mind.

You should keep your minds open to receive and assimilate new thoughts and ideas. Their influx bring about freshness in brain and help its growth. Exactly the same principle works in developing the fertility of the brain as in the

1. Speech while inaugurating the Lucknow University Students' Union, Lucknow, 28 October 1957. From *National Herald* and *The Leader*, 29 October 1957.

development of physique. It is dangerous to shut the doors of the brain feeling that whatever one has learnt is the final goal of achievement.

You should equip yourselves to share the burden of responsibilities to run the future administration of India. Nothing could be achieved through rowdyism and indiscipline. The days of slogan mongering are over. You should work hard keeping before you high ideals.

I congratulate you on the occasion to which you students seem to attach great importance as is obvious from the messages which you had secured from abroad. I have not only come myself in response to your call but also brought along with me Dr Radhakrishnan, who has great and varied experience of the Universities and the students and who, remaining above party politics, is like a seer eminently suited to give his blessings to you.

35. To Govind Ballabh Pant[1]

New Delhi
October 31, 1957

My dear Pantji,

Maulana Sahib spoke to me today about Bahadur Shah's tomb in Rangoon. He told me that Bahadur Shah expressed a wish in his last will, that his remains should be buried in Delhi in Humayun's *Maqbara* where his ancestors were buried. Maulana suggested that it would be desirable to bring these remains to India for this purpose. At present, they are in a very simple and out of the way tomb in Rangoon, which I visited some years ago.

I see no particular objection to this, and I suppose the Burma Government will not object. I referred this matter to some of our colleagues in the Cabinet today, and they did not object either. I should like your reactions to this proposal. After that, we can enquire further into it.

Yours affectionately,
Jawaharlal Nehru

1. JN Collection.

AT A MASS SPINNING HELD ON THE OCCASION OF GANDHI JAYANTI CELEBRATIONS, NEW DELHI, 2 OCTOBER 1957

ADDRESSING THE CONFERENCE OF THE STATES' MINISTERS OF INFORMATION, NEW DELHI, 30 AUGUST 1957

IV. LANGUAGE ISSUE

1. To Algurai Shastri[1]

New Delhi
16 September 1957

My dear Algurai,

I am sending you a letter received from 88 Members of Parliament belonging to the Congress Party. This is on the language question.

Please inform them that I have received it and read it. I shall certainly give opportunities in the Party for a discussion on this issue. We are not going to decide anything without the fullest discussion and I am sure that we shall endeavour to have decisions by agreement rather than by just a majority of votes.

As a Parliament Committee has been appointed to consider this matter,[2] perhaps the discussion might take place at a somewhat later stage.

Yours sincerely,
Jawaharlal Nehru

---

1. File No. 52 (12)/57-63-PMS. Also available in JN Collection.
2. A 30-member Joint Parliamentary Committee was constituted to consider the Report of the Official Language Commission which was submitted to the President on 6 August 1956 and presented in both Houses of Parliament on 12 August 1957.

2. Urdu and Hindi—Regional Languages of Delhi[1]

I received a deputation on behalf of the Anjuman-i-Tarraqqi-i-Urdu of Delhi this afternoon. It was headed by Shri Gopi Nath Aman.[2]

2. They came to me to urge that Urdu, in addition to Hindi, should be declared the regional language of the Delhi State.

3. They told me that in 1952 Delhi Assembly had decided to have three languages for the Assembly in accordance with Article 345 of the Constitution. These languages were Hindi, Urdu and English.

4. In 1955, the Delhi Assembly formed a Language Committee under the Chairmanship of Dr Yudhvir Singh[3] who was also the Chairman of the Hindi Sahitya Sammelan of Delhi. Among other members of this Committee were Shri Gopi Nath Aman and Prof. Ram Singh of the Hindu Mahasabha. This Committee recommended unanimously that Hindi and Urdu should be the regional languages of Delhi State. Further that Hindi should progressively take the place of English. These recommendations made under Article 347 were sent to the Centre by the then Chief Minister of Delhi, Shri Gurmukh Nihal Singh who added a note to the effect that if Urdu was made a regional language, so also should Punjabi be made one.

5. The request, therefore, is now that Urdu and Hindi should both be made the regional languages of Delhi State. I understand that a deputation also went to the Home Minister on this subject and was told that this question would be considered together with similar questions.

6. This note may thus be rather unnecessary. Nevertheless, I am sending it because, I think, it is of the utmost importance, both from the Delhi point of view as well as from the larger point of view of India, that Urdu should be one of the regional languages of Delhi State. There can be no doubt that at present Urdu is the best known and the most spoken of languages in Delhi State. Most of the leading newspapers here (apart from English ones) are in Urdu. Delhi has been the home of Urdu where Urdu had its origin, took shape and grew. It is the

---

1. Note to Home Ministry, 24 September 1957. File No. 40(132)/57-60-PMS. Also available in JN Collection.
2. (1899-1983); Urdu writer and journalist; former Minister in the erstwhile Delhi State; author of *Karnano Manzil*, *Naya Chaman*, *Urdu aur Uska Sahitya*, and biographies of Subhash Bose, Jawaharlal Nehru and Sardar Patel.
3. A Minister in the Delhi Government, 1955-56.

home of Amir Khusrau, Ghalib and Khan-i-Khana[4] and so many eminent poets and writers in Urdu. It would indeed be a tragedy if Urdu was not made one of the regional languages in Delhi.

7. A special reason for my writing this note is that at present Urdu is not, I think, being given a proper place in Delhi. There are seldom arrangements for teaching Urdu in the schools and if adequate arrangements are not made, Urdu naturally suffers and the people who wish their children to learn Urdu are put in a difficulty. In this matter, Delhi compares very unfavourably with Bombay. In Bombay, it is well known that the regional languages are Marathi and Gujarati. Nevertheless, arrangements have been made for teaching Urdu in the schools in the city and these arrangements are adequate. It is surprising that Delhi, the home of Urdu, should lag behind Bombay city in this respect.

8. There is another development in Delhi which is painful, and can almost be described as vandalism. In new signboards that are put up in streets, etc., not only is the name not written in Urdu, but sometimes where it was in Urdu this is removed. As a matter of fact, even now most people, like *tongawalas*, taxi drivers, etc., know Urdu much more than any other language and they are rather lost when the signboards are not in Urdu. I do not know who is responsible for this unhappy innovation. I doubt if any old resident of Delhi could have approved of this.

9. Then again new boards are put up with instructions such as the "No Entry" sign. "No Entry" is now represented in some places by *Pravesh Nishedh*. I consider this a linguistic horror in Delhi. I should like some test to be made of any odd 100 persons picked in the streets. They might be asked if they understand this.

10. I really am alarmed at this tendency of gradually ruining our rich language and making it completely artificial and largely not understood by the common folk. Certainly, I do not understand it. Surely some steps should be taken to prevent the spread of this horror.

4. Abdur Rahim Khan-i-Khana (1556-1627); son of Bairam Khan; a literary figure and a contemporary of Akbar and Jahangir; led many military campaigns; translated Babur's memoirs into Persian.

3. To Govind Ballabh Pant[1]

New Delhi
October 2, 1957

My dear Pantji,

...In regard to the Official Language Report[2] it appears that the Communists are very worried. Indeed, they are having a special meeting of the Politburo in Delhi just to consider this. Namboodiripad had come for that purpose.

I told Ajoy Ghosh that I was not prepared to express any definite opinion at this stage about this matter. I proposed to consider the Report fairly carefully soon and to discuss it with my colleagues. But I really did not see any necessity of passion to be raised on this issue. In a matter of this kind, it would be improper to impose any decision by a majority of Hindi-speaking votes on the non-Hindi areas. We could only win them over. We should make it clear to them that there is no desire to impose. Within the limits of that assertion, we could encourage Hindi to spread. There could be an intervening period, when Hindi was being used for official purposes at the Centre, but English was also being used. If any State Government wished to correspond with us in Hindi, naturally, we would accept it then. But, if any State Government preferred English, we should not force it to correspond in Hindi.

As for the Central Services, I thought that the resolution passed by the Working Committee some two or three years back was a good one. That stated that we should not do anything to put a burden on the non-Hindi-Speaking areas in this

---

1. File No. 52 (12)/57-63-PMS. Also available in JN Collection. Extracts. For the first two paragraphs of this letter see *ante*, p. 122.
2. The measures suggested by the Commission envisaged that (i) English would be replaced by Hindi after 1965 depending on the efforts made in this direction; (ii)English would continue as the subsidiary official language; (iii) Devanagari script should be used for Hindi and other Indian languages; and (iv) a national academy should be established for development of Hindi and other regional languages. The Report attached considerable importance to the development of Hindi by the Central Government. However, in a dissenting note, two members of the Commission, Suniti Kumar Chatterji and P. Subbaroyan said that the target date of 1965 for changeover from English to Hindi would not be adequate. Chatterji thought that this attitude was far from democratic as it would mean imposing Hindi on the non-Hindi speakers. He detected an incipient "Hindi Imperialism." Subbarayan expressed concerns of the Southern States and called Hindi enthusiasm as "militant chauvinism" which was creating "misgivings and opposition among the speakers of other languages."

respect. People could be taken in even if they did not pass in Hindi. But, they should learn Hindi subsequently.[3]

This was the broad burden of my argument. I am just passing this on to you for your information....

Yours affectionately,
Jawaharlal Nehru

3. This resolution was adopted on 5 April 1954 at the CWC meeting in New Delhi.

V. TRIBAL AFFAIRS

(i) The Nagas

1. To Bisnuram Medhi[1]

New Delhi
August 1, 1957

My dear Medhi,[2]

I have your telegram. I am sorry that you are having so much trouble to face. I would very gladly help you to the best of my ability.

In so far as the refinery question is concerned,[3] you know that we have gone very far to meet your wishes. We have reopened the whole question and we shall consider it with every sympathy for Assam. Indeed, as I have told you, I want Assam to be the principal beneficiary from this oil; but, obviously, we cannot do something which is entirely unreasonable. We cannot say now that we are going to have the refinery in Assam.

1. JN Collection.
2. Chief Minister of Assam.
3. Since August 1956 there was an agitation in Assam in protest against the reported decision of the Central Government to set up an oil refinery outside Assam. Also see *post*, pp. 347-350 and 353-354.

It seems to me that your opposition is exploiting the situation and is more concerned with the political aspect of it than the economic. Unfortunately, the situation has been created to their advantage. There is no way to meet this but calmly and firmly going on explaining the position to the people and making them realize that any other course would be very injurious to the future of Assam's development. This may take time, but there is no other way.

I realize that *The Statesman* has not been at all helpful and in fact some of its comments have done harm.[4] We have drawn the attention of *The Statesman* people to this matter.

As for the statement made in *The Statesman* about the withdrawal of our forces from the Naga areas, this is wrong and mischievous. We are trying to correct it.

The Naga problem has now got to be solved. As I told you, it can only be solved in the manner we discussed. There should be no weakening on this issue; otherwise we shall get entangled in it to our grave disadvantage. It may be that some people in Assam will not like this, but neither our basic policy nor our resources can permit us to go on suppressing a people.

Yours sincerely,
Jawaharlal Nehru

4. On 26 July 1957, *The Statesman* reported that the military operations against the Nagas in Assam, which have been conducted on an extensive scale for over a year, would be ended in the next few weeks to prepare the ground for a political understanding. Two main reasons had led to this decision. Firstly, the military operations were never intended to be the substitute for a political settlement. Secondly, the Government felt that it was imprudent to allow an armed force of that size in a small area of Assam. The Government was willing to go far enough to give the Nagas a large measure of autonomy by constituting the areas inhabited by them into a union territory.

2. Towards a Peaceful Settlement[1]

Please write to Shri Triloki Nath Purwar[2] in Hindi, and tell him that I have seen his letter.[3] The policy that is being pursued and will be pursued in regard to the Nagas is laid down by the Government of India, and we are taking direct interest in this matter. Naturally, we want others concerned and more especially the Assam Government also to cooperate in this policy. But the direction of the affairs is in the hands of the Central Government and we shall pursue that policy which, we hope, will result in a peaceful settlement of these problems to the satisfaction of all concerned. We have made our policy quite clear, and the Governor, as the Central Government's representative, is doing his best to carry out that policy. If the Naga leaders are at all cooperative, as we hope they will be, I am sure that there will be a peaceful settlement.

1. Note to M.O. Mathai, Private Secretary, New Delhi, 12 August 1957. JN Collection.
2. A social worker of Allahabad who enjoyed the confidence of the underground Naga leaders.
3. Letter not available.

3. Cable to Saiyid Fazl Ali[1]

Your telegram G/4 August 23.[2] I have had further report separately about yesterday's meeting and resolutions passed.

1. New Delhi, 24 August 1957. JN Collection.
2. Fazl Ali, Governor of Assam, informed that a Naga conference with delegates representing all tribes had commenced at Kohima on 22 August 1957. At the same time, the hostile propaganda against delegates intensified though it was reported that hostile high command had ordered no interference with delegates. According to Fazl Ali, the resolutions drafted at the conference stressed the necessity for bringing hostiles into final settlement, appealed for cessation of violence and asked for the formation of Naga Hills, Tuensang and the reserve forest into a separate administrative unit under the Central Government. Fazl Ali enquired whether he should ask the Naga delegates, who were coming to see him, to meet Nehru in Delhi.

2. First point to be considered is how far this Naga conference[3] can be said to wield authority over various Naga tribes. Can they control hostile elements in any large measure? Their appeal to us amounts to our taking some unilateral action without any guarantee that violence and troubles will end. Hostile elements may well say that they have already forced our hands and if they continue their struggle they would push us still further back.

3. On the other hand if conference really representative hostile elements can be greatly reduced and isolated and thus made ineffective.

4. As you know, so far as we are concerned, we are prepared to consider Central administration for Naga Hills and Tuensang, but we cannot possibly consider transfer of reserve forests as suggested. I hope that we shall get Assam Government to agree, however reluctantly, to transfer to Central administration of Naga Hills. Any suggestion about forests being added would raise a furore.

5. You will be seeing the delegates. You may tell them that should they desire to see me, their representatives can come to Delhi. But it might be pointed out to them that they should convince us of their ability to put an end to the activities of hostile elements.

3. The Naga People's conference, held at Kohima from 22 to 26 August 1957 at the initiative of liberal leaders and with the approval of Governor Fazl Ali, was attended by more than seventeen hundred delegates representing 15 Naga tribes and over 2000 visitors. Proceedings were started with the unanimous election of Dr Imkongliba Ao, as Chairman and John Bosco Jasokie as Secretary of the Conference. A Select Committee of fifty representatives were elected to finalize the resolutions to be put up before the General Conference.

4. To Saiyid Fazl Ali[1]

New Delhi
August 25, 1957

My dear Fazl Ali,

I received your letter of 22nd August two or three days ago. Since then I have had your message about the Naga meeting. I have also had some details of it from our Intelligence. I sent you a telegram in reply to your message.

I need not repeat what I said in the telegram. I suppose we shall have some difficulty with the Assam Government about the proposals made. As I said in my telegram, the question of transferring any forest areas from Assam proper is something which we cannot agree to. Whatever possibility there is of the Assam Government agreeing to the proposal for Central administration will be knocked on the head if this is included.

The one thing we should be clear about is the influence of this meeting over the Nagas, and the hostiles especially. If the hostiles in any numbers continue their hostility in spite of our even accepting, broadly speaking, the demands of the Naga conference, then an odd situation arises. It will not matter much if a very small number creates trouble, but if this small band has still marked influence they could make a difference.

When you meet the Naga representatives you should make this point clear to them. We want peace and we want a friendly settlement. But how can there be a settlement if a considerable number of Nagas continue to give trouble and persist in violent activities?

As for the Assam Government, you will remember that even their Cabinet more or less agreed to the Central Government coming into the picture and this area coming, at least for the time being, under Central administration. They preferred a reversion to the pre-Independence state, that is, treating the Naga Hills as an excluded area. Basically, however, they agreed to this proposition. Even when Medhi talked to me, he had to agree more or less to this, although he was reluctant. He cannot go back on this. I hope that you will tackle Medhi and the other Ministers in a friendly way and explain the situation to them. They will not profit at all by taking up a non-cooperative attitude. I need not point out our difficulties in regard to military operations which you and Medhi know well. But, quite apart from this, we have to follow certain principles. We cannot deal

---

1. JN Collection. A copy of this letter was sent to Subimal Dutt, the Foreign Secretary.

with a part of our territory as a colonial area to be conquered and kept down. This will have a disruptive effect all the time all over Assam. Unfortunately, a feeling has been created amongst some of these tribal areas, and more especially the Naga areas, against the Assam Government. That has to be removed. The only way to do so is to have some friendly arrangement and then gradually work in an unobtrusive way, to bring about closer contacts and integration with Assam.

In Sashimeren Aier's[2] note that you have sent, details are given about the future administrative organization. I suppose that when the main subjects are settled, the details may not be very difficult to work out. These details should not be discussed at this stage. Indeed, there can be no real reorganization till the basic political set-up is decided upon and the violent conflict is ended.

The change in the political set-up will require an amendment of the Constitution. It is obvious this amendment cannot take place suddenly; at the earliest we could take it up in the November session of Parliament, provided a settlement has been arrived at before. Of course, given the settlement, many small things can be done to give effect to it.

I would certainly like some sort of relationship with Assam State to continue such as representation in the Assembly though it is not quite clear to me how this is to be brought about.

Yours sincerely,
Jawaharlal Nehru

2. 1. Sashimeren Aier was Assistant Commissioner, Scheduled Castes and Scheduled Tribes for Assam, Manipur and Tripura.

5. Cable to Saiyid Fazl Ali [1]

Your telegram G/5 August 28th.[2] Naga Delegation can come to Delhi. But I would prefer meeting them not earlier than 4th and preferably on 5th September, as I am fully occupied on previous dates.

2. Before we meet them here, we should meet Assam Chief Minister or other representative Minister or, alternatively, have their broad agreement. I am, therefore, telegraphing to Chief Minister, copy to you.

3. I should like your appraisal of position of hostile elements and how far any agreement will stop activity of hostiles and produce peaceful conditions over this area.

4. Constitutional amendment can earliest take place in November session of Parliament. It might perhaps be possible to take some other action earlier under Constitution on plea of emergency.

5. Government will bear journey expenses of Naga Delegation and will look after them in Delhi.

1. New Delhi, 28 August 1957. JN Collection.
2. Fazl Ali informed that he was going to suggest to the Naga delegation to proceed to Delhi and present their proposals to Nehru. In that case the Government of India should bear journey expenses of the delegates both ways and they should be well looked after in Delhi. Announcement about the separate Administrative Unit should be made on about 15 September. Meanwhile, delegates should be told that it would take a little time to set up a separate Administrative Unit as it required a Constitutional amendment. But if the delegation returned empty handed, repercussions would be extremely serious, Fazl Ali added.

6. Cable to Bisnuram Medhi[1]

You must have followed closely proceedings of Naga Convention held at Kohima. Understand their delegation meeting Governor tomorrow and will probably come to Delhi on September 4th. I would naturally like to meet you or some other representative Minister of your Government before I meet the Naga delegation here. I would also like to meet Kapur[2] who could give us first hand information about Kohima proceedings.

2. Situation is a delicate one and has to be handled with great care, so as to achieve adequate results now and in the future. Failure now might have serious consequences. I am sure you have all these aspects in view.[3]

---

1. New Delhi, 28 August 1957. JN Collection. Extracts.
2. Balbir Chand Kapur (b. 1915); joined IAS, Assam Cadre, 1948; Commissioner, Naga Hills Division, 1956-58; Commissioner, Plains Division, 1958; Officer on Special Duty, State Electricity Board, Assam, 1958, and its Chairman, 1958-59; Advisor, Hill Areas (United Khasi, Jaintia and Garo Hills), Assam, 1969-70; Vice-Chairman, Bharat Heavy Electricals, Bhopal, 1970, and its Deputy Chairman, 1970-72; Additional Secretary, Department of Agriculture, 1972.
3. Medhi replied on 2 September that in the preamble of the resolution adopted by the Naga Convention, Government was condemned for measures taken to quell the rising without any criticism of underground hostile activities. Inviting Naga delegation in face of such a preamble meant that the Government accepted the criticism and the charges levelled. Medhi further wrote that if the Government accepted the Naga demand for a separate administrative unit, it implied reopening of the decisions based on the recommendations of the States Reorganization Commission. Medhi felt that the entire region to the north-east of East Pakistan should form a homogeneous administrative unit to serve as a strong bulwark of defence. The interim arrangement in pursuance of the resolution was also likely to open a floodgate for agitation demanding a separate Hill State as well as for the constitution of Purbanchal State, Medhi added.

7. To Saiyid Fazl Ali[1]

New Delhi
3 September 1957

My dear Fazl Ali,

...I rather wish that the Naga leaders come here before the 25th. However, that does not matter very much. Yesterday in Parliament, I made a brief reference in answer to a query to the visit of their delegation here. I expressed the hope that our talks would lead to satisfactory results.

This morning, I received a telegram from Arthur Lall, our Permanent Representative in the United Nations. He informed me that *The New York Times* had published a letter from Phizo dated Kohima, August 7. This letter gave a long list of so-called atrocities committed by the Indian Army in the Naga Hills. It laid stress on the fact that many of the Nagas were Methodist Christians. I have not seen the actual letter yet, but I shall no doubt see it soon.[2] Arthur Lall was rather upset at the publication of this letter, more especially just at this stage when the UN General Assembly is going to meet. This will be utilized by all those countries that are hostile to us. We shall try to issue some kind of a general contradiction through our Embassy in Washington.[3]

Someone told me that Kochhar,[4] in the course of a press interview some time ago,[5] had said something to the effect that our policy in keeping the Nagas grouped together in special places was on the lines of what the British had done to the Mau Mau or the French were doing in Algeria. I do not know if Kochhar

---

1. JN Collection. Extracts.
2. In this letter written to *The New York Times*, which was published on 2 September 1957, A.Z. Phizo, also wrote, "Between India and Nagaland there is no complicated issue. The historical problem of 'master servant' question does not arise. And we do not have common tradition or even culture. Neither is there immigrant minority issue present for free India to contend with—a problem which so often stand in the way of a happy solution in a political controversy. Like any other self-respecting nation we love our democratic freedom and national independence. We would rather die in the defence of national honour as a free people than be slaves of a foreign nation. This is why we are fighting without entertaining the thought of defeat."
3. Arthur S. Lall also wrote that the Naga leaders should be requested to issue a statement to all UN Missions against Phizo's letter and that statement might be handed over to all Foreign Offices by our representatives.
4. Raj Kumar Kochhar was General Officer Commanding, Assam.
5. On 31 July.

said anything of this kind. If so, it was a very foolish thing to say. It was factually incorrect because what was done to the Mau Mau was infinitely worse. But, apart from the facts, to make any such statement was exceedingly unwise.

I shall expect the Naga Delegation here on the 25th September.

Yours sincerely,
Jawaharlal Nehru

8. To Saiyid Fazl Ali[1]

New Delhi
September 3, 1957

My dear Fazl Ali,

I have already sent you one letter today. Since then I have had a talk with Pantji. We feel that it would be desirable for you to come here before we see the Naga delegation. It is not particularly necessary for you to be here when the delegation meets us, though there is no objection to it. But, I think, it is necessary for us to discuss with you the new situation that has arisen in all its aspects. There is not very much to discuss so far as the major approach is concerned. Broadly speaking, we agree with what you have said and advised us.

But, having accepted this major approach, what follows has to be worked out too with some precision. Thus, accepting the Naga contention that the Naga Hills District should be directly under the Centre, what follows? We may presume also that we accept the Naga District and the Tuensang Division to be lumped together. What kind of internal administration will there be? Will it be uniform for both these areas which are joined together?

You have built up some kind of administration in the Tuensang Division. Will that continue or will that be changed to fit in with something that the Naga Hills District will have? In the Naga Hills what kind of autonomy can we have? All these and many other questions arise and I think that we should be fairly clear in our minds about them, even when we talk to the Naga deputation.

Then there is the separate but allied question of the other Hill States. What steps should we take in regard to them? It is obvious that we cannot leave them where they are. This means amending the Sixth Schedule in so far as those

1. JN Collection.

214

States are concerned, apart from the amendments necessary for the Naga Hills. You have mentioned somewhere that a Commission might be appointed for these Autonomous Hill Districts. I confess that I react adversely to proposals for the appointment of Commissions. Apart from the time involved, the whole procedure becomes too involved and drawn too much attention. The Commission would no doubt visit all the Hill Districts and take evidence and there will be excitement and large numbers of papers presented and so on and so forth.

Would it not be better for you, first of all, to draw up some scheme for the amendment of the Sixth Schedule (apart from the Naga Hills question). This matter, of course, intimately concerns the Assam Government. You could discuss it with them and then we can consider it.

The whole point is that we have arrived at a stage when we must give some concentrated attention to the details. As a matter of fact, you have been thinking about these matters for months past and you have often written to me about them. There can be no better person than you to suggest what should be done. I do not want you to do this in any formal or official capacity, which might perhaps prove embarrassing. But I would like you to help us.

The amendment of the Constitution in so far as the Naga Hills are concerned will have to be considered in the November-December Session of Parliament. Will it be possible to bring in amendments affecting the other Hill Districts also then? Perhaps that might be difficult because the second subject may require closer consideration. It would be better, of course, to take the whole thing together.

I would request you therefore to give thought to both these questions that I have suggested above, namely, (1) the content of Naga autonomy and how far that would apply to the whole of Tuensang Division, and (2) the changes to be made for the other Hill States which will continue to be associated with Assam.

So far as the Naga Hills District is concerned, even after it is put under Central Administration, the possibility of its representation in the Assam Legislature has to be considered. This would not be logical, but if both parties agree, it would be desirable as a link.

I would, therefore, like you to come here. I have already informed you that I shall be away from Delhi from the 20th September till the afternoon of the 23rd. It would, therefore, be desirable for you to come here before the 20th September so that we could have our talks before we leave for Mysore.

I am writing to Medhi suggesting that in addition to his coming here on the 9th and 10th September, I should like him to be here, if that is convenient to him, when we talk to the Naga delegation on the 25th September.

Yours sincerely,
Jawaharlal Nehru

9. Need for a Political Settlement with the Nagas[1]

All of us have fully realized the importance of political settlement with the Nagas. Some progress to that end has been made on the Naga side. The Convention held recently at Kohima was undoubtedly a representative of the general body of the Nagas, though it cannot be said to represent all the hostile elements. Our information is, however, that some even of the hard core of the hostiles was secretly cooperative of the convention people. Anyhow, it may be said that if there is an agreement between us and the representatives of this convention, it will be very difficult for the group of hostiles to carry on.

2. After the convention, Naga representatives from the Convention went to see the Governor. Their meeting was quite satisfactory and they have gone back on the whole pleased. They will be coming to see me here in Delhi on the 25th September.

3. On the 9th or 10th September, the Chief Minister and some other Ministers of Assam are coming here to discuss this matter.

4, The present discussions will not deal with details of autonomy but mainly with this area being joined on to the Tuensang Frontier Division of the NEFA and both being under the Centre. Of course, a large measure of autonomy is presumed. So far as we are concerned, we are prepared to go pretty far in that direction.

5. Any present agreement will be in regard to these basic matters and will be followed by more detailed talks later. Some kind of provisional arrangement has to be made. The Constitution will have to be changed. At present there can be no doubt that the Governor of Assam would be the proper person in charge. He is trusted by the Nagas. He is in charge of NEFA with which the Assam Government has nothing to do. What the future set-up might be can be considered later.

6. I am surprised to read of the press conference given by Major-General Kochhar on July 31st. Much that he is reported to have said is rather foolish. I think he should be told that he should not indulge in press conferences.

---

1. Note to Defence Minister, New Delhi, 3 September 1957. JN Collection.

10. Reply to A.Z. Phizo's Letter[1]

This letter does appear to me rather too long.[2] Otherwise I have no particular objection to any part of it. I suppose it will go by post. There is no point in sending it by telegram to save two or three days. It should go by fast airmail to our Embassy in Washington. Copy could be sent to Indiadel, New York. But the letter should be issued from Washington.

It is stated in the letter that the tribal people are safeguarded by our Constitution in every possible way. I think, it should be further stated that they have the full rights of citizenship and voting for election of Members of Parliament as well as to the State Assembly. It is in addition to the normal citizenship right that certain safeguards are provided to prevent alienation of their land or any interference by others. There is also a considerable measure of local autonomy.

Where it is stated that the revolt is restricted to the Naga Hills District, I think you should say that it is restricted to a portion of the Naga Hills District.

I am not quite sure if Phizo's wife and children have sought our protection. I believe, they were in some kind of detention, but I am not sure.

Where you state that the letter is from A.Z. Phizo, I think you might say that it purports to come from A.Z. Phizo.

When you refer to the different languages of the Naga tribes, you might add that the common lingua franca for the North Eastern Tribes is Assamese, because they do not understand each other's dialects.

Phizo's mother is reported to have made a statement the other day. Perhaps some brief quotation from it might be helpful.

Where you deal with the recent Naga Convention and refer to the 1765 delegates, you might say that they were elected delegates from every tribe and village. You might perhaps further say that the Naga Convention has requested the Prime Minister to receive a deputation from them and the Prime Minister has agreed to meet them.

Paragraph 12 does not seem to me to be very necessary, at any rate, in the form it is given.

Defence Minister might see this draft and my comments.

---

1. Note to Defence Minister and Foreign Secretary, New Delhi, 6 September 1957. JN Collection.
2. These comments are on the Government of India's reply to Phizo's letter dated 7 August which appeared in *The New York Times* on 2 September. See *ante*, p. 213.

11. To Saiyid Fazl Ali[1]

New Delhi
16 September 1957

My dear Fazl Ali,

Thank you for your letters of September 12 and 14. The latter letter deals with the case of T. Rongsenchiba Ao. I had not heard of this previously. I am referring this matter to the Defence Ministry.

I am sorry that you have not been feeling well and had to go to hospital for a while. I do not want you to inconvenience yourself by coming all the way to Delhi. It is only if you feel well enough to do so that you should come here.

My dates are as I have informed you already, that is, I shall return to Delhi on the afternoon of the 23rd September. I shall leave Delhi again on the 27th morning. I shall again return to Delhi on the 28th midday. I shall then remain here till I go to Japan on October 3.

I have had talks with Medhi. He is not at all happy about recent events but he realizes that there is only one course open to us at present. I pointed out to him that it would be unbecoming for me to argue with the Naga Delegation that is coming here. They come bringing me a certain proposal which briefly is that the Naga Hills and the Tuensang Division should be formed into one unit and placed under the Centre. Further, of course, that this should be within the Indian Union. If we made any reservations, their answer will necessarily be that they are not empowered to deal with any changes. Anyhow, we do not want any changes. Therefore, my answer will have to be a simple and straightforward 'yes' to this particular demand of theirs.

In saying this 'yes', I shall lay stress on two factors. One is that throughout these years we had made it clear that we were prepared to discuss matters with the Nagas, and to amend the Sixth Schedule. But we would not have discussions unless the campaign for independence was given up. Now that this has been done clearly, I am happy to meet them and discuss matters with them. Secondly, I shall naturally lay stress on peace and order being established in that region.

I do not know if the delegation will be prepared to discuss any other matters with me, such as local autonomy, etc. I take it that they would like these matters to be discussed later. I do not mind. Probably it will be better, however, to discuss it later. Otherwise what we agree to with these people might be criticized by certain hostile elements.

---

1. JN Collection.

I agree with you that the type of administration we build up in these areas should be entirely free from red tape and should be largely based on local autonomy.

I do not quite understand what you mean by saying that the interim government might last a few years. I was under the impression that this should be a question of months. I should not like matters to remain hanging over for years.

The question that we shall have to decide immediately is the exact form of amendment to the Constitution in order to create this new unit of Naga Hills and Tuensang Division under the Centre. The amendment can be simple enough. Could it be done within the Sixth Schedule itself? It may not be necessary to have any constitutional provisions about autonomy, at any rate, at this stage. The President may be authorized to take such steps in this regard as he may think proper.

If you could send me some draft amendments, we could have them examined in our Law Ministry. As a matter of fact, this question will really arise afterwards. There is no immediate hurry, though one should like to be clear about it. Medhi has said that he will come here on 24th or thereabouts.

Yours sincerely,
Jawaharlal Nehru

12. No Reprisals on the Nagas[1]

I am glad that the house of Dr Imkongliba[2] has not been destroyed. That is some comfort.

2. I do not understand, as you do not, the reference to "the policy of the Civil Administration". In a matter of this kind, the Army has to follow the general directions given from the Government of India through Army Headquarters. If there is a conflict between them and any instructions issued by the Civil Administration of Assam, the matter should be referred to the Government of

1. Note to Defence Secretary, New Delhi, 23 September 1957. JN Collection.
2. Dr Imkongliba Ao was an elderly medical practitioner from Mokokchung who was later assassinated by underground hostile elements.

India and, till some other decision is made, their directions must be carried out.

3. In any event, now that a change is likely in the Naga situation, it should be clearly stated that no reprisals should be indulged in and, more particularly, that there should be no burning of villages or houses.

13. Inaccessibility of Home Ministry Officials[1]

As you know, the Naga deputation is here and I shall meet them tomorrow. Meanwhile, various Naga officers have also come here and we have been talking to them.

2. In the course of these various talks one fact has emerged. The Nagas insist that when one unit is formed of the Naga Hills and the Tuensang Frontier Division, this should be put under the control of the External Affairs Ministry. They were asked why it should not be put under the Home Ministry. They replied that they said that from their experience of the External Affairs Ministry in NEFA and the Home Ministry in Manipur. In NEFA, the officers were much more accessible and often visited the people. In Manipur, the ordinary people have no access to the officers. Bureaucracy is strong there (whatever that might mean). When Moon[2] was Chief Commissioner, he toured extensively in Manipur and came in direct touch with the people. Since then, Chief Commissioners and other officers have become quite inaccessible to the common people and are looked upon as outsiders and strangers, while in NEFA the people have a feeling that the officers are with them.

3. I am merely mentioning this to you, so that an attempt might be made to induce the Chief Commissioner of Manipur and other officers to move out of their offices and shells and meet the people more.

1. Note to Home Minister, New Delhi, 24 September 1957. JN Collection.
2. Edward Penderel Moon (b. 1905); entered ICS (Punjab Commission), 1929 and worked in Punjab Government in various capacities; resigned from ICS, 1944; served in Yugoslav Commission of UNRRA, 1944-45; Secretary, Development Board, Government of India, 1946; Revenue Minister, Bahawalpur State, 1947; Deputy Chief Commissioner, Himachal Pradesh, 1948-49; and Chief Commissioner, 1950-51; Chief Commissioner, Manipur, 1951-52; Adviser, Planning Commission, 1952-60; author of *Strangers in India, Divide and Quit, Gandhi and Modern India*, (ed.) *Wavell: the Viceroy's Journal* and *The Transfer of Power, 1942-7*.

4. The position in regard to the Nagas is not as simple as it appears. The hostile elements have been doing a good deal of propaganda against any settlement.

14. Peaceful Political Settlement[1]

The Prime Minister received a delegation of Naga leaders on the morning of September 25. This delegation was chosen by the Naga People's Convention held in Kohima from the 22nd to the 26th August 1957. It was led by Dr Imkongliba Ao, President of the Convention, and consisted of eight other members,[2] including Jasokie Angami, Secretary of the Convention.[3]

The leader of the delegation handed to the Prime Minister a copy of the resolutions passed at the Kohima Convention. The Prime Minister said that he had, on many previous occasions, made it clear that the Government of India were prepared to consider proposals involving changes in the Constitution to meet the reasonable wishes of the Naga people. They were not prepared to discuss any scheme based on independence. He expressed his satisfaction that this question had been cleared up in the resolutions passed by the Kohima Convention and he was happy to meet the members of the delegation.

The Prime Minister emphasized the need for putting an end to the troubles and disturbances in the Naga areas. He welcomed the assurance of the Kohima Convention that every effort would be made to this end and for the establishment of peaceful conditions.

The Prime Minister further stated that the proposal made in the resolutions of the Convention was that the Naga Hills District and the Tuensang Frontier Division should be constituted into one administrative unit within the Indian

---

1. An External Affairs Ministry statement on the discussions between the Prime Minister and the Naga delegation, 25 September 1957. Foreign Secretary, Subimal Dutt and Joint Secretary, B.K. Acharya were also present. From *The Hindu* and other daily newspapers, 26 September 1957.
2. The other members of the delegation were (1) R.C. Chiten Jamir, (2) Lhouthipru Chakhensang, (3) Thanwang Konyak, (4) Luzhukhu Sema, (5) Tokiho Sema, (6) Vizol and (7) Etssorhomo Lotha.
3. John Bosco Jasokie was one of the pillars of the Naga People's Convention as its Secretary. He later became the Chief Minister of the State of Nagaland.

Union, directly under the President of India. This unit would be administered by the Governor of Assam on behalf of the President under the Ministry of External Affairs.

The Prime Minister accepted this proposal on behalf of the Government of India and agreed to give effect to it as early as feasible. Since, however, the implementation of the proposal would involve an amendment of the Constitution, the necessary amendments could only be considered by Parliament during its next session in November-December 1957.[4] The Prime Minister did not anticipate any difficulty in securing Parliamentary approval.

The leader of the Naga delegation thanked the Prime Minister for his statement accepting the proposal contained in the resolution of the Naga People's Convention. He promised that his delegation and those whom it represented would try their utmost to bring about a cessation of hostilities and the restoration of peace. He hoped that there would be a general amnesty and that the villages that had been grouped together (for the maintenance of law and order) would be degrouped as this grouping had caused much suffering to the people concerned.

Then Prime Minister replied that he was anxious to see normal conditions being restored in those areas where troubles had taken place. As soon as hostilities stopped normal conditions would return. He hoped that this would take place soon.

So far as an amnesty was concerned, the Government of India will grant amnesty in respect of all offences committed against the State in the past. This amnesty will not cover offences that might be committed hereafter.

So far as the degrouping of villages was concerned, this would naturally take place as hostilities ceased and peace and order were established. The principle of degrouping was accepted and it would be progressively given effect to wherever Government were satisfied that in a particular area peace and order had been restored. Meanwhile, orders were being issued that there should be no further regrouping of Naga villages.

The Prime Minister hoped that this progress to normal conditions would be rapid and that the members of the delegation and those who had met in the Kohima Convention, as well as others, would cooperate in restoring peace to the troubled areas. The first task for them as well as for Government was to restore peace, the second was to rehabilitate the people who had suffered, and the third was to cooperate for the betterment of the Naga people.

---

4. Finally, a separate administrative unit known as Naga Hills Tuensang Area (NHTA), under the Ministry of External Affairs and administered through the Governor of Assam acting in his discretion as the Agent of the President, was formed on 1 December 1957 by an Act of Parliament.

The delegation thanked the Prime Minister and withdrew. They will see the Prime Minister again tomorrow to say goodbye to him before their return.[5]

5. Soon after the meeting both Imkongliba Ao and Jasokie told pressmen, who met them at Hyderabad House, that they had a very cordial and successful meeting.

15. Cable to V.K. Krishna Menon[1]

I am happy to inform you that a major step forward has been taken towards solution of Naga problem. There are still many hurdles in the way. But, I feel sure that the sting has been taken out of this problem and we shall gradually make progress in the right direction.

2. I met Naga delegation today and accepted their proposal to make Naga Hills District and Tuensang Division as one administrative unit directly under Centre. Some other matters were also agreed to. The delegation which was a mixed one, containing some people considered to be pro-hostiles, is happy at this outcome. There is no doubt that the great majority of the Nagas will welcome this. It is true, however, that Phizo and a small hard core may continue to resist. Phizo, according to reports, is half paralysed and has to be carried about. I think, he is mentally unsound and is very angry at these developments towards peace.

1. New Delhi, 25 September 1957. JN Collection.

16. To K.S. Thimayya[1]

New Delhi
September 26, 1957

My dear Thimayya,

I hope you met the Naga representatives today. They had complained to me that some of the delegates to the Kohima Conference were arrested by our Army folk as they were returning and ill-treated. I hope you will see to it that no such incident occurs in future.

They laid stress again on the degrouping of villages as well as on the removal of restrictions on movement. They said that unless this was done they could not meet the hostiles and others and convince them to give up their violent activities. I told them that we would gladly remove these restrictions, but we must be sure that they will not be misused. We shall, therefore, have to proceed a little cautiously and would naturally have to rely on the advice of our civil and military advisers. I told them further that we would gladly give full facilities for movement to them and to any others they might name.

I am asking the External Affairs Ministry to send you the full notes of my conversations with them.

Yours sincerely,
Jawaharlal Nehru

1. JN Collection.

17. Steps for the Implementation of the Accord[1]

You spoke to me today about the arrangements to be made for the future set-up of the Naga Hills and Tuensang Division. I agree with you that it is necessary to give thought to this matter now. We have the advantage of the presence of the Governor of Assam here for a few days and this gives us an opportunity of consulting him.

2. We have given some thought to the constitutional changes required, but thus far the administrative changes have not been considered in any detail. I think, it will be advisable for you to arrange an informal meeting first of representatives of the Ministries of External Affairs, Home Affairs and Finance. Also of the Army. This informal meeting can lay down the nature of the problem and the possible steps to be taken.

3. Thereafter a formal Committee could be set up of these Ministries plus a representative of the Assam Government to work out these matters in some detail so that we might be prepared for the changeover, which is likely to take place about the beginning of December. We might keep in view the 1st of December as the date for this changeover.

4. A paper should be prepared for submission to the Cabinet. For the present this paper need not go into any detail but should merely record what has thus far happened, that is the visit of the delegation to me and what I agreed to on behalf of Government. Some brief mention might be made in the paper of the new problems that arise.

5. I think that Cabinet should be kept in touch with every development. The next meeting of the Cabinet is on October 1, and I should like this paper to be presented then.

1. Note to Foreign Secretary, New Delhi, 26 September 1957. JN Collection.

18. To Saiyid Fazl Ali[1]

New Delhi
October 31, 1957

My dear Fazl Ali,

Your letter of October 28. As Pantji has already reached Shillong, I need not discuss the various points raised in your letter. You will no doubt talk to him about them. Also you will be coming here soon after.

You must have seen the final resolution passed by what is called the Select Committee of the Naga People's Conference which met at Mokokchung on 23rd October. I do not particularly like this resolution and the special stress they have laid repeatedly on the interim nature of the steps we are taking. I do not think, however, to say much about it in public. But I do think that these people should be left in no doubt about the basic decisions. We are prepared to consider later about measures of local autonomy. That has been made clear repeatedly, but we are not prepared to consider anything infringing in the slightest degree with the unity of India, nor can we go repeatedly to Parliament to change the Constitution. What we propose doing will be flexible enough for any internal changes later.

Yours sincerely,
Jawaharlal Nehru

1. JN Collection. A copy of this letter was sent to Foreign Secretary.

(ii) NEFA and Other Matters

1. Preserving the Tribal Culture of NEFA[1]

...S.C. Samanta:[2] Last year a party of tribal representatives was invited to the Republic Day demonstrations in Delhi. May I know whether it is a solitary feature or whether they will be invited every year to show their feats?

Jawaharlal Nehru: It was not last year only. I believe, every year since these functions were started on the Republic Day, a contingent has come from the NEFA.

Hem Barua: Besides exhibiting these tribal cultural items as museum pieces during the Republic Day celebrations, do Government propose to institute Folk Art Museums in those areas and encourage cultural exchanges between the plains and the hills and adopt other measures so that this culture is not destroyed by the automobile civilization of the plains?

JN: I do not know what the honourable Member means by museum pieces. A museum piece is something which is dead and gone. There is more life in these things than in most other things that I see in India. They are vitally living, full of exuberance and it has been one of the amazing things in India in the last five or six years. The revival of folk art, folk dancing, folk singing is one of the most promising features. Who would put folk dancing in a museum, I do not know, maybe somewhere, or folk dancing. The honourable Member is probably thinking of some limited form or maybe of something which may be exhibited. It is not a matter for a museum.

The honourable Member also said something about cultural exchanges between the plains and the hills. One of the major exchanges is that they are coming here to Delhi. They have this experience. But I am rather anxious, if I may say so with all humility, to avoid cultural exchanges between the plains and the hills. My reason is that certainly the hill people suffer by that exchange; normally, not always. Because the plains people take their mill economy there

---

1. Reply to questions in the Lok Sabha, 9 August 1957. *Lok Sabha Debates*, (second series), Vol. V, cols. 7708-7709. Extracts.
2. Satis Chandra Samanta was Congress Member from Tamluk constituency, West Bengal.

with their culture; they take various other things and they replace the too fine artistic woven products there with some cheap mill-made goods and very cheap things, and spoil the whole artistic background and the handicrafts of these people....

> Mahanty: May I know whether it is a fact that a UK-born anthropologist, Dr Verrier Elwin,[3] is associated with the NEFA Administration so far as this cultural anthropology is concerned? If so, may I know if there is a paucity of Indian anthropologists in this country to fulfil that role.

JN: Professor Elwin is associated and is likely to continue to be associated. We have Indian anthropologists in various places. I do not know what the questioner means. Is it an objection to Dr Elwin because he is a non-Indian? We do not accept that also.

3. British anthropologist; worked amongst tribals in Central and North East India, became an Indian citizen in 1954.

2. Situation in NEFA[1]

I have been discussing various matters pertaining to the NEFA with the Governor of Assam who has been in Delhi for the last few days. We are passing through a very difficult period in Assam. There is great excitement over the location of the oil refinery and, indeed, matters have come to a head there with frequent hartals often verging on violence. Then there is the trouble in the Naga Hills which, apart from its grave consequences, is something which has a powerful effect on Assam.

2. The state of mind of the people in Assam is thus at present rather peculiar and it is a bit difficult to discuss matters with them dispassionately. It is possible that some developments may take place in the Naga Hills situation in the future. That again will require very careful handling by the Assam Government.

3. What has all this got to do with NEFA? There is a great deal in it because of geography and the reactions of anything happening in one part of that area on

1. Note to Secretary General, Foreign Secretary, and Joint Secretary, New Delhi, 10 August 1957. JN Collection. A copy of this note was sent to the Governor of Assam.

another. But the trouble in the Naga Hills is intimately related to Tuensang Division. It is quite conceivable that some new constitutional arrangements might be made in the future. We have thus to proceed very cautiously in regard even to NEFA matters. Many of our principal NEFA officers are in Shillong and Shillong is a seat of agitation and trouble. I learn that on the 29th of July, the Director of Education for the NEFA, Shri Shamlal Soni, got a bad beating on the public road. That was a day declared as a hartal day on the refinery question. Because the Director wanted to go to his office, he got a beating. In a few days' time, there are likely to be further hartals on August 14, 15 and possibly 16.

4. We, of the External Affairs Ministry, have got rather used to sending out various directions in regard to the NEFA. They are carefully worked out and there is a great deal of noting. But I have a feeling that we are functioning in a way which is somewhat isolated from the facts of the situation and decide on some admirable basis of logic. Logic always does not help.

5. Thus, we have issued instructions about teaching in the schools in Hindi. This is greatly resented by the Assamese and, I think, to some extent at least their resentment is justified. There are certain areas of NEFA which have been much influenced by Assam and the Assamese language. In fact, the Assamese language is, more or less, the lingua franca of considerable areas. In such areas, it is clear that Assamese should be taught (after the tribal language) in preference to or earlier than Hindi. This does not mean that Hindi should be struck off the curriculum. I think, Hindi should be taught but as a second or third language.

6. In the areas of NEFA which are quite virgin, in so far as any foreign language influence is concerned, and where Assamese has not infiltrated, the question is a more open one. But even there, I think that Assamese cannot be ignored because we must remember that it is the lingua franca of all that broad region.

7. In this matter, we should not issue any hard and fast rules from here but leave it to the judgment of the Governor and his advisers as to where Assamese should be given preference over Hindi.

8. Another question that arises is what type of Hindi is to be taught. I am told that the Hindi teachers who have been sent there use difficult and intricate Hindi. This is most unfortunate and we must take every care that the language taught is simple and not some kind of ornate literary language. In fact, this also makes me feel that we should rather lay stress on Assamese than on Hindi.

9. The Governor told me of conflicts between these Hindi teachers and Assamese teachers and of demonstrations and all that. The Hindi teachers were looked upon as foreigners imposing themselves. There has been trouble at Margherita where there is an excellent institute for the NEFA. Because of this trouble, it is being considered that the institute might be removed to some other place.

10. These are some thoughts that have occurred to me. Another aspect which is always coming up before me is that we are setting up in the NEFA too top heavy an administration, various Directors of Education, Agriculture, etc. Our enthusiasm is laudable but I am not quite clear in my mind if it is suitable in the circumstances prevailing there.

3. NEFA—a Problem and a Challenge[1]

In dealing with human beings anywhere, a superior-person approach is a wrong approach. This is wrong even when it is well-intentioned and wanted to do good. Our treatment of human beings, whoever they might be, must not have the taint of that superiority. It should be one of respect for another human being, so that he or she does not feel in any sense ashamed or unhappy or frustrated. It is only through respect and affection that people react in the proper way.

I am proud of the work being done by our officers in the NEFA. Those I have met, have been full of enthusiasm and a spirit of adventure, which one often misses in India. NEFA offers adventure certainly, but the adventure should be of human spirit and the human approach, so that we win over the minds and hearts of people. This is the true victory and true development follows this.

To me and to all of us, NEFA is a problem and a challenge. The question it raises are different from those that we have to face in other parts of the country. We have, therefore, to find different answers. The first thing to realize is this difference in approach. Any attempt merely to copy methods used elsewhere would be unfortunate both for us and for the people of NEFA.

Any attempt to try to make them like others would also be wrong. They, like other people, should develop themselves and should not be imposed upon. This is important, as there is a big gap between the social fabric of the people of NEFA and our other countrymen and there is the danger that in trying to substitute another social organization, we break up the old and have nothing in its place.

We are anxious to help the people of NEFA to develop according to their own genius. But it must be according to their own genius and not something that

1. Message for an Independence Day brochure, giving a brief account of administrative and development activities in the North East Frontier Agency since Independence, New Delhi, 12 August 1957. From *The Hindu*, 13 August 1957.

they cannot absorb or imbibe and which merely uproots them. I would much rather go slow in our plans for development than risk the danger of this uprooting.

I feel, therefore, that it is unwise to try to do too many things at the same time there, which may result in disturbing the minds of the people or in upsetting their habits. I have no doubt that development and change and so-called progress will come to them, because it is becoming increasingly difficult for any people to live their isolated life, cut off from the rest of the world. But let this development and change be natural and be in the nature of self-development with all the help one can give in the process. After much thought I have come to this conclusion and I should like our officers and others working in NEFA to bear this in mind.

4. Permits for Entering NEFA[1]

Achaw Singh Laisram:[2] Will the Prime Minister be pleased to state who is the authority for issuing permits in regard to the entry of outsiders into North East Frontier Agency?

Jawaharlal Nehru: In the case of Indian nationals living outside North East Frontier Agency, the permits for entry are issued by the Political Officers for the respective Divisions under their charge, under the general instructions of the NEFA Administration.

In the case of foreigners, permits are issued by the NEFA Administration in consultation with the Government of India and the Ministry of External Affairs.

1. Reply to a question in Lok Sabha, 21 August 1957. *Lok Sabha Debates*, (second series), Vol. V, cols. 9080-81.
2. Socialist Party Member from Manipur.

5. To Bisnuram Medhi[1]

New Delhi
September 26, 1957

My dear Medhi,

I understand that you have gone to Puri. I hope that the rest there will do you good.

Now that we have passed over the first hurdle in regard to the Naga problem, we have to think of the autonomous tribal Hill Districts in Assam. You will remember writing to me at some length on this question sometime ago and suggesting that a Commission might be appointed.

Pantji and I have considered this matter. We agree with you that something has to be done fairly soon. We feel, however, that a Commission is too cumbrous a procedure and attracts too much attention and often leads to agitation. An informal approach is likely to be better. I am going away to Japan soon. I have suggested to Pantji, and he has been good enough to agree, to visit Shillong at a convenient date. He could confer there with you as well as the representatives of these Autonomous Districts. This, I think, will be a much better way of proceeding in this matter, at any rate, in the initial stage.

I had a telegram from some of the tribal people. I have sent an answer to them telling them that this matter is very much in our minds and we hope to have opportunities of consulting their representatives as well as, of course, the Assam Government. I have mentioned that our Home Minister is likely to go to Shillong. I rather doubt, however, if Pantji can go there before I return from Japan as his presence in Delhi will be required during my absence.[2]

Yours sincerely,
Jawaharlal Nehru

1. JN Collection.
2. G.B. Pant arrived in Guwahati on 30 October 1957 on a four day visit to Assam. His visit was mainly in connection with granting of greater autonomy to the Hills people by amending the Sixth Schedule of the Constitution.

6. Pace of Development in NEFA[1]

Please see the attached letter from the Governor of Assam about NEFA. I do not remember anything about the budget of NEFA except that I have been asking, as you will remember, for its curtailment and for our programme to be spread out over a longer period.[2] If that is so, then the question of asking for fresh grants surely does not arise. What might arise is that present allocations may be rearranged differently.

2. I agree that roads are very necessary, more necessary than anything else. Is it not possible for this road money to be found from other allotments for NEFA work?

3. There is a reference in the Governor's letter to hospitals, offices, residences, etc. I suppose all these are necessary though I would prefer going slow with the construction. So far as hospitals are concerned, I do not quite know what is meant. We should put up small hospitals there, not exceeding 25 to 30 beds. I do not know how much these cost there, but recently a hospital with 25 beds and some light equipment has been built not far from Delhi with Rs 45,000/-.

4. I am rather hesitant to ask for more money from Finance, even though I can, as acting Finance Minister, tell them to do so. I should like you to look into this matter and, if necessary, consult Finance. If you and they are agreeable, then I shall have no difficulty in recommending something. Or, perhaps, then my recommendation will not be necessary.

1. Note to Foreign Secretary, New Delhi, 2 October 1957. JN Collection.
2. In this regard see Nehru's note dated 6 March 1957 in *Selected Works* (second series), Vol. 37, p. 253.

7. To J.J.M. Nichols-Roy[1]

New Delhi
October 23, 1957

Dear Shri Nichols-Roy,[2]

On my return from Japan, I have received your letter of the 8th October. As you perhaps know, our Home Minister, Shri Govind Ballabh Pant, is going to Shillong soon. The purpose of his visit is, more especially, to discuss with representatives of the Hill Districts about any possible changes in future.

Our broad policy has been to encourage local autonomy as far as possible. We shall, of course, keep this in view. Further, that these Hill District areas should maintain, in so far as they wish it, their own customs. Thirdly, of course, that they should progress on their own lines.

The demand that used to be made some time ago about a separate State for these Hill Districts, seemed to me to be misconceived. This would have come in the way of their development. But, it should certainly be possible to increase autonomy in a number of ways.

Yours sincerely,
Jawaharlal Nehru

1. JN Collection. A copy of this letter was sent to G.B. Pant.
2. James Joy Mohan Nichols-Roy, a Christian missionary and Minister in Assam Government periodically till 1956, was Member, Advisory Committee for Minorities, and the Sub-Committee of Partially Excluded and Excluded Tribal Areas of Assam.

VI. SCIENCE AND TECHNOLOGY

1. To Mohanlal Sukhadia[1]

New Delhi
August 10, 1957

My dear Sukhadia,[2]

Please refer to your letter of the 20th June, 1957. This is rather a belated answer. When I received your letter, I referred it to our Ministry of Steel, Mines and Fuel, who consulted the Atomic Energy Commission. It is only now that they have sent me their note on the subject. Hence the delay.

In your letter, you had referred to the discovery of uranium ore in the Udaipur Division and to smelting of zinc ore from the Zawar mines. Your suggestion was that the sulphuric acid which you expect to get from the smelting process, might be used in uranium mills.

I am informed that low-grade uranium ore has been found at a few places in Udaipur Division. It is, however, too early yet to say whether this will lead to any major result. It will take another eighteen months before we know whether the ore deposits are worth exploiting, and another two years after that before any uranium mills can be set up. In the event that all goes well, it appears to be possible for uranium mills to use sulphuric acid from the zinc smelter. This will have to be considered by the people in Departments concerned at a later stage.

The information about the uranium prospecting is confidential, and I hope you will keep it secret.

Yours sincerely,
Jawaharlal Nehru

1. JN Collection.
2. Chief Minister of Rajasthan.

2. Atomic Energy and Fertilizer Production[1]

I sent you a note by Dr Homi Bhabha[2] a few days ago. In this he suggested that the Department of Atomic Energy should be represented on the different Boards of fertilizer undertakings. I had sent copies of that note to some of the Ministers concerned. I have received replies from the Finance Minister and the Minister of Commerce & Industry, which are enclosed.

I do not think it is necessary to put this matter up before the Cabinet. You might correspond with Dr Bhabha and suggest to him that we are agreeable to the appointment of a representative of his Department in any fertilizer undertaking where the manufacture of heavy water is included in the programme. If at any time this is included in other undertakings, his representative could be added to that Board also.

Of course it may be said that wherever there is a fertilizer project, the question of heavy water should be considered. In order to help in this consideration, a representative of the Atomic Energy Department could be asked to help even in the initial stages, although he is not, to begin with, a member of the Board.

You may also ask Dr Bhabha as to who will be the representative of the Atomic Energy Department on these Boards. It would not be fair to ask Dr Bhabha to add this work to his present burdens and to take him away from his research and other work. No doubt his representative will keep him in touch.[3]

1. Note to M.K. Vellodi, Cabinet Secretary, New Delhi, 15 August 1957. JN Collection.
2. Homi Jehangir Bhabha, Secretary, Department of Atomic Energy, and Chairman, Atomic Energy Commission, Government of India, wrote that there was a possibility of a considerable market for heavy water in future in different countries and India could earn large amounts of foreign exchange as it produced heavy water cheaply. Since it could be produced most economically as a by product of fertilizer production, it was desirable that the Department of Atomic Energy should be associated with all the fertilizer undertakings and also with the upcoming projects at Sindri, Trombay, Rourkela and Neyveli, Bhabha added.
3. In his note to the Cabinet Secretary on 30 August 1957, Nehru enquired whether it was possible for Bhabha to be appointed to the Board, but with the proviso that somebody else could represent him whenever necessary.

3. To S.K. Patil[1]

New Delhi
August 16, 1957

My dear SK,[2]

In my latest fortnightly letter to Chief Ministers,[3] which you will probably get tomorrow, I have referred to the importance of conserving our natural resources, which include fauna and flora, apart from other things. I have pointed out that a certain economy has developed in nature which is easily upset by some new intrusion and, as a result, unexpected consequences flow from it. Therefore, it is desirable to have some kind of a survey of these various factors before a major scheme is undertaken.

In this connection, there is an organization called International Union for Conservation of Nature and Natural Resources, with its office at Brussels (Belgium).[4]

I think it might be desirable for us to associate ourselves with this Union. For the present, I would suggest that your Ministry might get particulars from them as to what they are and what they have done. Information can be obtained from the Secretary of this Union, Dr Tracy Philipps,[5] 31 rue Vautier, Brussels, Belgium.

Yours sincerely,
Jawaharlal Nehru

1. JN Collection.
2. Union Minister of Irrigation and Power.
3. For Nehru's letter of 15 August 1957 to the Chief Ministers see *post*, pp. 796-806.
4. It was set up in 1948 for two purposes: (i) to promote international cooperation in scientific research and in applying ecological concepts for conservation of nature and natural resources, and (ii) to ensure the perpetration of biological diversity and genetic resources of wild animals and plants in their natural environment.
5. (1890-1959); Assistant Commissioner, Indian Expeditionary Force, 1914; British Relief Commissioner for South Russia (Red Cross), 1921; *The Times* war correspondent, Greco-Turkish war, 1922; Deputy Provincial Commissioner, East Africa, 1930; Foreign (Diplomatic) correspondent on Peoples of Moslem Mediterranean and East Europe, 1936-39; Adviser to Canadian Government on Immigrant European communities in War Industry, 1941-43; Chief of Planning Resettlement of Displaced Persons, UN Administration, 1944-45; Chairman, British Group of Union of Christian Democrats of Europe, 1947-56; Vice-President, International Institute of Differing Civilizations, Brussels, 1949-51; Member, International Centre for Cultural and Art Exchanges, Rome, 1958-59; Secretary-General, International Union for Conservation of Nature and Natural Resources at this time.

4. To T.T. Krishnamachari[1]

New Delhi
August 26, 1957

My dear T.T.,

An Indian Medical Association Deputation came to see me today and gave me a sheaf of papers which are enclosed.

As I have told you, I dislike the idea of discouraging research or the acquisition by doctors of equipment etc. We should encourage their possession of their tools of trade or profession. The equipment has little selling value. We should encourage initiative and love of research and the building up of laboratories etc., by them.

How exactly this is to be done is not clear to me. Some kind of line has to be drawn. Whether it is possible to do so by executive action later, I do not know. It will be a pity to discourage something that is essentially right.

Yours sincerely,
Jawaharlal Nehru

1. File No. 37(60)/57-58-PMS. Also available in JN Collection.

5. To Ajit Prasad Jain[1]

New Delhi
September 30, 1957

My dear Ajit,

I enclose a note about what is called "Hygeiopacking".[2] I saw M.A. Kazmi today and I asked him to see you as also Morarji Desai and Thacker.

From these papers, it appears that his invention has been accepted in the United States and, in fact, a plant is being put up there. If there is any validity about this invention, as there appears to be, then, of course, it is of great value to us. The first step we should take is to put up a pilot plant which, according to Kazmi, will cost about fifty thousand rupees. The plant would have to be manufactured probably in Germany or England. In fact, he is in contact with some people there for this purpose.

I suggest that you send for him and have a talk. He is here for a few days. His address is 134, Constitution House.

Yours sincerely,
Jawaharlal Nehru

1. File No. 17(265)/57-58-PMS. Also available in JN Collection.
2. In his note to Maneklal S. Thacker, Director, CSIR, on 29 September (not printed), Nehru explained that hygeiopacking, an invention by M.A. Kazmi, was for the preservation of milk and other perishable liquids without using preservatives or chemicals. It was recognized by USA and other countries, who wanted to take advantage of it.

6. International Atomic Energy Agency[1]

This Agency has come into being as a result of the initiative of President Eisenhower and the cooperative endeavours of a number of countries from all parts of the world to promote peaceful uses of atomic energy and to divert the fissionable material which now goes into the production of atomic weapons to peaceful and constructive purposes.

The success of this Agency will depend not only on its own efforts but also on the united efforts of all countries to build and ensure a lasting peace.

All those participating in the conference will, I am sure, join with me in hoping that a world climate of peace and security will be created soon in which the Agency can realize its full potentialities.

If an agreement is reached on disarmament, this Agency may well become the most important Agency of the United Nations as a possible custodian of fissionable material.

---

1. Message to the foundation conference of International Atomic Energy Agency held at Vienna from 1-23 October 1957. The conference, attended by 59 countries, was opened by the President of Austria, Adolf Scharf. Karl Gruber, Austrian Ambassador in Washington and former Foreign Minister of Austria, was elected as president of the conference. Nehru's message was read by the Indian delegate, Homi J. Bhabha. From *National Herald*, 3 October 1957 and *The Hindu*, 4 October 1957.

3
ADMINISTRATIVE MATTERS

I. GENERAL

1. To V. Veeraswamy[1]

New Delhi
August 3, 1957

Dear Shri Veeraswamy,[2]

Your letter of the 31st July.[3] As I wrote to you previously, this is a matter which has been examined by our Law Officers and advisers, and they have no doubt about it. It is, therefore, not a question of any sympathy from me, but of how our Constitution is interpreted.

You refer to the Sikhs. Their case is completely different. Right at the beginning of the Constitution, there was a question as to whether some castes which are in-between Sikhism and Hinduism, should be included in the list of Scheduled Castes. Four such castes were included then, and I think, two were added to it a little later.

It is perfectly true that by change of religion, one's material conditions are not changed. But, this rule has been applied previously to people of the Christian religion also. Anyhow, it is a matter for law and not for me.

Yours sincerely,
Jawaharlal Nehru

---

1. File No. 2(172)/57-63-PMS.
2. A resident of Tiruchirapalli.
3. Veeraswami urged Nehru that the facilities and privileges to Buddhist converts from Scheduled Castes should continue which they were enjoying before embracing Buddhism. He added: "When a section of the Sikh people are allowed to enjoy the special privileges of the Scheduled Castes why not those who embrace Buddhism from Scheduled Castes?"

2. To K.C. Reddy[1]

New Delhi
10 August 1957

My dear Reddy,[2]

I am writing to you about the All India Medical Institute. I understand that the Central PWD is in charge of the buildings there, though the architects are a British firm.

I understand that the original estimate for the main buildings was 172 lakhs. This was subsequently raised to 211 lakhs. Now, this has gone up to 625 lakhs. This very big jump is said to be due to better flooring, air conditioning, increased area as well as, presumably, higher prices. I think, these repeated jumps require careful consideration and explanation. In present circumstances, more particularly, we have to think in terms of economy.

There has been very considerable delay. I gather that a part of the delay is due to the fact that the British firm of architects have to refer every matter to their head-office in London and that perhaps there is not too much coordination between them and the CPWD.

None of the main buildings are ready yet. In fact, only the Pre-Clinical Block is under construction and is supposed to be ready by the end of 1957. The rest of the main buildings have not even received administrative sanction yet. As for the Hospital, which is going to be of 650 beds, this is supposed to be a part of phase-4. We are now only half way through phase-1.

While these main buildings are mostly in the air yet, most of the residential area has been built up. I understand that the residential quarters, big and small, have been built up to accommodate 688 persons. In addition, hostels have already been built for 207 and three more hostels are under construction. These will give accommodation to 173 more.

In addition, the Nursing College building is ready and quarters for 400 nurses have already been constructed.

---

1. File No. 40 (127)/57-61-PMS. Also available in JN Collection.
2. Union Minister of Works, Housing and Supply.

This is the information that I have received from Dr B.B. Dikshit,[3] Director of the Institute.

It seems rather odd to me that all this construction should have taken place for residential quarters etc., and the main buildings should have been ignored completely. Normally, the main buildings should have the precedence.

Altogether, it appears to me that there has been a great lack of any planned approach with the result that there is waste of time and money. The original foundation stone for this Institute was laid about five years ago. I think it had to be removed to a new location.

All this seems to me very odd. We are spending large sums of money without any benefit now or in the near future. I should like to know if the information given to me is correct and what the CPWD thinks about these various matters.

Yours sincerely,
Jawaharlal Nehru

3. (1902-1977); graduated from Grant Medical College, Bombay, 1925; joined School of Tropical Medicine and Hygiene, Calcutta, 1926-30; Professor of Pharmacology, Medical College, Vishakhapatnam, 1930-31; joined Royal College of Physicians, 1931 and obtained MRCP and Ph.D. in 1933; worked in Haffkine Institute, Bombay, 1934-46; Principal and Professor of Physiology, B.J. Medical College, Pune, 1946-51; Surgeon-General, Government of Bombay, 1951-56; Director, All India Institute of Medical Sciences, 1956-64.

3. To Lal Bahadur Shastri[1]

New Delhi
August 10, 1957

My dear Lal Bahadur,
You know that I have been much interested and concerned with the state of our Civil Aviation. Very soon after you took charge of your Ministry, I spoke to you about it. Since then I have spoken to you and Humayun Kabir[2] as well as written to you on this subject.

1. JN Collection.
2. Union Minister of State for Civil Aviation.

My immediate concern was that the technical aspect and the lack of discipline etc., and I had then suggested that a high grade technical man should be brought in at the top. I had further suggested that such a person could be obtained from our Indian Air Force. This was many months ago. I do not know if anything has been done about this.

Recently, we have had the threat of a strike by the Civil Aviation personnel. This brings out another aspect of this question. I have long heard about the discontent in the Civil Aviation staff. Whatever this discontent may be due to, the fact that there is all this trouble in Civil Aviation is patent. This requires very close and urgent attention and we cannot allow matters to drift either on the technical plane or the other. I hope you and Humayun Kabir will deal with this soon.

Yours affectionately,
Jawaharlal Nehru

4. To B.K. Gaikwad[1]

New Delhi
August 10, 1957

Dear Shri Gaikwad,[2]
I have your letter of the 8th August.

I need not tell you again that, so far as I am concerned, I have not the least objection to people belonging to the Scheduled Castes embracing the Buddhist faith. As you perhaps know, I am a great admirer of the Buddha and his faith. The one thing that I am concerned about is that this conversion should not be a superficial and political one but should really bring us nearer to the great teaching and practice of the Buddha. Unfortunately, it seems to me that sometimes this is treated, both by friends and opponents, as something political.

---

1. File No. 2 (172)/57-63-PMS.
2. (1902-1971); Member, Nasik Municipality and District Board, Nasik for several years; Scheduled Castes Federation Member of Bombay Legislative Assembly, 1937-46; SCF Member of Lok Sabha, 1957-62.

The question you raised in your previous letter was about certain special privileges given to the Scheduled Castes. In this matter, as I informed you, there are certain constitutional and legal difficulties which we cannot get over. We cannot amend our Constitution for this purpose. Indeed, it is difficult to amend it for any purpose. We must, therefore, function within the terms of our Constitution.

It may be that in some States the action taken is in excess of requirements. That should not be done.

Personally, I hope that the special political privileges given to the Scheduled Castes will cease fairly soon, though I want them in any event to have scholarships and other help for progress in various ways. I dislike the idea of any group being labelled as Scheduled Castes. We should not have such labels in India.

I am sending your letter to the Home Ministry.

Yours sincerely,
Jawaharlal Nehru

5. To Mona Hensman[1]

New Delhi
August 12, 1957

My dear Shrimati Mona Hensman,[2]
Thank you for your letter of August 8th.

I do not know anything about the subject of your letter, that is, about Mrs Parthasarathi's[3] professorship in the Presidency College. I knew, of course, that she had been a Professor or a Principal there previously. But, you have raised a question of principle. You say that the wife of an accredited Ambassador of ours serving abroad, should not be retained as a Professor in Government service. I

1. JN Collection.
2. Principal, Ethiraj College, Madras.
3. Saraswati Parthasarathi was wife of G. Parthasarathi, Indian Ambassador in Indonesia.

247

do not understand this. The fact of a person being the wife of an Ambassador may in practice come in the way of her service here. But, that is for her to decide, or for her husband, if you like. Where does the Government come in? The fact that she is the wife of an Ambassador does not mean that she has got a greater pull than others.

We have got some women in the Indian Foreign Service. At the instance of the All India Women's Association, we removed a rule that marriage should lead to resignation, although, obviously, marriage might come in the way of service and posting. In a case a year ago, one of our young women in the Foreign Service asked for leave to marry another person in the Service. We told her quite clearly that she could marry if she wanted to, but she should not expect her postings to be affected by the fact of her marriage. She agreed to this condition and, in fact, she has often been posted away from her husband. That is her lookout.

The point is that we cannot come in the way of the wife of an Ambassador or any other Government servant from doing any kind of work or service that she may get. That is the theory of it. In practice, of course, other questions may arise. I am not acquainted with the facts in this particular case, to be able to express any opinion.

Yours sincerely,
Jawaharlal Nehru

6. To Govind Ballabh Pant[1]

New Delhi
August 15, 1957

My dear Pantji,

You were good enough to send me a copy of a letter from the Chairman of the Law Commission dated August 8th.[2] I have read this letter and the note[3] attached to it.

1. JN Collection.
2. M.C. Setalvad, Chairman of the Law Commission, informed G.B. Pant that the Commission had very carefully considered the question of accumulated arrears in the High Courts and urged to implement its recommendations immediately.
3. The note contained the recommendations of the Law Commission.

The Commission criticizes in strong language the selection of Judicial personnel for the High Courts and hints that persons are appointed for reasons other than those of merit, such as personal considerations or those of a political or communal character. High Court Judges are, I believe, appointed on the recommendation, first, of the Chief Minister and the Chief Justice of the High Court concerned. Then the Chief Justice of India is consulted and, finally, the Home Ministry decides and makes the recommendation to the President.

Whose fault is it that wrong names are suggested? Is it suggested that the initial recommendation is wrong, or that at the other stages these irrelevant considerations come in? This is a serious charge. Perhaps, it might be worthwhile for you to have a talk with the Chairman of the Law Commission on this subject and to find out exactly at what stage, according to them, some error crept in.

What do you propose to do with this preliminary report of the Law Commission? Is this matter going to come up before the Cabinet?

The Commission expresses its views in a fairly strong language about the limitation by law of High Court vacations. A day or two ago, I saw a paper sent by your Ministry dealing with this matter, in which it was suggested by the Home Ministry that the vacation should be limited to nine weeks. Alternative suggestions were that it should be limited to eleven weeks. In view of the Law Commission's strong opinion, would it be worthwhile to have a law on this subject? It might perhaps be better to have a period fixed for the vacations in consultation with the Chief Justice of India and other Chief Justices, without having recourse to the legislature. I do think that the present vacations are much too long. I do not quite know what the suggestion made by the Law Commission, two hundred working days of five hours each, would work out in a term for vacations.

Our Law Minister[4] sent me a letter the other day with some enclosures. Perhaps, he has sent them to you also. In case he has not done so, I am enclosing them.

Yours affectionately,
Jawaharlal Nehru

4. Asoke K. Sen.

7. The Question of Abducted Persons[1]

Mridula Sarabhai's[2] opinions or criticisms are well known to be completely irresponsible. Indeed, that is a very mild way of describing them. Her activities in regard to Kashmir and connected maters have been deplorable in the extreme and have done much injury to our cause. I attach no importance to what she says. In fact, I rather doubt if she is behaving with any sanity. More than a year ago, I had informed her that I was not prepared to receive any of her messages and circulars. When they continued to come, I had returned them often unopened. Since then most of the circulars ceased to come to me, but sometimes still some odd letter comes. As I have said, I attach no importance to her views and usually react rather strongly to them.

We need not trouble ourselves therefore, nor the Ministry of Rehabilitation trouble itself about the allegations made by her.

So far as the question of the work relating to abducted persons is concerned, the only thing that I had in mind was that in these concluding days of this work, any changeover from one Ministry to another might lead to a lack of continuity and therefore delay, etc. Although the work is in charge of External Affairs Ministry, I have personally had very little to do with it. At my request, Sardar Swaran Singh had been good enough to look after it and has, therefore, been in intimate touch with it. It seemed to me that it might be desirable for him to continue this for the time being and gradually bring it to a close. The matter is entirely for Sardar Swaran Singh to decide, as he is best acquainted with the work and therefore under best position to judge. I shall abide by his decision.

Copies of this note should be sent separately to Sardar Swaran Singh and to the Ministry of Rehabilitation.

---

1. Note to Joint Secretary (AD), New Delhi, 15 August 1957. File No. 6 (25)-A.P./57, MEA. Also available in JN Collection.
2. She was a freedom fighter and organized relief and rehabilitation of refugees including abducted women after Partition.

8. To Jagjivan Ram[1]

New Delhi
August 17, 1957

My dear Jagjivan Ram,

Somebody was telling me that the average rate of movement of goods trains in India was very slow. This average is apparently worked out on a twenty-four hour basis, including stops etc. Could you find out what this is and ask your people to try to raise this average and bring it nearer the average of other countries? Obviously, if this could be done, movement of goods would be faster. It is in these matters that improvement pays good dividend. The same wagons can be used again and again much sooner.

Yours sincerely,
Jawaharlal Nehru

1. JN Collection.

9. To S.K. Patil[1]

New Delhi
August 17, 1957

My dear SK,

In this morning's papers, I read a report about your having said something in favour of what are called "sponsored programmes"[2] from the All India Radio. I was surprised to read this for a variety of reasons. First of all, you were dealing

1. JN Collection.
2. The sponsored radio programmes were a kind of community service by private individuals or concerns for recreation and instruction of the community.

with another Ministry and normally it is not the practice for one Minister to criticize another Ministry.

Secondly, the basic policy of AIR has been, right from the beginning, that they should not accept any advertisement, paid or unpaid. This has been their policy ever since the beginning and is not something introduced recently by the present Minister. To say that "the Central Government had not yet finalized its policy on the desirability of permitting sponsored programmes on AIR",[3] therefore, is not correct. We have a firm and fixed policy which has been pursued for the last dozen years or more. At no time that I am aware of was even a suggestion made that this policy should be changed. If this question had to be considered, this could be done in the normal way by discussing it with the Minister concerned and later in the Cabinet. The question is important enough to be dealt with by the Cabinet itself. It is not fair to your colleague in the I & B Ministry for you to refer to this matter publicly when no question of changing this policy has yet even arisen. Nor is it correct to say that the Government of India has no policy about it. Indeed, it has had a definite policy ever since AIR was started.[4]

You will appreciate that it is very embarrassing for a Minister to have his policy criticized by a colleague in another Ministry. This tends to put an end to the collective responsibility of the Cabinet or the Government.

Yours sincerely,
Jawaharlal Nehru

3. Patil replied on 18 August that Nehru was confusing 'sponsored programmes' with advertisements on the radio. He wrote that he was aware that the official policy of the AIR was not to accept advertisements. He emphasized: "Whatever my views may be on that subject, it would be a folly on my part to criticize that official policy. Please be assured that I never said a word about it in my speech." He added: "I agree with you that it is positively embarrassing to a Minister if his policy is criticized by his colleague. Believe me any idea of criticizing the Ministry was far from my mind."
4. To illustrate his point on "sponsored programmes", Patil cited the example of Standard Vacuum Company which sponsored the most popular programmes on music, sports news and cultural aspects of American life. Similarly, Four-H programme, sponsored by many private agencies, focused on farmers. This was done without any advertising for these concerns.

10. To Jogendra Nath Mandal[1]

New Delhi
August 19, 1957

Dear Shri Mandal,[2]
I have your letter of the 14th August.[3]

There is no question of taking any penal action against any student. The only question was whether, under our Constitution, members of the Scheduled Castes who are converted to Buddhism, will be entitled to any privilege which is reserved for Scheduled Castes. We have consulted eminent lawyers on this and they have given a clear opinion that they will not be so entitled under the Constitution. We cannot commit a breach of our Constitution. We have to follow it or to amend it.

This does not come in the way of scholarships being given to converts to Buddhism because of economic conditions or other worthwhile reasons. The point is that when certain scholarships are reserved according to our rules for a particular group, can we go beyond that group for these scholarships? Legal opinion is against it.

So far as I am concerned, I have not the least objection to anyone being converted to Buddhism. I have a great admiration for Buddhism myself.

Yours sincerely,
Jawaharlal Nehru

---

1. File No. 2 (172)/57-63-PMS. Also available in JN Collection.
2. Minister in Pakistan Government till 1950.
3. Mandal wrote that the press in Calcutta reported on 11 and 12 August 1957 that, "the State Government have issued instructions to the heads of all the educational institutions to take penal action against those Scheduled Caste students who, even after their conversion to Buddhism, have been enjoying the privileges and scholarships reserved for the Scheduled Castes." He informed Nehru that he was astonished and shocked by this news because their case was no way different from the Scheduled Caste Sikhs of the Punjab who were enjoying their previous privileges.

11. To D.P. Karmarkar[1]

New Delhi
19 August 1957

My dear Karmarkar,

The representative of the British architects who are in charge of the All India Institute of Medical Sciences came to see me today. I had a brief talk with him. He gave me a paper which I enclose. He said that work was held up because of various factors. Even Administrative approval had not been given for the future phases. He was also not very satisfied with the contractors. He said that their work required a great deal of supervision; otherwise the quality suffered. In his opinion, what was necessary was to have a few very competent young men to supervise this work. This would expedite it and ensure quality. He said such men could easily be found here.

I suppose the Central PWD people will be sending you or me a note about these various estimates for this Institute.

Yours sincerely,
Jawaharlal Nehru

1. File No. 140 (127)/57-61-PMS.

12. Approach to Technical Manpower[1]

Reading through this exhaustive note,[2] it appears that repeated and persistent attempts have been made to get information about our students abroad, more

1. Comments on the note "Indians with scientific or technical qualifications, receiving training or working, in foreign countries," New Delhi, 20 August 1957. JN Collection.
2. The note was prepared by the Directorate of Manpower and was submitted to the Manpower Committee of the Cabinet on 17 August.

especially, those studying technical subjects. On every occasion these enquiries yielded some results. These results presumably did not include all the students taking technical courses. But anyhow, we received information about several hundred Indians working or receiving training in other countries.

2. It is now sought to make a fresh and more comprehensive and perhaps a more methodical attempt on the same lines to collect information. This is certainly to be encouraged. But I am wondering what the poor Indian student abroad will think of these repeated questionnaires issued to him. He fills them in, sends them and then waits for a reply or some indication as to what is lying in wait for him. Instead of that, after some time he gets a fresh questionnaire from some other authority. It would not be unnatural for him to feel a little desperate about these repeated questionnaires which produce no result. Indeed, I have had several letters from Indian students abroad asking me why they are repeatedly asked questions and nothing happens.

3. The object aimed at is presumably not merely the preparation of lists of Indians abroad but a more positive one of finding work for them. As we have already received adequate information about some hundreds of Indians abroad, this attempt should have been made or at any rate for some of them who fulfilled the requisite qualifications. I am not aware of any such step being taken. Now, in the exuberance of our enthusiasm for preparing registers, we are sending out another questionnaire.

4. In this note for the Manpower Committee, some kind of a special procedure is laid down for recruitment of these persons. That may be good in so far as it goes. But even that appears to be rather long drawn out and might not perhaps suit all cases. I remember that when this matter was discussed in the Manpower Committee or in the Cabinet, it was suggested that if a person was obviously good and outstanding in any of the principal subjects required by us, we could immediately give him an assurance of employment. This would not relate to any particular post. It would simply mean that on his return to India with the necessary qualifications, if he did not immediately find suitable work, he would be put in a pool and would receive some kind of a moderate salary. We could utilize him in such ways as we wanted him or attach him to any of our industrial or other concerns for further training. As soon as a suitable post was available for him, he would go there. The whole idea was that we should get hold of such a person right at the beginning even though we do not have any post to which he could be appointed.

5. This procedure would not apply to everybody. It could only apply to some persons who prima facie satisfy us in regard to their training. Thus we want men in our steel plants by the hundred, I suppose. Those who undergo this training and qualify themselves could immediately be assured of work. This would apply

to other branches of work too.

6. This kind of approach cannot be made by lists being circulated all over India, although such lists should certainly be circulated. A Committee at the Centre consisting of representatives of the Ministries more especially concerned, and a member of the Public Service Commission could look through these lists and make a preliminary choice. Our Ambassador in the country concerned should be asked to report on the persons concerned. If his report is favourable, the Committee could accept this man temporarily. Perhaps no other interview is needed at this stage, as his appointment would be temporary and subject to his satisfying us later on. But he would be assured of a moderate salary anyhow and some kind of work. He would not be stranded and go from door to door in search of employment. If unfortunately, he does not come up to our expectations later, then we may have to deal with him in some other way. I think, we should ultimately point out to him that we cannot employ him.

7. What I have suggested above may not be a particularly good way of dealing with this situation, but I do think that some such method has to be evolved. In the United Kingdom and the USA, business firms send their representatives to the various universities trying to pick out bright young students. They engage them even before they leave the universities. In England it is becoming difficult to get candidates for the Foreign Service because the bright people are picked out by industrial firms even before they finish their studies.

8. We have therefore to be a little more alert in getting hold of these people. As we have fairly competent Heads of Missions in most of these countries with adequate staff, they could help us in picking them out first for the consideration of the Committee here and secondly for a more thorough interview if the Committee so suggests.

9. The question of Indians actually working abroad now is of a different kind. There can be no general effort to pull them away. The effort needed there is first to have full lists of them, secondly to separate the really competent men among them, thirdly to try to get them as individuals whenever we feel this worthwhile.

10. I would request that in official documents the word 'job" should not be used.

11. The note prepared for the Manpower Committee of the Cabinet can be sent to that Committee for discussion. A copy of this note of mine should be attached to it.

13. To Jagjivan Ram[1]

New Delhi
August 20, 1957

My dear Jagjivan Ram,

A deputation of the workers of the Shahdara-Saharanpur Railway came to see me today and gave me the attached memorandum. I have never heard of this Railway. It appears that it is some small light Railway run by Martins who, no doubt, have been making a good deal of profit out of it. The dispute concerning the workers has been referred to adjudication.

I was wondering why this little Railway was left in private hands. Probably, it is not worth acquiring and its rolling stock etc., is in the last stage of decay. But it passes through some very rich areas of UP.

Yours sincerely,
Jawaharlal Nehru

1. JN Collection.

14. To K.C. Reddy[1]

New Delhi
August 21, 1957

My dear Reddy,

I am told that some thought is being given to having mural paintings and frescoes on the outer and inner walls of the Vigyan Bhawan. I should like to be kept in touch with developments in this respect. Perhaps, you might know that when a famous Mexican mural painter came here last year, we discussed this matter with him.[2] We even thought of commissioning him to do part of this work.

1. File No. 28 (21)/56-59-PMS. Also available in JN Collection.
2. David Alfaro Siqueiros was in India in November-December 1956.

There is no question of his coming here now. But the ideas he put before me then appealed to me.

Yours sincerely,
Jawaharlal Nehru

15. To Lal Bahadur Shastri[1]

New Delhi
August 23, 1957

My dear Lal Bahadur,

I understand that Air Commodore Lal[2] of the Indian Air Force has been selected for appointment as General Manager of the Indian Airlines. I am glad that this step has been taken. Lal is one of our best officers in the Air Force. He is not only competent but is studious and conscientious young man. He has a big future in the Air Force. I hope that you and Humayun Kabir will meet him and have a talk with him.

Air Marshal Mukherjee[3] came to see me today and he was discussing the Indian Airlines. Now, that he and one of his special officers are going to be closely associated with Indian Airlines, he was anxious to make them a thorough success. There are three points that he mentioned to me.

One was that there should be a rebate on petrol. The second was about postal rates for the carriage of airmails which he said were very low and should be raised. The third was stoppage of sub-places where there was no traffic at all.

So far as rebate on petrol is concerned, this really is rather a paper transaction so far as Government is concerned. As for postal rates, I think that the normal

1. JN Collection.
2. Pratap Chandra Lal (1916-1982); commissioned in the IAF, 1939; absorbed into permanent cadre of IAF after War and held several posts till 1957; became General Manager and concurrently member of Board of Directors of Indian Airlines and Air India, 1957-63; returned to IAF, 1963 and held important posts; took over as Managing Director, Hindustan Aeronautics Limited, 1966-69 and its Chairman, 1969; Chief of Air Staff, 1969-73; Awarded Padma Bhushan, 1966 and Padma Vibhushan, 1972.
3. S. Mukherjee.

charge should be made. There is no reason why the Postal Department should get any special favour shown to it at the cost of the Airlines.

Yours affectionately,
Jawaharlal Nehru

16. To Humayun Kabir[1]

New Delhi
August 23, 1957

My dear Humayun,

I had a visit from an American from the State of Nebraska of the USA this afternoon. Evidently, he was connected with aviation there. He presented me on behalf of his State a gold plaque. Why I should have been presented with this, is more than I can understand. However, there it is.

This gold plaque is in recognition of our achievements in the advancement of global aviation. This means really the achievements of the Air India International.

I am sending this gold plaque to you and I suggest that you send it on with my compliments to J.R.D. Tata, the Chairman of the Air India International Corporation.

Yours sincerely,
Jawaharlal Nehru

1. JN Collection.

17. To Rajendra Prasad[1]

New Delhi
August 24, 1957

My dear Rajendra Babu,

It has just come to my knowledge that a committee has been formed in Delhi to sponsor a World Conference of All Religions in Delhi, and that a meeting of this committee was held in Rashtrapati Bhavan on 23rd and 24th June this year. I was in Europe at that time.

It is stated in the proceedings of this committee that you have been requested to inaugurate the Conference and the Vice-President has been asked to preside over it.

The objects of this Conference are entirely worthy. But we are put in some difficulty about it as some Foreign Missions are enquiring from us as to what this Conference is and whether the Government of India are sponsoring it or not. Apparently, the organizers have been approaching the Foreign Missions here and they have asked us to arrange to have some publicity given to it through our Missions abroad.

All this was done without any reference to the Ministry of External Affairs and it is only in the last few days that the Ministry has been approached; and Seth Achal Singh, MP, has seen some of our officers. He wants us to help in arranging for the accommodation etc., of the people who will come here from abroad.

It is rather unfortunate that all this was done without any reference to us and we do not quite know what to say in answer to the Foreign Missions who ask us about this Conference. Any international conference requires a great deal of organization as well as funds and I doubt very much if the Managing Committee of this Conference is capable of making any of these arrangements. On the other hand, it would be difficult for the Government of India to sponsor it. It has, therefore, to be treated as a private Conference which can be attended by invitees, arrangements for whom will be made privately.

Yours sincerely,
Jawaharlal Nehru

---

1. JN Collection.

18. Delegation to FAO Conference[1]

We have obviously to send a delegation to the FAO Conference. The delegation as suggested consists of six persons, that is, four officers, the leader and the alternate. That does not seem to me too big a number. We should, of course, keep to the minimum number.

2. I agree that in the circumstances the Minister of Food & Agriculture might lead the delegation. Perhaps he may not be able to stay there all the time.

3. As for the Maharaja of Mysore,[2] normally speaking I would welcome his being associated with this Conference and being included in our delegation. But a certain difficulty arises. He is the Governor of Mysore and Governors should not be, as a rule, included in our delegations because we do not wish them to leave their charge. It is stated, however, in this note that the Maharaja will anyhow be in Europe. I was not aware of this, and I do not quite see how he can go to Europe and leave his charge in Mysore. For him to go away would involve someone else functioning for him as Governor during his absence. If, however, he is anyhow going to Europe, then I would personally see no objection to his functioning as alternate. What an alternate means is not clear to me. Does it mean alternate leader? Or is there just one delegate and the other is the alternate delegate, the remaining members of the delegation being officers attached as associates? In that event I take it that if the Food & Agriculture Minister comes back before the Conference is over, then the alternate will be the leader of the delegation.

4. I think that the Home Minister should be consulted about the possibility of the Maharaja of Mysore going to Europe and joining the delegation if he is there.

---

1. Note, New Delhi, 25 August 1957. JN Collection.
2. Jaya Chamaraja Wodiyar.

19. Create Conducive Conditions for Tourism[1]

I have read the letter from the Transport Secretary.[2] With some matters I agree; with others I do not agree. However, I shall not go into all that at this stage.

2. The Transport Secretary should draw up a paper for the Cabinet containing recommendations of his Ministry. This paper should be considered by the Ministries affected such as Home, External Affairs, Finance, I & B, and Railways. When the comments of these Ministries have been received, the matter should be reported to me. Probably, it will be better at that stage to have a meeting of the representatives of the Ministries concerned to consider this matter. Then it will be ripe for Cabinet decision.

3. I have no doubt that tourism is most important for us from the foreign exchange point of view and should, therefore, be encouraged by us. The figures given in the Transport Secretary's letter, though perhaps satisfactory from some points of view, are really far short of what they should be. I do not consider fifteen crores an impressive sum.

4. I should like some calculation to be made about the net effect on our foreign exchange situation of foreign tourists coming here and Indian tourists going abroad.

5. There is no point in my referring to this matter in my fortnightly letter. What is necessary is that conditions should be created in all the States for facilitating tourist traffic. I do not think that the appointment of committees and officers with high-sounding titles yields results. In fact, I am beginning to suspect that this is a way of not getting anything done. In particular, I dislike "Directors-General" and the like. We are getting into the habit of having these big titles all over the place. It is not a title that creates a man. If we have got a good and competent man for this he will do the job whether he has a high designation or not. If we have not got that man, then all the designations in the world will not make him better than he is.

6. I am quite certain that tourist traffic in India can be increased very greatly. Among the difficulties are the visa system, which is restrictive and delaying, also Customs is a formidable barrier which only the brave and fearless can face.

7. As for publicity, I have had several instances of Americans coming to me and saying that they were surprised to find such a fine hotel as the Ashoka Hotel here. They had never heard of it before. Otherwise, they would have liked

1. Note to Principal Private Secretary, New Delhi, 25 August 1957. JN Collection.
2. R.L. Gupta.

to stay there. They were, in fact, staying in some other hotels in Delhi. On enquiry I found that the travel agencies normally booked these people for the other hotels in Delhi and not the Ashoka Hotel. Obviously, this requires closer touch with the travel agencies.

8. In the various places of tourist attraction, what is required is not a luxury hotel, but clean and comfortable rest houses with tolerable food supplied. Also, of course, good communications.

9. Please send a copy of this note to Transport Secretary.

20. To Govind Ballabh Pant[1]

New Delhi
August 25, 1957

My dear Pantji,

I enclose a letter I have received from Amrit Kaur,[2] with which there is a letter from the Church Missionary Trust Association Limited. I think that we should expedite this process of transfer of property to Indian hands from the foreign missionary organizations, and should advise Bihar and Madras Governments accordingly. The sooner this is settled, the better it will be for all concerned.

I shall be meeting Mr Measures[3] who has written the letter. But, before I do so, I should like to have your advice as to what we can do in this matter. When you write to me, could you kindly send back these papers?[4]

Yours affectionately,
Jawaharlal Nehru

1. JN Collection.
2. In her letter of 23 August 1957, Amrit Kaur, Rajya Sabha Member from Punjab at this time, requested Nehru to help J.B. Measures in his efforts to transfer the properties of Anglican Church to the Indian Church.
3. J.B. Measures, who belonged to Ireland and worked for Anglican Church in India.
4. Pant replied on 2 September that in August 1954 the Home Ministry had issued general instructions, 'to all State Governments to the effect that it would be desirable to facilitate the transfer of such properties from foreign missionaries to the Indian Church." He added: "I have asked the Home Ministry to address a general letter to them again emphasizing that every reasonable assistance and facility should be extended for having the necessary deeds executed without delay."

21. To Ajit Prasad Jain[1]

New Delhi
August 25, 1957

My dear Ajit,

I enclose a letter which came to me a few days ago.[2] Although it is signed, it might be considered really anonymous. I do not know what can be done about it. I think that you should bring it to the notice of Krishnappa and ask him about the two cases mentioned in it and any other information that he chooses to give.

Yours sincerely,
Jawaharlal Nehru

1. Ajit Prasad Jain Papers, NMML.
2. In a letter dated 10 August 1957, N. Krishnaiah, Ramakrishna and Ramakrishna Rao informed Nehru that they know two cases that when M.V. Krishnappa was Union Deputy Minister of Food, had taken bribe i.e., (i) Krishna Floor Mills were allotted the highest quota of wheat for which Krishnappa received a bribe of Rupees 40,000/-; (ii) similarly he received Rupees 13,000/- from Srinivasa Roller Mills.

22. Construction of AIIMS Buildings[1]

I have seen through these papers. It is beyond me to go into and understand these figures. All I can say is that I am alarmed at the way the estimates have gone up. I suppose that if we wait a little longer, the CPWD will revise their last estimate and add a few crores to it. Not being an engineer I can say little in criticism. But being, I presume, an intelligent human being, I dislike this extravagant approach to public funds and public buildings.

2. So far as the architects are concerned, I think it should be made clear to them that foreign articles are to be avoided. We have to get Indian products even though the foreign articles might be a little better or more shining.

3. As for the air conditioning, I am not clear as to what buildings are being air conditioned as a whole. That is , does this apply to the principal block of buildings

1. Note to Minister of Health, New Delhi, 25 August 1957. File No. 40 (127)/57-61-PMS. Also available in JN Collection.

housing the main Institute and Hospital or does this apply to other buildings such as residential buildings? I think that so far as the main Institute is concerned, and more especially the Hospital and research rooms, there is no escape from air conditioning. In regard to residential accommodation this is not so necessary. I am, therefore, inclined to agree with the architect and the CPWD people that it would not be desirable to drop air conditioning at this stage when the framework of the building is nearly complete. It may be, of course, that while we allow for all this air conditioning, the actual machine need not be fitted in now.

23. To Govind Ballabh Pant[1]

New Delhi
August 26, 1957

My dear Pantji,

I mentioned to you today a passage from Trotsky's book *The Revolution Betrayed.*[2] This was, of course, about the Soviet Revolution under Stalin. A part of the passage is as follows;

"....The actual establishment of a socialist society can and will be achieved, not by these humiliating measures of a backward capitalism, to which the Soviet Government is resorting, but by methods more worthy of a liberated humanity—and above all, not under the whip of a bureaucracy. For this very whip is the most disgusting inheritance from the old world. It will have to be broken in pieces and burnt at a public bonfire before you can speak of socialism without a blush of shame."

These words were used for Stalin's Russia. To some extent, though far less of course, they have a lesson for us. It is a lesson of human relations and human contacts between the governmental apparatus and the people, more especially, the police and the jail staff. I do not blame the police. They have to face very difficult circumstances. But, I do think that the mental approach has to be changed. Otherwise, we shall be constantly in trouble.

Yours affectionately,
Jawaharlal Nehru

1. JN Collection.
2. The book, written by Leon Trotsky in 1936, was published in 1937.

24. Removal of Statues of Foreigners[1]

Jawaharlal Nehru: I was venturing, Sir, to place before the House what the general policy of Government is in regard to this question of statues put up during the period of the British rule in various parts of India. There are various kinds of statues—some may be considered historical, some may be considered artistic and some may be considered, well, rather offensive in themselves, and of various types. Our general attitude has been, first of all, to remove such as might be considered offensive, and that too, gradually without making too much fuss and without doing anything to raise ill will between countries. We have removed some of those statues and we propose to continue doing that. There are those which have been historically significant without causing offences; we shall also remove them and put them in historic museums. There are those that are not important historically or artistically. I do not know what we will do with them; if somebody else wants them, we will make a present of them. In particular, regarding such statues as may be considered in a sense offensive to our national sentiment, we have taken them up and we do propose to take them up; but, we wish to do all this in a manner so as not to create international ill will and raise up old questions which are dead and gone.

S.A. Dange: On a point of clarification will the Government take census of statues in the three categories, those which are offensive, those which are historical and those which are artistic, and make a statement to this House at a later stage?

JN: I may mention to this House that these are not all statues. There are numerous paintings, some of high artistic value. Sometimes we have exchanged them for valuable articles of Indian art. So, we proceed in this way to benefit ourselves as far as possible and not to be burdened by them.

1. Statement in the Rajya Sabha, 26 August 1957. *Rajya Sabha Debates*, Vol. XVIII, cols. 1518-19.

25. Approach to Publicity[1]

Language does not consist of intricate long words. Language does not possess

1. Speech at the Conference of the States' Ministers of Information, New Delhi, 30 August 1957. PIB files.

powerful ideas being conveyed rapidly to a person. It should be simple and powerful.

How do you test the language you are using in your broadcasts, in your radio, which reaches the man who is a peasant, and produces a reaction on him. Language should not cause a burden on him, burden of difficulty and understanding.

These questions should be borne in mind. Any approach, let us say, to plan publicity must, first of all, be a thought out approach, not an odd approach. I suppose it can be thought out here and what you add to it in the States can be brought out here. It has to be thought out in an organized plan of campaign. While generally talking about the plan you should take bits of it, you may try to explain them, you may compare them with what is happening in other countries. That will be a process of education. If it is a book it should be in the simplest of language, with simple similies and metaphors and comparisons. If you are addressing the rural people, do not talk some thing which does not concern them except that which might be of interest to them.

When you read the Five Year Plan you see the importance that is attached to what is called public cooperation. I am not quite sure that public cooperation is a happy phrase. It is as good as any I suppose but I do not quite know. Not that we have not achieved good results. See labour, *shramdan*, all kinds of things.

The Community Development movement depends in the final analysis on public cooperation, and public response. If we don't have a large measure of public cooperation we disappear—that is much more true in the case of the Five Year Plan. The biggest thing we are tackling in this way is the Community Development programme, biggest in area because it touches or will touch the whole of our rural areas soon. It touches almost the type of persons whom you want to touch particularly.

Now, therefore, any publicity organized for the rural areas must be intimately correlated and coordinated with the Community Development programme. It must be part of it. It should not be considered as separate from it because that will be overlapping or pulling in different directions. In Community Development programme we have gradually built up an organization which is very big and far reaching and going down to the village level. You can almost immediately or quickly reach your village level workers. How far the organization works, well or badly, it is another matter but it is an organization and it is the biggest organization in India so far as I know and is becoming bigger and bigger. Now that organization should be utilized for this purpose in so far as it can be, I do not know how that can be done. It seems to me that a huge organization like this can be utilized for this purpose and we need not build up a new organization that will be wasteful.

When you are dealing with the public what is to be done is to create an impression on the mind of the person. Unless that impression is created nothing works out. While dealing with the people we are always telling them to be good. Personally, my own reaction is to get exceedingly angry if I am told to be good. I do not want to be told to be good. It is a habit in India of lecturing others to be good. Even if you have to tell them to be good, you have surely to tell them in a way that it does not appear that you are lecturing to them. That creates wrong reaction.

The main thing is when you think of public cooperation or of publicity you have to know at every step the reactions that are being produced, otherwise you are, by just talking through the air, imagining that you are doing things but actually they are producing very little results.

I am not an expert in advertising. But one thing which I try to do with or without success, is to try to understand, be receptive to public reactions, and try to have my hand on the pulse of the people. I do not always succeed, that is a different matter, but if I am before an audience—I seldom go to an audience with a thought out address because I do not wish to impose myself on them. I want to react to their looks, to their thinking. Of course, I have some broad ideas in my head but I want to fit into their thinking as far as possible. It cannot always be done because one goes off from one thought to another, but the deliberate attempt is to react to the audience; deliberately to be receptive to the audience and thus to impress your own mind on them. It is mutual effort. If you are merely telling them, without being receptive, they will not be receptive to you. In the same way, the individuals and the Government have to function in the way—with mutual receptiveness. If Government is to teach to the people, it has to be receptive to the people.

26. To Ahmad Said Khan[1]

New Delhi
September 3, 1957

My dear Nawab Sahib,[2]
This is with reference to your donation of fifty thousand Rayals to the Mecca University.

1. JN Collection.
2. The Nawab of Chhatari was the Congress Member of Rajya Sabha from UP.

268

I have been assured by the Central Board of Revenue that this will not be in the scope of the new taxation. It was the previous intention to exempt such cases but, in order to make the position quite clear, I think, an amendment is being sponsored to give power to the Central Board of Revenue to direct that a particular charity outside India should be exempt from the Expenditure Tax.

Would you now like me to forward your cheque to our Ambassador in Saudi Arabia?[3]

Yours sincerely,
Jawaharlal Nehru

3. Mustafa Kamal Kidwai.

27. Effects of War Predictions[1]

I think you should draw particular attention of the Home Ministry to effect of war predictions in some newspapers. Also to astrologers' forecasts of a coming war. Is it not possible to do something to stop this kind of thing? The least that can be done is to tell them forcibly that this must not be done. The astrologers should be warned that any publicity about war predictions will get them into trouble.

1. Note to Commonwealth Secretary, New Delhi, 5 September 1957. File No. 2-4/51-Pak I, p. 128/corr., MEA.

28. To Govind Ballabh Pant[1]

New Delhi
September 9, 1957

My dear Pantji,
I am told that the behaviour of some of our young men in regard to girls is becoming worse and worse, even in Delhi. Cases have been reported to me of

1. JN Collection.

girls working in the Arts and Crafts Emporium being insulted and asking for protection to be taken home when the shop closes. Even inside the shop offensive remarks have been made to them. Could we not do something about this matter?

Yours affectionately,
Jawaharlal Nehru

29. To T.T. Krishnamachari[1]

New Delhi
September 15, 1957

My dear T.T.,
Your letter of the 15th September about Pathak and the Dalmia[2] case.[3] I quite understand what you have said and how undesirable it is to go on postponing this important case. My difficulty is that I am responsible for sending Pathak with the UN Delegation to New York. If I had known much earlier about this Dalmia case, I would probably not have sent him, although he has been very

---

1. JN Collection.
2. Ramkrishna Dalmia (1893-1978); founder of the Dalmia-Jain Group of Industries which included banks, insurance and investment companies, cement and sugar factories, jute and paper mills, aviation, railways, collieries, and newspapers; propagated "one world government"; crusaded for a ban on cow-slaughter.
3. The Government of India promulgated an order on 11 December 1956 setting up a Commission of Inquiry to investigate into the working of a number of concerns managed by the Dalmia-Jain Group. Dalmia filed a writ petition in the Bombay High Court praying that the order be declared null and void. The High Court upheld its validity except a portion of the terms of notification which dealt with "securing redress or punishment" to act as a preventive in future cases. Dalmia filed an appeal in the Supreme Court against this judgement. The Government of India also appealed against the decision of the High Court holding a portion of the Notification invalid. These appeals were now pending before the Supreme Court where G.S. Pathak had to appear. Dalmia had also moved the Supreme Court for a stay order against the Commission proceeding with its work. The Supreme Court granted injunction restraining its work pending final disposal of the appeals.

helpful to us in the various matters that come up there. His coming back rather suddenly after having been there just for three or four weeks would be very upsetting for our work there.

While we should avoid, as you say, a long adjournment, it might not be perhaps difficult or harmful from the point of view of our case, for a relatively short adjournment to the end of November. In any event, I suppose the case will hardly be taken up before the middle of October. You gave me to understand the other day that it might be possible to arrange this in this way.

I shall write to Pathak and tell him that he will have to come back as early as possible.

The question of bearing the cost of his passage to India and back to the USA hardly arises, as that may be just the time when he is required there.

Yours sincerely,
Jawaharlal Nehru

30. To Bakhshi Ghulam Mohammad[1]

New Delhi
September 16, 1957

My dear Bakhshi,[2]
I am writing to you about that piece of land south of the Banihal, which you promised to give to Kailash Nath Kaul,[3] the Director of our National Botanical Gardens, for growing medicinal and like plants. The spot was chosen and, as you told me, everything was fixed up. On enquiry from Kaul, I find that he got a letter from your Government asking him to pay ten thousand Rupees for it, which he was not in a position to pay. Therefore, the matter has hung up.

I think, there must be some misunderstanding about this. Kaul does not want to buy the land or to own it. That will remain the property of the Kashmir

1. JN Collection.
2. Prime Minister of Jammu and Kashmir.
3. Brother of Kamala Nehru.

Government. All he offered was to utilize that wasteland for productive purposes, from which the Kashmir Government would profit. Will you kindly look into this matter and finalize it, so that work can start there.

Yours sincerely,
Jawaharlal Nehru

31. Autonomy for Indian Statistical Institute[1]

...3. The Institute is a public registered body which is largely carried on by Government grants.[2] There is a good deal of Government control over it, though not in the details of its working. I think, this is, on the whole, a satisfactory arrangement. Merely to make the Institute a Government Department would not be desirable. An autonomous institution basically controlled in regard to its policies, etc., by Government is much more satisfactory. If that is so, then how does it profit Government to have the satisfaction of saying that one or two buildings out of a large group of buildings of the Institute belong to Government? I should have thought that the arrangement made in paragraph 4 would be equally applicable to these buildings also.

4. I do not fully understand all this. You might perhaps discuss this question with Professor Mahalanobis who is due back in Delhi from the Soviet Union tonight and will probably spend a few days here. You need not tell him what I have written, but just find out how he feels about it. I am inclined to think that he will not like this proposal of the Finance Ministry. However, you can find out.

1. Note to Cabinet Secretary, New Delhi, 17 September 1957. Extracts. Also available in JN Collection.
2. Cabinet Secretary's note said that the assets representing the Government grant would not be mortgaged or disposed of by the Institute without Government's prior approval. It also said that the assets created by these grants should be treated as belonging to Government.

5. Anyhow, I should not like this matter to be hung up for long. The on-account payment suggested might be made immediately. The other matter is one of adjustment which we can deal with later.

32. Karan Singh's Proposed Visit to Soviet Union[1]

The Yuvaraj of Kashmir saw me the other day and he referred to the invitation issued to him long ago and repeated early this year from Mr Khrushchev to visit the Soviet Union. I told him that I saw no objection to his going to the Soviet Union. But, of course, this question should not be raised for the time being. We should wait till the Security Council meeting etc., was over. In any event, he will not be able to go there till April or May next year. There is plenty of time to wait and see.

2. Perhaps, you might write to our Ambassador in Moscow,[2] reminding him of this invitation and telling him that the Yuvaraj might be able to accept it early next year. For the present, the Ambassador need not mention this matter. But, later, if all goes well, it may be mentioned to the Soviet authorities. The Ambassador should wait till we write again on this subject. The Yuvaraj, if he goes, will be accompanied by his wife.[3]

1. Note to Foreign Secretary, New Delhi, 18 September 1957. JN Collection.
2. K.P.S. Menon.
3. Karan Singh and Yasho Rajya Lakshmi visited USSR in April and May 1959.

33. Subscription of Foreign Periodicals[1]

Shri Sunder Lal[2] of the India-China Friendship Association saw me today. He said that as Dr Zakir Husain had been appointed Governor of Bihar, he could not continue as president of that Association. Dr Zakir Husain had suggested that Dr Tara Chand[3] might be chosen for that post. I told Shri Sunder Lal that I had no objection and that this was entirely a matter between Dr Tara Chand and the members of that Association.

2. Shri Sunder Lal then showed me a letter he had received from the Editor or Publisher of *China Reconstructed* magazine which comes out in English. This letter stated that 20,000 copies used to come to India every month and that there were 105 distributing agencies in India. Recently, however, the import of this magazine had been suspended for three months, namely July, August and September, and it was probable that this suspension may continue later. The letter put forward a plea for the magazine to be allowed to come to India and pointed out that the foreign exchange involved was only about Rs 2,000/- per month.

3. I should like to know what steps have been taken about this magazine and whether they apply to other foreign periodicals also. Has action been taken on the basis of foreign exchange or on any other ground?

4. Some time back I wrote a note on the very large number of periodicals, mostly English or American, that are subscribed to by our Ministry.[4] I was astonished to see a list which ran into several pages. I doubted very much if most of these periodicals were read by anybody. Quite a number of them were third rate and not worth reading. Why should we subscribe to this very mixed

1. Note to Foreign Secretary, New Delhi, 18 September 1957. JN Collection.
2. (b. 1886); a revolutionary initially and later a follower of Mahatma Gandhi; participated in the national movement; established Hindustani Cultural Society at Allahabad, with the aim of promoting communal harmony; leader, cultural delegation to China, 1951; author of *China To-day*, 1952; editor of the monthly magazine *Naya Hind* in Hindi and Persian from Allahabad.
3. (1888-1973); Vice Chancellor, Allahabad University, 1947-48; Secretary and Educational Adviser, Ministry of Education, Government of India, 1948-51; Ambassador to Iran, 1951-56; Member, Rajya Sabha, 1957-68; author of *Influence of Islam on Indian Culture, History of the Freedom Movement in India*, Vol. I and Vol. II, *State and Society in the Mughal Period* and *A Short History of the Indian People*.
4. Nehru wrote to P.N. Haksar on 8 August that the list of foreign periodicals should be strictly scrutinized and revised.

fare? It seems that somebody has just ticked off every paper in a list without thinking as to what is useful or not. I suppose we spend a fair amount in subscriptions alone.

5. Also sometimes more than one copy of the same periodical reaches us here. I have received the airmail copies of the *Times Literary Supplement* and the *Manchester Guardian* and some weeks later the ordinary (non-airmail) copies of the same papers have come to me. Could not something be done to revise and limit this list only to worthwhile papers?

34. Law and Judiciary[1]

Mr Chairman,[2] friends and colleagues,
I think that to begin with I should pay my homage to the majesty and dignity of the law before I venture to say something more about it. We all agree, I hope, about the importance that this dignity and independence of the law should be maintained and kept up. We all agree, at any rate I am of that opinion, that law courts should protect the freedom of the individual, even against executive action, even against my own Government's action. These are basic principles in a democratic society with which we agree or should agree.

Now, having cleared up this basic position, let us examine how all this functions. The most dominating fact that stands up before us is the number of pending cases, the arrears. I have been looking through some of the papers distributed to you and I tried to add the numbers, and if my arithmetic is correct, it was 1,64,000. These are the pending cases, many of them for years. Now, this requires some explanation, some understanding. The Law Minister has just said that trying to cope with this the Home Minister has been adding to the strength of various High Courts. I should like the Home Minister or the Law Minister or the High Courts or the Supreme Court to undertake an investigation as to whether the appointment of new Judges lessens arrears or increases them. My own impression, not founded on any close analysis of facts, is that more the Judges,

1. Speech at the State Law Ministers' Conference, New Delhi, 18 September 1957. JN Supplementary Papers, NMML.
2. A.K. Sen, the Union Law Minister.

more the work, more the litigation, more the arrears. If that is even partly true, then the mere appointment of additional Judges, important as that is, of course, does not meet the situation at all. In fact, it might make conditions worse.

The other day in dealing with our normal governmental work, secretariat work, I ventured to circulate to many of my colleagues a certain article about what is called Parkinson's Law which shows how work grows, the more and more people you put there. Work expands always. Whether the work is worthwhile or not is another matter, but work grows. You go on putting officer after officer and the work will grow and you will always be shorthanded.

So, I was wondering if that Parkinson's Law, which is supposed to apply to governmental officers generally, also apply to this judicial and legal apparatus, and the more persons you have to deal with it, the more the work and the more the arrears. Surely, therefore, something is required to tackle this problem in some new way, and not merely by the simple process of adding to judges. I am not against adding to them at all. I am merely saying that that itself does not apparently help in solving the problem. I believe, again—I have just been adding in these lists—there are at present about 150 High Court judges in India. It is a substantial number. And I suppose that if all the proposals to add to them were accepted, there will be many more, and I suppose that the more the judges, the more the arrears of work later on, and the more the litigation.

There is something wrong about our whole approach to this problem. It may be that, quite apart from the ways in which the judicial machine works, we have done something which has created more offences, which has made people more litigious, or whatever it is. For instance, I have the greatest respect for our Constitution. But, undoubtedly, the Constitution has increased the work of the courts tremendously, with all kinds of writs coming in every time and holding up other work. All this requires examination, because the purpose of the law, and the purpose of the judiciary, is not merely to sit in wig and gown for a number of hours a day and look very learned. They supply a social purpose, that is, to bring about justice, to deliver justice to the people. That is the purpose obviously.

Or, let us take it further back. Law, as represented, let us say, by the judiciary, chiefly, apart from others, is meant to give a certain stability and continuity to a social order, more specially, the laws that are based on common laws and precedent and the like. But, obviously, every social order is a changing one. It may change rapidly or slowly, but it is a changing one. Obviously, you see the social structure changing. You see the machine civilization coming, a commercial civilization developing, and all kinds of new matters coming up before the courts. All that is happening, so that, while law gives a certain stability and dignity and protects people, it has to be flexible to meet the changing times, to meet the changing social order. Otherwise, something suffers; either society suffers, or the law suffers; one thing cracks up or both crack up.

You see how, even in a rather traditionally-minded country like the USA, great judges have really expanded the scope of the Constitution tremendously by judgments, because they wanted to bring that Constitution or the interpretation of that Constitution into line with modern conditions. The American Constitution was framed—I forget when, I think, it was about 175 years ago—a long time ago. America, as the rest of the world, but more than the rest of the world, has changed. A tremendous industrial fabric of civilization has grown up in these 175 years. Is it conceivable that if the old Constitution was rigidly interpreted in terms of the social structure of 1775 today, life or business or anything could be carried on in America? The whole thing would collapse. But great judges interpreted the Constitution in terms of these social changes, widened the scope of it and thereby gave it greater dignity and greater permanence. Otherwise, it would have cracked up.

So, the purpose of the law is not merely to give individual justice, which it is, but to keep pace with the social and economic structure of the society and of the nation. Otherwise, both suffer. Of course, the legislature keeps pace, is presumed to keep pace, by the laws it makes etc., and the judiciary is supposed to carry out what the legislature lays down or to interpret it. There has to be a great deal of coordination between all these different branches.

I have stated, to begin with, that I do believe absolutely in the independence of the judiciary—so, I am not criticizing that in any sense—but believing that one has to deal with this problem of the judiciary living in an ivory tower, unconnected with the world, unconnected with social developments, social forces, and everything that is happening, and thereby getting isolated from what is happening, from the facts of life. It was from that that the great American judges rescued the Supreme Court of America, rescued it by taking the facts of life, the facts of social growth of the USA into consideration.

It is patent that in India today, as in many other places, there is fairly rapid change going on in the social and economic structure. We are industrializing our country, we are doing this and we are doing that, all the time creating new social relationships and new problems. In order to meet these new problems, we legislate and we legislate a great deal, and we legislate often in a hurry. And then we bring forward amendments, because the drafting is bad or we have forgotten something. But all that indicates the pressure in which we live, the pressure of circumstances, the pressure of demanding fresh legislation and fresh this and fresh that. It is a changing society we are living in. That fact has to be recognized and understood by the judiciary, because whatever the law, the judiciary is meant to interpret the law. But whatever law the Parliament may pass, there is always a good deal left for interpretation, a considerable scope for it. It can be interpreted in a way which brings out the understanding of the social forces at play, or it can be interpreted in a reverse way. The first interpretation will make things smoother, in a changing world, while the second one will make it rigid and either bring about new laws, compel new laws to be brought or the cracking up of the social structure somewhere or other.

Now, the Law Minister referred to the practice which had grown up in various industrialized communities and countries, due to the tremendous growth of administrative, social and labour problems and the like, and the practice of having administrative tribunals, which are rather specialized. They are supposed to know their job a little better than others. Secondly, they keep in view not the rigidities of the law, but rather the object of achieving a certain successful result.

Suppose there is some labour trouble. Your object is not merely to punish this or that party by interpreting the law. That does not help you. You want to settle the dispute or settle something. Merely to say that this man has erred or that man has done this or that does not solve the matter in this complicated social framework where all these things are coming in. The administration itself is constantly becoming more complex and it is developing. The average court of law may not always be suited to consider these specialized problems.

I am not for an instant doubting the ability of the presiding officers, not at all. But, I am rather thinking of the procedures involved and the rigidity of those procedures and the time-consuming factor of these procedures. Here is an industrial dispute or some dispute where every day's delay may bring a crisis to the nation—an economic crisis or something. That factor, normally speaking, does not create the slightest impression on the high judicial authority which sits in majesty and dignity in its court regardless of the crisis occurring in the world or in the country. But it is of vital importance to the community and to the Government that this crisis should be avoided and the question has to be settled quickly.

The judicial system is excellent, the laws may be excellent, but the temper may be out of date. The temper may have suited a very leisurely time; it may not suit the time when people have to rush, hurry, tumble, fall, get up and go on.

All these factors make us think of how to meet this. I think, this is one of the reasons for this delay and arrears too. It is the temper which somehow reflects a very leisurely age and therefore, it is rather out of keeping with the storms and tempests of today. Therefore, it is worthwhile for you to consider this question of socialized administrative tribunals to deal with socialized administrative problems. That tribunal would have the same high quality person. It may be that a High Court Judge himself sits there or a Supreme Court Judge. Whatever it may be, it is not the man but it is rather the procedure which is involved and it is worth considering.

Of course, what is worth considering basically is how to get out of this outlook—vast number of petty and big cases coming and lasting years and costing a lot to the individuals and to the community and to everybody. It is something absolutely wrong. It is patent. It is a fundamentally bad thing and if it cannot be remedied in one way, you have to try another and I do not think that the way to remedy it successfully is merely to go on adding Judges. It is merely a palliative. It may lessen the work here and there but I will tell you the work will go on increasing that way and you have to approach it in other ways also.

I think that in this matter we have a right to request our senior and leading members of the judiciary system for their advice—Judges of the Supreme Court and the High Court—because, after all, it is for them to decide the merit of these things.

Having said something about this basic approach, I would say one or two matters which are important in a narrow sphere as well as bigger sphere. Delay is bad for a variety of reasons. It is also bad, because I think, it is because of delay that much of corruption takes place. As the Law Minister has said for every little thing—if you want to present a petition or want to expedite something—you have to give some kind of a gratuity or whatever it may be called.

If you want to deal with corruption, certainly deal with it directly as the Law Minister said, with the cooperation of the Bar and others. But the best way to deal with it is to avoid delay.

Then, as things come up, the room for corruption is necessarily much less than it might otherwise be. Sometimes, as Prime Minister, references are made to me, or they come to my knowledge. Take the income tax case. It is quite extraordinary how in an income tax case, where normally a man may pay income tax or not pay, decisions are kept pending for years. Where we have almost come to an agreement, the person concerned—of course, I am talking about the large payers of income tax and not the small ones—suddenly gets a bright idea to put in a writ or something of that sort. He puts in the same and the case is hung up for three years and nothing happens. I do not understand all the small details about law, but the fact is that large numbers of people can by some simple process in the law courts hang up the working of our laws regarding tax and so many other things.

What is wrong about the system? There is something wrong about it. I do not wish to deprive a person of the protection of the law; far from it. But law should not become the refuge of the, well if I may use a strong word, scoundrel. I do not say how to distinguish between the two, how to give every facility to the individual, this protection against executive action, against, if you like, the income tax authorities. Certainly, let him be protected but also, let that not be used by the wrong kind of person for wrong purposes. Of course, you can take action to that effect, but if things could be done rapidly it cannot be so used. It is the delay that always come in round and round whichever way you go. It is the delay which is at the root of all things.

Again, I am myself, to some extent, bred up in law and I have a certain sneaking regard for it and the processes etc., simply because one gets used to them. It is to be considered whether those processes which were quite suitable, as I said, in a 'leisurely age' do not miss their purpose and become obstructions in another age. Much depends, of course, on the quality of the judicial officers, whether they can do work quickly or not. I am not for a moment talking about the ways and processes only. It is important that judicial processes should be quick and should not be costly. Both these things are very important, and today they are both terribly costly and terribly long drawn out and, therefore, the whole purpose of that judicial system is not attained. We have lost it. The fellow is dead by the time you decide a case and he receives justice. The fellow is frustrated and does not care what happens.

Another thing about delays is the way our people are harassed by constant postponing of cases. The poor fellow comes to the court after spending some money travelling a long distance. He is made to stand in the court from ten o'clock in the morning to four o'clock in the evening and then he is told that the case has been postponed to another date, some ten or twenty days later. He walks back all the distance to reach his residence. This kind of thing happens again and again. I think, it is perfectly scandalous, this casual behaviour to individuals making them come and go like this, spending money and energy every time to see their cases being casually postponed. I do not know how to deal with it. That is a thing for you to consider.

Take even the election cases. I know my colleagues in Parliament travel from here 500 miles in connection with their election cases. They come back the next day because the Presiding Officer did not have time to attend. This happens half a dozen times. I just do not know how anybody in any country can carry on business in this way. It is scandalous, the casual way in which these matters are treated. Our busy men are made to run about because a person of leisure does not care to hurry up things and he takes his own time to do things. I think, it should be said so and known as such, that there is an amount of forbearance which the public can show to all these kind of things, but there is a limit to that forbearance and we have to change the procedure so as at least to make justice something which people can get and not merely dream about or talk about.

So, I am glad that you have all met here, and I hope you will find some way out of this tangle.

35. To Raja Mahendra Pratap[1]

New Delhi
19 September 1957

Dear Raja Mahendra Pratap,[2]
Your letter of the 15th September.

Accommodation for Members of Parliament is entirely in the hands of the House Committee of Parliament appointed by the Speaker and the Chairman. I have nothing to do with it and it would be considered rather improper for me to interfere in one of the prerogatives of Parliament. Apparently, you wrote to the Lok Sabha Secretariat who have sent you an answer from which it appears that the Accommodation Sub-Committee considered the matter.

I am afraid I can do nothing in this matter. My own Ministry is in urgent need of accommodation and we cannot get it.

Yours sincerely,
Jawaharlal Nehru

1. JN Collection.
2. Independent Member of Lok Sabha from Mathura at this time.

36. To Sukumar Roy[1]

New Delhi
September 19, 1957

Dear Shri Roy,[2]

I have your letter of the 17th September.

I have no doubt that the Dandakaranya Scheme[3] has great possibilities. Also, it will take some time to develop. We have to proceed in sections. We have also to take great care about the Adivasi inhabitants there. Otherwise, there will be much trouble.

What the future shape of this scheme may be, is difficult to decide now. There are obvious difficulties as there are three State Governments involved. We are at present investigating certain parts and a very good officer has been appointed as the Chief Executive for this purpose. He comes from the Punjab.

We should like the displaced persons who go there to be associated with this development right from the beginning.

Yours sincerely,
Jawaharlal Nehru

1. JN Collection.
2. A resident of Calcutta.
3. With a view to resettle a sizeable number of displaced persons from East Pakistan, an area of 80,000 square miles in Orissa, Madhya Pradesh and Andhra Pradesh was contemplated. However, the actual area was confined to 30,092 square miles comprising the Koraput and Kalahandi Districts of Orissa and Bastar District of Madhya Pradesh. For the expeditious execution of the Scheme, a Central Authority known as the Dandakaranya Development Authority had been set up.

37. Confiscation of an Art Object by Karachi Customs[1]

Yuvaraj Karan Singh of the Jammu and Kashmir State recently went to Europe.[2] He bought a marble figure[3] from some firm in Italy and asked them to send it on to him later. He did not indicate the route by which this should be sent.

2. This firm sent it via Karachi. It appears that the Karachi Customs, when they saw the Yuvaraj's name on it, decided to confiscate it and, I believe, it was sold.

3. This was about a month or six weeks ago. When I heard about this from the Yuvaraj, I was surprised and I felt that something should have been done by our High Commissioner in this matter. Do you know anything about this? I think, you should ask our High Commissioner[4] to enquire into it. This was a private purchase by an individual and it is very extraordinary that the Karachi Customs should confiscate it and sell it simply because of the Kashmir dispute.

1. Note to Commonwealth Secretary, New Delhi, 19 September 1957. JN Collection.
2. In July 1957.
3. It was a female head. Finally it did not reach him.
4. C.C. Desai.

38. Extension of Service Period[1]

Some four-five days ago, I passed this list which contains suggestions for several posts of Head of Mission. Subsequently, the President has been pleased to approve of it.

2. I have been reconsidering one aspect of it. Unfortunately, SG is not here as I should have liked to discuss it with him. I have had a talk, however, with the Foreign Secretary.

1. Note to Secretary General, New Delhi, 19 September 1957. JN Collection.

3. The question of extending the service period of a person who has reached the prescribed age of limit has often been considered by the Cabinet. We decided that in regard to scientific, medical, and technical personnel, the period should be extended wherever considered necessary, subject to fitness. In regard to others, extension might be given but this was to be not so usual.

4. I see that two of the persons mentioned in this list, namely, Shri C.C. Desai and Shri Venkatachar,[2] are both reaching their retirement age within the next few months. Appointing them will, therefore, mean automatically extending their period of service. I had some idea that Shri Venkatachar would be reaching his age limit soon, but I have no clear idea in regard to Shri C.C. Desai.

5. I think that we should avoid extending this period of service in this way. In special cases we may do so. But we should not make it a normal practice. Even if we want to continue the services of a particular person who has reached retirement age, the proper course would appear to be for him to retire from the Service and then to be engaged afresh.

6. I would, therefore, suggest that we should follow this course in future whenever we want a person to continue in our diplomatic service after he has reached the normal age of retirement. This should, of course, only apply to men in the regular Services. In the present case, it would apply to Shri Venkatachar, that is, Shri Venkatachar would retire normally from his present Service and we appoint him afresh to a new post.

7. The same would apply also to Shri C.C. Desai. But I feel that he is not particularly suited for diplomatic posts. He has a good deal of energy and ability and some use might well be made of this. For us to extend his period in the Foreign Service after his age of retirement would, therefore, not be advisable.

8. I should like SG to see this note; also FS, CS and SS.

2. C.S. Venkatachar, Secretary to the President of India at this time.

39. The Case of Helen TenBrink[1]

I met Miss Helen TenBrink[2] today and had a talk with her for about forty minutes. As a result, I was much impressed by her earnestness and desire for service. It may be that because she is of a type which does not think too much of personal benefit or comforts, that more worldly people do not approve of her. It may be that because of this the rich and comfortable missionary organizations in India do not like her, for indirectly her life is a criticism of the life of the average missionary here. It may be also that some of our officials also find it difficult to believe that a person can have no other object than the simplest forms of service without any reward.

2. Possibly, Miss Brink is rather an unusual woman. Some people might call her a little cranky. I like such cranks who do not think of themselves but of the work they do.

3. She has been in India now for four and a half years or more. No one has accused her of having done any harm to anybody. Accusation has come from the missionary organization which originally brought her out. Her brother is part of that missionary organization. In this conflict of views between the missionary organization and her brother on the one side and Miss Brink on the other, I am on the side of Miss Brink. I admire her attitude and sympathize with her.

4. I am particularly interested in the new concept of child welfare which the Poonamalle Child Guidance unit has put forward, that is, child welfare units can be started without much money and without even a building. Where there are children there can be children's welfare units. The way we have been looking at these things is always in terms of large sums of money and big buildings. It is refreshing to see children being looked after in villages with very small sums of money involved.

5. I cannot understand why a woman like Miss Brink should be ordered to leave the country. She does harm to no one, except perhaps to the reputation of some missionary organization. She is a competent trained person. She is actually

1. Note to Home Ministry, New Delhi, 19 September 1957. JN Collection.
2. Helen Dorothea TenBrink-Wyngarden (b. 1921); public health nursing educator from USA; worked in Kalamazoo City-County Health Department, 1948-50, Poonamalee Child Guidance Unit, Madras, 1952-59, Allegan County Health Department, Allegan, Michigan, 1960-62; instructor; pediatrics, Hagerstown Hospital, School of Nursing, 1962-63; public health nurse consultant, Wisconsin, 1963-67; Assistant Professor, University of Arkansas, 1969-70; public health nurse consultant, WHO, South East Asia Region, New Delhi, 1970-78; Associate Professor, public health nursing, Weslayan College, Buckannon, 1978-84.

doing some good work among children. No doubt, because there is not a big building labelled "child welfare unit", her work is not thought of much.

6. I am not in the least interested as to what her brother in India might say because he is himself a missionary.

7. Miss Brink told me that she used to get a large number of letters weekly from her family and friends in America. For some time past she has hardly had one letter a month. The post office people actually told her that they were returning her letters to America. Why is this persecution taking place and under what law is the post office behaving in this way? It seems to me that it is deserving of enquiry as to why this woman has been treated as she has been treated by our police or intelligence. Have they been influenced by the missionaries or are they incapable of understanding a person who has devoted herself to this ideal of village service?

8. I think that Miss Brink is an acquisition to India. Far from sending her away, I would be prepared to invite her to come to India if I met her in the United States. To think of deporting her at the Government's cost seems to me a fantastic idea. The Madras Government should be told our opinion. If they still have any doubts on the subject, please ask them to write to me directly giving me all the reasons. In any event, Miss Brink is not going out of India, whether the Madras Government likes her or not. If they do not want her in Madras, I shall see to it that she goes to some other part of India. On no account is she going to be deported from India.

9. I should like to find out from or through the Madras Government why this apparent persecution is taking place on this woman. Also, another matter which I mention below.

10. I understand from Miss Brink that a member of the Association which runs the Poonamalle Child Guidance Unit and a brother of the Director, namely S.I. Mathews and his son David applied for passports to go to England seventeen months ago. Mr Mathews has another son living in England. He wanted to go to see him. These passports have not been issued and he has been waiting for them for seventeen months. I should like to know from the Madras Government why this delay or refusal to issue passports has been taking place.

11. This case has rather upset me. It shows how some of our State Governments and even our Home Ministry can function on reports of some junior officers or intelligence people without any real enquiry.[3] I think, in future every case of

---

3. In a note (not printed) to A.V. Pai, the Home Secretary, on 16 September, Nehru pointed out that the charges against Helen TenBrink, "are based on vague allegations which can hardly be substantiated. I see that the District Magistrate of the place she worked in stated that her presence would be a great advantage to India. He is presumed to have known what her work was."

proposed deportation from India should be sent to External Affairs, or indeed should be reported to me. I hope also that the Home Ministry will not come to decisions on the basis of vague allegations and the opinions of some very junior and inexperienced officers.

40. Security Arrangements[1]

I am sorry for the delay in dealing with these papers that were sent to me nearly three weeks ago. I have now looked through them and I am noting some points. I have not yet had the time to go through these very carefully.

2. The notes give the number of security staff, both plain clothed and armed police, who are engaged at the Prime Minister's House, etc. Previously I received a detailed note about the security staff. The numbers given there varied very considerably from the present numbers. Possibly, some people who were engaged in this work have been omitted from the new list because they were not supposed to be dealing with the actual security of the Prime Minister.

3. In the note sent to me, it is stated that the rules included in the Blue Book for the protection of the Prime Minister have the consent of the Prime Minister. This is not correct and, in any event, it is not desirable to say anything about my consent. My whole approach to this question is different. I accept fully the idea of effective security. I am inclined to think, however, that the tendency is far too much on the side of numbers and building up what might be called Maginot lines of security. Maginot line has failed repeatedly in other places. Therefore, I feel that large numbers do not add to security. They are, not only politically and from the public point of view unwise, but they produce a false sense of security based on numbers only. In any event, it should not be stated in these rules that my consent has been obtained.

4. The rules deal with the Prime Minister's House and journeys in New Delhi and separately with the rules to be followed when I go out of Delhi. I do not think that these two sets of rules should be put together. It is not necessary for the rules relating to the Prime Minister's Residence and journeys in Delhi to be

---

1. Note on security arrangements for the Prime Minister's House and journeys, New Delhi, 27 September 1957. JN Collection.

sent all over India to various States who are not concerned with this matter. Therefore, the only rules that should be sent to the other States in India should be in regard to my journeys outside Delhi and not those relating to my residence.

5. In Chapter I, containing general principles, it is stated in paragraph 3 that 'the rules lay down the minimum precautions that normally should be taken, and it is left to the State Government or the local administration to decide if any additional precautions are necessary at place due to exceptional circumstances'. This precaution gives a wide latitude to the local people to do much more than is indicated in the rules. I know from experience that normally they go much beyond the rules, much to my inconvenience and annoyance. If they are actually urged to go beyond them, then my troubles will be all the greater. I can understand that in very special circumstances the local authorities might make some special arrangements. All that is necessary is to say so and not to lay down what has been said in paragraph 3.

6. In paragraph 6 of Chapter I, it is said that these rules cover all functions attended by Prime Minister. This is redundant and repeats in a different form what is said in paragraph 3. Also, to talk about "all functions" in this connection is not quite correct. There are public functions and entirely private functions. A private function is ruined by this excess of security personnel.

7. In paragraph 9, it is rightly said that display of large bodies of uniformed police or the stoppage of traffic for a long period does not improve security. That is correct. Large bodies of police, I repeat, do not add to security and are an irritant. Security does not mean a preparation for a pitched battle. It means dealing with odd individuals or possibly a small group. Further, traffic should normally not be stopped at all.

Chapter II—Prime Minister's Residence, etc.

8. The remarks I have made above about numbers apply here especially. An attempt should be made not to have too many people about. More especially, this is objectionable inside the house. It is stated in the rules that an armed orderly will guard the rooms occupied by the Prime Minister and, further, the armed orderly is to move about when I am walking in the garden. This is an infliction which I would be grateful if I could escape. I do not mind the orderly to be present opposite my study when I am working there in the day time or the evening. But I do object to the orderly accompanying up and down the corridor or hovering roundabout when I am walking in the garden.

9. In journeys in New Delhi, traffic should on no account be stopped and on no account should the route be lined by constables.

10. Para 21 of Chapter II. It is not clear to me how it is proposed to prevent what are called unauthorized persons coming within thirty feet of the Prime

Minister. If I go along a road, the distance between the footpath and my car can never be thirty feet. At a public function, also, it is quite impossible to keep this area of thirty feet clear and I would not like it to be so kept as I am likely to go right upto the people if I feel like it.

11. This thirty feet distance is even more undesirable and almost impossible in what are called private functions.

12. Private functions are of two kinds. One might be a small private dinner party. I do not think it will be right for any policemen to be hovering roundabout me in a small room at such a party.

13. In Chapter II, reference is made to New Delhi. But, as far as I have seen, thus far there is no reference to visits to Old Delhi. Broadly speaking, the same rules should apply to these visits to Old Delhi. There should be no stoppage of traffic or lining up routes by policemen. There might be extra pilot motorcycles when considered.

Chapter III

14. As I have said above, this Chapter should be quite separate.

15. Railway travelling. When the Prime Minister's train stops at a station, armed guards should not be too much in evidence in front of his carriage or saloon.

16. When the Prime Minister is travelling by special train, there is a tendency for this train to be a very long one and with crowds of people, mostly police personnel, or attendants, to be on it. This should be avoided. The fewer the persons, the better. Unless absolutely necessary, the restaurant car should not be attached as this adds to the length of the train and the number of people going in it. This also adds to the work of the security personnel and the railway staff.

17. Very special instructions should be issued that the normal railway is not upset and more particularly passengers are not caused inconvenience.

Chapter IV

18. Paragraphs 42 and 43. It is not clear to me why there should be both a warning car and a pilot car. Surely a pilot car is adequate on such occasions. If some kind of a previous warning is necessary, a motor cycle outrider can give it.

19. I am glad that it is stated that no large truck full of armed men should follow Prime Minister's car, This is one of the things which I have found most objectionable. I would, therefore, suggest that an attempt should be made to avoid too many cars following the PM's car, that is, there should not be any big convoy.

Chapter V

20. Paragraph 50, sub-para (iv), says that as a rule barriers should not be erected for roadside halts. I agree. I would go further and say that such barriers should not be erected at any time along the roads except near a meeting place where large crowds may collect.

I have not been able to read very carefully all the rules which have been sent to me. I have mentioned above, however, some of the points that strike me.

41. To B.B. Bhalla[1]

New Delhi
29 September 1957

Dear Shri Bhalla,[2]

I have received your letter of September 25th and have read it with interest and appreciation. You say in this that you are thinking of going to your old province, the Punjab, more especially, for some social and public service. There can be no doubt that East Punjab is suffering greatly from frustration and misguided leadership. It requires badly persons who could quietly work there and help in turning people's minds in right directions. I have always felt that Punjabis are splendid material. Unfortunately, they tend to faction. Fortunately, they recover soon also.

It is not clear to me from your letter what you mean by going to the Punjab. Does this mean that you are leaving your present work or whether you will continue your work and yet spend some time in the Punjab?

You have suggested that you should divide your income in some parts and send me one part every month for some public purpose. That is very good of you and, of course, whatever you send me, I shall gladly accept. But in sending this money you should indicate how you will prefer to have it spent.

I am leaving Delhi on the 3rd October for a visit to Japan.

Yours sincerely,
Jawaharlal Nehru

1. JN Collection.
2. General Manager, Hindustan General Electric Corporation Limited.

42. To Govind Ballabh Pant[1]

New Delhi
29 September 1957

My dear Pantji,

I think, I wrote to you sometime ago forwarding a copy of a letter from Maulana Azad about Maulvi Fazal Haque[2] of Khairabad. The Maulvi was a prominent figure in the rising of 1857 and was sentenced to life imprisonment and died in the Andamans. His grandson, Hakim Zafarul Haque, is now living, though he appears to be fairly old. It is said that he is in very straitened circumstances. Maulana has recommended that an allowance be given to him amounting to Rs 200/- per month.

I find that a reference was made to Hafiz Muhammad Ibrahim[3] about two years ago when the Maulvi was in considerable difficulty.

I do not know if any step was taken in this matter. Anyhow, I am sending you some more papers in this connection including Maulana's letter. I am inclined to think that we should help this man. At one time we were a little afraid of a number of applications like this coming in. But as a matter of fact very few have come. The only persons to whom we have agreed to give pensions are the descendants of Maulvi Liaquat Ali from Allahabad.

I think, therefore, that we might agree to give an allowance to Hakim Zafarul Haque. What we should give might be considered by you, if necessary, after some inquiry. The man is pretty old. I would suggest giving a thousand Rupees as a lump sum and Rs 150/- a month for life.

Yours affectionately,
Jawaharlal Nehru

1. JN Collection.
2. (1797-1861); eminent Islamic scholar from UP; served for sometime at the Delhi Residency as Cutchery Chief; resigned from service and signed a fatwa, denouncing the British; took active part in the 1857 uprising; mobilized the people of Delhi and Mughal princes against the British; captured by the British and transported for life to Andaman Islands.
3. Minister in the UP Government at this time.

43. To B.V. Keskar[1]

New Delhi
September 29, 1957

My dear Balkrishna,

Shiva Rao[2] came to see me this evening. He spoke about a number of matters, but his main purpose was, of course, this Price Page Schedule[3] business. He naturally looked upon it from the point of view of *The Hindu* of Madras. He said that *The Hindu* would inevitably have to withdraw some of its foreign correspondents which it could not afford to keep in future. He said that their New York correspondent and office cost *The Hindu* a lakh of Rupees a year and they had some other correspondents in important places. In Delhi, they had three full-time and one half-time correspondents. The half-time man did some reporting about the Supreme Court. They were trying to economize here and this half-time man was told that his services may not be needed in future and some other arrangement would be made. He was told this forenoon and a few hours later, Abid Ali, Deputy Labour Minister, telephoned to say that *The Hindu* should not take this step about this man. I do not quite understand all this business.

However, this is only the background. Shiva Rao's complaints were twofold: one was that inspite of repeated assurances about consultation, decisions are arrived at without consultation, and secondly, the final authority which Government takes in fixing this Schedule would give it the power to penalize papers it did not like and this would be a bad thing. He was not saying anything about the present Government, but rather about the future.

I do not know what consultations there have been, but obviously in a matter of this kind, there should be the greatest amount of consultation with those concerned. That, indeed, should be the normal practice. In a highly controversial matter of this present type, this practice is even more necessary. One should always give the impression of seeking cooperation even though we cannot always

---

1. JN Collection.
2. B. Shiva Rao, Member, Rajya Sabha at this time.
3. The Newspapers (Price and Page) Bill empowered the Government to issue from time to time an order providing for the regulation of the prices charged for newspapers in relation to their maximum or minimum number of pages, sizes or areas and for the space to be allotted for advertising matter in relation to other matters. This was in accordance with the recommendations of the Press Commission.

accept other people's ideas. Therefore, I suggest to you to keep this in view and give a chance to others to be consulted.

The other criticism of his may have some force under certain circumstances. I would not like Government to be directly responsible for fixing these rates and schedule in regard to individual papers, or, at any rate, they should do so on somebody's recommendations. I do not quite know how this can be done. But I suppose it should not be difficult to device some method so that some impartial authority could make recommendations to Government.

Shiva Rao mentioned another matter. He said that the whole idea behind this was the avoidance of unfair practices and unfair competition. That was good. But what competition is there between, let us say, an English newspaper in Delhi and a Hindi newspaper? They serve different clienteles. Or what competition is there between two papers serving different geographical areas? There is something in all this, but I do not know how it works out.

I do not want to delay this matter. It has become a headache and delay does not solve anything. But I am anxious that steps should be taken after an opportunity for consultation, so that no one can have a grievance about this. This should not delay much. Or else, is it possible to fix these schedules in parts, that is, one can deal with one part which is more or less accepted straightaway and a few days later the rest after consultation.

Yours sincerely,
Jawaharlal Nehru

44. To B.V. Keskar[1]

New Delhi
September 30, 1957

My dear Balkrishna,

We had an informal meeting of the Cabinet today. In the course of our talks, I mentioned this affair of the Price Page Schedule. We were all rather distressed

1. JN Collection.

at the turn events had taken and the difficulties that had arisen. It was clear, however, that we had to go on with this business and we could not leave it in mid air.

It was pointed out then that at the last Cabinet meeting when this was discussed, it was stated that the actual proposals for the Price Page Schedule will be put up before the Cabinet. If so, then it should be done. In any event, in view of the heated discussions that have taken place outside, it is desirable to have the backing of the Cabinet. You should, therefore, put them up before the Cabinet. You need not wait for my return from Japan for this.

Before you put them up before the Cabinet, I suggest that you might consult Pantji, Morarjibhai and Gulzarilal Nanda. I suggested this to them, and they have agreed to help you in this matter.

I understand that there is going to be a demonstration in front of my house tomorrow by some "journalists".[2]

Yours sincerely,
Jawaharlal Nehru

2. See *post*, p. 335.

45. Issuing of Passport[1]

If it is possible for you to see Chaudhari Mohammad Shaffee,[2] you should send for him and ask him if he applied for a passport and, if so, does he still wish to have it. Ask him why he applied for it, that is, to what countries he wanted to go and for what purpose. We were naturally intrigued that he should want to go to so many countries which should involve not only considerable expenditure, but a good deal of foreign exchange. It was difficult for us to understand how this

1. Note to Commonwealth Secretary, New Delhi, 30 September 1957. JN Collection.
2. (1918-1988); National Conference leader and an associate of Sheikh Abdullah; Editor, *Sach* (Jammu), 1940; Principal, Oriental College, Jammu, 1944-46; deputed by Mahatma Gandhi on peace mission in Mirpur district, 1947; worked for the restoration of abducted women and children and rehabilitation of displaced persons; Nominated Member, Lok, Sabha, 1952-57.

heavy expenditure could be met and we should like him to explain this to us.

Because of the above reason as well as because it was reported to us that he was likely to carry on anti-Indian activity abroad, the passport was previously refused. If he can explain the matters referred to above satisfactorily, the matter will be put up again for consideration.

Chaudhari Mohammad Shaffee has, I suppose, ceased to be an MP now.

46. To Balvantray R. Patel[1]

New Delhi
October 2, 1957

Dear Dr Patel,[2]

I have received your letter of the 30th September. I agree with you that conference should not be held in places which add to the expense. But, apart from this, there are usually other reasons to be considered too. I cannot say what the particular reasons were or are to have a meeting in Srinagar to discuss agricultural problems. The State Governments sometimes bring a lot of pressure to bear and want these conferences to be held at their headquarters.[3]

I do not think Srinagar is a very costly place for a conference, apart from the expenses of travel.

Yours sincerely,
Jawaharlal Nehru

1. JN Collection.
2. A resident of Ahmedabad.
3. Patel referred to the forthcoming conference of State Ministers of Agriculture scheduled to be held at Srinagar from 11 to 13 October 1957.

47. Concentration of Offices in Cities not Advantageous[1]

During the past few years, attempts have repeatedly been made in Delhi and, I suppose, in other cities also, to remove some offices to other places. The obvious reason for this was to lessen the congestion of the big cities and also to utilize unoccupied buildings elsewhere.

2. In spite of these efforts, little has been achieved. The principle of dispersal is always agreed to, but when it comes to giving effect to it, each office concerned objects on various grounds and the Minister-in-charge of that office supports the objection.

3. In the same way, attempts are made to avoid new industries being started in places where there is already a heavy concentration. But, again, these attempts fail and because of certain conveniences, a new industry is often started in the same concentrated area.

4. I feel that we have to consider this matter from the wider point of view and take effective steps. A particular reason for doing so now is the necessity for avoiding the construction of big buildings as far as possible for reasons of economy.

5. It is perfectly true that this concentration of offices and industries in particular places has some apparent advantages and is understandable. Once a major centre has come into existence, whether it is official or industrial, it tends to perpetuate its own growth. One office attracts another, one industry attracts cognate or related industries. A pool of common services and facilities is built up to meet the needs of the official world or the group of firms established there. A reservoir of skilled labour is established. There are probably some arrangements there for technical education. An official atmosphere is created or an industrial or business climate is built up. Because the area is big, producers of some goods and services are attracted to it. Thus, step by step, concentration grows and ultimately a giant city results.

6. All these have manifest advantages and attractions. To this we have to add the social and cultural attractions as well as the amenities offered by a large city.

7. A time comes, however, when the disadvantages begin to outweigh the advantages and, as growth continues, efficiency suffers. There is traffic congestion and a long time is taken by workers on journeys from their houses to

---

1. Note, New Delhi, 2 October 1957. V.K. Krishna Menon Papers, NMML. Also available in JN Collection.

the offices and back. Production, in general, and official work, in particular, suffer, and slums grow up. Disease and accidents take their toll.

8. These disadvantages are very obvious today in the really big cities of the world which have to face almost insurmountable problems. Sometimes, faced by these problems and difficulties, firms and offices have moved out to new towns where their employees and workers live near to their work place. It has been found that this has resulted in striking improvements.

9. As a city becomes more and more crowded, the cost of maintaining services rises sharply. Road improvements and traffic control become big problems. It becomes very difficult to widen roads because this involves the acquisition and destruction of existing buildings. The cost of land goes up and public housing becomes terribly expensive. Ultimately, all this high expenditure falls on the tax-payer. The cost of living in the big cities is usually much higher than elsewhere. Transport services may have to be subsidized.

10. We are undertaking in Delhi a comprehensive scheme of town planning. We have some excellent planners, architects and others engaged in this. In addition to our own people, we have been fortunate in getting the assistance of an expert team through the good offices of the Ford Foundation. This is not only helping in this major planning of Delhi for the future, but is also building up planners. Thus, we shall have an efficient team which can be used anywhere in India. It should be remembered that town planning is no longer confined to engineers or even architects who can lay down what appears to be a beautiful scheme. City planning has to take into consideration the life of the cities, so that it may move along smooth channels, each part of the city being to some extent self-contained. A school, a playing ground, a market place, a library, etc., should be within easy walking reach and should normally avoid the main avenues of traffic. All this becomes impossible in this unplanned growth of cities. Having once grown, the city becomes unmanageable and it is difficult to break it down to improve it. Sometimes the city spills over and satellite townships grow up round about. Usually, these satellite townships are not self-contained at all and are entirely dependent on the main city. They are residential suburbs and their residents go to the city for their various vocations in large numbers. A satellite township, therefore, is not a remedy. In fact, it makes matters worse. There is seldom local employment or local amenities. The perpetual dominance of the parent city over its satellite comes in the way of the development of the latter.

11. All these problems and disadvantages are now very evident in the great cities of the world. In India, perhaps the worst city from this point of view is Calcutta. But many others, like Bombay, Delhi, Kanpur, etc., are notorious for their slums. Probably, Madras suffers least from these disadvantages.

12. The question that now arises for our urgent consideration is how to halt

this progressive deterioration and to take steps in the other direction. This is no longer a matter of convenience, but of urgent and inescapable necessity. We must, therefore, try to put an end of this type of growth and, at the same time, organize a properly planned dispersal of offices and industries. The dispersal of industries is called for also from the point of view of a balanced growth of various areas in the country.

13. We must, therefore, consider afresh and with this new outlook of urgent necessity, the removal of certain offices from Delhi, even if this causes some inconvenience to persons or to work. That inconvenience will be temporary and I am sure that work will profit by this change as well as the individuals concerned. If we have to build up new townships, they should not be satellites, but self-contained townships. For the present, however, we should try to utilize existing housing accommodation in other places wherever it is available.

I am sending this note, so that this matter might be considered by all the Ministers of the Central Government as also by Chief Ministers. I hope that we shall take this up in earnest soon.

48. To K.C. Reddy[1]

New Delhi
October 2, 1957

My dear Reddy,

I am told that the External Affairs Ministry suffers from the fact that I am in charge of it. I cannot go about pleading their cause as perhaps other Ministers might in regard to their own Ministries.

External Affairs is desperately in need of accommodation. At present, what it has, is not enough, and even this is spread out all over the place. Our Special Secretary has just sent me a note which gives some indication of our difficulties. I am enclosing this note in original.

A proposal was made to me that the Ministry might use Hyderabad House for its offices. They are already using a small annexe to Hyderabad House. I have not agreed to the use of the main building, as I think, it is not fit for an office and do not wish it spoiled in this way.

1. JN Collection.

I hope you will be able to do something for my Ministry because work is suffering greatly. When I come back from Japan, I shall talk to you about this matter.

Yours sincerely,
Jawaharlal Nehru

49. In Absence of Prime Minister[1]

As you know, I am going abroad tomorrow morning and returning after two weeks. I am not issuing any special directions for the period of my absence. My old directions will hold good now.

2. In my absence, the senior Member of the Cabinet, who is present in Delhi, will function in any matter requiring his attention. Any really important matter will have to stand over till my return or, if it is necessary, it should be referred to me.

3. I hope that Cabinet meetings will normally be held weekly as heretofore.

4. I have been in formal charge of Defence and Finance Ministries in the absence of the Ministers. I have requested the Home Minister to take this formal charge during my absence and the absence of the Ministers concerned.

1. Note to Cabinet Secretary, New Delhi, 2 October 1957. JN Collection.

50. To Lal Bahadur Shastri[1]

New Delhi
24 October 1957

My dear Lal Bahadur,

Neogy[2] came to me today. He started by reminding me of a circular I had issued to Members of the Cabinet on the 8th June, 1957. In this, I had emphasized that no major step should be taken or commitment made without previous reference to the Planning Commission and later to the Cabinet.[3]

He then told me that in spite of this procedure laid down, you had made certain statements about a Shipping Development Fund being started without any previous reference to the Planning Commission. You had apparently referred the matter to the Finance Minister who had agreed and then you had apparently gone ahead with the proposal.

Neogy also showed me your letter to him of the 30th September on this subject.

I am sure you did not mean to bypass the Planning Commission, but in effect the procedure you adopted was wrong. This particular matter may not have great importance but I am sure that in future we have to be very careful. There has been far too much of separate decisions, sometimes after a reference to Finance, and this comes in the way of any corporate thinking and any real planning.

Because this matter was brought to my notice, I am sending a general circular letter to Members of the Cabinet emphasizing the procedure to be followed in future. You will get a copy of this.

Yours affectionately,
Jawaharlal Nehru

1. JN Collection.
2. K.C. Neogy was Member, Planning Commission.
3. For full text of Nehru's note see *Selected Works* (second series), Vol. 38, pp. 60-62.

51. To D.P. Karmarkar[1]

New Delhi
October 28, 1957

My dear Karmarkar,

I have your letter in which you have referred to the Defence Ministry's request for the services of Lt. Colonels Rao and Iyer. I wanted to speak to you about them myself. I would regret their having to leave Delhi. I should have thought that they would make excellent professors in the All India Institute. Indeed, I mentioned this briefly to Dr Jivraj Mehta[2] yesterday at Baroda. He said something about private practice not being allowed in the Institute. Further he said he was coming to Delhi soon and would look into this matter.

Yours sincerely,
Jawaharlal Nehru

1. JN Collection.
2. Finance Minister in the Bombay Government at this time.

52. Leakage of Finance Minister's Report[1]

The Prime Minister expressed concern at the publication of the Finance Minister's report of his foreign tour to the Cabinet in the issue of the *Amrita Bazar Patrika* dated 28th October, 1957.[2] He enquired whether, after the Cabinet meeting, any

1. Minutes of the Cabinet Meeting, 29 October 1957. JN Collection.
2. *Amrita Bazar Patrika* carried Krishnamachari's report to his Cabinet colleagues that the UK was not in a position to give substantial financial aid but West Germany had assured him to help India to tide over this foreign exchange crisis. Krishnamachari was understood to have revealed that much more aid was likely to materialize later in the form of Government and private loans, wheat loans, deferred payment credits, World Bank loans etc., to the tune of Rs 200 crores for one year. Assistance worth Rs 60 crores would come from West Germany and Rs 140 crores from the USA. Added to this was the assistance that was expected from Japan. According to him, the core of the Plan would be saved.

of the Ministers had met Dr Krishanalal Shridharani, Special Representative of the Paper. One or two Ministers had met him, but it was not between the date of the Cabinet meeting and the date of the publication of the report. The Prime Minister directed the Cabinet Secretary to investigate whether the leakage could have occurred from one of the officials after the preparation of the draft minutes.

2. The Prime Minister informed the Cabinet that the Australian High Commission had invited Shrimati Lakshmi Menon, Deputy Minister in the Ministry of External Affairs, to visit Australia for a period of two weeks. The Cabinet agreed that the invitation might be accepted.

53. Intelligence for Foreign Countries[1]

I have seen some of these papers. I think that the general question of our Intelligence set-up in foreign countries deserves careful consideration and revision. You have indicated that this is being done.

2. For the present I am, therefore, considering only this limited proposal of sending a new man to Peking. I think, there is much force in what our Ambassador[2] has written, though one of his points about the language has been met. A great deal would depend on the type of person who is sent. Thus, a real observer should be a trained economist and should also have political training. Mere intelligence training is very far from adequate for an appraisal of a situation.

3. In order to judge of a situation in a great country, the facts to be considered are more or less public, though occasionally information about some private reports or meetings would, no doubt, be useful. It is the capacity to judge of these public changes that is important. Intelligence is often far too apt to look at matters from a much narrower point of view and thus in the wrong perspective. Sometime certainly it supplies useful information.

4. However, what I have said above really applies to the broader consideration of the subject. For the present, as Home Ministry are anxious that someone should be sent and arrangements have already been made, I think that we should agree to the Home Ministry's request. We should, however, tell them that we

1. Note to Foreign Secretary, New Delhi, 30 October 1957. JN Collection.
2. R.K. Nehru.

consider that this entire question of our Intelligence set-up in foreign countries should be reviewed.

5. Our Ambassador in Peking should be informed that we have fully considered his criticisms and partly agree with them. We are considering the general question more fully, but for the present, in view of the desire of the Home Ministry, we think that we should send someone to Peking. The Shanghai post is, of course, dropped.

54. Lenient View Necessary[1]

Apparently this matter has been examined by you already. At first the Railway Ministry was inclined to give some kind of an extension to this man for various reasons. Subsequently, a police report stated that he was engaged perhaps in some communal activities. I have seen some of these papers and, to some extent, that accusation might be justified. As far as I am able to recount, the main charge is that when the book about *Religious Leaders* came out a number of these people put on black badges in protest.[2] That was undesirable. But it was a moment of excitement when, because of exaggerated and false propaganda by some sections of the press, the feelings of the Muslims were greatly excited and it is possible that some people may go astray because of this. That by itself, I think, should not be a bar. We know that at such moments of excitement Hindus or Muslims or Sikhs are greatly worked up. Even those who normally function correctly lose their balance. We have seen this happening in the Punjab when both Hindus and Sikhs who are supposed to be nationalists, have behaved wrongly. Yet we have put up with them and tried to win them over except in very serious cases.

2. I should like you to look into this matter again and, particularly, to ask for a report from Nagpur where he has been functioning for some time. If there is

---

1. Note to Jagjivan Ram, Minister of Railways, New Delhi, 30 October 1957. JN Collection.
2. Actually, the book entitled *Living Biographies of Religious Leaders* by Henry Thomas and Dana Lee Thomas, was first published in the USA in 1940, and later by Bharatiya Vidya Bhavan, Bombay, in 1955 under Bhavan's Book University Series. For more details, see *Selected Works* (second series), Vol. 35, pp. 253-271.

nothing more against him, then perhaps some leniency might be shown to him and an extension of a year or so might be given.

3. This is entirely for you to decide. But my suggestion is that you might have this more fully examined before coming to a final decision.

55. To Govind Ballabh Pant[1]

New Delhi
October 30, 1957

My dear Pantji,

Thank you for your letter of October 30th about Nagarvala[2] who is in charge of the police force on the Goa border.[3] At our request, Nagarvala came here some days ago and had long talks with our Foreign Secretary and others.

It seems to me that Nagarvala is a competent officer though he has occasionally tended to go a little further in the exercise of his duties than he might have done. The chief difficulty appears to be that he has not got on well with the Mysore authorities. In this matter I am not at all sure that the Mysore authorities have been completely in the right. We have suggested to Nagarvala that he should go to Bangalore and develop adequate contacts with the Chief Minister and others there. Some other instructions have also been given to him. I think that for the present at least he might be kept on the Goa border. Any change now might not be desirable. We may, however, consider this matter again later.

Yours affectionately,
Jawaharlal Nehru

1. JN Collection.
2. Jamshid Darab Nagarwala (b. 1914); joined Government Service, 1937; worked as Assistant Superintendent of Police and Deputy Superintendent of Police at several places before Independence; on deputation to Government of Hyderabad, 1948-49; Deputy Commissioner of Police, Bombay, 1949-50; Principal, Police Training School, Nasik, 1950-53; Deputy Inspector General of Police, Belgaum, 1953-54; Deputy Inspector General of Police, Bombay, 1954-61; Inspector General of Police, 1961-63; Officer on Special Duty, 1963.
3. Nijalingappa, the Chief Minister of Mysore, and Violet Alva, Union Deputy Minister for Home, had criticized Nagarvala. The Goa border was now shared by two States—Bombay and Mysore.

56. To Humayun Kabir[1]

New Delhi
October 30, 1957

My dear Humayun,

I have your two letters of 29th and 30th October.[2] I am afraid you are raising questions which would add to our difficulties. It is unusual and not to be encouraged for a Minister to go abroad for subjects which have nothing to do with his particular work. It is even more unusual, and in fact there is no precedent for it yet, for a Governor to do so.

The other day I mentioned this casually to some of my colleagues and the impression I gathered from them was that it would not be proper for a Minister to go in this way. As for the Maharaja,[3] I am quite sure it is undesirable for a Governor to leave India in this way. There was another invitation to him for a Philosophical Congress next year somewhere in Italy. In fact, I have written to the Maharaja about it. This is a year hence and I did not wish to decide now.

Tomorrow we are having an informal meeting of our Cabinet and I shall consult them about the possibility of your going.[4]

Yours sincerely,
Jawaharlal Nehru

1. JN Collection.
2. Humayun Kabir had expressed his desire to visit Australia to attend the Philosophers' Conference which was to be held there in December 1957 and sought Nehru's consent for the same.
3. Maharaja of Mysore, Jaya Chamaraja Wodiyar.
4. After consulting some of his colleagues on 31 October, Nehru wrote to the Cabinet Secretary: "...we felt that, in the circumstances, Shri Humayun Kabir might go to this conference."

II. EMPLOYEES' UNREST

1. Firing on Municipal Sweepers[1]

...Jawaharlal Nehru: May I say a few words?

    Ananthasayanam Ayyangar: The Leader of the House will have preference over others normally.

JN: The motion for adjournment to consider the matter, I take it, means that this matter—what has happened—should be discussed properly in this House.[2] Then the House may decide as it chooses. Now, if it is a question of looking into this matter thoroughly, every aspect of it, so far as Government is concerned, we are entirely in agreement with it. There is no question of a matter of this kind being passed by, by-passed, hushed up or anything. The question is what will be the best time when this House has as full possession of the facts as it can be, so that it can discuss it?

Whether it is this motion or any other motion—it is immaterial what form the motion takes—Government would like this matter to be considered by this House. But all I would say is that it would be desirable, I take it, to consider it when as many facts as possible are available.

Now we are just within less than 24 hours of this very unfortunate occurrence. As honourable Members know, only yesterday I said something about it. Within an hour of what I had said yesterday, my colleague, the Health Minister, met the representatives of the Sangh[3] and in fact the matter appeared to be—so far as the demands were concerned—well on the way to a settlement.... That was my information. Then late in the afternoon, he informed me of the present occurrence.

Now, nobody can doubt that it is a tragic occurrence. There is no doubt about it, and it deserves the fullest and the most impartial inquiry and any action that

---

1. Speech in the Lok Sabha, 1 August 1957, *Lok Sabha Debates* (second series), Vol. IV, cols. 6389-6390. Extracts.
2. This refers to the firing on the striking Municipal sweepers on 31 July 1957 leaving one worker dead and two injured. The workers were demanding revision of pay scales, provision of gratuity and medical facilities etc.
3. The representatives of the Delhi Municipal Workers' Sangh met D.P. Karmarkar, Union Minister of State for Health.

may come out of that inquiry. We are all agreed about that, whatever side of the House we may sit. The point is, how best to approach, to go into this matter, and in what circumstances the House can consider it fully. Government is prepared to give full time to the House. I do not mind whether the discussion is in the shape of this motion—adjournment motion—or any other motion. It is immaterial. It is not that we shirk the discussion.

But I would submit for your consideration what would be the proper time for such a discussion in this House. I think, it would probably be better if we had fuller facts. Neither my colleague, the Home Minister, nor anyone who has been inquiring, has been able to get all the facts. Some of the honourable Members have visited the place. I intended visiting the place this morning, but I was told that it would not be a suitable time. I am going probably sometime today. But my going there and seeing the place, of course, is not an inquiry. It is just satisfying an urge that I may have. That is all. But I can assure the House that nobody wants an inquiry into this matter in a hush-hush way. We want a full consideration of it, a full inquiry. It is not that the prestige of Government is involved in this matter so that Government may foolishly try to hush up something or postpone something. We want the fullest inquiry, as the House wants it, and we want action taken as a result of that inquiry. We also want this House to consider this matter fully. As to when it should consider it, and in what form, it is for you to consider.[4]

4. See also *post,* pp. 369-372.

2. To M.D. Tumpalliwar[1]

New Delhi
August 5, 1957

My dear Tumpalliwar,[2]

I have received the telegram signed by you and others in which you suggest that the Rajya Sabha should be summoned immediately to consider the Essential Services Bill. The Rajya Sabha will, of course, be meeting before long. Even if it is summoned forthwith, it will take some days for it to meet. The difference between the two dates will not be very great. I do not think, therefore, that it will serve any useful purpose to upset our present arrangements by summoning the Rajya Sabha just a few days earlier.

In the event of a strike, we have to take action soon. We cannot even afford to wait a few days for that. If the strike does not take place, then the need for immediate action is much less. So, in either event, it will not be helpful to change the date of the summoning of the Rajya Sabha.[3]

Yours sincerely,
Jawaharlal Nehru

1. JN Collection.
2. M.D. Tumpalliwar (1910-1971); imprisoned during freedom movement; General Secretary, Nagpur Pradesh Congress Committee, 1948-51 and its President, 1956; Member, Rajya Sabha, 1956-62.
3. As the call to strike by the P & T Employees' Federation was withdrawn on 8 August 1956, the Essential Services Maintenance Bill was not taken to Rajya Sabha, after it had been passed by the Lok Sabha on 7 August.

3. On Posts & Telegraph Employees' Strike[1]

Comrades and friends,
I have not spoken to you on the radio for a long time. I am sorry for that, because I should like to keep in touch with you as much as possible. I prefer the personal touch to the radio and I take advantage of this personal approach whenever I can. But even so, the radio is increasingly becoming a way of reaching large numbers of people. It is important that our people should take interest in the vital problems that affect them and the nation. Every problem that affects India as a whole, affects each one of us, whatever our station or occupation. Thus, the Five Year Plan and the Community Development Schemes and so many other things that we are doing in the country affect everyone, the farmer, the industrial worker, the technician, the scientist, the engineer and so many people engaged in transport, administration and the manifold activities of a great country. If prices rise, they affect all of us, more especially, those of small means. We face today critical situations both internally and externally, and it is in the context of these situations that every problem has to be considered. That indeed, is the essence of planning and of an integrated approach to our problems. Otherwise, an isolated step, however desirable in itself, might well have grave results on our economy. Perhaps, it is to some extent, due to our lack of success in our planned approach that the difficulties of today have arisen even though some of them are due to factors beyond our control.

I am addressing you today, more especially, in regard to the threatened strikes by the Posts and Telegraph workers as well as others. First of all, I should like to say that it is not by threats or the language of threats or by counter-threats that we can resolve our problems at any time, more especially, when we face critical situations. We must give up this approach and develop the cooperative attitude and the objective approach. Strikes may be legitimate or not in particular circumstances, and the strikes has been the old and well-recognized weapon of industrial labour to better their conditions. But I would earnestly suggest, that the time has come when other methods should be evolved both for the benefit of labour as well as of the community at large. There can be no doubt that strikes not only impede production, which is so essential for us today, but also bring about an atmosphere of conflict and ill will which we must avoid. If we are to avoid strikes, lockouts and the like, we must have effective steps of solving disputes equitably as they arise. At present, these methods require great

1. Broadcast to the nation, New Delhi, 5 August 1957. AIR tapes, NMML. Original in Hindi.

309

improvement and I recognize that. So far as Government is concerned, its methods are often cumbrous and slow-moving. We must improve them.

Recently, a conference of representatives of Government, employers and employees in industrial concerns was held and the resolutions of this conference broadly pointed in the right direction.[2] I welcome them. So far as industries are concerned, we are moving I hope towards a progressive participation of workers in the management. These industries are the joint concerns of all, and the workers have a special interest in them, and they should have their say. In the administrative services, the position is different; but even there, there should be a great deal of cooperation.

During the few minutes at my disposal now, I cannot go into the past history of the demands and disputes relating to the Posts and Telegraph workers. In the main, their demand was for a Pay Commission. There were also a number of other demands. About two weeks ago, speaking on a resolution on a Pay Commission in the Lok Sabha, the Finance Minister and I stated that we were agreeable to having a full enquiry into the pay structure in the context of today, keeping in view the economic situation and our development plans.[3]

A few days ago, I met a large deputation of the National Federation of Posts and Telegraph employees.[4] We had a friendly talk for over an hour and discussed various matters. In particular, I explained to them our decision to have a Pay Commission and the context in which we thought this should function. On an enquiry being made about interim relief, I told them clearly that this matter would also be considered by the Pay Commission who could make interim reports containing such recommendations as they thought fit and proper. About other matters, I told them that they could be discussed by us fully in the manner suggested. I was happy at this meeting and I came away with the firm belief that the proposed strike would be called off. The next morning I found that I was mistaken, and in fact, the strike decision was confirmed. I was much pained at

---

2. After two-day deliberations, the Indian Labour Conference suggested on 12 July 1957 the setting up of tripartite wage boards for fixation of fair wages for certain industries. The Conference also discussed the issues of model rationalization, discipline, industrial peace etc.

3. Nehru spoke on the resolution on 19 July 1957. See *Selected Works* (second series), Vol. 38, pp. 62-70.

4. On 26 July 1957. See *Selected Works* (second series), Vol. 38, p. 345. Nehru met several representatives of the employees such as Nath Pai, Chairman of the Confederation of Central Government Employees' Unions and Associations, on 4 August and B.N. Ghosh, Secretary-General of the Federation of Posts and Telegraph employees, on 6 August, after this broadcast.

this and more particularly at the fact that this had been done after our friendly talk and without any further reference to me.

I do not wish to argue this matter or to blame anyone. But both as a member of the Government and as an individual, I am concerned, together with my colleagues, to prevent such an unhappy development taking place, and if unfortunately, it does take place, then to take such measures as become necessary for the protection of this vital service of essential importance to the community and the whole country. We have, therefore, regretfully had to introduce a Bill in the Lok Sabha for the maintenance of essential services. This Bill need not and will not come into effect, if there is no strike.

I realize that the rise in food prices and the cost of living has hit our people hard, not only the Posts and Telegraph and the other employees of Government but even more so, large numbers of others. It is up to us to find ways and means to help them, but the method we adopt must not be one which might ultimately aggravate the disease. The whole object of our development plans is to raise the standard of living of our people. That is, the real wages should go up and not merely the artificial wages which are countered constantly by a rise in the price level of essential commodities. I have no doubt, that we shall achieve this objective but sometimes we have to go through periods of strain and difficulty as today and then we have to be careful not to take a false step. It is for this reason, that we are appointing a Pay Commission headed by an eminent Judge of the Supreme Court, which will go into these questions in all their aspects and make such suggestions as are not only helpful to employees of Government but also keep in view the whole community and our economy and future development. As I have said, they can make interim reports about relief or other matters. I do not know, what more the Government could do in these circumstances. If there are other problems apart from pay and allowances, these should be dealt with separately and, I hope, as speedily as possible.

As I have said above, I am most anxious that we should evolve suitable methods of frequent consultation to consider problems as they arise. We are trying to evolve such methods in our various departments of Government. I hope that these methods will bring about a meeting of the people concerned as equals and as partners in a common undertaking and not as superiors and inferiors or as those in conflict with each other. Our objectives are the same and there is no reason why our methods should not be friendly and cooperative in order to realize those objectives and avoid methods of strikes and conflicts involving ill will and injury to all concerned. I do not understand how and why the Federation of the Posts and Telegraph employees or other organizations should think in terms of a strike now. A strike can only do harm to them as well as to the community. I still hope that they will change their minds and put an end to this wrong approach. I am sure, the great majority of the Government of India employees in the Posts and Telegraph Department as well as others do not wish to strike and would much prefer that their problems were dealt within cooperative ways. If, however, unfortunately the strikes take place, then it must be remembered that these are not ordinary strikes in industrial undertakings but they concern the essential services of the community and affect its intimate life. No Government and no citizen can remain as a helpless spectator to this injury done to the community. It becomes everyone's duty, therefore, to help in meeting the situation and to maintain these essential services. I repeat the hope, however, that such a contingency will not arise.[5]

I have referred to the grave problems that confront the country both internally and externally. We have the problem of foreign exchange, which is casting a heavy burden on us and which is coming in the way of our development schemes, which means so much to our people. There are many internal problems. As you know, various taxation measures have been proposed which cast a considerable burden on our people. Our determination to proceed with our Five Year Plan and build up the resources of our country and increase the people's living standards has compelled us to take these measures. There are external dangers also and grave risks against which we have to be constantly on the guard. This is the situation that confronts us and this requires unity and common endeavour and hard work above everything else. I do earnestly hope that our people who have endured so much in the past and who are anxiously looking forward to the better days to come, will rise to this great occasion and decide to face the problems and perils that confront us with unity and determination, setting aside the smaller problems of the day.

We live in an age of revolutionary changes, technical and other, and the dreadful symbol of this change is the hydrogen bomb. The old order changes yielding place to the new. If we are to succeed in this changing revolutionary age, as we must and will, we shall have to get out of the old ruts of our thinking and the old ways of action and conflict and build up an unbreakable front of unity of outlook and endeavour. Thus we shall serve India and progressively bring happiness to our people, who have suffered from poverty so long.

---

5. While reacting to Nehru's broadcast, V.G. Dalvi, President of the National Federation of the Posts and Telegraph employees, laid down three conditions for the withdrawal of the proposed strike: grant of interim relief, withdrawal of Essential Services Maintenance Bill, and an assurance that the recommendations of the Pay Commission would be accepted and implemented.

4. Action Regarding Strikes[1]

The Prime Minister briefly referred to the talk he had with the representatives of the Posts & Telegraph employees on 6th August, 1957. Their demand was for an immediate interim relief of Rs 15/- per month. Conceding this demand would have committed Government to an expenditure of several crores of Rupees. The Prime Minister, therefore, merely referred them to his broadcast talk of 5th August, 1957, in which he had clearly stated Government's position in regard to interim relief.

2. The Cabinet then decided that the Essential Services Maintenance Ordinance should be promulgated in the afternoon of today and the Ministry of Home Affairs should address the other Ministries with regard to the amendment of the Civil Services (Conduct) Rules, already approved by the Cabinet, and the warning to be given to Unions and Associations of Central Government employees against joining the Confederation which has not been recognized by Government.

3. It was decided that, for the present, only the two Departments of Posts & Telegraph and Civil Aviation should be notified under the Ordinance as "essential services". There was some discussion whether the President himself should sign the orders to be issued under the Ordinance. In order to avoid risk of controversy, it was decided that the President should be requested to sign these orders.

4. The Minister of Defence suggested, and the Cabinet agreed, that the Prime Minister might make a statement in Parliament on 8th August giving a gist of the talks that he and other Ministers had with the representatives of the Posts & Telegraph employees. It was desirable to keep Parliament in touch with the efforts made by Government to come to a settlement and the assurances given by them in respect of the employees' demands.

5. The Minister of Home Affairs suggested that the Ministry of Defence might issue general orders to their local Commanders to give such help as they can to the State Governments in respect of these strikes. The Cabinet agreed that such orders would be helpful.

---

1. Minutes of the Cabinet Meeting, New Delhi, 7 August 1957. JN Collection.

5. To Abul Kalam Azad[1]

New Delhi
August 7, 1957

My dear Maulana,

I enclose a copy of a letter from the Delhi State Teachers' Association.[2] It appears that the Delhi State is not doing anything in this matter. I hope your Ministry will take interest in it before the situation gets worse.

Yours affectionately,
Jawaharlal Nehru

1. JN Collection.
2. Ram Prakash Gupta, General Secretary, Delhi State Teachers' Association, conveyed on 5 August 1957 their decision to observe the chalk down strike for four days from 20 to 23 August in view of failure of the Government to redress their grievances. To make matters worse, the Directorate of Education, Delhi issued a circular reducing their salaries.

6. To Sampurnanand[1]

New Delhi
August 7, 1957

My dear Sampurnanand,

Thank you for your letter of August 6th, about the Posts and Telegraph strike etc.[2]

During the last two or three weeks, while we have discussed the question of this strike and other strikes of Central Government employees, we have had

1. JN Collection.
2. Sampurnanand referred to the open support from certain political parties to the call to strike and resentment among the lower paid Government servants about the disparity between their emoluments and Central servants'. He mentioned the Intelligence reports which indicated that "various classes of State employees, not excluding the police, feel that the Government puts on a bold front in the beginning...the only way to make it see reason is...the threat of a powerful strike."

constantly before us the question of State Government employees and the reactions on them of any decision affecting the Central Government employees only. The whole position is illogical and undesirable. As you have noticed, we have mentioned this matter in the terms of reference. It would have been difficult to enlarge this enquiry, so as to include everybody. But, I have no doubt that this whole question has to be reviewed in some way or other.

I think you are right that this matter has not been handled as well or as wisely as it might have been. We are at fault, not so much in regard to the Pay Commission matter, but because our procedures are terribly cumbrous. The P & T demands have been before our Communications Ministry for months and months. Some of them had been accepted, but final sanctions could not be given because of delays in other Ministries, notably Finance. Sometimes, the Home Ministry comes into the picture also. We shall have to evolve better methods.

As a matter of fact, however, we announced our general agreement to the appointment of a Commission of Enquiry right at the beginning of this session of the Lok Sabha. This was done in the course of a discussion on a resolution.

You refer to the judicial enquiry in a recent case of police firing in Delhi, when a sweeper met his death.[3] I hold rather strong views about police firing. I think, it is hardly ever justified, and almost always it produces harmful results. If one judges from the actual situation immediately before the firing, it might be justified. But that means that a situation is allowed to arise, out of which there is no escape. I have no doubt that in the Delhi case, any intelligent person could have handled it without firing, even though at the last moment firing might have been justified.

I think that most of our problems in the last year or more, have been due to police firing at crowds, whether in Bombay or Ahmedabad or Patna or elsewhere. Nothing injures the reputation of Government more than recourse to firing. Personally, I think that policemen should not have firearms. Armed police might have them, but not the ordinary policemen. Tear gas is the most they should use, apart from batons.

I also think that we should never hesitate to have an impartial enquiry whenever there is a firing by the police.

You must have followed the course of the Save Hindi agitation of the Punjab. It has been pretty bad, and large numbers of policemen have been injured, some badly. But, the Chief Minister there has made it perfectly clear that he will not tolerate firing, and his orders have been obeyed. I think, he has done a wise

---

3. See *ante,* pp. 306-307. Sampurnanand wrote that this would make it difficult for the State to resist demands for judicial enquiry in cases of police firing to maintain law and order. This "makes the police nervous..."

thing, not only from the point of view of Government, but of the police also. It is really the police who suffer ultimately in all these cases of firing, and it is not fair to put them into this difficult position.

Yours sincerely,
Jawaharlal Nehru

7. Impending Stoppage of Work in Certain Essential Services[1]

Mr Speaker, Government and I am sure this House are deeply concerned about notices and news of impending stoppage of work in various essential services in the country. This matter has come before the House in different forms on several occasions during the last two weeks or more. I should like to keep the House informed of recent developments and what the Government have done in this matter and propose to do.

While it is the duty of the Government to take necessary powers to maintain essential services and take steps to that end, it is equally their concern to deal with the problems that have arisen, taking into account all the aspects involved and the demands of the workers affected.

During the last three weeks or more, I have myself been intimately connected with this matter, and so have indeed my other colleagues in Government. On the 26th July I met a deputation from the National Federation of Posts and Telegraph Employees. My colleagues, the Ministers of Labour and Communications, were also with me. We had long and friendly talks in the course of which I explained to the deputation more fully our ideas about the proposed Pay Commission. The question of interim relief was then raised and the deputation was informed that this would also be referred to the proposed Pay Commission.

I came away from this meeting feeling that an atmosphere of friendly cooperation had been created and the proposed strike would not take place. I was, therefore, much surprised and distressed to learn the next morning that the strike decision had been confirmed by the Committee of P & T Federation.

1. Statement in the Lok Sabha, 8 August 1957. *Lok Sabha Debates* (second series), Vol. IV, cols. 7530-7532.

On the 3rd August, the terms of reference of this Commission were announced in the House by the Finance Minister. These terms were to form part of the subsequent notification to be issued by the Government of India.

On the 5th August, I made a broadcast to the country in the course of which I spoke about the Pay Commission and referred to their function. In particular, I stated that the question of interim relief would be referred to the Commission.

I was informed later that some representatives of the P & T Federation wanted to meet me again to seek some clarification. I met them on the late afternoon of the 6th August and had a long talk with them. The principal subject discussed was that of interim relief and I explained again that this would be referred to the Commission. Thereupon, I was pressed for some immediate grant of relief. I pointed out that as this matter was being referred to the Pay Commission, it would neither be desirable nor possible for us to accept any such proposal of immediate relief. This would naturally affect many others, apart from the P & T people.

The question of a dateline or time limit being fixed for the Commission to present their interim proposals had also been raised. I made it clear that in our opinion it would not be proper nor suited to the dignity of the high-level Commission that we were appointing.

Thus, Government already announced that a high-powered Commission with an eminent Judge of the Supreme Court as Chairman will be appointed soon. In the notification appointing this Commission, reference will be made to the question of interim relief being considered by them and they may make interim reports. I have no doubt that the Commission will consider with care and expedition all problems brought to their notice.

It will appear that Government are well seized of these problems and have made it clear as to how they should be met. It is in the interest of the workers themselves as well as the country as a whole that there should be no stoppage of work in our essential services and that these problems should be dealt with by peaceful approaches and methods of conciliation to which Government are committed.

If, however, there is a stoppage of work in these essential services, then it is the duty of Government to see that the essential services are maintained, and we seek the cooperation of the public in this matter.

In view of the reaffirmation of the strike threat, in spite of the efforts that Government have made, Government have been compelled to advise the President to issue an Ordinance on the lines of the Essential Services Maintenance Bill passed by the Lok Sabha on the 6th August. I trust, however, that there will be no stoppage of work and that it will not be necessary, therefore, for this Ordinance to come into operation.

8. To Gulzarilal Nanda[1]

New Delhi
August 25, 1957

My dear Gulzarilal,

About 200 workers from Modinagar came to my house today. I saw a few of them and they gave me the memorandum enclosed. They also gave me one or two other papers which are enclosed.

I told them that I knew nothing about this matter, but I would enquire from our Labour Ministry as well as from the UP Government who were principally concerned. I told them also that it was absurd for them to go on hunger strike in this way. Thereupon, I think, they went away and there will be no hunger strike.

I understand that their chief complaint is about the Union they had established. Whenever any member of this Union applies for registration, he is dismissed by the management and the Registrar says that the people applying or most of them are not active workers and so he refuses to register them. According to these people, a large number of workers have thus been dismissed. Apparently there is already a Union there which is sponsored by the management and is associated with the INTUC.

It appears also that some matters in dispute were referred to Abid Ali for enquiry and settlement.[2] I hope that Abid Ali will deal with this matter early.

Something also was said about the Conciliation Committee which had not been formed according to the wishes of these people.

I hope you will look into this matter and see that it is settled properly and fairly soon. It is no good delaying these quarrels which then are likely to become bigger ones. The workers who came to me said that they were accused of being communists. They had nothing to do with communism or the Communist Party.

Yours sincerely,
Jawaharlal Nehru

---

1. JN Collection.
2. Final settlement of the amount of bonus and cases of dismissed *mazdoors* were to be referred to Abid Ali, Deputy Labour Minister, Government of India.

9. Demands of Indian Rare Earths Employees' Association[1]

Vasudevan Nair[2] and two others: Will the Prime Minister be pleased to state:
    (a) whether the management of Indian Rare Earths' Factory at Alwaye have recognized any union of their employees;
    (b) if not, the reasons therefore;
    (c) whether the Indian Rare Earths Employees' Association, Alwaye, has submitted any memorandum of Demands to the management of the factory; and
    (d) if so, what are the demands and the action taken thereon?

Jawaharlal Nehru: (a) and (b). Indian Rare Earths (Private) Ltd., have not recognized the union of its employees known as "Indian Rare Earths' Employees' Association." The Company deals with products of strategic importance for the development of atomic energy and as the office bearers of the Association are dominated by non-employees of the Company, the Board of Directors of the Company have decided not to recognize the Association.

(c) and (d). A copy of the Memorandum of Demands received from the Indian Rare Earths Employees' Association in April 1957 is laid on the Table of the House. The matter is at present before the Conciliation Officer (Central), Cochin.

---

1. Reply to a question in the Lok Sabha, 5 September 1957. *Lok Sabha Debates* (second series), Vol. VI, cols. 12034-35.
2. P.K. Vasudevan Nair was Communist Party Member from Thiruvella, Kerala.

10. Grievances of Hindustan Aircraft Limited Employees[1]

I had an interview with some representatives of the Hindustan Aircraft Employees Association at Mysore on 22nd September.[2] Shri Shrinagesh,[3] the General Manager, was also present. The interview lasted for about forty minutes.

2. They gave me a paper which I subsequently handed to Shri Shrinagesh and asked him to return it to us with his notes on it and with a brief report of the interview I had with these people.

3. I told the Employees Association representatives that they had my full sympathy in many ways and we were anxious to deal with them fairly and so as to have a contented body of workers. They were employed in a highly important Government industry dealing with defence, and in such an industry there can be no question of strikes, lockouts or the like. At the same time, any suggestions they might make should always be considered speedily and wherever possible given effect to. There should be a proper machinery for this so as to avoid delays. Unfortunately, there had to be delays because of references having to be made to Delhi and in Delhi various Ministries having to be consulted.

4. As for some matters, I told them that these involved questions of principle about which I could not say anything and which will apply not only to them but to other undertakings also. So far as dearness allowance was concerned, we were prepared to refer it to a tribunal. When they asked for temporary relief, I said that any decision of the tribunal should be given effect to from that date (that is, the date of reference).

5. In their statement, they had said a great deal about lack of amenities and also about the workers in Sindri and Chittaranjan having far greater facilities. I got the impression that what they said was largely true and this matter would have to be looked into soon.

6. It seems to me that these Hindustan Aircraft employees deserve better conditions and amenities. They should be treated on the human level and every effort should be made to make their life more agreeable. They seemed to spend a great deal on transport. In this matter I have specially asked the General Manager to report to us immediately what can be done.

1. Note to Defence Secretary, New Delhi, 24 September 1957. JN Collection.
2. Representatives of 11,000 employees of the Hindustan Aircraft Factory, Bangalore, presented a memorandum to Nehru, which demanded, among other things, appointment of a wage board and interim relief pending final consideration of their demands which were submitted to the management in October 1954.
3. J.M. Shrinagesh.

7. It is also to be considered how far we can give different treatment to our workers in Bangalore from what people get in Sindri and Chittaranjan. There may be some minor differences here and there but it will not be possible for us to keep up any markedly differential treatment.

8. You will probably get a note from the General Manager. As soon as this comes, I should like to see it and we shall consider it.

11. Reply to Bank Employees' Memorandum of Demands[1]

Please reply to this letter from the Bank Employees' Association as follows:
"Dear Sir,

Your letter dated 29th September has been received by the Prime Minister. He has asked me to say that he has read it. He cannot go into the merits of this dispute,[2] or to express any opinion about it. He has in fact discussed this matter to some extent with a number of people concerned.

He is perfectly aware of the difficulties being experienced by many people in the country because of a certain rise in prices. These difficulties are probably much greater in the case of many people other than the Bank employees. Government has already taken action in various ways to check the price rise and definite results have followed. The actual price of foodstuffs is lower now than it has been for some time, although at this time of the year usually there is a rise.

It is not clear to him how any person's interests are served, least of all the interests of the Bank employees, by the present strike which can only do harm to them as well as to the general public. Apart from the reference to the Tribunal, if necessary, other methods can be adopted to consider this

---

1. Note to Private Secretary, New Delhi, 29 September 1957. JN Collection.
2. Bank employees in Calcutta were agitating on the issue of compensation allowance for rise in prices of essential commodities including food, equivalent to 25 per cent of their monthly pay with a minimum of Rs 20.

matter peacefully and cooperatively. A strike of this kind cannot be a right method more especially at the present time.[3]

Yours sincerely,

Send a copy of this letter as well as the Bank Employees' memorandum to the Law Minister, Shri Asoke Sen.

3. The All India Bank Employees' Association communicated in its reply that the bank employees were most anxious to settle the matter in a tripartite conference and requested Nehru to depute Gulzarilal Nanda, the Labour Minister, to finalize the terms of agreement. The AIBEA assured that the bankmen were prepared to call off strike immediately provided the Government withdrew all the prosecution cases launched by it and the bankers honoured their commitment for making ad hoc cash payment towards the compulsory allowance. The AIBEA also said that the bankers had always taken full advantage of the adjudication machinery and the employees got no opportunity to place their viewpoints. The strike ended on 19 October.

12. To Lal Bahadur Shastri[1]

New Delhi
September 29, 1957

My dear Lal Bahadur,

Bidesh Kulkarni[2] is an MLC of Bombay. He is a man of wide contacts, especially in the labour field. He came to see me today and said that labour or workers in Banks, Insurance, Transport, Civil Aviation, Communications, etc., were drifting away from responsible methods and wrong hands were progressively controlling it. I told him I knew this, of course, to some extent.

He will probably see you about this matter. I suggest you have a talk with him. He has often helpful suggestions to make.

Yours affectionately,
Jawaharlal Nehru

1. JN Collection.
2. Bidesh Tukaram Kulkarni (1905-1988); General Secretary, Forward Bloc; Congress Member, Bombay Legislative Council, 1949-56; Member, Rajya Sabha, 1962-74; Lt. Governor, Pondicherry, 1976-79; President, Foreign Affairs Association of India, and Member, Indian Institute for Strategic Studies.

13. The Case of Hindustan Aircraft Employees[1]

I am writing this note on the eve of my departure for Japan. I am anxious that the questions relating to the Hindustan Aircraft employees should not be allowed to drift, as is the usual practice in many other Departments. It is only when this process of drift leads to critical developments that steps begin to be taken. We should learn from past experience and deal with a matter at a much earlier stage.

2. On my return from Japan I shall go further into these questions. I take it that the question of Dearness Allowance and one other matter have been referred to the Tribunal. There should be no delay about this and no continuous references and cross references between Ministries.

3. I do not think anything else can be referred to the Tribunal.

4. The Jagannatha Das[2] Pay Commission will not directly deal with such industrial undertakings as HAL. But, of course, whatever their decisions will be, they will in many ways apply to such undertakings and influence our policy towards them.

5. I do not think we should have a Wage Board specially for HAL or indeed for a larger group. But I certainly think that this question has to be considered by us in all its aspects. I believe that wages, etc., in all the Government of India factories in Bangalore are less than those at Sindri and Chittaranjan. I do not suggest that there should be an identity of wages all over India because conditions differ. But it is difficult to maintain a system where there is too great a difference for the same type of work. Therefore, we shall have to make adjustments not only in regard to wages, but other amenities also to avoid this marked difference.

6. It should be remembered that HAL is, from the national as well as security points of view, a much more important undertaking than most of the others owned by the Central Government, whether in Bangalore or in Sindri or in Chittaranjan. Therefore, we should have a contented labour force. This does not mean that we should accept wrong demands. It does mean that we should not wait for pressures from all round before we deal with the questions raised.

7. I cannot give any opinion about the various demands contained in the employees' memorandum. I have not got that with me nor have I the time. I have sent all the papers back to the Defence Ministry. The General Manager, however,

1. Note to Defence Secretary, New Delhi, 2 October 1957. JN Collection.
2. Bachu Jagannatha Das (b. 1893); enrolled as an advocate, 1917; practiced in the Madras High Court, 1917-48; Permanent Judge, Orissa High Court, 1948-51; Chief Justice, Orissa High Court, 1951-53; Judge, Supreme Court, 1953-58.

is well seized of this problem and I would value his advice in the matter. We should be prepared to go some distance to indicate that we want to ease the life of the workers as much as possible.

8. In your note you have said that important changes cannot be made without obtaining the approval of the Board of Directors and later of the Defence Ministry after consulting the Labour, Finance and possibly Home Ministries. That may be so, but this does not mean that we should go round and round various Ministries until everybody's patience is exhausted and matters come to a crisis. If we are clear that something has got to be done, the Board of Directors can meet almost in a few days notice and, as for the other Ministries, they can also be requested to meet immediately to discuss the matter. I do not wish long drawn out correspondence to be carried on in such matters.

9. The real thing is to decide what we think is proper and fit. Anything decided for HAL must necessarily apply to the other Central Government undertakings in Bangalore. Therefore, this question should be viewed from that point of view and the Ministries concerned with these undertakings will have to be consulted. Further we shall always have to bear in mind what the conditions are elsewhere, say, at Sindri, Chittaranjan, etc., though we need not copy them.

10. I should like these various preliminaries that I have referred to above to be gone into during my absence from India so that we can take up the matter afresh on my return.

14. To S.R. Vasavada[1]

New Delhi
October 23, 1957

Dear Vasavada,[2]

Thank you for your letter of the 21st October, with which you have sent me a note on the recognition of unions. I have read this note. Broadly speaking, I agree with your approach to this question.

I do not know all the facts, but the recent notice of a strike by some section of the Railwaymen, struck me as being exceedingly irresponsible.

Yours sincerely,
Jawaharlal Nehru

1. JN Collection.
2. President, National Federation of Indian Railwaymen.

III. APPOINTMENT OF SECOND PAY COMMISSION

1. To S. Nijalingappa[1]

New Delhi
August 2, 1957

My dear Nijalingappa,[2]
Your letter of 31st July.

We are fully aware of the great disparity between the pay scales of Central Government employees and State Government employees. We propose to mention this fact in any terms of reference to a Commission of Enquiry, but it is difficult for that Commission to deal with this subject in its entirety.[3]

Yours sincerely,
Jawaharlal Nehru

---

1. JN Collection.
2. Chief Minister of Mysore.
3. The Finance Minister, T.T. Krishnamachari announced in the Lok Sabha the appointment of the Second Pay Commission under Justice Jagannatha Das of the Supreme Court on 3 August 1957. According to the terms of reference, the Commission should (i) examine the principles governing structure of emoluments and service conditions of Central Government employees; (ii) consider and recommend changes in the same keeping in mind the historical background, economic conditions, implications and requirements of developmental planning, disparities in remunerations and conditions of service of the employees of Central and State Governments, local bodies, aided institutions and other relevant factors; and (iii) recommend benefits to Central Government employees in the shape of amenities and facilities.

2. To B.C. Roy[1]

New Delhi
August 4, 1957

My dear Bidhan,

Thank you for your two letters dated the 3rd August. I think, they were brought here by Morarjibhai.

One of these letters is your reply to my letter of the 31st July.[2] The other deals with the Pay Commission and the possible consequences on the salaries and allowances of State employees.

You will have seen, I hope, the terms of appointment of this Commission, which have been announced in Parliament. These terms lay particular stress on the economic situation in the country and the implementation of the Five Year Plan. Further, there is some reference to the emoluments of State employees, although these employees do not come directly within the purview of the Commission's enquiry.

It was after prolonged consideration and debate amongst ourselves that we agreed to the appointment of this Commission. There was no escape from it for a variety of reasons. In fact, even the last Pay Commission laid down that a new one should be appointed within ten years. It is eleven years now. Also, there is no doubt that the present pay structure has many anomalies and is not very satisfactory. Further, there is no doubt that an immediate situation has been created by the rise in prices of foodgrains and the general cost index.

The situation had to be faced in all its aspects and we could not merely say 'no' and refuse to recognize facts. We have, therefore, laid emphasis on all the surrounding circumstances which are to be kept in view.

Exactly what we can afford or not, is more than I can say at the present moment. But, what you have stated about the effect on the emoluments of State employees is obvious. How far it will be within the capacity of the Central Government to help in this, is a very doubtful matter. I am afraid we have arrived at a stage when we may well have to give up some of our schemes.

1. JN Collection.
2. See *Selected Works* (second series), Vol. 38, pp. 348-349.

It does not appear to be certain yet as to whether there will be a P & T strike or not. The chances of its taking place or not taking place are about even. Anyhow, we shall probably know in the course of the next day or two.

Yours,
Jawahar

3. To B. Shiva Rao[1]

New Delhi
August 6, 1957

My dear Shiva Rao,

Thank you for your letter of the 6th August.[2]

I certainly have in mind the setting up of some machinery to improve staff relations in Government Departments. But I rather doubt if the Pay Commission should be entrusted with this task. This will merely add to their work and this might well mean our waiting a long time for their report before we take this question up. I think, therefore, that we should deal with this separately.

---

1. File No. 35 (42)/57-66-PMS. Also available in JN Collection and T.T. Krishnamachari Papers, NMML.
2. Shiva Rao wrote about the desirability of devising some machinery for Government employees to discuss their problems and difficulties in an informal and friendly manner in order to improve staff relations in Government departments. Shiva Rao had received some useful literature from London giving details of the manner in which staff relations were regulated. Rao mentioned Civil Service Associations, Whitley Councils and Welfare Officers in this connection. He suggested that the Pay Commission under Justice Jagannatha Das might be asked to consider this aspect of the problem and an expert adviser with practical experience from Civil Service Associations and Whitley Councils in Whitehall might be associated with the Commission.

As you are so much interested in this subject and have a good deal of material too, why not let me have your own views in the form of notes, etc.?[3]

Yours sincerely,
Jawaharlal Nehru

3. Shiva Rao sent a note on 2 August 1957 giving details of the mechanism in Britain. According to the note, there were "recognized" Civil Service Associations with certain rights; Whitley Councils in all departments and a Civil Service National Whitley Council at the top, which were set up in 1919, to deal with all matters affecting the service conditions of the staff including provision for arbitration in case of disagreements. Shiva Rao wrote that while there was no law forbidding civil servants in Britain from striking work, seldom there had been strikes, mainly because of the procedure adopted.

4. Functioning of Staff Committees[1]

These questions will have to be considered more fully not only in our Ministry but to cover all other Ministries and Departments of the Government of India.

It is clear from the notes in this file that these committees have not functioned properly and are very quiescent. We should not only activise them but give them a different direction. I have no personal experience of these committees and I would like to have that not only in regard to the IFS Association but to other committees also.

The committees presumably consider grievances. That is necessary, but this gives a limited outlook to the committee. They should be encouraged to discuss methods of work and improvements for greater efficiency and many other matters.

I imagine that the senior and junior staff committees, under the Chairmanship of Senior Officers, are reluctant to say much. They are not used to it, unless some particularly important point arises. The question is to make them feel at

1. Note to Secretary General, Foreign Secretary, Commonwealth Secretary and Special Secretary, New Delhi, 8 August 1957. JN Collection.

home so that they may not be overawed by the presence of their Senior Officers. I believe that in England it is often the practice for the Chairmanship to be rotated so that others have a chance also and feel more at level.

I am thinking about these matters and I shall probably write a separate note on them and discuss with SG, FS, CS and SS.

5. Utility of Staff Committees[1]

I agree with you that no formal staff committee appears to be necessary for the PM's Secretariat. But in a department, small or big, there should be contacts between various people there and full opportunities of discussion of any problems that might arise. This is not a question of complaints being considered, but something more to introduce a cooperative atmosphere and an opportunity for suggestions to be made for better efficiency or waste being stopped or for any other purpose.

2. Therefore you might see that

(i) there is every opportunity for any person in the PM's Secretariat to have access to you;

(ii) you should let it be known to all that we welcome suggestions in regard to the working of our office or any kind of improvement either to add to the efficiency of the working or generally to the conveniences;

(iii) periodically you should meet different groups of people of varying grades just to have a talk with them and discuss matters with them.

3. The point is that there should be a sense of cooperative effort and partnership in considering any problem or difficulty or suggestion whenever it arises or is made.

4. You might, therefore, write to the Home Ministry that we are following these lines and that we do not think that in a relatively small Secretariat a formal staff committee is necessary or desirable. In fact, we are prepared to treat the whole Secretariat as a committee whenever necessity arises and from time to time we propose to meet them in separate groups also to discuss matters that arise.

---

1. Note to Kesho Ram, Principal Private Secretary, New Delhi, 10 August 1957. JN Collection.

5. What I want to make clear is that even these staff committees, where they exist or are being formed, should not be committees merely to voice complaints, but to discuss matters of common concern in the office in a cooperative way.

6. To E.M.S. Namboodiripad[1]

New Delhi
August 12, 1957

My dear Namboodiripad,

Your letter of 9th August.

You must have seen the terms of reference of the proposed Pay Commission. Soon I hope the Government Notification appointing it will be issued.[2]

These terms of reference are confined to the All India Services, but reference is made in them to the States' Services. It was difficult to enlarge the work of the Pay Commission so as to include all the Services in India. That would have been a terrific job and would have delayed their work much. But, as a matter of fact, the indirect reference to the States' Services brings out the intimate connection between the two and this will help us to consider the other matters also. If the State Governments appoint similar committees or commissions, they will no doubt help.

Yours sincerely,
Jawaharlal Nehru

1. JN Collection.
2. On 21 August, the concerned papers were laid on the Table in the Lok Sabha.

7. To Govind Ballabh Pant[1]

New Delhi
August 18, 1957

My dear Pantji,

Shiva Rao has sent me another note dealing with the working of the Whitley Councils in England.[2] I understand that a copy of it has been sent to A.V. Pai. Nevertheless, I am sending you his letter together with his note for facility of reference.

I think, we can learn much from the working of the Whitley Councils and might follow to some extent their procedure. Of course, it will have to be adapted to our own needs.

As Shiva Rao says, it would be desirable to give effect to some of these proposals without waiting for the Pay Commission Report. In fact, you have already taken steps to appoint Welfare Officers.

Yours affectionately,
Jawaharlal Nehru

---

1. File No. 35 (42)/57-66-PMS. Also available in JN Collection.
2. B. Shiva Rao reported his conversation with J.S.P. Mackenzie, Labour Adviser to the UK High Commissioner in New Delhi, on the functioning of the Whitley Councils in Britain. There were the National Whitley Council, consisting of 26 members on each side, which operated mainly through two Committees; local Whitley Councils in a city; regional ones for particular regions; and countrywide Councils. Agreements were sought by informal discussions which were recorded for being implemented. Problems, which had not been settled by discussions, were referred for arbitration by a tribunal of three, composed of staff side, official side and a chairman. Shiva Rao suggested staff councils for India on these lines, and welfare officers on the pattern of Information Bureau. He also referred to the recommendations of the First Pay Commission in 1946 on employees' grievances.

8. To N. Sanjiva Reddy[1]

New Delhi
August 26, 1957

My dear Sanjiva Reddy,

I am sorry for the delay in replying to your letter of the 16th August.[2] Since you wrote, the terms of reference of the Pay Commission have been announced.

I quite agree with you about the State Services. Indeed, only a day or two ago I received a deputation representing the non-gazetted officers of Andhra, Madras, Mysore and Kerala. I told them that what they said was logical and reasonable and I had no answer to it except certain practical difficulties. It seems to me quite absurd for people doing the same type of work to be paid so differently and I have no doubt that gradually these differences will have to be removed. How exactly this is to be done I cannot say immediately. We have some hard years ahead.

Some reference has been made in the terms of reference to the State Services. But it is true that the Pay Commission has not been asked to enquire into these State Services conditions etc. We felt that any such enlargement of their work would have made it much too wide. But the mere fact of some reference brings it to the fore.

I suppose the State Governments can certainly make representations to the Pay Commission.

Yours sincerely,
Jawaharlal Nehru

---

1. File No. 18/22/57-SR (R), MHA. Also available in JN Collection.
2. Sanjiva Reddy highlighted the disparities in emoluments of State Government and Central Government employees and sought to remove them through the newly-appointed Second Pay Commission. He pointed out that major sources of expanding revenue were allocated to the Centre whereas Sales Tax was the only elastic source of State revenue. He hoped that the State Governments would be given opportunity to make representations to the Pay Commission.

IV. DECISIONS OF WAGE BOARD FOR WORKING JOURNALISTS

1. To B.V. Keskar[1]

New Delhi
August 30, 1957

My dear Balkrishna,

I understand that as a result of the recent decisions of the Wage Board for Working Journalists,[2] the *National Herald* and the associated newspapers may well have to close down.[3] Probably, some other newspapers will suffer the same fate. This seems to me rather an unfortunate outcome of the long negotiations and legislation that we have passed.[4] I do not quite know what the position is now. Could you enlighten me?[5]

Yours sincerely,
Jawaharlal Nehru

---

1. File No. 43(103)/57-62-PMS. Also available in JN Collection.
2. The Wage Board for Working Journalists in its decision announced on 11 May 1957, classified the newspaper establishments into five groups, namely, A to E, on the basis of their gross annual revenue. It also classified the working journalists into four groups, and fixed minimum basic pay scales for each group. Consequently, all the employers were required to file with the appropriate authorities the returns for the years 1952, 1953 and 1954 within a period of one month from the date of the publication of the decision of the Wage Board. The Board also asked for payment of arrears of increased wages from 2 May 1956 to 10 May 1957.
3. The *National Herald* including its Hindi and Urdu editions, and a large number of newspapers, specially the medium and small units, were adversely affected by the Wage Board's decisions.
4. The Government of India enacted a legislation in 1955, namely, the Working Journalists (Conditions of Service and Miscellaneous Provisions) Act 1955. The Wage Board was constituted under this very Act.
5. B.V. Keskar, in his reply of 1 September 1957, suggested minor verifications in the Working Journalists Act, 1955, such as increase in working hours but cautioned that overall granting of amenities and wages could not be modified. He also suggested that Price Page Schedule might provide some relief in the shape of lessening unfair competition and bringing in a slightly better quantum of advertisements to the less favoured newspapers.

2. To Gulzarilal Nanda[1]

New Delhi
6 September 1957

My dear Gulzarilal,

I wrote to you some days ago about the Wage Board decisions about newspapers and mentioned that the *National Herald* and its associated newspapers were in considerable difficulty.[2]

Today, I had a visit from B.N. Sanyal, Assistant Editor of the *Amrita Bazar Patrika*, who gave a paper which I enclose. This deals with another aspect of the question.

I confess I have sympathy for what B.N. Sanyal has written. The *Amrita Bazar Patrika* and its associated newspapers are very prosperous and, I think, they pay their Editors, etc., of the Hindi and Bengali editions very low salaries.

Yours sincerely,
Jawaharlal Nehru

1. File No. 43 (103)/57-62-PMS. Also available in JN Collection.
2. On 30 August 1957 (Not printed).

3. To B.V. Keskar[1]

New Delhi
October 1, 1957

My dear Balkrishna,

I have read your three letters, one dated September 30th and two of October 1st. As I told you at the airport, I am afraid that Shiva Rao indulges in exaggerations and does not always stick to the facts.

1. JN Collection.

I agree with you that much delay in this matter is not desirable. Naturally, I want the decision to be such as will be generally accepted and will not cause any major upsets. As I suggested to you, you can consult Pantji, Morarjibhai and Gulzarilal Nanda. At our informal meeting of the Cabinet, this was suggested.

I do not think a large conference now is desirable.

I enclose a memorandum which was given to me this morning by a crowd of Delhi journalists who came here.[2]

Will you come and see me tomorrow, the 2nd October, at 3.30 p.m. at my house?

Yours sincerely,
Jawaharlal Nehru

2. Over 500 working journalists, press workers and their sympathizers, led by the Delhi Union of Journalists, protested against the alleged victimization by newspaper establishments of some of the working journalists connected with the trade union movement. They also demanded the implementation of the decisions of the Wage Board.

4. To Gulzarilal Nanda[1]

New Delhi
October 31, 1957

My dear Gulzarilal,

Tushar Kanti Ghosh of the *Amrita Bazar Patrika* came to see me this afternoon and talked with great distress about the impending fate of his and other papers in India. I told him that I was not going to interfere. I recognize that some mistakes had been made in the drafting of the original Bill and then we had been embarrassed by some interpretations by High Courts. It is unfortunate that an assurance given to Parliament on behalf of Government had been ignored by the High Court. If Government could do so, we would certainly honour that assurance.

1. File No. 43 (103)/57-62-PMS. Also available in JN Collection.

It may be desirable later to have some amendments to that piece of legislation. But we could not touch it at present, nor can we delay its implementation.

I told him further that this was a matter entirely in your hands and that of Keskar and that you two should deal with it together and settle it as soon as possible. I have informed Keskar of this also and told him to keep in touch with you.

Tushar Kanti gave me a piece of paper containing his suggestions. I enclose this.

Yours sincerely,
Jawaharlal Nehru

V. A NEW HOUSE FOR PM

1. To Raghu Vira[1]

New Delhi
August 3, 1957

My dear Raghu Vira,[2]

Your letter of August 2nd. The information that the newspapers gave of an estimate for my new house is completely wrong. The actual estimate was not Rs four lakhs, but about Rs one lakh, and the accommodation provided was considerably more than what you have mentioned in your letter. Therefore, the difference in price was not so great as is made out. The house in which I have to live has to have a study and some office rooms, apart from other accommodation.

Anyhow, for the present, I am not proceeding with this matter as I am too busy otherwise.

Yours sincerely,
Jawaharlal Nehru

1. JN Collection.
2. Congress Member of Rajya Sabha from Gujarat.

2. Arrangements for the New House[1]

Some time ago, I decided to postpone consideration of this matter. A general impression was created, quite wrongly, that I was giving up the idea of having a new house. As a matter of fact, I had no such intention. But, at the time, I was overburdened with so many other things that I just did not want to add to this mental burden. Now, I am a little freer and my mind has, therefore, reverted to this subject. Vaguely, I have thought about it all this time and I am quite convinced that a new house is desirable not only for me, but for any subsequent Prime Minister.

2. So far as the location of the house is concerned, and the broad plan of it, I have nothing further to say. We have approved of these and, subject to minor modifications which may be agreed upon, these may be finalized. I should like this to be done before we leave for Japan, so that the necessary preparations for starting building as well as the actual building itself may be taken in hand.

3. What I have been thinking of has rather been the new arrangements after this house is built and we move into it. The present Prime Minister's House is used by us not only for residential purposes, but as office by me, by Indiraji and by Shri Mathai.[2] Shri Mathai, Mrs Atal[3] and Srinivasan[4] live here also. There are some big functions here from time to time, garden parties, banquets and other semi-official meals, etc., apart from private guests. I meet many people here in the mornings and also in the course of the day. So does Indiraji.

4. We have, apart from a collection of personalia and books, a large number of official papers stored here as well as many other things. It will not be easy to remove these to the new house. In fact, there will not be room there.

5. It has also to be considered how far I can meet people officially or semi-officially in the new house, more especially the crowds of people who come to the present PM's House, usually in the mornings. It is clear that these crowds cannot be invited or accommodated in the new house.

6. I should like to use the new house, as far as possible, as a private residence. This does not mean that I will not see people there or occasionally have a few guests for meals, even official guests like Ambassadors. But, broadly speaking,

---

1. Note to Indira Gandhi and M.O. Mathai, New Delhi, 8 September 1957. JN Collection.
2. M.O. Mathai.
3. Uma Vati Atal (1905-1997); wife of Brij Mohan Atal, a cousin of Kamala Nehru; in charge of Prime Minister's Household till 1964.
4. C.R. Srinivasan was Private Secretary to the Prime Minister.

they will be individuals who will be invited there and not groups. Gradually, I wish to have more and more my official interviews in my office in South Block or in Parliament House. But, as things are, something else will have to be provided for for groups and others to see me.

7. I think, therefore, that the process of moving to the new house cannot be a sudden one, except that Indiraji and I go and stay there. For some time, a part of our work will necessarily have to be carried on in the old house. We shall gradually adapt ourselves to the change.

8. Thus, it will be simpler and more feasible for me and for Indiraji to meet people, when desired, in the old house. I think that my study room in the old house as well as the sitting room down below should be reserved for this purpose. I think also that Shri Mathai, Mrs Atal and Srinivasan might well continue to stay here and Shri Mathai can have his office too as at present, for some time at least. If necessary, some minor arrangements might be made to make this part of the house rather compact, so that it might not come in the way of guests staying here. If necessary, also, and if Indiraji so desires, another room might be kept for her. I shall not, of course, require my bedroom here or any other room, except the study and the small sitting room below for meeting people occasionally. Naturally, the hall down below will also be of some use to meet people.

9. For the rest, the old PM's House will be used for State guests. As a rule, no private guests will stay here. In the new PM's House, there is not much room for private guests. There will be one guest room which will be used only on special occasions for special people.

10. The whole idea is that the changeover should be gradual and we should see how it works. There is no need to go away from this house bag and baggage suddenly. Even from the point of view of the old house, it will not be desirable to leave it completely empty except for the occasional guests who come here. Also, if Shri Mathai, Srinivasan and Mrs Atal have to move out, that will create a new problem of finding accommodation for them as well as for our papers, files, etc. They can easily stay on here.

11. Most of the pictures etc., can well be left in the old house, even if some of them belong to us personally. Such as are required in the new house will be taken.

12. As for the furniture in the new house, I would suggest that only the built-in furniture should be provided for now. Once this thing is out of our way, we can think of the other furniture. If necessary, we can, to begin with, have a make-shift arrangement and get such furniture as available to carry on with and then replace them with particular things that we desire which should be relatively simple. Big carpets are neither necessary nor desirable. I would prefer small carpets thrown about, where considered necessary.

13. This is the way my mind works at present. It will not be necessary for the kitchen establishment, as it is here now, to be maintained, but it will have to be used when guests come here.

14. In the new house, I should like as small a complement of domestic staff as possible. If necessary, an extra man or two can come for any particular purpose, but, as a rule, I should not like that house to be cluttered up with domestic staff.

15. I should like Indiraji and Shri Mathai to consider this matter and what I have written, and give their comments and discuss it with me. As soon as we are clear in our minds, we should have another look at the plan of the new house and finalize that also. All this should be done before we leave for Japan.

3. Security and Other Considerations[1]

This is in reference to Shri Mathai's note of 9th September.

Location of the house. So far as I can make out, there is no other feasible site in the compound of the present Prime Minister's House. It is essential that the new house should be so placed that it can be separate from the old house and its compound. Otherwise, it becomes just an annexe to the old house. It is for this reason also essential that it must have a separate entrance.

I do not think it is at all desirable to locate the new house in the pine area. That would either mean cutting down some of the pine trees or we shall have to change the whole construction of the house so as to straggle about in between the pine trees. That would also spoil that pine area.

I have been unable to understand Shri Mullik's[2] line of reason, nor can I understand how this new house will involve additions to the present bloated strength of security personnel.

I do not think it has been quite understood why I want this new house. I want a private house, quite separate from the present Prime Minister's House. I do not propose to encourage anybody to come to the new house on business. That is why I have said that I shall meet people either in my office in South Block or possibly in a room in the old Prime Minister's House. No demonstration should be encouraged near the new house. I shall absolutely refuse to see any

1. Note to M.O. Mathai and Indira Gandhi, New Delhi, 9 September 1957. JN Collection.
2. B.N. Mullik was Director, Intelligence Bureau, Government of India.

demonstrators there. If they come, they will be told to go round and come to the old house or in front of it.

It is immaterial whether the existing pathway through the present PM's House Estate is made into a pucca road or not. That will not make any difference to the other proposal. In any event, that pathway should be in a fit condition for a car to go on it.

It was not my intention to continue my office in the present house. What I had said was that for some little time, it may be a month or two, this room may continue more or less as it is. It may be locked up. I shall not use it as an office. But the process of moving out will be a gradual one.

This applies to the other arrangements you have suggested also. I do not wish to be hustled into this business.

Srinivasan can stay where he likes.

STATES AND UNION TERRITORIES

My immediate concern was that the political aspect and the facts of discontent... and it had then suggested that at a suitable stage of the... anything to... and what is of more... This was many months ago... been decided upon later.

Anyway, we have had... this brings out another aspect... incident in the Coast Wireless staff. Whatever this discontent may or may be due to, the fact that there is at this trouble in Civil Aviation is patent... This requires very close and urgent attention and we cannot allow matters to drift either on the technical side or the other. I hope you and Humayun Kabir will deal with this soon.

Yours affectionately,
Jawaharlal Nehru

4. To D.K. Gaikwad

New Delhi,
August 10, 1957

Dear Shri Gaikwad,

I have your letter of the 6th August.

I agree not with you again that, so far as I am concerned, I have not the least objection to people belonging to the Scheduled Castes embracing the Buddhist faith. As you perhaps know, I am a great admirer of the Buddha and his faith. The one thing that I have suggested... that this conversion should not be a super-religion... something... trying to deprive the great teaching and influence of the Buddha. Unfortunately, it seems to me unfortunately that it is treated, both by friends and opponents, as something political.

File No. 2(80/57)-53-PMS.
4. (1902-1971), Member, Nasik Municipality and later on Board... Chief Executive of Scheduled Castes Federation; Member of Bombay Legislative Assembly 1937-46; SCF Member of Lok Sabha, 1957-62.

I. ANDAMAN & NICOBAR ISLANDS

1. To Govind Ballabh Pant[1]

New Delhi
August 28, 1957

My dear Pantji,

From time to time my mind goes to the Andamans and I have a feeling that this is a forgotten part of our territories. Apart from its other problems,[2] etc., the main thing that has always struck me is the enormous forest wealth of the Andamans and yet we find that our highly placed officers of the Forest Department manage to work the forests at some deficit. The contractor who has another part of the forests makes some profit though not much. Inspector-Generals of Forests pay State visits to the island and write long reports, and we remained where we were. A place like the Andamans in Europe would be a tremendous earner of foreign exchange. In fact, Finland and Norway have good revenues from their forests.

I know that in order to do this we have to invest money. But I do not think it is money that comes in the way. It is the lack of competent and eager human beings who have some technical knowledge. I am told that the Planning Commission has allotted four and a half crores of Rupees in the Second Five Year Plan, but it simply cannot be used under existing circumstances. Four and a half crores of Rupees is a fairly large sum. I should have thought that a much smaller sum would make the Andamans hum with activity.

Of course, the first thing is communications. Nothing can be done to the Andamans till it is possible to have easy communications by air and sea. There has been talk of some kind of an airfield in North Andamans for a long time, but it has yielded no result. There has been talk also of ships, and a new ship was recently built. Just when it was ready, I understand that Lal Bahadur paid a visit

---

1. File No. 17(250)/57-64-PMS. Also available in JN Collection.
2. Although, the Government of India had approved various measures in 1952 for the development of these islands, there had still been lack of road and transport system, medical care and schools. Besides, no proper survey of mineral and forest resources had been undertaken as yet.

to it at Visakhapatnam. Just then it was discovered that the ship had some serious defect. There is, I understand, some kind of an enquiry. Meanwhile there is no ship.

I gather that there are two Executive Engineers in the Andamans. What they do I do not understand, because precious little is done there. But according to our complicated and expensive system, we have to appoint two there. However, between the two very little is done. I am told that they cannot do much because they have not got junior officers, and if the junior officers are there, they have not got assistants. Is this not typical of the unfortunate bureaucratic outlook that we have developed in this country where every chauffer wants a cleaner before he can work a car?

The Chief Commissioner[3] of the Andamans saw me today. He was telling me of some little PWD structure which was made recently. He said the PWD charged almost exactly three times as much as anybody else would have done there. Fancy schools and hospitals are put up for a tiny population.

The Andamans seems to me a symbol of a wasteful and unprofitable administration which yields practically no results except to keep itself going. I am not blaming any individual. It is the system that is all wrong.

But I come back to communications because nothing can be done till communications improve. I think, there should be an airfield there. But even more important than an airfield is a good ship. Also, surely there should be one or two launches there which can go about between the islands. Every little firm by the seaside in Bombay has a launch, and yet we cannot provide a launch to go between the Andamans and the Nicobar islands.

I think, we have got into a complete rut and think of the Andamans as some out-of-the-way place which can be dusted occasionally and forgotten. As a matter of fact, it is a mine of wealth and should be a fine place for colonization. In fact, the only good that has been done thus far is that it has absorbed some of our East Bengal refugees.

Yours affectionately,
Jawaharlal Nehru

3. S.N. Maitra.

II. ANDHRA PRADESH

1. To Bhimsen Sachar[1]

New Delhi
September 19, 1957

My dear Sachar,[2]

I sent you today a letter with which I enclosed a communication from Basheer Yar Jung, the son of Begum Walliuddowla. This Begum is one of the claimants to the funds deposited with the Hyderabad State on behalf of the three big jagirs known as *Paigahs*.

I had received a letter from Begum Walliuddowla. On enquiry made from the Home Ministry here, I have been told that the facts are as follows:

"Begum Walliuddowla is one of the claimants to the funds deposited with the Hyderabad State on behalf of the three big jagirs in the former Hyderabad State which were known as *Paigahs*. About 28 years ago, the Nizam issued orders on the basis of the recommendations of an Investigation Commission that surplus income of the *Paigahs* should be invested and one-third of the interest earned should be appropriated for administrative charges. He also directed that the principal should not be disturbed without his express orders. Now that the *Paigahs* have been resumed by the Government under the Jagir Abolition legislation, the question of the disposal of the investment has been raised. The Hyderabad Government, had tentatively issued orders that one-half of the principal at credit should be paid to such of the claimants as were willing to accept the condition that they would waive all claims to the rest. The remaining half of the invested amount was intended to be retained by the State Government for being utilized for the development of the *Paigah* areas which had been neglected in the past."

On receiving representations from the parties concerned, the Ministry of Home Affairs referred the matter to the Ministry of Law.

"The Law Ministry's view is that, since the *Paigah* deposits were of the nature of trust money, there is no justification on the part of Andhra Pradesh

1. JN Collection.
2. Governor of Andhra Pradesh.

Government to retain any part of them. The Ministry of Home Affairs asked the Government of Andhra Pradesh to reconsider the matter in the light of the opinion given by the Law Ministry. As the amounts in dispute were in the possession of the Andhra Pradesh Government, the Ministry of Home Affairs could not, obviously, issue any directive to the State Government. All that they could do was to advise them about the appropriate course in the light of the examination of the case by them in consultation with the Ministry of Law."

I am told that our Home Ministry wrote to the Chief Minister of Andhra Pradesh, who replied to say that, in his opinion, the stand taken by the Hyderabad Government was justified.

I do not quite understand how this matter can be disposed of by mere assertion when our Law Ministry has definitely given an opinion. If our Law Ministry's opinion is not considered correct, we can take the Attorney-General's opinion or somebody else's. We have to follow the law.

I am enclosing the original letter I received from Begum Walliuddowla. You will see that she is very anxious to have some money because of weddings etc. I would suggest that the Andhra Government might make some considerable payment to her without necessarily committing itself about the rest. This would be an ad hoc payment.

Yours sincerely,
Jawaharlal Nehru

2. To N. G. Ranga[1]

New Delhi
October 19, 1957

My dear Ranga,[2]

I have seen a press cutting in which you are reported to have said that there was a conspiracy by the Central Ministers, newspapers and the town people against

1. File No. 32 (5)/59-61-PMS. Also available in JN Collection.
2. Congress Member of Lok Sabha from Tenali, Andhra Pradesh.

Andhra millers and ryots.[3] I do not understand this. Where is this conspiracy? The Congress has a clear policy which we are trying to further. I take it that you agree with that policy. Anyhow, it is odd for you to say that the Central Ministers are conspiring against the Andhra ryots.

Yours sincerely,
Jawaharlal Nehru

3. His speech was reported in *Madras Mail* on 15 October 1957. The call given by Nehru, U.N. Dhebar, Vinoba Bhave, Jayaprakash Narayan and others at the *Gramdan* Conference at Yelwal near Mysore for a united effort to solve the land reform problem was interpreted by Ranga as a conspiracy of all political parties including the Congress against the *kisans*. He reportedly encouraged ryots to be prepared for breaking the law.

III. ASSAM

1. To B.P. Chaliha[1]

New Delhi
August 1, 1957

My dear Chaliha,[2]
I have your letter of the 31st July. From your letter as well as a letter from the Chief Minister and the press reports, we have had full reports of the situation in Assam and what has happened there recently.[3]

1. JN Collection. Also available in AICC Papers.
2. President, Assam Pradesh Congress Committee.
3. In July 1957, it was reported in the press that a fifth oil refinery was going to be set up in Assam in association with the Assam Oil Company. It was also reported that the Government of Assam had appointed a French oil expert who was going to submit a report regarding location of the refinery. These reports created much confusion among the leaders at the national level and they raised questions in the Parliament on this issue.

I quite realize all your difficulties and it was, in fact, because of these difficulties that we have gone a long way to meet your wishes. We have, in fact, as you know, kept this question of the location of the refinery open for further consideration after all the facts have been received in the project reports. In the statement we issued, we made it clear that final decisions will only be taken then.

It is manifestly not possible for us to go any further or to declare that in any event a refinery must be located in Assam. It may be that this whole project is postponed if the people of Assam do not want it. There is no other way to deal with this situation which has largely arisen because of a weak and confused attitude adopted in the past.

You know that we want to do everything we can to meet your wishes and to ease the situation in Assam. But, surely, no Government can be asked or coerced into a vital decision without the fullest consideration of all aspects. All I can suggest is that the Assam Government and the Assam Congress should calmly but firmly face the situation and explain to the people that this matter is fully under consideration, and that the Central Government has every sympathy with Assam's views. Just to give into clamour, however widespread it might be, is to ruin the chances of Assam's development in the future.

You know that we invited even the Leader of the Opposition to come and talk to us.[4] He did not come. I think that fact should be mentioned in the public.

Yours sincerely,
Jawaharlal Nehru

4. Hareswar Goswami.

2. To Hareswar Goswami[1]

New Delhi
August 13, 1957

Dear Shri Goswami,[2]
I have received your letter of the 9th August.[3]

It is true that I did not write to you on this subject. I wrote to the Chief Minister of Assam inviting him to come here to discuss the question of the oil refinery. In my letter I suggested to him that he might invite you as well as the President of the Pradesh Congress Committee to come to Delhi with him. Apparently, he did suggest to you to come with him, though he did not perhaps mention that I had made this suggestion. I am sorry if there has been any misunderstanding. I would have been glad to meet you.

Yours sincerely,
Jawaharlal Nehru

---

1. JN Collection.
2. (1918-1968); freedom fighter from Assam and was imprisoned during the Quit India movement, 1942; left Congress and joined Socialist Party, 1947; Leader of Opposition, Assam Legislative Assembly, 1952-62; rejoined Congress, 1964; became Speaker, Assam Legislative Assembly, 1967-68.
3. Goswami expressed surprise at the last paragraph of Nehru's letter to Chaliha dated 1 August (see the preceding item), which appeared in *The Assam Tribune* on 8 August. Goswami clarified that he did not receive any communication from the Prime Minister's Office in this regard, but B.R. Medhi suggested this in July last and said that he would arrange it. However, no invitation to Goswami was issued.

349

3. Oil Refinery in Assam[1]

It is very difficult to deal with this oil refinery problem because of the high excitement in Assam.

2. I agree with you that it would be quite improper for a junior officer of the Assam Government to roam about the various Embassies in Delhi. In fact, this will not serve the Assam Government's purpose. You should, therefore, tell that officer that this is neither the right procedure, nor will it be helpful in any way. But, if the Assam Government so desire, they can send us a note stating what they wish us to do. Is it their desire to invite experts from foreign countries to come here? As a matter of fact, a single expert coming here can only give the vaguest of opinions.

3. If the Assam Government want to know the names of prominent experts, we can try to get these names for them by reference to our Embassies abroad, or perhaps even to the Embassies here. But, this will have to be done by External Affairs Ministry.

4. The first point to be clear about is what the Assam Government want to be done in this respect. It seems that they want to bypass the enquiries being conducted by the Government of India and to have an independent investigation. This is odd. But, nevertheless, we do not wish to come in their way, if they are keen on it. But, that investigation must be worthwhile, if it is to help.

5. Please keep in close touch with the Ministry of Steel, Mines and Fuel in this matter.

---

1. Note to Foreign Secretary, New Delhi, 13 August 1957. JN Collection.

4. To V.T. Krishnamachari[1]

New Delhi
August 23, 1957

My dear V.T.,

I am worried about Assam. Of course, the immediate reason for this worry is the refinery question. But I am not for the moment thinking of that. I am thinking that we have rather ignored the development of Assam chiefly because of the difficulty of access to it. The Railway line was feeble. No private industrialist would like to set up anything there if communications were as they are now.

I think that we must take this matter of Assam in hand in a comprehensive way, quite apart from the refinery question. The first thing that stares one in the face is the improvement of the Railway line. We are told that the Railway Administration have decided to strengthen and stabilize this line, whatever this may mean. I am writing to the Railway Minister about it and telling him that this is an urgent matter.

The trouble with the Nagas has also demonstrated how important it is that we should have better communication with Assam. Then there are many kinds of fruits which are wasted and rot away there because of lack of transport. Everything seems to depend on the Railways.

I think that it might be worthwhile for a small committee to be formed to consider schemes for the industrial development of Assam. In that Committee or in some supervisory committee we might have to get Medhi associated with it. Whatever we do we shall require the cooperation of the State Government.

Meanwhile, couldn't the Planning Commission draw up a paper on this subject? Neogy is, I believe, fairly well acquainted with the problems of Assam. Will you please share this letter with him?

Yours sincerely,
Jawaharlal Nehru

1. File No. 17 (259)/57-68-70-PMS. Also available in JN Collection.

5. To Jagjivan Ram[1]

New Delhi
August 23, 1957

My dear Jagjivan Ram,

I am much worried about Assam. The more I think of it, the more it appears that the whole future of Assam depends upon the improvement of the Railway connections. No industry will start there unless it is assured of good connections with the rest of India both for raw materials and finished products.

As you know, the people of Assam have worked themselves up to a high pitch of excitement and have become almost neurotic over the question of the refinery. I think, they are quite wrong about the refinery, but they have reason to feel frustrated about the past. Quite apart from this question of refinery, which should be dealt with separately, I think that we must pay attention to the development of Assam in various ways. Here we come back again to Railways. Indeed, quite apart from the industrial development of Assam, the Naga trouble has demonstrated how important it is to have proper Railway connections.

This, of course, has been mentioned many times and I have been told by the Chairman of the Railway Board, and you yourself have said it, that steps are being taken to stabilize and strengthen the Railway link, whatever that might mean. I want to know precisely what it is proposed to do and how soon it will be done, because all this has become an urgent matter.[2] I am thinking of appointing a committee to draw up a plan for the development of Assam. This committee, among other things, will have to consider the Railway aspect also. It might be desirable to have Medhi on that committee, or on some other supervisory committee.

Yours sincerely,
Jawaharlal Nehru

---

1. File No. 17(259)/57-68-70-PMS. Also available in JN Collection.
2. Jagjivan Ram replied on 30 August 1957 that he had decided to create a separate Railway Zone in Assam covering entire North Eastern Railway from Barauni eastward to Tinsukia and beyond. He gave a brief indication of the works, approximate cost and time required for their completion. Approximately Rs 32 crores were required for stabilization of the existing route, providing alternative alignment to cover the foothills, doubling of tracks where necessary, construction of a bridge on the Brahmaputra at Amingaon, and rolling stock to complete between one to five years' time.

6. To Hareswar Goswami[1]

New Delhi
September 6, 1957

Dear Shri Goswami,

Thank you for your letter of the 26th August.[2] I am sorry for the delay in answering it. I have been very heavily occupied.

It is difficult for me to discuss all the matters referred to in your letter except to tell you that your information in regard to some of them is not correct. So far as the question of refinery is concerned, no final decision was arrived at at any stage. At one stage we were told that it was not possible to prepare project reports unless some indication was given about the possible locations of the refinery. It was at that stage that Barauni was mentioned in this connection. This was a provisional decision to enable various reports to be prepared for consideration.

There is no question of accepting or rejecting the Location Enquiry Committee's report. That is merely part of the data before us.

I do not know when the project reports will be ready. They will probably take some months. A project report contains a detailed working out of all aspects of the scheme with estimates, etc. Normally, this is done by large firms who specialize in this kind of thing and who utilize different types of engineers for the purpose. An individual expert can hardly prepare a project report unless he has a large group to assist him.

I have not heard that the Bihar Government is doing anything in Barauni in connection with the possible location of the refinery there.

You say that in the case of the location of the refinery it should not matter much if the Central Government suffers some loss and that economic and technical considerations need not be given too much importance. So far as this

---

1. JN Collection.
2. Expressing concern about economic development of Assam, Goswami wrote that location of an oil refinery in Assam would improve communication, facilitate growth of subsidiary industries, remove shyness of capital etc. He pointed out that the refinery agitation had made the people of Assam quite industry-minded which would not have come about even ' with 20 years of usual propaganda. He sought clarification on the location of oil refinery (Barauni or Guwahati) and criterion of economic and technical considerations or special situation in Assam for it, Government's decision on the report of Location Enquiry Committee, and proposed gas and fertilizer plants in Assam.

refinery is concerned, as we are going to consider the whole question fully later when all the facts are before us, I need not discuss it now on inadequate data. But apart from this, there are certain aspects in general which we have always to bear in mind.

Unless the production and distribution of oil is economically profitable and competitive, this will not enable us to meet the arguments of the oil companies in regard to price which we consider quite unsound. At present, the major oil companies in the world have laid down methods of calculating prices which, we think, are wrong and which should be modified greatly. If our own production is expensive, then we cannot meet the case of the oil companies. The result is not loss of some money but an obstruction in the way of our developing our oil exploitation and profiting by it as Assam should.

It is thus not a question of suffering some initial loss but of satisfying a number of considerations from various points of view, including, of course, the good of Assam. If a refinery, wherever started, does not make good economically, this will have repercussions adverse to Assam and will come in the way of future development of oil exploration in India, and more particularly in Assam. We think, there is a great future for the development of oil in Assam and that we are likely to find much more of it there. This is fortunate for Assam because this will lead directly and indirectly to many avenues of progress. But it becomes necessary that the initial step should be a marked success. Otherwise future progress will be delayed.

Any success in the exploitation of oil in Assam can only result from hard work and cooperation of the Government and people of Assam with those who are working on this oil. If that cooperation is lacking, then it might be better to postpone this exploitation till better times.

Independently of this oil, there are various proposals for encouraging industrial advance in Assam.

Yours sincerely,
Jawaharlal Nehru

7. To Bisnuram Medhi[1]

New Delhi
September 19, 1957

My dear Medhi,

Some time ago I had a visit from Hoover Hyuniewta, a person coming from Khasi and Jaintia Hills. He gave me some copies of correspondence with the Assam Government, which I enclose. He also spoke to me of the great difficulties which they had been experiencing on the Pakistan border. You know these well and I need not repeat them. But one thing I should like to tell you. He complained that they had addressed the Assam Government and had received no reply. I hope, you will remedy this omission and in fact treat these people with every courtesy. We should try to do what we can for them. There is much that we cannot do at present, but personal contacts and courteous behaviour is always good. I suggest, therefore, that some of their representatives might be sent for and their problems discussed.

Yours sincerely,
Jawaharlal Nehru

1. JN Collection.

8. Tribal Problems of Hill Areas[1]

Yesterday, I received a telegram from some tribal leaders in Shillong.[2] I want to send an answer to it. Please find out the telegram. But in today's *Statesman* there is a mention of that telegram. Send the following answer. This should be

1. Note to Private Secretary, New Delhi, 26 September 1957. JN Collection.
2. In a statement issued on 24 September, B.M. Pugh, Captain Williamson, T. Cajee, R. Thanhilira, MP and B.M. Roy, MLA, said that the tribal problems in the eastern frontiers of India would remain "not only unsolved but in fact will be aggravated if consideration of the problems of other hill people is not taken up simultaneously with the solution of the Naga problem."

355

sent to Mr B.M. Pugh, President, Eastern India Tribal Union, Shillong. Send copies of your reply to Captain Williamson, Vice-President and Mr T. Cajee, Secretary. Send copies of your reply to the Home Minister and to the Governor of Assam, Rashtrapati Bhavan:

"Dear Sir,

The Prime Minister has received your telegram. He has asked me to acknowledge it and to inform you that he and his colleagues are giving thought to the problems of the Hill States in Assam. He hopes to deal with this matter in consultation with the representatives of the Hill States as also of the Assam Government. He is leaving for Japan soon and will return in the third week of October. Meanwhile he has requested his colleague, the Home Minister of the Government of India, to go to Shillong at a date convenient to him to discuss this matter with the representatives of the Hill States in Assam. Both the Prime Minister and the Home Minister are anxious to deal with this question at an early date and to find a satisfactory solution of the problems connected with it.

Yours sincerely,"

IV. BIHAR

1. To Jayaprakash Narayan[1]

New Delhi
August 2, 1957

My dear Jayaprakash,

Thank you for your letter of the 28th July, which reached me today.[2] I am glad you have reverted to our normal method of addressing each other.

1. JN Collection.
2. Jayaprakash referred to buying of legislators and the case against Mahesh Prasad Sinha, Minister for Industry, Transport, Information and Revenue, in Bihar. He wrote that the hush-hush manner, in which this case was dealt with, had done no good to the prestige of Congress in Bihar. He felt that a proper procedure had to be rethought for investigating charges against Congressmen holding public office.

As suggested by you, I have shown your letter to me as well as your letter to Sri Babu,[3] to Morarjibhai. I am sending both to Dhebarbhai.

You refer to legislators being bought up. I referred your previous letter, as I wrote to you, to Dhebarbhai. In this connection, I might tell you that we received complaints of exactly the same kind against Anugraha Babu.[4] The complaints came from a non-Congressman. I confess to being somewhat overwhelmed by these widespread complaints. I could not believe that either Sri Babu or Anugraha Babu could have anything to do with such a thing. It is possible, of course, that other people exploited their names.

It is always a difficult matter to hold enquiries when charges are made. The charges may be true or not. But it has become common practice to hurl the most serious charges against well known people, especially during election time.

Our practice in the Congress has been to consider such charges and, if they are not, on the face of it, frivolous, to have a private enquiry made by some leading and competent person. If we have a public enquiry or ask Government to conduct one into every charge that is made, then there is hardly anyone that I know of in India, who would not be constantly under enquiry. On the receipt of the report of the private enquiry, the parties concerned are asked for their replies etc. Sometimes, they are interviewed. The Disciplinary Committee of the Congress considers all these matters and papers at considerable length and comes to some decision. That decision, sometimes, may be based on giving a person the benefit of doubt or, in our opinion, he may have cleared himself or, in some cases, action is taken by us.

In a recent case, when charges were made against a leading Congressman, we have requested Sardar Hukam Singh, Deputy Speaker, to be good enough to enquire. No one can challenge his impartiality or competence.

I am not trying to defend anybody in Bihar or elsewhere, because I have been greatly distressed at what I have seen and heard about Bihar. I am merely pointing out that we try not to be complacent and deal with difficult situations in the manner which appears to us to be feasible. In this and like matters, it is naturally the Congress President who takes the initiative. I know of few persons anywhere who are more anxious to maintain integrity in public life than Dhebarbhai.

Yours affectionately,
Jawaharlal Nehru

---

3. Sri Krishna Sinha, Chief Minister of Bihar.
4. Anugraha Narain Sinha, who was Finance Minister in Bihar Government, died on 5 July 1957.

2. To Jayaprakash Narayan[1]

New Delhi
September 7, 1957

My dear Jayaprakash,

Your letter of the 30th August 1957.[2] I am sorry for the little delay in answering it. I have been heavily occupied.

You have referred again to various allegations against the Chief Ministers of Bihar and Orissa. Anything coming from your personal knowledge naturally deserves consideration. But it is very difficult and rather improper, I think, to take any kind of formal action on the basis of gossip and vague allegations. In the case of any individual, it would hardly be right for me to have roving enquiries unless I had some specific facts to hold on to. In the case of a person holding the highly responsible office of Chief Minister, it would be even more extraordinary for us to have such a roving enquiry. That kind of thing may be done in authoritarian States. But I hope, we shall not hold up the secret service above the heads of people here, including our own colleagues.

If you will be good enough to let me have some particulars about the sums collected, with those who collected them and those who made the contributions, then it would be possible to start some kind of an enquiry. I would make a reference to the persons concerned and adopt other ways of ascertaining the true facts. A roving enquiry, I think, is hardly ever justified and certainly not in the case of persons bearing heavy burdens of responsibility in difficult circumstances.

Yours affectionately,
Jawaharlal Nehru

---

1. JN Collection. Also available in AICC Papers, NMML.
2. Jayaprakash Narayan wrote that in Orissa, some members of Ganatantra Parishad walked over to the Congress Party to enable it to secure a majority in the Legislature. According to him this was "engineered by a liberal distribution of bribe." He wrote that in Bihar also, a similar last minute walk over of supporters of A.N. Sinha was engineered to Sri Krishna Sinha's side. Jayaprakash recalled that U.N. Dhebar told him that while enquiring into Mahesh Prasad Sinha's case, Dhebar was handicapped because he could not ask for State papers and had to read between the lines of the replies sent to him by the persons concerned. Jayaprakash repeated his suggestion that Nehru should, through his own private or Government sources, satisfy himself about the truth and then take appropriate action.

3. To Sri Krishna Sinha[1]

New Delhi
18 September, 1957

My dear Sri Babu,

Your attention has already been drawn to the case of Dr J.C. Jain[2] who was selected by the Bihar Public Service Commission for appointment as Professor of Prakrit & Jain Learning in the Vaishali Institute. It appears that the Bihar Council of Ministers approved of Dr Jain's appointment and this approval was communicated to Dr Jain who appeared for medical examination and was passed as fit sometime in March 1957. Two months later, the Additional Under Secretary to Bihar Government addressed a note or memorandum in regard to Dr Jain to the Council of Ministers. A copy of this memorandum is being published. It is dated 17th May, 1957.

"I am not in a position to express any opinion about Dr J.C. Jain. But what I am concerned with is the fact that the Bihar Council of Ministers comes to a decision and then reverses it on the basis apparently of this note from the Additional Under Secretary which refers to a CID report and says that this report "has revealed that Dr Jain has very pronounced leanings towards communism since 1945. He is the Vice-President of the India-China Friendship Association, Bombay. His association with communism makes it very risky for the State Government to appoint such a person to an important post in Class I Bihar Educational Service as Professor in the Vaishali Institute".

The note goes on further to say "In the circumstances, it is proposed to appoint Dr Nathmal Tatia[3] (the second nominee of the Commission) to that post on a temporary basis".

As I have said above, I know nothing about Dr Jain. But I am surprised to read the Under Secretary's note and further to realize that the Bihar Council of Ministers reversed their previous decision on the basis of this note only.

1. JN Collection.
2. Jagdish Chandra Jain (b. 1909); Head, Hindi Department, Ramnarain Ruia College, Bombay, 1938-68; taught Hindi at Peking University, China, 1952-53; Vaishali Prakrit Institute, Muzaffarpur, 1958-59 and Kiel University, West Germany, 1970-74; received Soviet Land Nehru Award, 1966; some of his publications are *Prakrit Sahitya Ka Itihasa, Bharatiya Tattvacintana, Life in Ancient India as depicted in the Jain Canons.*
3. Professor of Pali, Prakrit and Buddhist Philosophy; Director, Research Institute of Prakrit Jainology and Ahimsa, Muzaffarpur in 1960s; author of *A Critique of Organ of Knowledge* and *Sarvastivada.*

I do not know what kind of notes Under Secretaries and others usually write to you. But the present note appears to me to be objectionable and if I received such a note I would ask for some kind of an explanation from the person concerned for writing in this manner. It was open to him to draw attention to a CID report. But to say that because of this it was proposed to appoint someone else was not proper. The second question is whether the Bihar Government comes to decisions about individuals on such flimsy evidence as in this case. The fact that Dr Jain was or is Vice-President of the India-China Friendship Association is supposed to reveal pronounced leanings towards communism. This is rather odd because quite a number of people, including your present Governor,[4] have been associated with the India-China Friendship Association. Your CID and your Under Secretary have not apparently understood what is happening in the world today and what the policy of our Government is. Further, the appointment was for a Professor of Prakrit and Jain learning which presumably has nothing to do with communism.

This entire case leaves a feeling of distaste in the mouth. It shows how third-rate people impose themselves in regard to important appointments. This is just the kind of thing which has raised a furore in some Western countries and has been called McCarthyism in the United States. I think that the prestige of your educational institutions will go down if it is known that their appointments have to be vetted by some Sub-Inspector of police or CID or some Under Secretary.

Yours sincerely,
Jawaharlal Nehru

4. Zakir Husain.

4. To Sri Krishna Sinha[1]

New Delhi
October 19, 1957

My dear Sri Babu,
On my return here from Japan, I heard of the dismal news about the failure of the rains in Bihar and elsewhere and the grave consequences that we have to

1. JN Collection.

face. I have also received your letter on this subject. Ajit Prasad Jain is going to Bihar. We are collecting all the facts of the situation, so that we can give it full consideration soon.

May I send you all my good wishes on the occasion of your birthday on the 21st October, when you will be completing seventy years. During these many years, you have carried a very heavy burden, and you have still to shoulder it. There is no escape for us, whatever the difficulties. I hope that your health is good now and that you will be spared to us for many long years.

Yours sincerely,
Jawaharlal Nehru

V. BOMBAY

1. To Gulzarilal Nanda[1]

New Delhi
August 7, 1957

My dear Gulzarilal,
Some papers have been sent to me about a case started by Paranjape against me. This matter should be looked after entirely by the Bharat Sewak Samaj, who know the facts.

Evidently, there is some case against you too. The two cases must cover more or less the same ground.

It is suggested that we should object to leave being granted to sue in *forma pauperis*. So far as I am concerned, I am certainly not prepared to take up this technical plea and to have an investigation made into his private effects. This is most undignified. And I do not see why the Bombay Government should go out of its way to do this. At the most, the Bombay Government's attention should be drawn to the matter. But, my name should not be dragged into this at all.

---

1. JN Collection.

It is apparently suggested that a Counsel be engaged, and the name of R.M. Hajarnavis,[2] MP, has been suggested. This is entirely for you to consider.

Yours sincerely,
Jawaharlal Nehru

2. (1908-1976); Advocate, Bombay High Court and Supreme Court; taught law in the University of Nagpur for some time; Member, Lok Sabha, 1952-67; Union Deputy Minister of Law, 1958-63; Minister of State for Home Affairs, 1963-64; Minister of State for Law and Social Security, 1965-66.

2. To Y.B. Chavan[1]

New Delhi
August 11, 1957

My dear Chavan,
I am told that the Indian Society of Agricultural Economics conducted a survey of the Surat District some little time ago and has presented a report of this survey to the Bombay Government. No doubt your Government is considering this report. I shall be glad if you will have a copy sent to me, because we are all interested in these surveys and what they reveal. We are anxious to tone up the administration and such reports often help us in doing so.

I am afraid most of us in the Central Government live rather far removed from district administration. It is good for our education, therefore, to see these reports so that we might appreciate what is happening at the District level.

Yours sincerely,
Jawaharlal Nehru

1. JN Collection.

3. To Sri Prakasa[1]

New Delhi
August 31, 1957

My dear Prakasa,[2]

As you perhaps know, Damodar Swaroop Seth[3] cited me as a witness for the defence in the case against him. I was supposed to be a witness of good character. The Commission came here some days ago, and took my evidence. In the course of this evidence, I was asked about a letter written by you to me in or about July 1953, and my reply to you. Also, the letter I wrote to the Finance Minister[4] then in the same connection.

I did not have these letters with me. I said that I remembered getting a letter from you and referring it to the Finance Minister. I was then asked if I would be prepared to produce these letters. I replied that communications between a Governor and a Prime Minister are confidential documents, and I would not like such secret papers to be produced in a Court of Law. That, of course, had no reference to the contents of these letters. When I was asked further if I would trace these letters and see what they were, I said I would try to find them and look into them.

Now, the Registrar of the City Sessions Court, Bombay, has written to the Secretary to the Government of India, Ministry of External Affairs, on this subject. He has asked these three letters to be placed before me for my decision whether I claim the privilege either under Section 123 or Section 124 of the Indian Evidence Act in respect of any of them. It is added that if I decided to claim privilege, even so the letters should be sent, under seals, through a responsible officer, apparently so that the Judge may look at them and decide on the question of privilege.

I have got copies of these letters out from my old file. I enclose a set of copies for you to see, although you must have the original or copies of some of them. These copies are :-

(1) Your letter to me from Madras, dated July 24th, 1953.

(2) My letter to Deshmukh, dated July 28th, 1953. (This was a forwarding copy of your letter to me).

1. JN Collection.
2. Governor of Bombay.
3. Congressman from Uttar Pradesh.
4. C.D. Deshmukh.

(3) My brief letter to you, dated August 11th, 1953, with which I enclosed a copy of Deshmukh's letter to me, dated August 10th, 1953.

On reading your letter of July 24th again, I find there is reference to Satya Ranjan Bakshi[5] having seen me and further that I had given him some impression that I would be prepared to intervene in case someone could be found, who would be willing to invest the necessary money. In reply to you, I did not deal with this matter. Indeed, I did not deal with your letter at all, except to send it on to the Finance Minister. It was rather a pity that I did not write to you on this subject myself, because evidently Satya Ranjan Bakshi must have told you something which was not correct. I have no recollection of his seeing me in this connection, but, of course, I might have forgotten this and he may have come to me. He saw me sometimes, and wanted me to get some kind of employment for him. It is possible that he might have mentioned Shankar Lal's or Damodar Swarup's case to me, though I do not remember. But, I am quite sure that I could never have told him that I would intervene if someone could be found to invest the necessary money. That is a course I could not have adopted. I am very careful about these matters. It is just possible that when he said this to me, I would have said that this was a matter for the Finance Ministry to consider or some such thing.

I am merely mentioning this matter to clear up my mind and, perhaps, your mind on this subject, although this does not arise now.

The question now is about my producing these letters in Court. I am reluctant to do so, as it is a bad precedent for confidential letters from a Governor to a Prime Minister to be so produced. At the same time, the letters really deal with rather personal matters and can hardly be said to be on Government business as such. If I sent them, as I suppose I must, to the Judge, even if I plead privilege he might well write to me that, in his opinion, there is nothing to suggest privilege in these letters. I can hardly have an argument with him on this subject, more especially, as no Government secrets are involved.

It is my intention to have copies of these letters sent to the Registrar of the City Sessions Court, Bombay. My Principal Private Secretary[6] will do so and, in a covering letter, he will state that the Prime Minister thinks that secret and confidential letters exchanged between Governors and Prime Ministers should not be disclosed or produced in Court unless, of course, some grave public interest is involved. The Prime Minister thinks that it would be desirable under Section 124 of the Evidence Act, not to produce these letters. But, he is having

5. An associate of Subhas Bose.
6. Kesho Ram.

copies of the letters referred to, sent for the Additional Sessions Judge of Greater Bombay to consider them. If the Judge thinks that it is necessary in the wider public interest to disclose these letters, the Prime Minister will abide by his judgment, even though he would prefer not to produce these letters.

Something to this effect might be written to the Registrar. We would then await his reply and, naturally, if the Judge decides the letters should be produced, they will be produced.

I am, however, not taking this step till I hear from you. I understand that you are also going to be examined in this case, and I have little doubt that you will also be asked about these letters. You will be asked anyhow, whether I send them or not. If I send them, then of course, you may be asked in regard to their contents. Your answers will naturally be, as more or less mine were, that you know nothing about the cases in which Damodar Swarup is involved. All you knew was the person himself, and you could not conceive that such a man was likely to go in for these major frauds, having regard to his previous life etc.

In the event of your being asked as to what Satya Ranjan Bakshi said to you about me, you might well say that he told you what you had written, but you have no other knowledge as to what Satya Ranjan Bakshi is reported to have said to me or what I said to him in reply.

I am inclined to think, as I have stated above, that the best course would be the one I have suggested above, that is, for me to have these letters sent to the Judge, claiming privilege, but, at the same time, telling him that I will abide by his decision in this matter.

I might just mention for your information, that Satya Ranjan Bakshi is not at all a reliable person. These persons connected with old revolutionary activities have a curious bent of mind. Please let me have an answer soon. As a matter of fact, we were asked to produce these letters on the 3rd September. Patently, this is not possible, and we have told them so. But, nevertheless, we have to send an answer soon.

Yours affectionately,
Jawaharlal Nehru

4. To Sri Prakasa[1]

New Delhi
September 3, 1957

My dear Prakasa,

A few days ago I wrote to you about the Damodar Swarup matter and the summons that had come to me to produce some letters. At that time I felt that I should claim privilege, but nevertheless leave it to the Judge to decide. I sent all these papers to our Law Ministry. The Law Minister spoke to me today that in his opinion I should definitely claim privilege and not send these letters to the Judge in Bombay. He is sending me a note to this effect. I have not seen it yet.

In view of the Law Minister's opinion, I shall probably not send these letters to the Judge and claim absolute privilege. I am writing to you immediately so as to let you know what I am likely to do. I shall write to you again after I have seen the Law Minister's note and have taken a final decision in this matter.

Yours affectionately,
Jawaharlal Nehru

---

1. JN Collection.

1. Expansion of Delhi not at the Cost of Peasants' Interest[1]

As I mentioned to you today, a fairly large crowd of peasants from roundabout Delhi came to my house this afternoon. They came to protest against some orders of land acquisition for purposes of housing scheme.[2]

2. Some two months ago or so, a few of these people had come to me and brought their complaint. I had told them that I would enquire into it. The matter was referred to the Chief Commissioner,[3] who sent me some particulars. On reading the Chief Commissioner's note, I felt that I should not interfere in this matter. It was difficult to prevent Delhi from spreading and, in any event, it would not be possible for these adjoining areas to be protected for long from this spreading city. I did not then go deeply into this matter.

3. Today, various points were raised. It was natural for the peasantry to dislike and to resist being turned out of their homes. Apart from this, there was the idea at the back of their minds, that their land was going to be handed over to some rich companies or housing societies, who will make a great deal of money out of it. Houses will be built for the rich etc.

4. I spoke to this crowd (which was led by Raja Mahendra Pratap, MP). I told them that they must realize that a big city grows, and nothing could stop the growth of Delhi. We did not want our cities to become bigger and bigger, but it was not possible wholly to stop this growth. If this growth occurred, it could either be planned or in a haphazard manner. Thus far, it had been of the latter kind mostly and, in fact, some housing companies had bought their land cheaply and sold it at a much bigger price, thus making a huge profit. I entirely disapproved of them and I hoped that nothing of this kind would occur in the future.

1. Note to Home Minister, New Delhi, 30 August 1957. JN Collection.
2. About one thousand *kisans* from four villages on the outskirts of New Delhi protested against the acquisition of their land for the purpose of a Government housing scheme and for constructing the Indian Medical Institute's building. See also *Selected Works* (second series), Vol. 37, pp. 330-31.
3. A.D. Pandit.

5. If we allowed this haphazard growth to go on, the peasants roundabout would suffer most by it. They would be induced to sell their separate bits of land, and no provision will be made for them. It was much better, therefore, that this matter be approached in an organized and planned way, attention being paid to the interests of the peasants and their future habitation etc.

6. I said that it was not possible for me to express any definite opinion to them at this stage, except what I had said above. I was naturally concerned to see that the interests of these people were looked after. At the same time, I did not myself see how the growth of Delhi in that direction could be stopped for long. However, I promised to look into this matter again and to find out what was proposed to be done and how far the interests of the peasantry were being looked after.

7. I am sending you this note as I understand you are discussing this matter with the Chief Commissioner soon. A copy of this note is being sent to the Chief Commissioner.

8. I enclose a note that these villagers gave me.

2. Removal of Unauthorized Construction[1]

You may forward this to the authorities concerned. But in this matter of unauthorized constructions, wherever they might be, I do not think it is easy for exceptions to be made. If exceptions are made, obviously other people will do the same thing again and again and we shall never put an end to this. The Chairman of the DDPA told me some time ago that it would not be possible for him to carry out any policy if exceptions were constantly made. The result was he never caught up with these irregularities and illegalities.

2. At the same time, there is always the human element and one does not want to create repeated crises with a large number of people wandering about or sitting at dharna in front of my house.

3. You should, therefore, send this on to the Chairman of the DDPA and tell him to consider all these various aspects and decide as he thinks fit.

---

1. Note to Principal Private Secretary, New Delhi, 5 September 1957. JN Collection.

4. The rainy season is now on, but it will be over. I suppose, within two or three weeks or so. It would certainly be undesirable to pull down these structures till the rainy season is quite over.

3. To D.P. Karmarkar[1]

New Delhi
24 September 1957

My dear Karmarkar,

I am told that the Delhi sweepers' organization is again having trouble with the Municipal authorities. They are harassed and victimized and large-scale transfers have taken place. Those workers who appeared as witnesses before the Judicial Enquiry are said to be victimized.[2] If these charges are true or even partly true, the attitude of the Municipal authorities is very wrong and objectionable. They are inviting trouble for themselves and they would have no sympathy from us. Could you please send for these Municipal people and find out what is happening and tell them of the complaints we are receiving.

Also, I should like to know how many of the old demands of these workers have been fulfilled.

Yours sincerely,
Jawaharlal Nehru

1. JN Collection.
2. See *ante,* pp. 306-307.

369

4. To K.L. Balmiki[1]

New Delhi
2 October, 1957

Dear Shri Balmiki,[2]

I have your letter of the 26th September. When you wrote to me some days earlier, I asked my Principal Private Secretary to go into all your complaints and to get in touch with the Delhi Municipal authorities. I also wrote to the Health Minister of the Government of India.[3] I was not only very busy but it would have served little purpose for me to meet any deputation till these matters had been enquired into fully.

I understand from Shri Kesho Ram, my Principal Private Secretary, that he has met you and discussed this matter with you very fully. He has also met the Health Officer of Delhi. I have further had other reports also.

The report that Shri Kesho Ram has made to me, after his talks with you, does not quite fit in with your complaints. Your letter talks vaguely about harassment and victimization etc. If there is any victimization, it is bad and I am certainly prepared to enquire into it. But I cannot enquire into a vague charge. We have been assured by the Health Officer that the charge is not at all correct.

The only specific instance that you have given is that instead of one full holiday weekly on Sundays, the new arrangements are to give two half holidays, one half day on Sunday and one half day on Thursday. This, I am told, is correct. I am further told, however, that this is generally approved by the persons concerned. I myself would have thought that this might be more advantageous but in this matter I am prepared to abide by the decision of the workers themselves. If they definitely prefer one full day's holiday to two half days, I shall certainly ask the Municipal authorities of Delhi to accede to their request.

I am leaving Delhi tomorrow for Japan but I shall come back within two weeks. Meanwhile, I am asking my Principal Private Secretary to keep in touch with these developments and to help the Municipal workers in every way to get any legitimate grievance removed.

1. JN Collection.
2. Trustee, Balmiki Temple, Delhi and Member, Lok Sabha.
3. See the preceding item.

I find from your letters that they are vague and contain general charges. Such letters are not at all helpful to me. Thus, you say that the demands which have been accepted have not been fulfilled. You do not mention a single one of these. I should like you to give me precise details about any complaints and not merely to write to me in strong language.

As you know, I am particularly interested in this question of Municipal workers in Delhi and I am going to maintain my interest and to see that justice is done to them. You will not help me in this by merely making complaints in strong language. There must be a cooperative attitude on all sides, that is, on the side of the Delhi Municipal authorities as well of the Municipal workers.

Yours sincerely,
Jawaharlal Nehru

5. Sweepers Require Courteous Treatment[1]

Please see the letter from Shri Balmiki and my reply to him. I have no doubt that Balmiki exaggerates and often behaves in a manner which is not very desirable. But it is not for the New Delhi Health Officer merely to criticize or condemn Balmiki whatever the latter's behaviour might be. We must remember that people who have been brought up, as many of our depressed class people have been, in very bad surroundings, and have been kicked and cuffed about for a long time, are apt to react strongly. They do not have the advantage of education nor have they been trained in restraint. We, who have had these advantages, have no business to criticize these people because they do not come up to our standards.

2. Further, Shri Balmiki is a Member of Parliament, apart from being the Secretary of the Municipal Workers Sangh. He has to be treated, therefore, with consideration, whatever any of our officers might think of him.

3. You will see from my letter that I have made it clear that if the Delhi sweepers prefer one full day's holiday to two half days, their wishes will have to be accepted, whatever we may think about it. It is they who are concerned and who have to

1. Note to Principal Private Secretary, New Delhi, 2 October 1957. JN Collection.

make this decision. This should be made perfectly clear to the Health Officer and to the New Delhi Municipal Committee. If this means addition of some staff, we shall have to accept this. It is no good our trying to impose our own opinion on them in a matter which affects them intimately. I do not know what many of our officers in Government Departments would say if we suggested to them two half holidays in a week instead of the Sunday full holiday. I rather doubt if they would like to change.

4. I do not like references in Balmiki's letter to the Health Officer's behaviour. These references may be exaggerated but the mere impression created of such behaviour is bad. It is up to the Health Officer to create a different impression on his workers. He has to remember that it is not right to treat even sweepers in the old way. Their cooperation is to be sought and the language used towards them should always be courteous.

5. Please keep in touch with this situation and I shall go into it again on my return.

6. To Mehr Chand Khanna[1]

New Delhi
October 2, 1957

My dear Mehr Chand,[2]

Your letter of September 28th about the various markets in Delhi.

I quite agree with you that we should adhere to our previous decision in regard to some of these markets and retain Government ownership and control over them. This has nothing to do with the financial aspect. It is intimately connected with the planning of Delhi. We dare not take any step now which will come in the way of this planning. After the full plan is ready, we can consider this matter and see how far it fits in with it.

Yours sincerely,
Jawaharlal Nehru

1. JN Collection.
2. Minister of State for Rehabilitation and Minority Affairs.

VII. HIMACHAL PRADESH

1. To S.K. Dey[1]

New Delhi
August 14, 1957

My dear Dey,

I met a deputation from Himachal Pradesh today who complained that all development work was held up there and the administration was hardly functioning. More particularly, they referred to roads, where work had been stopped and the men working there were unemployed. The roads were gradually deteriorating. There were jeepable roads, but not good enough for trucks and so they could not be used for the potato season.

They also referred to dispensaries and hospitals gradually being given up. In particular they mentioned that a small hospital at Konihar of six beds had had its beds taken away. Also that health centres were locked up.

In the course of conversation they said that they had spoken to you and you had expressed the opinion that the administration of Himachal Pradesh was irresponsible.

Would you let me know what your own opinion is about the conditions in Himachal Pradesh, more especially, in the Community Development areas.

Yours sincerely,
Jawaharlal Nehru

---

1. JN Collection.

2. To Bajrang Bahadur Singh of Bhadri[1]

New Delhi
September 18, 1957

My dear Bhadri,[2]

I have been wanting to write to you for some time past. In the course of the last session of our Parliament, some MPs from Himachal Pradesh as well as a number of other people connected with Himachal Pradesh have seen me from time to time. Most of those spoke highly of you and your work, but they had a number of complaints. I know well about the party factions in Himachal Pradesh, and it is not easy to sift the truth from various statements made. I have no doubt that you are fully seized with the position in Himachal Pradesh.

I think, however, that I should let you know what many of these people have been telling me. Most of them feel that the popular element is not given much chance and that the officials still behave in the old way and do not cooperate with this popular element. These officials, many of whom belong to the old *Riyasti* Services, find it difficult to fit in into the democratic structure. They tend, therefore, to restrict or give an illiberal interpretation to the Acts or Rules framed.

There is a Territorial Council now and, in all such organizations, a great deal depends on the human factor and on the spirit of cooperation between various elements. The political element in Himachal Pradesh is not very bright and has little training. But, there it is, and we have to accept it and try to work with it. The only way to do so is to give them a sensation of frequent consultation and thus enable them to develop.

In so far as the powers given to the Territorial Council are concerned, they should be liberally interpreted in favour of the popular element. In regard to the reserved subjects, more especially such as dealing with public activities, panchayats, cooperatives, developments, etc., frequent consultation is desirable,

I have been told that developmental work under the Second Five Year Plan has long been held up, and progress has been slow, even though there is no lack of money.

I am passing on these complaints and suggestions to you for your consideration, not knowing myself what the exact facts are. But, in any event, I would suggest to you to confer with these popular members of the Territorial Council and

---

1. JN Collection.
2. Lieutenant-Governor of Himachal Pradesh.

others as frequently as possible, and also to tell your officers to do this, so as to create a sensation among these people that they are parts of the governing apparatus and not outsiders who are just tolerated.

Yours sincerely,
Jawaharlal Nehru

3. Working of Cooperatives[1]

Please see the attached letter from Dr Parmar.[2] You should write to the Himachal Pradesh authorities and enquire from them as to what the Committee appointed to enquire into the cooperatives has been doing and when it is expected to present its report. Tell them that this Committee was appointed especially at my instance. I am, therefore, interested in its work. Tell them also that I have received some complaints that this Committee is not receiving the cooperation it should from the Cooperative Department of the State. You might quote the passage from the *Tribune*, which I have marked in the attached letter.

2. Do not refer to Dr Parmar's letter.

1. Note to Principal Private Secretary, New Delhi, 19 October 1957. JN Collection.
2. Congress Member, Lok Sabha from Mahasu, Himachal Pradesh.

VIII. KERALA

1. To Govind Ballabh Pant[1]

New Delhi
August 10, 1957

My dear Pantji,

I have received a telegram from the Mayor of Trivandrum, copy of which is enclosed.[2]

As the President has already agreed to lay the foundation stone of the proposed Freedom Hall, there is not much more to be said about it. I do not know who the Mayor of Trivandrum is, that is, whether he belongs to the Communist Party or not. If he belongs to the Party, then this may be said to be sponsored and approved by the present Kerala Government. If he does not belong to the Party, then it might be some kind of a move independent of the Kerala Government.

I should like your advice. I suppose there is no harm in my sending a message.

Yours affectionately,
Jawaharlal Nehru

---

1. JN Collection.
2. In his telegram of 9 August 1957, the Mayor requested the Prime Minister "to send a message to be read out on occasion of foundation stone (of Freedom Hall) laying by *Rashtrapati* on morning of Wednesday Fourteenth August." The Freedom Hall was intended to be "an architectural edifice" depicting freedom struggle, paintings on patriotic themes and India's basic cultural unity, tolerance and goodwill. The Hall would also provide open forums for free expression of opinion, political and cultural."

2. To E.M.S. Namboodiripad[1]

New Delhi
August 31, 1957

My dear Namboodiripad,

On the 24th August, I sent you a letter, with which I enclosed a copy of a resolution passed by a Muslim organization.[2] The charge made in this was about the kidnapping of an unmarried Muslim girl.

I have now received another letter on the same subject. This is from the Secretary, Thabligul Islam, Nadukunnu, Pathanapuram, Kerala State.[3] I enclose a copy of this also.

I shall be grateful if you would let me know what the facts are and what steps have been taken in this matter. It appears that there is considerable excitement among the Muslims.

Yours sincerely,
Jawaharlal Nehru

---

1. JN Collection.
2. The resolution, passed by the Muslim Jamaat of Erinjalakkuda on 16 August 1957, stated that "the Honourable Minister Shri P.K. Chathan of Kerala State has kidnapped an unmarried girl by name Mymoon Beebi, daughter of late Mr Kattal Abdul Hameed Khan, belonging to a respectable Muslim family of this place, when he visited this place on 10th August 1957." Further, it "requests the authorities to inquire into the matter and prevent recurrence of such disgraceful incidents from persons wielding high authority and power."
3. In his letter of 27 August 1957, the Secretary complained to Nehru that P.K. Chathan, Minister of Local Self-Government, Kerala, had kidnapped a young Muslim girl on 10 August from Alwaye "while the Minister was camping in the Erinjalakkuda T.B." He added: "After spending the whole night in the T.B., he left for Trivandrum along with her. This incident has created great vibration among the religious attitude of the Muslims of this place.." He requested Nehru to take necessary steps in this regard.

IX. MADHYA PRADESH

1. To Padmavati Devi[1]

New Delhi
September 3, 1957

Dear Padmavati,[2]

I have received a letter containing various complaints.[3] It is stated in this letter that a large area of forest having bamboos and teak and other timber of good quality has been granted to you free of royalty. This area is said to measure over eight thousand acres and is about 40 miles from Khairagarh. I have received details of this forest area and how large sums of money have been realized from it by the sale of timber etc., I am not giving the details here.

I am surprised to read this and I am, therefore, writing to you about it. This would have been important in any event, but as you are a Minister of Madhya Pradesh Government, any such charge becomes even more important.

I am drawing the attention of your Chief Minister, Dr Kailas Nath Katju to this. But I should like you to write to me also about this matter.

Yours sincerely,
Jawaharlal Nehru

---

1. JN Collection.
2. (b. 1918); former Rani of Khairagarh; Member, Madhya Bharat and Madhya Pradesh Assemblies, 1952-67; leader, Indian Delegation to the 12th International Conference of Social Work, Athens, 1964; Minister in the Government of Madhya Pradesh, for Public Health, 1956-62, Social Welfare, 1963-64 and Local Government 1964-67.
3. The employees of the Bortalao, Dongargarh Government Forests, South Eastern Railway, Madhya Pradesh, wrote to the Prime Minister that Padmavati Devi had been granted a vast area of forest having the best quality wood. They reported about smuggling, stealing and felling of unapproved teak wood of the Government forest with the help of Forest Department personnel. They requested Nehru to enquire and intervene in the matter.

2. To Kailas Nath Katju[1]

New Delhi
September 19, 1957

My dear Kailas Nath,[2]

Your letter of the 18th September.

The meeting of the Congress Parliamentary Party that I addressed, was, of course not open to the press, but when hundreds of people are present, it can hardly be called a secret meeting. I spoke to the meeting for nearly an hour. Addressing them on various subjects, towards the end of my speech, I referred to the incidents at Raipur.[3] I expressed my great sorrow at them and said that this aggressive communalism and intolerance was bad. I do not think I said anything about seventy Christian families having left Raipur, because I did not know anything about this. But I cannot be sure what the actual words I might have used then. I did lay stress on the Christians there being frightened and the repercussions in other parts of India especially the South.

Yours affectionately,
Jawaharlal Nehru

1. JN Collection.
2. Chief Minister of Madhya Pradesh.
3. The reference is to an attack on a Christian gathering at Raipur. For details see *post,* pp. 471-472.

3. A College Without Students[1]

Will you please find out from the Education Ministry as well as from the Madhya Pradesh Government what the present position is of the Janata College at Sanchi?

2. I want this enquiry to be made because a friend who visited Sanchi recently has written to me that this College was completely deserted when he went there a few days ago. There was not a single student in that institution although there

1. Note to Principal Private Secretary, New Delhi, 19 September 1957. JN Collection.

was a Principal, lecturers, clerks, etc. I visited this place some time ago and at that time some students were produced. I am now told that they were enrolled only for my reception.

4. Grant of Forest Areas[1]

I received a complaint some time ago, in which it was stated that Rani Padmavati Devi of Khairagarh had been given a vast forest area from which she was deriving enormous profit. (This lady is now, I think, a Minister of the Madhya Pradesh Government). Thereupon, I wrote to Dr Katju, Chief Minister of Madhya Pradesh, and I also wrote to Rani Padmavati. She has now replied to me.

I have no time to go into these matters. But, prima facie, I do not understand or appreciate these vast grants, even though they might have been made just before the merger; nor do I understand why the merger took place in 1948 and not earlier at the time of Independence when most States were merged.

I think, this requires further enquiry. Will you please find out the previous papers and refer this matter again both to the Home Ministry and to the Chief Minister of Madhya Pradesh?

Further, please acknowledge this letter and write to Rani Padmavati. You can give her the substance of the complaints received by me previously.

1. Note to Principal Private Secretary, New Delhi, 1 October 1957. JN Collection.

X. MADRAS

1. To C. Subramaniam[1]

New Delhi
19 September, 1957

My dear Subramaniam,[2]

I am getting quite a large number of messages about the riots and killings and shootings roundabout Madurai. Some new ones I enclose. I have some general idea of the situation there and of how Muthuramalinga Thevar[3] and his followers have terrorized people in that area, more especially the Harijans. Evidently, the worm has turned.[4]

But one thing mentioned in the telegram I am sending you is rather upsetting. It is stated that five men were taken by the Ramnad police and were shot down in cold blood, their hands tied behind their backs. Further this was done by the entire village population.

Whether those five men were guilty or not, this kind of procedure by the police is most objectionable.

Yours sincerely,
Jawaharlal Nehru

1. JN Collection.
2. Minister of Finance, Education and Law in Madras Government.
3. Pasumpon Muthuramalinga Thevar (1908-1963); belonged to an ancient warrior community of Maravars; scholar in Tamil and English; well-versed in Saiva Siddhanta Philosophy; joined Congress, 1927; labour leader of the Mahalakshmi Textile Mills, 1936-37; arrested for stirring up labour trouble, 1938; Member, Madras Legislative Assembly, 1937-39; influenced by Netaji and organized the Forward Bloc in Tamil Nadu, 1939; started a Tamil Weekly, the *Netaji* and associated with its publication, 1940-42; Member, Lok Sabha, 1952-62; imprisoned for instigating communal riots in Ramanathapuram District in 1957 and acquitted in 1960.
4. About forty persons were killed in the clashes between Maravars and Harijans in this area and consequent police firing.

2. To G. Ramachandran[1]

New Delhi
2 October, 1957

Dear Ramachandran,[2]

Srinivasan has shown me your letter of the 27th September.

If you so wish it, I can try to reach Gandhigram earlier, i.e., by 8 a.m. As for your second point, I do not think there should be two public meetings within five miles of each other. If there is a big meeting at Dindigul, that might be considered the principal meeting and you could have some smaller function at Gandhigram in the evening. It is difficult for me to fix these matters as every engagement has to be dovetailed into another. Therefore, this can be only done in consultation with the Madras Ministers. Whatever they and you agree to, I shall accept.

But another and unforeseen difficulty has arisen. I have been told that the Madras Government does not particularly fancy my going to the area roundabout Madurai or near it because of the disturbed state of affairs in the Ramanathapuram area. (In your letter you say that your own Shanti Sena was doing work there). Therefore, they want me to postpone my visit entirely to some other date and it is quite possible that they might approach you to change the date of your function.

I have been put in a great difficulty because of this. I do not want to be a burden on the Government or on others and if my going to Gandhigram or the neighbourhood means upsetting the Madras Government's arrangement in Ramanathapuram and their collecting large numbers of policemen etc., wherever I go, then I become a nuisance, and the main purpose of my visit is lost.

I am writing to Subramaniam, the Finance Minister, Madras, about this matter and asking him to get in touch with you. Tomorrow morning I am leaving for Japan.

Yours sincerely,
Jawaharlal Nehru

1. JN Collection.
2. (1904-1995); noted Gandhian from Tamil Nadu; associated with the Hindustani Talimi Sangh and All India Spinners Association for several years; participated in freedom movement and was imprisoned several times; elected to the Travancore Legislative Assembly, 1946 and became Minister but soon resigned; nominated Member of Rajya Sabha, 1964-70.

3. To K. Kamaraj Nadar [1]

New Delhi
October 23, 1957

My dear Kamaraj,[2]

I enclose a press cutting in which E. V. Ramaswami Naicker[3] is supposed to have called upon his followers to kill Brahmins and set fire to their houses. This is really amazing, and this must result in tension and strong communal feeling and may be even murder. I do hope that you will take adequate notice of this.

Yours sincerely,
Jawaharlal Nehru

1. JN Collection.
2. Chief Minister of Madras.
3. Popularly known as "Periyar," he was leader of Dravida Kazhagam; he initiated anti-Hindi movement in Madras.

XI. MYSORE

1. Dussehra Celebrations in Mysore[1]

During my recent visit to Mysore, I had some talk with both the Governor, that is, the Maharaja, and the Chief Minister about the Dussehra celebrations. No mention was made then about the participation of the military. In fact, our talk was chiefly concerned with some conflict of opinion that had arisen between the Chief Minister and the Governor.

1. Note to Defence Secretary, New Delhi, 23 September 1957. JN Collection.

2. The Chief Minister is new, not only to his present office, but also to some extent to the customs of Mysore. The previous Chief Ministers there were Mysoreans and knew about these customs. It appears that an important part of these Dussehra celebrations are religious ceremonies in which the Maharaja plays a central part. The Chief Minister, not aware of this, had suggested that the State should organize these functions. The Maharaja did not like this idea at all, and insisted on the religious part of the ceremonies being a private affair of his own. The Chief Minister ultimately agreed. Apparently, the State will, nevertheless, organize something apart from these religious ceremonies inside the palace.

3. There is another aspect to these Dussehra celebrations and ceremonies. The Maharaja, according to old custom, receives *Nazars*, also the participants of the religious ceremonies go in a special dress or undress. Our advice to the Chief Minister was that, while the Maharaja was free to do what he liked in his personal capacity, the Ministers should not present *Nazars* or go in that special dress to these religious ceremonies. Evidently, the Maharaja did not like this. However, this has been agreed to.

4. In view of all this, there appears to be some lack of cooperation between the Maharaja and the State Government in regard to these celebrations. I am not quite clear as to what the State as such is going to do about them, and I had no occasion to discuss this.

5. I do not know how many of our soldiery previously participated in these celebrations. I would have little objection to any soldiers stationed in Mysore City itself participating, but I do not like the idea of large numbers being sent from Bangalore to Mysore for this purpose. Perhaps, a small number might go.

6. I suggest that you communicate with the Mysore Chief Secretary[2] by telephone and enquire from him what the position is in regard to the State's part in these celebrations. Tell him that it does not appear desirable for a number of reasons, for large numbers of soldiers to be sent from Bangalore to Mysore. If, however, the State so desires, a small number could be sent. We would, however, prefer the Army as such to keep out of it.

2. P.V.R. Rao.

XIII. ORISSA

1. To Harekrushna Mahtab[1]

New Delhi
September 8, 1957

My dear Mahtab,[2]
Jayaprakash Narayan has written to me accusing you or your colleagues of unfair practices and in fact of bribery in getting some members of the Ganatantra Parishad to join the Congress Party.[3] I told him that I could not believe any such thing. He is functioning in a very peculiar way and he has written to me again. I am, therefore, writing to you and would like to have your definite reply to this.

Yours sincerely,
Jawaharlal Nehru

1. JN Collection.
2. Chief Minister of Orissa.
3. See *ante*, p. 358.

XIV. PUNJAB
I. Save Hindi Agitation

1. To Atmanand Saraswati[1]

New Delhi
August 10, 1957

My dear Swami Atmanandji,[2]
I have received your letter of the 8th August 1957.[3]

1. JN Collection.
2. Arya Samaj leader and President of Hindi Raksha Samiti, Punjab.
3. Atmanand Saraswati wrote that Nehru's letter of 22 July 1957 shattered all hopes of his colleagues to get a fair deal to their demand to use Hindi in all educational and administrative matters. He apprised Nehru of the developments in Punjab and the State Government's handling of peaceful agitating volunteers during the two-month old agitation. He mentioned that the Hindi Raksha Samiti had not so far been declared an unlawful organization and the Government had not enforced Section 144 anywhere, therefore, they had not committed any illegal act so far.

I have twice written to you on the subject of the agitation started by the Hindi Raksha Samiti in the Punjab.[4] I have ventured to write at some length in order to try to put before you my own viewpoint and to convince you that the agitation with which you are connected is doing a great deal of harm to the cause of Hindi that you espouse, apart from the other national injuries it causes. It would serve little purpose for me to repeat those arguments, but I would like to say again that it passes my comprehension how the cause of Hindi is being helped in any way by your agitation.

You say in your letter that you think that my mind is a closed one on this subject. It is not for me to judge my mind, because I cannot take an objective view of myself. But I try always not to have a closed mind, even in regard to matters about which I feel strongly. Perhaps it would be equally justifiable for me to say that your mind and the mind of your colleagues in this agitation is a closed mind which does not take into consideration the good of India or the Punjab or of Hindi, and is actuated evidently by other motives.

I have ventured to suggest to you in my previous letters that this agitation, whatever its motives, could only be a communal one and would raise communal passions. It is clear now, even if there was some doubt previously, that this has developed into a purely communal agitation and that some of the well known communal elements in the Punjab are intimately associated with it. Indeed, it appears to be conducted much more now by the Jan Sangh in the Punjab than even by the Arya Samaj which started it. It is a matter of deep regret to me that the Arya Samaj, which has such a great record of social and educational work behind it, should now tie itself up with something that is narrowly communal and which does injury to both the nation and our culture. Whatever the outcome of this agitation, it is an unfortunate reflection on the Arya Samaj.

You say in your letter that I am not prepared to hear you or to discuss with you the pros and cons of the Hindi Raksha movement. May I say that this is hardly correct? I have always been prepared to discuss any subject with representatives or indeed with any fellow-countrymen of mine, whether I agree with them or not. I have indeed not only discussed this with representatives of the Arya Samaj but have corresponded at some length on this subject. That surely does not mean that I am not prepared to hear or discuss it. But I would be doing an injustice to you as well as to myself if I did not tell you how my mind works and that it is my firm conviction that this agitation is not only misconceived but injurious to the causes which I presume you, as a leading citizen of India, and I have at heart. Nothing has happened, since I wrote to you my letters

4. See *Selected Works* (second series), Vol. 38, pp. 216-222 and 227-231.

previously, which has changed my basic opinion on this subject. Indeed, subsequent events have confirmed it.

You refer to the shackles placed on Hindi in the Punjab. I am still unaware of any such shackles. Hindi is the honoured language of India and the Punjab, and I have no doubt it will progress. Apparently, you wish us to put shackles on the teaching of Punjabi in the Gurmukhi script. That, I think, is not only wrong from the point of view of our Constitution and broad policy, but is also harmful from the point of view of Hindi.

You have referred at some length to the treatment given to your volunteers at the Secretariat in Chandigarh[5] as well as Rohtak.[6] There is no mention in your letter of the violence committed by your volunteers, the way large numbers of policemen were injured and beaten, how offices have been entered and damage done there. Obviously, I cannot say what any individual policeman or officer might or might not have done. But I should like you to place yourself in the position of any Government or authority and try to think what you would do if violent attacks were being made on the police force, on public buildings and on many people. Whatever this may be, it is as far removed from the Gandhian way, to which you refer, as anything I know of, nor do I see any *sadbhavana* in this.

This conflict was none of our seeking. It has been deliberately brought about, to begin with, by the Hindi Raksha Samiti and is being now carried on, chiefly by the Jan Sangh. Nobody has ever considered the Jan Sangh as an organization

5. Atmanand Saraswati wrote that they started this movement with *sadbhavna* mission on 30 May 1957 when he and five others went to Chandigarh to meet the Chief Minister and were told that the Government would not change its policy in this regard. After a few hours, they were bodily lifted and sent to their Ashram. This happened thrice on the same day. In the second phase, the volunteers started going to the Ministers to place their demands, but they were stopped outside the Secretariat, bodily lifted, dragged on the road, beaten by police and put forcibly into the vans. He wrote that the Sikh officers and constables wrecked full vengeance on peaceful satyagrahis. He also referred to the Punjab Police raid of the Arya Samaj Mandir at Chandigarh on 7 August. According to him, the police broke open windows of the Mandir, assaulted the volunteers and insulted and badly handled the ladies who had gathered there.
6. He wrote that the Punjab Police was controlled by officers who had communal prejudices and were determined to crush the movement with an iron hand. Since 30 July when the movement started in Rohtak, agitationists including MLAs, were publicly slapped, beaten up and mercilessly assaulted by the police. He wrote that a batch of respected and venerable ladies from Delhi, who had gone to Rohtak to offer satyagraha, were arrested without warrants and let off at midnight in a jungle near Narela.

following Gandhian methods, or indeed, peaceful methods. They have a different reputation and are considered a narrowly communal body.

I deeply regret that the cause of Hindi, to which we are so much attached, should be made to suffer in this way and should be allied to narrow communal and political issues. A language does not prosper by this kind of unworthy alliances.

I regret also that at a moment when we have to face grave and critical problems in India and in the world, those connected with the Hindi Raksha Samiti should be oblivious of them and should continue an agitation which has already become violent and thus create an atmosphere of grave communal tension in the Punjab.

Yours sincerely,
Jawaharlal Nehru

2. To Algurai Shastri[1]

New Delhi
August 10, 1957

My dear Algurai,

I have received two letters from you dated August 8. One is a protest from the Arya Samaj about the so called police atrocities, and the other is from some people in the Fazilka tehsil of Ferozpur District.

So far as the latter is concerned, I am forwarding it to the Home Minister.

As for the protest from the Arya Samaj, all the information that we have from many sources goes to show that the police have behaved with quite extraordinary restraint in this so called Save Hindi agitation. Scores of them have been badly hurt and wounded. The whole agitation is more or less in the hands of the Jan Sangh now, and the Arya Samaj is playing a secondary role in it. It is becoming increasingly a violent agitation and is obviously anti-Sikh in character, apart from being anti-Government. The Sikhs are now beginning to rouse themselves

---

1. JN Collection.

and there are grave dangers of considerable communal clashes. I receive complaints from Sikhs. I am afraid the Arya Samaj has no sympathy from me in this matter. They are doing something which is wholly indefensible and anti-national.

The Sikhs have complained that they were not being protected against Jan Sangh agitators who had gone inside their houses and done lot of damage.

Reference is made in the telegram you have sent me to Shri Mangal Sen, a Jan Sangh MLA.[2] I gather that he was a declared absconder. On attempts being made by the police to arrest him, the police force was attacked. Even the police station was later attacked, injuring many policemen. Subsequently, in the speeches made by Jan Sangh people, it was said that Sikhs should be looted and killed. The Punjab Government is being accused by the Sikhs of being too lenient towards this agitation. More particularly, the Sikhs of Rohtak have complained.

Yours sincerely,
Jawaharlal Nehru

2. From Rohtak.

3. To C.P.N. Singh[1]

New Delhi
August 11, 1957

My dear C.P.N., [2]

Your letter of August 10th.[3] Yesterday, I sent you a letter I had received from Swami Atmanand and my reply to him.

If the Arya Samaj people wanted to send a deputation to meet you, it is quite right for you to arrange a meeting. We should never refuse a meeting to discuss matters. The situation is undoubtedly a difficult one, not only on the side of the Hindi agitation people, but, on the other side, the Akalis. You know my views and how senseless and objectionable, I think, this Hindi agitation is. But, we have to proceed with caution and with wisdom. We cannot go behind the Regional Formula.[4] Minor arrangements can certainly be made without offending that Formula. But, it would be unfortunate if we gave the impression to the Akalis that we were going behind what we agreed to.

Yours sincerely,
Jawaharlal Nehru

---

1. JN Collection.
2. Governor of Punjab.
3. C.P.N. Singh wrote about his meeting with a delegation of the Hindi Raksha Samiti led by Atmanand Saraswati on 8 August. They mentioned their grievances about the raid on the Arya Samaj Mandir in Chandigarh and explained at great length what led them to undertake the Save Hindi agitation. Singh informed Nehru that he had arranged a meeting between representatives of the Samiti and Punjab Government for 12 August 1957. He referred to the attitude of the Akalis also in this matter.
4. For details of Regional Formula, see *post*, p. 468.

4. Agitation in Haryana[1]

I received a deputation today of Congress workers from Rohtak District. This deputation consisted of :
Shri Daulat Ram Gupta,
Shri Murarilal Pennar,
Shri Amar Singh Pandu,
Shri Om Prakash Bhatnagar, and
Shri Bipin Chandra.

2. They spoke to me about the language issue which had shaken Hariana thoroughly. Caste panchayats had adopted it and were organizing and leading groups to offer Satyagraha at Chandigarh. It was astonishing that Hariana which was a great stronghold of the Congress, had turned away and become in this matter so very anti-Congress. It was difficult now even to explain anything to them or to argue with them.

3. Of course this was not a sudden development connected merely with the language issue. There has been growing frustration in Hariana for years past and there is now no faith at all left there in the State Congress leadership.

4. In the 1952 General Elections Hariana was solid for the Congress. In the General Elections this year, only five Congressmen were elected out of eleven. This was chiefly due to Congress tickets being given to wrong persons and old Congress workers being ignored. Indeed tickets were given to persons who were outside and opposed to the Congress till only a short time previously. The Chhotu Ram's[2] party was encouraged.

5. In the past Congressmen in Hariana had put up a good fight and had won against the nominees of the Government or of the Zamindara League of Chaudhuri Chhotu Ram and others. There was no place for the Jan Sangh in Hariana. Now it had come to this that even the Jan Sangh raised its head in Hariana. Many other disintegrating forces were concentrating on Hariana.

6. Old Congress workers had lost influence in the organization there and the organization had lost influence in the people. It has come to this that even a man like Chaudhuri Ranbir Singh[3] who represents the Congress organization now

---

1. Note, New Delhi, 22 August 1957. JN Collection.
2. Lawyer and Kisan leader from Haryana.
3. (b. 1914); Member, Constituent Assembly, 1947-50; Provisional Parliament, 1950-52, Lok Sabha, 1952-62; Member, Punjab Vidhan Sabha, 1962-66; Minister, Government of Punjab; Member, Haryana Vidhan Sabha, 1966-67 and 1968-72; Minister, Government of Haryana, 1966-67; Member, Rajya Sabha, 1972-78; Chairman, House Committee, Rajya Sabha, 1974-76.

there, cannot open his mouth because of his unpopularity. In fact, the other day he was insulted and humiliated by a crowd.

7. The last date for making Congress members is the 31st August. Very few members will be made by this date or even later. The Congress offices are closed. Nobody is working for this or dare work because the whole atmosphere is against it.

8. Even now, however, the Hindi agitation can be dealt with satisfactorily and largely stopped if old Congressmen were encouraged. At the time of the last elections Kaushik was sent from the AICC Office to Hariana. He created a good impression and made recommendations which were based on a correct appraisal of the position. His report and recommendations were, however, set aside and decisions were made by the leaders of the Pradesh Congress Committee. People were given tickets who had no influence or position in Hariana and more especially who had carried no weight with Congressmen. The result has been that these persons who got the ticket and who are MLAs and MPs, etc., cannot even face the situation that has arisen.

9. These mistakes have been made. Now soon there is going to be a second Chamber in the Punjab, the Legislative Council. It is hoped that on this occasion the old procedure will not be repeated, leaving everything to the local Congress which has bungled things so badly in the past. The High Command should itself choose real representatives for this Council.

10. The Deputation referred to some other matters also.

11. Some time ago the Punjab Government had issued a form in connection with the licensing of coal depots. It was made out in this form that a person who had gone to jail might be preferred. In fact there was a column for this in the form. But no attention was paid to this matter and people at Chandigarh just decided in favour of refugees getting all these licences. This had also irritated greatly people in Hariana who were not against the refugees but who certainly thought that other people should also be given a chance.

12. The Hariana Cooperative Sugar Mills was in a bad way. It was incompetently run at a loss. This also affects the prestige of the Congress.

13. Development Blocks: Little work being done in spite of plenty of money being available. Reports being sent are not correct and some things are reported again and again. The *Gramsevaks* had no real contact with the people.

14. I have put down above what this deputation from Hariana said to me. No doubt this is exaggerated. But the mere fact of such ideas being allowed to spread is significant.

15. I spoke to them about some of these matters and more especially about the Hindi agitation and told them that it was their business not to remain passive in face of this harmful agitation. Thereupon they said that they would like me to

meet a larger number of workers from Hariana, say about thirty or forty, so that I can tell them what they should do in regard to this Hindi agitation. I told them that subject to time I was always prepared to meet people. But in this matter they should go to the Congress President and discuss it with him and with the General Secretaries of the Congress.

5. To C.P.N. Singh[1]

New Delhi
August 25, 1957

My dear CPN,

Thank you for your letter of August 22.[2]

Vidyalankar[3] has also sent me a fairly full report of the meetings of the Government representatives with the Hindi Raksha Samiti people. Broadly speaking, it seems to me that the Government's attitude was correct, but even a correct attitude has to be maintained without loss of temper. All this business of this agitation has been most distressing.

---

1. JN Collection.
2. Singh wrote about the meeting between the representatives of the Samiti and members of the State Government on 21 August. He wrote that the talks started well but ended badly. At one stage it looked almost 80 per cent of the differences had been adjusted except on three points: (i) one formula for both erstwhile PEPSU areas and Punjab; (ii) the word "compulsory" for teaching of Punjabi only or passing of an examination; and (iii) language of notings on files at district levels and below. C.P.N. Singh suggested a further meeting between Ghanshyam Singh Gupta, President of the Sarwadeshik Bhasha Swatantrya Samiti and the Chief Minister. He expressed concern about growing communal tensions in the State and migration of minority communities to safer areas. He felt that the tension was penetrating the services also. He was skeptical of the effectiveness of the suppressive methods and instances from the past made him apprehensive about the Punjab Police.
3. Amar Nath Vidyalankar was Minister of Education, Labour and Languages in the Punjab Government.

I am much upset by what you have written about the Superintendent of Police of Karnal, Grewal.[4] If what you say is correct, then I am quite clear that very serious notice should be taken of this and it is not merely enough to demote the person. This has to be done in the interest of the police themselves. It would be a very bad day if we go about protecting policemen who commit crimes themselves.

Yours sincerely,
Jawaharlal Nehru

4. Daljit Singh Grewal (b. 1922); Superintendent of Police, Punjab Armed Police, Ferozepur, 1954; officiating Superintendent of Police, Karnal, 1957; Assistant Superintendent of Police, Jalandhar, 1957 and Kangra, 1957; Commandant Superintendent of Police, Punjab Armed Police, Jalandhar, 1965; officiating Deputy Inspector General of PAP, 1965; Chairman, Punjab Road Transport Corporation, Chandigarh, 1974.

6. To Amar Nath Vidyalankar[1]

New Delhi
August 25, 1957

My dear Amar Nathji,

Thank you for your letter of the 22nd August which I have read with interest. I am glad you have sent me a full account of what happened at your meetings. I think that the attitude taken up by you and your colleagues in the Government was eminently right.

Apart from its being right, we have always to remember that in our anxiety to settle one problem we do not raise other and more difficult problems. If Government breaks its own word, then nobody will accept its word in future.

Yours sincerely,
Jawaharlal Nehru

1. JN Collection.

7. To Partap Singh Kairon[1]

New Delhi
28 August, 1957

My dear Partap Singh,[2]

I am afraid there appears to be no end to your difficulties. The recent incident at Ferozepore Jail has been peculiarly shocking.[3] Whatever the result of the enquiry might be,[4] this is a small matter. The harm has been done.

Another thing that has rather upset me are the accounts we have received about the behaviour of the police in some Rohtak villages. Quite a number of people from here have visited these places and have carried back reports and impressions. You must have received Mauli Chandra Sharma's[5] reports of some kind of an enquiry carried on there.

The impression I get from all these reports is that the police is becoming brutal. Also, of course, jail officers. The reputation of the Punjab Police has always been that they were somewhat tougher than the police in other parts of India.

The other day I heard that one of your DSPs shot down some people in cold blood. These people were probably dacoits. Nevertheless, this business of cold-blooded shooting, if true, indicates a mentality which will ruin any State. I think that if any such case is proved, there should be a criminal trial. No amount of admonition is adequate and he must be made to leave the service forthwith.

What is worrying me greatly is this increasing tendency to violence, both on the people's side and on the Government's. When this occurs, quite apart from the merits of any particular incident, it is the Government that suffers and must inevitably suffer.

In the early days of this agitation, your instructions were that there should be no violence or beating of any kind by the police. That was right. Subsequently, apparently this has changed. I do not mind people being arrested quietly and put in prison. But beating, whether in public or private, is degrading and even

1. JN Collection.
2. Chief Minister of Punjab.
3. More than 100 Hindi Raksha Samiti prisoners and 26 Jail Warders were injured after a scuffle between the storekeeper of the Central Jail, Ferozepur, and the prisoners on 24 August.
4. Justice S.B. Capoor, Judge of the Punjab High Court, was asked to conduct a judicial inquiry into the incidence.
5. Vice-President, Hindi Sahitya Sammelan.

on the practical plane brings discredit to Government. Our public is tremendously affected by it, as we know to our cost in Calcutta, Bombay, Ahmedabad, etc.

I hope, therefore, that you will be strict with your police in this matter. Any person who really misbehaves must be held to account and general direction should be that they are dealing with our own people and not some enemies.

These are the directions we gave to our Army in the Naga Hills. Even though the Nagas were in active rebellion and shooting our people down, on the whole the Army obeyed them.

I wonder if you are coming here for the AICC meeting.

Yours sincerely,
Jawaharlal Nehru

8. To Indra Vidyavachaspati[1]

New Delhi
September 3, 1957

Dear Indraji,[2]

Thank you for your letter of the 3rd.

You are right that this movement for Hindi is unfair. It has adversely affected the Hindi language and its influence has reached even Tamilnad. I have written two-three letters to Swami Atmanand on this subject. These letters have been published in newspapers also. You might have seen them. In these letters, I have clearly expressed my views.

You have written that no language should be taught forcefully. This principle, perhaps, has not been followed in any country. Yes, it is important that they should be taught at the right time. In European countries, generally three languages are taught apart from the mother tongue. This is necessary also.

If there are two viewpoints on this issue, a decision should be arrived at after peaceful discussion. I am sure this entire movement is political and meant to harm the Punjab Government.

1. JN Collection. Original in Hindi.
2. (1889-1960); Vice Chancellor, Gurukul Vishwavidyalaya, Kangri; editor, *Vaibhava, Vijaya, Nav Rashtra, Jana Satta, Vir Arjun*; Member, Provisional Parliament, 1950-52 and Rajya Sabha, 1952-58.

I know how much damage it has done in Punjab and how much poison it has spread there. In my view, we should all try to solve this problem. I made my efforts for this, but they have failed.

Yours sincerely,
Jawaharlal Nehru

9. To Baburam Saksena[1]

New Delhi
September 19, 1957

Dear Dr Baburam,[2]

I am sorry for the delay in acknowledging your letter of the 26th August. I read that letter with interest.

I am afraid I do not agree with you when you say that this Hindi agitation in the Punjab is not political or communal. I think, it is fully recognized now that the agitation has little to do with Hindi or with any cultural matter. In fact, some of the leading people in it have said as much to me.

You say that it is wrong to force the medium of one language on a speaker of another language. No such attempt is being made. It is open to anyone in the Punjabi speaking areas to choose the medium of Hindi or in the Hindi speaking area to choose the medium of Punjabi. It is true that in spite of this facility, when passions are roused, the authorities of schools create difficulties. That is a practical matter which can be dealt with. But these difficulties become greater and greater when these passions are roused. No amount of legislation or rules can deal with a situation when people are excited.

Yours sincerely,
Jawaharlal Nehru

1. JN Collection.
2. A resident of Allahabad.

10. To Chandra Bhan Gupta[1]

New Delhi
September 19, 1957

Dear Chandra Bhanji,[2]

Thank you for your letter of the 7th September.

I entirely agree with you that the worst aspect of this Save Hindi agitation in the Punjab is the way many Congressmen have forgotten their principles and been led away by this agitation. I spoke on these lines at the Congress Parliamentary Party meeting. I think that the time has come when we should stick to our principles, whatever the circumstances.

Yours sincerely,
Jawaharlal Nehru

1. JN Collection.
2. A pleader from Rohtak.

11. To U.N. Dhebar[1]

New Delhi
September 24, 1957

My dear Dhebarbhai,

I enclose a letter from the Punjab PCC. I think the AICC should inform Prabodh Chandra[2] that the statements he is issuing and in fact his general conduct in regard to the Hindi agitation is unbecoming for a Congressman and encourages communal tendencies.

Yours sincerely,
Jawaharlal Nehru

1. JN Collection.
2. (1911-86); Member, Punjab Legislative Assembly, 1946-67; also Minister and Speaker of Punjab Legislative Assembly; Member, Lok Sabha, 1967-77.

12. To N.C. Chatterjee[1]

New Delhi
September 24, 1957

My dear Shri Chatterjee,

Thank you for your letter of September 22nd, which I have received today.[2]

I am naturally much concerned at what has happened and is happening in the Punjab. I would gladly help to put an end to this trouble. But there is no point in my taking any step, till I see my way clear, and I do not see the particular point of calling what is called a Round Table Conference.

I have, as a matter of fact, made several attempts in my own way, but they have not been successful. I am quite clear in my mind that the Arya Samaj and the others who are carrying on this so-called Save Hindi movement, have done enormous injury to Hindi and, of course, to the Punjab.

When I was in London, I heard about your visit there and the good effect of your meeting people and what you told them.

You refer to an international press agency. It has been a basic approach of ours that Government should not sponsor an agency. A subsidized press agency is not looked up to in other countries. We can, of course, help an agency in other ways. There is the PTI which can develop into a bigger agency.

In Shri H.B. Bhide's report, reference is made to charges of corruption, high-handedness, communalism, etc.[3] Such vague references do not help. We have,

1. JN Collection.
2. Chatterjee, a prominent leader of Hindu Mahasabha, expressed deep distress over the widening gulf between the Hindus and the Sikhs in Punjab. He was convinced that this tangle could be solved if Nehru took initiative, and that something drastic was required to be done to reorganize the Punjab Administration which had forfeited the confidence of the Hindus. He appealed to Nehru to call a conference, before going to Japan, of Hindus and Sikhs, to impress upon them the desirability of solving the problem in an amicable spirit to avoid further disaster. He referred to anti-India and anti-Nehru propaganda in the international press and the desirability of having an international press agency under the auspices of the Government.
3. H.B. Bhide of *Kesari* toured Punjab for a week in September and met Hindu and Sikh leaders and local workers to study the situation. His findings were: the movement was being conducted in a peaceful and non-violent manner; the gap between the two groups was widening; sympathizers of the movement were opposed to the compulsory teaching of Punjabi in Gurmukhi script and to the communal, high-handed, corrupt, inefficient administration of Punjab Government; spread of communal tension would lead to communal disturbances; and the psychological effect might be detrimental to the national interests in case of any possible invasion by Pakistan.

in fact, investigated many such charges and the Punjab Government is itself constantly doing so. Many people have been punished because of this and many charges have been found completely groundless. I doubt if any State Government is taking so much interest in rooting out corruption as the present Punjab Government. But, in the circumstances existing today in the Punjab, every person makes wild charges against others. Those who are most communal call others, whom they do not like, communal.

Yours sincerely,
Jawaharlal Nehru

13. To Partap Singh Kairon[1]

New Delhi
September 26, 1957

My dear Partap Singh,
Information reaches me that Giani Kartar Singh[2] is functioning more and more as an Akali leader and less and less as a member of your Cabinet, who should deal with all groups and peoples. That is not a good development. If the report to me is right, I think, you should speak to him and tell him that this kind of thing is not proper and will create grave difficulties.

Yours sincerely,
Jawaharlal Nehru

1. JN Collection.
2. Minister for Revenue, Local Self-Government, Relief and Rehabilitation, Cooperative Societies and Cottage Industries in the Punjab Cabinet.

14. To N.C. Chatterjee[1]

New Delhi
September 30, 1957

My dear Shri Chatterjee,

Thank you for your letter of the 30th September.

There is no question of my being too busy or too much occupied with other problems and, therefore, not being able to spare the time for the Punjab and its affairs. That would be a poor excuse indeed. I realize fully the importance of what has happened in the Punjab and what is happening there now. To begin with I sought to interfere in a friendly way. The result was not good. I decided then not to interfere any more unless I felt clearly that such intervention would be desirable.

My impression still is that any intervention by me at this stage is not desirable. I am quite convinced that the Arya Samaj agitation is utterly wrong and misconceived, and that it deserves no sympathy whatever. I propose to take no action which goes contrary to this conviction of mine.

If the situation in the Punjab is bad, as it is, surely this is the result of the Arya Samaj agitation. Who started this agitation and, having started it, why is it not stopped? If it is said that Government's decision in regard to the language question was wrong and this led to the agitation, I suggest that this is a very feeble excuse. I do not think that decision was wrong and, even if people do not agree with it, it seems to me absurd for any individual or organization to upset the peace of the province because they disagree with a decision of this kind. Also, nothing actually had been done, to which objection could be taken. In any event, there can be no democratic or peaceful functioning of a State if any group which dislikes some decision of Government, chooses to break the law and create conditions of violence and insecurity. If one group can do it, so can another. Government might as well abdicate its function and leave decisions to armed bands in the streets.

You mention Bahu Akbarpur and the Ferozepore jail incidents. I regret very much both these incidents. But, may I say that they have nothing to do with the main issue which the Arya Samaj agitation has raised. The Ferozepore incident has been under enquiry by a High Court Judge, and I understand his report will be out soon.

1. JN Collection.

It seems rather extraordinary to me that to bolster up this agitation in the Punjab, people are being brought from other States and money is being collected all over India. The fact of the matter is that the Arya Samaj leaders have made mistake after mistake, and have got themselves stuck in a morass. Instead of acknowledging their error and stopping this agitation, they are prepared to go on with it even if Punjab is ruined. If this is their idea of culture and protection of Hindi, then I beg to differ from them.

Yours sincerely,
Jawaharlal Nehru

15. To Algurai Shastri[1]

New Delhi
22 October, 1957

My dear Algurai,

Thank you for your letter of October 21 and copies of some telegrams. I am not impressed by these telegrams. I still continue to think that this so-called Save Hindi Agitation is the most futile that I have ever seen, apart from the injury it is causing to Hindi. To persist in it is a sign of lack of wisdom. To try to draw in the students in it is something much worse.

I do not propose to intervene or interfere in any way.

Yours sincerely,
Jawaharlal Nehru

---

1. JN Collection.

16. To Mauli Chandra Sharma[1]

New Delhi
31 October, 1957

My dear Mauli Chandraji,

I understand that you will be seeing me tomorrow morning, as arranged. I am surprised, however, to find references in the press to your meeting me in connection with the Punjab language agitation. Because of this, I should like to make it clear that I am not at all interested in what might be called compromise formulae being evolved.

I have expressed myself often on this subject and made clear what I think. It is my conviction that there has seldom been in India anything so vicious and harmful as this so-called Save Hindi agitation in the Punjab. Quite apart from the merits, and I do not think they are many, the whole background of this agitation has been utterly irresponsible and I am surprised that any organization should sponsor this kind of thing, much less an organization which claims to be religious and cultural. This Save Hindi agitation has shown how we go from error to error when once a wrong step is taken and there is no courage to correct it. I do not understand why I should be asked to cover up that wrong step and to give it any kind of legitimacy when it was and continues to be completely illegitimate.

Another aspect that has rather distressed me, and I mentioned this at a public meeting a few days ago, is the dragging in of the President's name in this matter. Newspapers stated that I had written a "moving" letter to the President and the President had thereupon sent for Shri Ghanshyam Singh Gupta.[2] All kinds of speculations were indulged in. As a matter of fact, I have never written to the President about this and when I met the President later he expressed his distress at the wrong type of propaganda that was carried on. He said, quite rightly, that he would not interfere in any way in this business except, of course, to advise the withdrawal of this agitation. He was not anxious to see anybody, but as President if anybody wants to see him, he is available.

I am writing to you to make my attitude to this agitation perfectly clear. Unfortunately, in spite of my efforts to clarify my own attitude, attempts continue to be made to confuse the issue.

Yours sincerely,
Jawaharlal Nehru

1. JN Collection.
2. President, Sarwadeshik Bhasha Swatantrya Samiti.

II. OTHER MATTERS

1. To C.P.N. Singh[1]

New Delhi
August 17, 1957

My dear CPN,

I do not know how you have been getting on with the Committee appointed for talks with the Arya Samajists.[2] The situation in Hariana troubles me a little. The Jats of Hariana are tough people and they have had some kind of a grouse for a long time because they think they have been neglected by the Punjab Government. Added to this, this language agitation, which really does not concern them much, might well create difficulties.

I wrote to you a few days ago about the various allegations and defamatory statements that had been made against Partap Singh's son.[3] I do hope that he will go to court about it. Partap Singh told me when he came here, that his lawyers had advised him that there was nothing very actionable in the charges made. I cannot understand this and I told Partap Singh to change his lawyers. But, whether such a case would be good or not, not to proceed in the courts of law is, I am certain, very bad indeed.

Today I saw a paper which I enclose. This is about Lachhman Singh,[4] who, I think, was nominated by you to the Punjab Council. Giani Gurmukh Singh Musafir[5] is also mentioned. I am told that Lachhman Singh has served a notice for defamation.

1. JN Collection.
2. On behalf of the Government of Punjab, following Ministers were to meet the Hindi Raksha Samiti representatives and explore possibilities of some understanding in the matter: Amar Nath Vidyalankar, Giani Kartar Singh, Rao Birendra Singh, Brish Bhan and Yash Pal. The delegation of the Hindi Raksha Samiti consisted of Virinder (Editor of *Pratap*, Jalandhar), Jagdev Sidhanti (Samrat Press, Delhi), Bhagwan Das (Principal, DAV College, Ambala), Krishan Lal (Vice-President, Provincial Jan Sangh Office, Jalandhar), Raghbir Singh Shastri (Sarvadeshak Sabha, Shraddhanand Bazaar, Delhi).
3. The PSP had alleged that Kairon's son, Surinder Singh Kairon, was involved in smuggling of gold. See also *Selected Works* (second series), Vol. 38, p. 233.
4. Congressman from Ferozepur District.
5. Congress Member of Lok Sabha from Amritsar.

Whatever the truth may be in these allegations, and probably there is very little, there is no doubt that they are doing a lot of injury to the Punjab Government as well as to the Punjab Congress. At any time this kind of thing would have been harmful; and in the present excited state, it is even worse. The only way to deal with these matters is to go to court and challenge the defamators.

Yours sincerely,
Jawaharlal Nehru

2. To Govind Ballabh Pant[1]

New Delhi
August 26, 1957

My dear Pantji,

Raja Mahendra Pratap and Pratap Singh[2] the Communist Lawyer MP from Rohtak, came to see me today. Although they came together, they spoke in a rather different key.

Mahendra Pratap showed me a letter he had received from Suraj Mal,[3] Health Minister Punjab, inviting him to tour in the Punjab. In fact, the tour dates were fixed earlier in August, but he had not gone there.

Mahendra Pratap then told me about the tremendous growth of communalism in Hariana. His remedy was that the Jats should be organized, that is, both the Sikh and the Hindu Jats and thus to meet the communal danger by some kind of a caste organization. I did not argue with him.

He then said that because of the proposal to acquire some lands round about Delhi near Hauz Khas etc., the Jats were greatly excited. They were going to hold a meeting on the 30th August and then to march to Parliament House. He asked me to say a few soothing words when they came to Parliament House. I

---

1. JN Collection.
2. Pratap Singh Daulta (Sekhon) (1918-1985); lawyer; associated with Unionist Party, Punjab; imprisoned a number of times in connection with Kisan movements; President, Punjab Young Zamindara Association, 1943; Vice-President, Punjab Kisan Sabha, 1953-55; CPI Member of Lok Sabha from Jhajjar constituency, 1957-62.
3. Minister for Health, Medicine and Panchayats in the Punjab Cabinet.

told him that I completely disapproved of people demonstrating in front of Parliament House. If any person wished to see me, it was always open to him to come to my house. Mahendra Pratap said that he would tell them to come to my house and not to Parliament House.

(Some time ago I believe a deputation came to me about the acquisition of land round about Hauz Khas. I think, I referred the matter to the Chief Commissioner.)

Pratap Singh, the Communist, then spoke and said that both Congressmen and the Communists were being ousted by the communal elements, the Hindu Sabhaites and the Akalis. Communalism was triumphant. The position was particularly bad in Hariana. Shri Ram Sharma[4] was misbehaving greatly and had made life difficult for him (Pratap Singh). His home had been surrounded by communal groups and he had to escape somehow. Most of the Congressmen were not facing the situation. Only Chaudhuri Ranbir Singh was doing good work. The police cannot suppress this movement. In fact police action has the opposite effect.

Pratap Singh then appealed to me to tour in Rohtak and Hariana. My visit there will do a lot of good. I said nothing to him about this.

Pratap Singh also pointed out that many of the Jat soldiers and Jat policemen were being affected by this agitation.

Presumably Mahendra Pratap will bring a crowd of Jats to my house on the 30th August. I do not know when and how many there will be.

Yours affectionately,
Jawaharlal Nehru

4. Congress MLA from Sonepat.

3. To Master Tara Singh[1]

New Delhi
August 27, 1957

My dear Master Tara Singhji,

I have received your letter of August 24.[2]

I am afraid there is so much difference in our views even in regard to facts that it will serve little purpose for us to carry on this correspondence. I do not agree with much that you have written in your letter.

I should like to say especially that it is not true that any commitments were made to Sardar Gian Singh Rarewala[3] or inducements held out to him for him to leave the Akali Party.

You refer to certain charges and allegations about gold smuggling. I understand that these matters have gone to court on a criminal charge of defamation.

Yours sincerely,
Jawaharlal Nehru

---

1. JN Collection. Also available in AICC Papers.
2. Tara Singh, the Akali leader, made several charges against the Congress. He referred to Gian Singh Rarewala's role during and after the merger of Akali Dal and Congress and accused Congress of applying "double standards" and of committing a breach of faith with Tara Singh. He reminded Nehru of the definite reassurances regarding the position and status of the Akali Dal while awarding Congress tickets to the Sikhs from the Sikh majority seats. This promise was never fulfilled which made his position very awkward among the Sikh masses. Tara Singh was against awarding of tickets to corrupt and undesirable leaders including Partap Singh Kairon. He referred to the charges of gold smuggling against Kairon's son levelled by the General Secretary of the Punjab Pradesh PSP, who was prepared to establish his charges in an independent enquiry. But the Central and the State Governments were quiet on this episode.
3. Minister for Irrigation and Community Development, Punjab Government.

4. To Govind Ballabh Pant[1]

New Delhi
August 28, 1957

My dear Pantji,

A senior Congressman from the Punjab came to see me today. Apart from many other things that he said, he spoke about smuggling on a big scale.

He mentioned one particular case, that of Hazara Singh Gill of Village Ratoke, Police Station Valtoha, District Amritsar. He said that this man was the chief of the smuggling operations, but for some reason he was protected and, therefore, the Police could not touch him. He asked me to send for the Police Station Officer and enquire from him. This Officer would be able to tell us a great deal about smuggling racket which, it is said, includes some members of the Punjab Legislature.

I think, it is worthwhile your asking the Intelligence people to conduct a secret enquiry into this. It is obviously better for them to do it without any reference to the Punjab Government. In fact, the enquiry appears to be just to meet this Police Station Officer at Valtoha. I do not know if it is desirable to send for this Police Station Officer here.

It was also stated by this man who saw me that some recent changes in the Police organization in the frontier have also led to smuggling being facilitated. There was one Police Range called the Jullundur range. In July 1956 this was broken up. Previously, Ashwani Kumar was in charge of the full Range. Now Chowdhuri Ram Singh has been put in charge of the Border Range and this, it is said, has given a great fillip to smuggling.

Another case was mentioned to me. This was the murder case of Village Bilga, Police Station Nurmahal, District Jullundur. The murder took place about April-May 1957. Some relation of Darbara Singh (Secretary of the PCC) was murdered. The Superintendent of Police, Bijwa, investigated through Malik Sundar Lall, Inspector, who arrested some members of the family. Darbara Singh[2] objected to the investigation. Bijwa, SP, was transferred to Singrur and the Inspector was demoted and transferred to Kangra. The case faded out.

Yours affectionately,
Jawaharlal Nehru

1. JN Collection.
2. Congress Member of Punjab Legislative Assembly from Nurmahal Constituency.

5. To Partap Singh Kairon[1]

New Delhi
September 5, 1957

My dear Partap Singh,

The Congress President has written to me and sent me a note on the problem of landless tenants in Gurdaspur District. I believe, he is going to publish it in the *AICC Economic Review*. This will not be very creditable to the Punjab Administration. I hope, therefore, that you will take immediate steps in this matter.

I am addressing a letter to all Chief Ministers in regard to all ejectments.[2] I enclose a copy.

Yours sincerely,
Jawaharlal Nehru

1. JN Collection.
2. See *ante*, p. 95.

6. To Partap Singh Kairon[1]

New Delhi
6 September 1957

My dear Partap Singh,

"General" Mohan Singh[2] came to see me today after a long interval. We discussed various matters. As you know, I like him and I think that he is a disciplined and

1. JN Collection.
2. (b. 1909); belonged to Sialkot, West Pakistan; joined Indian Army, 1927; fought against the Japanese on Malaya-Siam borders, December 1941; organized the First Indian National Army in Malaya with a view to freeing India with the help of Japan; fought against the British on the Singapore front, 1942; developed differences with the Japanese and disbanded the First Indian National Army; when Singapore was re-occupied by the British, he was arrested at Pungal, sent to Red Fort, Delhi, from where he was released in 1946; joined the Forward Bloc and became its President; later joined the Indian National Congress; organized the Desh Sevak Army.

effective worker. He appears to have been a little hurt at the way his name was put forward for the Rajya Sabha and then was struck out in favour of somebody else. He had no objection to the fact that a person from Hariana was chosen which, he agrees, was quite right. But what has hurt him was the way this was done and the comments in the press about it.

Mohan Singh spoke highly of you and said that you had been treating him in a friendly way. I had a feeling, however, that he was at a loose end and did not quite know what to do. Surely, he could be utilized to great advantage. I suggest that when you have the time, have a talk with him and make him realize how much you value his work.

I think, it has been a good thing that you have taken Dr Gopichand[3] in the Ministry. But it is obviously important that there should be full cooperation between you and him. I say this because I have not quite fancied some of the statements that Gopichand has recently issued. There was nothing wrong in the statements, but they might have been better worded. They are apt to create a wrong impression in people's minds. I am writing to Gopichand about this also in a friendly way.

I think that you should keep in close touch with him and have frequent talks so that mischief-makers may not come between you two. So far as I am concerned, as you know well, I rely upon you more than on anyone else in the Punjab. This is not only because you are Chief Minister, but also for personal reasons because I have faith in you and your great capacity for good work. I know that there is a deliberate attempt being made by many people, including some of our friends, to discredit you. I do not like this at all and whenever an opportunity offers itself, I shall make my views clear on this subject.

Mohan Singh spoke to me about some kind of a land army. I think, this should be considered further. The idea rather appeals to me.

Yours sincerely,
Jawaharlal Nehru

---

3. Gopichand Bhargava was Minister for Planning and Community Projects, Social Welfare, Jails and Justice, Excise and Taxation in the Punjab Government.

7. To Gopichand Bhargava[1]

New Delhi
6 September, 1957

My dear Gopichandji,

The other day you came to see me and I was glad to meet you after a fairly long interval. I am glad also that you have joined the Punjab Ministry. This is a difficult time in the Punjab and I am sure your presence will be of great help.

There is one matter which has been troubling me a little and I wish to write to you frankly about it. It is clear to me that this Hindi agitation is a cloak for other objectives. The real objective is really to weaken the present Punjab Government and, more particularly, the Chief Minister, Sardar Partap Singh Kairon. In fact, the movement becomes more and more an anti-Partap Singh Kairon movement. I regret to notice that even some Congressmen, directly or indirectly, encourage this. This kind of dubious loyalty or in some cases dual loyalty is most unfortunate. I see this both among the Sikhs and the Hindus. That is our misfortune.

So far as I am concerned, I have the highest regard for Partap Singh Kairon—for his integrity and selflessness, his capacity for hard work, his contacts with the masses and his being quite above communalism. No doubt he, like all of us, has his failings. But my regard for him and faith in him are strong. Even ordinarily, it is my practice to support the Chief Minister who is the head of the Government. In addition to this, there is my regard for him.

Your coming into the Government was welcomed by me, but it is clear that the good that this will do will depend largely on the close cooperation between you and the Chief Minister. I am sure both of you will try to bring about this cooperation. But I notice that there are some people who want to create mischief. Some members, even of our Congress Party in the Punjab, appear to me not to be functioning in the right way. I do not like this kind of thing and that is the reason, I thought, I should write to you.

You have issued some recent statements in the press about the possibility of a round-table conference in regard to the Hindi agitation and the release of prisoners etc. There was nothing wrong about these statements but, as they dealt with matters of broad policy, I wondered how far your Government as a whole had

1. JN Collection.

considered them. In such matters, it is essential that there should be a united approach and no impression should go abroad that there is any lack of this.

Yours sincerely,
Jawaharlal Nehru

8. To C.P.N. Singh[1]

New Delhi
September 8, 1957

My dear C.P.N.,

On the 6th September I sent you a copy of a letter I had sent to Dr Gopichand. Today Dr Gopichand came to see me. He had not received my letter to him, as he had been travelling about. So, I showed him a copy of it. He told me that he was himself troubled at the kind of gossip that was going on about him and the Chief Minister. It was absurd and very wrong for people to create trouble in this way. He had come into the Ministry to help Partap Singh and not to hinder and he did not wish to do anything which might not be approved of by Partap Singh.

As for the statements, he had intended to make no statements, but some pressmen had put questions to him and he had answered them casually.

Apparently, this matter was raised at one of the Punjab Cabinet meetings and he explained this.

Then Dr Gopichand told me something which surprised and distressed me. He said that at his house in Chandigarh he is shadowed by the Police, who apparently want to see who visits him. When he went to Ambala and stayed in his own personal house, there also he found this shadowing was going on.

This really is extraordinary and most objectionable. Could you please speak to Partap Singh about it or any other person who may be responsible.

Yours sincerely,
Jawaharlal Nehru

1. JN Collection.

9. To C.P.N. Singh[1]

New Delhi
September 14, 1957

My dear C.P.N.,

I enclose a copy of a letter I have received. I do not know if the signatory of the letter is a real person or not.[2]

It is a fact that before the Amritsar Congress, the local Congress people took me to a party given by Bijli *Pahalwan*, and he gave me a cheque for the Congress. That has nothing to do with any charge of smuggling now. I think, it is worthwhile while finding out from the police or from any other quarter why the case against Bijli *Pahalwan* has not been proceeded with.

Yours sincerely,
Jawaharlal Nehru

1. JN Collection.
2. The letter dated 11 September from Anant Ram from Amritsar informed that Madan Lal, popularly known as Bijli *Pahalwan* of Amritsar, was arrested on charges of gold smuggling but within two days all the charges against him were withdrawn under political pressure. The letter said that it was believed that in 1955 Nehru visited his house for the sake of Rs 1,10,000/ donated by him for the Congress Session. It was also believed that Indira Gandhi, U.N. Dhebar and Partap Singh Kairon also collected money from him for election funds. This incident had caused great resentment among the people. The letter also said that smuggling of gold had again started on old scale.

413

10. To Partap Singh Kairon[1]

New Delhi
26 September, 1957

My dear Partap Singh,

Thank you for your letter of September 23rd, 1957, in which you give me particulars of the present state of the Save Hindi agitation and the arrests made.

You will remember my mentioning to you about Dr Gopichand's charge that he was being shadowed. You denied it naturally, but he still says that this continued. I hope you will have this matter enquired into thoroughly. I find that the Police of Punjab sometimes think of themselves as a State within a State and do what they like. They have to be pulled up.

The other day I wrote to your Governor and sent him a copy of a letter I had received making strong allegations against Bijli *Pahalwan* of Amritsar. The Governor writes to me that he mentioned this matter to you and you said that you had already explained it to me. I remember your saying something to me, but I did not connect it with this man at the time. I am rather worried over this matter because Bijli *Pahalwan* has had an unsavoury reputation all this time. It was with the greatest reluctance that I went to his house at the time of the Amritsar Congress. The idea that we protect those who give money for Congress purposes has to be checked.

Normally, when a charge is made and the person is arrested on that charge, it is far better for the courts to decide about the adequacy of the evidence or not than for any executive action to be taken to withdraw the case. In fact, the executive should interfere as little as possible at this stage. Even when these actions are right, they are likely to be misjudged by the public.

Yours sincerely,
Jawaharlal Nehru

---

1. JN Collection.

11. To C.P.N. Singh[1]

New Delhi
October 22, 1957

My dear CPN,

Your letter of 21st October about Tara Singh from Jullundur District.

This young man saw me twice. He impressed me in some ways and, on the first occasion, I told him to go and see Sardar Partap Singh and others. Later he came and told me that he had met Partap Singh and others. He even mentioned that Partap Singh had suggested getting him nominated to the Punjab Council. I told Tara Singh that while I had no particular objection to this, I disliked this business of a young man who had just returned from the United States being nominated to the Second Chamber. The idea that a person can only serve by being put in the Legislature was quite wrong. Further, a person should serve some kind of an apprenticeship before he was nominated or elected. I had no doubt that he had learnt much in the United States, but I attached greater importance to what he had to learn in India. It was no good trying to reproduce the United States in India. The first thing for him to understand was India or the Punjab specially and to learn from the people there before he tried to teach them anything or put across anything to them. A person who was always trying to teach others did not appeal to me because usually he did not know much himself.

I have repeated above what I told Tara Singh and I hold to that view. I have no objection to his being nominated to the Council and he might do good work. But this sudden pushing of a young man freshly returned to India, might not produce good results on him. This will instill a tendency in him to think in superior American terms about India.

I repeat, however, that I have no objection to his nomination as such if Partap Singh is anxious to have him. I do not know what the reaction of my colleagues here in the Congress Parliamentary Board will be.

Yours sincerely,
Jawaharlal Nehru

1. JN Collection.

13. To C.P.N. Singh[1]

New Delhi
31 October, 1957

My dear CPN,

I enclose a copy of a letter I have sent to Mauli Chandra Sharma,[2] as this might interest you.

Partap Singh Kairon came to see me yesterday and, discussing my programme for Chandigarh, said that he would very much like to have some kind of a party or reception at Chandigarh where the local citizens could come and meet me. As I am not going to Pinjore, perhaps this might be feasible. It might have some good result for me to meet a larger number of people in this way.

I asked Partap Singh about the Ferozepore Jail Inquiry Report. He said that this had been received by Government some three weeks or more ago and was under consideration. I told him that in a matter of this kind I would have expected Government to express their views and take action within two or three days of the receipt of the report. To deal with it in a leisurely way and allow weeks to pass was neither right nor helpful in the circumstances. I urged him, therefore, to issue Government's decision on it very soon.

He told me that, as he had previously announced, Government would accept the recommendations of the Judge. If this was so, then there was still less reason to delay the decision.

He asked me about the publication of this report. Normally, I am always for publication of reports because it is better to put such reports before the public rather than allow unauthorized versions of it to appear in the press. We must always give the public an impression of taking them into our confidence even when this might appear to harm us.

In the present case, however, I suggested that the Government's decision and action taken should be announced. In this decision the recommendations of the Judge would be quoted and accepted. Because of this, it might not be necessary to publish the report. If later, the question still arose about its publication, this could be considered separately.

Yours sincerely,
Jawaharlal Nehru

1. JN Collection.
2. See *ante*, p. 403.

XII. RAJASTHAN

1. To Mohanlal Sukhadia[1]

New Delhi
4 September 1957

My dear Sukhadia,[2]

I have received a letter from Niranjannath Acharya,[3] Deputy Speaker, Rajasthan Legislative Assembly, from Udaipur. He tells me that on account of many breaches of tanks etc., in Udaipur District, hundreds of families have been rendered homeless, without food and property. Further that this loss hits chiefly the Scheduled Tribes and Scheduled Castes people and other poor peasants who are reduced to a sorry plight and are near starvation. He asked me for some help from the Prime Minister's Relief Fund.

It reminds me that the Udaipur District collected about Rs 22,000/- for the Prime Minister's Relief Fund at the time of the Bihar floods in 1955.

I think that we should help these poor people. It is not our practice to send money for such help normally to local people. I am, therefore, enclosing a cheque for Rs 10,000/- from the Prime Minister's Fund in your name, but this is earmarked for Udaipur relief. Will you please inform Niranjannath Acharya about it and see that the money is spent for relief of people affected in Udaipur District?

Yours sincerely,
Jawaharlal Nehru

1. JN Collection.
2. Chief Minister of Rajasthan at this time.
3. (b. 1911) Congress Member of Legislative Assembly, Rajasthan, 1957-72 and Independent Member, 1972-77; Deputy Speaker, Rajasthan Legislative Assembly, 1957-62 and Speaker, 1957-62.

2. To Satya Narayan Sinha[1]

New Delhi
September 7, 1957

My dear Satya Narayan,

I have received complaints from Palana Colliery Mazdoor Union of Bikaner against certain activities and behaviour of Shri Panna Lal Barupal,[2] who is apparently a Congress MP. It is stated that Shri Panna Lal Barupal frequently misuses his position for the purposes of accepting illegal gratification. Among the charges made against him briefly are:

He has written to the Chief Minister of Rajasthan trying to defend Shri A.B. Mukerjee, Mine Manager, Palana Colliery, in spite of the fact that Shri Mukerjee is involved in a number of cases of defalcation of accounts, bribery, corruption etc., and has numerous accounts in various banks in different names.

It was stated by a close associate of Shri Panna Lal that the latter was meeting me, the Home Minister and the Minister of Railways on the 7th and 8th August to further the cause of Shri Mukerjee, the Mine Manager. Also that he was meeting C.D. Pande, MP.[3]

The charges made are rather indefinite and the only fact that comes out is that Panna Lal Barupal is trying to help the Mine Manager, Shri A.B. Mukerjee in various ways. However, I should like you to speak to Panna Lal Barupal and tell him that we have received complaints about him in this respect and find out what he says.

Yours sincerely,
Jawaharlal Nehru

---

1. JN Collection.
2. (1913-1983); Congressman from Rajasthan; worked for upliftment of the downtrodden; Secretary, Harijan Sevak Sangh, 1949; Member, Lok Sabha, 1952-77.
3. (1906-1988); Congressman from UP; Member, UPCC, 1926-36; Member, AICC, 1927-35; Private Secretry to G.B. Pant, 1937-39 and 1946-51; Member Provisional Parliament, 1950-52, Lok Sabha, 1952-62.

XV. UTTAR PRADESH

1. To Sampurnanand[1]

New Delhi
August 1, 1957

My dear Sampurnanand,[2]

There have been many references in the press and some even in Parliament to the scarcity conditions prevailing in the Eastern districts of UP. Some say it is near famine. Whatever the conditions may be, it is obvious that they are not good and help is required. Your Government is, no doubt, doing its best.[3]

I am sending you a cheque for Rs 50,000/- for such help. You can spend this at your discretion. But my preference would be that it might be used, as far as possible, for children.

In the past when Orissa suffered greatly from drought and scarcity, it was a great help to them to organize the feeding of children. In this we helped them.

I can send you some more money, if you so wish for this purpose.

Yours sincerely,
Jawaharlal Nehru

---

1. JN Collection.
2. Chief Minister of Uttar Pradesh.
3. In a reply on 2 September, Sampurnanand explained that the problem of the Eastern districts of Uttar Pradesh had recently been spot-lighted by the hunger strike of Genda Singh, a PSP leader, and movements started by the Socialist Party, the PSP and the Communist Party which centre round the economic condition of the people of these districts. These movements included taking possession of regional grain godowns and distributing the stored grain among the destitute. The PSP also demanded the setting up of a commission to inquire into the measures for developing the area.

2. To Sampurnanand[1]

New Delhi
3 September, 1957

My dear Sampurnanand,

Your letter of September 2nd.[2]

It is surprising that in an area of the UP which is so full of sugar mills, there should be this acute poverty. However, there it is and I agree with you that we must do something to it. What exactly we can do now I cannot immediately say. I am sending copies of your letter to the Finance Minister and the Deputy Chairman, Planning Commission and asking them to give thought to this matter and to confer with the Ministries concerned.

Yours sincerely,
Jawaharlal Nehru

---

1. JN Collection.
2. Sampurnanand wrote that the "permanently deficit areas" of Eastern districts of Uttar Pradesh were a problem. According to him, the main reasons were: heavy pressure of population, fragmentation of land into small holdings, lack of development and irrigation facilities, haphazard growth of sugar factories and no attempt to improve the yield of cane and provide roads for its transport. In addition, floods were a regular feature. He wrote that the provision for flood control for UP had been cut down in the Plan and asked for Rs 5.12 crores for flood control, roads, cottage industries and minor irrigation works for 9 districts in Varanasi and Gorakhpur divisions. He wrote that the hills were another problem areas in the State and required special development measures. He also mentioned that release of foreign exchange would be very helpful for schemes like Rihand Dam.

3. To V.T. Krishnamachari[1]

New Delhi
3 September, 1957

My dear VT,

I enclose copy of a letter I have received from Sampurnanand, Chief Minister of UP. I am sending a copy to the Finance Minister also.

There is no doubt that these districts of UP are in a very bad way and the PSP and the Communist Party are exploiting the situation. But apart from this, the fact is that these people have been neglected in the past. We would all like to help them. What exactly we can do in our present circumstances, I do not know. I should like you, however, to consider this matter and discuss it with Finance and other Ministries concerned.

Yours sincerely,
Jawaharlal Nehru

1. JN Collection.

4. To Sampurnanand[1]

Raj Bhavan, Lucknow
27 October, 1957

My dear Sampurnanand,

Some of the foreign delegates to the Youth Congress gave me a number of gifts. I am leaving most of these behind here and I should like you to send them to the Bal Sangrahalaya which I opened today.[2] The following articles are being left :-

1. A clock in wrought-iron frame. This was given to me by the Russian delegate.

1. JN Collection.
2. See *ante*, pp.198-199.

2. An Uzbek cap given by the lady delegate from Uzbekistan.
3. Three polar bears with a black seal also given by the Russian delegate.
4. A wooden lacquer round box given by the delegate from North Vietnam.
5. A box (in case) with silver work on top and two sides probably also given by the North Vietnam delegate.

(The cap and the three bears are inside the lacquer box).

Please hand them over to the Children's Museum.

Yours sincerely,
Jawaharlal Nehru

5. Investigations into Riots[1]

Last year, at the time of the *Religious Leaders* agitation, there was some trouble at Orai in Uttar Pradesh.[2] As a result of this, I am told that twelve Muslims and two Hindus were killed. According to the report I have received, no step was taken against any Hindu, although so many Muslims were killed. A case was, however, started against the Muslims, and recently judgement has been given in this case, convicting about nine of them.

2. I should like you to get full particulars of this case from the Uttar Pradesh Government. A copy of the judgement should also be obtained. You should enquire from them also, if any steps were taken against any Hindus because of these disturbances at Orai.

1. Note to Principal Private Secretary, New Delhi, 31 October 1957. JN Collection.
2. For details of this issue see *Selected Works* (second series), Vol. 35, pp. 253-271.

XVI. WEST BENGAL

1. To B.C. Roy[1]

New Delhi
August 3, 1957

My dear Bidhan,

I have your secret letter of the 1st August, with all the papers attached to it.

In this letter, you say that the representatives of the CPI came and told you that some of them had seen me in Delhi and that I had felt that I could do nothing unless the State Government agreed to the proposition of releasing Kansari Halder[2] and others.[3]

I remember Renu Chakravarty and one or two others coming to me and mentioning this case. I knew nothing about it and I told them, naturally, that this was a matter for the State Government and not for me.

Now that you have written to me about it, I shall express my own opinion about this set of cases. You have also written to Pantji on this subject. He will, no doubt, let you have his views.

Broadly speaking, I do not see any reason why we should show any special leniency to people convicted of murder, armed dacoity, etc. Some of these cases, as you have pointed out, were peculiarly horrible. You may, if you like, give the normal remissions to them as suggested by the Home Ministry. But, to treat people who have committed murder etc., as politicals worthy of lenient treatment, seems to me quite wrong.

I can conceive of some individual case in which you are satisfied that there has been a real conversion and change of heart, to be treated somewhat differently. But, that is a matter for an individual case and for you to decide. The general rule should be to treat them as ordinary criminals.

---

1. JN Collection.
2. (1910-1997); Communist leader from West Bengal; Member, Lok Sabha, 1957-62 and 1967-70.
3. Halder and some other CPI members were involved in organizing the peasant uprising in Kakdwip in the Sunderbans in 1949-50.

As for the case of Kansari Halder, who has become an MP, although he was an absconder, I do not quite know what to say. There is a legal aspect of it, apart from any other. I am, therefore, sending these papers to our Law Minister, Asoke Sen, for his advice.

Yours,
Jawaharlal

2. To B.C. Roy[1]

New Delhi
14 August 1957

My dear Bidhan,

You wrote to me on the 1st August about Kansari Halder, MP, and others against whom warrants were out in the Kakdwip case.[2] With that letter, you sent me particulars of all other cases also.

I replied to your letter on August 3. In that I mentioned that I was referring Kansari Halder's case to our Law Minister for his advice.

Our Law Ministry and Asoke Sen have now examined this case from a purely legal point of view. The fact that a person is an MP does not absolve him and does not give him any immunity from any prosecution. The question, however, is whether considering all the facts, it is desirable to have a prosecution against Kansari Halder. Asoke sen has written the following note on this case:

"I have seen the papers, including the letter of the PM dated 3rd August, 1957, to Dr B.C. Roy. It is difficult to say whether any prosecution at this stage of Shri Halder, MP, after the lapse of so many years would end in conviction or not. I doubt seriously any chances for a successful prosecution. In these circumstances, I should personally advise that the Government should not proceed any further against Shri Halder, especially

---

1. JN Collection.
2. B.C. Roy informed that there were 36 persons against whom charges of conspiracy were brought; 6 remained absconders, and of the remaining 30, 21 were acquitted and 9 were sentenced to transportation for life.

in view of the fact that the people of the locality have voted him to Parliament. The case against the other absconders may proceed."

I had a talk with Asoke Sen also and he told me that he had not only seen the papers that I had sent him but that he had occasion to see the evidence in this case and connected papers. From this he felt that the case against Halder was very weak. Even normally, he would not advise that this should be proceeded with. Added to this were two facts that eight years have passed and that he has been elected a Member of Parliament. If we proceed against him now and, as is very likely, he is acquitted, then that will not redound to the credit of the Government. His advice is really based on the evidence in the case.

In view of this advice, I think, it would be better to withdraw the warrant against Kansari Halder.

So far as the cases of other absconders are concerned, they might be examined also from the point of evidence etc. If their cases stand more or less on the same footing as that of Kansari Halder, that is the cases are considered weak, then these warrants might also be withdrawn. That is each case should be judged on merits and only cases which are considered strong in regard to the particular individual involved should be proceeded with.

I had a deputation today from some Communist Members of Parliament including Hiren Mukerjee and Renu Chakravarty. They gave me a representation which I am sending you for your information. This contains nothing very new but still I thought you might have it.

I told them that I saw no reason why serious crimes and indeed some crimes which were peculiarly brutal and made my hair stand on and should be treated lightly or should be considered as political cases. I could understand amnesty in cases which were not so serious or in which the evidence etc., against an individual accused was not so strong. Thus each case had to be considered on merits.

They told me that this morning papers announced that the West Bengal Government had released four persons in the Dum Dum-Basirhat case.[3]

This matter is, therefore, for you to consider on the merits of each case, distinguishing very serious ones from the others.

Yours,
Jawaharlal

3. On 26 February 1949, the Dum Dum airport, the nearby ammunition factory and an engineering workshop of Messrs Jessops Ltd. were raided by a group of Revolutionary Communist Party of India. This was followed by armed raids on Gowripur police outpost, Basirhat Police Station, a sub-jail and a sub-treasury. See also *Selected Works* (second series), Vol. 10, pp. 13 and 214.

3. To Govind Ballabh Pant[1]

New Delhi
14 August 1957

My dear Pantji,

I enclose a copy of a letter I have addressed to Dr Roy. In this you will find that I have referred to Asoke Sen's opinion about Kansari Halder.

As I have mentioned in that letter, I saw a deputation of Communist MPs today. There were some people from Madras also. These people referred to some old Madras cases. I made a note which I attach. They said that the Madras Government was agreeable to release the convicts but that the Central Government was apparently not agreeable. I gave them the same reply as I had given to the Bengal people, that is, we cannot consider serious crimes as political and treat them differently. Each case had to be considered on merits and in relatively lighter cases, amnesty could be thought of.

I enclose the representation that this Communist group made to me.

Yours affectionately,
Jawaharlal Nehru

1. JN Collection.

4. To Ila Palchoudhuri[1]

New Delhi
August 15, 1957

Dear Ila,[2]

Thank you for your letter of August 13.

The question of the prisoners and convicts connected with some conspiracy case in West Bengal has been before me for the last few days. Naturally we want

1. JN Collection.
2. (1908-1975); Congress leader from West Bengal; Member, Lok Sabha, 1952-62 and 1967-70.

the amnesty to apply to as many prisoners as is possible. But when I read the account of these conspiracy cases, I was horrified at the brutality which was committed by some and which the Courts found to be proved. I do not think it is right for brutal murders committed allegedly for political purposes to be considered on a different plane from other crimes of that type. There would be no justification for that and this would be a bad precedent.

The question, therefore, is an examination of all these cases and amnesty to be exercised wherever it is possible keeping in view of what I have said above. I cannot give any personal opinion about any individual case without going to it fairly deeply and looking at the evidence etc. I am sure that the West Bengal Government is doing this. In fact, they have already, I believe, released some people.

You have already written to Dr Roy and I am sure he would give every consideration.

Yours sincerely,
Jawaharlal Nehru

5. To Lal Bahadur Shastri[1]

New Delhi
18 August 1957

My dear Lal Bahadur,

I enclose copy of a letter from the Governor of West Bengal[2] to the President. A good part of this letter deals with the congestion in the Calcutta Port, and I thought you might be interested to read this. I have marked the passages. There is also a passage at page 5 about dock labour.

There is a reference in this letter to the criticism of trade union officials, Calcutta. Among other things, it is stated that the outmoded arrangements for clearance of cargo without adequate mechanical aid to workers is one of the defects. There is also reference to the heavy machinery which is difficult to handle with the present equipment.

---

1. File NO. 27 (32)/57-PMS. Also available in JN Collection.
2. Padmaja Naidu.

I think that it is quite inevitable that we should fix some modern methods for this purpose. There was some trouble in Bombay because workers objected to this automatic methods of unloading. I believe, we have now decided that these automatic machines should be used.

Apart from this, I think that we are short of cranes. It is worthwhile to look into this matter because obviously suitable and big cranes are essential and other mechanical appliances to speed up loading and unloading.

Yours affectionately,
Jawaharlal Nehru

6. To B.C. Roy[1]

New Delhi
August 19, 1957

My dear Bidhan,

Thank you for your letter of August 16.[2]

The Kakdwip case was undoubtedly a horrible one, as the Judgement of the Court says. The question is whether a person like Kansari Halder, as an individual, was obviously concerned with it or not. Asoke Sen told me that he had looked through the evidence and was clearly of opinion that this was a weak case in so far as Halder was concerned.

Also, of course, the fact that he is a Member of Parliament, although it does not absolve him by any means, is something to be taken into consideration.

---

1. JN Collection.
2. B.C. Roy quoted from the judgement of the Tribunal which convicted the persons who were guilty of conspiracy in the Kakdwip case. The judgement called the criminal conspiracy "a most heinous offence" which became doubly aggravated by the fact that "a number of murders and also mischiefs by setting fire to a number of dwelling houses and *kutchery* houses were committed," by some of the conspirators. The judgement said that "ordinarily such an offence calls for the capital punishment to its perpetrators" but in this case a departure was warranted by "the extraneous circumstances that these accused are unsophisticated *bhagchasis*...."

Only the strongest and clearest case against such a man should be proceeded with at this stage. Otherwise we would be discredited. After all he is supposed to have been elected by a large number of persons.

Thus, the case of Halder stands on a separate footing. I do not know about the cases against the other absconders.

Yours,
Jawahar

7. To B.C. Roy[1]

New Delhi
22 August 1957

My dear Bidhan,

Thank you for your letter of 21st August which has reached me this morning. This is about Kansari Halder.

I understand that Halder was arrested in New Delhi last evening on a warrant from West Bengal.

If your advisers are quite clear of the issues, then there is nothing further to be said and you should exercise your own judgment. I can form no opinion about the evidence. As for Asoke Sen, I was wrong in saying that he had looked through all the evidence. He had looked at some of the evidence and the judgment. On the basis of that he had come to the opinion that the case was a weak one. The only two other matters that had to be considered were the length of time that had elapsed and the fact that Halder had been elected as a Member of Parliament. Neither of these rules out the prosecution. All that they do is to make us a little more careful so that we might be more or less certain of the result of such a prosecution.

Yours,
Jawahar

1. JN Collection.

8. To B.C. Roy[1]

New Delhi
October 23, 1957

My dear Bidhan,

I have just received your letter of the 22nd October.....

In your letter, you refer to Raja Rammohan Roy's ashes. Rammohan Roy deserves every honour that we can pay him. He was one of our greatest men. But I do not myself see the need or the desirability for his ashes to be brought to India. They have rested in the Bristol Cemetery for over a hundred years. Some years ago, our High Commission in London spent some money in some repairs etc., there.

Let us by all means have a suitable and fine memorial for Raja Rammohan Roy. But, why bring the ashes?

Yours,
Jawahar

1. JN Collection. Extracts.

5
DEFENCE

1. Foreign Exchange Demands for Defence[1]

I am afraid it is becoming progressively beyond our capacity to meet demands for Defence, especially those involving foreign exchange.[2] With the best will in the world, there are limitations to our ultimate capacity. As you know, very large additional expenditures on Defence have already been accepted. It is true that much of our equipment and especially vehicles require replacement. I do not, however, understand how it is even possible for us to spend the large sum demanded during the next half year.

Our present position in regard to foreign exchange is a very difficult one indeed and at tomorrow's Cabinet meeting drastic cuts are going to be made even in regard to the most vital items. I cannot, therefore, ask the Finance Ministry or the Cabinet to add the large additional sum demanded by Defence when every other Ministry is asked to cut its quota down rigorously. At any rate, for the next two or three months we cannot do so. We shall examine the position then.

I have had a talk with the Finance Minister and we have agreed that for the present the sum of Rs 20 crores should be increased to Rs 30 crores. The matter should be reconsidered on his return from his trip abroad.

---

1. Note to Defence Secretary, New Delhi, 16 September 1957. JN Collection.
2. Defence Secretary, O. Pulla Reddi, wrote a note justifying the estimate of Rs 66 crores foreign exchange required for the Defence Services for the half year from October 1957 to March 1958. He emphasized that the re-equipment plans of the Services had been approved by the Defence Committee of the Cabinet and the proposed allotment of Rs 20 crores was "wholly insufficient for meeting the requirements of the Defence Services."

2. Stay Arrangements for VIP Aircraft Crew[1]

I travel, as a rule, by an IAF VIP aircraft. My tours are rather rushed affairs and I seldom stay in one place for more than a day. The crew thus have a fairly difficult time and require rest so as to be fresh for the next day's flight.

2. I have sometimes found that no proper arrangements are made for their stay and they spend a good deal of time in trying to make arrangements for their own stay. Apart from this, I have been surprised to learn that, according to the present rules, they have to pay their own expenses. They get, I suppose, some kind of daily allowance, but the expenses are often much more than that. The result is that they suffer an actual loss by coming with me—a loss which they can ill afford. In addition, they are put to a great deal of worry and often cannot take the rest which they should so as to be fresh for the next day's flight.

3. Obviously, the rules governing them for such occasions are not suitable and should be revised.

4. To give you an instance, I reached Mysore on the 20th September in the afternoon. The aircraft immediately went to Bangalore as they had to bring the President to Mysore from Bangalore the next morning. When they reached Bangalore, the crew found that no accommodation for them had been arranged. The IAF Mess in Bangalore is a small one and there was no room there. They wandered about for a long time and ultimately got some unsuitable accommodation which was fairly expensive. Instead of resting they got more tired in the process, and then had to pay more than they could afford. They came to Mysore the next day with the President. Here also they had the same difficulty.

5. I should like you, therefore, to look into this matter and revise the rules so that at least the out-of-pocket expenses of the crew should be paid to them and proper arrangements made for their stay wherever they go. They should not be left to themselves. Sometimes they do not even have transport from the airfield to the nearby city. Any rules framed should be simple and not complicated. Sometimes, though rarely, they can stay where I stay. This is not always practicable, and other arrangements have to be made for them. It would be desirable to request the State Government concerned to be good enough to make these arrangements and to send the bill direct to the Defence Ministry, where payment has to be made by Defence. Anyhow, this burden of finding accommodation and paying heavily for it should be removed from the crew.

---

1. Note to Defence Secretary, Lokaranjan Mahal, Mysore, 22 September 1957. JN Collection.

3. Reported Discourtesy of Brigadier Wilson [1]

I have read these notes. Also the report of Lieut-General Thapar[2] and the letters received by him from the four members of the Cantonment Board.[3]

2. My first impression is that Lieut-General Thapar's report is extraordinary, casual and unsatisfactory.[4] It is patently based on statements of Brigadier Wilson only, though Lieut-General Thapar had the four letters of the members of the Cantonment Board. His saying that because Dr Dube,[5] MP, had not replied to him, he could not take any further action in regard to an official enquiry, is odd and without any justification. Whether Dr Dube deliberately or accidentally did not reply, I do not know. As a matter of fact, he was attending Parliament and he might well have not been in a position to reply. But one person's lack of response should not have come in the way of General Thapar's enquiry. There can be no doubt of what Dr Dube feels about this matter because he came to me himself and was greatly excited about these incidents.

---

1. Note to K. Raghuramaiah, Deputy Minister for Defence, New Delhi, 25 September 1957. JN Collection.
2. General Pran Nath Thapar, General Officer Commanding-in-Chief, Southern Command, 1957-59.
3. Thapar enquired into allegations of discourteous behaviour of Brigadier Wilson, President of Jabalpur Cantonment Board, when a public deputation accompanied by two elected members of the Board went to his residence on 19 August 1957 which happened to be a gazetted holiday on account of *Janmashtami*. This led to the resignation of five elected members of the Board. Thapar asked them to relate the specific instances of alleged misbehaviour of the President.
4. After making verbal enquiries from Brigadier Wilson regarding these allegations, Thapar observed that as the subject matter of the deputationists was not of a pressing nature and could be discussed on a working day, the President was upset and acrimonious talk appeared to have taken place; that the word "Hell" was only used during his conversation with one member inside his house and not in the presence of the whole deputation; that the Brigadier did not intend any discourtesy to the Prime Minister himself. Thapar opined that both sides could have exercised greater restraint and discretion, and this incident was not serious enough to justify the resignation of five elected members.
5. Raghunath Prasad Dube (1896-1961); medical practitioner; President, Bharat Boys Scouts and Guides and Jabalpur Medical Association; Vice-President, Faculty of Medicine, Nagpur University; Member, Rajya Sabha, 1952-60.

435

3. Even from the report of General Thapar, it appears that the remarks attributed to Brigadier Wilson are correct and he admitted them, though he said he did not mean any particular disrespect to the Prime Minister. Further, for Brigadier Wilson to say that part of his choice language was used to Shri Agarwal inside his house and not in the presence of the whole deputation, appears unaccountable to satisfy General Thapar.

4. Even on the record as it is, it is clear that Brigadier Wilson was grossly discourteous and insulting to the members of the Cantonment Board who visited him. To say, as General Thapar says, on the basis of his talk with Brigadier Wilson, that there was acrimonious talk between the President and the deputationists and, therefore, both sides were to be blamed, is rather remarkable conclusion. Even Brigadier Wilson has not stated, as far as I can make out, what the deputationists said to him. If the mere fact that they went to his house on a holiday is considered enough justification for his loss of temper and abuse of language, then I am unable to agree with this conclusion.

5. There are two aspects of this case: (1) the discourteous behaviour of Brigadier Wilson to the deputationists, and (2) the various charges brought by the deputationists against Brigadier Wilson's administration of the Cantonment Board. Both should be properly enquired into and investigated. General Thapar has not taken the trouble to have an enquiry into either. I am dissatisfied with this way of dealing with matters and General Thapar should be so informed. Discourtesy is always reprehensible. In the special circumstances of this case, it seems to me to have been particularly so.

6. Although even on the record it is clear that Brigadier Wilson's behaviour was unworthy of a military officer and a President of the Cantonment Board towards its members, I think that a further and proper enquiry should take place before a final decision is taken. Further that the other allegations in regard to various matters should also be enquired into properly and a report sent to us.[6]

7. The Chief of Staff, Army, should be informed of this note.

6. Thapar suggested that for further consideration, Director, Military Lands and Cantonments, might be deputed to personally investigate.

4. Army: Equipment, Training and Education[1]

Some days ago, the Foreign Secretary passed on to me a copy of the report by General Thimayya on his recent visit to the Soviet Union. I do not know what you or the Chief of the Army Staff have done about this report and to whom it has been circulated. I think, it is an important report and I am asking the Cabinet Secretary to send copies of it to the members of the Defence Committee of the Cabinet.

2. I do not want this report to be sent to too many people as we must avoid any kind of leakage. At the same time, our Army General Staff as well as other senior officers of the Army and the Air Force especially should consider it. There are some points in it which deserve our particular attention.

3. I suggest, therefore, that General Thimayya be asked to confer with his senior colleagues in the Army and discuss some of the suggestions made in this report and let us have his reactions. To some extent these suggestions, are more or less, on the same lines as those which Marshal Zhukov[2] made when he came to India. But there are some other matters too which deserve consideration.

4. There can be no doubt that the Soviet Defence Forces are efficient and well-equipped. I do not think any army in any other country at present can be compared with them from the point of view of general efficiency and capacity. It may be that the US Army has better equipment in some respects. But even so, the Soviet Forces are not much behind and, in a technological sense, have advanced far.

5. So far as we are concerned, we do not and cannot aim at these high technological developments.

6. We have fashioned ourselves in the past and, to a large extent even now, on the British model. That model was good in its own way. But it is an expensive way. The Russians have adopted methods which appear to be less expensive. How far they are applicable to us I do not know. Thus, stress is laid on standardization and on some limited types being developed, whether in armour, aircraft or in other ways. Obviously, this is something which should suit us.

7. Then again there is the question of airfields. We spend a lot of money on them, and yet the Soviets can get on with airfields which are not even cemented except in a very few places like Moscow, Leningrad and Tashkent. Whether we

---

1. Note to Defence Secretary, New Delhi, 28 September 1957. JN Collection.
2. G.K. Zhukov, Minister of Defence, USSR.

can follow this line in our climate I do not know. Further, the Russians do not put up huge buildings in the airfields. They can do without these expensive structures. Why then should we spend so much money on them?

8. From the report of the COAS, it is clear that he has a high opinion of the training that is being given to the Army and apparently this applies to the other Services also. Stress is laid, especially, on the practical aspect of this training and on the highest efficiency. The Service rules apparently are to honour suitability and capacity, and seniority is of minor account.

9. The Russian soldier is fully educated while in service.

10. It is interesting to note that there is no retirement age for their senior officers if they are considered good enough.

11. It might also be noted that many of the military units have built their own barracks for summer quarters.

12. In regard to teaching, apparently the most eminent men are brought in to teach, that is to say, not only are there the normal military teaching personnel but eminent civilian authorities are brought in to deal with particular subjects. I think, this is a good idea.

13. There is some reference in this report to Indian officers or men being sent in small groups for brief courses of training in the Soviet Union. This again has to be considered. As I have stated elsewhere, I think that our sending people to the Imperial Defence College in London for training does not yield adequate results for the expenditure incurred.

5. Message to Territorial Army[1]

The magazine of the Territorial Army is named *Savdhan*. The Territorial Army and, indeed, all of us could not have a more appropriate motto.[2] In this world of storm and conflict, we have to be ever ready and vigilant and this readiness

---

1. Message on the eighth anniversary of the Territorial Army, New Delhi, 29 September 1957. JN Collection.
2. Raised by the British in 1920, the Territorial Army was reorganised on 9 October 1949. Its role is to assist the civil administration in dealing with natural calamities, to maintain essential services in times of crisis and to provide units for regular Army as and when required.

demands from us training and unity and always to think of the larger things and not of the small ones.

On the occasion of the eighth anniversary of the Territorial Army, I send my greetings and good wishes to all ranks in it. I would wish that more and more people in our country could take advantage of this training that the Territorial Army gives. This force is a reserve force. It does not interfere with peaceful vocations and, at the same time, it trains a person for national service, thus not only preparing them for emergencies but making them better citizens.

6. Training in the Imperial Defence College[1]

I have no doubt that a person undergoing this training must benefit by it. The question is; to what extent he benefits and whether the amount spent on him for this purpose is worthwhile.

2. It has been stated in the above notes that the principal advantages of the course are that it creates an interest in current affairs and that it develops a capacity to understand the other man's point of view. No doubt, this must be true to some extent. But, for a person to go from India to the Imperial Defence College for this purpose, seems to me very odd. British officers are not particularly known for their knowledge of current affairs or for their flexibility of thought, though, of course, there are always exceptions.

3. As we have already gone far about the arrangements for 1958, I suppose, we should honour our commitments so far as the military personnel are concerned. But, I still see no reason, whatever, why a civilian should be sent.

---

1. Note to Defence Secretary, New Delhi, 17 October 1957. JN Collection.

6
PARLIAMENTARY AFFAIRS

1. Privileges of the Vice-President[1]

It seems to me that the Vice-President should not and cannot be placed, in this matter, in a position of less privilege than the Governors. If the Governors have that privilege, the Vice-President should also have it. But, I would be quite happy if the privilege was taken away from the Governors. I really see no reason why they should have it in present circumstances. You may send your note as well as my note to the Home Ministry.[2]

1. Note to B.N. Chakravarty, Special Secretary, MHA, New Delhi, 3 September 1957. File No. 19/52/57-Public I, MHA.
2. Chakravarty wrote that the President and the Governors of States, were entitled to exemption from Customs examination and payment of Customs duty under the Government of India (Governor's Allowance and Privileges) Order, 1950. In 1952, the Vice-President was also exempted from Customs examination. Chakravarty suggested that to extend the privilege of exemption from payment of Customs duty to the Vice-President, an executive order or a notification under Section 23 of the Sea Customs Act might be issued on a proposal of the Home Ministry.

2. To Raghunath Singh[1]

New Delhi
September 4, 1957

Dear Raghunath Singh,[2]

Your letter of September 3rd about the Bill restricting the terms of the President to two terms only.[3]

I understand that the Law Minister has already opposed this Bill on behalf of the Government.[4] I think, it is right that we should not press this Bill, whatever the merits there might be in it. It serves no particular purpose at present.

As a matter of fact, this question was raised at the time of drafting the Constitution, and we decided not to put any such restriction.

Yours sincerely,
Jawaharlal Nehru

1. JN Collectioin.
2. (1910-1982); Congressman from Varanasi; imprisoned several times during freedom movement; Member, Lok Sabha, 1952-67; Convener, Congress Party Study Group on Kashmir in Parliament.
3. During the discussion on the Bill, presented in the Lok Sabha on 23 August, Raghunath Singh cited many such examples and argued that more than two terms might lead to autocratic behaviour.
4. A.K. Sen, the Law Minister, opposed the Bill on 6 September on the basis that the Bill would impose fetters and destroy flexibility which "every democratic constitution must possess." He argued that a democracy like India functioned with the aid of conventions as well as written letters. The Constitution of India did not confer any important functions on the President, who acted on the Prime Minister's advice. However, in extraordinary times a third term might become necessary.

7
INDIAN NATIONAL CONGRESS

I. NEW DELHI SESSION OF AICC

1. India on the March[1]

I take it that we are interested in three things: (1) the broad policies that have been laid down or that should be laid down; (2) the implementation of these policies; and (3) something entirely apart from all these, what a Congressman individually should do.

In the old days, because of our struggle for freedom, almost all the resolutions of the Congress or the AICC were concerned with what Congressmen should do. The broad policy was to get Swaraj. That was a broad thing. It might vary somewhat here and there, but, all our thinking and all our resolutions in the old days related to what Congressmen should do—what an individual Congressman should do. That broad policy had been accepted, sometimes it was Satyagraha, sometimes something else. I find that now we concern ourselves a great deal, and quite rightly of course, with broad policies or with criticism as to how they have been implemented or not implemented, but not so much as to what we have to do about them. Let us take a simple example. We talk about corruption and there is no doubt that something of corruption, and specially lower down the scale, is there, something that exists, something that has to be fought out. It seems to me that if a large body of men, i.e., Congressmen and Congresswomen, set about putting an end to this, that will make a vast difference. I do not say that they can do this by themselves. But that can make a terrible difference. In fact, whatever we may undertake, the fact that a large number of organized human beings want something to be done, or want to suppress something that is wrong, it can make a tremendous difference. Do we do that? Do we think in terms of our own individual concurrent duty and obligation to face the problems of the day or to suppress the wrong tendencies of the day? I am mentioning this because, I think, it is important that we should do so. I think that it would make a great difference itself to set about it. We should consider that to be our primary job.

---

1. Speech during a debate on the economic situation at the closed door sitting of AICC, 1 September 1957. File No. G-23(A), AICC Papers, NMML. The AICC session was held at Sapru House, New Delhi, from 31 August to 2 September 1957.

So much for that particular matter. The first two points are the broad policies and the implementation of them. The broad policies may be said to have been laid down in the Second Five Year Plan. Naturally, they may vary here and there. Difficulties arise and they have to be faced under the broad policy that has been laid down in the Five Year Plans. Most of you are acquainted with the Second Five Year Plan. You have read a large part of it. Speaking of myself, I am surprised how wisely that Plan was laid down. After this three years' experience, I can say that, it is a fine Plan and a wise Plan.

I commend to you to read the Plan; read the Plan about our resources, about where our resources may not come upto expectations; read the Plan about the crisis that we may have to face two years later, something like the crisis in foreign exchange, etc., unless we make good. See what the Plan-makers say about prices. The Plan may have stability. The Plan may go to pieces if the prices go to pieces. I am amazed and surprised that people go on arguing about subjects which have been dealt with, and disposed of in the Plan. We still go on arguing and sometimes argue in opposition to that. It depicts an extreme confusion in our corporate mind and sometimes in individual minds too.

The Plan is not a sacrosanct document not to be touched or changed at all. When necessary, we can change it. That is alright. But we cannot change a document over which years of thought have been given; to which not one person but a large number of persons have given thought. So, it should not be treated lightly. It is this confusion which has to be cleared in dealing with the Plan. The Plan could not foresee what was going to happen in the international sphere. Suppose a war may come off in the course of a plan. We are facing a number of difficulties, e.g., foreign exchange. Well, what are they principally due to? Much has happened in other countries and much has happened here which we cannot and could not control in the economic sphere, in the financial sphere, and in the military sphere. The whole world, as a matter of fact, ever since the last War, is in a state of acute tension, a continuing tension. We talk about inflation in India. The tendency, of course, is there. Two things have affected us. We have internally raised our obligations, over food and defence. We did not want or expect that to happen or to spend to the extent as we are going to spend on defence, etc. Imports of food mean burden on foreign exchange. There are hindrances. One cannot absolutely foresee natural disasters, e.g., the vagaries of monsoons are there. We are not in an assured position to produce food. Of course, the reason may really be a bad monsoon. It fails in one part and may be good in another. That is a different question. After all, we have to build up large stocks. That is possible only by compulsory procurement. Let us be clear about it. It surprises me, some people talk about socialist pattern and about nationalization. We talk about nationalization of industry and socialism and the like. On the other hand, the moment controls are mentioned, there is an outcry: 'never again'. Has it occurred to you that socialism is all controls and nothing but controls? But, I do not understand this confusion of thinking.

Socialism is thought to be apparently chopping of the heads of some tall persons and cutting at the pockets of some persons who have money. That is, a childish way of thinking of socialism. If money is required, why not put higher taxes, get more money and solve the problem? With all respects I may say that it is not clear thinking. Whatever money we may have in our country, and I believe, there would be a good deal, it is a good thing, it is there. But the main thing that we are concerned with is not some money underground but the production of money, the production of goods which means money. That is the main thing. To create an atmosphere in the country which produces wealth and an atmosphere which helps you to get it, is important. Can this be done by slashing to the right and to the left? I believe, we can raise money in the country. We are committed to build up this country into, I use the word, a 'Welfare State'. There can be no socialism without a Welfare State.

The important thing is how to produce more wealth. How to apply the resources to our advantage, so that they may produce more wealth, that is what planning is. It is the best application of the resources at your disposal and the training up of human beings. Ultimately, it is human beings that count, not our laws and resolutions. It is trained engineers that count, trained agriculturists that count, and technicians that count. If we want to take advantage of the modern world, we might presume justifiably that the countries of the West, Europe, and other countries too, have become more or less Welfare States or wealthy countries, because they adopted certain scientific techniques of production; and I am saying that whether a country is communist, socialist or capitalist, the techniques are all the same. We seem to imagine Russia as something utterly a new world, but it is the same machine that functions in America or in Russia. They have the same technically-trained engineers in Russia or in America, and there is the same type of training. You have to accept that and, in India too, you have to have, more or less, the same type of trained men. You may have more public sector and all that. That is a different mater. But basically, the basis of society in Russia and America is the same, it is a technical society. It is based on scientific achievement. The difference comes in distribution, later on. The first thing is a technically advanced society having the means of production, better production from land, more factories, more factories producing factories, plants producing plants, that is the technical apparatus of modern economic growth, modern civilization.

The whole purpose of our Second Five Year Plan or any Plan is to produce that technical apparatus for growth, apart from other policies that we pursue.

449

That requires obviously investment on a huge scale. You cannot produce that, however, heavily you may tax your people, because if you can, I do not know how long it will take, that will take a mighty long time. In fact, meanwhile, you may be overwhelmed by your increasing population or by increasing demand. Therefore, no country, except USSR, industrialized itself without considerable help from abroad in the shape of investment. USA had large investments from abroad, and therefore, it went ahead. Russia did not do so, not because it chose not doing so, but because for 20 or 25 years, after the Revolution, it was boycotted, and other countries would not deal with it or help it. They were forced to raise themselves up from the bootlace. They went through a terrible period of starvation, famine and death by the millions. But apart from USSR, I know of no other country, no underdeveloped country, which has crossed the barrier of underdevelopment fairly rapidly without considerable foreign assistance in the shape of investment. China too is getting a good deal of help from Russia. If that is so, if we want to progress rapidly, we have to utilize our internal resources as well as external resources to our best advantage.

I am not talking in terms of gifts from anybody, but in terms of honest, call them business transactions, investments, where we give inducement to the industrialists and where we give guarantee that they are safe to invest. But I do not mean to say, we cannot advance without this type of large-scale investment, and even with this, apart from our taxation, etc., the process may be slow. Naturally, it has got to be slow.

When you yourselves become a producing country, producing in the sense, when you can export more and more goods and satisfy your own wants, when that initial barrier is passed, then there is a spontaneous element of growth in the economy, and your principal difficulties are over. The difficulties will continue, of course, but the principal difficulties are over. Now, we are at this very critical state of being on this barrier. I think, we have done fairly well. But in our attempts to go fast—and ours are justifiable attempts, whether right or left, which were laid down in our Plan—we have gone a little farther than outwardly our present resources would justify. It is nothing to be terribly alarmed about. But it is certainly a serious thing and requires looking after. It requires tightening of the belt in many ways. There is nothing to shout about. It is, as the Finance Minister says, a sign of growth and development. Of course, if we grow complacent about it, then we are doomed. A complacent society is doomed at any time. Some people imagine: oh, we are a democratic society, therefore, we cannot adopt the methods that authoritarian societies have adopted and so we look very virtuous and democratic, and we will not succeed even if success lies somewhere near. It all tantamounts to saying that we prefer virtue even to quick success. Now, this presumes the idea that those other countries which are not democratic in this way are making a great success in all their efforts. It presumes that these authoritarian methods, however bad they may otherwise be, at any rate, will lead to success. I challenge this. I am not prepared to accept that proposition in thinking, as some people do. I am not criticizing any country and it is none of my business to criticize other countries. But I know that these authoritarian countries are facing their own difficulties. I am leaving out Russia; Russia took 40 years to work its progress.

Russia has achieved that very vital thing, which is the common factor between it and America, a technical and scientific civilization. It is a technical and scientific civilization that has been built up in those countries. Every boy in America or Russia is taught how to use machines. The child plays with machines and has no other toys. At the age of 12 or 13, boys and girls are trained about making hydroelectric works. They are brought up like that. It is the machine civilization that they have built up and that has brought them the results in agriculture and industry. Communism is a method of organizing it, but the real thing is the machine civilization. Our people seem to think that it is by some law or by some process of taxation that we can bring about socialism, or maybe communism, and are not realizing the base of it. It is something very hard, hard steel, huge machines, cranes and all sorts of things that these countries have built up and that is the base which is required. It is only then that you get going. We are trying to make that base in our own way. We do not want to bring about similar machine age in India, but we cannot progress without machines. Therefore, we have to use machines and try to adopt them in our own way.

You may know, or you may be surprised to learn, that the type of difficulties we are facing in India today are exactly the types, oddly enough, which are being faced by other countries like China and some countries in Eastern Europe. The facts of life are the same in China and India; both are huge agricultural communities, not industrially well-developed, trying to make progress and facing all kinds of disasters, natural calamities, floods, etc. We face them, they face them, but the facts of life are the same and difficulties are the same in China as in India, their difficulties often are sometimes much greater. For instance, take food; the food situation is very difficult there in spite of all the controls in the world. People sometimes imagine that by control, we will solve everything provided they are efficiently worked out, you do spread out what you have got. Obviously, if you have not got enough, you do not spread out enough and there the matter ends. You cannot merely by controls produce something that is not there. You have to produce goods and then spread them out or distribute. You might have seen in the newspapers rationing of cloth in China—6 or 7 yards per capita. In India it is at the moment 18 yards and this is going up. It is already nearly 3 times of theirs. That is a measure of the hardships the people there are

451

experiencing. And China is a cold country, a good part of China is frightfully cold. Here a large number of our people can live without clothing, without acute discomfort. Take some countries in the Eastern Europe. Ten years ago, they started at a much higher industrial level and level of general living standard than ours. They wanted to increase their agricultural production and they got into the most hopeless mess and as a result of that, there have been troubles there for the last two or three years. I admire them for the courage with which they are facing their difficulties. I am sure they will get over them. But what I am pointing out is that the difficulties which we are facing in this country are the difficulties inherent in a country trying to go ahead, and such difficulties are common to a capitalist society, to a communist society, a socialist society or a mixed society. Your sticking to democracy is not merely a question of virtue, but your leaving it does not bring in any adequate gain with regard to success in solving your problems. Therefore, let us have a true perspective of our problems and the world's problems. I do not think, India as she is situated today, is economically even remotely in an unsound position. In the type of economy we are living, all kind of crises may come and go and may create a great deal of troubles and sufferings.

People talk about controls. I remember that in 1948, when the cloth control was removed, the amazing spectacle that we witnessed then was just piracy. It was let loose all over India as soon as cloth controls were removed. Enormous profits were made here and there, it was an astounding sight. Ultimately, we had to bring some checks in. It is no good talking of controls or lack of controls, as if one is good and other is bad. It depends on circumstances which may induce you or compel you to do this or that. It is not some theoretical proposition. If there is scarcity, under a modern capitalistic society, some people profit by scarcity. It is bad that some people should profit by exploiting scarcity in essential commodities, whether it is food, cloth or any other essential thing, and the State must come down and protect the people from this kind of exploitation instead of thinking about socialism, capitalism or any such thing. Every State has to come down to protect the people, and the real thing is not to have scarcity.

People talk about communism. Apart from the old definition of Lenin, in which he said communism was electricity plus Soviets, with the technical mind having come in power; another definition of communism is production to the extent that there is abundance. It is, of course, abundance in everything that succeeds. Call it communism, socialism or any ism. It functions because abundance functions. It is the scarcity that gives the trouble, and the justification of a communist theory or a socialist theory is that you will have abundance by adopting that method or theory and not by living in conditions of scarcity and not merely controlling it. That is only a trivial way, trivial path to it. Let us forget these national idealistic conceptions. Let us think of the problem as it is, as the Planning Commission has sought to think. They do not talk about socialism and communism. There is some reference to socialism. They have to have some picture of where we are going to. For the rest they take the problem in hand as it is.

We are said to be living under, what is called, a mixed economy. A public sector and a private sector are essentially combined in such a mixed economy. It is a capitalistic economy with a great deal of State control or a capitalistic economy plus a public sector directly under the State. But it is essentially a capitalistic economy. We have stock exchanges, and other such things. You do not have stock exchanges in a communist country, because there is no question of stock exchange there. We have deliberately accepted, for the moment, this mixed economy, which we say will gradually go more and more towards the public sector, and gradually change into a socialist economy. Why have we done so? Not because we are afraid of some vested interests or some groups, not because we want to show favour to some people, but because under the existing conditions, we thought that this is the best way to attain our objectives—the immediate objective being to stir up the machinery of production, and to build it up which may lead to more and more wealth in production in every way. That is the essential thing because we do not want distribution of poverty in India. Poverty is never socialism. Therefore, we thought, by having this mixed economy, we shall be able to encourage production in India in the largest measure. We want to utilize every possible method of production, whether public or private enterprise, and not to do anything which comes in the way of increasing our production. Because, whether you produce or do not produce goods, you produce some 50 lakh human beings every year. However, you see, there is an overwhelming problem for India and other countries of human beings produced all the time by the millions—wanting food, shelter and clothing. The least you can do is to produce enough for them. If you produce merely enough food for them to eat and cloth to live in, you never catch up to your poverty. You have to produce much more. Therefore, you must have a productive apparatus. All the laws passed by Parliament or all the taxation, etc., do not produce a productive apparatus. The taxation brings you money which can be utilized, by investment or otherwise, in producing that productive apparatus—whether in land or in the factory.

Many of our people go about with long drawn out faces and bemoaning the lot that was happening to India and the difficulties we are in. Some people who are our opponents seem to be very pleased about it. Some people in other countries, newspapers and others, are constantly harping on India's precarious position. They all are trying to create an atmosphere of depression, fear and apprehension, and, I am afraid, some of our own people sometimes help in this process, not realizing what it means. It is not our custom in the Congress to try to cover up facts which we do not like. We have to face facts and we face our difficulties and do not cover them up. But, it is equally more wrong to exaggerate things and help in producing an atmosphere of fear and apprehension, because in a matter of this kind, the faith and confidence of our people are all important, infinitely more important than money, it is the man that produces money. Money does not necessarily produce faith or confidence. Take in this context, for example, foreign aid. I have been saying that we do realize the importance of foreign aid. By foreign aid I mean not grants, but investment, whatever it may be, credits or loans. We welcome foreign help as has been customary in all countries. We shall welcome it with gratitude. But I have always laid stress on the fact that we are the people who must stand on our own feet. The moment we get into the habit of imagining that our problems are going to be solved by foreign efforts or foreign money, then it is a bad thing for us. We want foreign aid and we are not ashamed to say so. We accept it with thanks, provided that the terms are good and we are not tied up in any way. But the fact remains that we have to rely upon ourselves. We can look around to some of the neighbouring countries to understand how in relying all the time for everything on foreign aid, they have grown weak, economically, politically, psychologically and emotionally, in every way.

We must not do anything to cultivate or to encourage this atmosphere of defeatism. It does not matter if not a rupee comes from outside. We shall fight this crisis, and win it. It is quite clear and I want the world to know it. I have been tired of being told that India is going down because somebody does not help her. We shall fight this in our own way. We issue this challenge to the world that we shall fight it in our way, instead of constantly being afraid of what another country does or does not do to us. That is not an unfriendly statement I am making to other countries. We want help from abroad for meeting our difficulties and we are asking them in a friendly way. We are not hiding our position nor trying to appear something that we are not. We are a poor country and I am never ashamed to say that. We go in a friendly way and ask for help, but at the back of our mind and heart, there must be the firm resolution that whether there is any help from outside or not, we are going to face our difficulties, come what may. Naturally, if help is lacking, our difficulties will be infinitely greater and we shall have to cut down the Plan here and there, but we shall have the enormous satisfaction of doing it ourselves, whatever it is.

Now, all this leads me to the last part of the three problems posed in the beginning: what is the business of a Congressman? And that is the most important of all. We have to remember that a great responsibility falls on Congressmen at this moment to meet this trouble and face this responsibility. By doing that we will not only discharge the duty and obligations to the country, but also to the Congress to which we have the honour to belong. We pass resolutions which are good ones. We shall give them new roots and new life. We have to set an example. People talk about austerity and all that. I want something more positive and not negative austerity. I want Congressmen to go out with confidence and tell people about our Five Year Plans and our present achievements and all that, and make people understand it, instead of merely complacently watching or just allowing your opponents to go and run down the Government and the Congress, as is being done today. You cannot be in this defensive position. You have to be in an aggressive position; by aggressive I do not mean vulgar tactics. Communist and other parties are going to encourage the young people to indulge in agitation which degrades our culture. The whole foundation of our society will disappear if this kind of thing happens, whether it is socialism, capitalism or whatever you call it. It is the human being that counts. Therefore, it becomes our business and duty to understand this and go ahead. I do not care if sometimes you take wrong step but show some spirit about it. Explain things to people and tell them our difficulties. We are on the march. We have to pass through deserts, etc., before we reach the fertile land—the promised land. We shall have to do it and it is no good merely stopping each other or trying to curse each other. We have to do it together. If some people are not prepared to do it and are only prepared to condemn, let them do so. Why should we fall into line with them? Tell them that no nation is going to progress if they stoop to vulgar violent tactics.

2. Cooperative Farming Should be Introduced[1]

The opinion and policy laid down by the Planning Commission is correct. I believe in the fixation of ceilings. Whatever steps we may take, we should always aim at increasing foodgrain production. It pains me very much that even now I am receiving several complaints of ejectments. Immediately hundred per cent ejectment should be stopped. The representatives of the World Bank had opined that the per acre yield in India is the least in the world. Those representatives

1. Speech at the informal session of the All India Congress Committee, New Delhi, 1 September 1957. File No. G-23 (A), 1957, AICC Papers, NMML.

had suggested that there is the scope of increasing food production from three to four times in India. The most advanced countries have the tremendous machine power for production. The other essential unit is the man himself, the physical, mental, and the training capacity of man played vital role in production.

The United States of America, is the most advanced country these days. In the same first category we can place England, Norway, Sweden, Canada and Denmark etc. In the second category countries like France and Italy can be placed and the third are the countries like Spain etc. The manpower in those countries has been trained and applied to increased production. Increased production has become more and more a trend day by day. The advancement of a country is indicated by the rise in the standard of living of the common man and his health, literacy and the physical power.

Poverty makes a country more poor while the well-being of a country helps to advance it more and more. The present population of India is nearly 37 crores, but it was not so much before two or two hundred and fifty years ago. There was no scarcity of land then and with the increase of population the people who lived on land became poorer. At the time of advent of Englishmen in India, majority of our population was business-minded. Ours was then a mercantile civilization. 63 to 64 per cent of our population depended on agriculture, while nearly 36 per cent of the population carried on trade. After the advent of Englishmen, the pressure on cultivation of land increased and now 80 per cent of our population is based on agriculture. It is impossible for India to develop and advance unless we lower the pressure on land. The Indian peasantry is the poorest as compared with any peasantry of the world.

We must introduce cooperative farming without which it is impossible to develop.[2] The cooperation method should immediately be introduced by making available better seeds, irrigation facilities, and distribution and marketing on cooperative lines. It is a minor work where the cultivator ploughs the land in bigger farm or small one. The cultivator loves the land, but at the same time, he loves money more. The cooperative farms should not be so big that the cultivators will not recognize each other. We must introduce service cooperatives on bigger scale in our country. This will result in increased food production and use of scientific instruments. We can also run the cooperative dairy farms successfully. The ultimate aim of the cooperatives is increased foodgrain production. With the help of increased production we can develop our industries also. The cooperatives develop an individual and aim at socialist society.

2. K.D. Malaviya, who spoke before Nehru, said that the cooperative farming should have a minimum unit involving ten to fifteen familities having an average of half to one acre land. The problem was not of pooling and totaling of land, but of pooling efforts and integration of resources.

3. Membership Issue of the CWC[1]

The old members like myself need not be nominated on the Congress Working Committee year after year. If we are dropped, the other people will be able to come in and shoulder responsibilities. The trouble arises when a few people try to remain in a place always, thereby closing the door for new elements.

I oppose the proposals made by some members that the Congress Working Committee should be elected. It is necessary for harmonious functioning that the Congress Working Committee should continue to be nominated by the President. However, there is no reason why I should be thrust into it as a nominated member all the time. My not being nominated would not reduce my status. What I mean is that I will come whenever the Working Committee calls me to attend its meetings. But I warn you against adopting the system of proportional representation by means of the single transferable vote for conducting any elections. This is a dangerous system and is not conducive for the smooth working of any organization.

These days there is a lot of talk about democracy. Every kind of thing is brought forward in the name of democracy. Every kind of crime and stupidity and procession is undertaken in the name of democracy. What is this democracy behind whose screen all kinds of things are happening?

Mr Tyagi has talked in the name of democracy.[2] Mr Banarasi Das[3] and Mr Gadgil[4] have also brought in democracy in their speeches.[5] The big democracies

1. Speech during a debate in the AICC whether the Congress Working Committee should be a nominated body or a partially elected one, New Delhi, 2 September 1957. From the *National Herald* and *The Hindu*, 3 September 1957. Also available in File No. G-23 (A), 1957, AICC Papers, NMML.
2. Mahavir Tyagi, Member of Lok Sabha from Dehradun Constituency in UP, said that if the present system of nominating the Working Committee was retained, there would be no democracy in the Congress set-up. And the AICC though considered to be the supreme body, would become a "pocket borough" of the Working Committee as out of 120 ex-officio members of the new AICC, 99 would be nominated by the Working Committee. This would fortify the Working Committee to face the AICC on any issue boldly and such a situation would amount to a "complete denial" of democracy.
3. Congressman from UP.
4. N.V. Gadgil was a leading Congressman of Maharashtra.
5. Banarasi Das said that under the present set-up "ministers are dominating the organization with the result that there is a craze for position and the organization is suffering from intellectual bankruptcy." Gadgil asked the Congress leadership to "come forward with something progressive instead of sticking on to worn-out system and policies." If the leadership refused to "change their outlook today, they would have to do it tomorrow."

in the world are the United States, England and France. There are other democracies also like Holland, Belgium and the Scandinavian countries. There is a lot of difference in their constitutions, rights and system of elections. The President of the United States has a lot of powers and rights. He can do what he likes. He has more rights than anyone else. If in Russia there is a dictatorship, the President of the United States has even greater powers than any dictator in Russia. The difference is that the US President held these powers only for four years. But during these four years, the President has more rights than anyone else.

In the United Kingdom, the system is a little different. But if members are conversant with the history of England, they would know that the office of Prime Minister there has acquired great significance. The rights of the British Prime Minister have increased tremendously and in a way compared favourably with the rights of the US President. The British Prime Minister has acquired these rights not by law, but by conventions.

In France nobody has any rights there. But according to Mr Tyagi's conception of democracy, it has gone very far in France. One result of it is that no stable government exist there. In my opinion, the French people are more intellectual than any people in the world. Even the air of Paris is intellectual. All kinds of debates and arguments about things political and artistic are held in France on a high level. But as far as the question of running the government goes, no government usually lasts for more than three or four months there.

In the Scandinavian countries, things are different. In Sweden, a Government has been in existence for more than ten years. On the last day of my visit to Sweden, at a banquet given by the Swedish Prime Minister,[6] I had said that in these revolutionary times, the pattern of things changes fast in the world, Governments fall and Prime Ministers change, but the Governments and Prime Ministers of Sweden and India have not changed in these last ten years.[7]

Mr Gadgil displayed a lot of intellect, but it is of the "college class room" variety. It has no relation with fact. It is a fact that determines ultimately what has to be done. Facts do not remain static all the time. This is true of the Congress Constitution also. It has changed from time to time to suit the changing conditions. In 1920, the Constitution was changed at Nagpur under Gandhiji's guidance. The Working Committee was made by Gandhiji. Even the Congress President was chosen by him. Now, nobody could say that this was a good practice from the point of principle. In my opinion, it is not a matter of high principle whether a president is elected or nominated. The question is of the way things are done. We have to adopt the way which gives the best results.

6. Tage Erlander.
7. See *Selected Works* (second series), Vol. 38, p. 592.

Before Gandhiji, the Working Committee was elected. But this election had not put any life or soul in it. It merely passed resolutions. We have now to see what Congress has to do and which is the easiest way of doing it. Members must beware of the system of proportional representation. It always produced an "adulterated" thing with all kinds of elements and groups coming into a committee. I have always been an opponent of this election by proportional representation by a single transferable vote.

If Congress is losing respect and regard in the eyes of the people and getting a bad name it is because of the inefficient functioning of the Congress Committees at the city, district and provincial levels. The Congress name has been kept high only by the Congress at the upper level.

I do not like the new provision that the Congress Working Committee would nominate a number of members to the AICC to represent certain interests like women, minorities, tribal people and Scheduled Castes. But if nomination is not a good thing, election of every member is not good either. In an election many good people are not returned. Often sensitive people wish to remain out of election turmoil. But it is very desirable that these people who could render service should be taken in. We have to see facts. The primary consideration is not of any 'ism', democracy or autocracy. These systems follow their own path. If we do not follow facts, we may face defeat.

There is criticism that any resolution drafted by the Working Committee has to be passed and no change could be made in it by the AICC members. But the Working Committee of late has started consulting very many people. The Congress President often held consultations with Pradesh Chiefs and others. Its resolutions, therefore, embodied the considered views of all sections.

No principle is involved in either the Working Committee being nominated or elected. It is a question of doing work. But members should be vigilant to see that the Working Committee do not sit tight on them. Whoever is elected as the President should be given the right to nominate the Working Committee. This would enable the Committee to work in a harmonious and smooth manner. It is better to follow a wrong path rather than not following any path.

There are dangers inherent in a procedure of nomination. But there are dangers in democracy itself. But I agree that old members who had been nominated to the Congress Working Committee from year to year need not be nominated in the future. They could attend its meetings whenever they are called to do so. This would enable other members to come in and shoulder responsibilities.

II. OTHER MATTERS

1. To U.N. Dhebar[1]

New Delhi
August 2, 1957

My dear Dhebarbhai,[2]

I have read your letter which you gave me today.[3] With much that you write, I agree, and anyhow this is a matter to be discussed rather than for me to reply at length.

In your letter you suggest that we should take a hundred to two hundred selected workers into our confidence. I entirely agree. It is not necessary for you to give me any kind of list. You can invite those people and we shall discuss matters with them fully.

You will remember that at the meeting of the Party Executive today, we fixed a meeting on Sunday, August 4th, at 4.45 p.m. at my house for the Party Executive to meet the Congress Select Committee members. I hope you will also come then.

Yours sincerely,
Jawaharlal Nehru

1. JN Collection. Also available in AICC Papers, NMML.
2. President, Indian National Congress.
3. Dhebar wrote that the present economic crisis was not a crisis that could, if not rightly handled, weaken India. It was a healthy crisis in the sense that the investment made by India in the past few years would enrich the country by increasing production. The complaints that proper care was not taken in issuing the import licenses and that the private sector was eating away the resources of the public sector could be answered by curbing for the time being the investments in private sector and by applying a rigid curb upon avoidable expenditure involving foreign spending. Dhebar further made a series of suggestions to contain the crisis namely, (i) the entire nation must face it as one entity, (ii) to resolve the labour unrest, a commission should be appointed for an overall national and rational pay structure, (iii) as per taxation, there was a need for evolving procedures of recovery based upon trust of the people including business community, (iv) a group of hundred or two hundred Congress workers should be selected, taught them the facts about the economic situation so that they spread awareness among people, (v) the unavoidable calls on foreign exchange must be met by giving Defence and Food Production the foremost priority and, (vi) financial assistance should be secured on the basis of a clear picture of our needs.

2. To U.N. Dhebar[1]

New Delhi
2 August 1957

My dear Dhebarbhai,

Your letter of August 1st.[2] I am sending you the file containing correspondence on this subject. I would particularly invite your attention to my letter dated July 21st addressed to the Auditor-General[3] and his reply dated 23rd July. Kindly treat this file as secret and return it to me after you have gone through it.

Yours sincerely,
Jawaharlal Nehru

1. AICC Papers, NMML.
2. Dhebar wrote about his meeting with Sri Krishna Sinha, Chief Minister of Bihar, and his discussion with the Liaison Committee, to advise both the Congress Working Committee and the PCC on the steps to be taken to eliminate casteism, to create proper atmosphere for free elections and to instill a sense of discipline in the members of the Congress organization and the members of the Legislature. He also told Sinha that if there was a proper approach on the part of the members of the Liaison Committee and the PCC, the organization in Bihar would again be stabilized to a reasonable extent.
3. For Nehru's letter to Asok K. Chanda on the Constructive Wing of the Assam Pradesh Congress Committee, see *Selected Works* (second series), Vol. 38, pp. 338-340.

3. Fight Narrow-Minded Bigotry[1]

This is the last meeting of this session. There is no specific agenda. Anybody, who wants to speak, can speak and I would also like to say something. But first, let us condole the passing away, two-three days ago, of an old member, Dr

1. Speech at the Congress Parliamentary Party meeting, New Delhi, 14 September 1957. Tape No. M-27/c (ii), NMML.

Choithram Gidwani;[2] let us stand and observe silence for a while.....sit down.

Now I shall speak in English so that you can all understand.

This session, although it has lasted little under two months, has been a heavy session[3] and it has dealt with and passed very important legislations[4] which might be considered very controversial also. As you know, most of the legislations were introduced in the previous session and even then we had party meetings to consider each in its broad aspects. On this occasion, in this session, we had also held numerous Party meetings and the meetings of the Executive Council and in addition to that the Finance Minister, who was dealing with these important measures, met groups of members of our Party to discuss it with them and as a result of all this a considerable number of amendments were introduced. Some people wanted more amendments, and some people disliked these amendments and said that they went too far and took away much of the benefits expected to get from these measures. Well, to begin with, in any democratic assembly, one has to find a common measure of agreement. The result often is that some people are not satisfied, they think it should be more this way or that way. But the main thing about these measures that we have passed is not so much about some minor change here or there, but that we have taken certain steps in the direction of taxation which are out of the common rut. They are not very revolutionary steps but certainly they are novel steps and if you think novel, it rather tends to create apprehensions in people's minds who do not quite know what it is and what they know about it or what they are used to. That is the main thing and, I think, as I have said often in this House, that the direction in which we are now going regarding taxation etc., is a correct direction. No doubt, we shall profit by experience, we may make some possible changes later when we gather experience but the fact remains that we have taken a major step in a new direction, and this has attracted not only the attention of our people who will be affected but of other countries too and we should try to make that a success as it is, and then improve upon it later. But one aspect of this, not only this but of our economic situation, is that while we have to raise our internal resources as much as we can, but even all the internal resources that we raise cannot meet the

---

2. Choithram P. Gidwani (1889-1957); Congressman from Sind; joined Tilak's Home-Rule League; organized hartal in 1919 in Sind against Rowlatt Act; imprisoned during freedom struggle; elected Member of the Sind Legislative Assembly, 1937; engaged in the rehabilitation work for the displaced persons after Partition; Member, Lok Sabha, 1952-57.
3. The Lok Sabha session was held from 15 July to 13 September 1957.
4. The reference is to the Essential Services Maintenance Bill, the Wealth Tax Act and the Expenditure Tax Act.

difficulty of foreign exchange, except by export, except by loans, credits, etc., and we need that foreign exchange in a considerable quantity. It is not a question of getting an odd crore or two here and there by taxation and otherwise. We have to think in terms of hundreds of crores. Some people have criticized that we planned or calculated in a bad way and that has brought us into this deadlock or impasse now. That criticism may be to some extent justified but you will have to remember that even in the Second Five Year Plan we anticipated this, but not in this measure and not quite so soon. But, apart from the Plan, it is not so much our calculation that has gone wrong but events happening in the world that have affected us and that are likely to affect us in the future. And in any event it is better, I think, to go wrong, shall I say, while aiming higher than to remain more or less where we are. The First Five Year Plan proved a success in the sense that we realized, more or less, our targets and this produced a sense of self-reliance that we have done what we aimed at. That was a very good thing, but the fact is that the First Five Year Plan was a very modest one and really did not stretch or strain our resources and our progress was very slow and very limited. In fact, it is in the Second Plan only that we have really planned, you might say. Why do we plan? We plan because there are scarcities, because people have not got the thing that they want, because we want to produce them, because we want to invest for their production, and because we want to utilize our limited resources in the best possible way. Otherwise, if there is abundance in the country, there is no need for planning because everybody has got what he wants. It is the lack of things, and the lack of resources that forces us to plan. And that means stretching our resources to the utmost, even with some pain in the process, and we are now experiencing that pain and difficulty as a nation and as groups and as individuals. That has resulted in discomfort. It has also resulted in one good thing and that we have been brought face to face with, well, the facts of life in this country, the conditions in this country, and we are forced to think, think outside our ruts.

Some people seem to imagine that we could solve many of these problems by more stringent measures in the country, higher taxation, this, that, and other. That is a question of, well, balancing various factors because the ultimate factor to be balanced is, how we can increase the productive capacity of this country. It is only that that will give us the advantages, gradually to get on, and if any step that we take reduces the productive capacity, then we get stuck in a morass, it is that we have to keep in mind. The productive capacity of a country depends on many factors. One very important factor is the human being, his training, his capacity, his training for specialized work, his capacity for the hard work. Besides this, the atmosphere in the country, the techniques that we employ, the machinery that we use and all these factors are also important. The productive capacity of a country and the countries which have this high capacity has grown because of

463

high techniques of producing wealth, of investment and right things, hard work and all that. So, taxation has to be brought in to get as much revenue as possible, to try to equalize burdens as much as possible, but even the revenue that you get cannot be adequate for fast progress because of the patent fact that our country is a relatively poor country. Well, we are trying to get loans and credits abroad and as you know the Finance Minister is going abroad for among other things, for that purpose. What we shall get or not get I do not know, neither does he. We must be prepared for everything whether we get anything or not or whether we get some thing which is not adequate for our purpose but help a little. But having said that we must realize that in the final analysis we have to stand on our own feet and if we do not get the help that we want, as much as we want, obviously we are not going to give up our job, and we are not going to give up our Plan. If we are forced into that contingency, we have to work harder, may be we have to slow down here and there because of that, I hope not. The rate of progress in the First Five Year Plan was not adequate, there is no doubt about it. It did not even deal with the problem of our catching up with our fresh population, unemployment, this and that. In a sense it just did some good certainly but pace of that good is not enough, therefore, we have to go faster. I do not know whether even now there is quite an adequate realization of, well, the complexities that we have to face in this planning business, whether it is foreign exchange or internal but one good thing again of these difficulties that we face has been that we are forced to think now. It is no good our repeating merely some good slogans of yesterday whatever policy we may pursue, socialist, capitalist, communist, or whatever it is. The old slogans of all these are out of date except that they may indicate a right direction of our thinking, that is all right. Some people imagine that it is only strength of mind and enthusiasm that will produce results and both these are no doubt desirable. What is equally necessary is clear thinking and trying to keep our mind not in a rigid condition. Now, it is obvious that in spite of all the talk, we indulge in, of somewhat critical conditions, what is our response? What is the country's response? Let us take one measure of it, say savings, say loans, obviously the first thing that should be done is for the country, to show that we meet this challenge by pursuing these campaigns of loans, the savings campaigns, etc. Here is the money the country requires, more of it, that is an effective answer partly at least. There are other methods also of doing it. So, now that you are going back from here, I hope that in your constituencies and in other places where you may go to, you will explain to them positively, effectively, what the situation is here today. Also, the new legislation that has been passed, and how we are trying to meet this challenge and we hope and expect the country to meet it too because we do not want to fail in this great adventure that we have undertaken; and explain to them our difficulties, explain to them our failures, explain to them that we did not hide anything from them. Explain to them also that we are determined to pursue this line that we have adopted and to make it a success, make the Five Year Plan a success and not allow even external happenings, whatever they may be, to affect it much and that while we welcome and try for aid from outside, it is ultimately on ourselves that we rely. The moment we depend completely on outside then we are done for, then we have lost that spirit of determination that makes a country grow. And I hope you will do that.

You know, yesterday, I came back from Jammu and Kashmir after two days there. I went there after more than four years. I had not gone there during this period, as I said in Kashmir itself, because I had felt unhappy and uncomfortable at the thought of going there when an old colleague, Sheikh Abdullah was in prison.[5] It was quite apart from the fact of the merits of the question, and I am not going into the merits, and sometimes situations are created which are very painful and one has to take painful decisions, but it is always a matter of deep regret to me when a break comes between an old colleague and myself and I feel that whatever possible wrong the other party might have done, there is something lacking in me that that break has come. Why could not I hold the faith and affection of the other person? So, I did not feel like going there to Kashmir during these years. I went there now because of the floods, etc., and I am glad I went because meeting various people there gave me some more intimate acquaintance of things there as they are. I hope that some of the people including Sheikh Abdullah, will not continue indefinitely in prison. They will be released in due course. I cannot say when, of course, because ultimately the responsibility must lie on those who are carrying on the Government of Kashmir. But, you know that while on the one hand the State of Jammu and Kashmir has made very good progress in the last few years, it is still living in the shadow of these armies and the ceasefire line and constant threats from Pakistan of war, jehad and subversive activities. Since the last three months, there has been a fairly concentrated attempt at creating trouble by explosions, etc., in both Jammu and Kashmir and this is not a secret thing, it is probably proclaimed. It has done damage, it has killed some people. What happens when some kind of an attractive looking box is lying about and somebody naturally goes, looks at it, opens it, unties it, opens the lid and off it goes. It is interesting to see that one was placed in a mosque, another of these was placed in a temple, just to create communal friction and a number of boys, children have died, one or two of our officers, just by opening the box they were blinded. And all this kind of activity is rather a mean type of activity neither war nor anything, just low-down meanness but,

5. Abdullah was arrested on 9 August 1953.

it shows how alert we must be and prepared for all this kind of thing and, I believe, the Jammu and Kashmir Government and our Army and the people there generally realize this and are fairly alert. But it brings to your mind this background in which principally Kashmir State and to some extent all of us in India have to function unfortunately in regard to these activities from Pakistan and this has led us to add to our present burden considerably in defence. Just at a moment when we talk about foreign exchange we have to get new types of weapons costing us a good deal of money.

Now, there is one other matter, I should like to refer to. It is for the moment concerned with the developments and the situation in the Punjab. But I used that more as a symbol and an example than by itself. During the last three or four months since this agitation started in the Punjab,[6] I have naturally been concerned with this, I have taken deep interest and to some extent I have tried to help in putting an end to these difficulties. I am afraid neither I nor my colleagues in the Central Government, nor our colleagues in the Punjab Government, have succeeded in that, that is our misfortune. But what has troubled me much more than anything else is not that particular development or agitation there, by itself bad as it is, but rather the way it brings out, unveils, some failings among our own people. I am told that some days ago, maybe a week, maybe ten days, a meeting was held here of Congress MPs from the Punjab. I was not present, but I got some kind of a report of it and I was told that there was a heated argument and someone present there said that I came in the way of their expressing their opinions frankly, in a sense, I throttled their expression of opinions and they felt very frustrated about it. Well, I do not know perhaps that might be somewhat true, although I have not actually come in the way of any expression of opinion, but I will admit this, I am not talking about MPs as a whole or any individual but broadly speaking, what Congressmen have said and done in connection with this Punjab agitation, has not only astonished me but distressed me greatly. And without meaning to give offence to anybody I should like to say truthfully what I feel, that there are very few persons in the Punjab whether they are in the Congress or outside, whether they are Hindus or Sikhs, who have not functioned, to some extent, communally in this matter.

Now, I am talking about Congressmen, not others, who have been pulled away from such moorings as they might possess as Congressmen, principles etc., and drifted away, both certainly in their expressions of opinion or in their feelings and sometimes even in action in communal directions. Now, that becomes rather a symbol to me of the Congressmen not in the Punjab only but everywhere, and I want you to think and feel and analyze your own thoughts

6. On 30 May 1957.

about this matter, how far do we really accept certain basic principles of the Congress. I do not wish to throttle anybody's expression of opinion, but I would not be the leader of this Congress Party and a person who has had the privilege of being associated with this great organization for the last 40 years or so. If I was not pained and distressed at a violation of the very basic ideals of the Congress, and what is more this kind of thing being not an aberration of a moment but a way of thinking that develops a way of action, the way it is taken for granted, that well, this is so. It is a bad thing and a far more serious thing than that of the foreign exchange difficulties or taxation difficulties or anything else. We can make good with an effort the money that we want, maybe a painful effort, but what are we to do if our organization loses its soul and its ideals and its principles and an innerrot sets in, it is a painful thought. It is astonishing to me to see the extreme narrow-mindedness which many people in the Punjab have exhibited. I am not here to discuss the merits of this controversy. Although I am convinced that this so-called Hindi agitation has nothing to do with Hindi or saving Hindi, and that in fact it has done more injury to Hindi than almost anything I can think of. In the Punjab it has brought Hindi into controversy and hatred, which always is a bad thing. It has encouraged all the bad tendencies in other parts of India and in the South in regard to Hindi. We saw last year how this linguistic provinces agitation led to fierce passions, conflicts, firing, deaths and all kinds of things.[7] That was a bad exhibition of how we feel about it, how easily we are swept away regardless of the merits of the question. Let us fight for any principle but fight without losing our principles and without misbehaving and without forgetting that something much more important than any minor question is the unity of India.

Now, see this Punjab example. I wonder if I asked you, who are sitting here, to put down on a piece of paper exactly what people are quarrelling about in the Punjab, how many of you could do it, or you may broadly say that Hindi is being crushed and Hindi is being discouraged and people are being forced to swallow Punjabi and some such broad thing you may say but that is not enough. If I ask you to put down exactly what the trouble is there, I doubt if anyone of you could put it down correctly. I have asked people who were bravely going to take part in what it is called Satyagraha or whether the Hindi agitation, they did not know, except they had been told Hindi has been squashed, well of course, that is completely untrue. Hindi is not only the language of India but the State language of the Punjab. It is true that in addition to that we have said Punjabi is also a State language. Everybody has got to learn Hindi there, has to pass. Now,

---

7. See *Selected Works* (second series), Vol. 31, pp. 153 and 209, Vol. 32, pp. 180-181 and Vol. 35, p. 41.

opinions may differ about some minor thing as to when it should be taught, well this or that, these are minor matters. But even supposing for a moment that the decision that we made, that is, the Congress Executive, and the Government ultimately, about that formula which is called Regional Formula,[8] whatever it is called, even suppose that it was not an ideal decision that some parts of it might have been bettered, admitting that, is that a thing for which people upset the peace of a province and carry on a bitter strife in this way and create a situation where hatred and bitterness spread more and more, surely there must be some element of balancing the importance of things. I cannot imagine that any reasonable person would create so much trouble about this matter which, for my part, I do not even see the difficulty except very minor ones here and there. What then is this trouble about? I have not a shadow of doubt that it is the trouble by the people who were defeated in the Punjab in the elections against the present Government which was formed after the elections by the majority party,[9] it is purely political. Having been defeated in the elections, they seek other methods to discredit it, to weaken it, and rouse up people's enthusiasm just as in old days the Muslim League raised a religious issue which had nothing to do with politics, a purely communal issue and upset politics by that, and it is exactly comparable to the old Muslim League tactics. Instead of a purely religious issue this is called a cultural issue, and even behind that some suspicions of religion if you like, comes in. The Sikhs said they are not going to live under *Hindu Raj,* the Hindus would say they are not going to live under *Sikh Raj.* Nothing to do with Hindi and Gurmukhi. That is the statement. Some of the Sikhs had, as you know, demanded wrongly, I think, a separate state in the Punjab, and we thought and we still think that it would be highly objectionable and harmful to have a separate communal state like that in the Punjab. Why did the Sikhs or why did the Akalis want that? Well, presumably, for two reasons, one that they should not be bossed over by Hindus, second was the idea that they should be in a majority and the others should be in a minority so that they can control them. Now, you see, what is happening in the Punjab today, the opposite

---

8. As a result of the negotiations between the five-member Akali delegation led by Tara Singh and Nehru, Azad and Pant, a compromise formula known as the Regional Formula was evolved for reorganization of the Punjab. It merged PEPSU with Punjab; provided for one legislature, one governor, one council of ministers for the whole of the reorganized state; and constituted two Regional Committees consisting of MLAs belonging to the two language regions to deal with legislation on the specified subjects. See also *Selected Works* (second series), Vol. 32, P. 209.

9. The Congress won 118 seats in the Assembly and the Government was formed on 9 April 1957 with Partap Singh Kairon as Chief Minister.

of this exactly. People complain of *Sikh Raj* because Sardar Partap Singh is the Chief Minister and there are some other Sikhs too, here and there, of course, there are many Hindu Ministers too, and it seems they are not putting up with this. Now, they are wrong in demanding that and we resisted that demand, equally wrong are those who take up the exact opposite, and I say both are functioning on the exact lines laid down previously in India by the Muslim League. Therefore, I am distressed much more so because so many Congressmen get led away by passion and prejudice and anger because of all this and given their sympathies or sometimes even their active support to this totally misconceived agitation which can lead nowhere. If the agitation, let us say, succeeded, what would be the result? It would lead to a counter-agitation on the other side. It does not bring peace of mind to you, and if it fails, it also brings unhappiness. It is odd either way, you see when an individual or an organization pursues a wrong method, the result is bound to be wrong, whatever the result, victory or defeat, that is what we are facing in the Punjab. What has also pained me very much is that this agitation has been initiated and is largely carried on, no doubt by the help of others, by a great organization which is supposed to be essentially religious or cultural. Now, the coming down of an organization which is essentially religious or cultural into the political field is bad and that is the essence of communalism, and that is again what the Muslim League did in India.

So, you see what is happening and we, because of our religious affiliations, naturally are affected, some of us and get swept away, not realizing the basic wrongness of that approach. Now, always, when such an agitation takes place some time or other, there is conflict with the apparatus of the Government, people are arrested, come in conflict with the police, lathi charges and what not, most unfortunate but there it is. In this particular agitation, I think, for about six weeks or two months the police, no doubt under orders from the Punjab Government, behaved with very considerable patience, although they faced violence, although they were hit and spat upon by people, curious kind of satyagraha which goes about spitting at people and throwing stones and bricks at them. After that, sometimes, the police retaliated with lathi charge etc. I am glad that at any rate that most unfortunate thing, that sometimes happens, did not take place, that is firing, but there were lathi charges and all that. Now, the events occurred which shock everybody, all of you, all of us, more particularly one. One a relatively lesser one, was in Rohtak, where some people came in conflict with the police, stopped them what they were doing and then the police came and tried to arrest and, I believe, misbehaved with the people there. But the other was in Ferozepore Jail where really a very grim tragedy was enacted. There is no doubt about it, whatever the provocation, the fact is that the warders inside the prison hit out and did very great injury to these prisoners there whose number was 150 or 170 or may be 200. It is a very grim tragedy and I have no doubt that those people who were guilty of this should be fully punished. Immediately, the Punjab Government appointed a High Court Judge to enquire and the enquiry is carrying on and the Punjab Government stated that they will punish everybody found guilty by the Judge, and in fact they took away, removed, transferred or suspended some people immediately. Now, this was a very grim tragedy, I say, and a very sad one, but it is not quite logical or right to blame the Punjab Government for it, though responsibility is of the Government you may say, because this thing happened there. It is said that the warders were jeered at by the prisoners, made fun of and very annoying remarks were made, but that is no justification. Anyhow that was a bad show, very bad show, and people should be punished for that. Let us not mix up that with the other part of the main agitation. Now, in this Ferozepur Jail incident one young man died because of lathi blows etc., and he was brought to Rohtak. Now, I understand in Rohtak, not only in Rohtak but in other parts, in the UP etc., his poor ashes or bones are carried about in processions to excite people, and to enroll fresh satyagrahis. Now, I call that indecent, bad, this kind of exploiting of the tragic death of that poor boy in this way. You see, to what levels we have sunk and—what is the question, an educational question—when something should be taught and when it was not taught; these are the questions which are sought to be decided in this way.

Now the question arises where are we, men and women, who are members of the Congress? Do we firmly believe in what the Congress has stood for, that is against communalism, against factionalism, etc., or are we not swept away by these times, whether we are Sikhs or Hindus or Muslims? It is a very serious question for us to consider because if one thing can break up the Congress, it is this inner rot that comes in, when we do not stand by the basic principles which the Congress has stood for all these long years. Apart from the Congress, see logically how this kind of thing affects everybody. We see, in the Punjab and any of you who come from there or who have acquaintance of conditions there will know, how deeply this has affected public life, private life, every life in the Punjab, there it is. And how it brings about disruption, how it works against the basic conception of the unity of India. If I am not prepared to serve under somebody not of my religion or caste etc., then the other fellow is not prepared to serve under me. You see, the whole conception is one of spreading up whether you apply it to religion or caste or other forms of community or language groups. The moment you say, that all right I am not going to cooperate, or serve other religion or code, well, you deny the basic quality of nationality and nationalism and at the back of your minds more important than nationalism is caste feeling,

470

group feeling, and some kind of distorted religious feeling. Then we come back to that which has been the bane of India for these many long years and which was the chief function of the Congress to fight and overcome and if the Congress succumbs to it, then what happens? Who stands up for it? Individuals maybe. We saw in 1947 in the months of August, September and October, when those troubles occurred after Independence and with the coming of Partition. We saw terrible things happening. It is all very well for us to blame Pakistan for what happened in Pakistan. Pakistan is blameworthy. What about the things that happened in Delhi city or in other parts of northern India, in bits of UP and bits of Eastern Punjab? If you say that well, this was in retaliation of what was happening, that is a poor answer. Retaliating in that way was a wrong doing. It shows how we break up, how easily we break up, and revert to our primitive state of narrow-mindedness and communal feeling. It was a dangerous thought. So, I wish you to consider this and I wish you to consider again, I repeat. Take this Punjab agitation, it is an agitation whatever the result, success or failure, breaks up the Punjab either way. But the question can be considered in other ways. It is patent, that if under threat of that agitation, we in the Central Government or in the Punjab Government merely surrender, then first of all, we break the pledged word, our pledged word which we have given when we come to an agreement. Then what would be the worth of the Government of India's pledge word in future on any occasion? No value at all. Nobody will care two pins for it. We do not want to come in the way but we cannot break our word in this way, come what may. It is quite clear. And if we did, we face another agitation sometimes bigger or smaller and so you go on doing this. Is this the way for any country or even, if I may say so, a second rate country to behave and we presume and take pride of the fact that we have high ideals all that. So, it is very distressing.

There is one of the incidents I should like to mention, quite different and yet essentially the same. Some weeks ago, in Raipur in Madhya Pradesh, there was an attack on Christian gathering and not only an attack, much damage was done so far as I know, the poor Christians had done nothing, a pure communal frenzied attack just to frighten them, just to injure them. And the MP Government has appointed a Judge for enquiry and I hope the enquiry will bring out all the facts. But why should this kind of thing occur in this country? We call ourselves by all kinds of high-sounding names but yet the beast comes out. We talk about our culture and our *Samskriti* and all that, where is it? And see the results, the results go far. The result of what happened in Raipur shocked every Christian in India and there is a large Christian population in the South of India specially. It shocked me. If this kind of thing occurs we are not safe in this country. This story is spread in all the newspapers of the world by newspaper correspondents here and elsewhere. There are plenty of people who do not like India as it is, plenty

471

of people who want to take advantage of our failings and they give great publicity and sometimes exaggerate the incidents. So, these are the basic failings and the basic questions we have to think about, not merely foreign exchange or anything else. We have faced big problems and solved them in the past and we will face these problems again and solve them, but if our hearts and minds collapse and if there is no anchorage left which holds us to our principles, then the situation is a pretty difficult one and a bad one. So, I have ventured to place these thoughts before you, for you to consider and ponder over and when you go home or wherever you may go to, to fight this tendency, this narrow-minded bigotry, which is corrupting our public life.

4. Task Before the Youth of India[1]

The youth of the country should learn discipline, self-restraint and dignity of labour as you have to bear the brunt of the battle for reconstructing the edifice of a prosperous India in the near future. You should also equip yourselves physically, intellectually and emotionally to shoulder this task. India lives in villages and you are to spread out to villages, as India will progress only if the villages prosper. You have to help in the silent revolution that is taking place in the villages through the Community Projects.

Self-discipline is very important and without self-control energy becomes a liability. India has a massive population of 37 crores but unless the people are united and worked in a disciplined manner, mere enthusiasm will lead to confusion.

There is lack of discipline among the people particularly among young men. I am surprised to learn at what had happened in Lucknow yesterday when groups of people almost ran amuck, disturbing traffic and forcing people to close their shops, all because something has happened somewhere else.[2]

---

1. Speech while inaugurating the second all India Convention of the Youth Congress at the sports stadium, Lucknow, 27 October 1957. From *The Hindu* and *National Herald*, 28 October 1957.
2. In support of the linguistic agitation in Punjab, the students of Lucknow organized a hartal and as a result all commercial activities came to a standstill.

I think you should draw the particular attention of the Home Ministry to effect of war predictions in some newspapers. Also to astrologers' forecasts of a coming war. Is it not possible to do something to stop this kind of thing? The least that can be done is to tell them ... forcibly that this must not be done. The astrologers should be warned that any publicity about war predictions will get them into trouble.

J. Nehru
- 5/9/57

FACSIMILE OF A NOTE TO COMMONWEALTH SECRETARY ON WAR
PREDICTIONS, 5 SEPTEMBER 1957

THE AICC SCENE

At the 1957 AICC Session. Among the recumbent leaders are Lal Bahadur Shastri, Krishna Menon, Kamalapathi Tripathi, Morarji Desai, B.C. Roy, Maulana Azad, Govind Ballabh Pant, Jagjivan Ram and Gulzari Lal Nanda.

"THE AICC SCENE", A CARTOON FROM *SHANKAR'S WEEKLY*, 8 SEPTEMBER 1957

India has a long history and tradition and the present generation has inherited the glories of a thousand years along with certain weaknesses also. The most important question now is—how is the country going to survive with peace and can go ahead.

Do not be victims to mere slogans and nothing is ever achieved by mere shouting. How can the people tolerate *tamasha*, that is going on in Punjab in the name of Hindi when the country is facing a crisis. National strength lays in unity and history shows how India suffered in the past because of disunity.

The people of our generations are reaching the evening of their lives and so the youth of the country should realize the responsibilities which are to devolve on them. You are to mould yourself for taking up the future responsibilities. Linguistic quarrels, provincialism, casteism and narrowness of outlook will weaken the country. The youth of India should protect themselves against such weaknesses and bring round the misguided elements with love. If people indulge in internecine quarrels and indiscipline, India will become weak and her Independence will be in jeopardy.

The linguistic controversy in the Punjab and the sympathetic hartal organized by students in Lucknow yesterday should be deplored. The country is faced with many problems and hence the people should concentrate on eradicating all weaknesses.

The world has advanced to a stage of inventing a new moon and further progress may be made in the near future. In this context it is a pity that in India people harped on the age-old, outdated traditions and prejudices. Gandhiji had taught us many lessons, but we did not learn from him much. If the people had learnt those lessons better, the country would have gone much ahead. The Independence of the country should not be threatened through rowdyism and slackness. Independence can be maintained only through sacrifices at every stage.

The world is fast changing today on account of technological and scientific advances, but people have to remember that mere technological and scientific advancements will not go a long way in solving the problems of the world. Development of atomic energy and technological advancement without a corresponding development of the spirit of cooperation and tolerance will crush humanity.

The people should judge these technological advancements from ethical plane, the plane of cooperation and democracy. Democracy and civilization are behaviours of humanity. We in India grew up under the leadership of Mahatma Gandhi who told us to stick to ethical principles.

In the international sphere, India has adhered to principles of *Panchsheel* because India dislike war which produces only hatred. Our policy should be for peace and non-violence, tolerance and compassion. That is what was taught by our leader, Mahatma Gandhi.

You should understand the implications of India's foreign policy. We have befriended many countries, through *Panchsheel*. We have looked to their merits and ignored their weaknesses. In Japan, I followed the same policy of commending their achievements. I found both areas of agreement and disagreement, but I laid emphasis on the areas of agreement.

India has no atomic weapons but her potentialities lay in right understanding and non-violence. The history of the country has taught the people that India was subjugated on account of disunity. The youth of the country should try to understand their country and the unifying force behind it. If they want to assess the position their country occupied, they should go abroad.

Recently, Dr Radhakrishnan visited Cambodia, Mongolia, Vietnam, Laos, Thailand and China.[3] I also went to Japan.[4] We have seen a replica of ancient India in those countries. We found the reflection of India's thought, culture and language in those countries, which are the indications of the real strength of India. Indians in the ancient days went to other countries with great risks to their lives. They did not go to those countries with any aggressive designs but with a missionary zeal to win over the people of those countries with love. They had spread Indian language, fine arts and culture and gave the message of tolerance, love and mutual cooperation. Then Indian society was not moribund as it became later, when sea travel became a religious taboo, and inter-dining and inter-marriage led to excommunication.

It is a complicated problem to run the administration of a country. Some mistakes might have been committed, but we are rectifying them. The country has made great progress during the past ten years. In the coming years, the youth should prepare themselves increasingly for the service of the nation. India is yours and I cannot give any better gift than this. You are to run the administration in any way you like, but before making the claim of running the administration, you have to discipline yourselves. The country is passing through a period of reconstruction. It is your duty to uplift the peasantry in the countryside and for that we are to extend a helping hand to the Community Development Schemes, which are revolutionizing the rural economy.

The Youth Convention may pass pompous resolutions, but such resolutions by themselves do not serve any specific purpose. Sometimes, resolutions are passed advancing their Government and criticizing the policies of other

3. Radhakrishnan left New Delhi on 8 September 1957 for a three week tour of South East Asia.
4. Nehru was in Japan from 4 to 13 October 1957.

Governments, as if they have become so capable as to understand the world. These things do not benefit them at all. In my youth days, students devoted themselves to doing their work and did not try to meddle with the affairs of others. They mostly concentrated in their own sphere without giving sermons to others.

India is passing through a crisis today. If the country has to exist not merely in the physical and geographical sense, it must grow and prosper with dignity and freedom. The present state of poverty in which millions lived without adequate shelter, food or education has to be banished. And towards that end the people of the country, each and every individual and not merely ten or twelve people who sat in Delhi or Lucknow, will have to take an active interest.

Freedom cannot be secured until people are eternally vigilant and prepared to make sacrifices. Freedom was the first step towards greater progress and happiness. India do not want gifts or donations from others. She only wants loans which she will pay back. Every nation requires foreign assistance for speedy development but this does not mean that foreigners will be sharing the hardships in building up another nation's prosperity.

8
KASHMIR

1. Inaccurate Canadian Report[1]

The High Commissioner for Canada[2] has sent me the attached report. I have briefly acknowledged it.

On glancing through it hurriedly, I came across a sentence on page 17, which says:

"Then on Republic Day, January 26, 1957, India accepted formal accession of Kashmir into the Indian Union."

I think that you might informally draw the attention of the High Commissioner to this sentence and say that it is not correct. India accepted accession of Kashmir in October 1947. That accession was complete. On January 1957, nothing was done by India to accept accession. In fact we have taken no action at all. All that happened was that the Kashmir Assembly, having finished its Constitution making in October or November 1956, formally dissolved itself on January 26th.

1. Note to M.J. Desai, Commonwealth Secretary, New Delhi, 6 August 1957. File No. 11-KU/57, pp. 49-50/Note, MEA. Also available in JN Collection.
2. Escott Reid.

2. Repetition in the Canadian Publication[1]

I have seen your previous note dated 15th July. That, presumably, was based on some bulletin issued by the Canadian Government and you were quite right in drawing the attention of the Canadian High Commissioner to the inaccurate statement made therein.

Now, we are dealing with another publication called *Canada and the United Nations*,[2] where the wrong statement is repeated. It is true that this book is probably just a collection of the bulletins and no correction could be made in it in time. Nevertheless, I think that the attention of the Canadian High Commissioner should be drawn to this particular passage in this book and our

1. Note to Commonwealth Secretary, New Delhi, 7 August 1957. File NO. 11-KU/57, pp. 49-50/Note, MEA. Also available in JN Collection.
2. *Canada and the United Nations 1956-57.*

regret expressed at a factually wrong statement being repeated again and again. We should request him to ask his Government to get it corrected in the book itself.

In such matters, we should not take anything for granted and we should draw attention to an error again and again if necessary, so that they may know that we attach importance to it and they should change their methods in future.

3. To Bakhshi Ghulam Mohammad[1]

New Delhi
August 7, 1957

My dear Bakhshi,[2]

Thank you for your letter of August 7th, which I have just received.[3] I have not read the bundle of correspondence that you have sent me, but I have glanced through your letter of August 5th to D.P. Dhar and the draft resolution submitted by D.P. This resolution, as drafted, certainly is not acceptable.

1. JN Collection.
2. Prime Minister of Jammu and Kashmir.
3. Bakhshi wrote about the developments preceding the resignations of G.M. Sadiq and five others from the Working Committee of National Conference. Their differences began with the formation of the new Cabinet after the elections. Bakhshi wanted to include Sadiq and Mir Qasim in a broad-based Cabinet, representative of various regions and interests, but Sadiq took an irrevocable stand for inclusion of the whole group. Several attempts to persuade him by various people, including Karan Singh and Krishna Menon, failed and finally, Shamas Din of Anantnag was inducted in the Cabinet. On 27 July 1957, Krishen Dev Sethi and Ram Piara Saraf of the Sadiq group subjected the National Conference party and Government to wild criticism during a discussion in the Assembly. The Working Committee of National Conference met from 31 July to 6 August to sort out these differences. On 5 August, a draft resolution by D.P. Dhar suggesting drastic changes in the organization, was discussed. However, it was decided to draft a new resolution and include portions of Dhar's draft. All this while, Sadiq and his group held deliberations with Comrade Surjeet of the Communist Politburo, who had been staying in Srinagar. On 6 August, Sadiq and five others sent a joint letter of resignation containing wild allegations against the party and the Government. Earlier they revealed the story to the local press correspondents. Bakhshi wrote that a campaign of vilification had been let loose against the Government in anticipation of the proposed changes envisaged in the budget in regard to State's food policy and taxation.

I am sorry for the developments that have taken place in Kashmir in recent weeks. As you know, I tried my best to avoid any kind of a split and I was glad to find that you were also trying your hard to avoid this development. It seems to me clear, however, that Sadiq, D.P. and others had made up their minds on this issue.

The burden on you must be much greater now and you will have in your Assembly and otherwise continuous criticism from this group. This criticism will no doubt be answered. But the best way to answer it is to see that the work of the Government and the organization is done efficiently and in a manner pleasing to the public.

Yours sincerely,
Jawaharlal Nehru

4. To U.N. Dhebar[1]

New Delhi
August 10, 1957

My dear Dhebar Bhai,
I wonder if you saw in *The Hindustan Times* of the 9th August a report of an interview given by G.M. Sadiq of Kashmir to a local paper there.[2] He is reported to have said that the proposal for an investigation of irregularities committed by any National Conference worker during the recent general elections by any representative of the Indian National Congress, as has been suggested by Bakhshi Ghulam Mohammad, is unacceptable to him because it would provide an opportunity for the Congress to meddle in the internal politics of Kashmir. Further that the proposal was misleading and could result in the merger of the National Conference with the Congress.

Yours sincerely,
Jawaharlal Nehru

1. JN Collection. Also available in A.I.C.C. Papers, NMML.
2. The interview with Sadiq, leader of the dissident group in the National Conference, was published in the *Sandesh* (Jammu) on 8 August 1957.

5. 'The Kashmir Story'[1]

I have glanced through this rough script of 'the Kashmir story', which you have no doubt seen. I do not understand film scripts.[2] But, there is one thing which, I think, should be stressed more. And, that is the material progress made by the State. I do not think enough propaganda has been done of this in foreign countries or even in India, although people talk vaguely about it. This is not merely a question of rice prices being low, but of big schemes of hydro-electric power, control of floods, great advance in education, in handicrafts, cottage industries, etc. etc.

1. Note to Commonwealth Secretary, New Delhi, 11 August 1957. JN Collection.
2. This was a factual documentation of India's case on Kashmir.

6. To Bakhshi Ghulam Mohammad[1]

New Delhi
August 17, 1957

My dear Bakhshi,

I met Sadiq and D.P. Dhar this morning for some time and later, in the afternoon, I met D.P. Dhar separately. I told them clearly and strongly that I thought they were completely in the wrong in the way they had acted recently in regard to Cabinet formation, etc. They had put themselves in the wrong by the attitude they had taken up. Sadiq spoke at length. I need not repeat what he said. In the main, his complaint was about the organization which, he said, was losing its hold on the people. He said that quite a considerable number of good workers had resigned recently and more might resign. These persons might drift in wrong directions and he hoped that, in the circumstances that had arisen, he might be able to keep them away from the wrong courses. He complained about the vilification that was going on against him, not by you, but by others. Also about

1. JN Collection.

numerous pinpricks—meeting not being allowed to be held, Sadiq being stopped on the road. One fact surprised me, that D.P. Dhar had been served a notice to quit his house within forty-eight hours, or otherwise force would be used to remove him.

He mentioned further that many of the members of your new Cabinet were hardly known to the public and could not exercise much influence there. Altogether, he seemed to think that the position was very unsatisfactory. He said that it was his wish to strengthen the organization which was more important than being in the Cabinet. But, unfortunately, he was not allowed to do so.

I told him that whatever justification there was in some of his complaints, the way he had acted was not the way to meet the situation. In fact, it was likely to do much more harm. As it was, there were difficulties enough before us in Kashmir and he had added to them.

I was rather worried to learn about D.P. Dhar being asked to quit his house suddenly. This by itself does not mean much. But it becomes symbolic of an out and out conflict. It also appeared to me to be lacking in courtesy to a colleague of long standing. Here, in Delhi, we allow a full month and indeed much more, if necessary, for old Cabinet Ministers to stay on in their houses even after they resign. What I am worried about is that we should avoid personal recrimination and pinpricks. You will remember that when Shaikh Abdullah was arrested, I was anxious that there should be no attacks on him. This kind of thing never does any good and often does much harm. Arguments or charges can be answered soberly and without the personal element coming in. It is bad politics to indulge in personal attacks or pinpricks. I am sure you will not do it, but others might. I hope you will look into this matter.

Sadiq told me that no meeting of the General Council of your Conference had been held for a long time and many *Tehsil* committees of the Conference were breaking up. If this is so, it is unfortunate, because ultimately it is the organization that counts. I presume that, in the near future, Shaikh Abdullah will be released. You may well have to meet a difficult situation then. If the organization is not in proper trim, then it will be even more difficult to face this. new situation. An organization is not merely something isolated from the public. It has to command the confidence of the public and to have intimate contacts with all sections. This is the problem which has been worrying us in regard to the Congress here. We have a huge organization, but its public approach has become weak, so we are doing our utmost to strengthen this. There is a great deal of psychology about this, as there is about everything connected with the public. If we have the public confidence, it is well; if not, then even a well-knit organization cannot produce a good effect. I am, therefore, anxious that the organization should be such as commands the confidence and faith of the public,

483

both in its integrity and its manner of working. The question is not of putting down Plebiscite Front or any other opposing group. That is a minor matter. The real objective has to be to win the goodwill of the public and to make them feel that it is their organization and not something isolated from them.

I would particularly like you to see that the split that has taken place between you and Sadiq and others is not widened, and therefore, no bitter words should be used or other action taken which might tend to widen it. We cannot afford to increase our opponents.[2]

I am writing to you immediately and rather in a hurry because I wanted to tell you about my meeting with Sadiq and D.P. Dhar. It always pains me to lose a colleague because, I think, I ought to be capable of holding everybody together with me. Sometimes circumstances are too strong for us. Even so, I struggle against them.

Yours sincerely,
Jawaharlal Nehru

2. However, a formal split occurred in the party resulting in the formation of the Democratic National Conference on 6 September 1957 under Sadiq. The new party demanded closer integration with India and criticized the ruling party for suppressing civil liberties, resorting to authoritarianism, generating corruption and nepotism.

7. To Jainarain Vyas[1]

New Delhi
August 24, 1957

My dear Jainarainji,[2]

Thank you for your letter of the 22nd August about Kashmir. I have been much disturbed at the developments there. As a matter of fact, I have been unhappy ever since Sheikh Abdullah was arrested and detained, though perhaps that was inevitable. I have not gone to Kashmir since then. Recent development also

1. JN Collection.
2. Congress Member of Rajya Sabha from Rajasthan.

have not been at all happy, though, I think, that in this matter Sadiq has taken up an unreasonable attitude.

I hope we shall meet in the near future and have a talk about these matters.

Yours sincerely,
Jawaharlal Nehru

8. Alleged Soviet Air bases in Kashmir[1]

Awadheshwar Prasad Sinha: [2] Will the Prime Minister be pleased to state:
  (a) whether Government's attention has been drawn to a statement reported to have been made by Mr Feroz Khan Noon, Foreign Minister of Pakistan, in answer to a question in the Pakistan National Assembly that "Russian planes are known to have been landing in Kashmir and the whole of India can be considered a Russian base";
  (b) whether there is any basis for the allegations made; and
  (c) if the answer to part (b) above be in the negative, what steps Government have taken to counter the allegations?

Jawaharlal Nehru: (a) Government's attention has been drawn to certain press reports of the statement.

  (b) There is not an iota of truth in the allegations made and it is surprising that the Foreign Minister of Pakistan should make statements which have no basis whatever. The statement that "Russian planes are known to have been landing in Kashmir" is completely untrue. No Russian plane has landed there except when the Soviet leaders, Mr Khrushchev and Mr Bulganin and their party visited Srinagar during their visit to India in 1955. They went there on their own aircraft Ilyushin 14.

  The statement that the whole of India can be considered a "Russian base" is so fantastic and perverse that it is difficult to imagine that even the Foreign Minister of Pakistan believes in it.

1. Reply to a question in Rajya Sabha, 28 August 1957. *Rajya Sabha Debates*, Vol. XVIII, cols. 2038-39. Extracts. A similar question was answered by Nehru in the Lok Sabha on 26 August 1957.
2. Congress Member from Bihar.

485

(c) We have contradicted these allegations publicly and are bringing this also to the notice of the Pakistan High Commission....

9. Alleged Settlement of Non-Muslims in Kashmir[1]

...Jawaharlal Nehru: I have not got the exact letter which my colleague has.[2] But the apprehension or the complaint was that by pushing other outsiders into Kashmir, we are changing the proportion of the population. That was the charge made and which is denied completely, because as a matter of fact, as the answer says, nobody under the Kashmir laws which I confess are rather peculiar, can get land unless he is in a particular list of Kashmiri citizens.

V.K. Dhage: Is it the allegation made in the letter that the property that is left by the Muslims there is being given over to non-Muslims ?

JN: The first thing is that non-Kashmiris, i.e., non-residents of the Jammu and Kashmir State, have been settled there. That is denied. But a large number of refugees came from those parts of Kashmir State which are occupied by the Pakistan Government. Those refugees have been settled there, in those parts of Kashmir State, and it may be that they are Hindus and Muslims—all Kashmiris. They are not from outside Kashmir State. That is the point.

Jaswant Singh:[3] The complaint also says that the properties left behind by the Muslims in Kashmir State are being declared as evacuee property. Knowing as we do the conditions in Pakistan, is it true that the Kashmiris have left Kashmir to go into Pakistan?

JN: When this trouble arose in Kashmir, a large number of Kashmiris went over to Pakistan or later, to the Pakistan-occupied areas of Kashmir and a large number of Kashmiris came from that side to this side of the ceasefire line. Many people went in either direction.

---

1. Reply to a question in the Rajya Sabha, 29 August 1957. *Rajya Sabha Debates*, Vol. XVIII, cols. 2270-2272. Extracts.
2. V.K. Dhage, Independent Member from Bombay, asked whether it was a fact that Pakistan's Permanent Representative in the UN, Ghulam Ahmed, had written to the President of the Security Council, indicating that India had recently settled a large number of non-Muslims in Kashmir and that the properties left behind by the Muslims in the Kashmir State were being declared as evacuee property.
3. Independent Member from Rajasthan.

D.A. Mirza:[4] Does it make any difference between a Kashmiri and an Indian? Is not a Kashmiri an Indian?

JN: A Kashmiri is an Indian national. But no non-Kashmiri Indian national can get land there.

Jaswant Singh: How does the question of the property left behind arise if the people have not left Kashmir to go into Pakistan? Then how does the complaint speak of the properties left behind?

JN: Surely, Sir, if people leave their land and go away, they leave their property behind—that is, a land or maybe some house, whatever it may be.

Jaswant Singh: That is what I wanted to know exactly—whether Kashmiris have left Kashmir to go into Pakistan?

JN: Hundreds of thousands have gone to this side and that side of the Pakistan-occupied Kashmir.

Maheswar Naik:[5] May I know whether the honourable Prime Minister can give us any idea of the Muslim refugees coming from the occupied territories of Pakistan to this side?

JN: I do not think....

Chairman:[6] He is talking about the other question in the United Nations, not about Kashmiris there. Can you give any answer?

JN: Yet, I can say something, but I do not know if this is the answer. One must remember that these parts of Kashmir State, because of the invasion by Pakistan, were war areas. Armies marched this way and that way and quite a considerable number of people went to the area which was originally invaded by Pakistan. Quite a large number of people went towards Pakistan, towards that area. Now, when the Pakistani armies were pushed back by the Indian armies in those particular areas, for the moment, those areas were empty. When they went to the other side, the Pakistanis told them, "If you will remain here, your heads will be cut off". Two or three months later, most of them were returned. Therefore, there was this coming and going within the Kashmir State....

4. Congress Member from Madras.
5. Congress Member from Orissa.
6. S. Radhakrishnan.

10. To Ajit Prasad Jain[1]

New Delhi
August 30, 1957

My dear Ajit,

As you must know, Jammu and Kashmir both have had terrible floods.[2] The damage caused has been colossal. Almost every village in the Valley and many in the Jammu area have been swept away. Bridges have broken down and all the crops in the Valley have been destroyed. We have not really had any full accounts of this yet. But General Kalwant Singh[3] came from Srinagar today and gave us an account which was alarming.

This inevitably puts a great burden on us in many ways. But apart from everything else, the question arises of feeding this destitute population. I have just spoken to Bakhshi Ghulam Mohammad on the telephone. He asked plaintively for any kind of food that could be sent to him, rice, wheat, maize, in fact anything. He wanted this to be sent to Jammu. From there he would transport it to Kashmir Valley. I suppose we must do our best.

Yours sincerely,
Jawaharlal Nehru

1. JN Collection.
2. Devastating floods in Jhelum, Chenab and Tawi rivers hit Jammu and Kashmir in the last week of August 1957. Described as the gravest in the history of the State, the floods inundated thousands of acres of paddy fields; uprooted about half a million people; breached the Jammu-Srinagar road, Srinagar-Pathankot highway and smaller roads interconnecting it with smaller towns, Srinagar-Awantipur-Anantnag road; and communications were disrupted. Thirty-eight people were reported to have lost their lives in the State.
3. Lt. General Kalwant Singh was GOC-in-Chief, Western Command.

ADDRESSING THE NATIONAL CONFERENCE WORKERS, SRINAGAR, 11 SEPTEMBER 1957

(Courtesy: HT Photo Library)

WITH AIICHIRO FUJIYAMA, JAPANESE FOREIGN MINISTER AND
NOBUSUKE KISHI, JAPANESE PRIME MINISTER, TOKYO, OCTOBER 1957

11. Cable to Bakhshi Ghulam Mohammad[1]

I am very glad to learn that the flood danger is now a little less. What a terrible time all of you have had. We have felt a little helpless here not being able to do much for you, but we are glad that the Army was doing everything possible.

2. I sent you a telegram two days ago enquiring what you would suggest we should do from here. I have had no reply as you must have been very busy.

3. I shall, of course, send you money from the Prime Minister's Fund for relief.

1. New Delhi, 30 August 1957. JN Collection.

12. To T.T. Krishnamachari[1]

New Delhi
August 30, 1957

My dear T.T.,
The floods in Kashmir have been something quite extraordinary in extent and ferocity, not only in Kashmir Valley but in Jammu also. The damage done has been colossal and almost every inhabited village in the Valley has ceased to exist. The immediate need is of food of any kind, rice, wheat, maize, and I am asking Ajit Prasad to send what he can immediately to Jammu.

I feel that in the circumstances I should pay a brief visit to Jammu and Srinagar. I have not been there for about four years, but this particular calamity deserves a visit at least. It is no good my delaying the visit. But the earliest I can go is on the 3rd September. Tomorrow and the day after is the AICC and on the 2nd September is the Foreign Affairs debate in the Lok Sabha. From the 5th onwards there are visits by various Foreign Ministers.

I am, therefore, provisionally, thinking of going to Kashmir on Tuesday, September 3rd, morning, and returning the next day about midday.

1. JN Collection.

489

On Tuesday you have fixed your informal tea for Ministers and 4th morning there is a Cabinet meeting. I would suggest the postponement of the Cabinet meeting to the 5th September afternoon and I would request you to postpone your tea to the 4th September 6 p.m. I hope you do not mind these changes. I shall confirm them tomorrow afternoon after I have finally made up my mind that I am going.[2]

Yours sincerely,
Jawaharlal Nehru

2. Nehru's plane could not cross into the Kashmir Valley on 3 September due to poor visibility and landed at Ambala. An hour and a half later, it again took off for Srinagar but had to fly back to Delhi owing to bad weather.

13. Refugees from "Azad" Kashmir[1]

I have read these papers including the note on the condition of refugees from the Jammu and Kashmir State. If you like, you can send that note to the Rehabilitation Minister for his comments, and so that he might give the facts of the case.

It is true, I think, that refugees from "Azad" Kashmir were not treated in the past on a level with refugees from Pakistan. I believe, it was thought that if we treated them as refugees from Pakistan, this might mean some kind of admission that "Azad" Kashmir was part of Pakistan.

After some time, however, I think, some privileges were given to these Mirpur refugees, though I do not exactly remember what they were. I know that I wrote about them on more than one occasion to the Ministry of Rehabilitation.

If you would like to see my correspondence on this subject, I can have it brought out from the files. But perhaps the best course would be for the Minister of Rehabilitation to be requested to send his comments on the note from the Mirpur D.P. Association.

1. Note to Defence Minister, New Delhi, 31 August 1957. JN Collection.

14. Radioactivity in Kashmir[1]

Harish Chandra Mathur[2] and two others:
Will the Prime Minister be pleased to state:

(a) whether the attention of Government has been invited to the reported statement by Kashmir Government's Director of Fisheries that a larger number of fish in Kashmir's springs and lakes have been found dead or dying owing to radioactivity;

(b) if so, what is the extent and source of this pollution; and

(c) what steps Government have taken or propose to take for protection from this menace?

Jawaharlal Nehru: (a) Yes.

(b) and (c). The radioactivity reported by non-official scientists in Kashmir is certainly not sufficient to cause the death of fish. The Department is not aware of any other measurements of radioactivity in Kashmir. Nor has the Director of Fisheries, Kashmir, indicated how he measured the radioactivity of the fish or how he came to the conclusion that radioactivity was responsible for their death. Government are awaiting a detailed report from the State Government. Samples of the affected fish are being obtained and necessary investigations will be carried out. Until the results of these investigations are known, it is not possible to express any definite opinion on whether the fish were killed by radioactivity.

1. Reply to a question in the Lok Sabha, 2 September 1957. *Lok Sabha Debates*, (second series), Vol. VI, cols. 11291-92.
2. Congress Member from Pali, Rajasthan.

15. To Vishnu Sahay[1]

New Delhi
September 4, 1957

My dear Vishnu Sahay,

I enclose a telegram[2] and a note.[3] What the actual facts are, I do not know. But I am distressed at the idea that my visit should be the occasion of any arrests or beating. I now intend going to Srinagar on the 11th. I hope I shall not be responsible for this on that day.

I had received telegrams from Plebiscite Front, Political Conference, etc. seeking interviews with me in Srinagar. I suppose they shall try to do that again. I have no intention of giving them any interview.

But I have written to Bakhshi Sahib that I should like to meet for a few minutes Maulana Masoudi[4] who had also sent a telegram to me asking for a brief interview to pay his respects.

Yours sincerely,
Jawaharlal Nehru

---

1. JN Collection.
2. Ali Mohammad Naik, President of the Jammu and Kashmir Plebiscite Front, telegraphed from Srinagar on 3 September 1957 that on the eve of Nehru's arrival, a number of Srinagar Plebiscite Front workers were detained in *thanas*, molested and ruthlessly beaten. He appealed to Nehru to stop this lawlessness and hooliganism.
3. The note dated 4 September 1957 by Mridula Sarabhai referred to *The Times of India* report that all political parties including Plebiscite Front and Praja Socialist Party, went all out to give a reception to Nehru. When it was known that he had returned due to bad weather, the police went wild and started indiscriminately beating up those whom they suspected to be associated with the Plebiscite Front. Their action at Amirakadal was specially severe. She wrote that about 200 persons were beaten up and 65 were taken into custody. They were released at night in small groups and warned "to be away from any reception activity if Nehru visited again."
4. Maulana Mohammad Saeed Masoudi was Member, Lok Sabha, till 1957.

16. The Kashmir Case[1]

There is no difficulty about our seeing any papers in the Yuvaraj's possession.[2] He might be informed immediately that such papers as are with him, might be kept ready for us to see them when we go there.

2. As for ex-Chief Justice Mahajan, I think that someone should go to see him and ask him such questions as are considered necessary.[3] I do not know where he is at present. If he is in Delhi, then there is no difficulty. If he is somewhere in the Punjab, then someone will have to make this journey. Obviously, some person of senior status and who knows this case, should go. Commonwealth Secretary might do so.

3. Before anybody sees ex-Chief Justice Mahajan, a note might be prepared as to the papers we would like to see and the questions which we should like to be elucidated.

1. Note to V.K. Krishna Menon, New Delhi, 5 September 1957. JN Collection.
2. In a note on 5 September, Krishna Menon wrote that he had seen a reference to some notes by the Maharaja of Kashmir, which might be in the Yuvaraj's possession. These papers "may well be against us, but it is well to know what these papers are about" and decide what use to make of them.
3. Krishna Menon marked certain portions of an article on Kashmir by Justice M.C. Mahajan, ex-Chief Justice of the Supreme Court, which he thought, could be used against India by Pakistan in the Security Council. For example, Mahajan wrote that Chitral, Hunza and other dependencies while swearing loyalty to the Ruler were pressing him to accede to Pakistan. Krishna Menon thought that this could be "argued as evidence that these areas have been part of Kashmir. It could equally be argued as evidence of the protest by part of Kashmir against accession." Further, Mahajan said in the article that "we have not got the necessary convincing evidence." Krishna Menon's view was that Pakistan could argue that the facts on which India based her historical claims were less than convincing. Mahajan's position as a former Chief Minister of Kashmir and as an ex-Chief Justice, if cleverly utilized by Pakistan, could bring difficulties for India. Menon enquired if Mahajan could help India's case.

17. Pakistan's Intervention in Kashmir[1]

I have not been to Kashmir for the last four years because I have been pained and hurt by the arrest and detention of Sheikh Abdullah. I cannot say this step was wrong, but since he was our companion for years and had earned a name for himself in the freedom struggle of India, his arrest has deeply pained me. Sometimes, we have to take actions that we do not relish, but circumstances make us helpless. Sometimes, we are faced with questions whether we should follow ideals and principles or continue to respect and honour friendship. I still do not know what caused him to part company with me! What was it that was lacking in me? I have not understood that, but the way Sheikh Abdullah was going then was a dangerous way and was harming the interest of Kashmir and the whole of India, and therefore, the arrest has been correct.

It is always painful for old, trusted colleagues to part company. Nevertheless, when basic ideologies are same, that is the State's accession to India, those who have fallen apart should not go far against each other. But I do not understand what has led G.M. Sadiq and his group to leave the National Conference. I had met them in Delhi and advised them to sink their differences and work within the framework of the old party and try to resolve their differences from within rather than without. People should remain united and work shoulder to shoulder for the welfare of the State which is passing through a critical period, with the armies of India and Pakistan facing each other on the ceasefire line.

Some people here cry for closer relations with India, but in fact, do things that create an adverse effect. The real relation of Kashmir with the rest of India is that of the union of hearts. If that is not there, then all laws are useless.

Freedom has only opened doors to progress. Our Community Projects are our biggest enterprise, aimed at rousing people living in five lakh villages to the tasks of national construction. Half of rural India has so far been covered by Community Projects and the other half will be covered in another four years. Real prosperity does not lie in the possession of wealth in the shape of silver or gold but in the total production. This is what the Five Year Plans are designed to achieve.

India has made spectacular progress during the past 10 years. Even foreign countries have acknowledged this. But it is unfortunate that Pakistan is carrying on "Jehad" propaganda against India, threatening her with war and trying to

---

1. Address to the National Conference workers in Jammu (morning) and Srinagar (evening), 11 September 1957. From *The Hindu, The Hindustan Times, The Tribune,* 12 September 1957 and the *National Herald,* 13 September 1957.

harm her in every possible way. Now, it is getting arms from America. America assures us that the arms supplied to Pakistan will not be used against India. America is our friend and we respect that country, but when once arms fall into wrong hands, who can stop them from being used anywhere.

The Kashmir problem is a simple one. Pakistan had attacked Kashmir which is in every respect part of India. This simple problem has been so much complicated that the real facts are being forgotten. We are prepared to face the situation in any manner: if it comes to armies, we shall face them by armies. But such questions are usually not solved through armies and it is the force of the people which is final in such things. Unity among people is a fundamental thing. Pakistan is trying to create disruption by exploding bombs and killing children in the State.[2] It is sheer nonsense to kill and endanger the lives of the people of Jammu and Kashmir by exploding bombs, and for this Pakistan is responsible.

The attitude adopted by some Big Powers towards the Kashmir problem has very much pained me, because they are sleeping over the fact that Pakistan has committed aggression in Kashmir and is in illegal occupation of a part of the State. I am sure world opinion could not be misled for ever and facts are steadily asserting themselves. The State's case is in the Security Council and now after ten or eleven days it will again be discussed. Last time when the Security Council discussed the Kashmir issue, certain nations amazingly enough did not support India. Mr V.K. Krishna Menon, the Defence Minister, who represented India in the Security Council, presented India's case with great ability and courage.[3] The problem of Kashmir is not that of holding a plebiscite but that of Pakistan's aggression. The problem of Kashmir is: what right has Pakistan to be in this State? What right has she to have her troops in Kashmir? What right has she to intimidate the people of this state? The answer to these questions is not plebiscite.

Behind this big problem of Kashmir is a bigger problem—that of Pakistan inheriting the mentality of the Muslim League in undivided India—the mentality of creating difficulties, of organizing fights and feuds and intimidation. Pakistan has harboured a feeling of jealousy and malice against India. It is this attitude of Pakistan that has led to the problem of Kashmir, that has led to the invasion of the State and destruction and devastation in Kashmir.

Having committed aggression in Kashmir, Pakistan is attempting to present the case in a different angle altogether. She is presenting facts the world over about Kashmir which are far from reality and truth. This attitude of Pakistan has surprised India and even pained her. The basic facts of the Kashmir problem are

2. For instances of bomb explosions in Jammu and Kashmir State, see *post*, pp. 498-499.
3. See *Selected Works* (second series), Vol. 36, pp. 349 & 356.

that Pakistan attacked the State. Her troops were found in the State by the UN Commission, when it came here some years ago to negotiate a settlement of the dispute. Even the UN Commission had admitted that the presence of troops of Pakistan in Kashmir is a new situation, a new development in the dispute.

Keeping these facts in view, India had fought Pakistan in Kashmir and cleared most of the State of raiders and troops of Pakistan. But India, believing in peace and friendship with all, and more so with her neighbour Pakistan, has attempted to settle the dispute through other means. India is contented to have a settlement of the dispute in a peaceful manner at a time when her forces were triumphant and well poised to clear the entire State of intruders and the aggressor. We had the strength to complete this task but that attitude would have only further poisoned the atmosphere and led to bitterness.

I do not understand how Hindi, which is the national language, is in danger in the Punjab. It is funny that such an uproar is being raised to save the national language which everyone is required to study. Hindi agitation in Punjab is having adverse repercussions in the South. Such agitations rather give rise to sentiments against Hindi. It is a national disruption which weakens a country, and in India certain language controversies have harmed the national cause. Also I warn that Hindi cannot be forced, and those not knowing it should be persuaded to read it. The result of mixing religion and politics is always dangerous. Years before, the Muslim League had pursued this policy which resulted in disunity and rivalry with consequential establishment of Pakistan, which is again trying to harm us. When outsiders play some mischief it can be countered, but when our own men do undesirable things, it pains us and affects our minds.

I appreciate Bakhshi Ghulam Mohammad for shouldering the heavy responsibility of the State's administration when it is passing through hard times. There is fear of war and other troubles created by Pakistan, but Bakhshi Ghulam Mohammad has faced everything with courage, ability and confidence.

I have come here to see the great damage caused by the recent floods. I appeal to you to devote yourself to the task of more and more production in the country.

18. Commendable Services of the Armed Forces[1]

Indian Armed Forces had come to Kashmir at the invitation of the people of this part of India to defend them against raiders and marauders who had laid waste the State during their attack on Kashmir. I also appreciate the heroic resistance of the people of Kashmir who had met the aggressors with all their might and made tremendous sacrifices. You are soldiers of a great and glorious country whose efforts to serve the world peace during the troubled times in Korea, Indo-China and Egypt are well known the world over. With such peaceful traditions, India and her armies will not attack any country but if we are attacked, we will repulse them with all our strength. India has made it clear to Pakistan and the rest of the world that she will deem any attack on Kashmir as an aggression against her because Kashmir is part of India.

India has agreed to ceasefire in Kashmir because she has been prompted by the desire to find a peaceful solution to the dispute. This desire cannot be construed to indicate her weakness or inability to face aggression or an attack on her territory.

You have come to Kashmir to help the Kashmiris and not to rule over them or to interfere in their administration. You are here to serve the local people. I am happy that you have rendered splendid services to the people of Kashmir during the recent floods. Your contribution in fighting floods in Kashmir has not only heartened Kashmiris but has made the rest of the country proud of you. The principal role of the Armed Forces is, of course, the defence of India but it is also your function to render a helping hand to the people in facing natural calamities like earthquakes and floods. This new role of Army is unlike what it was during the British days. The Armed Forces are today part and parcel of the whole nation and not a separate entity.

I am visiting Kashmir after a span of four years. Before this I used to visit Kashmir about once a year. I have thought of coming to Kashmir now because I have heard about the devastating floods. I have considered it necessary not only to come and see the flood areas for myself but to congratulate you on your yeoman service in flood relief and rescue work.

A number of your equipment needs are being met by the ordnance factories, but still several articles have yet to be imported from industrially advanced countries. Imports drive wealth out of the country and make people depend on

1. Address to the Indian Army and Jammu and Kashmir Militia, Srinagar, 12 September 1957. From *The Hindu, The Hindustan Times* and *The Tribune*, 13 September 1957.

outside supplies. Such dependence also makes the country helpless at the time of an emergency when supplies are stopped. Therefore, India wants to manufacture all the goods she requires. This will not only produce more wealth but will also create more employment. In order to advance industrially, India has to invest large sums of money. She has, therefore, to save money. It is, however, rather difficult to save much money. Therefore, people have to be taxed and money has to be otherwise raised to invest in huge plants to produce iron and electricity.

Britain and America are rich today but they have taken more than 200 years to become wealthy. India cannot afford to wait for so long. But it will certainly need 25 to 30 years to become rich. While India is making strides in the production of iron, electricity and other things, there is yet no sign of producing wealth. When the huge plants will go into production, wealth will be produced and the country will be rich. In the meantime, it has to bear the burden and make sacrifices.

19. Explosions in Kashmir[1]

K.T.K. Tangamani[2]: Under rule 197, I beg to call the attention of the Prime Minister to the following matter of urgent public importance and I request that he may make a statement thereon:-

"The recent explosions in Kashmir".

Jawaharlal Nehru: The recent series of explosions in Jammu and Kashmir State started in mid-June 1957. Previously in 1956 there had been two explosions.

In June 1957 there were five explosions, three in Jammu and two in Srinagar. As a result, one person was killed and four injured.

In July 1957 there were four explosions, two in Jammu and two in Kashmir. Three persons were killed and two injured.

In August 1957 there were five explosions, two in Jammu and three in Kashmir. One person was injured.

Up to the 8th September there have been two explosions, both in Kashmir. Two persons were killed and three wounded.

1. Reply to a question in the Lok Sabha, 13 September 1957. *Lok Sabha Debates* (second series), Vol. VII, cols. 13754-55. Extracts.
2. CPI Member from Madurai, Madras.

Thus, from the 18th June to the 8th September 1957, there have been sixteen explosions in Jammu and Kashmir. These have resulted in damage to property and six persons being killed and ten injured. The explosive devices employed are of various kinds. Some of these are complicated and intricate and have Army markings. It is clear that they cannot be locally made and they can only come out of the stocks of some organized army.

From other information gathered by us from various sources, including the statements of people arrested in this connection, it appears that these explosive devices have come from Pakistani sources across the ceasefire line. In addition to these explosive devices, considerable sums of money are known to have come from Pakistan as well as notices, posters, etc. It also appears that the persons sending this material from Pakistan were maintaining contacts with an organization in the Jammu and Kashmir State. The purpose apparently is to have a campaign of sabotage and violence in order to create panic and confusion. Indeed, this objective has sometimes been publicly stated.

A deliberate attempt appears also to have been made to create communal trouble as some of these explosive devices have been placed in a mosque and some in a temple.

A number of persons engaged in this traffic have been arrested and are being prosecuted by the State Government. Their cases will come up for hearing before the courts of law at an early date....

20. Great Powers' Attitude on Kashmir Issue[1]

The UK High Commissioner[2] came to see me this afternoon and gave me the attached message from the Prime Minister of the UK.[3] This deals with Kashmir.[4] Earlier I had received another message through him from Mr Macmillan dealing with the situation in the Middle East.[5]

1. Note, 15 September 1957. File No. 155-KV/57, pp. 2-3/note, MEA. Also available in JN Collection.
2. Malcolm MacDonald.
3. Harold Macmillan.
4. See the succeeding item.
5. See *post*, p. 671.

2. I spoke to him first about Kashmir. I told him that, during the past many years, we had given enough evidence of our patience and our desire not to humiliate Pakistan in any way. We had not asked at any time for a specific condemnation of Pakistan as an aggressor, although we had repeatedly made it clear in the UN and elsewhere that Pakistan had committed aggression. We followed this policy because of our anxiety not only to settle the Kashmir issue, but so as not to embitter our relations with Pakistan insofar as we could help it. We looked to the future when we hoped to live in friendly cooperation.

3. The result of this policy has been to make Pakistan more and more aggressive and to cloud the basic issues. Unfortunately, Pakistan has been encouraged in this attitude by other Powers. We saw what took place in the UN last year, where, to our amazement, we were treated as if we were in the wrong and in the dock in spite of the fact that Pakistan had been the aggressor and it continued its aggression. We came to the conclusion then that the only way of dealing with this Kashmir issue was to keep the basic facts before us in the UN all the time, that is, the original and continuing aggression of Pakistan and the accession of Kashmir to the Indian Union. If those facts were admitted, as they must be, then one could discuss the matter on a secure foundation. Otherwise, we would have the same deadlocks that we have had during the past few years and India would have to face the extraordinary situation of being almost put in the dock.

4. Not only has this aggression continued throughout this period, but, lately, another and a different type of aggression was now being indulged in by Pakistan. This was the campaign of sabotage which was openly admitted by some of Pakistani leaders. Therefore, we cannot discuss this issue except on the basis of the facts of the situation. It has never been our desire to humiliate Pakistan or to make things more difficult. Difficulties have arisen from Pakistan's attitude and its support by some of the Great Powers, which has encouraged Pakistan in its intransigence. Even now, it is not India that has asked for a meeting of the Security Council to consider this matter. It is Pakistan which has done so.

5. It is, to some extent, true that the attitude we have adopted now is a clearer and stronger one than sometimes in the past, although throughout these past discussions, we have always based our case on Pakistan's aggression. We have been compelled to adopt this attitude because of Pakistan's activities and threats and the support Pakistan has got from other countries. It is not possible to proceed with this matter any further except on a basis of facts and reality.

6. Some reference was made by the UK High Commissioner to the Jarring Report.[6] I pointed out that the Jarring Report itself recognized the many changes which have occurred. Towards the end of it, there was a reference to some kind

6. For Jarring Report see *Selected Works* (second series), Vol. 38, p. 411.

of an arbitration to decide whether Pakistan had carried out its obligations under Part I of the UN Resolution. I did not understand how this matter was suitable for arbitration. Nobody doubted the fact that Pakistan was in illegal possession of a larger part of the territory of the Jammu and Kashmir State. If that was so, as it was, then the Security Council had to determine whether Pakistan had committed a violation of that resolution or not or if it had failed to implement it. As a matter of fact, some of the UN Representatives had expressed their views on this subject previously already. In addition to this was the new aggression and violation taking place now.

7. The UK High Commissioner said that there was no question now of having any arbitration, but perhaps someone on behalf of the UN could report on this present position. I said that was a matter for the Security Council to consider, but I did not see what additional facts, which were not known, were required for a decision on this primary issue.

8. The High Commissioner reminded me that Mr Macmillan was anxious to keep this Kashmir issue 'ticking on" so that the other major issue, namely, the Canal Waters, could be proceeded with. Any success in the latter would create a favourable atmosphere. I said I would welcome any progress made in that respect.

9. I am sending you a separate note on the talk I had with the High Commissioner about Syria and the Middle East.

10. I shall be sending a telegram to Shri Krishna Menon about these two notes I have received from Mr Macmillan. I shall also have to answer these two notes. I propose to send an answer about Syria first, as this appears to be a more urgent matter.

11. I suggest that copies of both the messages from the UK Prime Minister as well as a copy of my notes on my interview with the UK High Commissioner might be sent by air mail to Shri Krishna Menon, so that he might have the full text of these papers.

21. Message to Harold Macmilan[1]

Thank you for your personal message on Kashmir.[2] I am glad you read the memorandum which I gave you in July. That memorandum was rather a general one and not prepared especially for you. Should you so desire it, we can have a more precise memorandum prepared.

2. You know our broad position about Kashmir. We have felt very deeply the aggression by Pakistan in Kashmir, accompanied as it was by loot and massacre of large numbers of innocent people. In spite of this, when we went to the Security Council, we did not specifically ask for condemnation of Pakistan as an aggressor, and all that we asked for was that the Security Council should ask Pakistan to prevent Pakistan personnel and nationals from participating or assisting in the invasion. We chose Article 35 of the UN Charter, which is meant for conciliation. Even then, in spite of our strong feelings, we were anxious not to humiliate Pakistan in any way and to keep a way open for a friendly settlement. We had in view our future relations with Pakistan. In spite of this, Pakistan not only did not stop its nationals from participating and assisting in this invasion but sent its regular army into Kashmir. Pakistan's attitude then and ever since has been aggressive and violent and based on prevarications and false propaganda.

3. Our basic position has always been that Pakistan committed aggression and, in fact, was continuing it. This was accepted by the UN Commission when it said that a new situation had been created by Pakistan armies occupying the Jammu and Kashmir State territory and calling upon them to withdraw. We had accepted the UN Resolutions of August 1948 and January 1949 on the explicit assurances given to us by the Commission, which were published.

4. In the course of the past many years, we sought earnestly for a peaceful settlement and entered into long discussions which proved fruitless. We became

---

1. New Delhi, 18 September 1957. JN Collection. Also available in File No. KS-53/57, MHA and File No. KU/57, pp. 6-7/corr., MEA.
2. In a message dated 15 September 1957, Harold Macmillan referred to India's concern about the principle regarding aggression. He interpreted that India now wanted that Pakistan should give effect to Section A of Part II of the August 1948 Resolution. He realized the difficulties about demilitarization in Kashmir and about the prolonged controversy as to the precise meaning and effect of the UNCIP Resolutions. Although he wanted to see a settlement of the Kashmir dispute acceptable to both countries, he was equally anxious that public controversy and acrimonious debate should be avoided which could only harm the common cause. He wrote that "controversies about events in 1947 and the revival of disagreements in 1948 will be sterile."

convinced that no notifications, which ignored the basic facts of the situation, that is, Pakistan's aggression in Kashmir, and Kashmir's accession to India, could succeed.

5. Pakistan's aggression has continued and has been further consolidated and, now, another type of aggression has been started. This is well organized campaign of sabotage through Pakistani agents. I hope you will appreciate our position and the difficulties we have encountered in our attempts to find out a peaceful settlement. These difficulties have been largely due to Pakistan not carrying out the basic provisions of the UNCIP Resolutions. I regret to say that Pakistan has been encouraged in this intransigent policy by great countries. We have no desire to condemn Pakistan. Indeed, it is not we who have asked for the coming meeting of the Security Council. But, we cannot accept any position which is not based on the essential facts of the situation. Nor can we go back to the interminable arguments and discussions which have taken place during the past years and which have led nowhere.

6. Apart from the basic facts to which I have referred, I must confess that it is very difficult for us to deal with a country and its leaders who continually indulge in violent abuse and untruths, and deliberately aim at propagating hatred and ill will and adding to the tensions that so unfortunately exist between our two countries. Feeling in our own country is very strong, and our Parliament has often expressed it. We have, however always tried to restrain this and to give expression to our views in moderate language, always expressing our goodwill to Pakistan and her people.

7. You refer to the importance of giving effect to Parts I and II of the UNCIP Resolution of August 1948. Nine years have passed since this Resolution, and the facts are patent that Pakistan has not carried out her obligations even as regards Part I. It is for the Security Council to accept this position, which does not require any detailed enquiry. The documents and admitted facts in the case are enough to establish this. We are, however, always ready to give careful consideration to any suggestions for constructive approach which are consistent with the stability and integrity of our country and which might help in the reduction of tension and conflict.

22. To Govind Ballabh Pant[1]

New Delhi
September 29, 1957

My dear Pantji,

Bakhshi Ghulam Mohammad came to see me this afternoon. He will be seeing you and so I need not repeat what he said to me. But I should like to mention two matters.

One is about the case to be started in Srinagar in connection with these bomb or cracker explosions.[2] There has been talk of this case for a long time, but it does not take shape. I asked Bakhshi about this. He said the delay was due at our end here and not in Kashmir. I think, this matter should be expedited. I believe, you are going to Kashmir in a few days' time. These cases have a certain important political aspect also.

The matter about which Bakhshi was considerably agitated was the food situation. About this I have written a letter to Ajit Prasad, a copy of which I enclose.[3] Bakhshi said that the situation was really bad. In many places he has not been able to send foodgrains at all or less than one-tenth of the need. The situation is worsening.

In this matter of food, I have spoken to Bakhshi rather strongly in the past because of his habit to make sudden and ever-increasing demands. He has, I believe, done something in the direction of our recommendations. He has increased the price and reduced the ration. There can be no doubt that at present there is grave difficulty there and in view of the possibility of Sheikh Sahib's release, it is not wise to allow the food situation to worsen.

Unfortunately, Ajit Prasad has spoken to him in such a way in the past that Bakhshi is not at all inclined to go to see him. As you will see, however, I have asked Ajit to invite him and have a talk with him. As I am going away to Japan soon, I should like you to keep this matter in mind.

Yours affectionately,
Jawaharlal Nehru

1. JN Collection.
2. Jammu and Kashmir witnessed a series of bomb explosions, 16 in number, between 18 June and 8 September 1957. See *ante*, pp. 498-499.
3. See *ante*, p. 488.

23. To Bakhshi Ghulam Mohammad[1]

New Delhi
October 2, 1957

My dear Bakhshi,

I am sending you these few lines on the eve of my departure. Yesterday, you mentioned to me that there will be big assemblies at Hazratbal in the third week of November. You suggested that it would not be advisable to release Sheikh Abdullah at the time of these assemblies. There was force in that argument. As I understood you, your intention was that his release should take place immediately after.

A few days normally do not matter, but it is rather embarrassing to have to extend the period of detention formally. However, perhaps it cannot be helped. There is one thing, however, which has troubled me and continues to worry me. For the last two years or more, there have been repeated decisions or, at any rate, expressions of opinion that Sheikh Abdullah should be released soon. But some thing or other has intervened and an argument could always be raised against his release at that time. There was the Constitution being finalized, there were elections either local or for the State, there was the tourist season, etc. etc., and so this matter has gone on being discussed and nothing being done. It is my conviction that this delay has done you harm and every day's delay adds to it. There is no doubt that our position vis-à-vis the world has suffered greatly on this account. However, it is no good thinking of the past. We have to see the future. I do hope that no further occasion will arise for delay and that, as suggested, very soon after the Hazratbal celebrations, this will be done. Since we have to do it, we should not hesitate to do so and we should be prepared for the consequences. There should be no further reasons for postponement.

As, in any event, Sheikh Abdullah is going to be released, it is obviously desirable not to take any step which makes it more difficult to deal with him at the time of his release. That is to say, a special effort should be made to avoid any personal criticism of him or his family or any other step which will irritate him without doing any good to us. I think, it is necessary for you privately to tell your colleagues and others about this attitude.

With all good wishes to you,

Yours sincerely,
Jawaharlal Nehru

1. JN Collection.

24. Cable to M.J. Desai[1]

I have received copy of Indiadel, New York message from Krishna Menon to you about British manoeuvres regarding Kashmir.[2] Hope you have made position quite clear to UK High Commissioner. We are greatly surprised and grieved at the way the British give us certain assurances and then act contrary to them and in hostile manner to us. We shall have to resist these to the utmost.

1. Tokyo, 7 October 1957. JN Collection.
2. In a cable to M.J. Desai on 5 October, Krishna Menon wrote from New York that Pierson Dixon, Permanent Representative of UK in the UN, was already drafting a resolution on Kashmir and would not allow its copies to get around; the British were acting as spokesmen of Pakistan inspite of the honeyed words; and the British attitude was one of hostility to India in spite of what Macmillan told Nehru and the merits of the Kashmir case itself. Krishna Menon asked Desai to tell MacDonald firmly that India was aware of what was going on and that this tactic would not work.

25. No Intention of Using Force in Kashmir[1]

I think you should send a letter to our Ambassador[2] conveying your reply to the Imam.[3] It is not necessary to send a long telegram. In this letter you will state that his information that India threatens to use force in Kashmir is completely wrong. In fact, we have avoided doing so, although Pakistan has committed aggression and occupies part of our territory. Further that we have repeatedly offered a No War Pact with Pakistan, which she has refused to accept. The main

1. Note to Commonwealth Secretary, New Delhi, 22 October 1957. File No. 23-KU/57 (Pt. I), p. 4 6/Note, MEA.
2. R.S. Mani was India's ambassador in Iraq.
3. Shaikh Mohammad Khalisi, Imam of Grand Mosque of Kazimiyah, Baghdad, sent telegrams to Maulana Azad and Nehru and complained about Krishna Menon's alleged threat to use force in Kashmir.

aspect of the Kashmir question is that Pakistan has committed aggression and is continuing to do so, although the territory is in law part of India.

Show your reply to Maulana Saheb before sending it.

26. Uncertainty in Kashmir[1]

The Kashmir situation is so uncertain that there appears to be very little chance indeed of Bakhshi Ghulam Mohammad being able to visit the Soviet Union in the foreseeable future. Apart from possible developments in the Security Council[2] and after, there is the expectation of Sheikh Abdullah being released before long. That will create a situation which will have to be carefully watched and Bakhshi Ghulam Mohammad cannot be expected to leave at that stage. Indeed, it is difficult to say when the Yuvaraj and the Yuvarani will be able to go.

This question can only be decided early next year. But Shri K.P.S. Menon might inform Mr Khurshchev that the Yuvaraj and Yuvarani hope very much to be able to visit the Soviet Union next year in the early summer. This will, however, depend on developments that may take place in Kashmir. As for Bakhshi Ghulam Mohammad, he is also very anxious to go to Russia, but it would be a little more difficult for him to leave till matters are more settled down.

---

1. Note to Foreign Secretary, New Delhi, 25 October 1957. JN Collection.
2. The discussion on the Jarring Report on Kashmir had started in the Security Council from 24 September 1957.

27. Cable to V.K. Krishna Menon[1]

Your telegram 588 26th October received at Lucknow.[2] I shall reply more fully tomorrow from Delhi.

2. I have no objection to your referring to any British intrigues. But too much past history obscures present situation. Main question appears to be refusal of British to accept or even consider Pakistani aggression and Kashmir's accession to India. This is extraordinary attitude.

3. In any event, please do not repeat not refer to Chitral. Even reference to it irritates Afghanistan very much.

4. United States Ambassador[3] has urgently asked for interview regarding Kashmir question. I shall see him tomorrow evening.

1. Lucknow, 27 October 1957. JN Collection.
2. Krishna Menon enquired if he could refer to the British machinations on India during the debate in the Security Council.
3. Ellsworth Bunker.

28. Cable to V.K. Krishna Menon[1]

American Ambassador saw me this evening to convey a message from State Department. He referred to Wadsworth's[2] talk with you and Lall[3] on Tuesday last. Object of talk was to tell you as a matter of courtesy, what he proposed to say about Kashmir.

2. Your reply then and general tone had caused them distress as it was such as to hinder understanding. You had accused United States of being hostile to India and ganging up against her, both UK and USA unfriendly to India and presenting accomplished fact, US military assistance to Pakistan had caused starvation of thousands of Indians which would be on US conscience.

1. New Delhi, 28 October 1957. JN Collection.
2. James Jeremiah Wadsworth was Deputy US Representative to UN.
3. Arthur S. Lall was India's Permanent Representative in the UN.

3. These charges had grieved them. There was no hostility to India and no intention of ganging up. They tried to help in finding way out and to narrow area of disagreement. They could understand our not agreeing with their approach but to ascribe motives to them, and especially of hostility to India, was distressing to them. More particularly, mention of thousands of Indians being starved because of US action, was most unfortunate, when they were trying their best to send food here.

4. They had been working hard for greater friendship and sympathy between India and US. My visit to US and subsequent developments had helped greatly in this. All this good work would be gravely imperilled if motives were ascribed and charge of starvation raised.[4]

5. This is summary of what he said. He added that he recognized fully our right to express our opinion firmly.

6. I told him that we must separate this Kashmir issue from broader relations of India and US. I was glad that these relations had improved and were improving, and there was no question of our considering US as hostile to India, even though we disagreed in some matters. We were anxious to have friendly relations.

7. So far as Kashmir issue was concerned, there was strong feeling in India on this subject, and we had been deeply hurt by attitude taken up previously, more particularly by United Kingdom, in this matter. During past few months, we had some reason to hope that they would adopt a different and more understanding attitude. Our surprise and distress, therefore, was considerable to find that British attitude continued to be hostile in this matter to us. When Wadsworth and Dixon jointly met you and Lall and explained the line they were likely to adopt, this undoubtedly produced a shock because we did not expect it after all that had happened. Also, this joint statement of decision already made, was upsetting. Subsequently, speech made by Dixon, though in relatively moderate language, included some statements which seemed to us extraordinary and totally unjustifiable. More particularly, his statement that questions of aggression and accession had never been pronounced upon and therefore, should be bypassed. This attitude seemed to us to be utterly wrong and unfriendly to India. It was to some extent this approach had created so many difficulties in the past. Now it was openly proclaimed. We could never accept it.

---

4. Krishna Menon replied on 29 October that with regard to Kashmir, "we have to proceed on the hard fact that the stakes are high" and "the State Department is hard-headed and is trying to create divisions in the hope that they will get you to remove me from the international sphere, as quite frankly, they feel they can deal with others better in their own way. Hope you will not think this egoistic." He also pointed out some inaccuracies in their account.

8. Bunker said that he understood our attitude and he had conveyed it fully to his Government. They were trying their best to find a basis for fresh approach. In your comments, you had made no constructive suggestion to Wadsworth.

9. I replied that no constructive approach can be made unless basic facts are recognized. We do not wish to accuse any country of motives but, unfortunately, attitude taken up by UK Government must lead our people here to think that they were very unfriendly to us in this matter.

10. Another telegram in regard to Kashmir will follow.

29. Cable to V.K. Krishna Menon[1]

Your telegram 588 October 26th.[2] You will, of course, reply to Iraqi and Formosan speeches and generally follow the line you have suggested about Graham Report.

2. I am inclined to think that your going back to early British intrigues about founding of Muslim League and subsequent encouragement of Partition will not be helpful. Present issues will be obscured by past history and people will think that our real objection is to Partition and we want to undo it. This will give handle to our opponents and might also weaken the case which you have put forward with such force and ability. Main stress should continue to be on aggression, accession and subsequent developments. In particular, you should deal with Dixon's statement that Pakistani aggression and Kashmir's accession to India not having been pronounced upon by Security Council, must be ignored or bypassed. Entire approach of UNCIP and Resolutions of 1948 and 1949 was indirectly based on these facts. Dixon's present approach is thus contrary to this. Anyhow, it is impossible to ignore these facts in any consideration of this issue.

---

1. New Delhi, 28 October 1957. JN Collection.
2. Krishna Menon wrote that the Iraqi speech was written by the Pakistanis and was not liked by the Arabs. Formosan Chinese delegate made a number of misstatements. Regarding Graham Report, which was referred to in the Jarring Report, India had said that it was exploratory and until the whole scheme was agreed to, any agreement on any part of the scheme was purely tentative. He proposed to argue that since there was an established Government in Jammu and Kashmir, the idea of plebiscite at any time would be to "seek endorsement of existing position."

3. I agree that it is better to deal with British attitude and to separate this from that of Americans and Latins. But even in regard to British attitude, it might be desirable not to impute long distance motives to them. You might bring out some of the favourable points in Dixon's speech, such as his references to Jarring Report. Our case should be presented firmly and objectively, dealing with criticisms made. We need not go out of our way to attack other countries.

9
EXTERNAL AFFAIRS

I. FOREIGN POLICY

1. Reply to Arthur Aibinder[1]

Please reply to this letter as follows:-
"Dear Sir,
    Prime Minister Nehru has received your letter of July 27.[2] He asks me to say in reply to you that the policy of India is not pro or anti-any country, nor is it what is called neutral. It does not divide the world's problems up into two sets. At the same time, India's policy is to be friendly to all countries and, therefore, it may be said to be pro-all other countries without being anti-any country. This, of course, does not mean agreement in every matter. India's policy in regard to any matter is determined by India and is, it may be said, pro-India with friendship towards others.
    The world is much bigger than any single country or group of countries and the policy of a country is determined by many factors, its history, background, geography, stage of development, objectives, etc. India's broad political and economic structure is indicated in the Constitution of India, and this is a democratic Constitution. Further, India's Five Year Plan indicates the objectives which India has."

---

1. Note to C.R. Srinivasan, Private Secretary, new Delhi, 2 August 1957. JN Collection. Arthur Aibinder was in the editorial staff of *New York Mirror*, which published Nehru's letter on 11 August 2006.
2. Aibinder had asked Nehru whether he was "pro-American, pro-Russian or just neutral. I am well aware, Sir, that you and your people desire to see and contribute to reality of peace and harmony."

2. International Situation—I[1]

Jawaharlal Nehru: Mr Speaker,[2] Sir, I beg to move:
"That the present international situation and the policy of the Government
of India in relation thereto be taken into consideration."

I am afraid, this has become rather a stock motion which I move regularly and
periodically before the House. The international situation naturally changes
somewhat from time to time. The present one is not quite the same as it was
yesterday and yet, fundamentally it is more or less the same. In the same way, as
regards the policy of the Government of India, as this House is aware, we have
tried to follow the same basic policy adapting it to changing circumstances.

The two questions that directly affect us in regard to international policy are
our relations with Pakistan and with that, of course, is inevitably included, more
especially, the question of Kashmir, and secondly, the question of Goa. These
two, I say, affect us directly, because they affect the integrity and sovereignty of
India; of course, the other questions which are really much bigger in their world
significance affect us very greatly, for the simple reason that whatever happens
there affects us as it affects the world. In fact, almost all our problems are affected
directly or indirectly by what happens elsewhere in the world. If the Suez Canal
is closed, we are affected; our Five Year Plan is affected. If something else
happens, our defence budget is affected on account of external factors. If military
aid is being given to Pakistan, well, our defence, our position, is affected, and a
greater burden is cast upon us if something happens which gives solace and
help to Portugal in its holding on to Goa, and that affects us.

So, although the two immediate and important points directly affecting us,
affecting the sovereignty and integrity of India are, Kashmir and Goa, the real
matter, which concerns this House, no doubt, is this, the international situation
which seems to be balancing itself on the edge of some sword for a long time
and without finding any solution to its many problems. It is true that there is no
immediate crisis of possible war. That is a good thing. But, at the same time, it
is also true that no basic problem has been solved. They all remain where they
are and suddenly new crisis erupts. In the recent months, the biggest crisis perhaps
has been in what is called the Middle East, and in fact since the last year.

---

1. Statement in the Lok Sabha, 2 September 1957. *Lok Sabha Debates* (second series), Vol.
   VI, cols. 11318-11330 and 11429-50. Extracts.
2. M. Ananthasayanam Ayyangar.

Last year, when we discussed these matters, the Suez Canal crisis was dominant. Well, fortunately, the Suez Canal is functioning now, working: not that the problems of all have been solved but they have gone a long way towards a solution, and the declaration that the Egyptian Government has made in regard to Suez Canal appears to us to be a fair and good declaration, acknowledging the Suez Canal as a waterway in which other nations participate and it should function as an international waterway in that sense. And we hope that that declaration will be the basis for the final settlement of this problem, if any matters still remain to be settled.

But, after that, we see this crisis shifting a little from the Suez Canal, from Egypt, to Syria and other parts of the Middle Eastern countries. It is not for me to discuss the position in Syria or any other parts of the Middle East, but I do feel more strongly than ever before that the types of approaches which are made to many of these countries in the Middle East or to other parts of Asia are approaches which do not facilitate a solution of any problem and which have progressively made conditions worse there.

We have a record of a few years now, a few years of this policy of military pacts—well, these are attempts to gain influence or power over various parts of Asian or African territory, one move leading to a counter-move with the result that instead of some kind of security, insecurity prevails, in Western Asia—especially the Arab nations which are split up—and generally Asian conditions, conditions in Western Asia are much worse than they were two or three years ago. I do not think anybody can doubt that conditions in Western Asia are more insecure than they were two or three or four years ago.

In these years, the chief development has been the development of these military alliances, the Baghdad Pact and the rest. NATO was a little far off; the Baghdad Pact comes nearer to us. The result was, this has been, what we see; these pose in different directions, and because one Great Power attacks the other, another Great Power tries to counter that step by some other step that it takes. Unfortunately, this policy continues and these conflicts continue. Behind all this, we see this development of terrible new weapons of warfare. The Disarmament Conference and its committee meet somewhere in London and they work hard[3] and I believe, they are earnestly bent on having some way out, but the fact remains that the world really is conditioned today by these rival power conflicts and there are attempts—I would not say balance of power politics,

---

3. The UN Disarmament Commission was to meet in New York on 30 September 1957 to consider its sub-committee's report on the discussions held in London between 18 March and 6 September.

because the old idea of balance of power which existed in the 19th century no longer exists, when there were a number of countries which tried to find some balances with alliances—today, when these two huge countries, very powerful ones, each if I may say so, with all respect to them, trying to become stronger than the other. There is a phrase now—"negotiating from strength". Well, if one party tries to do so, the other party also tries to do so, and the result is strength, as measured by the latest type of nuclear or super-nuclear weapons and the piling up of these weapons goes on.

We have just heard of a ballistic weapon which the Soviet Union has produced. A little before, the United States were experimenting with some such weapon. No doubt, whatever one country produces in the shape of horrible weapon, the other will produce a few months later if not sooner. And now, we have got at the stage of what is called the ultimate weapon. Evidently, there is some stage, presumably, in the ultimate weapon but there appears to be no stage about the ultimate folly of human beings!

So, we have to face this, and we have to face this not in a spirit of being wiser than others or in any sense better than others. I would like to make that clear. It is not that we try to tell others what to do. We are very conscious of our own failings and all that, but we are absolutely conscious of this, that in our own interests—if you like, call it opportunist interest—peace is better than war. We are convinced that for the world, peace is better than war. We are convinced that peace is not going to be preserved by policies which hover round war by these military alliances and the like. And in our own interests, we are naturally concerned with the techniques when cold war comes right upto our borders and attacks us, which it has done as the House knows. It is done because of these alliances.

SEATO—NATO did not concern us—did concerns us; it comes up to our borders on the eastern side. The Baghdad Pact concerns us infinitely much more so, and added to that, when the other bilateral agreements for arming our neighbour country and thus upsetting all the balances that exist there, are made, well, they concern us very much. It is not a question of some kind of theoretical opinion, but it is a practical proposition before us which is concerning us and which is casting great burdens upon us in the shape of defence and other matters.

So, in this world situation as we see it, all I can hope is that the experience of the last two or three years at least will convince everybody that the approach that has been made through military alliances and through Great Powers pushing themselves into the concerns of other nations is not successful. In the Middle East, we find that—I have not a shadow of doubt about it—conditions in the Middle-Eastern countries would be much better if they were left to themselves. If those countries, either of these great military blocs, whether it is the Soviet

Union or whether it is the Western nations, if they left matters to take their own course, without military interference or without any other type of interference, things will gradually settle down.

Certainly, they can be helped. But when there is this cold war going on and they declare that if any of these blocs takes a step in the Middle East or anywhere else, then the other one naturally thinks of taking a similar step itself to counter the other one and so it goes on. Either one party should be powerful enough to crush the other by military means; that means a great war, a world war and that is ruled out. Then, if you rule out a war, if a war is not there, are threats of war going to do it? Surely not. If wars and threats of war have to be ruled out too, why adopt an attitude which just irritates and which induces the other to do something irritating to you, without producing any other good result? So, that is, broadly speaking, if I may say so, the analysis of this continuing crisis, which changes here and there, but basically remains the same.

Last year, there was the trouble in Hungary. We understand that this matter is going to be brought up soon before the General Assembly of the United Nations, which is being convened again. In regard to Hungary and in regard to other matters, our general approach has been one—we have declared our general policy in regard to it. For instance, we said then and we have repeated it often that in our view the rising in Hungary was essentially a nationalist rising; in our view foreign forces should not be kept in a country; in our view, the people of the country should be left to fashion their own destiny. We said it then and we said it repeatedly. At the same time, all our efforts had been bent during the past year to help and not merely to condemn. We want to help Hungary. We want to help the Hungarian people. We want to follow a policy which will help in removing some of the tensions, some of the burdens from which the Hungarian people suffer and not merely to condemn loudly the many things that we do not like.

There are many things happening in the world from year to year, and day to day, which we have disliked intensely; we have not condemned them. Sometimes when circumstances have compelled us, we have expressed our opinion in the United Nations or here or elsewhere. But generally speaking, we have avoided this business of condemnation, whether of small powers or Big Powers, not because we thought that we would gain anything thereby ourselves, but because when one is trying to solve a problem, it does not help calling names and condemning. Our effort whether in Asia or in Europe has been to the extent we could do something to create an atmosphere for solution. That has been our general approach to these problems.

That is going to be our approach now if this matter is discussed in the United Nations. I have no idea what form it will take, in what form the discussions take place and in what form the resolutions come up. But the main approach is there.

We are not anxious merely to have a discussion there. In fact, when this Commission was appointed, we were not clear in our minds if in those circumstances the Commission would be very helpful. The Commission has now presented a report,[4] which is an able document, a well-argued document, but which inevitably is a document which is based on a good deal of evidence of one side. It is perfectly true that the other side did not facilitate the enquiry; that is perfectly true. But the fact remains that from a purely judicial point of view they looked at this picture, from the point of the number of refugees. That may, to some extent, vitiate some of their conclusions or not, but that is a small matter. As I said, we ourselves believe that this rising was essentially a nationalist rising; that is the main issue; the other things may follow. But the problem has been before us since the last year.

How can we be of any help? We cannot do much, of course, situated as we are. But we did wish to help to some extent and we have tried in our own way through diplomatic exchanges and in other ways to try to lessen the tensions there and to bring about a normal atmosphere as far as possible. It is obvious that in the circumstances that exist there, a country may go on and condemn the Hungarian Government or the Soviet Government or others. But having condemned, is one going to take armed action? No. It is obvious that by condemnation—it is just conceivable and it depends on how it is done—tensions still further increase and the burdens on the poor Hungarian people become worse, instead of relaxing and lessening. There is that difficulty one has to face in all these matters. So we shall approach this matter in the United Nations, as we have done in the past, by making our attempts to find a way to help the Hungarian people. We shall express again our views, as we have expressed, that we do not approve of foreign powers remaining there and the people should control their own destinies. I do here also express the hope that the Hungarian Government will also work towards normalizing conditions there and lessening the burdens which, to some extent, should exist on many people who are arrested or who are imprisoned and the rest.

Coming back to some of our own problems, I referred to the two major problems that affect us, that is, Pakistan's relations in Kashmir, and Goa. Pakistan's relations means many things, but essentially the question of Kashmir. This question is coming up, I suppose, soon before the Security Council. So, I do not wish to say anything about it, except to repeat what I have said very often and the House knows that very well, that in spite of the confusion about Kashmir that is sought to be introduced, the issue is an exceedingly simple one.

4. This refers to the Report of the UN Special Committee on Hungary. For other details see *post*, pp. 656-657.

The issue is one of aggression, committed, abetted and continuing aggression by Pakistan. I did fail to understand—I hope I am not rigid in mind not to see an argument against me, to close my mind to an argument against me—but I have yet failed to see an atom of justification even put forward, much less accepted, as to why Pakistan is there except by invasion and aggression. Whatever justifications may be placed about matters, Pakistan's position there is clearly by aggression and invasion. That has been stated repeatedly on previous occasions, and in fact the United Nations Commission proceeded on that basis. And the Resolution they passed was clearly on that basis. The first thing they said was that Pakistan should vacate that aggression.[5] There it is. And all the subsequent arguments—no doubt due to the fact that partly we ourselves were anxious to explore every possible avenue of settlement, and other countries were also anxious to help us—cannot cloud this basic issue. Therefore, there is this basic issue, and I cannot imagine the United Nations, or any country in fact, calling upon us to do something which no self-respecting country can ever do, that is, tolerate aggression and submit to aggression and invasion.

Apart from the big arms race that is going on in the wide world, of atomic weapons and all that, we are faced and we have been faced in the last two years with this development of Pakistan getting very large quantities of military aid; maybe that they get it because they are in the Baghdad Pact and other Pacts, but principally they have got it by bilateral agreements with the United States. According to our information—and our information is fairly accurate in this matter—the aid that they have received is very considerable. It is not a small aid, as is sometimes said; it is very considerable. And we view that with great concern.

Now, we are not going into an arms race with Pakistan or with any other country. Nevertheless, as the House knows, we have been compelled, at a moment of great difficulty, to spend much more than we ever intended to on defence, and the House has accepted it. Because, in some matters one can never take a risk.

I should like in this connection, to show how conditions have changed, to read a sentence or two from the report of Dr Gunnar Jarring, the UN Representative who came here some months back.[6] He wrote:

"In dealing with the problem under discussion as extensively as I have during the period just ended, I could not fail to take note of the concern expressed in connection with the changing political, economic and strategic

5. The reference is to the UNCIP Resolutions of August 1948 and January 1949.
6. Jarring was in India from 24 to 28 March and 6 to 9 April 1957. For his talks with Nehru, see *Selected Works* (second series), Vol. 37, pp. 428-435./For his report see Vol. 38, p. 411.

factors surrounding the whole of the Kashmir question, together with the
changing pattern of power relations in West and South Asia"

that is, these military pacts and this military aid to Pakistan have changed the
whole position, the whole pattern of power relations in this area, and changed it
in a manner which gives us concern.

So, whatever reasons we had—and we had adequate reasons—to take up a
particular attitude in regard to Kashmir, which is our basic attitude, these new
developments have strengthened and solidified that attitude. And it seems to me
clear that any person or any organization like the United Nations considering it
must take this factor into consideration.

Now, in regard to Goa I confess that I have not said much—I can say very
much—to my satisfaction or to the satisfaction of the House. There can be no
doubt that the Indian Revolution will not be complete till Goa is part of India,
and we can never accept the fact that Goa or any other part of India can remain
or fall into some other power's dominion. Obviously when we talk about Goa,
our struggle or our trouble is not with the people of Goa, it is with the Portuguese
Government. The people of Goa according to us are, well, our own people. Our
quarrel is with Portugal. Now, it should be remembered that because our approach
to the question of Goa is a peaceful one, that does not indicate a lack of
determination; nor does it indicate that this question is not going to be solved in
our favour. It is possible that the Government of Portugal, living in some past
century, does not understand modern developments and may not quite understand
this; it functions in a peculiar way. But so far as the Government of India is
concerned, and I am quite sure, so far as every Group and Party in this House is
concerned, there is this fixed determination on our part to see that this outpost
of Portugal in India must be freed, must be liberated, and that no foreign power
should ever be allowed to have any kind of outpost in India.

We have recently, in the last few months, relaxed some of our rules, because
we felt that they were bearing down rather heavily on the people of Goa, and we
did not want them to suffer, in so far as we could help. Of course, we are not
fighting those people. Therefore, as a result of experience, and on compassionate
ground, we have relaxed some of those rules. We are continually watching the
position and if we think that some other rule has to be relaxed so as to bring
some comfort to the people of Goa, we shall do so.

We believe, and I should like to repeat it, we believe in conducting this affair
in a peaceful way. We do not want violence, sporadic or other. And it is not
merely a question of some high theory or moral approach to this problem, but
the very practical approach. Because, Goa may be a very small part, a corner of
India; and Portugal is not considered, obviously, among the Great Powers of the
world. But the fact is that all these things get tied up with other international

questions. You cannot separate it, and any approach of violence is not a violence limited to that particular issue but is likely to spread and likely to entangle us in all kinds of difficulties. Therefore, even from the point of view, if you like, of narrow practical reasons, we have to do that.

Now, we have been greatly interested in the disarmament, in the efforts made for disarmament. And perhaps this House will remember that it was at our suggestion that the Disarmament Sub-Committee of the UN was formed, that is as a result of India's initiative in the General Assembly in 1953. Last year we suggested in the UN some initial steps for this purpose. These steps were, firstly, that experimental explosions of nuclear and thermo-nuclear bombs should be suspended pending their abandonment; secondly, there should be at least total dismantling of some bombs—at least of some bombs—and thus, a reversal of the process of piling them up; thirdly, the parties concerned should publicly declare to the United Nations and to the world their willingness not to manufacture any more of these dreadful weapons; and fourthly, military budgets should be published in all countries, no further expansion of military strength should be made and any possible reduction should be immediately effected. These were our suggestions.

It is true that any real settlement about disarmament will have to be a comprehensive one. You cannot have it in one corner and leave the other free. But it is equally true that, I think, it is better to have a comprehensive agreement or none at all instead of simply making it difficult to have another agreement. The fact that you have a partial agreement does not rule out the comprehensive agreement; it is a step to that; it produces the atmosphere and the confidence to go further. Therefore, we have always suggested that a partial agreement is better than no agreement, provided that is a step towards the larger agreement.

Another thing is that if any agreement on disarmament is tied up with political issues, then we are likely to solve neither the political issue, nor the disarmament issue. Disarmament must be considered separately. Now, we find an extraordinary state of affairs in regard to arms. All kinds of new horrible weapons are coming out one after the other and unless all wisdom has left humanity, some way out has to be found.

I should like, and I am sure the House will agree with me, to welcome the advent of the new independent State of Malaya which came into being day before yesterday. We welcome it for a variety of reasons. We welcome it because this is one more step, slowly and laboriously taken, in freeing Asia, or partly freeing Asia, from foreign control. We welcome it because Malaya is a country which has thousands of years of association with India. Even now, if you go to Malaya like the other places in South East Asia, you will find evidence of India or Indian culture all over the place. And in the past few years also our friendship and cooperation in some matters have grown. Now, that is a good thing, Malaya joining the ranks of independent nations, just like Ghana joining them some months previously.[7]

But we have to remember that there are many other countries still struggling for freedom and the one which comes foremost in this connection is that of Algeria, which has suffered tremendously in the past two-three years—everybody has suffered at that—in that internecine war. I had always a great deal of admiration for the French nation and the French people, for the past history, struggle for freedom, for their tremendous brilliance and I do earnestly hope that the French people and the French Government will get out of this country, getting out of it by accepting the full freedom of Algeria.

This matter came up last year in the United Nations and will come up again, I suppose. Naturally, we stand for their freedom. What else can we stand for? That does not mean that we are against France or anybody. We are not. But we are for the freedom of Algeria, as we are for the freedom of other countries.

One thing more before I end. I referred to the political aspect of the Kashmir problem. At the present moment, Kashmir is experiencing something which is quite unprecedented in its long history—the new floods that have come there which are tremendous and colossal. So, I beg to ask leave of absence for tomorrow and day after from the House to go to Kashmir and I hope—and I am sure you will permit me—to convey to them the feelings of this House, the anxious concern of this House and the assurance of this House that we shall be most helpful. Sir, I move....

I have not got the United Nations Charter in front of me. I think, it must probably apply to a country against which the United Nations has acted, not in regard to a country about which a dispute is pending.[8]

Now, Mr Speaker, I have had the advantage of listening to various viewpoints and comments in regard to our foreign policy. I have been told on the one hand that we should cease to be crusaders or messiahs of peace, and the same honourable Member two or three minutes later said that India should play her role in bringing about peace in the Middle East.[9] Now, it seems to me that there is some slight contradiction between these two statements. Another honourable

---

7. Ghana became independent on 6 March 1957 and Malaya on 31 August 1957.
8. Mulchand Dubey, Congress Member from Farrukhabad, UP, said that according to an article in the UN Charter, any member of the UNO or of Security Council "shall not render any military aid to a party whose dispute is pending before the Council."
9. Atal Bihari Vajpayee, Jan Sangh Member from Balrampur, UP, said so.

Member went a little further and said India's role should not only be to support national interests but to support peoples' demands in other countries.[10]

Now, these statements require little consideration. So far as we are concerned, it is entirely wrong, if I may say so with all respect, to say that we go out anywhere as crusaders of peace or with any idea. It is true that when we go out or when we remain in our country, we talk about peace, because that is dear to us, because we consider that of vital importance in the world and to our country.

Now, it so happens that in many parts of the world, indeed I would say, in every part of the world, the idea of peace appeals to people and, therefore, there is talk of it. It is not that we go out to convert people or to carry on any kind of a campaign in regard to it. Because I do not think that that is the right approach to this question, for a Government—I am not talking about people—to adopt, if I may use the word, an agitational role in other countries. If that is so, even in regard to what I might call the propaganda for peace, to which we are so intimately attached, the second idea that we should support peoples' demands in other countries simply means that we should support, encourage and help agitational demands. I am not using the word 'agitational' in a bad sense at all. Of course, obviously, it has a good sense too, but such demands in other countries are presumably made against their governments; obviously, peoples' demands are made against their governments. Now we are asked by at least one Member here to support people's demands in other countries. How would that honourable Member like some other government supporting somebody's demands in India? If that kind of policy is adopted by governments, that is a policy of continuous and persistent interference, to which we certainly, our Government, would take the strongest exception; and I am quite sure this House would object. And if that is so, surely we cannot play that part in other countries, apart from the fact that we are not made that way. We have not got the resources which other countries may have, but it is not a question of resources; it is a question of doing something which we do not want others to do. It is a bad example to set.

We talk about *Panchsheel*. In *Panchsheel*, there is a very definite clause to the effect that there should be no interference—apart from external interference—in the internal affairs of a country. I forget the exact language, but even ideological interference is mentioned there—any kind of interference, including ideological interference.

So, I just do not understand how we are asked to go and support peoples' demands. Let us admit that we in our hearts and minds sympathize with those demands; they fit in with our policy and ideals. I can understand that. And, it is

10 P.V.G. Raju, Socialist Party Member from Visakhapatanam, referred to Muscat and Oman, and said India must also support people's demands, "if it is to have historical validity."

not for me to say what individuals may do or private groups may do but for Government to go about supporting peoples' demands against their Governments in other countries would be really an extraordinary proposition which would land us into great difficulties and land other countries too in difficulties if they do so.

I know and I regret that some countries do this kind of thing, sometimes overtly and sometimes otherwise, and our voice is raised here and elsewhere against this kind of thing and we say that it is far better for the peace of the world that every question of interference is put an end to, interference of one country in another.

There are world forces at play and today they cannot be kept away by any kind of barriers even if Governments want to put up barriers thoughts flow, ideals flow and all kinds of things flow; and there are economic forces at play and political forces at play, and all kinds of forces. Well and good. If we agree with some force we encourage it in our own way but not, I submit, by interfering in the slightest degree in the country's affairs.

If we look at the countries of the world, there are 70 or 80 countries—I forget how many there are—which are supposed to be independent, of all kinds. Some are more powerful, others are, well, more or less strong but middling; many are weak and they have all kinds of governments. Many or some are communist governments which are supposed to be authoritarian. Others are what are called parliamentary democracies, a very few of them. Some are called democracies which, on closer analysis, have not much of democracy about them in their country; yet they are called democracies. Some, I need not mention names, call themselves democracies with no elections and nothing. They simply carry on.

Now, we do not go about criticizing them. There are monarchies which may be called free monarchies so far as the people are concerned. There are authoritarian monarchies; all kinds of countries and States in the world. Are we to set about telling them which of them is good and which are bad and criticizing everybody? That would be extraordinary presumption, apart from its being extraordinary folly. So, we really do not try to criticize other countries. As a Government I am talking about it. If I am Prime Minister, unfortunately I cannot wholly disentangle myself from my position in Government. Even in private, I cannot go about criticizing other countries because immediately it will be difficult for me to say, "I did so in my private capacity and not as Prime Minister". So that point should be borne in mind.

Our policy has been, as I stated in the morning, to express our viewpoint. When we have to do so, whether in the United Nations or here in Parliament or elsewhere, we are trying as far as possible not to criticize other countries. It is true that sometimes we have to do it, inferentially, indirectly, or sometimes even directly.

But, broadly speaking, we do not want to do so because there is today far too much, not of criticism only but something much worse between countries, and that has spoiled the atmosphere of any problem being considered objectively.

The first thing, therefore, is to remove this tension, this new type of diplomatic and public language which is coming into play and we try to avoid it. I do not say that we are virtuous or that we always succeed or that we are better than others. I certainly do not say this. But, we have had a certain, first of all, a certain kind of training in restraint of expression under our leader Mahatmaji. We tried to avoid it in the days of our struggle, tried it against our opponents, the British, against whom we felt so strongly.

So, now, as a Government surely, it is not merely Gandhi's teachings but the normal practice of Government which, I am afraid, is not normally followed now, but still it has been the practice of Government. But apart from that, looking at it purely from a narrow, personal, our own country's point of view, there is no reason why we should allow ourselves to get entangled in the conflicts and troubles of the world. To some extent we cannot help it, because the world is becoming more and more inter-related, and we have to deal with problems in the United Nations or elsewhere—our chanceries have to deal with them. Nevertheless, we do not wish to get entangled in these problems as far as we can help it. Sometimes it is not possible to keep away from them. We express an opinion. Even then we express an opinion in a more or less restrained language.

The honourable Member who spoke just before me referred to what I sometimes said about me personally—I am sorry to refer to a personal matter—that I am so involved in world issues that I forget my own country.[11] Well, it is not for me to talk about myself or to judge myself. But, my own feeling about this is that I rather not have anything to do with world issues; we have enough problems in our country to solve. And, also, I know very well, and this House knows that, if we want to play any part in world affairs, that part is completely dependent not on our loud voices but on the internal strength, unity and conditions in the country. By purely just criticizing others we may for a moment create some impression here and there but, ultimately, the country finds its own level and other people know exactly in what depth of water it is and what strength it has, and only attach that much importance to its voice. Therefore, both from the point of view of our primary needs and primary concern being our country and, secondly, from the point of view that if we wish to play any part in world affairs it can only be by developing the strength and unity of our own country, we have to pay the first attention to our own country's affairs.

11. Again, it was Atal Bihari Vajpayee.

Having said that, I should also like to say that apart from our general inheritance in the past, it is our inheritance, let us say, against colonialism, in favour of freedom—that is there—we feel that still; we have not forgotten that, and our sympathies go out. Apart from that, it has become obvious that if certain things happen in the world, more especially, of course, if the war occurs, then it does not matter what our internal problems may be; everything is subordinated to this great disaster. All our problems, all our planning etc., go to pieces because the whole world goes to pieces, and we are part of that world. Therefore, it has become necessary and incumbent on us to see what is happening in the world. The world and world affairs are impinged upon us all the time. It has become impossible for us to take, if I may use the word, a parochial outlook. We cannot understand our own problems, if we look at them that way. Therefore, we are interested.

Now, take, for instance, the situation in, what is called, the Middle East, and which really is for us the West, Western Asia—those countries. At the present moment, probably, that is the most difficult and explosive part of the world surface. Now, it will be untrue if I said that I am not very much interested in what happens there. I am not only interested as I was interested, as this House was interested, in what happened last year in those very Middle Eastern regions, in Egypt etc., in connection with Suez Canal or intervention of other powers, in which we were interested, if you like, emotionally interested, psychologically interested but, ultimately, politically interested, but it affected us—what happened there. Whatever consequences they had, they had far-reaching consequences. So, we tried to help there insofar as we could, there too. Although we took up a fairly clear and unequivocal line, we tried to avoid just condemnation of any kind even though we felt strongly about matters. I believe, we were of some little help in finding some solution, whether it was subsequently about the Suez Canal or other matters, what happened then affected us. It affected our Five Year Plan and our economy and all that. Something happens, let us say, in the Middle East, in Syria. Even if they are small beginnings of a conflict, it will affect us. But there is hardly such a thing now that we can think of, that it is a small conflict. However, a small conflict has the shadow of a big conflict behind it and the big conflict has a shadow of a world war behind it, and if there is that danger there, we are interested, every Member of this House is interested, this country is interested, because it will affect us and affect the world.

Therefore, we are concerned about it, and therefore we venture to say, and in this matter it is no good my criticizing any country or condemning any country's action. I may have some views and perhaps I have more information at my disposal than most Members of this House, obviously I do not know what is happening there behind the scene, what has happened or what is happening.

Some bits come to us and we have to pick and choose what is true and what is not true, and we form some kind of notion which is checked as we have further knowledge.

But the main thing is that there is a dangerous and explosive situation in Syria. We have seen previously how things happen in the Middle Eastern countries and we should be warned by what has happened and what has been happening in the past and other countries should also be warned and should not make any country in the Middle East a plaything of their policy. It is a dangerous thing, dangerous from the larger viewpoint of even major wars developing.

I said this morning there is no immediate crisis in the sense of war. That is true, but, nevertheless, there is plenty of crises brewing all round which may suddenly burst out. And, therefore, I should like to repeat my appeal which I said in the morning about conditions in the Middle East, that it is unsafe, it is dangerous, for policies to be pursued in which those particular countries become merely playthings, chequerboards, for other major conflicts to be played out. It is a dangerous policy as things are today. The major power groups are each too powerful to be sat upon by the other. That is a practical fact which you may like or dislike.

If that is so, if something is done by one, the other responds to it by doing something to counter that; and so, step by step, one may be drawn into the conflict. Therefore, we have seen in the past how one led to another; it is quite extraordinary. If you look back at the history of these Middle Eastern countries including Egypt and Western Asia and the roundabout countries, if you look at their history for the last three or four years—not very long—you will find how one step has led to another and how one step which was meant to protect, presumably, the interests of one group of power, has actually led to an injury of that interest, because somebody else is taking some other step and then they are worried and then they take a third step and so it has gone on, step by step, whether it is Baghdad Pact or something else. It has not brought peace or security or any measure of freedom from conflict there. Conditions in the Middle East countries, since three or fours ago, may not have been what might be called ideal. They were not ideal. They were not ideal anywhere. But will not everybody admit that conditions today and the last year or two have been worse than before? They have been. So, there has been progressive deterioration.

So, all these things, the Baghdad Pact and various other pacts, intrusions, etc., have worsened the affairs. That is obvious. One might say, "Oh! Yes, it is true, but other facts have occurred too". I admit it. One fact has led to another. One interference has led to another. Here we are, therefore, instead of learning from this and keeping out, leaving those countries to work out their own destiny, with our goodwill, with our help, if you like, but not this military help, not this military intervention, not military threats, not all kinds of pressure tactics being exercised. I do earnestly hope that these words, which I say with all humility and respect, will have some effect on those who may hear them.

We do not wish to interfere in international affairs, except where we feel that we might be able to be of some help, or except where we cannot help it. But where something affects us directly, then naturally, we have to say something. For instance, what has happened in regard to Pakistan, the military help given to it, is not an international matter about which we may have some views. We have views, of course, but that is a matter that has an immediate direct effect, an adverse effect, on us. Then we have to express our views clearly, strongly and unequivocally. Or, when something is said about Goa—Goa affects us. Goa may be a small thing in the world context, but Goa affects us and if something is said in regard to Goa which, we think, is not only wrong, but offensive to us, well, we have to reply to it.

So, you have to test our policy from that point of view, not a crusading policy or a seer-like policy; we are too humble for that. We know our limitations. We do believe in something stoutly and we express our opinions in a friendly way, but I hope, clearly when occasion arises. Where world peace is concerned, naturally we want to have our say as a member of the world community. Where India's interests are directly threatened, whether in Goa or in Pakistan, we must have our say, a loud say, a positive say. There we cannot remain quiet. So, you have to balance all these things.

Somebody said about Kashmir. One honourable Member said, it has been suggested, "Withdraw your complaint from the UN". I do not understand this. I should like honourable Members to realize that there is no such thing done. It cannot be done simply. Also, somebody said, "withdraw your plebiscite offer". I do not know where the question of withdrawal comes in, continuing the offer or withdrawing it. Originally the plebiscite offer was made to the people of Kashmir by us, if I may say so. I do not call them a plebiscite, I am not trying to juggle with words, but in the course of the last few years, we have had two general elections in Jammu and Kashmir State, except that part which is under the illegal and unlawful occupation of Pakistan. I do not call them a plebiscite. But anyhow, the people of those territories have been given a chance to elect their representatives. Some people say that these elections were bogus. Well, I think that charge is wrong. I do not say, and I cannot say naturally, that all those elections were perfect elections; there were no mistakes or no errors committed. I cannot say that. But I do say that, by and large, those elections were good elections in the circumstances and even now an Election Commission, consisting of some Judge, I believe, is there. I speak from memory—a retired Judge from India has been asked to look into this matter; a High Court Judge, I think. Now, election petitions go before them and they will be decided. There can be no doubt at all—barring some irregularities or mistakes—that in the main those elections represent the viewpoint of the people of Jammu and Kashmir. There is not even a shadow of doubt about it. If many of them were uncontested elections, well, I would submit, Sir, that the persons who did not wish to contest had no chance and therefore, they did not contest. Maybe, some people had a chance, but they did not. Whatever the reasons they are there.

What I wish to point out here is that in the course of the last five years or so, there have been two elections, general elections. On the other side, there have been no elections, no attempt at elections. In fact, conditions in the Pakistan-occupied part of Kashmir have been very extraordinary. News does not come very frequently; sometimes it does come and in today's papers there is something about that.

Then again it was said by an honourable Member that the accession of Kashmir was not only accession of the ruler of the State, but accession of the people. Well, I agree. Further it was said that it was accession to the Constitution of India. That is a wide statement, which is not quite clear to me.

When the accessions took place, not of Kashmir only, but of the other States of India in those days in 1947, the accessions were on three subjects only at that time: defence, foreign affairs and communications. The accession documents of all the major States of India contained only these three subjects. It was then thought certain States, at any rate the big ones, will have their own Constituent Assemblies to frame their constitution, naturally in line with our Constitution, but not necessarily adopting it completely. That was the original idea. Some months later Sardar Patel discussed this matter and, in fact, some Constituent Assemblies were formed in some of the States.

Some Honourable Members: Mysore.

JN: I am told that seven Constituent Assemblies were formed in the other States. Meanwhile, of course, our Constituent Assembly for the whole of India was functioning here. Later Sardar Patel and many of us discussed this matter with the then representatives of the States as they were and it was felt unnecessary, and perhaps, if you like, undesirable for all these Constituent Assemblies to function, because their representatives had been imported to our Constituent Assembly; they were there. So, the idea of these separate Constituent Assemblies was given up. Their representatives functioned in our Constituent Assembly and helped us in making our Constitution.

While all this was happening, something else had happened in Kashmir. First of all Kashmir did not come in before Independence or even at the time of Independence. Then came the Pakistan invasion and aggression and war was being carried on. It was a completely new situation. Kashmir acceded to us and acceded to us on these three subjects. And in fact, it was made clear even then—I forget now, I am speaking from memory, I hope I do not make a wrong statement—certain provisional matters were even then incorporated in the Constitution in regard to Kashmir.

From the very beginning it was clear that the accession of Kashmir, complete as it was, as the other States' accession was, did not mean that everything in our Constitution automatically applied to it. In the course of the next year or two further amendments and changes were made in consultation with the then Kashmir Government and their representatives. So, that to say that Kashmir acceded to the Constitution of India is an incorrect statement. The House may remember that subsequently there was a Constituent Assembly in the Jammu and Kashmir State. It really would have functioned long before it did, but because of military operations and other difficulties it was postponed. Ultimately, when nothing came of these talks in the United Nations, we could not leave Kashmir in mid-air and, therefore, with our willing approval, they elected their Constituent Assembly.

The first thing that that Constituent Assembly did was to change the nature of the Head of the State there. The ruling family there of the State was removed—although the son of the Maharaja was elected, was chosen as the Head of the State, the Sadar-i-Riyasat. That is the very first thing they did. And this was reported to the Parliament and to the President, because the President came into the picture; and we made necessary amendments to fit in with that in our own Constitution. Later, other changes came in. As their Constituent Assembly went on making changes, they were reported to us, and we accepted those changes after discussion etc., and they were engrafted on to our Constitution.

Their Constituent Assembly finished their Constitution-making in October last year, I believe—about a year ago, maybe October or November. Meanwhile, of course, that Constituent Assembly had also functioned as a Legislative Assembly and carried out very far-reaching land reforms and other reforms. So that, this Constitution-making has legitimately gone on there in conformity with our Constitution, and we have frequently adopted, made some changes, to fit in with that, in our own Constitution.

At the present moment it has come very near to our Constitution in many matters, only in a few matters they have kept apart. One matter to which they attach great importance and which has come up in the shape of questions here is about their ownership of land. It is an odd thing against our Constitution. I cannot go and buy land or possess land in Kashmir. It is restricted to, well, if I may use the word, genuine Kashmiris.

Hem Barua: What about you Sir?

JN: They have got, I believe, certain definitions—people, that is generations, who have been there, who have been born there, and all kinds of things. There are two or three groups or classifications of them. I can very well understand this. It is an old rule, not a new rule, from the old Maharajas' time—not this Maharaja, but from his father's or grandfather's time. And the rule was framed, I am told, firstly because of their fear that, Kashmir being such an agreeable place for foreigners, for English people specially, English people will come and practically physically take possession of it, start living there and take property. No Englishman, not even the biggest Englishman—they could go there, of course as tourists—could get any property there. A great favour was shown to them about thirty, forty or fifty years ago when they were allowed at Gulmarg, which was a very favourite place, to build a cottage there for ten years after which it lapsed to the State. Because, I remember one of the Maharajas, thirty or forty years ago, telling us that he had failed in many ways but at least he had kept out the British people from settling down in Kashmir, because it was such an attractive place climatically. The rule applied, of course, apart from the British, to people from other parts of India, monied people who could go and buy up property there, because Kashmir is a poor place with poor people, and they were afraid these moneyed people would buy all the delectable spots in Kashmir. So, they made this rule, and when this matter was put to us about their desire to continue it, we agreed. We said: "No, we do not wish to come in your way, certainly continue it" and as indeed in quite another place we ourselves in our Constitution have made a rule, if you remember it. In some of the Hill Districts of Assam there is a definite rule that land cannot be transferred to outsiders etc., because we wanted to protect that land so that it may remain with the tribal people there.

Therefore, in regard to Kashmir, I would beg of this House to remember always that all these nine, ten years, there have been two armies facing each other on the ceasefire line. There have been frequent attempts by Pakistan to create trouble inside Kashmir. Recently, there have been almost deliberately organized attempts to do so.[12] As the House knows, in answer to some questions I have said so. Because of all this you cannot treat Kashmir as a place which can be completely normal. As a matter of fact, as far as the common man is concerned, normalcy has returned. He does business, he has much more business than he has ever had, he has more food and all; but nevertheless, there is this danger hovering over it of spies, espionage, sabotage and all that, and if the Kashmir Government takes some special measures to meet the situation, I do not quite see how we can blame them or ask them to remove some of the special powers that they have taken.

12. This refers to the recent bomb blasts in the State. See *ante,* pp. 498-499.

There was a reference to Sheikh Abdullah. I have often said in this House that few things have disturbed and pained me so much as the arrest and detention of Sheikh Abdullah. I would not go into the past history. Sometimes, we have to take steps which are exceedingly distasteful. This is one of them. I did not take the step, but certainly indirectly—not directly, but indirectly—we were approving or consenting parties. I shall be very happy indeed when this state of affairs is ended.

I was referring to Pakistan. Now, there are two or three matters which I should like to mention. It is really quite extraordinary, the kind of false statements that are made now with greater frequency than before from Pakistan. The other day a statement was made with a great air of secrecy by the Foreign Minister of Pakistan that Russian planes were landing in Kashmir, and that Kashmir or India, I forget which—India, I think—had become a Russian base.[13] Now, one would expect of a Foreign Minister some slight adherence to truth. It is really quite extraordinary. India is not a closed land, nor is Kashmir. It is not particularly easy for people to go to Leh. It is physically difficult, and otherwise we do not encourage people going there either, but there are thousands and thousands of tourists in Kashmir and in India, of course. I gave a very specific denial to each single fact. I invite Pakistan, and I am prepared to do the same, to give the names of every foreign person employed directly or indirectly in our defence services or in the construction of anything connected with defence like air fields, like barracks, like anything. I am prepared to give every name, to publish them. Let them publish the names of all the foreigners they are employing there in their defence services, not only actively in the defence services, but—of course, what happens is they do not have an exact position in the defence—of the advisers, the builders, the trainers, the vast crowds of them that function there.

One thing we can never forget, and that is the exodus from East Pakistan into India, this tremendous exodus which shows the state of affairs in East Pakistan, and in Pakistan generally, a fact which we know very well, but which few foreign countries realize; that mere fact brings out the picture of our relations with Pakistan and the conditions in Pakistan much more vividly than almost any argument that we could put forward.

Some honourable Members said something to the effect that our Defence Minister had said something. What did he say? It is about Goa. The Defence Minister had made some kind of an appeal to the United Kingdom and the United States of America about Goa. I understand from him that he made no appeal. What he had said was—I speak subject to correction—that the case of

13. See *ante*, pp. 485-486.

Goa was such that countries like the UK and US should express themselves clearly as to where they stood. Am I right?

V.K. Krishna Menon: Did they support colonialism or oppose it?

JN: Yes. Did they support colonialism there or not? It was a kind of an enquiry. I have said previously in this House that the case of Goa is incontestably a colonial domain of Portugal; it does not matter how long they have been there. It is colonialism functioning, and functioning very badly.

Now, when people in other countries talk about colonialism vanishing and their being opposed to colonialism, we are justified in asking them, in all politeness: how does this fit in with your anti-colonial declarations, this continuation of Portugal in Goa? We are entitled to ask them this question. Apart from the major questions with regard to Goa, one continuing pain and torment for all of us is the continuation of hundreds and hundreds of Goans in prison there. There are a few Indian nationals too still there, whose nationality is challenged by the Portuguese. I think, there are about 5 or 6. But there are hundreds of Goans suffering tremendous, long terms of imprisonment, quite apart from those who have been put to death or who have had to submit to all kinds of torture in the past. It is a horrible thing and it surprises me that this is ignored by these Great Powers and small powers.

It does not surprise me that in the context of world events Pakistan and Portugal in Goa are closely knit together and are close friends. And yet, it is rather extraordinary. There was the Bandung Conference[14] which talked about colonialism and all that. And partly Pakistan had actually supported it. We did not expect Pakistan to stand out as a crusader of anti-colonialism. They could well have remained silent over the issue. But no, they have gone out of their way to support Portuguese dominion in Goa. Their newspapers supported it. The present Prime Minister, before he became Prime Minister,[15] was the advocate for Portugal—I believe, the legal adviser and advocate for Portugal. It is an extraordinary thing that simply because of their hatred of India they should descend to such levels.

An honourable Member referred to Indians abroad, in Burma, East Africa and Mauritius. In some places Indians have to suffer some disabilities, I think, in Burma, except the one common factor in many places about facilities for sending money which are not easily granted. Now, we do not grant them easily to others. So, we cannot very well complain. Most of these countries are in

14. For Nehru's speeches at the Bandung Conference (April 1955), see *Selected Works* (second series), Vol. 28, pp. 100-125.
15. H.S. Suhrawardy became the Prime Minister of Pakistan on 10 September 1956.

difficulties about foreign exchange and we can hardly call upon them to adopt a policy in regard to Indians which they are not adopting for their own people.

But the major fact is that Indians spread out in the past because they were to some extent more adventurous people, whether they were business people or others or they went in search of employment. And, wherever large numbers of people go to another country, a certain problem arises there subsequently. Everywhere there is this question of unemployment and the tendency of that country is to reserve its employment for its own nationals. It is difficult to criticize that tendency. And, Indians get into some difficulties. The way we look upon it is this. Where the country has slightly to face difficulties we advise our countrymen to put up with those difficulties, the other country's difficulties. We cannot ask for special privileges. But where any unfair treatment is given to our countrymen, then, of course, we protest. But even there we have to protest in a friendly way, we cannot issue any threats. We refuse to do that. That is not the way to deal with such matters because there is a case. And again where there are Indians abroad, we have left it to them entirely whether to continue to remain Indian nationals or to adopt the nationality of that country. It is entirely for them to choose.

If they remain Indian nationals, then all that they can claim there is favoured alien treatment. They are aliens and they should get as good treatment as any other alien gets. They cannot vote there. Obviously, the aliens have no right of vote. But they have all civic privileges; they have the privileges as friendly aliens. If they adopted the nationality of that country, then, they should be treated as citizens with all the rights of citizenship. But then, we have no concern with them. Sentimental concern, of course there is, but politically, they cease to be Indian nationals and we have no concern. The problem is of people who are not Indian nationals.

There are two problems clearly. There is the problem of Indian nationals. Admittedly, Indian nationals who have gone there with visas, many of them have come back. Now, if Indian nationals who went there for a period are asked to go back we cannot object. We can say, well, do this in a phased way. Do not push too many people back. But they are people with visas and the Government concerned has the right not to renew the visa. But we ask them to exercise that right in a way so as to cause the least inconvenience and injury to the people concerned.

Then, there are the other people; that is, those whom we do not consider our nationals, who have been there 50, 60, 30 or 40 years, whatever the period may be, and they have settled down and many of them have been born there. Their problem is there. So far as we are concerned, strictly, legally and constitutionally, it is none of our problem. They are not our nationals. It is a problem of Ceylon.

But we do not take up that particular attitude although it is the correct attitude because we are interested in their welfare and we are interested in finding a solution because there is a history behind this.

For the last 30 or 40 years, before we became independent and before Ceylon became independent, all kinds of agreements and other things were being made. We are independent. But fundamentally it is a problem of Ceylon dealing with its own people.

Finally, Sir, Shri Mukerjee again appealed to us to break the old moorings of thought and action which tie us to the Commonwealth. I do not think it is necessary for me to repeat what I have previously said. It is perfectly true that there are certain old moorings of thought which necessarily affect our action sometimes, not in regard to England only but in regard to so many things. Those old moorings have carried us to this Parliament, which is largely modelled after the British Parliamentary system. There are so many other things. That is true, but so far as the Commonwealth is concerned, I think that it should be considered entirely apart from any sentimental point of view—that is, our association—but purely from the point of view of whether it is good for us and for world peace or not, whether we can balance the advantages or not. I feel I have been convinced, and I am still convinced that our association with that serves some useful purpose for ourselves and for the larger causes that we support in the world. That has grown. The fact of new countries coming in like Ghana, like Malaya, possibly a little later Nigeria—I do not know—brings about continuous changes in the complexion of the Commonwealth and makes it, I think, even more desirable and necessary for us to remain associated with it.

One of my young colleagues, I believe, in the course of his maiden speech here, said something about the Nagas.[16] Of course, this is not a problem of international affairs at all. It is entirely a domestic problem for us and, therefore, the question does not arise. But, since he mentioned this I should like to say to this House what I have said previously, that our approach to this Naga question is, has always been, one of friendship and of dealing with our own countrymen, some of whom may have gone astray but whom we have to win over and make friends. Even if they are not our friends today, we propose to continue that approach.

---

16. Dinesh Singh, Congress Member from Banda in Uttar Pradesh, hoped that the Naga demand for placing Naga Hills District and NEFA under one administration would find favourable consideration from the Government so that blood-shed there could be stopped and 17 battalions of the Army freed from their duty.

Recently, some kind of a convention was held at Kohima. It was held with the permission of the governmental authority, otherwise it could not be held, and large number of representatives or delegates of the Naga tribes came to it. They, ultimately, after two or three days, passed a number of resolutions. I have received some brief telegraphic information about them, and I was asked if I would accept a delegation from those Naga representatives. I replied that I would be glad to receive them, talk to them, discuss matters with them. Presumably, in the course of the next few days, I do not yet know when, such a delegation will come here, we shall discuss matters in a friendly manner and I have every hope that these discussions will lead to satisfactory results for us, for them and for India.[17]

Sir, we discuss these various matters, internal and external, especially external matters, and I have no doubt that every Member of the House feels their importance. It is not merely a question of our discussion or of our indulging in debate and answering each other's points, but the basic realization that for us and perhaps for other countries also, it is a question of survival of what happens in the world, what happens in our country. It is from that point of view that we have to look at it and bend our energies so that we might survive and nothing may happen in the world which affects our survival and other people's survival.

May I say that I gladly accept the amendment moved by Shri Jaganatha Rao?[18]

17. An agreement was reached between the Government and the Nagas. For more details see *ante*, pp. 221-223.
18. R. Jaganatha Rao, Congress Member from Koraput, Orissa, replied to disagreements of H.N. Mukerjee and others. He expressed support to the policy followed by the Government of India and moved an amendment to that effect.

3. International Situation—II[1]

Jawaharlal Nehru: Mr Deputy Chairman,[2] I beg to move:
"That the present international situation and the policy of the Government of India in relation thereto be taken into consideration."

1. Statement in the Rajya Sabha, 9 September 1957. *Rajya Sabha Debates*, Vol. XVIII, cols. 4192-4207.
2. S. V. Krishnamurthy Rao.

I have spoken on this subject, Sir, on many occasions in this House and elsewhere, and I feel a little unhappy to relate the same story again and again, to go through more or less the same ground and to confess that all the major problems of the world still remain unsolved problems. It is possible that progress is being made behind the scenes or in the hearts and minds of men, which will give results in future. But, for the present, the outlook is very far from bright.

I suppose that the basic issue which perhaps governs other matters is that of disarmament. During the last 18 months or perhaps a little more, an impression has been created, I think, with some justification, that we were getting somewhere near to some form of disarmament. I have no doubt that all the great countries concerned—the United States, the Soviet Union, the United Kingdom, France and Canada—have all worked hard towards the same goal and wanted to have some measure of disarmament. All kinds of proposals have been made. but the fact is that, at the present moment, again the Disarmament Commission faces a deadlock. It may well be that they will come out of that deadlock and start discussing again. But it is a somewhat frustrating experience to expect something to happen—something that you are eagerly and anxiously looking forward to—and be repeatedly disappointed. Meanwhile, while these Great Powers discuss questions of limiting atomic, nuclear tests or limiting the use of these bombs or of the manufacture of them, the fact is that both the tests and the manufacture go on and in some measure vitiate world's atmosphere and make it more and more dangerous for human beings. The measure may be small at the present moment, that is, it does not actually affect people, but nobody quite knows how it is affecting gradually not only children, but still unborn children, all kinds of genetic aspects. I do not know what part we in India can play in this matter. We have in the past made certain proposals in all humility for the consideration of the Big Powers and I believe, some consideration has been given to them by the Committee. But we seem to be where we were. It is obvious that this question cannot be solved by some majority voting. It has to be solved ultimately by the Big Powers who are dealing with these bombs, more particularly, the United States and the Soviet Union, and secondarily, by the other Powers that possess these weapons, like the United Kingdom and some others may possess them soon.

Occasionally, it has been stated that India might play a greater part in the Disarmament Sub-Committee or elsewhere. Last year or earlier this year, we offered to appear before the Disarmament Sub-Committee in support of a memorandum that we had given. The Committee thanked us for that memorandum and said they would consider it carefully, but pointed out that it would be difficult for them to make an exception in favour of one country, as requests might be made from many other countries too. Well, there was some justification for that statement. Anyhow, it is not our decision or our desire to push ourselves in these Committees or Commissions, but naturally, we would like to help, we are prepared to do so.

The House knows that recently we had some of the latest developments in these weapons. On the one hand, there is the development of the nuclear bomb or the hydrogen bomb; on the other, of the ballistic weapon which carries it to some other place—there are two different types of developments—and thirdly, some method of guiding that weapon and by some means making it hit the target. Every day, we hear of more and more progress being made and I should imagine that perhaps this might shake up a little more than before, the conscience and the mind of mankind. I suppose it does do so because, I believe, the people of every country are very much exercised over this possibility and in effect, all our problems—every problem in the world and every problem that we face in this country—become very secondary in the face of this major world problem. It is an extraordinary thing how the sphere of each other pervades in the world. An opportunity has come to me during the last few years of visiting many countries in Europe, in America, in Asia and some in Africa. Wherever I have gone, I have been welcomed not only officially but by the people, and welcomed not as an individual, but as some kind of a representative of India, and welcomed with affection that astonished me. Everywhere I noticed this tremendous desire for peace and friendship with other countries. Now what strikes me as very extraordinary is that here are these people in every country, decent, desiring peace, desiring living their lives without interference from others and desiring to better their prospects and their standards, and yet being driven by some uncontrollable fate in the direction of conflict, bitterness, hatred and violence. It may be that some honourable Members here might, in their judgment, criticize one country or the other. It is not for me to criticize other countries. We have enough of our own failings and our own errors and mistakes to account for, and it is not becoming of us to go about criticizing and condemning other countries. Occasionally, it becomes inevitable to express our opinion in regard to a matter, whether in the United Nations or elsewhere. Even so, we try to do it as far as possible without condemnation. There is plenty to condemn in the world today in our thinking as possibly there is a good deal to condemn in India today. I do not suppose we would like it very much if foreigners went about condemning things that happen in our country, even though they may have some justification for it. And similarly, I do not suppose others would like it very much if we go about condemning what they do; and in any event, the atmosphere we seek to further, the atmosphere of, well, lesser tension, lesser fear and cooperation, is driven away by this match in mutual condemnation. We avoid that.

There has been an instance—there have been many instances, of course, but there has been one particular instance—which has given us much trouble and much thought, and which is still troubling us greatly. This has been the case of Hungary. Now, the House knows that a Committee was appointed by the United Nations, and that Committee presented a report. The Committee consisted of able men, and I am quite sure that they tried their utmost with the material before them to arrive at some conclusion as to what had happened. Their material was not complete for no fault of theirs, but nevertheless, it was incomplete. Now this matter is coming up before the United Nations. There was a question answered here today about this matter, about India's attitude towards the consideration of this Report. Naturally, when a Committee has been appointed by the UN, its Report has to be considered by the UN. What we were concerned with was that it should be considered, as far as possible in an atmosphere which would help the people of Hungary, and which would help in lessening tensions and fears in Hungary, and not merely to add to them. We were of opinion then— it is of no consequence now—that it might have been better for it to be considered in the regular way by the new session of the United Nations and not by reconvening the old session. It makes no great difference—perhaps a month or some weeks—but the old session has been reconvened. And if so, there is no particular difficulty about it, but the main thing is how this matter is to be dealt with there, and there is this great difficulty, because many things have happened in Hungary which most of us have disapproved very strongly. It has been one of the biggest tragedies that have occurred in recent years, and yet the question is how we can help, not how we can condemn. I believe that India has played some effective part in helping the people of Hungary. During the past few months we tried to continue to play that part. Now, if in the United Nations we join, let us say, in some kind of repudiation of the Hungarian representation in the UN—I mention this because sometimes it has been suggested, although I do not know whether anybody is going to do it—and deny the right of the Hungarian representatives to come to the United Nations, what would be the result? How exactly do we help the Hungarian people by not recognizing the present Government functioning there? I do not quite know by what standards we judge, because there are many Governments, at any rate, some Governments in the world which probably would not come up to any standard of judgment. We acknowledge them as a fact, and there the matter ends. And sometimes, some Governments which, from every standard are justified, are not acknowledged like the Government of the People's Republic of China. But whatever measure you may employ, if a proposal is made, as I said, to deny the present Government of Hungary from being represented or from their representatives being accepted, what is the significance of that? How does that help in dealing with the problem of Hungary? The Government of Hungary does not disappear by that act. It functions and it functions in hostility and it functions possibly with greater rigidity than it otherwise would. If we take some such step, it is to be followed by many other steps. Yet nobody is prepared to follow the step which leads to war, and rightly so. Therefore, this kind of a step or any similar step of condemnation which cannot be followed by outright war, because nobody wants that, does not help in these circumstances. I am troubled not only about the past happenings, but also about the present happenings, and I want to help in those present happenings.

I believe that in Eastern Europe all kinds of forces have been at play, liberalizing forces and democratizing forces, and that some progress has been made, and indeed a great deal of progress has been made in some countries. Left to themselves and helped a little, they would go further, but if they are restricted and hindered and are upbraided and condemned, then you stop those forces from functioning properly and yielding results. That is our broad attitude in regard to Hungary. But I must confess that in a matter of this kind, whatever attitude one may take, it is not wholly satisfactory. It can be criticized. Every middle attitude of trying to seek peace when people are excited is not welcomed. Take the case of one of the most explosive parts of the world today, Western Asia or the Middle East or whatever it is called, and more particularly Syria.

Now, the story of these Middle East countries during the past year or a little more has been quite extraordinarily interesting, fascinating, and to some extent, tragic, how step by step conditions there have become worse, not better. We are told from time to time that the situation has improved there because of this military pact or that military alliance. But the fact is that the situation has become progressively worse. If the Western Powers have disliked any interference by the Soviet Union in the Middle Eastern countries, and if they have made these alliances to prevent that happening, well, the very thing they disliked and the very thing, they wanted to avoid by those alliances has taken place, and because of those alliances and because of that policy. It is an obvious thing. Apart from the fact, of course, that the Soviet Union is a great country, if a country is sitting there geographically, you cannot wash it away, and it cannot be ignored in any settlement about the Middle East, or just you cannot ignore China in any settlement about the Far East, because geographically it is there, and it cannot be pushed out of its place on the surface of the earth. But as I said, it is interesting to see that during the course of the past two or three years, the situation in the Mid Eastern Region has progressively become worse. There was a measure of Arab unity there. That has been broken up and split and then these Arab countries, some of them, look at each other with extreme dislike, and possibly they even arm against each other. We read that Syria has been armed by the Soviet Union. We read further that Syria's neighbours all around are being supplied with arms by air lift from the United States. Tanks are going by air from all over the place, from some European places where they are stocked and from America itself. It is an extraordinary world where each country has to take steps to prevent the other country outstepping it in arms aid. How one wishes that this competition was in economic aid and not in arms aid. But it is an extraordinary thing that here, these countries, not big in size, not big in population, occupying a famous part of Asia where Asia joins Europe, with a tremendous history behind them, with great cities, with a common culture so far as Arab countries are concerned, with a common language and living in a state of high tension, spending all their substance on arming themselves and thereby, I have no doubt, restricting and limiting the freedom they posses. We cannot put ourselves under another country for the arms they supply, for the free arms they supply, without somehow affecting our own freedom. It is a grave situation in the Mid East, and especially in Syria. If a wrong step is taken, even if a small conflict somehow unfortunately begins there, the consequences may well be for a bigger conflict to occur and the bigger conflict may lead to a still bigger one. Therefore, it is a dangerous situation. These things affect us because they affect the world. We are not intimately connected with what happens in West Asia or let us say, in Germany. That is one of the bigger questions of the world in Europe. The two Germanies, whether they unite or don't unite, is a very big question and, if not at present, an explosive question. It is not our lookout but inevitably we are interested in it because it affects the world. In that sense we are interested in every major question, more especially disarmament which I mentioned. But really the issues of immediate importance to us are those which directly affect us. Our relations with Pakistan and more especially involving the Kashmir issue and Goa—these two are the questions which affect us directly and intimately. They affect the integrity of India and they affect the security of India. As I have said often, so far as Kashmir is concerned, a part of Kashmir territory has been invaded, aggression has been committed and is still in hostile possession.

So far as Goa is concerned, it is true that Goa has been under Portuguese possession for a considerable time, for hundreds of years, but the freedom of India and the political revolution of India will not be complete however long it may take, till Goa is part of India. That is patent to anyone who sees it. If we disapprove, as we do, of colonialism in North Africa, in Algeria or in South East Asia or somewhere else in the wide world, would anyone expect us to permit colonialism in our very lap, sitting here in India, our own territory? It is an astounding idea and presumption that people seem to have. Nobody in India, I say, no party, no group, no individual in India can ever accept a foreign power sitting in any corner of India: because we have deliberately and with painful effort arrived at a conclusion that we must restrain ourselves and not allow any military effort in regard to Goa, perhaps some people imagine, perhaps the Portuguese Government imagines that they have settled this problem or dealt with it to their own advantage. I think, they are very much mistaken because a problem of this kind, as I said, can never be settled till it is settled in one way and that is till Portuguese domination ends there completely.

There is one small matter, not small but small only in the sense that it is whispered now, but very important and vital. I would like to mention this. It is sometimes said that Goa might be made some kind of a base for other powers. Portugal is a Member of the NATO alliance and it seeks to preserve its colonies under cover of that NATO alliance. A year or two ago there was some reference to NATO in connection with Goa and we referred to the NATO countries. The replies we got were more or less satisfactory. I would not say, they were 100 per cent satisfactory but they were more or less satisfactory. The replies broadly were that according to the NATO treaty, the Portuguese colonies did not come into it directly but under the Treaty and they could discuss them. What they did afterwards, was another matter. So, I said, they were not completely satisfactory, though that question and answer did serve as a warning to all these countries as to what we feel about Goa and what we feel about the application of any alliance to Goa. Now, if Goa is made any kind of a base for larger purposes of any alliance, that would be a move of the most serious character. It would be an unfriendly act to India and every country that helps or supports that move would thereby be committing this unfriendly act towards India and India will not tolerate it whatever the consequences. We have shown enough patience in regard to Goa by tolerating in the sense of not taking any aggressive steps so far as Portuguese are concerned but if that concept is widened so as to make Goa the base of other powers or alliances or make Goa as the agent of other powers functioning in that way, then the situation is much worse and we cannot possibly admit that and accept it.

I referred to the Kashmir issue which unfortunately has long been with us and is still with us, for no fault of ours. Sometimes, you will find that the outside world and even the world of Pakistan rather forgets Kashmir. Sometimes, you find all the newspapers and many leading personalities in Pakistan having Kashmir on their lips morning, noon and night, and shouting at the top of their voice. It is a kind of cyclical movement. Whenever anything happens, if the Security Council is meeting, then this propaganda goes up tremendously. During the past year or so, this propaganda has been at its highest pitch and I feel and I confess it with regret that it produced last year some considerable effect in the minds of other countries. Why it did so is another matter. There are many reasons, maybe the effectiveness of repeating falsehoods with great force again and again, maybe because the minds of some other countries were conditioned that way to begin with for various reasons. However, it did produce a certain effect and honourable Members will remember, when this matter came up before the Security Council last year, we had to face a very considerable opposition. It was an astonishing opposition, because it seemed to ignore some obvious, basic and patent facts. I hope I am not so blind to any viewpoint that I cannot even understand an opposition viewpoint or an opposing viewpoint. I may not agree with it. But the kind of arguments that were raised, then the kind of speeches that were delivered and delivered by the representatives of Great Powers who are supposed to know about this matter, by the representative of England, by the representative of the United States of America and by other countries were so far out from facts, from truth and from even a fair appraisal of the situation that we were astonished. My colleague, Shri Krishna Menon dealt with the situation there at very considerable length. Then the argument was raised that India's case is weak and so it has to be argued at length, the idea being that if we admitted the weakness of the case, then they would be generous with us and just put us on the back. I confess that during a long period of dealing with these matters, I have seldom come across something so astounding as the attitude last year in the Security Council of some of these Great Powers and other powers. They never dealt with this question. I do not mind their having other opinions, but I do expect and, I think, it is reasonable to expect that a question should be faced and all the basic factors considered and answers framed and enquiries made. But not a word of it. And they passed a resolution then about the accession of Kashmir not taking place and nothing being done with regard to it on the 26th January 1957. They were told repeatedly that the accession of the State of Jammu and Kashmir to India had taken place in October 1947, and nothing was happening in January 1957 except the winding up of the Constituent Assembly of Kashmir. They were told further that even though the Constituent Assembly of Kashmir drafted the Constitution, it had been finalized months before in the previous year. Nevertheless, they passed that resolution with all pomp and circumstance. Well, nothing happened on the 26th January. Nothing happened. We did nothing then. Parliament did nothing. After all, if there are any steps to be taken constitutionally, Parliament will take the step. A public parade was held there. We normally have it on the 26th January. In Kashmir all that happened was that on the 25th midnight, their Constituent Assembly met and they delivered some valedictory speeches and stopped functioning. Then these representatives of countries, their chanceries and newspapers started writing articles that India had disobeyed, had flouted the Security Council and Kashmir had acceded to India on the 26th January 1957. It is perfectly extraordinary how if a lie is embedded in a person's mind, how difficult it is to uproot it and take it out.

They talk about plebiscite. Again and again we have pointed out that in terms of the Resolution passed by the United Nations Commission in the Security Council, the first thing to be done was for Pakistan to get out, that Pakistan was there by virtue of invasion, of aggression, and it has been practically admitted, and until it goes out nothing else is going to be done. Instead of going out, it has entrenched itself. Instead of going out, in the name of maybe fighting communism or whatever it may be, it has got enormous aid from the United States of America, it may be getting it from the Baghdad Pact or the SEATO, I do not know. But what they get from the United States of America is very considerable. I make no vague or general statement, and I say so, because we have enough information in our possession to show that the military aid, the air aid and the other aid that is coming from the United States to Pakistan is very considerable, and is a menace to India unless we deal with it. And here, because of this menace we have had to do something which has hurt us and given us a tremendous deal of pain, that is, to spend more and more on armaments. The House knows that on the economic plane, especially on the foreign exchange plane, we are not very happily situated. Just at this moment, we have had to add to our burden of foreign exchange. It was a difficult decision; but in the final analysis where the security of India is concerned, there can be no two decisions on the matter. We took it. And I should like other countries, our friendly countries concerned, to realize how by some of their policies of military alliances, military aid, they have added to the burdens of India, creating a feeling of insecurity and thereby coming in the way or some other thing, of our working out our Five Year Plan and our developmental schemes. We are very grateful for the help, financial, loans or credits or otherwise, that we have received from other countries and— I speak in all honesty—I am grateful to them but it is an odd thing that while we are helped, other conditions are produced which wash out that help. We have to carry greater burdens. Now, therefore, so far as Kashmir is concerned, let there be no doubt in peoples' minds as to what our position is. We have not repudiated any direction or decision of the Security Council to which we agreed. We went to the Security Council ourselves complaining of a certain aggression of Pakistan. We went there under an article of the Charter which is a kind of mediatory article. The Security Council passed two main resolutions to which references are made, one in 1948 and the other in January 1949. We accepted them; we stood by them and we stand by them but they have to be interpreted in terms of today. Apart from that, the question remains that the two things those resolutions laid down were that Pakistan had brought its Army into Kashmir and that it must withdraw, it must go out of that territory. That should be the first thing but they have never done that. Their aggression, indeed their occupation of Jammu and Kashmir territory, continues still. While that continues, we are asked repeatedly by some of the Western Powers to make it up with Pakistan, to agree to what

Pakistan says or for a plebiscite or for other things. Whatever may be the rights and wrongs in regard to some steps that we may have taken, I fail to understand how anybody in the wide world, including in Pakistan, can justify the presence of Pakistani armies, troops, civil personnel, in Jammu and Kashmir territory. There is no explanation, no justification, no pretext except that of armed invasion and aggression. Nothing more and, if they say: "Oh, we came here because Muslims are in a majority in Kashmir. The hearts of Muslims in Pakistan bled because they were suffering under foreign yoke and we came over to free them". Then let that be put forward and no other argument. We shall answer that. The more I think of it, the more surprising it becomes as to how these statesmen of the Western world cannot see the facts as they are and go on repeating something which has no basis and will have no basis. Now, we do not propose to forget facts as they are. Facts remain facts whether a person forgets them or not and the Kashmir issue is going to be treated on the basis of those facts and on none other. The House knows how constantly attempts are being made in Kashmir, attempts at sabotage. Members may have read this morning about bombs bursting and little children being killed. Of course, these bursting of bombs and crackers do not solve the question of Kashmir. It is absurd but this is the extent to which people in Pakistan are going. Having failed in their major efforts, now they are sending their emissaries with all kinds of bombs, etc., with money and so on. We have got the money and we have often got the material which was sent by Pakistan. We have often got the material which they sent, the pamphlets that they had sent. After all, it is not easy to guard a huge frontier, to see that nobody comes in. This kind of very unseemly activity is going on, of trying just to frighten and to unnerve the people of Kashmir and, in fact, training people to do this.

N.R. Malkani:[3] This aggression is open and is increasing day by day. Could you do nothing about it?

JN: I do not know what the honourable Member means. We certainly deal with them. We have captured many people who came and some people, I believe, are going to be tried in open court. It is being done but it is not exactly easy to guarantee that nobody will throw a cracker or a bomb especially when this apparatus is helped by a neighbouring Government which has great resources at its command.

I mentioned casually about Algeria. I do not think I need say much about it except that it is today one of the major colonial issues in the world. It is a difficult issue. We have always recognized that difficulty for France because of the presence of a million and a half or a million and a quarter Frenchmen there.

3. Nominated Congress Member.

Because of this, it does become a little difficult issue but the fact of the presence of the Frenchmen there cannot possibly be made an excuse for continuation of this colonial regime as a colony. They have suffered very greatly and I do earnestly hope that they will gain their freedom with the cooperation of the French because this injury is harming both terribly.

I do not wish to say anything more at this stage because, I would like honourable Members here to help us in considering this problem in all its aspects. After all, this question of international affairs becomes more and more difficult and intricate because we cannot control the world. We cannot control our own country as we would like to much less the world and we cannot presume to control the world. We can only influence world events a little by our weight and by our influence do what we can. Ultimately, one comes to the conclusion that the only way wherein one can influence any event in the world is to increase one's own strength, the country's strength and unity and purpose. Then only it is that its voice counts; otherwise, it is just shouting in the wilderness. So, we try to do our best in our humble way in world affairs. It is really in our own country that we have to build up our position in the world.

4. Cable to V.K. Krishna Menon[1]

Your telegram 510 September 17.

There has been no question at any time about any change in our basic policy of non-alignment nor is there any question of our retreating in any matter of foreign policy because of economic conditions. What has happened is greater attention being paid in India to these economic questions which are frequently discussed. We are not going to change our any basic policy in order to get economic assistance.

2. The question of defence expenditure has not been mentioned often here. I have spoken about it more than anybody else. Anyhow, it is a fact which we cannot hide from others.

3. What I said to you about our not getting entangled in foreign matters had

1. New Delhi, 18 September 1957. JN Collection.

nothing to do with any basic policy, political or economic. It was and is a personal reaction to events all over the world, which have distressed me. Also perhaps a feeling of tiredness. We were quite right in the attitude we took up in the UN about Hungary, but the fact remains that I am unhappy about present conditions there. So also Algeria which distresses me greatly. We cannot help playing our part in world affairs in the manner we think best and I am sure that our past activities have been helpful. But I do not want to appear as a crusader on the world stage.

5. Cable to V.K. Krishna Menon[1]

Have just returned to Delhi. Your telegram 522 September 25th. I know that newspapers abroad are trying to show that we are gradually changing our approach in foreign affairs because of our necessity for aid. This is without basis. I am quite clear that we must adhere to our basic policy of non-alignment as also in regard to disarmament. Any change in it would be harmful to us as well as to wider causes which we advocate. In adhering to our policy, however, we should avoid criticisms of other countries which do not help and only irritate.

2. I have nothing to suggest to you about Kashmir. Noon's speech has angered people here and press comments have been very strong.[2]

3. Your telegram 523 September 26th. Naga developments are much more favourable to us than *The New York Times* report indicates, though, of course, we cannot speak with certainty about future. Naga Delegation that came here represented not only so-called loyalist elements but also pro-hostile elements.

---

1. New Delhi, 28 September 1957. JN Collection.
2. Feroz Khan Noon said in Karachi on 23 August that since India had consistently refused to have a plebiscite in Jammu and Kashmir, it might be "presumed that the people of the State have already acceded to Pakistan."

II. THE ASIAN TOUR

(i) Japan

1. On Arrival in Tokyo[1]

Mr Prime Minister[2] and friends,

Arriving here this afternoon on the soil of Japan, I feel very happy, because it has long been wished to come here for many long years past and I am happy that that wish is lastly fulfilled.[3]

I come to you as a representative of my country, bringing you greetings of my Government and people. I come to you also as an individual citizen of India who has had for long admiration for the people of Japan and who has wanted to come here. So, I am happy to come as a friend, and I hope, as a messenger of goodwill and affection for the people of Japan. I hope that my visit here as the visit of you, Mr Prime Minister, to India will help in adding to mutual understanding and the ways of cooperation.

Thank you for your friendly welcome.

---

1. Speech at the Haneda airport, Tokyo, 4 October 1957, *Journal of the Indo-Japanese Association of Japan,* Vol. 6, No. 1. This issue is available in JN Papers, NMML.
2. Nobusuke Kishi.
3. He was in Japan from 4 to 13 October 1957.

2. Talks with Nobusuke Kishi—I[1]

According to the Kyodo news agency, today's talks between the Japanese Prime Minister Mr Nobusuke Kishi and Pandit Nehru "did not touch upon questions concerning China or the Japanese proposal to set up an Asian Development Fund."

The Japanese news agency's account of the talks said: "At their first formal talk this morning Prime Minister Nehru and Premier Kishi are believed to have mainly taken up the question of banning nuclear tests. Informants indicated that the talks on the atomic issue did not go into specific details. Their discussions of other topics were also of a broad and preliminary nature."

"The Indian Prime Minister did most of the talking."

The agency quoted Mr Aiichiro Fujiyama,[2] the Japanese Foreign Minister, who took part in the talks, as having said that Pandit Nehru's "basic ideas" of a neutral bent of mind appeared to be the result of his "clear understanding of the West", his occidental studies and his experience during the fight for Indian Independence.

The Secretary General, Mr K. Aichi, who also took part in that talks, was quoted by Kyodo as having said that "no proposals on specific questions were made either by Mr Kishi or Pandit Nehru during the talks."

"Mr Aichi said that they agreed that efforts should be made by both countries to stop nuclear tests. The two leaders agreed that in the interest of world peace, Japan and India should act so as to bridge effectively the differences between Russia and the United States."

1. An account of the first formal talks between Jawaharlal Nehru and the Japanese Prime Minister, Nobusuke Kishi in Tokyo on 5 October 1957, based on the reports by the Kyodo news agency. From *National Herald* and *The Hindu*, 6 October 1957. No official record of the talks is available.

   The Japanese Prime Minister was accompanied by the Foreign Minister, A. Fujiyama; the Deputy Minister for Foreign Affairs, K. Ono; Parliamentary Vice-Minister for Foreign Affairs, Takizo Matsumoto; Secretary General for Foreign Affairs, K. Aichi; Japanese Ambassador to India, S. Yoshizawa. The Indian Prime Minister was accompanied by the Secretary General, MEA, N.R. Pillai, and C.S. Jha, Indian Ambassador in Tokyo.
2. Aiichiro Fujiyama (1897-1985); Japanese businessman and politician; President, Dai Nippon Sugar Manufacturing Company, 1934 and Nitto Chemical Industry, 1937, Japan Air Lines, 1951, Japan and Tokyo Chambers of Commerce, 1951-57, Society for Economic Cooperation in Asia, 1954-61; Foreign Minister, 1957-60; State Minister in charge of Economic Planning Board, 1961-62, 1965-66; President, Association for the Promotion of International Trade, 1973.

"Mr Aichi also said that there was no move to combine into a single proposal of the drafts on nuclear tests which Japan and India have separately submitted to the UN General Assembly."

The agency continued: "Although Mr Aichi said that the two leaders did not go into the possibility of combining the Japanese and Indian proposals on nuclear tests, informants believed that the talks on this subject actually went deeper. They understood that after he had heard Pandit Nehru's exposition of India's attitude towards nuclear tests, Mr Kishi indicated his readiness to revise the Japanese draft proposals at the UN if thereby the objective of ending nuclear tests could be more speedily achieved."

The Kyodo news agency said that the two leaders also expressed views on the international situation with particular reference to West and East Asia.

The agency said that on West Asia, Pandit Nehru dwelt on the supplies of arms by one side or the other and expressed the view that such supplies should be stopped.

Pandit Nehru was also reported to have touched on the Baghdad Pact.

Kyodo said that there was also a reference to the attitude to International Communism, Pandit Nehru, according to informants, declared that he was an Indian and, therefore, he would think and act as an Indian throughout his life. Pandit Nehru added that he was trying hard to maintain a balance in India's relations with the two power blocs.

He was also reported to have said to Mr Kishi that Japan, India and China have emerged as the leading nations in Asia. He did not specifically say what they should do for the sake of Asian people and world peace. His view was that the three nations would have a major influence in this region.

Mr Nehru, according to a Japanese spokesman, analyzed the Syrian situation and India's views on the Baghdad Pact. He added that without touching upon concrete problems of recognition of the People's Republic of China, Mr Nehru emphasized the importance and the forceful role China was playing in Asia.

He said that the two Premiers were endeavouring to pool their efforts to bridge the gulf in the approaches of the Soviet Union and the Western Powers on the question of banning nuclear weapons.

3. Talks with Nobusuke Kishi—II[1]

The Japanese Foreign Minister, Mr Aiichiro Fujiyama, told correspondents at the conclusion of the second round of Nehru-Kishi talks at Hakone tonight that the two Prime Ministers were agreed on the broad issue of a ban on nuclear tests but differed on the "methods and details" of bringing it about.

The Foreign Minister, who was present at the talks, said most of the talking was done by Mr Nehru who explained India's stand on international problems. Mr Kishi also outlined Japanese stand on these problems.

The main subject at the talks, Mr Fujiyama said, was ban on nuclear tests. Economic questions were not much discussed, he added.

The Minister disclosed that Mr Nehru in the course of the talks gave reasons which led India to recognize the People's Republic of China.

He said that Mr Nehru's detailed analysis of India's policy on international questions would enable the Japanese Government to have a better understanding of the Indian policies.

The Japanese Premier Mr Nobusuke Kishi told Mr Nehru that Japan was not and could not be interested in military alliance involving the dispatch of Japanese troops abroad.

This view was communicated to Mr Nehru during the second meeting between the two Premiers which took place here last night and lasted two hours. Mr Kishi is understood to have told Mr Nehru that the Japanese Constitution prevented Japan from sending troops abroad. Japan, therefore, could not undertake any commitments to send troops abroad.

At this meeting, which was again held in cordial and friendly atmosphere, Mr Kishi, it is understood, spoke about his visit to the United States following his visit to India. He also explained at length the present position of Japan in the international field. Mr Kishi is stated to have emphasized that Japan's foreign policy was based on three things: the UN Charter, Japan's position as a free nation and its position as an Asian country. He also referred to Japan's relationship with Korea, China and Taiwan (Formosa).

Questions relating to "broad aspects" of East-West relations were also discussed by the two Premiers.

---

1. Report of the second round of talks between Nehru and Nobusuke Kishi held at Fujiyama Hotel, Hakone, 5 October 1957. From *The Statesman*, 6 October 1957 and *The Hindu*, 6 and 7 October 1957. No official record of the talks is available.

Mr Nehru gave an account of what he called 'local problems'—India's foreign relations with Pakistan and problems such as those of Goa and racial discrimination in South Africa. The two Premiers also discussed the question of cultural, commercial and economic relations including the exchange of professors and students as well as films between the two countries. The discussions were stated to have been in general terms. Present at last night's talks were Mr Nehru, Mr Kishi, the Japanese Foreign Minister, Mr Fujiyama, the Japanese Ambassador to India, Mr Yoshizawa, the Japanese Vice-Foreign Minister, Mr Matsumoto, Mr N.R. Pillai, Mr M.O. Matthai and the Indian Ambassador, Mr C.S. Jha.

4. First Step Towards Disarmament[1]

Motoo Hirooka: Does India require economic aid at this point?
Jawaharlal Nehru: We do not want any aid, but we want loans and loans only. Both the countries, Japan and India are competing in certain economic fields. But in the long run, it is in their mutual interest to have a dovetailed economy so that economic exchanges between India and Japan could be established.

Indian economy is very sound. Our present difficulties are only due to the fact that we have to buy machinery and capital goods. This is, however, an investment and money not spent on trivial matters. We make a very good investment.

MH: What is your advice on Communist China?
JN: I have no advice to give to any Government about recognition of the People's Republic of China. I simply think that a policy which does not take any account of facts, patent facts, is a weak policy.

MH: Japan has put forward a proposal for setting up an Asian Development Fund. What is your opinion?
JN: Asia is so vast and so varied that bilateral agreements would be preferable. There are countries in Asia which are not connected with any military alliance. It seems, therefore, difficult to talk of any Asian Development Fund which does not take into consideration these facts.

---

1. Interview with Motoo Hirooka, Chief Political Editor of *Asahi Shimbun*, Hakone, 6 October 1957. From *The Hindu* and *National Herald*, 7 October 1957.

Besides, I am not in favour of creation of blocs. But I feel that it is advisable to have an area which is not aligned to any existing bloc, an area where preservation of peace will be the sole considerations. I think, we should work for the unification of the ideals of Asia.

MH: What do you think of the relations between the US and Communist China?

JN: Although India has no plan to mediate in Communist Chinese-United States relations, I believe, the American people are realistic and businesslike. They will recognize the futility of their position towards China in the near future.

MH: Is there any possibility of holding a second Afro-Asian Conference?

JN: The possibility of holding another Afro-Asian Conference cannot materialize at present. Indeed, if we organized such a conference, it would only create more confusion.

MH: Japan is trying to get nuclear tests banned.

JN: Nuclear weapons should be completely banned without any restrictions or reservations. Japan knows more than anyone else the devastating effects of atomic weapons. The weapons can be banned only step by step. That is why we want first to stop the tests and then discuss ways and means of banning them altogether. The Indian people consider that a ban on these weapons is a matter of principle.

India favours the immediate cessation of tests followed by the organization of an effective control system which can be extended at a later date to cover general world disarmament.

MH: What are, in your opinion, the prospects of world peace?

JN: Events show the prospects for world peace are becoming better. There still remains, however, a lot to be done.

There is no doubt that the people of the world want genuine peace but there can be no genuine peace as long as nations continue the cold war.

The existence of military blocs places the world in an uneasy situation. This situation is compounded when some nations persist in criticizing the peaceful efforts of other nations.

We in India are democratic, constitutionally and by disposition. We respect individual freedom. We also feel that India can best serve the cause of world peace by not joining any bloc.

The development of democracy in the world is being hampered by the formation of blocs serving the selfish interest of groups of nations.

Generally speaking, recent events in the Soviet Union show the present regime is becoming more liberal and stable. There is more freedom in Russia today than there was three years ago. Because of this liberal movement no single leader in the Soviet Union will be able to establish a new dictatorship.

5. India's Foreign Policy[1]

Question: Mr Prime Minister, we are very happy to have you here tonight. Professor Abe's question was rather long. So I should like to summarize it. He said, first of all, that he was very happy to have this opportunity to talk with you. He only wished that this was not for the television but only a private talk. He said that you are a politician as well as a philosopher, an idealist as well as a realist, and when he was reading Socrates he said that he would never be involved in politics. He quite understands why anyone who is a thinker does not want to be involved in politics and he feels that there is a great deal of conflict which he must face and you are also educated in England and with this tradition of India, which you must face every day, and when you take your ideals to your masses of people and then have them implemented, this must also be difficult, and if he is permitted to ask a very personal question, he would like to do so.

Jawaharlal Nehru: Well, Professor, you have asked a very difficult question. But first of all I should like to make it clear that I am no philosopher. I happen to be a politician by force of circumstances, not by choice. I have spent the greater part of my life working under Mahatma Gandhi for the freedom of India and the last ten years as Prime Minister of India, because of the affection and faith of my people in me. But that does not make me a philosopher or very deep thinker and I have to face these problems you have mentioned from day to day. It is very difficult to combine idealism with practical affairs. Too much idealism makes one out of touch with reality. Too much, what is called, being practical is even worse, I think. So, one has to keep one's ideals as far as one can, and work up towards them, even though sometimes the pace may be slower than one wants to. The point is one should not be diverted from them. If one is clear about the objective and the ideals, then one can go even a little slow because one has to carry one's people. One has to convince them, especially in a democratic society. So, there is always this tussle and this attempt in balancing between these two and sometimes one goes wrong, one tries to retrace one's step. That is inevitable. So, I do not know what better answer I can give you.

1. Record of a television interview with Professor Yoshishige Abe, President of Peers University, Professor Shintaro Ryu, editor of *Asahi Shimbun* and Ms Yoko Matsuoka, a critic and the interpreter, Geihenkan (State Guest House), Tokyo, 6 October 1957. AIR tapes, NMML. Also available in the *Journal of the Indo-Japanese Association of Japan*, Vol. 6, No. 1.

Q: He quite agrees with you and he has read in one of your books that in tying to reach the essence of the same thing you find happiness, and perhaps in this conflict that you also find time for happiness.

JN: Happiness is rather a difficult thing to describe, or to realize. The best happiness, I think, comes from a feeling of thought and action combined together. Then there is a certain personal satisfaction.

Q: May I also summarize this question. As Professor Abe[2] has stated before, it is true that we all know of your education in England and your very modern ideas. But how do you also face this Indian tradition in yourself?

JN: What Indian tradition?

Q: Do you feel that you have in yourself the ancient Indian philosophies and thinking?

JN: I do not know. I suppose, to some extent they do influence me. But when people talk about the Indian tradition or the Asian tradition, I think, they are judging from recent happenings in the last few hundred years. People think that Asia is passive, is decadent, India is passive. Well, I do not think history, that is not the last two or three hundred years or before that, shows that Asia was passive at all, or India was passive. These are periods that come in the life of every nation. It is true that many countries in Asia, not the Japanese, in the last 100 years or so have tended to be passive. That was a sign of weakness, because I do not think that being passive is a virtue at all. For instance, peace is not passivity. For me peace is an active virtue. A person who is just passively peaceful is no good to me. And Mahatma Gandhi was very particular.

Gandhi was a man of peace above all, but he was a man of action all the time. He did not believe in a man just sitting quietly and calling himself peaceful. He wanted India to be active and yet peaceful. So, I do not know what you would say about the Indian tradition, because in a country with a long history, it has so many traditions of passivity, of activity, of everything. But there is a certain philosophical element in India which might be called—the feeling of philosophical detachment, being in action and yet not being swept away by it. Further, something that Mr Gandhi laid great stress on was that means are always very important. Ends by themselves are not good enough. The means to be followed must also be good. So, if I may say so, the philosophy that I endeavour to follow, not always to win success, and that means should always be remembered

2. Yoshishige Abe (1883-1966); Japanese educator and philosopher; taught at Hosei University and Keijo Imperial University, Seoul; Member, House of Peers; Minister of Education, Janaury 1946-May 1946 and worked for educational reforms; Chairman, Special Committee on Bill for Revision of the Imperial Constitution; President, Gakushuin University.

which should be good and that one should actively pursue and not merely passively wait for things to happen.

Q: You just mentioned about peace. Now in that connection, he would like to ask the following question. You do not like the word neutralism. But that is the word which is used to describe India's foreign policy. Now you have used the term 'non-alignment' or 'third area' or 'peace area'. Now Mr Ryu[3] feels that there is a development of thinking between these words and there are slight differences also between these words. Now, if you would clarify this we should be grateful.

JN: Mr Ryu was quite right in saying that I do not like the word 'neutral' in connection with India's policy. I do not like it, first of all, because in public affairs one talks of being neutral as opposed to belligerent. If there is a war some countries are belligerent, some are neutral. I do not understand why that term should be used in peace times. Am I to call the countries that are not neutral belligerent? No, they are not. But it shows a mentality of belligerence to talk about neutrality. Although they may not be fighting, they think in terms of war and fighting. Therefore, I do not like the word.

Secondly, I do not like the word because it is a passive word. And I do not approve of passive policies. I want an active policy.

The word 'non-alignment' describes our policy better. It simply means we do not tie ourselves up with any bloc of nations in any alliance. But we are friendly to them. We try to be friendly to all countries and follow an independent policy, that is to say, we judge everything on the merits, in so far as we can, and without trying to condemn any country, because condemnation creates difficulties and makes it more difficult to deal with those countries. So, I think that the very use of the word 'neutral' shows a mentality which does not think of peace so much, but of the possibility of war.

We are not neutral about any matter of principle to which we attach importance. We are not at all neutral. We are against something which we consider wrong. Even in our struggle with England for our Independence, we were against British imperialism but not against England. It is difficult to distinguish. But we did not want to condemn the British people, but we did condemn British imperialism.

Q: Mr Prime Minister, in connection with your active policy of non-alignment, may I ask one question? This morning's papers reported that in your talks with our Prime Minister, and Foreign Minister you have mentioned that India, China and Japan are three big powers in Asia. Not it

3. Shintaro Ryu (1900-1967); Japanese economist, worked in Ohara Institute of Social Research, and Showa Research Association; member, editorial board of *Asahi Shimbun.*

seems to me that neither China nor Japan is exactly following, what you call, the non-alignment policy. But if these are the three big powers—and I think they are—and they have to work for peace and stability in Asia, what do you suggest are the steps?

JN: I suppose you are referring to my conversation with Prime Minister Kishi. What I said to him was that China, Japan and India are three big countries in Asia. There are many other important countries too. And undoubtedly what they do, or what anyone does will affect the future of Asia and, in a sense, the world. Further, I did not say this to him what I am saying now, that these countries, as well as some other countries of South East Asia have an old bond in the message of the Buddha. I am not talking about the religion as such, but the broad message of compassion and friendliness, which, I think, is very much needed in the world today. And, naturally, I said that it is desirable for all these countries, as well as others, to try to develop friendly relations, even if they disagree. The essence of coexistence is, even if you disagree with another country, still not be hostile to it. You may be hostile to a policy, but not to the country. Otherwise, the only alternative is conflict. One cannot make all the world alike. People think differently, act differently. But it is important that one country, any country, should not interfere in the affairs of another country, otherwise there is conflict.

Q: Professor Abe wanted to add that he completely agrees with your view and that he feels that if the five principles of peace, which you and Prime Minister Chou En-lai talked about, were really implemented, then he thinks that peace can be brought about.

JN: That is perfectly true, if they are implemented. I would say that for fear that they might not be implemented, one should not stop working for them, because the way to get them implemented is to go on pressing for them, and then gradually world opinion is created, which rather compels people to implement them and any country that does not, is, well in a sense, if I may say so, become an outcaste.

Q: I cannot help having some sort of antipathy towards the communist countries, though we know that we must never have such antipathy against any people and must think and look at people more realistically. But frankly speaking, I cannot help thinking of communist countries especially Soviet Union, with dissatisfaction and fear. Of course, the same thing can be said to our attitude towards US.

JN: Well, that is true. As you know Professor, we ourselves follow a policy, political and economic, which might be called democratic. We also aim at a socialistic pattern of society. But our socialism is not doctrinaire or rigid. It grows with experience, and the main purpose being progressively more equality and equal opportunity to our people and better standards. Now, it is not for me to criticize other countries, but obviously, if we follow a democratic pattern, we prefer that for our own country. What other countries want, they can have, provided they do not interfere with us. I do not like many things that other countries have done, whether it is the Soviet Union, or whether it is England, or whether it is the United States, or whether it is France. Sometimes they do not like things that my country has done. It is a difficult position.

Q: Mr Ryu has read your book *Glimpses of World History* and in it you have praised Japan during Meiji Era, and particularly the statesmen of that period. Now, Japan has changed considerably since that time. He would like to know how you would assess the situation today, not as the Prime Minister of India but as the author of that book and, that is to say, from the point of view of a historian.

JN: That book was a book written for my daughter and does not pretend to be a scholar's book. But since those old days, it is obvious that Japan has undergone many changes, has experienced, well, great triumphs and great defeats and the people are powerfully conditioned by these experiences. So of one thing, I have no doubt, that the Japan of today is in many ways different from what it was previously. In what measure, and what the present conditions may be here, it is not for me to say. I do not pretend to know exactly. But naturally, I hope that Japan, after all these terrible experiences, will stand for peace and work for peace and cooperation among nations.

Q: The greatest task, which you as the Prime Minister of India and also as a world statesman have, he feels, is to avert war, and if we cannot do so, then there is no use in having satellites and all these scientific conquests, and we certainly hope and expect, that you would keep contributing towards this end.

JN: Well, Madam, you just reminded me of what I said of a meeting in India some years ago. When I said that I was a confused man in a confused world, I do not pretend to have any superior wisdom or deep insights. All one can do is to try one's hardest for something worth having, not to give way to hatred and violence, not to lose one's nerve and to carry on as best as one can.

Q: The last thing we would like to ask is something about the cultural exchange between India and Japan. I think, all of us in Asia have jumped over Asian nations and went over to the West for all sorts of teachings. We have certainly learnt a great deal from the West, but we have not tried hard enough to learn anything from the Asian nations. Where would you put the most emphasis on the direct cultural relations between the two nations?

JN: Well, there is not much time left, not a minute. But you are quite right in saying that the expansion of Europe into Asia cut off contacts between Asian countries. Now we have recovered from that. Therefore, we should develop these relations, cultural and every kind of relations, to know each other better, to pick up old threads, to understand each other, and more specially, well in every way, intellectually, professors, scholars and in every other way we should like to do it.

6. Views on the World Problems[1]

Question: As you know, Japan was recently elected to the United Nations Security Council.[2] What role do you expect Japan to play in the World Organization?

Jawaharlal Nehru: What role? Good role, a role for peace, a role to lessen tensions in the world and, generally, to bring about more and more cooperation between nations.

Q: Mr Prime Minister, can you give your reactions to the announced Russian launching of the earth satellite?

JN: Yes, my reaction is that scientific and technological advance has run far ahead of the capacity of human beings to adapt themselves to it. That is to say, to adapt themselves mentally, biologically. It is quite fantastic, I think, in this world of advancing science, for our politics to be concerned with petty conflicts, military alliances, armament races and the like. It is just out of date. It is almost like somebody coming and suddenly talking to you in terms of some stone age people, when we are living in this age, so that the gap between scientific and technological advance today and normal human thinking, I am not talking about special individuals, is very big and causes this inability for adjustments to be made. We have to adapt ourselves to the age we live in. We have not. Although we travel by air and we use radar and send ballistic weapons, but in a sense, psychologically, mentally speaking, we still live in a past age and talk in terms of it too, even in the United Nations.

Q: Mr Prime Minister, what is your opinion about extending Japanese long term credits to India? Has that been discussed in your tour so far?

1. Press conference, Tokyo, 7 October 1957. AIR tapes, NMML. Also available in *Journal of the Indo-Japanese Association of Japan*, Vol. 6, No. 1.
2. On 1 October, Japan, Canada and Panama were elected to the Security Council as non-permanent members.

JN: No, nothing of that type has been discussed here this time. India is very much interested in big credits or loans to cover her foreign exchange payment difficulties in the course of the next year or 18 months. You must remember that the very fact that our foreign exchange difficulties have arisen is a sign and a symbol of the fairly fast rate of progress that we are making. It is a sign of a sound and advancing economy. Maybe, we advance a bit too fast, maybe, but that advance too is represented by investments in machines, etc. It is not that we are wasting money. The thing is that we are going to produce money tomorrow. So, we want credits and certainly our Finance Minister, who went to the United States early for the World Bank meeting, for which he is a Director, has mentioned that there we welcome these long credits or loans from the United States or any other country too. It so happens that the United States is more in a position to grant big credits and loans than most other countries.

Q: Mr Prime Minister, would you tell us your opinion whether or not the launching of the satellite increases or decreases the chances of world peace?
JN: I do not think it has any very direct and immediate influence except, as I said, to force people to think in other terms, that is, gradually to make them realize that it is becoming rather absurd to talk about wars, armaments and the like in an age which really has gone ahead of all these. So, in that sense, you might say it takes humanity a little bit forward towards lessening of tensions and thinking differently.

Q: Mr Prime Minister, in this morning's papers, you said that nuclear disarmament should be done step by step. Is the first step mutual inspection?
JN: Well, if I may say so, that report is not 100% correct in the press. What I said was that disarmament, i.e., comprehensive disarmament, should be achieved step by step. One cannot bring about comprehensive disarmament by the way that one wants suddenly. It is a complicated thing. By step by step it may be brought about and each step facilitates, makes easier the next step. Of those steps, I said, the problem of nuclear arms is the most urgent and important, although it is tied up with other steps of convention, alarms and the rest. And I said, the first step should necessarily be a suspension of tests. I can very well understand the apprehensions of countries that if they stop, the other party will go ahead. But a suspension of tests for a period of time to allow matters to be discussed further, does not give any particular advantage to anybody. With the suspension immediately one should consider the inspection and the control. There will never be, if you start by saying that we shall inspect and control first before taking up any other step, you can take it from me there will never be any control or suspension or any thing. Because of the tremendous fears, nobody is going to allow people to come and peep into your back door and everywhere till

some lessening of apprehension is taking place. But the whole thing goes together. Obviously, inspection and control is the essence of disarmament, whether it is nuclear disarmament or any other. But, I think that the real first step is, and in fact we have stated in our resolution in the UN, the suspension of tests which is a small thing, because you remain where you are. Meanwhile, an immediate attempt, scientifically and technically is to find out what is the best way of inspecting and controlling and give effect to it. The rest gradually follows one step after another.

Q: Have you any specific number of months or years in mind for suspension without inspection to continue?

JN: There is no particular point in saying suspension for, let us say, six months. It has no meaning. Because normally each country suspends its activities for six or seven months, between one series of tests and another. They cannot go on day to day functioning. So, the period of suspension, to have any meaning, must be about, say two years or so. Of course when I talk about suspension I consider it a prelude to banning of the thing, after other steps have been made. It is a preclude and I do not expect a long period to elapse for mere suspension and nothing being done. That would be a failure. So that the moment it is suspended, at the same time you go ahead with the scientific examination of control and inspection. That may yield results in six months time, 7 months' time and 8 months' time. I do not know. I do not think it is easily possible to have any major experiment, atomic test explosion today, hiding it, I mean. I do not think it is possible. You can always know that something has been done, exactly what. So that for a country to bypass any suspension or to try to be clever, I do not think it is very easily possible, even now.

Q: I think you will agree that there is quite a difference between Japan and India in regard to their foreign policies or views on international political affairs; do you think it is still possible for our countries to cooperate closely?

JN: I believe, it is true that at present there are some differences in international affairs between Japanese and Indian policies. I do not know, to some extent, of course. Each country's foreign policy is not something evolved out of a vacuum. It is dependent on geography, on, well, past history, not distant past, I mean recent past history and all manner of other things. In that sense, it is inevitable that the conditioning factors of Indian policy at the present moment should be different from the conditioning factors of Japanese policy. Having said that, I do not think it would be correct to say that there are any very basic differences. Between Japan and India, there are no major problems of differences as between ourselves. We may differ about other matters, but as between the two countries there may be minor points. We discuss and come to an agreement. It is not necessary for two countries to have identical views to cooperate. If that was a

563

condition precedent, then it will be difficult to have any cooperation in the world. In fact the very idea that we hold of a country having an independent policy of its own, means that there are variations in policies and even so they cooperate.

Q: Do you think Russian troops should eventually leave Hungary, and if so, I would like to know how the Russians can be persuaded to do so?

JN: You are right in saying that I have repeatedly said that all foreign troops should leave the countries they are in. I do not think they serve any long term useful purpose. I do not know about any short term event happening. In that connection I certainly laid stress that Russian forces should not occupy Hungary, not be there.

You asked me how I am going to persuade them. I have no particular answer to that, except saying that there are only two ways, or if you like, persuasion or bringing about circumstances which lead to certain result. One is a peaceful way, the other is a warlike way involving war. If you rule out war, the other is only a peaceful method. There is no intermediate method, because with a method of half-war, half-peace, you fall between two stools. You have all the disadvantages of both. I suppose these questions are connected with the larger issues of cold war. If there is a lessening of tension or a lessening of the cold war, I imagine, it would facilitate the solution of many problems in Europe, as elsewhere.

Q: Mr Prime Minister, there has been a statement by your Dr Homi Bhabha, who is an authority on the matter of atomic fallouts, asking for Japanese scientists' cooperation with India in connection with investigation of the fallout problem?

JN: Well, I suppose there can always be scientific examinations, six months, less or more. There should be cooperation, but an examination of the fallout has to take place in every region, in every country—Japan, India, every other country and the results communicated to each other. The actual examination does not require two countries sitting together. Their scientists do it separately but they communicate their results to each other, as it is done all over the world.

Q: Mr Prime Minister, to go back for a moment to the previous question regarding the presence of Russian troops in Hungary, do you draw any distinction between the presence of Russian troops in Hungary and Poland; and the presence of American troops in Japan or in Korea?

JN: Essentially, there is no difference, but there is practically. I understand that forces in Japan are in the process of being gradually withdrawn. That is a difference. Otherwise, there is no difference. Of course, it may be that the troops may get involved into civil conflicts, that is bad, as in Hungary. But the basic thing is that the very presence of foreign troops, I am quite sure, is never and will never be welcomed by any population, whatever the population may be, and however good or bad the foreign troops might be; no country likes foreign troops on its soil, of that I am absolutely certain. Judging from my own reactions to foreign troops in my own country and such as I know elsewhere, nobody likes it. It is such a visible symbol of another country dominating over you. In some way nobody can like it. The whole nationalist feeling, sentiment in a country is against it, and nationalism is a very strong sentiment, whether in Europe, or Asia, or anywhere else. It is, I believe, still the strongest sentiment, the strongest feeling in a country.

Q: Mr Prime Minister, do you see any evidence of more promising trends towards an understanding between the two Vietnams?

JN: I do not know exactly, but so far as we know, there is no great improvement. The position remains where it is.

Q: Do you find that there is any difference between the presence of American troops in Japan and Korea, and Indian troops in Kashmir?

JN: Yes, I am glad you asked that question. Kashmir is a part of India. I am not aware that Japan is a part of the United States.

Q: Did you speak of the admission of Mainland China into the United Nations with Mr Kishi or Foreign Minister Fujiyama. Do you think that you can succeed in persuading the Japanese Government leaders to pursue a non-alignment policy regarding Mainland China?

JN: Prime Minister Kishi knows our views very well on this subject and they have been mentioned to him previously and at this time. He has expressed his views. It is not a matter for a long discussion. We know each other's views very well.

Q: You said to have talked to Prime Minister Kishi and Foreign Minister about Mainland China; should we take it that you suggested that Japan should recognize China?

JN: Well, first of all, one does not like to talk about private conversations, but as a reference has been made in the press, what I said to Prime Minister Kishi was that there are many great countries in Asia, great and small. But it is obvious I said, and I was talking about the future, not about the present so much, that the three countries like Japan, China and India have an important role to play in Asia, and the future will be influenced by their relations to each other. If there are cooperative relations, the influence will be good. If not, then the influence will be bad for them and for others.

Now, your question was about my saying something about the recognition of the People's Government of China by Japan. Is that your question? When my country recognizes the People's Government of China and presses for its inclusion in the United Nations, it is obvious that I want every country to do so. If I consider my action right, I want others to follow the right action too. It would be presumptuous of me to go about telling other people what they should do. They know very well what I think about it and if in the course of the argument the matter comes, I mention it. But you observe certain decorum and proprieties even in political conversations.

Q: Sometime ago you made a statement to the effect that Russian troops are staying in Hungary against the will of the Hungarian people. Do you mean to say that American troops are staying in Japan against the will of the Japanese people?

JN: I did not say what you said first. In fact, I said the reverse. What I said was, that essentially where foreign troops are present in a country, that fact can never be liked by the people of that country. I again lay down that proposition, which cannot be challenged at any time, in any country, in history, not only today but in the past, and certainly in the present and future. I do not mean for a brief period, that is a different matter; there may be some development, some wartime development, and that is a different matter. But, broadly speaking, in peace time the presence of foreign troops in a country can never be liked by the people of that country, whatever the country and wherever it may be, Europe, America, Asia, Africa. Now, that has nothing to do with any comparison, that is a broad statement of my views on this subject.

Your question, I do not think, as far as I know, I do not think the great majority of the Hungarian people want the Soviet troops there. I think, it is obvious from what has happened; as to what the Japanese may feel about it, surely it is not for me to answer. There are plenty of Japanese in Japan to answer that.

Q: We understand that the South Koreans are opposed to the withdrawal of American troops; what do you think of this?

JN: Well, I should not like to discuss this matter in that way. But if a country wants foreign troops to defend itself, it is a weak country, unsure of itself or of its neighbours.

Q: Is there any possibility of any coordinated action in the United Nations between Japan and India regarding the banning of nuclear tests?

JN: I don't think it is a very difficult thing, but what we want in the United Nations is not some kind of propagandist resolution or propagandist approach. We want results. In achieving results in this matter the three countries that matter most are the USA, the Soviet Union and the United Kingdom. These are the three countries which at present possess nuclear weapons and therefore, our attempt is to find some ways of bridging the gap between the different viewpoints. Just two or three countries combining and delivering fine speeches, well, it may sound very nice, but it does not help.

Q: Is there any chance that during your visit here you would formulate a new plan to fill up that gap?

JN: I don't think there is any great difficulty in the statesmen of Japan, or me coming to a broad agreement on it. Broadly speaking, our views are the same. But, the question is about the agreement between the USA, the UK and Soviet Union. How can we, sitting here, bring about an agreement between the USA and the Soviet Union? That will have to be discussed with them, maybe, in the United Nations, not publicly in speeches, but privately. Some way out can be found because everybody wants to find a way out, and of that, I have no doubt.

Q: Would you care to comment on the idea proposed by Prime Minister Kishi of setting up of an Asian Development Fund?

JN: Well, I have been asked this question the other day too. I might say we have not discussed this matter on this occasion. Prime Minister Kishi did mention it when he came to Delhi.[3] I said then that the matter was not quite clear to me. I could understand bilateral agreements between countries, Asian countries or others, but conditions in Asian countries naturally vary, they are different. I should like to know a little bit more about this proposal so as to understand it. Perhaps you may remember that at the Bandung Conference, there was a resolution passed about cooperation between the countries of the Bandung Conference. That is a very big area and we found that although we were very friendly and cooperative to each other, it is not very easy to find a common measure of different countries coming together on the economic plane. Well, two countries can, or three countries might, but a broader range becomes a little more difficult to organize.

Q: Should we understand that your answer will be negative?

JN: How can you take it that way when I say that I am trying to understand it? It may be that our answer may contain some suggestions, etc. There are many ways of approaching. There is no basic negative in such matters because, broadly speaking, we aim at the same thing. The question is how to achieve that thing and we discussed that and maybe we will come to some agreement about it.

Q: Is there any possibility of having another Bandung Conference?

JN: Last November, we discussed this matter with some of the Prime Ministers who sponsored the Colombo Conference, and, I think, we said then that the second Bandung Conference should be held some time in 1958. Well, of course, we did not fix a date and we left matters rather vague and they are vague still. It depends on circumstances. There is no talk of holding it; no date has been fixed or even discussed. So, I don't think there will be any such conference in the near future. Certainly, it takes a good deal of organizing.

3. For Kishi's visit to India from 23 to 25 May 1957 see *Selected Works* (second series), Vol. 38, pp. 736-739.

Q: The Communist Party has been winning elections in your own country and to a very large extent in Indonesia. Can you comment on this?

JN: I can only speak about my country. It is difficult for me to discuss conditions in other countries. In my own country the success of the Communist Party in the elections has not been, of course, striking. It has been a little more than the previous elections. Partly, I suppose, due to the fact that any Government which is functioning year after year has an effect on the people of being stale—some people among the vast electorate. The Communist Party in our country puts on the most proper and decorous constitutional clothing and tries to make out that it functions strictly within the four corners of the Indian Constitution and, in fact, they are following the policies laid down in our Second Five Year Plan Report and nothing more. The other day we had a curious conference in India. India is an odd country in some ways. I suppose no other country could produce a man like Mahatma Gandhi. There is another man in India, a very chosen disciple of Mr Gandhi. His name is Vinoba Bhave. He is physically a weak man, but with an amazing spirit and somehow when you see people like this you feel that the spirit is stronger than many other things. Anyhow, he invited a small group of 30 to 40 persons including our President, myself, some other Ministers and including two or three Communist Ministers of the Southern State of Kerala. We all went there. It was a curious gathering, to discuss land reforms, because Bhave is leading a movement which is called the land gift movement.[4] People give their land, not to somebody, but they give it to the village community. That is, they remain there but the ownership goes into the common pool of village community. Of course, he is wedded absolutely to non-violence, peaceful approaches and truth. Now, all of us—communists, non-communists, capitalists, wherever they were, subscribed to a statement issued from there about our adherence to the truthful and non-violent approach to the solution of the land problem. So, you see, we function rather oddly, isn't it?

Q: You said that Kashmir is part of India. When did it become part of India?

JN: A few hundred years ago. Kashmir has always been in history for thousands of years, not always a political part but essentially a part of India. For hundreds of years a political part of India, long before the British came. It has been essentially and culturally one of the biggest seats of Indian culture and learning throughout history—2000 years. So, the finest books about Indian history have been written in Kashmir. Then came the Partition of India. And certain rules

---

4. This refers to the *Gramdan* Conference held at Yelwel near Mysore on 21 September 1957. See *ante*, pp. 12 and 114-115.

WITH EMPEROR HIROHITO, INDIRA GANDHI, EMPRESS NAGAKO AND CROWN PRINCE AKIHITO, IMPERIAL PALACE, TOKYO, 7 OCTOBER 1957

AT THE ANCIENT SHRINE OF HEIAN JINGU, KYOTO, 7 OCTOBER 1957

were laid down about the Partition of India. According to the rules, Kashmir acceded to India and became part of the Indian Union, as an autonomous state of the Indian Union. That is why I say that Kashmir is as much a part of India as Calcutta, or Bombay, or Madras. At that time, Kashmir was invaded through Pakistan, and later by Pakistan.

I don't think it is possible for anyone, even a Pakistani, to say that that was not aggression. There have been a number of cases of aggression in the world in the last 10 years or so. There has been no case of more clearer and more flagrant aggression than that of Pakistan over Kashmir territory, which was Indian Union territory. Now, whatever legal or other arguments one may have about Kashmir in the Indian Union, there is not a shadow of doubt over the argument in favour of the presence of Pakistani troops in Kashmir and that aggression is continuing today. Over one-third of the territory of Jammu and Kashmir State is in the occupation of the Pakistan Army. My friend reminds me that one third in population and nearly one-half in area, is in the possession of Pakistan. It is a continual aggression, and there is absolutely no kind of justification. One justification Pakistan has raised is that the majority of the people in Kashmir are Muslims. Now, that is a very odd argument. Once we admit that states are formed on the basis of religion, we go back to the middle ages in Europe or elsewhere. It is an impossible argument. If we admit it, then, within India, as it is today after Partition, there are 40 million Muslims. Are they Pakistani citizens? Do they owe allegiance to Pakistan? Every village in India has Muslims. There are Christians. Is there Christian nationality, or Muslim nationality, or Buddhist nationality, a Hindu nationality? It is an impossible proposition. So, the present position in Kashmir is, undoubtedly that is, legally speaking, historically speaking, constitutionally speaking, a part of India, a part of the Union of India. The Jammu and Kashmir State has been invaded, aggression committed against it by Pakistan forces who are still continuing that aggression by occupying it. It is only a country like India, peacefully inclined, that would have stopped its military operations against the aggressor and decided to deal with it peacefully. I would be very much surprised if any other country would have done that. In keeping with our tradition of peace and what Mr Gandhi taught us, we were anxious to stop it. We stopped at ceasefire even though the aggression is continuing, and we said that we would decide it by peaceful methods and that is our present policy. We wanted to decide every question by peaceful methods but that does not mean, and will not mean our submission to aggression, and I regret that this fact is not adequately appreciated by some of the Great Powers, who talk about aggression in other places. But in Kashmir, where there is an act of international gangsterism, they support; I am astonished. I wish to make it perfectly clear that whatever happens, we shall never submit to this aggression and does not matter what Powers in the wide world support it, we will not accept it. I think, it is a shameful thing that this fact is slurred over. The matter is coming up before the Security Council in a day or two and I want, therefore, to make it perfectly clear that this fact is slurred over, and privately we are told one thing and publicly another attitude is adopted by some of the Great Powers. I have seldom come across more double standards than in this matter of Kashmir. Here is the barest and the most blatant piece of aggression and continuing aggression and we are told; "Oh, forget the past, forget the past, whatever it was." Well, well, if we are prepared to forget the past, the history of the world today will be very different from what it was.

Q: What is India's position in regard to the Pakistani offer to withdraw its troops from Kashmir if there is an United Nations supervised plebiscite in both parts of the country?

JN: It is very kind of Pakistan to make offers. The only thing I am interested from Pakistan is to get out of Kashmir. I want no offers from them. They have committed aggression on my territory, on India. What business they have to tell us that you do this or that? We will admit no foreign troops in any spot of India, one inch of India, it does not matter whatever happens to India and whether you call them United Nations troops or any other troops. I have just explained to you that we have had enough experience of foreign troops in India, and come what will, we will not admit foreign troops. Just because Pakistan commits aggression, has it got the right to invite other foreign troops to aid its aggression or to shelter its aggression? We admit no foreign troops, whether in Pakistani part or any other part. We will not be willing to do that. As for the national plebiscite, it is up to us to decide what is going to happen in Kashmir. We have had two elections in Kashmir—two general elections in our part of Kashmir. Pakistan talks about the plebiscite in Kashmir and for the last 10 years it has not had any election in Pakistan itself. I think, it is monstrous the way this question has been dealt with by some people without understanding it.

Q: In the case of Hungary, the Russian troops are in Hungary and the Hungarians, as you have stated, do not want the Russians there. Don't you think on the same basis that it would be fair for the Hungarians to get help to get the Russians out?

JN: I will tell you. That question raises a practical issue, apart from any theoretical issues. That means world war. If you are prepared to face world war, you don't fear anybody, you have a world war on that issue alone. What the result of the war will be is anybody's guess, but the Hungarian people do not benefit by it. Therefore, the step taken to aid the Hungarian people may well mean their further ruination and not help. It is no good. If you want to settle it by force of arms, Hungary is not the field of battle—it is world, because there are two huge rival blocs concerned and if we do not want to settle it that way, then surely it is better not to give hopes of settling it that way, because that is neither here nor there. So, practically speaking that does not help, in fact it hinders.

Q: Do you think that it is desirable that we have close relations in the field of academic research and industrial use of atomic energy between India and Japan?

JN: Yes, of course, so far as we are concerned, naturally. We are a very minor country doing atomic research. There is no comparison with the big countries, although, I believe, even now, barring maybe five or six countries, we are doing all very well in the atomic research, apart from a few leading countries and we are making good progress. Our scientists are good. The policy we have followed is that there is no secrecy in our atomic work. In our scientific policy we have no secrets to keep and we welcome cooperation. We are today cooperating with quite a number of countries and, for instance, we are cooperating closely with the United Kingdom. We had a good deal of cooperation with the United States, with France, with the Soviet Union, in a certain measure; and some other European countries. So, we will very gladly cooperate with Japan and we have got one reactor working in India and a very big one will be ready in about six months or eight months' time. We made it quite clear that we shall welcome scientists and students from Asian countries to come and cooperate with us in those reactors.

Q: Do you feel there has been any improvement in the Middle East situation?

JN: Well, it is quieter apparently. I do not know about any basic improvement. But it is an improvement, I think, in this negative sense that any danger of flare up seems to be far less.

Q: What is your opinion about the racial situation in the Little Rock in the United States?[5]

JN: I do not think it is a proper question. Well, about the Little Rock question, if I may say so with all respect, President Eisenhower has shown great courage in dealing with a very difficult situation. May I say that while, naturally, I am against all racialism, and when I say that, do not think I exclude my own country. It does not take the form of racialism as such in India, but casteism and the rest, was in the past a form of racialism, though now it is different. The supreme

5. Following the US Supreme Court ruling of 1954 for desegregation in schools, the school board of Little Rock, Arkansas, planned to implement it gradually beginning with high schools in 1957. However, warnings of riots and breach of peace were issued by the segregationists on 2 September just before the schools were to open. Units of Arkansas National Guard and paratroopers had to be called in to control the situation.

example of racialism today is South Africa, in the Union of South Africa, and, I think, it is terrible both in theory and practice. In the United States it is there and I regret it, but I believe that not only the Government of the United States but other social factors are fairly rapidly going ahead solving that problem. I should like it to be faster still, the process, but it is not for me to judge.

Q: I would like to ask if the issue of Kashmir in the United Nations controlled plebiscite would be an alternative to world war?

JN: You have made a statement or asking a question? It is an extraordinary position. An aggressor comes and sits in your house and then claims all kinds of privileges. I say I should discuss this matter only when the aggressor is out of it. I am not afraid of a plebiscite, but I will not have a plebiscite, or the threat, or to be this plebiscite branded about in front of me that unless you do this, we do this and that. You read the Pakistan press. It is full of threats of holy war. Well, I am a bit tired of these threats and I am a bit tired of gangster tactics employed against India.

Q: I would like to ask your opinion about the present position of Taiwan, in regard to the current relationship between your country and China?

JN: So far as we are concerned, we recognize the People's Government of China. Many other countries recognize that Government too. We do not recognize the Taiwan Government. That is to say, we do not recognize two Governments of China, only one. And so far as I know, every government recognizes only one, this or that. And I do not think even the Taiwan Government does not want to be recognized as the Taiwan Government, also as the Government of China, whether that is a fact or not is another matter. So, what is going to happen in the future I cannot say.

Q: What do you think about the provision in our Constitution renouncing war?

JN: I know of the provision that was introduced in the Japanese Constitution to that effect. But if you ask me, if I have any idea about them, I hope every country will be more disarmed in future, sometime or the other. What am I to say about the processes leading to it?

Q: What do you think of the chances of coexistence and of possibility of lessening of world tension at this stage?

JN: The chances of coexistence in the long term are admirable and inevitable because there is no other way, unless of course, there is widespread international suicide. There is no middle way in the long term. In the short term, of course, one may follow conflicting policies. There is no alternative between coexistence and international conflict, and no doubt this would be progressively realized. Any attempt by a country to impose itself on another country gives rise to conflict. Therefore, coexistence implies non-interference in other countries, whether it is

Communist interference or any other. You will remember the so-called five principles of coexistence: recognition of independence; national independence; integrity of a country; non-aggression and non-interference. If that is accepted, then you will see that many of the present day problems will disappear, not every problem, but many of them disappear, and then nations exercise their influence on other nations, not by force, by coercion or by interference, but by argument, by persuasion, by example, that is a good way of exercising influence and this fear, terrible fear, which grips the world today disappears or lessens and the minds are opened out. Coexistence is not a novel phenomenon or a novel approach. I think, you will find in a large number of edicts of the Emperor Asoka in India 2300 years ago, a very fine analysis of coexistence between differing groups, differing religions, and differing opinions. 2300 years ago, they were inscribed by him on huge rocks which are still there for you to see.

Q: Going back to the Middle East situation, you said there was some improvement in the Middle East situation. Do you think this applies to the Algerian question also?

JN: No, I don't think so.

Q: Do you think there has been a deterioration?

JN: Well, I think, it is pretty bad, the Algerian situation.

7. Respect the Doctrine of Coexistence[1]

Mr President and respected members of this University,

You have done me the honour of making me also a graduate and member of this University today by conferring this degree. I am deeply grateful to you, Sir, and to the University for this honour. I wish I could speak to you in your own language, Japanese, but unfortunately I cannot do so and, therefore, I have to speak in a language, which is neither yours nor mine. I do not say so in any narrow spirit of language nationalism. It is well to know languages as many as possible, but it is true that while language is a bond, language also becomes a barrier.

---

1. Speech at Waseda University where an honorary degree of Doctor of Science was conferred on Nehru, 7 October 1957. *Journal of the Indo-Japanese Association of Japan*, Vol. 6, No. 1.

I have been here only for three or four days, in Japan, and I have seen a little bit of this famous country and wherever I have gone, I have received warm welcome. I come here and, naturally, I discuss many problems of importance with the leaders of your nation. But it is not so much to discuss problems that I came. That can be done by our ambassadors and by communications. I came here for two purposes. One was to gain that personal and intimate feeling of knowledge which comes from personal acquaintance and meeting a country or a people. The second was to convey to you and to the people of Japan not in mere words only, but perhaps in a deeper sense, our affection for your country and your people.

Many of you are students of the sciences and you have made your country great in science and technology and industry, and yet we all know that great and important as science, technology and industry are—and we in India are working for them—by themselves and unless balanced by other things of the spirit, they need not, may not, yield right results. We have seen in the world of today tremendous achievements of science and technology—magnificent advances, and we should be proud of them; but we have also seen these very advances sometimes turned into wrong directions of conflict, hatred and warfare.

So, something else is necessary, something which above all a university can give, something embodying the feeling of the spirit, something humanistic, something which frees our minds from narrowness and hatred. The world has grown because of science and technology and we all live next to each other today. I come from India to Tokyo in 20 hours and maybe after a few years I may come here in three or four hours. Quite likely, we are all each other's neighbours now and if we are all each other's neighbours, we can either live in cooperation and in friendship or quarrel and destroy each other. That is the fate of the world.

Now, how is one to get a proper balance? Because it is more important today than anything else, for nations, for peoples, to get that balance, to fit themselves in this world of high science and technology. Because unless you do so, science and technology will rather weigh with you and rather weigh with the world and run away with them into the deep abyss of common disaster. After all, who is to find the balance. Surely, that is the duty of the universities of the world, because it is people like you studying in vast numbers of the universities in the world who will shoulder tomorrow the burden of solving the problems of the world. You represent tomorrow, the tomorrow of Japan, as the young men of the universities of India represent the India of tomorrow.

Now if that is so, it becomes exceedingly important what this young generation in our universities is thinking, what urges it, in which way it is looking, how it is conditioning itself and moulding itself to face the problems of the age? They are difficult problems. When I wander about India, I look into the eyes of the boys and girls to try to find out what tomorrow's India will be like. That is more important to me than heavy books of scholars. So, this is the great problem and I do not pretend to know a solution of it. You and you will have to find a solution, and people like you in other countries. But I do know one thing that there can be no solution unless we bring in the ways of the spirit and find the solution, unless we develop a wide humanistic outlook, unless we realize that through hatred and violence there is no solution of any problem. They only add to problems and create conflict. So, it is by putting an end to hatred and violence and by developing the spirit of friendly cooperation that we might go towards a solution. And if we do not do that, the alternative is common disaster.

Now, I just said to you that I come to you bearing a message of affection to the people of Japan and whether I say so in words or not, because I feel that affection, you will also feel it. You learn scientific laws of cause and effect. You read that if something is done, something follow from it. That applies to human relationships and to national and international relationships also. If your approach to a human being is friendly and of affection, the response of that person will also be friendly and of affection. If the approach of a nation to another nation is friendly and affectionate, same response will come to it. That, I believe, is as much a law of science as the laws of Physics and Chemistry that you study. Therefore, we shall not find peace and the solution of our problems in this world by hatred because hatred will bring out the hatred from the opposite party, violence will bring violence from that party, and there is an unceasing cycle of hatred and violence. We have had wars, you have had wars and destruction and suffering.

So, I want to put this idea before you. It is not a novel idea. There is nothing very special about it. The great sages have told us that and all the advance in science and technology which we value greatly, which is very important, does not make this basic law any less valuable. In fact, in this atomic age of ours, this is even more important than ever before, because we seek today, we have to choose today, the path we follow. And the paths have been very clearly defined. There are no middle ways. One is the path of peace, and the other of conflict and warfare. If it is the path of peace that you follow, as you must, then you must also think in terms of peace. It is not just enough to shout slogans of peace. You must think in a friendly way even of those who oppose you, even of those who think badly of you. That is the lesson that my great leader, Mahatma Gandhi taught us. I do not know if we have learnt the lesson because we are small folk and he was a great man. But at any rate, we learnt something of it. At any rate,

2. Earlier in the day, an honorary degree of Doctor of Law was conferred on Nehru by the Keio University.

in our limited and imperfect way we try to follow it. We often blunder and make mistakes, but whether we make mistakes or not, I am convinced that it is by following that path only that the world will prosper.

I remember we talked of coexistence. In India, we have all over the country great monuments, great stone pillars, on which are inscriptions carved 2300 years ago by the Emperor Asoka, a great Buddhist Emperor. And if you read those inscriptions today, 2000 years after, the original inscriptions on the original rock, you find the doctrine of coexistence there. You find the doctrine of respecting the opinion of the other, respecting the religion of the other, and of toleration. It is an old and wise lesson that came to the world.

Among other things that abound India and Japan has been another message, a great message which came from India to Japan, the message of the Buddha. I am not speaking in terms of religion as such, but rather the message of peace and compassion that came here and to other parts of the world. I do believe that in the present age, we cannot meet the hydrogen bomb by any other way except something quite different from that, not by a bigger bomb, but something which brings in this bomb of the spirit, if I may call it, which was the old message of compassion.

I ventured to say a few words to you of what I had in mind, because among you are the future leaders of this country and you will have great problems to solve.

I am grateful to you, Mr President, for this great honour that you have done me and I wish you all well.

8. *Panchsheel*—the Only Choice[1]

Mr Prime Minister, Mr Governor,[2] distinguished members of the Reception Committee, ladies and gentlemen,

I am greatly moved by the kind words that have been said and by this great gathering of welcome. I came to Japan not only to fulfil the long-felt wish of mine, not only to find out what this great nation and its great people are thinking

1. Speech at a civic reception jointly organized by the Tokyo Metropolitan Government, various political parties, and social and cultural organizations of Japan. Metropolitan Gymnasium, Tokyo, 8 October 1957. *Journal of the Indo-Japanese Association of Japan*, Vol. 6 No. 1.

2. Seichiro Yasui, Governor of Tokyo Metropolis.

and doing today, but also to bring the message from the Indian people as a whole to the people of Japan. This gathering, I am told, is under the auspices, joint auspices, of a number of parties and groups here in Japan. It is not confined to one party, it is a national gathering. May I say that if I come here today from India, I come certainly as the Prime Minister of India and as one associated with a great party in India. But I come not merely as that but also in this respect, at any rate, as the representative of every party and group in India, bringing to you, and to all the people of Japan, the affectionate regards and greetings of all our people. I am sure that when my people learn of the great kindness that you have shown to me, they will realize that it was not to me, as a mere individual, but to them, to India, to the people of India and they will also be greatly moved by it. So, I am grateful to you. It is a little difficult to express in words one's feelings on such occasions.

I knew that the Japanese people were able and clever. But, if I may say so, that impression has been confirmed by the way they have treated me. I came here to learn, not to preach or to teach or to say much, because, I believe, we have to learn much from the experience of Japan. But here I find myself repeatedly put in a position of speaking instead of learning, that is why I say that in the warmth of your affection, you have maneuvered me into a wrong position. But I cannot say no to this because it comes from your affection.

Reference has been made by the Prime Minister and the Governor, to the past, to the distant past and to the recent past. It is true that there have been bonds chiefly through the message of the Buddha for long ages past between India and Japan. For a long period those contacts were not direct but rather indirect. And then came a long period when the contacts between Asian countries were interrupted and almost put an end to by the coming of Europe into Asia. Now that independence has come to most of the countries of Asia including my country, we are naturally anxious to look at our neighbours and friends of old, to think again of those thoughts that brought us together in the past, to renew old connections between countries that have had common experiences. It is true that we are different from the Japanese people or the Chinese people or many other people in Asia. Each of our countries has a definite individuality, a past, a special culture. We have grown up and we have been conditioned by hundreds and thousands of years of history. That is true. But it is also true that we have much in common. That this very process of conditioning of thousands of years has moulded us to some extent in the same way. So, while we differ as nations differ, we also have a great deal in common and, in the present, certainly there are many things that draw us together and should induce us to cooperate for our mutual advantage as well as for the advantage of the causes, wider causes that we have at heart in Asia or in the world.

You asked me to talk to you not about, I suppose, just a few pleasantries, not merely expressions of my goodwill which I feel, but to talk to you about matters of importance which affect us in the world today. But then what am I to talk to you; because I am a learner myself, a seeker and a searcher for the right path and often, even in my own country, which I know better than other countries, I am not sure what we should do and what we should not do. How then am I to tell others, how then am I to be presumptuous enough to tell others what they should do? I do not propose to do so. Long years ago, I wrote a book called the *Discovery of India* and I said in that book that I was trying to find out what India was and is and I was constantly discovering new facets in India in the past and in the present and the more I saw, the more I felt that I did not know India very well. For we, like you, like many other races in Asia, have a vast racial inheritance, a tremendous background of history which has built us up and it is not easy to delve into that background and to understand it. So, as I approach my own country, India, its past, and its present, with a certain reverence, with a certain mystery, I also approach other great countries with long past with a reverence at the mystery of their build-up through thousands of years. I do not presume, therefore, to tell you what you should do, and I do not often know what I should do. All I seek from time to time is guidance from myself as well as others, as to decide what the general approach should be so as to avoid the wrong thing even if I am not sure of the right thing. And sometimes, often enough, when I am in grave doubt, I think of my master and leader, Mahatma Gandhi, and try to pick up courage from his thought and try to see what I should do, and sometimes my mind goes back much further to the message of the Buddha whose 2500th birth anniversary was celebrated last year. And sometimes I think of the greatly treasured volume in India, which has influenced generations in India of 2000 years or more, i.e., the *Bhagvad Gita*. I am not a religious man, I am afraid, but I do value much of the wisdom that our ancients possessed in my country or in other countries. For, after all, even though we may have failed as we have often failed in history in different countries, we have also survived these thousands of years and shown a certain stability, a certain equillibrium, a certain maturity of thought and a certain wisdom. We are not newcomers in the world—newcomers in the field of history or action. We are old hands—old actors in this stage of the world. But I know that we have often failed and I know that in the course of history although we have imbibed much that is good, we have also collected much that is burdensome and bad. So, we have to distinguish between these two; keep the good and get rid of the bad.

You know how during the last two or three hundred years, some of the countries of Europe, because of science and technology, went ahead, and the countries of Asia became passive, if I may use the word 'decadent' or non-progressive. Japan was the first country in Asia which shook itself out of this and went ahead on the path of science and technology. From the beginning of this century, Japan exercised a great influence on the countries of Asia. It became an example to be admired and to be followed in so far as possible.

In later years, if you will permit me to be frank, various countries in Asia did not like much of what was being done by Japan. Their admiration became tampered by other feelings, because to them Japan not only represented great capacity and ability, because not only did they admire the tremendous progress that Japan had made within a relatively short period, but they began to sense also that Japan was exhibiting the pride of power—the pride of a great nation which sensed its own strength and, to some extent, wanted to impose its strength on others. So, the feelings about Japan became rather mixed in other countries of Asia. But even so, they admired its great capacity and the way it had faced and solved many difficult problems.

You know all this and I am saying nothing new. You have experienced even during this present generation great trials and grave disasters, and people learn more from personal experience than all the teaching in schools and universities. You have gone through the hard school of personal experience and now you face, as we face, the world today as it is. Do you not feel that it is most important for you and for us and for other countries of Asia to catch up to the countries of Europe in science and technology, to raise the living standards of our people, and to give them some happiness and contentment? All that certainly. But also not to follow a mere past of technological advance, good as that is, but to have some moral standards, some tiny spiritual standards, some moral disciplines, and some inner concepts to our national lives. The world today is an example of magnificent progress. Well, as you read only two or three days ago satellite moons are created[2] and all kinds of new things are taking place from day to day. So, the world is an example of tremendous and magnificent achievement. The world is also an example today of tremendous and dismal failure, both at the same time—great advance in the physical, technological and scientific domain, and great failure in the moral, mental and spiritual domain. There is a big gap between the two and all our search for peace etc., fails because of this big gap, this big gulf, which has not been bridged so far. When we search for peace or talk about peace, it is not just a word—it is not just a slogan, which is sometimes hurled by one party at another. It is a deep conviction, a deep feeling, which has both its practical side of saving the world from disaster and its moral and spiritual side of saving the world from inner decay. Because nations and societies may sometimes be conquered by another country, more powerful, but in effect it might be said that countries fall not because of external forces but because of

2. The USSR had launched the first artificial earth satellite on 4 October 1957.

inner decay. If Asian countries fell in the past, it was because of inner decay, not because of Europe's power. We became pious, passive and static and if we are to rise again, it will be because we recovered from the inner decay, as we are recovering today in Asia. We are recovering, certainly, but at the same time not in Asia only but all over the world, there is this dangerous moral stupor, this dangerous acceptance of even the horrors of the atomic bomb or the hydrogen bomb about which the people of Japan know more by experience than any other. So, when we talk of peace, it is not a question of finding some resolution or formula. We may find it in the UN. When we talk of disarmament, we look for a formula to satisfy. It has to be done. When we talk about the stopping of nuclear experiments or banning nuclear warfare, it is not a question of balancing two forces and two armies or two groups of countries. It is something much deeper than that which is the world's ill. It is something absolutely and completely opposed to that mentality which produces cold war. Out of cold war, peace or goodness will never come. Because the cold war itself is a war of hatred. How can anything come out of hatred—out of an approach of hatred. Sometimes, I feel that even shooting war is better than cold war. At any rate, your hatred is out of you—you hit out; but this nursing the hatred in your hearts, and becoming angrier and angrier, and becoming more and more full of violence and hatred, it degrades the individual, it degrades the social rule, it degrades the nation. Therefore, this call for disarmament, this call for peace, this call for the stoppage of this horror of nuclear explosions is not only something that is absolutely necessary to save the world from disaster but it is something deeper than that which is a call ultimately to the conscience of the human race, to the minds of the human race, to all that civilization has sought to build up through thousands of years of so-called progress of humanity. It is all that and if humanity is not prepared to listen to that call, if it is prepared to forget the lessons of thousands of years of civilization and if it is prepared not to take heed to all the great sages and prophets and wise men of old or of the modern age, then all that one can say is that humanity is beyond redemption.

It has always struck me as an amazing contradiction that on the one hand we make this tremendous scientific and technological progress. On the other hand our political forms, our political theories, do not keep pace with it. We have various parties. I am not referring to your parties in Japan. I know nothing about them. But there are so-called capitalist countries, socialist countries, communist countries and various parties with various labels. I suppose that all these parties or all these theories have something worthwhile in them. But I have a strong feeling and I say so with all respect that all these various 'isms', whether it is capitalism or socialism or communism, are in the world of today rather out of date. Certainly, some of their principles are right. I call myself a socialist and I try to build up a socialist pattern of society in India; but when I say I am socialist, I am not a doctrinaire socialist. I follow nobody's strict or rigid theory. I want equality in India. I want equal opportunity for everybody. I do not want concentration of power, political or economic and I progress by trial and error, without tying myself up to any theory, any doctrine, whether religious or political or economic in that rigid way, certainly keeping principles in view—because principles do not change. So, I am a little surprised sometimes at the fears, conflicts and theories that are advanced today, which have little application to this world of atomic energy and ballistic weapons and artificial moons. The fact is that our thinking, our political thinking, has been left far behind by our scientific advance—and we have to catch up to them. And we have to approach all our political and economic problems from this point of view of this new world, this new atomic energy world, this new world where you can stretch out your hands possibly to the outer space, and to planets, and stars. It is a new world completely. We are not used to it and we go on thinking in our narrow ways and in our narrow concepts and 'isms' and this and that. I do not know what the new thinking should be, but I do know partly what it should not be. The new thinking cannot be based on violence because the moment you think of violence it is all destructive today and destroys the world. The new thinking even cannot be very much narrowly nationalistic. A nation becomes too small in the world of today. Of course, a nation has importance, a nation has a certain individuality and life, which is precious, but if it isolates itself and thinks of itself only and thinks the rest of the world as hostile to it, then it does not do any service to itself or to the rest of the world, for we are gradually approaching the idea of one world.

Therefore, I would like you to think of this. How backward our political thinking has become and many of our parties and many of our 'isms'. Some parties calling themselves very revolutionary, appear to me very reactionary, because violence is the most reactionary thing today. Any person who thinks or talks in terms of violence is utterly and absolutely reactionary. Therefore, we have to think in other terms, in terms of peace, in terms of cooperation and I will submit for your consideration that the only basis today for international relations is what has sometimes been called the five principles or the *Panchsheel*. What are those five principles? (1) recognition of the freedom, (2) sovereignty and integrity of a country; (3) non-aggression of one country over another; (4) non-interference of one country into the affairs of another country; and (5) mutual respect and peaceful coexistence. There is no other way. You have to choose in the world today as it is, in the atomic energy age, coexistence between nations even though they do not agree with each other or the alternative is conflict and complete destruction. There is no choice left. So, I earnestly trust that all of us will try to take ourselves out of the old ruts of thought—of the old theories of political action and try to think in terms of this new world which science and technology are building up. If we do not think rightly and control this new world, this terrible machine will kill us and destroy the world. That is the problem before us.

Anyhow so far as we are concerned in India, we do not claim to be wiser than others; we do not claim to be better than others. We are full of failings but we try our best to serve the cause of peace and cooperation. And I am here to offer you my hand of friendship and affection on behalf of our people.

Mr Prime Minister, Mr Governor, distinguished members of the National Committee, ladies and gentlemen, I thank you again for your gracious and cordial welcome.

9. Talks with Nobusuke Kishi—III[1]

Prime Minister Nehru and the Japanese Premier, Mr Kishi conferred on economic matters, for the first time in the present series of talks for over an hour and half today.

The talks, which were stated to be of a general nature, were held after dinner at the Indian Embassy here. No specific decisions were reached.

Apart from economic subjects discussed today the two Premiers dealt with resolutions now before the United Nations General Assembly on banning of nuclear tests.

Economic subjects discussed tonight included increased supply of iron ore by India to Japan and supply by Japan to India of equipment for mining, transport and development of port facilities, on deferred payment basis.

Supply of textile machinery, rolling stock and other equipment by Japan to India on the same basis was also discussed.

Other subjects discussed were: conclusion of a trade agreement between India and Japan, withdrawal of application of Article 35 of GATT (General Agreement on Tariffs and Trade), return of pre-war Japanese property in India, compensation for damage to Indian property in Japan, the Japanese proposal for establishment of an Asian Development Fund and Japan's offer to establish technical training centres in India.

The talks are likely to be continued in the next few days.

1. Report of talks between Nehru and Nobusuke Kishi, Tokyo, 8 October 1957. From *The Hindu*, 10 October 1957. No official record of the talks is available.

10. Hiroshima—the Indomitable Spirit of Man[1]

Mr Mayor[2] and the citizens of Hiroshima,

I am deeply moved, standing here on this platform at a spot which has become famous and historical. As I stand here the past comes before me and also all that has intervened in these last twelve years.

Coming here, I feel that I have come on a pilgrimage to a spot which represents many things not only to me but to men and women all over the world. It represents the end of an age and the beginning of another. It represents the ultimate violence that can take place. It represents also the hope of resurrection which has taken place.

Here, where twelve years ago was created a desolate waste, and death and destruction surrounded this area. This new city of Hiroshima has sprung up and all you citizens, men and women and children of Hiroshima, have built this and are living your lives and demonstrating that you can rise above every kind of disaster.

That day of August 1945, put an end to an age in human history and we started this new age with a very terrific bang which resounded all over the world. And now we are in the atomic age, as it is called; and you and I and vast numbers of people in the world wonder whether this atomic age is going to lead to peace and plenty for humanity, or to utter disaster.

You, Mr Mayor, have spoken about your wish and the wishes of the people of Hiroshima and Japan in regard to this atomic warfare and atomic test explosions. You have expressed the hope that these explosions will be put an end to, and that the terrible scourge and fear of warfare with atomic weapons will also be banned and ended. I entirely agree with that hope and I am quite sure that vast numbers of people in every country agree with that, because they have not only seen or heard the horror of the bomb that fell here, but ever since then greater horrors appear to be in store for humanity unless humanity has the wisdom to control them. Let us hope that this heartfelt wish of humanity all over the world will be fulfilled. Let us hope that the great statesmen who are considering these matters today in the United Nations and I am sure, all of them, want to find a way out of this terrible deadlock, that they will succeed in finding this way out

---

1. Speech at a public meeting, Hiroshima, 9 October 1957. AIR tapes, NMML. Also available in the *Journal of the Indo-Japanese Association of Japan*, Vol. 6, No. 1.
2. Mayor Watanabe of Hiroshima.

and remove this terrible fear of this new kind of warfare involving atomic and hydrogen bombs, and to remove this from the face of the earth.

Remember that in this matter you do not stand alone. The people of every country agree with you about banning and putting an end to this warfare—this new type of terrible warfare. But unfortunately, fear comes in the way, fear of each other, and fear is a terrible companion, and fear makes us do many things which we do not want to do. So, we must try to get rid of this fear all over the world and create conditions in which countries are not afraid of each other.

Let us hope, therefore, that not only these atomic explosions and atomic warfare but all kinds of warfare will be put an end to, so that there will be effective disarmament, so that the people of every country may live free from fear, live in freedom and live without an apprehension of other people's aggression or interference, and in this way cooperate with each other and build up one world which lives together in friendship and cooperation.

Those who have great power, have great responsibilities, because if that power is misused or not used rightly, then it brings dire results. If used rightly, then it helps mankind to progress. We have seen in the past centuries—history tells us—how countries in great power became proud of their power and used their power sometimes badly. If you do something badly, whether as an individual or as a nation, the results are bound to be bad and the consequences are bad. We have seen the evil consequences of violence, of war, of pride and of power. We suffer from them today. Let us hope that in future, countries will bear their responsibility in the right way and their power will be used to benefit mankind.

The past is over. Let us not think too much of the past or evil and fear and horror and destruction. Let us rather think of the future. When I see here, in this city of Hiroshima, large numbers of bright young faces of boys and girls and children, it is the future I think of. Not only here, but the future of the world with all these bright children going to school, training themselves. Let us build up a future where they can live in peace and happiness and not be tortured by hatred and violence for each other or for each other's nation.

The answer to the atom bomb, or the hydrogen bomb is not a bigger atomic bomb, or a bigger hydrogen bomb. You have to seek some other kind of answer. The world today has to choose between the two paths, the path of ever greater violence, symbolized by the nuclear bombs, or the path of peace and compassion, symbolized by the message of the Buddha.

The Mayor has presented me with a precious gift, the key to Hiroshima. May that key prove a key to the hearts of people all over the world, moving them to compassion, moving them to discard fear and to live in friendship and cooperation with each other.

I am grateful to all of you, men and women and children, for your affectionate

AT HIROSHIMA PEACE MEMORIAL MUSEUM, 9 OCTOBER 1957

INSPECTING A WIRE FACTORY OF METAL INDUSTRY COMPANY IN OSAKA, 10 OCTOBER 1957

welcome. I shall carry back this memory with me to my own country, and tell my people there of this city of Hiroshima which suffered so terribly and which has revived so brilliantly. That shall be a proof and a witness to them of the indomitable spirit of man which survives every disaster and goes forward. And so, I must bid you goodbye now and wish you well. *Sayonara!*

11. India on the Path to Progress[1]

Sisters and brothers,
I have had the desire to visit Japan for a long time for various reasons, and I feel a sense of wonder that I have been able to make it at last.

As you know, in the olden days, India had very close links with China and Japan and other countries in this region. The people of India in those days were full of vitality and a spirit of adventure. Then came a time when we lost that vitality and began to be afraid to set foot outside the country. A strange feeling developed that foreign travel was against the tenets of our religion. All our time and energy were wasted in kitchen rituals and taboos. The result was that the world advanced and we remained stagnant. So, it was quite obvious that downfall was inevitable in the circumstances. How could there be progress when we were so wholly absorbed in kitchen rituals and failed to take notice of what was going on in the world?

Anyhow, we were enslaved and so we fought for our freedom. India acquired a new vitality under the leadership of Mahatma Gandhi and we became free. India became independent by coming to an agreement with the British. But you must bear in mind the fact that the agreement took place at a time when it had become quite impossible for British rule in India to continue. There was no question of being beholden to anybody. The circumstances demanded it.

Well, once India became free another kind of problems confronted us, difficult problems, more complex than the ones we had faced earlier. We were faced with the task of governing this vast country not in the manner that the British did for the benefit of a handful but to ensure the progress of 36-37 crores of human beings, to reduce their burden and hardship and poverty. It is an enormous

---

1. Speech at a reception given in his honour by the Indian Community, Kobe, 9 October 1957. AIR tapes, NMML. Original in Hindi.

problem to uplift 36-37 crores of human beings. As you know, we have drawn up the Five Year Plans to tackle this problem. The First Five Year Plan is over and the Second Plan is going on. There is no doubt about it that we succeeded to a very large extent with the First Plan. But it is not enough because we want to achieve in ten or fifteen years what the West has achieved in 200 years or more. We cannot wait for 200 years to reach that position. Rapid progress implies a courageous bid to shoulder great burdens. We cannot achieve our goals by counting beads or consulting astrologers. It is only the good for nothing who believe in astrologers. A nation, a race grows by hard work, its intelligence and unity.

You have been living in Japan for a long time. You know better than me their qualities and defects. Every nation has its good points as well as bad. But we must always pay attention to the good qualities of other nations and to our own shortcomings. Very often it is the other way round which is not right. We must learn from the good points in others and try to get rid of our weaknesses. There is no doubt about it that there are many good qualities in the Japanese. For one thing, they have been able to achieve great progress in their country very rapidly. They have some shortcomings too. They have been punished for becoming steeped in pride because of their progress and the desire for domination that they developed. They suffered a terrible defeat in the Second World War and underwent an ordeal never suffered by any country before or since. The first atom bombs were dropped on two Japanese cities, Hiroshima and Nagasaki. I visited Hiroshima today.

Anyhow, Japan suffered a great deal as a consequence of their pride in the progress that they had made and their desire for domination. Ultimately, they entered the Second World War and were defeated. But what is praiseworthy is that they were not crushed by the misfortunes that befell them. Their country lay in ruins and yet they were undaunted. They began the process of rebuilding and you can see how prosperous Japan is within ten years or so. It is indeed praiseworthy. The true test of an individual or a nation is their behaviour in the face of adversity. Anyone can behave with equanimity when there is no crisis. It is only when danger threatens that a nation's mettle can be tested, whether it faces the crisis squarely, unflinchingly or gives way to fear and panic. There is no doubt about it that the Japanese have shown that they can weather any crisis and come out with flying colours. We can learn a great deal from this.

We are prepared to learn from everyone. But that does not mean that we should lose our identity in the process or become a carbon copy of someone else. We will be nowhere then. We must learn from others but remain firmly rooted in our own soil. If we lose our moorings, there is no salvation for us. It is true that the peoples of the world are becoming alike in many respects because travel and communication have become simpler and they learn from one another. It is a good thing that the world is becoming similar.

What is India's role in this modern world? It is a great testing time for us and the eyes of the world are upon us. Why is India held in great respect in the world today? It is because the manner in which we won freedom under the leadership of Mahatma Gandhi made a tremendous impact on the world. The sacrifices and the courage of millions of human beings made an indelible impression upon the world. We succeeded in the great task that we had taken up and the world began to realize that the path shown by Gandhiji had a strength of its own.

Anyhow, the world respects us for various reasons. One because of Gandhiji and two, for the manner in which we have dealt with the problems which descended on us after Independence. As you know, North India was rocked by violence and chaos in the wake of Partition. We agreed to Partition because we wanted to put an end to this long-standing quarrel and somehow get freedom. We agreed to it, rightly or wrongly and we want Pakistan to be happy. It is our neighbour. Unfortunately, there have been tensions between India and Pakistan ever since. Millions of people crossed over from one side to the other after Partition. This was in 1947-48, but even now refugees continue to pour into India from East Pakistan. Do you know that in the first few months after Partition, about 50 or 60 lakh people crossed over from one side to the other. So far 40 lakh have come in from East Pakistan alone. It is a great burden upon us to look after them, to provide homes and jobs and rehabilitate them. Most of them are Bengalis.

Well, we faced these complex problems of refugees, food shortage and a thousands and one difficulties squarely and gradually overcame them. The First Five Year Plan came to an end and we achieved all the targets that we had set for ourselves. It made for greater strength because when a nation takes a pledge to do something and fulfils it, it increases its self-confidence. As a matter of fact, the real strength of a nation lies not in gold and silver which are tools of trade, but in its courage, determination and self-confidence. Money is essential and without it there are obstacles in the way. But ultimately, it is human beings who produce wealth by their strength, skill, hard work and intelligence.

So, our self-confidence grew. Then we started on the Second Five Year Plan which is bigger, more ambitious than the First and casts a greater burden upon the country. In a sense it is a symbol of our progress. We are mid-way through the Second Plan. You may have heard about the difficulties that are cropping up. These difficulties are a sign of growth and development, not born out of our weaknesses or lack of courage. The problem is that we are progressing very rapidly and the resources are limited. There is a difficulty about foreign exchange which again arises because of the pace of our progress. In a sense such problems

587

are welcome though we have to face them today. As you know, efforts are being made to get over this crisis and there is no doubt about it that we shall overcome the problem. A nation is not so easily defeated. But I want you to understand that we are facing extremely complex problems in India today. The rest of the world looks on with great interest as to how we fare, how quickly we progress, and whether we will succeed or fail in our efforts. Then there are others who do not like India's successes. We have no enmity towards anyone. But there are some countries in the world which do not like the fact that India has progressed very rapidly in the last few years.

Well, we cannot help that. What can we do except to make an effort to be friendly towards all the countries? So much so that even with Pakistan we want to maintain friendly relations even though there are tensions between the two countries. After all, India and Pakistan are neighbours and must have cordial relations with each other. We cannot escape geographic contiguity. Why should there be any quarrel?

It will be our effort now and in the future, to be friendly towards Pakistan. But India is held in great respect elsewhere because people see what we are doing. India's stature has gone up in the world because of the successes that we have achieved in the last few years. The world has begun to realize that a great country has entered the world stage and will soon be a force to be reckoned with. There are many independent countries on the map. But not all of them are truly independent. However, people have realized that if not today, 10 or 15 years hence, India will without doubt become powerful and the masses in India will become prosperous which is bound to affect various international issues. India is held in respect because of what we are trying to do. I cannot go to other countries and forcibly demand respect. India has to show strength and determination. I cannot enhance India's stature by my visits abroad or by making speeches. Everything depends on the rapidity with which we progress.

I am very happy to meet all of you here. Your problems must be solved. But you must always bear in mind the need to enhance India's prestige and your own by your behaviour. You are India's ambassadors apart from those who work in the Indian Embassy and represent the country formally. But the fact of the matter is that every Indian—man, woman and child—who lives here is in a sense India's ambassador. Their actions will bring honour or disrepute to India. If you behave badly in India it is bad but it gets concealed to a large extent. Here in a foreign country, even the slightest misdemeanour comes under the glare of publicity. Therefore, all Indians who live in other countries, must always keep in mind the need to behave with decorum as the ambassadors of India. Every action of yours will be judged by the people of this country.

You must be loyal to the country in which you are guests, not indulge in malpractices for personal benefits. That would annoy the host country and think badly of us. All this is no doubt true. But your ultimate loyalty is to India. You must not forget that. No matter which corner of the globe you may be in, you must remember that you must strive to serve India's interest in any way that you can. One way in which you can do this is to set an example by your conduct. It is not difficult. I have often found that wherever Indians live, they form separate cliques and groups and do not live in unity. There are groups of Punjabis, Gujaratis, Marathis, Bengalis and others, all living like frogs in a well forgetting that India is not a well but a vast ocean. We have no use for frogs any more. We need animals of higher quality.

You will find that the Japanese, English, Germans, Chinese and others live as cohesive groups wherever they are. I do not know why we Indians have the unfortunate tendency towards sectarianism and disunity. It is partly due to the caste system and other reasons. But we must get rid of anything which acts as an obstacle to India's progress and unity.

This should be our first priority. Then the next thing is for you to think in what way you can serve India. You can consult our Ambassador and others about this because you ought to do something. For one thing, it is your duty. Secondly, if you do your bit by contributing money or in some other way, it will create a feeling of participation in the great task of nation-building. You stand to gain and India will also benefit in the process. You must explain to your children what is happening in India at the moment. After all, whatever we are doing today is for the future generations. We want that by the time our children grow up, India should have advanced very far. I want you to pay attention to all these things.

I want to say a few words about Netaji Subhash Chandra Bose. I shall go back to Tokyo today and then perhaps the day after tomorrow or so, I shall visit the Renkoji Temple where his ashes are kept. This is a tradition. As you know, Subhash Chandra Bose was my comrade for a number of years and our relationship was like that of brothers. We were very fond of each other and India had great hopes from him. It is true that we had differences of opinion. But that did not diminish our confidence in each other and mutual affection. We had some differences of opinion and the fact of the matter is that in those days we were often in jail. He established the Indian National Army which was a different path from the one which Gandhiji wanted to follow. I am not complaining, merely pointing out what happened. Yet our love and admiration for him were in no way affected. He was a brave hero and earned great fame. He has set an example which will be remembered forever.

Well, I am referring to him in particular here because he had close links with Japan in the days of the Second World War and ultimately by a strange coincidence he even died in an air crash in the Japanese skies. So ended the life of a great Indian of whom India had great hopes and who had fought bravely in the cause of freedom, in the prime of his youth.

Well, I have come to Japan for the first time. The welcome accorded to me by the people of Japan has overwhelmed me. I have seldom come across such spontaneous affection. I consider it my good fortune that wherever I go, the people welcome me with great affection as the Japanese have done. When I went to Hiroshima today, the spectacle of love that I witnessed there has made an indelible impression upon me. I hope that the bond between the two countries will grow stronger. That does not mean that we should always agree with one another. We are two independent countries with different perceptions. But so long as there is mutual trust and respect, a great deal can be achieved.

I feel that my visit to Japan would help in strengthening the bond between us. You can help us in various ways. I have come to Kobe specially at your invitation. I came to Japan because a large number of Indians are settled here. I did not come to see Kobe but to have the opportunity of meeting the Indian community, I am happy about that and thank you. I want you to remember that every one of you—man, woman and child—are soldiers of India and so you must behave with decorum and discipline as befits a soldier and serve our country. *Jai Hind!*

12. Cable to V.K. Krishna Menon[1]

We have had repeated and prolonged talks with Japanese Ministers about nuclear test explosions and disarmament. They are anxious that Japan and India should cooperate as far as possible in this matter in UN and are instructing their representative to keep in close touch with you. Please maintain contacts with him.

Obvious that Japan wants suspension or ending of test explosions but are anxious not to offend United States as far as possible.[2] Also they do not wish to line up with Soviet resolution in opposition to Western Powers.

I told them that it would be easy enough for India and Japan to agree but the question was of the party concerned agreeing. Our efforts were to get some

1. Tokyo, 9 October 1957. JN Collection.
2. See *post,* p. 739.

kind of agreement which would be effective. We were not tied down to any form of words but we were certainly anxious to stop nuclear test explosions as well as to make some progress about disarmament generally. If Nuclear Powers agree to any effective proposal we would be happy to agree also. We have no desire to put forward proposals for propagandist purposes or to support any such proposals. It would serve little purpose for resolutions to be put forward in General Assembly without some such agreement.

As Japan is rather specially concerned in regard to test explosions it would be desirable for us to cooperate with her in this matter.

Would it be advisable to suggest suspension of test explosions without mentioning period but asking for report at next year's General Assembly? In addition to this, of course, other proposals about Technical Committee etc., could be made.

Leaving Tokyo for three days. We are meeting Japanese Prime Minister again on the 12th and 13th. Would like to have your appraisal of situation by then.

13. So Much to Learn from Japan[1]

Mr Governor, Mr Mayor and Mr President of the Osaka Chamber of Commerce and Industry,

You have deeply honoured me by this joint function in this famous city of Osaka. I arrived here about two hours ago and I shall be leaving soon. My visit is, therefore, very brief but the visit has been highlighted and made memorable to me by meeting and seeing so many of the distinguished citizens of Osaka. You have rightly said, Sir, that this city of Osaka has been famous for a long time for the commerce and industry and for a long time also, it has had ties with India. Indeed, I suppose, that I have at least heard of Osaka from my boyhood. I may not have known many other cities in Japan, but Tokyo and Osaka have been known to me from boyhood.

You have mentioned Mr Governor, that my coming to Japan is for the message of friendship, of a mission of friendship. That is so of course. Nevertheless, why have I come to Japan? Well, many things have brought me here. My long-felt

1. Speech at the luncheon by the Governor of Osaka, the Mayor of Osaka and the Osaka Chamber of Commerce, Osaka, 10 October 1957. AIR tapes, NMML. Also available in the *Journal of the Indo-Japanese Association of Japan*, Vol. 6 No. 1.

desire to see Japan and meet people here, to form some personal impression of a country about which I had heard a great deal. That would have been enough to bring me here, but apart from that, I am anxious, if I may say so, to feel well the spirit of Japan. The present spirit of Japan is something, we cannot read about, is something you can feel if you are receptive to feelings.

Naturally, I am interested in the industrial Japan, in the big industries, in the middle industries and in the small industries of Japan—all of them. Because we are facing big problems in India, in trying to industrialize India at all levels, heavy industry, medium industry and small-scale and even cottage industry. So, we are deeply interested in what has been done and is being done in Japan and we feel that we can learn a great deal from Japan by long experience, and by contacts and cooperation with the Japanese people.

That is so, but as I said, I am even more interested in trying to find out what is happenning in the minds or the hearts of the people of a country. To find out, something of the sources of the tremendous vitality of the Japanese people. Not only in Japan but I have been to other countries in Europe, in America and Asia, trying to sense the spirit of the people there. I am interested, of course, in the great accomplishments of modern civilization. That is important and essential, but even more I am interested in the mind and spirit that lies behind it.

In travelling in these various countries of Europe or America and Asia, I have found a tremendous fund of goodwill not for me only, but generally. And I have found how exaggerated is what we read so much about, about international conflicts, people being angry with each other, of course, they are angry sometimes of course, they differ, but people basically in all the countries I have visited are full of goodwill; they do not live in an atmosphere of hatred and ill will. And because of this my faith in the future of humanity has risen high. It is true that we have grave problems to face in the world, grave difficulties, hostilities, conflicts and all that. But behind that all, I think, is a basic common sense of the people in every country, a basic fund of goodwill in every country, which, I think, will survive and win in the end, and then help in solving our world's problems.

We in India do not presume to offer solutions for any problems for others, we do not presume to offer advice to others or to judge others. We try as far as possible, to find out what our own failings are and try to remedy them. If we succeed in removing our own failings we have done some service not only to ourselves but to the world also.

So, please do not imagine that I go to other countries or come here with any presumptuous intent or telling others what to do in international affairs. I have no such intention. I come here to learn, to understand, to learn many things which we can learn from other countries. If our country has any kind of thing, which is worthwhile for others to learn, well, that is if they take interest in it, well and good. It is not for me to try to find out, to put across if I may say so, the ideas of our country. If they are interesting, others will try to be interested in them, but my special object is to learn and my country's special object also is to learn from others.

So, our approach to every country is an approach of friendship, even though we differ from it. I do not see why, people or countries who differ from each other should not have friendly feelings for each other. We learnt a great deal from our long association with England, although association was not a normal or a happy one—still we learnt much. We are learning a great deal of that country, of the magnificent achievements of United States of America, which is in many ways a leader in science, in industrial techniques and many other things. We have sought to learn even from the Soviet Union, as to how they have made progress rapidly. We do not agree with their policies, but it is to learn from others and seek to be friendly to them as to other countries.

So, that is our general approach. But, we are specially interested in learning from Japan and the Japanese people because to some extent, we are passing through phases which have already been traversed by Japan. Also in trying to understand how Japan and her people have balanced or tried to balance the industrialization of their country with their old culture. Inevitably, India is becoming and will become more and more industrialized but we do not want to become industrialized at the expense of our culture and our soul, we want to have both, if that is possible. A country today cannot exist, cannot prosper, without adopting the ways of science and technology. At the same time, if a country and a people is uprooted from its own culture, then it becomes rootless and cannot do much good. This applies to every country, but more specially to countries with a long and ancient past and long histories like India or Japan. We have our roots deep down into the past and if we simply cut them off or dig them out and throw them away, then we may adopt science and technology, but the creative spirit will gradually go and we will not have much branch and flower in our trees.

Each individual has a certain individuality. We value individuality and the individual, just as we value the freedom of the individual. In the same way, each nation has a certain individuality. We value that individuality. That does not mean that that nation should be hostile to another nation but each should develop itself according to its own genius and in cooperation with other nations. While this is so, it is also true, that in the modern world, communications have become so frequent and so fast; trade, commerce and so many other things bring us nearer to each other, that we move gradually to many common undertakings,

2. Nehru was elected Chairman of the Allahabad Municipal Board on 4 April 1923. For documents of that period see *Selected Works* (first series), Vol. 2, pp. 1-78.

common activities and ultimately to the idea of the one world. So, when I speak of the individuality of a nation, I do not mean a nation living in isolation or cut off from others but living in cooperation with others and gradually helping in the development of one world.

So, however, brief my stay might be in the city of Osaka or in Japan, I shall carry away with me many vivid impressions. I shall learn many things not so much what an expert may learn about industrial techniques. That is for others to learn. But, I think, I should learn something about the character and spirit of Japanese people, which is ultimately more important. And jsut as I have brought with me from India a message of affection and goodwill for the people of Japan, I hope, I shall carry away with me some of your affection. That is a surer basis of cooperation between peoples and Governments than formal documents. Although formal documents have a good place in their own way, but behind them, as we seek to develop, is this larger feeling of goodwill, affection and cooperation between our countries. I was Mayor of my own city of Allahabad about more than 30 years ago.[2] Of course, my city is a small city not so big as Osaka. It has only a population of two or three hundred thousand but nevertheless, I enjoyed that experience long ago of dealing with municipal administration; and, I think, it helped me a little to train myself in understanding many things which affect the people. May I thank you again Mr Governor, Mr Mayor and the Members of the Chambers of Commerce of Osaka for your gracious hospitality and the welcome that you have given me. Thank you!

14. Growth of Asian Consciousness[1]

Maurice Chanteloup[2]: What are your impressions of Japan?
Jawaharlal Nehru: I am no symbol but the people tend to imagine such things. I look upon the warm welcome I received in Japan as something more than ordinary courtesy, something deeper in search for I do not know what.

I heard a great deal about Japan even from my boyhood. I read Japanese history, met a number of Japanese in India or in foreign countries, but I had no

1. Interview with Maurice Chanteloup, UPI-AFP special correspondent covering this visit, Nara, 11 October 1957. From *The Hindu*, 12 October 1957.
2. Maurice Chanteloup (b. 1915); French journalist working for Agence France Presse, went to cover Korean War but was imprisoned from July 1950 to March 1953.

previous occasion to come into intimate contact with them. I have, of course, now seen them in masses. So, on this occasion of my visit to Japan, I had an entirely new experience, most specially of the Japanese masses.

Among the many things which impressed me in Japan, naturally have been the extraordinary warm welcome from the people, including all kinds of workers, students, intellectuals and others. I have wondered, why those masses of people have honoured me in this way. I felt that it was not an individual honour, but thus they looked upon me as some kind of symbol of their imagining. I am not a symbol but people tend to imagine such things. Why the Japanese people do so, I wonder. Perhaps, I felt, after the tremendous experiences of the last few years they were in search for something; they wondered that perhaps I could help them in that search anyhow.

I realized more vividly than ever the artistry and aesthetic sense of the Japanese people, their astonishing sense of duty in so many things, and beauty allied to simplicity in the way they treat arrangements of rooms, flowers and so many other things.

Then I noticed very great number of boys and girls in schools and colleges. They seem to form a good part of the population and they look jolly and cheerful. I was pleased and surprised that the Japanese were not quite so serious as I imagined, that they had exuberance of youth and even showed their emotions at times. I do not know if this is a new development or something continuing from old.

Another point which struck me is the amazing capacity of the Japanese to make things of beauty and utility from the simplest material. They are dainty and neat in little things of life which count so much. They have discipline and capacity, of course, for hard work. All these are great qualities but much depends on what direction they are turned.

The vitality of the Japanese people is also obvious, as past history shows. We come back, therefore, to the basic question as to the direction in which this vitality and these other great qualities were likely to be turned.

I have a feeling that the Japanese people are becoming more and more Asia conscious not like in the past but in a different sense.

I think, in the past they looked to Europe and America and rather looked down on the rest of Asia. I think, that attitude is changing. That does not mean any hostility to Europe or America, of course. Today, it seems to me that in many externals they certainly look to Europe and America but they are not quite sure they will find everything and hence the new type of Asian consciousness and search for something that leads to a desire of greater cooperation with nations of Asia.

My visit has been beyond my expectations in many senses. In nothing am I disappointed. I do not mean to say I like everything I have seen here. We all have our likes and dislikes. What I mean is my picture of Japan and the Japanese people has improved considerably as a result of my visit.

Japan-United States relations are perhaps a natural result of the Second World War. There have been progressive changes in these relations and Japan functions now as a fully independent country. I imagine that these changes will continue.

Military or like arrangements with the USA are part of this changing pattern. They are also part, I suppose, of the world situation and cold war. It is not for me to say much about them. It is for the Japanese people and America to deal with these matters. My views about cold war are well known and I earnestly hope that all over the world, nations will relax and cold war will end. This itself will bring in many advantageous changes.

The other day, I was asked in a press conference about American forces in Japan and my answer was, to my surprise, greatly misrepresented and misunderstood. Indeed something has been reported which I expressly deny, that is, comparison of American troops in Japan and Russian forces in Hungary. I said that conditions are totally different and that I could not make any comparison. This is for the Japanese people to consider. I added however, that no country to my knowledge, likes the presence of foreign troops on its soil. This may happen for limited period or because of special circumstances.

MC: What did you discus with the Japanese leaders?

JN: I cannot tell you about our talks but I can say that Premier Kishi and myself discussed many things among which were the proposal for the Asian Development Fund and the cultural relations between India and Japan.

MC: What is your reaction to the election of Japan to the Security Council?

JN: I do not think there are any anti-Japanese sentiments about the admission of Japan to the Council. I believe, Asian countries generally welcomed it. The difficulty arose because of convention and understanding in the UN that the seat should go to an East European country. That convention has now been broken. The present representation in the Security Council is unbalanced. Asia, of course, has always been poorly represented considering its size and importance. It is desirable to have much more balanced representation of various parts of the world.

Although I do not know whether Japan is strong enough economically to help others I think, she is developed enough industrially to be of assistance to underdeveloped countries. For example, three wheeled truck is one Japanese manufactured product which I would like to import into India.

I hope that my current visit to Japan has proved to be extremely fruitful and the results obtained so far have exceeded my earlier expectations.

MC: Do you have any successor in mind?

JN: I have nobody in mind.

15. Talks with Nobusuke Kishi—IV[1]

An Indian trade mission is to visit Japan "to discuss concretely" economic matters with the Government of Japan, the Japanese Foreign Minister, Mr Fujiyama, told pressmen here tonight.

A decision to this effect, he said, was taken at a meeting the Prime Minister Nehru had tonight with the Japanese Premier, Mr Nobusuke Kishi, and Mr Fujiyama. The meeting lasted one hour.

Mr Fujiyama, speaking to pressmen after the meeting, said Japan had agreed to supply capital goods to India to help implementation of her Second Five Year Plan and details of this would be discussed with the proposed Indian mission.

Japan had also agreed to set up two technical training centres in India, Mr Fujiyama said.

Mr Fujiyama said that the Japanese view about Mr Kishi's South East Asia Development Fund was explained in detail at the meeting.

Mr Fujiyama said that while there was no agreement on the proposed "Asian Development Fund," Pandit Nehru promised to give the Fund a further study.

Pandit Nehru was quoted by Mr Fujiyama as saying that he felt the proposed Fund was "a vast project" requiring careful scrutiny.

Pandit Nehru was told by Premier Kishi that the United States would not necessarily be the principal supplier of capital in the proposed Fund, that West Germany has also shown "considerable interest", and that therefore provision of capital by the USA did not involve any political strings being attached to them.

Mr Fujiyama said the Asian Development Fund took up most of the time at tonight's talks. Pandit Nehru was anxious to know of reactions of South East Asian nations to the Japanese plan and was told by Premier Kishi that only criticism so far has been fear of disappearance of bilateral assistance between Japan and respective Asian nations. Pandit Nehru himself did not venture any opinion on the idea which was originally conceived by Premier Kishi.

Mr Fujiyama said that size of capital or the forms of assistance were not discussed in detail but stated Japan will be exporting machineries and various facilities.

Other points on which both sides agreed included:

(1) The Japanese draft of the trade agreement and the request to India for

---

1. Report of talks between Nehru and Nobusuke Kishi, Tokyo, 12 October 1957. From the *National Herald* and *The Hindu*, 13 October 1957. No official record of the talks is available.

according the Most Favoured Nation treatment to Japan will be given serious consideration and an early reply.

Japan offered capital in Japanese currency and other favourable terms of capital assistance such as differed repayment. The size of the capital or the forms of assistance were not discussed in detail but Japan would be exporting machinery.

(2) Mutual claims to war-time properties should be settled as early as possible. Negotiations on property claims should be held at an early date between the Indian and the Japanese Governments.

(3) For promoting cultural exchange, Pandit Nehru proposed not only exchange of professors and students but also of musicians, dancers and films and the Japanese side agreed.

(4) Pandit Nehru agreed to give support to the Japanese plan of establishing "project consulting centre" in various South East Asian nations as part of the development of the region.

Mr Fujiyama said that Pandit Nehru invited Mr Kishi and Mr Fujiyama to visit India. Premier Kishi accepted the invitation and expressed hope that he would see places in India other than New Delhi where he spent a few days earlier this year.

Today's meeting was also attended by Mr N. R. Pillai, Secretary General of Indian External Affairs Ministry, and Mr C. S. Jha, Indian Ambassador here.

A joint communiqué on Pandit Nehru's talks with Japanese leaders is expected to be issued tomorrow before Pandit Nehru leaves Japan for India after concluding a ten-day goodwill tour.

Pandit Nehru and Mr Kishi will meet for the fifth time tomorrow to conclude the talks and finalize the communiqué.[2]

2. At the meeting on 13 October, the two Prime Ministers issued the joint communiqué which said that the talks covered a wide range of international problems with a focus on Asia and matters of special interests to Japan and India. Japan's recent election to a non-permanent seat on the UN Security Council had brought her new and heavy international responsibilities towards world peace. The communiqué referred to nuclear weapons and disarmament, dangers of piling up of arms especially weapons of mass destruction, space missiles, and urgency of prohibition of their manufacture and use. The Prime Ministers considered the suspension of nuclear tests as the first step towards creation of such conditions. It was decided to instruct their delegations at the UN to cooperate with each other for bringing about this among the Powers concerned. They discussed the economic development of Asian countries, promoting economic cooperation between the two countries and agreed on Yen credit to finance the supply of capital goods from Japan. Under the cultural agreement, the possibility of exchange of professors and students, scientists, artists, films etc., was also discussed.

16. Human Advance to Match Scientific Advance[1]

I am glad to have this opportunity of saying a few words about my visit to Japan, but the question you have raised for me to answer is a very big one—the impressions I have gathered from my visit to Japan. You have mentioned that I have met, as I have, the top leaders and industrialists and others, but you missed out one important fact that I have had the occasions to meet the people in large numbers also, to which I attach considerable importance.

Any person who has not visited a country but read about it or met people from that country, forms some idea of the country on the imaginative plane, no doubt based on facts. But a visit makes a great difference. It gives a realistic background. Also in the changing phase we live in today, what we may have had ten years ago, may be out of date today in every country. And we are going through all kinds of changes.

I came to Japan because I wanted to see Japan, and meet the leaders and the people here; most especially I wanted to form some idea of, should I say, the spirit of Japan today; what was moving people's minds here. Well, it would not be proper for me to say after nine day's stay that I know about this complicated question. But one does get impressions, and I have got many impressions.

First of all, of course, of the great vitality of the Japanese people. The way they have developed their industries is a past story, but the way they have reconstructed Japan in the last ten years is a present story. Now, that is so, and I know that. It did not require a visit. But how does all this fit in with the present problems of the world? How does Japan stand in regard to these problems, above all the problems of peace, all the related problems like, well, nuclear test explosions and the like? That too, more or less, we knew.

Another aspect comes up: Japan was the first country in Asia to industrialize herself in the last fifty, sixty, seventy years. I was wondering how far this process of industrialization had affected what might be called the old culture of Japan, because it is bound to affect it, but to what extent I did not know.

I always felt that if a country loses its old roots, its own culture, then it loses something very precious and valuable. It loses to some extent its individuality, and that is important for an individual as for a country. How to find a balance— when it has to go ahead in a modern world, when a country can't remain in an old world, and at the same time, when it has to, well, keep on the roots and the

---

1. Broadcast over Radio Japan, Tokyo, 12 October 1957. *Journal of the Indo-Japanese Association of Japan*, Vol. 6, No. 1.

old culture too, how to find its balance—is a problem before any ancient country. We in India are also a very ancient country with deep roots in the past; some of them are very good, and some of them bad, naturally. And we are in the process of industrializing ourselves very rapidly, and I am anxious that in this process we should not lose our footing, if I may say so, and keep firmly attached to our soil.

Now, while I see that, I realize also that a narrow nationalist outlook of a country is no longer good enough, although it is important in itself, but it is not good enough. The world moves on today to broader areas of cooperation, in effect, to what is called one world. And I wondered how far Japan was, if I may say so, narrowly nationalistic, always moving on, at the same time, to this broader conception of a world cooperation. I cannot obviously give a firm answer to that, but I have a feeling that today in the mind of Japan there are many questions being asked. These questions are occurring there, and I have no doubt that some answer will be found.

For my part, my visit to Japan has been not only of an exceeding interest, but a most exhilarating experience. And I am very grateful to the Government, the leaders of Japan, and even more, if I may say so, to the people of Japan for the warm and affectionate welcome they have given me, which is something much more than merely an official welcome. Affection always draws out affection, just as hatred draws out hatred. I wish in the world today there was less of hatred and cursing of the nations and more of friendly approaches, which would inevitably result in a friendly response. I think that is the law of nature, law of science, if you like.

So, I have been much affected by this welcome and by what I have seen—the tremendous artistry of Japanese people, their aesthetic sense, which is the old culture. I do not speak about the industries because we all know they made a great progress, and are going to make a great progress. But I should be very sorry indeed if they lost their artistry and the aesthetic sense in the process of industrial development, because I consider that very important and vital. Japan has obviously a very important part to play in Asia, and in the world, partly because in Asia, it has led in industrial rebounds and for other reasons also. I honestly trust that it will play it, not, if I may say so, in the narrow sense of looking after its own interests only, which of course it must, but in the broader sense of helping the cause of Asian solidarity and world's solidarity, because I do not conceive of Asia as hostile to the rest of the world. That is wrong, and does not fit in today's world.

So, I should like to express my deep gratitude to the Government and the people of Japan for their welcome to me and the affections they have given me.

17. Indians in Japan Should Know About India[1]

Friends and fellow countrymen,

On this last day in Tokyo and in Japan, I am grateful to you for having given me this opportunity to meet the Indian citizens, the Indians who reside in Tokyo, and who, presumably do business of various kinds here. I have just been speaking in Hindi and pointing out how we are entering a new phase of our national and international existence.

There was the first phase, a thousand and two thousand years ago when India had contacts with her neighbour countries, Asian countries; on the one side with China and Japan; then South East Asia with Indo-China, Siam, Indonesia, Burma, Malaya; and on the western side, Iran and the Arab countries.

Geography has given a place to India in the centre of South East Asia, and because of her geographic position, she became the meeting ground of people from Western Asia, from Central Asia, from North East and from South East Asia. As you know, apart from trade and commerce, a very special bond between India and all these countries was the bond of the message of the Buddha, which came from India and spread to China and Japan, to Central Asia, to South East Asia and even to Western Asia during those days. And in those days there was great traffic of hundreds and even thousands of persons going to and from India to the other countries including China and Japan. This continued for a thousand years or more. It carried not only the message of the Buddha but also it carried Indian ideas, in South East Asia, many influences of the Sanskrit language, Indian architecture, Indian dancing, and so many Indian trades, all over South East Asia. So, there was this great commerce of ideas for a long time, for a thousand, fifteen hundred years.

Then came Europe to Asia and that put an end to this, and we in India developed grater contacts with Europe and England than with our neighbouring countries in Asia.

Well, now things have changed again and since we have become independent, naturally we want closer contacts with our neighbouring countries. That does not mean that we want to lessen our contacts with Europe or America, certainly not. We want contacts with Europe and America but also the closest contacts with our neighbours in Asia.

---

1. Speech at a reception given by the Indian Association, Tokyo, 13 October 1957. AIR tapes, NMML. Original in Hindi. Also available in the *Journal of the Indo-Japanese Association of Japan*, Vol. 6 No. 1.

Now, Japan has a certain obvious importance in this matter because Japan was the first of the countries of Asia to take to industrialism and has much advanced on that line. We are passing through the phase of the industrial revolution in India now fairly rapidly. So, it is natural that we should have contacts and cooperation with Japan in this matter. And all of you who live here, Indian citizens, have an important duty to perform in your own sphere. You have represented India here and you have to see that in doing so you set up high standards so that people here may form a good opinion of Indian standards of behaviour, and of India. Because they will judge India from you, that is, all the India that they see here. Therefore, a great responsibility is cast upon you.

I have just referred to a problem which interests me much—that is the problem of Indian children abroad. The Indian children abroad will sometime or other return to India. If they return to India as strangers to India, as strangers to their own language, it will not help them at all. They will not be able to do much service to India. Therefore, it is important that you should take steps to keep them informed of not only their own language, so that they may learn it, but of developments in India. Otherwise they will know nothing about their own country and that will be bad. You should consider this matter and make arrangements for it.

I do not know whether you have arrangements here, for Indians here for proper reading rooms or libraries dealing with India specially, I mean. I am not talking about Japanese reading rooms, of course they are, but something that you should organize where not only a good selection of books on India, past and present should be there, but more particularly the numerous publications that are coming out today about our development schemes, about our Five Year Plans, about a thousand and one activities in India, whether they are industrial, commercial, cultural, and so many others. A nation that is growing, grows in all directions not in one, that is the sign of the life of a nation. And India is growing in all directions. So, a library where you could have all this material, where you could have many newspapers from India, periodicals, and this library and reading room not only for Indians but of course, for Japanese also, for others, for anybody, but more particularly for yourself, for your young men and women and children, you may know. Otherwise, you will get cut off from India. You may read newspaper accounts, but that is not enough. We should remain in intimate contacts and you should have such a library here open for all.

Well, thank you very much for your welcome, I wish you well. *Jai Hind!*

18. Change and Continuity[1]

Friends,

I am glad to have this opportunity of meeting not only the Indian students in Tokyo but also many others—Japanese and other students from Asia and other countries—who are studying here.

I have just been telling the Indian students that it is their function here not only to study well, to make themselves as experts as possible in their own subjects so that when they go back, they can serve their country to the best advantage, but also to remember that life consists of something that is very important. That is human relations, national relations between two countries. National relations are supposed to be looked after by Governments and Ambassadors. That is so, of course. But no Ambassador can go about meeting large numbers of people. It is ultimately the people of that country who have to do a great deal of work of being in their own persons, in a sense, ambassadors of their country, to interpret their country to the other country, to develop friendships, and to understand the other country. Those of you Indian students, who are here, have apart from your studies, obviously, to understand the Japanese people. Also, to some extent, you have to help them to understand India. So that on the basis of mutual understanding, cooperation should grow.

It is surprising how little understanding there is of one country about another, especially in Asia. You will remember that in the past two or three hundred years or even more, the contacts of Asian countries with each other stopped or gradually faded out. Long years ago, 1000 years or so, the contacts of these countries were far greater with each other.

Speaking of India, remember the geography of India, geography is very important. India is in the South of Asia. On the western side, it is connected with the countries of Western Asia and old countries like Iran etc. We have had contacts with Iran for thousands of years. On the North and North East, we adjoin this great block of nations—China and Japan. In the South East, we adjoin the countries of South East Asia. So, geographically India is so situated that in the past it has had intimate contacts with these various powerful cultures, which have influenced so much humanity, and we had a great intercourse, people

---

1. Speech at a meeting of Indian and Japanese students at the International House of Japan, Tokyo, 13 October 1957. AIR tapes, NMML. Also available in the *Journal of the Indo-Japanese Association of Japan*, Vol. 6 No. 1.

travelling to and fro, even in those old days, when travelling was very difficult. We had plenty of people coming to our country from China especially, also Japan, South East Asia, from Java, Sumatra, Burma, Indo-China, plenty of people going from India and coming from these countries from Central Asia, and also from Western Asia.

But when some two or three hundred years ago, European powers came to Asia, one of the effects of their coming was that our contacts with Asian countries stopped. Partly also that was the effect of the development of sea traffic. The old caravan routes across land did not function as much as they used to, though they continued for merchandise. But sea traffic developed and speaking of India, India had more contacts with Europe or with England especially, than with her neighbour countries in Asia, which is very odd, and for two or three hundred years. Therefore, our contacts and our knowledge of our neighbour countries in Asia became less and less.

Now that we and other countries in Asia have become independent, naturally, we think again of those old contacts. That is inevitable—a country thinks of its neighbours, develops contacts with its neighbours, especially when it has had those contacts in the long past. So, we try to pick up old threads and develop these contacts, and that is what is happening in other countries of Asia also. It is important that we should understand each other. It is important that more and more of our people should understand each other's languages. Because it is ultimately very difficult to understand the people unless you know their languages. It is a language which tells you of their feelings, their literature when you can talk freely to them. If you have translators and interpreters that does not bridge the gulf. So, those of you who come here should take advantage of this, to learn the Japanese language as well as you can and not merely learn the subject of your study.

The future of Asia and the world is difficult to say what it is going to be. But it is clear that the future is going to be different from the past. In the world itself, take these new developments, tremendous developments, whether it is atomic energy or now this attack on inter-plenetary space, satellites and others. All these tremendous changes are taking place which will affect all our countries ultimately, and we have to be prepared for all these in our own way. I am not for the moment talking about scientific preparation. That, of course, is a different matter. But we must realize that we are living in a changing world, rapidly changing world, and we have to understand this world. And we have to keep in mind two facts. One is the principle of change. The world changes, everything changes. A human being changes from day to day, from childhood to boyhood, from boyhood to youth, to middle age, to old age and death, everything grows. The world changes, society changes. That is true. Sometimes it changes more rapidly than at other times as now. So that is the principle of change. The other is the principle of continuity which is opposed to change. Continuity, because if there was no continuity, then everything would be completely new. That is not so. The Japanese people, in spite of change, remained the Japanese people. The Indians, in spite of change, remained Indians. A society remains, keeps its fundamental nature in spite of change. So, always there are these two principles at work, the principle of change and the principle of continuity in a society. If there is no change and there is only continuity, then society becomes static, it becomes half dead, because a thing that is not changing is half dead and may be completely dead. It becomes without life. On the other hand, if something is changing so suddenly and that continuity is broken, then you lose all the life-giving elements of that continuity.

In the old Buddhist philosophy, an analogy is given often of a flowing river. The river is the same but it is always changing. It is not the same water, the water is flowing but the river continues to be the same, but the water is always changing. So—or even like a flame burning—the flame is the same, but it is changing all the time. So, that in this period of great change that we are living in, we have to remember this principle of having our roots in our culture because if we are uprooted, then we cannot be transplanted anywhere, not easy. We can learn from others a great deal. We should learn everything we can from others. But if we learn it at the cost of uprooting ourselves from our own soil, then we shall have no depths in us. We shall only be superficial learners and imitators. Mahatma Gandhi once said to us: "Keep the windows of your mind and spirit open to all the winds from heaven and other countries—wherever they come from. Learn from them but do not allow yourself to be blown off by them. Keep your feet firm". Which is, if I may say so with all respect, perfectly true. We can only learn from others if we do not allow ourselves to be blown off our feet. If we are blown off our feet, then we have lost root, lost sustenance. We may learn something for show. But it will not grow within us.

Now, the world grows more and more, what shall I say, to one world and that is a good thing provided we approach each other with understanding, with charity, with compassion. If we approach each other thinking of ourselves only and in a narrow- minded way, then we do not profit by our experience of meeting others. We should be receptive, try always to lay stress on, emphasize the good qualities of others and remember always your own weak and bad qualities, and failings. Instead of emphasizing the bad qualities of others and your own good qualities, it is better to emphasize the good qualities of others and your own failings. Thus, you will get rid of your failings gradually and you will make friends and draw out the good qualities of others.

I am happy to meet all of you here. Thank you!

19. The Mind of India[1]

Mr Nyknorh, Dr Takagi,[2] ladies and gentlemen,

I am deeply honoured by this invitation here to speak to you and also somewhat embarrassed because this is not a gathering to which I can repeat some well known phrases of goodwill which one does often at public gatherings, but the one which consists of leaders of thought in Japan, it is not easy to say anything significant to people who think. Nevertheless, since you have honoured me, I shall endeavour to express some ideas to you. But I warn you that I am going to say nothing profound or very significant or anything that you do not know already.

In one of our very ancient books in India, written more than 2000 years ago, which has had a profound influence on Indian thought and philosophy, they are actually a number of small books, which are called the *Upanishads*. The word *Upanishad* means sitting nearby, in other words, of people to sit nearby, and discuss matters by question and answer, whether it is the pupil and his teacher or friends and thus by discussion try to elicit truth. It is, if I may say so, a scientific approach, not to lay down a dogma for acceptance but to search for truth.

Now, Mr Nyknorh wrote to me two or three days ago and suggested a subject for this afternoon. I think, the subject was 'The mind of India'. It is a very difficult subject and it is difficult for a variety of reasons. One is that the mind of a country whose roots go back thousands of years is likely to be a very complicated mind and not something that can be easily described. Then that mind of India comes into contact with all kinds of other minds and thinking from other parts of the world, with the modern changing world, and it is affected. Well, then again as you perhaps know in Japan and as, I think, it is a fact all over the world, the mind of one generation today is not exactly the same as the mind of the last generation. I do not know how far, for instance, I can speak of the younger generation in India. I try to understand it. But I belong to an older generation, I could speak with much greater authority on the mind of my generation in India; but my generation is a passing generation. Others come, we influence them no doubt, but they have their own springs of thought. So, it is

---

1. Speech at an assembly of Japanese and foreign scholars at the International House of Japan, Tokyo, 13 October 1957. AIR tapes, NMML.
2. Yasaka Takagi (1889-1984); started American studies in Japan; Professor Emeritus, Tokyo University; Member, Japan Academy; President, Japanese Association for American Studies, 1947-66; Chairman of the International House of Tokyo.

difficult to speak about the mind of India, but I can try to let you have some glimpses into some aspects of that mind, going back very briefly to ancient times.

Our contacts—I am talking about the period let us say before Christ, long before Christ, our contacts were considerable with Western Asia and with Southern Europe, by Southern Europe I mean Greece etc. That is, Grecian civilization, later with Roman civilization and in previous to that with Iranian civilization. You will be surprised to know perhaps that the old Sanskrit language, the old form of it is almost identical with the old Persian language, not the modern Persian, but the old one. It is almost the same. They parted company, one became modern Persian and the other became Sanskrit. Now, it appears that there was constant intercourse in so far as it could take place in those days between India and Greece, Rome, Iran etc. Now, no doubt, we were influenced by that intercourse in India. I am talking about the realms of thought, but I should personally imagine and I hope, I am not looking at this from any exaggerated Indian point of view, but that is a normal fact; that Indian thought had a greater influence on even parts of Greek philosophy, than on the whole Greek thought had on Indian philosophy. I am talking about the time of Pythagorus and others. But both acted and interacted on each other. But the point that I wish you to consider is that Indian thought was very sure of itself. It was not easily swept away. It was open and it did open the windows of its mind to thought from Western Asia, later from Eastern Asia and from Southern Europe. But it was so sure of its own foundations that while it absorbed much from outside, it never lost its footing on its own soil. Later periods, when Indian thought became perhaps less firm in its faith, although it is pretty firm still it became rather static, firm but became static, and not changing, advancing. Then the thought that came in from elsewhere affected it a little more. And you find in India's cultural history a constant attempt to find a synthesis between what comes from outside with itself. Some kind of balance. Gradually succeeding, a balance not, of course, imposed but rather growing up. There have been many leaders in India for the past thousand years or so, who were always trying to find a synthesis and balance—succeeding to some extent, not succeeding to some extent.

Then came a new type of impact not so much in the realm of thought directly but in the realm of modern industrial civilization as represented by European powers coming to India, coming to India in a political way and obtaining dominance over India. Now, it is well to remember a fact that probably there is no country in Asia, which has had such a long experience of Europe or parts of Europe as India has, in the main of course, British. English influence in some parts of India, French influence in some other parts and naturally a couple of

607

hundred years or more of that influence has left a very deep mark apart from the influence of industrial civilization. I am rather referring to the influence and thinking on the cultural aspect. We, quite a large number of our people, learnt the English language. We hardly learnt it as a foreign language, it was not our mother tongue, it became, if I may say so, our stepmother tongue. Though naturally, it was confined to people at the top, masses could not have it and through that we obtained access to, specially to English literature and political thinking; and to some extent, European literature either directly through French or German, or a little or indirectly through translations into English.

So that, there has been all these impacts in India of thought, of various kinds and throughout the 19th century, we were naturally attracted very greatly to English political thinking, even though we struggled against the British, British rule in India, we were attracted by English political thinking and influenced by it very greatly.

Now, that is why you see today that even after Independence and even after a tremendous struggle after Independence our political structure and forms are basically the British structure—our Parliament, our methods of elections and all that goes with it are basically the British structure, varied by one major fact that India is a very big country and England is a slight little country and we could not have a unitary form of government. We have had to have a federal government there with federal powers to the States. So, to some extent, we took the analogy of the United States Constitution, so far as federal structure was concerned or the other Commonwealth Constitution, but basically it was the English structure that we followed, and possibly even a little more in some details than some of the Commonwealth countries. Now, all this has happened and all this mixed thinking is there.

Now, in our struggle for Independence, a new force, there are many forces of course, but a new, a very and a very vital force came in into the picture about 40 years ago. That was Mr Gandhi. And he, well, made a very tremendous change and he made a tremendous change in a variety of ways. He was a man, well acquainted with Western thinking, with Western literature, specially English literature, at the same time, a man who was deeply religious and spiritual, whose foundations were, in what might be called, old Indian culture and thinking; and further who was utterly unlike, well, what I would call the English educated Indian. Not so much in thinking I mean, but in his ways and to some extent, in his thinking too. He noticed a basic fact that this English educated Indian had formed a class in India, which was separated by a big gulf from the common people of India and he said, that is no good. If you wish to raise the common people, if you wish even to understand them, you have to be more like them. You cannot have a gulf and sit in some ivory tower above and tell the others to follow him. So, everything that he did—Mr Gandhi, was based on thinking of the common people of India. If you read his writings, they may sometimes appear to you, well, as not very exciting or not very profound. The fact is that he is always addressing the common people of India and he does not want to complicate anything which may not be understood by the common people of India. Although he said very profound things, of course, but his thought was governed entirely by them. Once he said if you judge any policy whatever it may be—political or economic: think how it will affect the poorest people in India. Will it affect them for the good or not? If it affects them for the good, then it is a good policy, go ahead; if not, think again. So that was his basic thought and he spread our national movement from, you might say the middle classes who were too strong, it spread suddenly to our peasantry and workers and the mass of the population. And it became very strong. At the same time, he laid the greatest stress on certain aspects because without those aspects our political movement, our nationalist movement, would probably have gone to pieces by disrupting itself, by coming into conflict, violence and all that. As you know he laid the greatest stress on peaceful methods, non-violent methods and his meaning of non-violent methods was not merely not hitting a person but of thinking peacefully about it, of being friendly to him. I doubt, if you have an example anywhere of a nationalist movement, in its intense phase. Well, we had, let us say, our people being shot down in the street by the soldiery or large numbers of our people in prison or being attacked by the police with batons and all that and strong passions were roused. At the height of that movement an Englishman could march through a crowd without being touched. It is extraordinary, the discipline, which Mr Gandhi imposed upon us, gradually, he did it gradually, it could not be brought about suddenly. He took about 20-30 years, but it was astonishing how much he succeeded. I don't say that the Indian people became angels. Of course not. They are bad, as bad as anybody can be, but he did impress this fact, and he impressed this fact chiefly because in a sense, he reflected in saying so a basic thought of India. That is Gandhi's strength, which came not by repeating some new truth but drawing upon the reserves of Indian thought and putting them across as a modern thought, as applicable to the modern age also, not out of date as some of us intellectuals thought. And he spoke always to the people in language which they were used to, in language of parables, in language of stories, in language of simple ethical principles. It is that sort of thing he would say which is surprising. The freedom of India would mean nothing to him in fact, he would not work for it if India became a violent country or it was achieved through violence, because then he said India would lose her soul. Now, that kind of thinking repeated again and again sank into the people's consciousness.

Now, again I do not wish, I do not pretend to tell you that the Indian is better or more peaceful than other people. I do think, that in a sense, the average Indian basically is more gentle. The average Indian would step aside rather than tread on an ant or any insect—rather not do it, and yet that average Indian can misbehave and be violent at times, very violent, very inhuman. It is quite extraordinary, how decent people in every country, decent people, civilized people in a moment of passion how they can misbehave. It is astounding! I dare not criticize any people in other countries for that behaviour, when I have seen my own people behave in that way, when they have been swept by some gust of passion. Because, all of us appear to have, appear to be a strange mixture of the angelic or divine and the devilish or the satanic. And I suppose the process of, well, growth of real culture is to emphasize the angelic aspect, if I may call it so, the better aspect at the expense of other aspect, of the devilish.

Now, one very vital important aspect of Gandhi, Gandhiji's message repeated again and again was that means are even more important than ends. That right ends, even right ends do not justify bad means. That is to say, you may have a good objective, but in order to obtain that good objective, you must not adopt bad means. Apart from the ends being bad, they divert you, they take you away from the objective, is just like if you want to reach a place, if you have to go by the path leading to that place, that's end, that's the means. If you adopt, you say you want to go there and adopt a path which goes in other direction, you never reach there, you will go somewhere else. So, he was always stressing this about means and ends, and, I think, perhaps it may be said, that among the innumerable things he impressed us with, that was the basic thing: means and ends. Again I do not mean to say that the Indian people have become very much better because of this, but no doubt they are a little slightly better and it is another layer in their consciousness, which has had so many layers, layer upon layer through hundreds and thousands of years and I have no doubt, that it does influence their thinking and the rest.

Now, we come to this present day age , with this tremendously rapid developments and technology and science, when even we are venturing out into planetary space and atomic energy and all that. It is a good thing, we cannot, and we should not stop the advance of science, but one fact alarms me, and that is, with the advance of science are we keeping abreast of it in our advance of ourselves? Because, if not, undoubtedly science or technology or the big machine will overwhelm us and overwhelm civilization, whether it is, well, in the shape of, let us say, atomic warfare and other destruction or something even more deeper than that—producing an inner ethical rot in humanity which will ultimately be more harmful than some sudden bang destroys us. It seems to me, that history shows us that hardly ever has a race been conquered unless that race has itself gone through a process of decay, inner decay, spiritual decay, ethical decay, to pleasure loving and forgetting the other responsibilities of the human being. And, if modern science, as it threatens to do, will produce a civilization, well, less and less work has got to be done. I understand it is quite a possibility in America, the United States, or Canada for a four-day week to come in, three-day week later and so on. Some people will say a day or two days work will be enough. Very good. I have no objection to that. But how, people who are not adequately trained for the purpose will utilize the other four or five days, the leisure'days, is going to be a major problem. My point is that somehow, technical and scientific advance has outstripped human advance and therein lies danger in this world. There is no doubt, that Asian countries will be industrialized sooner or later. That is inevitable and that is a good thing, it will raise their standards. But how far will that affect their other inner cultures, I do not know.

I do not wish to compare the individual cultures of different countries. But I do wish to say that as with an individual human being, unless he is sure of himself, if he merely imitates others, he is not much good. He can learn from others, he must learn from others, but he must be sure of himself. So, a nation also unless it has some sure foundation and is sure of itself, by mere imitation, it does not gain real strength and yet we have to learn, of course. We cannot keep our minds closed. Mr Gandhi once said: I want my people and my nation to keep all the windows, doors and windows of its minds and spirit open to the winds from all countries, but I do not want our people to be blown up and blown away by those winds; which, I think, is a fairly good way of putting it. That we must accept, be open to everything, learn from everything but keep our feet on the ground upon our own soil. That applies certainly to all countries like India, which has a tremendously long period of experience, racial experience and other good and bad. If you uproot them from what they are completely and engraft them on something else, I have not a doubt that the grafting process will not be wholly successful. It will lead to a rather suspicious civilization. And if I may give you a very very different parallel, nothing to do with this—I have much experience of dealing with, if I may say so, primitive cultures, primitive tribal people who have not developed and very fine people but their state of society is primitive. We have seen all over the world, Pacific Islands and what not, so-called Western civilization going to improve them, sometimes missionaries, sometimes traders with the result often enough that those simple folk leading a happy life have been ruined completely. Their chief occupation becomes drinking gin and well something else. They have lost their old roots and found no new roots. Now, I do not compare them with the ancient civilization but nevertheless their analogy is useful. One cannot uproot a people, one should not try to do so. One should try, of course, to make them turn in this direction or that, keeping their roots in their soil, to learn from everything.

Then again finally, I should like to say, that when we talk in today's world in the political sphere of coexistence, that is no new thing for us and that is not a political slogan for us. It is something basic to our philosophy of life. If we did not have coexistence in India itself, we break up, in the past I mean, we would have broken up. India is such a big country, kind of a subcontinent, with so many varieties of human beings, religions, this that and other, if we did not have that tolerance, and approach to coexistence, we quarrel, we break up, destroy each other. It is essential for us to have that to live in India. There is a famous saying which has come down to us in numerous rock edicts and huge pillars of stone built by Asoka, the old Indian Buddhist Emperor. Now, all over India, he put up these pillars. There they are still, original pillars with its inscriptions and there are hundreds of inscriptions. Asoka was rather a unique kind of king because in the middle of the war of conquest, suddenly he felt compunction, the news was brought to him that so many hundreds of thousands of people have been killed, so many maimed, so many made prisoners and so on. He felt very unhappy. He said, in the middle of that conquest, he stopped the war. He said, no more war for me. It is very seldom that a victorious conqueror stops the war. He stopped the war and he has left his own inscriptions to describe how he felt. They are very interesting—how the news came to him, the sacred majesty was deeply hurt and he said: why should I do this, henceforth no war for me except the war for righteousness. Now, there is another famous inscription of his, because he tried to teach his people through these inscriptions. He said: if you honour your own opinion, or your own religion, that is good. If you honour the other persons' opinion and religion, which is different from yours, that is also important, because if you honour the other persons' opinion and religion, he will honour yours. If you do not, then he will not honour yours. Now, that is a fine way of putting the sense of tolerance and this is two thousand and three hundred years old; and that you can far more easily influence a person by friendly methods, than, well, by coercive methods. You do not after all change a person's mind by coercion, you may force him to do something. It is only by other and more peaceful and friendly methods that you influence the mind.

Now, in the world of today, where we have been brought so close to each other by these developments in communications and every country is, more or less, the neighbour of an other country, there is no choice left, but to have coexistence and live with each other, quite apart from the dangers of conflict and atomic weapons. That is, of course, inadequate argument, but I say apart from that, there is no real choice but to have this way of tolerating others who disagree with us. Of course, the basis of tolerance can only be non-interference with each other because if one interferes with other, there is no tolerance, the other has to do something to defend himself or to interfere with others. Therefore, if we realize that coexistence is not a theory to be accepted or not to be accepted, it is an inevitable development of the modern world, there is no way out of it, the only way out of it is war and war means utter destruction, not only physical destruction but destruction also of the human spirit. That is no way, that is no way. When we come back to the other idea of coexisting and trying to influence each other by friendly and peaceful methods and thereby first of all, trying to lessen tensions and to break down the barriers that have arisen and later when the barriers go down, to find, I am sure, that you will find, that after all, the differences were not so great as we imagined. There is much more in common among human beings, than one thought.

Well, ladies and gentlemen, as you will notice, I have said nothing profound. I do not know how far I have represented the mind of India, but I can say that I have represented one section of the mind of India. I am very grateful to you for this opportunity. Thank you!

20. On Departure from Japan[1]

I am returning from Japan, richer than when I came—richer with many unforgettable memories of this country and her people, richer with the happy burden of their welcome and affection. I am infinitely grateful to the Government and people of Japan for this welcome and this affection that they have showered upon me.

I do hope that my visit has served some purpose not only in bringing greater understanding between the people of Japan and the people of India, but in helping the cause of peace for which we all stand.

Thank you again, Good bye and *Sayonara!*

1. Speech at the Haneda airport, Tokyo, 13 October 1957. *Journal of the Indo-Japanese Association of Japan*, Vol. 6, No. 1.

21. Impressions of Visit to Japan[1]

Before I return to India, I am noting down some impressions of my visit to Japan, as these might interest my colleagues. I am doing so during my brief stay in Hong Kong. The fact that rain and cloudy weather has come in the way of my programme in Hong Kong and confined me to my house, has made it easier for me to dictate these notes.

2. The nine days we spent in Japan were very full and were crowded with impressions. I am not dealing here directly with political or economic matters but rather with other impressions of Japanese life. I went to Japan with some knowledge of the people and the country derived from reading and meeting people. I knew something of its history and, of course, we all knew about recent events which had powerfully effected the Japanese people. Some of my previous impressions I have had to change as a result of closer acquaintance. What I note down here is only a jumble of ideas and impressions and should be read as such.

3. We received an extraordinarily warm welcome wherever we went in Japan. The Government helped in every way in this and organized my programme. In addition, some kind of a Reception Committee was formed in Tokyo consisting of various parties, including Parties in the Opposition, like the Socialist and the Communist, as well as many other organizations. Apart from Governmental people, I met some leading intellectuals.

4. What impressed me most, however, was the exuberance of the popular welcome. I have had the good fortune to receive welcomes in many countries. I think it would be correct to say that, outside India, nowhere have I received such a big and spontaneous welcome as in Japan. The only other place which I can think of in this connection is part of Central Asia, more especially, Tashkent and Samarkand.

5. Students, both boys and girls, were particularly in evidence in the large gatherings in the streets. I was surprised to see the numbers of these students. They stood out because they wear some kind of uniform and, therefore, did not merge with the others. I think, I must have seen many hundreds of thousands of students in this way. They were students of all ages and grades, from the University, from senior schools and elementary schools, and sometimes even from the kindergarten. It struck me that when compulsory education is fully

---

1. Note, Government House, Hong Kong, 15 October 1957. JN Collection. Also available in File No. HC (S)-39/57, pp.1-11/Note, MEA and V.K. Krishna Menon Papers, NMML.

introduced in a country, what a large proportion of its population go to various educational establishments. I enquired about the figure for the number of students in Japan, and the following information was officially supplied to me:

May 1, 1957

	Primary School	Middle School	High School	University
Male	6,609,351	2,896,241	1,621,718	521,991
Female	6,346,934	2,821,942	1,275,931	115,600
Total	12,956,285	5,718,183	2,897,649	637,591

This totals 22,209,708. The total population of Japan at present is just over ninety millions. The number of students thus work out nearly at a quarter of the population.

6. Compulsory education begins from six to seven years of age. For six years there is elementary education and for three years some form of junior secondary education. All this is compulsory, that is, there is nine years of compulsory education. After that, there is no compulsion but anyone wanting to go to a University has to pass through another three years of senior or higher secondary education. While primary schools are almost entirely State run, there are many private secondary schools. The Universities are both private and State. Indeed many of the private Universities are of old standing and repute. Apparently, every major college is a University. Thus, in Tokyo city there are about twenty-six Universities. I visited two old private Universities of great repute as well as the National State University. Each one of these had about thirty thousand students on its rolls.

7. I was told that uniforms were introduced in schools and colleges long ago, in fact, as a part almost of compulsory education in the Meiji era. The idea was to bring about a feeling of equality among the students, so that the children of richer people should not feel superior. As I have said above, practically everyone, rich or poor, goes to the same type of school. They have the same education. They wore the same uniforms and all of them, in these primary schools, get a free meal in the middle of the day. It seemed to me that this must have a powerful influence in bringing about a certain feeling of equality and fellowship. I feel sure that so long as we have special schools for the children of the well-to-do classes, there will always be a difference, both psychologically and practically, in their bringing up, and it is only when the same quality of teaching and other conditions are provided for all children that we will raise the very poor standard of our primary schools.

8. I motored through hundreds of miles of country roads. I must have passed by hundreds of huge motor buses carrying school children or college students

on excursions. Probably this was because October is specially a month for excursions for students. Nevertheless, I was surprised to see these tens of thousands of students visiting famous places in Japan for their scenic beauty or historical interest. I was told that the students paid for these excursions and they saved money throughout the year so as to participate in them.

9. I have mentioned the fact that all these students wore a kind of uniform. This is, in the case of boys, black trousers and buttoned-up coats, cotton in summer and probably some warm material in winter. The cap varies with the school and there is some marking on the shoulder to indicate the school. The uniform is not particularly attractive and rather resembles that of a Railway Guard in India. So far as girls are concerned, they wore skirts and a short coat. Even the kindergarten children were often in some kind of uniform clothing. It struck me how a uniform helps not only in encouraging discipline but also a fellow-feeling. It would be a good thing if we could introduce some kind of uniform in our own schools and colleges. In course of time, I hope that we shall be able to give a free meal a day to every student of an elementary school. If we did this, we would give some relief to the parents and at the same time help in building up the children.

10. The idea came to me that we might make a beginning of this kind in some of the schools which we have started for the children of the employees in State industrial concerns. Thus, at Sindri, we have built up an amenities fund, but we are told that as every amenity is provided for, the fund is not being used. Why should not the children in the schools there be given uniforms and a midday meal? In this connection I might add that factory workers generally in Japan also appear to have some kind of suitable uniform. This is obviously necessary in factories for efficiency of working and for avoidance of danger. Loose clothing, whether for men or women, should not be allowed in a factory. I hope that we shall gradually introduce this among our factory workers.

11. In dealing with this question of students and others, I have rather gone off the main track. My previous idea of the Japanese was of an able, hard-working and serious-minded people, rather dour and not given to too much smiling, heavily disciplined, and blindly obedient to superior commands. I found them somewhat different. They were quite jolly, especially the young folk, and easily given to laughter. I suppose there has been a marked change in them since the breakdown of the old imperial regime. They have adopted, in the big cities especially, many external symbols of the American way of life, including the language and dress. They continue to be, as ever, amazingly courteous and polite. Indeed, their whole culture revolves round an exaggerated courtesy which is very pleasing, though sometimes it may be overdone.

12. I have referred to language above. The Japanese are not good linguists.

616

They have made English compulsory now for the second language. What interested us was the odd fact that long before the English language is taught, the Latin alphabet is taught to the children. This is supposed to be a kind of step towards learning English later on. The Japanese language has become a curious mixture of the ideographs which they have derived from China and some kind of alphabet. It is a very difficult language for the typewriter.

13. We knew all about the great development of the Japanese industry, The way the Japanese had converted Manchuria in the space of thirteen years into an intensively developed industrial area had often been cited as an example of rapid progress. I expected, therefore, a very developed industry. On the whole, I felt that actuality exceeded my anticipation. We must remember, of course, that the Japanese have been at it more or less for seventy or eighty years.

14. The Japanese have many qualities which are notable. I have referred to their extreme courtesy. They are hard-working and disciplined, and they carry punctuality to an extreme. My programme was a heavy one, but every attempt was made to stick to it to the minute. I was even hustled in finishing a meal so as not to be delayed by a minute or two. They take pride in their Railway trains running on split-second schedules. But there are two abiding impressions which remain with us about the Japanese. One is their vitality and the other is their extreme artistry and aesthetic sense.

15. I was constantly surprised and delighted to notice this aesthetic sense of theirs and their amazing capacity to bring about harmonious arrangement of flowers or furniture or pictures or indeed of a whole garden. Their sense of harmonizing colour is remarkable. So also the way they make a few things go a long way. I was happy to see no display of gold or silver anywhere in Japan as, to our misfortune, we often see in India. If there was wealth, it is shown itself in artistic ways of beautiful porcelain or lacquer-work. Even so there was never too much of it. From our standards, a room was very bare with very little furniture, very few pictures, even few flowers. There might just be a picture scroll on the walls, a single flower and the room looked perfect in its simplicity and artistic completeness. It was astonishing how small things were made to go a long way. A few small pebbles would be used to decorate a table. They would surround possibly a beautiful vase or lacquer bowl, and set it off.

16. I do not know how and why the Japanese developed their ideas of miniature gardens and other things done on a relatively small scale. Their houses are the simplest possible with moving screens instead of walls with no chairs or tables except sometimes some low table. The floor has a padded mattress. There is usually a slightly raised alcove where there would be a painted scroll on the wall and a flower or two in front of it. Shoes are not worn inside a house. They are left right outside. People may wear, however, special slippers which are provided

617

for the house. The idea is entirely to keep the house free from dust and dirt. Cleanliness and daintiness are evident everywhere. In the temples, of course, and even in Japanese inns and hotels shoes are left outside the building (not merely the room). This too is done methodically and there were several-tiered wooden racks for these discarded shoes to be kept. We might learn from this and not make a mess by piling up shoes outside a room as we do, often losing them in the process.

17. The Japanese Tea Room is famous. Indeed it is meant to symbolize Japanese ways of life. Simplicity, extreme courtesy and quiet converse about the beauty of flowers and poetry etc. The Japanese are nature lovers and nothing pleases them so much as a pleasant outlook of a garden with a pond and water flowing. The old tea ceremony is a highly complicated affair, as far removed from the rush and hurry of modern life as anything can be. The mere drinking of it is a minor element in it. It is the way things are done. An odd feature of the tea room is the entrance to it which is very low, about three and a half feet high. The idea is that a person should enter it with due humility and serenity and not in an excited frame of mind.

18. Japanese landscape gardens are famous and the more I saw them the more charmed I was with them. I saw big gardens built by the Emperors and tiny ones at the back of houses. It was extraordinary how a very small patch of land behind a house or a shop and in the heart of a city, was converted into a secluded and beautiful corner quite cut off from the city. The whole conception was totally opposed to our New Delhi idea of gardens with flat broad lawns soaked with water. Their ups and downs and mysterious turns and corners give an idea of space even in that very limited area. There would be a small pool and possibly a little wooden bridge and a golden fish in the pool. Trees would be trained in a particular way and sometimes dwarfed. I wish very much that we could learn something of this type of gardening and get rid of our present idea of flatness which seems to possess the minds of those in charge of our gardens in New Delhi. It is far more attractive to have ups and downs and even *maunds* of earth or stones sticking out. Indeed, the Japanese pay particular attention to stones. I am told that their idea is that a garden on the analogy of a human being, should have stones as the bone structure, flowing water as the blood stream and the trees and foliage as the flesh. Even when they have to dig to provide earth for some object, they do so with some sense of artistry leaving a big *maund* somewhere in the middle which is then made part of the landscape with foliage etc.

19. Conditions in India are different and we cannot reproduce Japanese landscape gardening on any large scale. But I do think that we can learn much from it about the utilization of space and having instead of flat lawns all over

something of grater variety. It struck me specially that in the memorial we are setting up for the Buddha Jayanti on the Ridge, we might make an attempt to have a Japanese landscape garden round about that memorial. That is particularly suited because of the presence of plenty of rocks there. Our gardeners dislike these rocks and would probably want to remove them. The Japanese method would be to leave them where they are and utilize them.

20. I think also that a corner in our zoological gardens in New Delhi might well be converted into a Japanese garden. It would be worthwhile to get a Japanese landscape gardener to come to India for both these purposes as well as perhaps to advise us in other matters also. I have mentioned this to our Ambassador in Tokyo and told him to try to find out a suitable person.

21. In regard to children going to schools, I might mention here that they are all supposed to go to the schools in their particular area. This means that they have to go to short distances and they walk to it. The question of transport and long distance conveyance does not arise. This also means a school should be situated so as to be easily accessible to children in an area.

22. I had an idea which turned out to be quite wrong, that Japanese food was not very appetizing. My first experience in a Japanese restaurant gave me an entirely different impression. The meal we had was not only very tasty but delightfully served. As in other matters, a great deal of attention was paid to the manner of serving the food. We sat on the floor on cushions with a low table in front which was simply and artistically decorated. The plates and cups were of porcelain or lacquer. Even the colours were carefully chosen so as not to conflict with the colour of the food. Indeed the arrangement of food itself was thought out to avoid a clash of colour. We ate with Japanese chopsticks which are used only once and then thrown away. Japanese girls in their old Kimono costumes served us daintily, quietly and efficiently. The furniture of the room was exceedingly simple with a painted scroll in the alcove and a few flowers before it. At another end of the room some kind of entertainment took place throughout the meal—Japanese music, dancing and jugglery. Altogether it was a very pleasant and soothing experience. On another occasion, in another place we were provided with separate low tables, the top being rather like a thali but in fine lacquer-work. Everywhere there was the attempt to create a harmony of colour.

23. Of the cities, Tokyo is a huge sprawling mass of small structures, either single storied or double storied. The business centre, however, has big modern buildings. There are huge Department Stores in all the big cities and these are supposed to be as good, if not better, than any Department Stores in other countries including the United States. What attracted me, however, even more were the small shops. I only saw them from the outside. But they were all

attractively arranged and inviting and neat and dainty looking. These shops are on a level with the pavement and open out fully, so that they appear to be almost an extension of the street on both sides. The result is that they give a decorative look to the street which is added by the streamers and signs in Japanese characters. While these shops are brilliantly lit, the Municipal lighting is very poor. The result is that the shopping district is bright and in some places a blaze of colour. Other streets are rather dark. Of all the cities Kyoto, the old capital of Japan before Tokyo, attracted me most. It was a little quieter than Tokyo or Osaka, which are great industrial cities, and it had an air of old charm. Of the small towns, Nara, an even older capital, was very attractive.

24. Most of the houses are made of wood and single storied or at most double storied. Partly this is due to the fear of earthquakes. The big heavy concrete structures, however, are multi-storied and are supposed to be strong enough to withstand earthquakes.

25. The roads in Japan were generally not very good. I was surprised to find that the drainage system also was not good. The central parts of Tokyo and other big cities had a proper drainage system. For the rest there were open drains. I do not know the reason for this except for the fact that the Japanese, like the Chinese, make full use of the night soil. Thus, the municipalities do not spend too much money on lighting or drainage or even on roads and yet municipal taxation is said to be very heavy and the revenues of the big cities are very considerable. I was told that most of their expenditure goes towards providing services for the people and especially for the children. Education with free meals is a heavy item of expenditure. Also there are all kinds of amenities for the people. I might mention that nowhere in Japan, whether in city or countryside, did I see a barefooted person, man, woman or child. Generally they were well clad.

26. There are far more cameramen in Japan than anywhere in the world. In fact there are swarms of them. Press cameramen are present in large numbers everywhere. But apart from them, there are innumerable others with cameras.

27. I motored for hundreds of miles through the countryside and saw the rice fields on both sides of the road, often coming right up to the road or within six feet or so of the Railway line. There was obviously a bumper crop. This was the third year running of a good crop and naturally both the Government and the people were very happy about it. I visited some farm houses. They were naturally selected and might not be considered to represent the normal farm house. One of these consisted of a farm of three and a half acres with one cow. There were some agricultural implements; four members of the family. Income, I was told, was equivalent to £400/- per annum. There was a radio and an electric washing machine. The second farm consisted of eleven acres and belonged to an old landlord family who had been allowed to keep more land. Normally, the holding

is four acres after the land reform. This eleven acre plot had a good deal of agricultural machinery, three cows and poultry, radio, etc. and seven members of the family. Income about £1700/- per annum. The houses were neat and clean of the old Japanese style with no chairs, etc. The income figures are surprisingly high. They were given by the farmers themselves.

28. At Nara we saw a fine bronze statue of the Buddha. This was the biggest in Japan. There is a smaller but more famous statue at Kamakura. We were told that when this statue was inaugurated many hundreds of years ago, India was represented by a learned monk, Bodhisena.[2]

29. We visited a small museum containing some old treasures, manuscripts, scrolls, etc. This was lodged in a wooden building, kept scrupulously clean. We had to take off our shoes so that no dust might go in. Very special steps were taken to protect this from fire and there were thermometers to measure the humidity of the rooms.

30. One of the things I noticed was a three-wheel truck. The streets were full of these trucks of Japanese manufacture. They were of half-ton and of one-ton. I was told that there were some of two-tons also. I learnt that the coming of these three-wheel trucks had brought about a small revolution in transport in Japan. They were cheaper, very easy to manoeuvre and could go into narrow roads. It struck me that such three-wheeled trucks would be very useful for us in India and we may well think of manufacturing them. The big heavy four-wheel trucks are, no doubt, necessary for us, but for innumerable small purposes, the three-wheeled trucks might be much more useful.

31. I visited a big ship-building yard at Kobe. They make ships of all sizes, big and small, there. We are putting up these ship building yards in India and launching biggish ships. I thought that it would be a good thing if we took up the manufacture of small ships or launches useful for inland waters as well as coastal trade, something from 500 tons to 1,000 tons. Also motor boats. There were the most delightful tiny motor boats dashing about the sea. I was told they were very cheap.

32. It is well known that Japanese cultivation is intensive and is terraced. These terraced fields indicated how every bit of land is utilized. What is more it added to the beauty of the scene.

33. The broad impression left upon me of Japan was of the capacity of the Japanese people to make use of the little things and make small things go far. They developed their industry towards the end of the 19th century and later tried to adapt it to conditions in Japan as they were, that is, they did not copy expensive European or American models, but tried to adapt them. The result was, not only

2. Bodhisena, an Indian Buddhist scholar-monk, visited Japan in A.D. 736 at the invitation of Emperor Shomu.

in industry but in administration, that they did everything on a less expensive scale. In India we tried to reproduce European models in administration and industry which were very expensive and far removed from Indian conditions of life. A huge gap was created between the two and this subsists still. Japanese living conditions have, of course, gone up considerably during the past two or three generations, but the rise has been general. There are rich people still. But I suppose the difference between the rich and poor is much less than in India. Since the War, this difference has become still less. I was told of many rich people parting with their big houses or renting them out because they could not afford to keep them.

34. What was the significance, I often wondered, of this very warm welcome that the Japanese people gave me. The personal element in it was not very great. To say that it showed an appreciation of India would also not be an adequate explanation. But I do think that it represented a broad reaction to India's foreign policy of peace and friendship. I have had this sensation in other countries also. Whatever Governments may say or do, it is heartening to find these reactions among the common people of various countries. Because of this, I become for the moment a symbol of that policy and was acclaimed as such.

35. Also in Japan there appeared to me a tendency to look a little more towards Asia. In the last half century and more, Japan's general attitude has been of some contempt for Asian countries. It considered itself as belonging to the superior European or American species. It is true that they talked of Asia or of co-prosperity in Asia, but there was no friendly or comradely intent in that. Asia for them was a country to spread their influence and their economic domain.

36. During the last fifteen years or so, the Japanese people have experienced the height of victory and the depth of defeat. The defeat has been even more significant and painful for them because it is apparently the first defeat in their long history. From a proud people looking down upon the world and considering themselves unconquerable, they became a conquered and occupied country. They suffered, but their discipline held and their pride prevented them from even exhibiting their suffering. They did not complain. They appeared even to submit voluntarily to many a humiliation. But behind it all, they were building themselves up again recovering their strength and independence, and, perhaps, waiting for the day when they were strong and independent enough to take the action of their choice. They have gone far in this direction and have made economic progress and have recently even become a member of the Security Council of the UN. It is true that American forces still remain in Japan and that the Japanese Government are anxious not to come in conflict with the United States in any way. They want to increase their economic strength and build up their industries still further.

37. In 1949, I think, at the request of some Japanese children, I sent an elephant

from India to the Tokyo Zoo. I visited this Zoo and in the course of an address to me made there, it was said that the coming of this elephant was almost a psychological turning point in the lives not only of the children but of the people of Tokyo and Japan. Till then they were desolate, suffering all the humiliation of the war. They had forgotten to smile. But when Indira, the baby elephant came, it was so comic and friendly that they had to smile and laugh at it. The tension was broken. This may have been a poetic way of expressing things. But, I think, there was some element of truth in it. Since then progressively that change has continued and now the Japanese are certainly a people who laugh and are prepared to enjoy themselves. While externally many of them have taken to American ways, I do not think that represents any internal turning towards American way of thinking. More and more people now think of Japan being essentially a part of Asia and look towards Asia, not in the old way but in a new way of fellowship rather than domination. It is true, I suppose, that the industrialists and others want to spread their businesses and their export markets. But there is something deeper about it and it was this something that added to the welcome.

38. Also, of course, there was the fear of the nuclear explosions that are continuing. In this matter I think that the Japanese Government lags very much behind public opinion in Japan. Not that the Japanese Government is itself of opinion that it should go slow, but it is anxious not to offend in any way the United States in this matter by taking up too extreme an attitude. Sometimes in speeches Japanese statesmen expressed themselves strongly, but when it comes to a formal resolution or memorandum on this subject, they are more cautious as can be seen from their resolution in the United Nations on suspension of nuclear test explosions. We discussed this matter at length during our talks. In the joint communiqué, it will be noticed that great stress is laid on the vital necessity of an immediate suspension of the nuclear tests, later further steps are envisaged. The actual Japanese resolution in the UN falls far short of what we have said in our statement.

39. Seeing and meeting these very courteous and friendly people, I often wondered how they could be so cruel as they were during the last Great War or in their invasion of China and Korea previous to the War. We have had long tales of atrocities and even though these stories might be exaggerated, there can be little doubt that there is much substance in them. I found it difficult to reconcile the two pictures, and then incidentally thought of our own people. I suppose that the Indians, by and large, are gentler than almost any people in the world. They dislike violence. Most of them will deliberately avoid treading on an ant or any other insect, and yet they are callous to animals. They may show reverence to the cow, but they ill-treat her, as they ill-treat other animals. Even more so, the picture came before me of the horrible occurrences and inhumanities committed by our own countrymen after the Partition, even as these atrocities and inhumanities

623

were committed on the other side of the border in Pakistan. How was it that these people who are essentially friendly and gentle, committed these inhumanities? I have no explanation except to say that all of us, individuals and peoples, have a double side of our nature, the gentle side and the brutish, the divine and the devilish. Circumstances bring out one aspect or the other. Civilization has not curbed sufficiently the devil in us. That devil may come out because of various reasons, but above all, was fear and hatred. And so it ill-becomes us to criticize others because we are all made of the same mixture of good and evil. We are apt to see the evil in others and to ignore the evil in ourselves. Charity and compassion are suppressed by outbursts of passionate fear and hatred. It has been my good fortune to see many peoples in many countries and to find them friendly and full of affection and goodwill,. In some other circumstances those very people might become brutish. In war this happens inevitably. In a war of extermination through nuclear weapons, there will probably be an extremity of fear and hatred which will reduce humanity to the lowest level of degradation, apart from the destruction it will cause. It is this inner decay and degradation that is more fearful than any outside damage or injury.

40. There is one rather local matter to which I should like to refer. In Tokyo we purchased for our Embassy building a house and a plot of land of about one acre for Rs 3,20,000. This is a good house with an attractive garden and I was astonished at the low price we paid for it. I was told that this was due to the fact that it was in a quarter which was not considered respectable. Last year we purchased some land in Tokyo for our Chancery. This is also about an acre and it has a small building in it too, not big enough for our purposes. The price was Rs 11,30,000. The difference between the two prices is astonishing. It is partly due to land values having gone up considerably and partly to the situation being a better one and, what was considered, more respectable. For my part, I would prefer a little less respectability if I had to pay a much smaller price. It was our intention to set up a Chancery building over this newly purchased land. This has not been done yet because we have stopped building operations.

41. Meanwhile, our Chancery in Tokyo is located on the fifth floor of a huge office building of seven floors. We do not even occupy the whole of the fifth floor as some rooms are occupied by other offices. We are paying a monthly rent of Rs 9,800 for this Chancery. This rent is likely to go up to over Rs 11,000/- a month soon when air conditioning is installed as it is being done. I was shocked at this exorbitant rent. I was told that for an expenditure of about Rupees four lakhs we could put up a Chancery building over our newly purchased land and thus save this heavy rent which is likely to amount to Rs one and a half lakhs a year. That is, in about three years' time, we will have paid more rent than the cost of the new building. I do hope that we shall be able to get rid of our very expensive Chancery

quarters in Tokyo as soon as possible. Apart from other reasons, situated as the present Chancery is, it is difficult to have security arrangements there.

42. This is a very long note I have dictated. It is not based on books and statistical material but on impressions and casual talks. It may not be accurate in some respects. But it will at least give some idea of what I have carried away from Japan in the shape of pictures and impressions. The country is an attractive one and there can be no doubt that the people are a great people who have made good in peace as well as in war. Speaking to the Japanese statesmen, I pointed out that it was inevitable in the future that three countries in Asia would play an important part, namely, China, Japan and India. I was not thinking in terms of great powers or the like. If these three countries cooperated with each other it would be for the good of Asia and the world as well as of peace. If not, it will be bad for them and for Asia and the world. Naturally, I spoke of the Chinese People's Republic and the obvious necessity of its being taken into the United Nations and have closer relations through trade and other ways being established with it. The Japanese realized this but were inhibited by their present position. There was much else that I discussed, but I need not go into that. So far as economic matters were concerned, although we discussed them, we left them for further consideration on the expert and official level. The Japanese Government thinks more of them than of political matters and obviously desires to develop close economic contacts with Asian countries which no doubt would mean the flow of Japanese goods and personnel to other countries.

22. Cable to V.K. Krishna Menon[1]

My visit to Japan was notable for extraordinarily warm popular welcome everywhere. I have received great welcomes in many countries I have visited. Nowhere has any welcome exceeded people's welcome in Japan.

Although Government organized my tour reception committee consisting of numerous parties including Socialist, Communist and many other parties and organizations were formed with their approval.

1. New Delhi, 15 October 1957. File No. 5 (9)-UN-II/57, Vol-II, P.454/C, MEA. Also available in JN Collection.

Our Joint Statement inevitably had to represent least common measure of agreement with Government. In our talk we had stressed our general viewpoint about China's admission to UN and inevitable necessity of Japan having trade relations with China. Japanese, however, said in circumstances they could not say anything about it. They were inhibited by fear of displeasing Americans in this and other matters.

About disarmament and nuclear tests suspension, we went as far as we could get Japanese Government to agree. It will be noted that in Joint Statement vital necessity of immediate suspension of tests explosion is referred to without any limitation or period.

About economic matters everything has been left to future discussion.

Generally speaking Japanese public opinion seems to be much in advance of governmental policy. I have sent message to Premier Kishi saying it would be unfortunate if after our Joint Statement, Japanese resolution on nuclear tests explosion is pressed in UN and we are compelled to vote against it as in our opinion it does not go far enough.

(ii) Hong Kong

1. Suspension of Nuclear Tests[1]

Question: What will be the effect of the launching of the Soviet satellite on the world situation? Is there any need of controlling satellites?

Jawaharlal Nehru: I should imagine that the universe has not been much affected by it as yet. As regards control there is obvious need for controlling all these developments, but the main thing is we first learn how to control ourselves instead of the satellite. If we do not control ourselves something always is going wrong with us or with the person we do not like. In other words, we have arrived at a stage where we have to think about all these matters in somewhat different terms.

Obviously, when these natural resources have been released or are capable of being released, which can destroy the world, are we to go on thinking in terms of

1. Press conference on arrival at Hong Kong airport, 14 October 1957. From *National Herald*, 15 October 1957.

626

petty power conflicts in view of these vast forces? It means man is much too small to even think about it. One has to think afresh about these matters and, perhaps, get a slightly different mind to do it.

We are entering, if I may say so, from this three-dimensional into a four-dimensional world. Our difficulty is in thinking strictly in third dimensional mind in fourth dimensional matters.

Q: What is the purpose of your visit to Hong Kong? Local papers have carried reports that you will discuss with the British Governor of Hong Kong[2] about the political future of this colony.

JN: Well, all I can say is it did not strike me that way. How my visit is going to affect Hong Kong's political future is not clear to me. I have come here for the very simple reason that Hong Kong is a famous place as a city and I am passing through Hong Kong and wanted to see it. There is an Indian community here of long standing. I thought I might see them too.

My main purpose in Hong Kong is to have a restful time. I was rather exhausted by Japan.

Q: What is your opinion about suspension of nuclear tests?

JN: I can only ask them (Powers possessing nuclear weapons) to suspend tests. I can argue with them, reason with them, beg of them, but it is for them to suspend. I cannot suspend on their behalf. Can I?

I do think there is a very strong feeling about suspension of nuclear tests among the people in every country—as much I could say, in England or America as in every other country.

Q: Will the talks at experts' level between Japan and India take place soon?

JN: I did not fix any date, but we discussed various matters with the Japanese Government. I have not suggested any place or date for the discussion.

Q: When is the next Asian-African conference?

JN: It is very difficult to say when it will be held. There were 30 countries last time (Bandung) and it is very difficult for me to answer on behalf of all these countries. In one sense, I should like (another) conference. In another sense, such a conference is not just an odd meeting of people. It has to be prepared for months and months. There has been no preparation thus far.

Q: Pakistan Prime Minister Suhrawardy has resigned.[3]

JN: It is not for me to discuss domestic affairs of Pakistan. So far as we are concerned, we are always eager to have very friendly relations with Pakistan. I have heard Mr Suhrawardy has resigned. It is not for me to say in direct answer to your question as to what would happen in Pakistan.

2. Alexander William George Herder Grantham.
3. Suhrawardy resigned on 11 October and I.I. Chundrigar was sworn in as Prime Minister of Pakistan on 18 October 1957.

2. The Fourth Dimension[1]

Technical advancement has outmoded war to an extent where war has become a ridiculous thing of the past.

Our thinking has now to be of the fourth dimension. The third dimension of thinking does not suit these problems. We have got to get out of it. The fourth dimension is the ethical dimension. Scientific advance and satellite moon do not change the ethical approach to problems. All technological advance does not make evil good or good evil.

All these tremendous and big machines that you may build up do not make hatred good. Hatred is bad and still remains, whatever happens. These are basic things and I have ventured to speak to you about them because it is time that people spoke about them and got out of this rut of violence and hatred which had submerged the world in the past and threatens to do it again.

Let us hope the world will become gradually civilized. It is not really civilized today. It is highly advanced technologically and scientifically but it is not civilized. It will become civilized when this technological advance is used for human betterment and not for human destruction.

Nuclear tests are a direct violence on human welfare and each nuclear explosion adds something to the atmosphere that might effect the present and the future generations—and people are putting up with that. Each Great Power making nuclear tests says to another: if you don't do it we don't do it, thus casting the burden on one another. It is an amazing thing. Surely the very first thing is to stop the nuclear tests. Let us not only say stop it but suspend it without qualification, without proviso, without limitation.

It is astounding and astonishing that this kind of thing goes on while people deliver high speeches in the United Nations on various proposals. There is nothing wrong in their arguing but before that the tests should be suspended completely and without reservations.

How our thinking has become, shall I say, divorced from every moral, ethical and human principle? What has this nuclear test to do with human welfare? It is a direct violence on human welfare.

People all over the world, irrespective of the blocs to which they might belong, hanker after peace.

I am fortunate to travel to many countries and receive words of welcome

1. Speech at a reception given by the Indian community, Hong Kong, 14 October 1957. From *The Hindu*, 15 October 1957 and *National Herald*, 16 October 1957.

from their peoples. People talk of cold war and rival blocs of nations opposed to each other. There is some substance in what they say, but I also know that: whether I visit the countries of this so-called bloc or that so-called bloc, I find friendly warm welcome there, and I find that people in all these countries hanker after peace. They don't want war, they don't want trouble, they don't want to interfere with other countries.

Yet, while all these people hanker after peace and peaceful development, we see this terrible race in weapons of war going on—atomic weapons, hydrolic weapons and ballistic weapons which is an extraordinary sight, and some times I wonder if we have not somehow rather lost the habit of thinking logically. All this seems to me so illogical, so much without meaning. Everybody knows in every country that war with nuclear weapons will bring utter disaster to the entire world. If that is so, why not act up to it?

The fact of the matter is that war, big war, is out of date today in the modern world. But the difficulty is that most of our minds are out of date. Science progresses, technology progresses at a record pace, but the power of our minds remain behind, unable to catch up with it. We still think in terms of a past age, though sometimes we have glimmerings of the future.

While I was in Japan, we read about this so-called satellite moon thrown out into outer space from the Soviet Union. What does all this mean? It means, I have no doubt, that very soon you will have one, two, three or four more satellite moons from the United States. If one country imagines that it has got a lead in science and technology over another country, the other country takes a jump and takes a lead. So, they (the Big Powers) go on like this. It would be a very good thing if countries enter a race in scientific and technological advance if it would be profitable to the entire human race. But if that is tied up with the cold war, tied up with the possibility of mass destruction of war, then it becomes a very terrible thing and vitiates invention and discovery.

One thing is quite clear that world problems are not going to be solved by a hot war or a cold war or any other type of violence or by hatred. The only result of all these will be universal destruction. If that is so, then why not try some other way, more specially when the peoples of the world, of every country, whether countries of Europe or America or Communist countries or non-Communist countries or anti-Communist countries, every country, I have been to, hanker after peace. Why then should we not get out of this cold war which leads nowhere?

We signed a joint statement—I and the Chinese Premier Chou En-lai—on the Five Principles (*Panchsheel*),[2] and later other countries also signed these five

2. For this Sino-Indian Agreement on Tibet see *Selected Works* (second series), Vol. 25, p. 468.

principles of international behaviour.[3] Now if these principles were accepted by nations and acted upon, surely there would be no war.

In following these principles there may be some difficulty. But everybody asks how to trust the other party.

I know you cannot be absolutely sure of trusting everybody but I say that the mere fact of accepting right principles creates an atmosphere in the world which makes it difficult for people to break these principles and if any country breaks them, it goes against world conscience. Anyhow, a right principle is a right principle. It is all right to say that we will not accept right principles, because somebody else does not accept them. That has no meaning. It amounts to saying: we don't speak the truth because somebody else may tell a lie. It is absurd, but absurd as it is, that is oddly enough the way in which world problems are being dealt with. Why? Because countries are afraid of each other, because of fear, and oddly enough fear grips great powerful countries.

A time will come when a new approach will have to be made to new problems. We must train our minds to think in a new way in this new age in which we live in, the atomic age, the inter-planetary age. If we don't, then the alternative is utter, absolute destruction. The alternative is not victory for this or that side. If people or countries think that they are going to force other people to act according to their wishes, well, then, it simply means that every party will try to force other people in that same way and we get back into an area of conflict—of each party trying to force another to function according to its wishes, which means conflict and war. It means destruction and total destruction. Is it clear to you that that is not the way of solving problems?

The only other way, the civilized way, is to create an atmosphere where these tensions and fears of each other go. Remember this, that nothing is more dangerous—there is no more dangerous companion for you or any one to have—than fear. Fear makes a person foolish, cowardly, makes one misbehave.

Individuals and nations do many things out of fear which otherwise they will not do. Therefore, we must try to lessen tension and fear, and when fear becomes much less, it becomes easier to consider problems in a friendly way and easier to influence in a friendly way. If someone comes to you with a big stick in his hand and asks you to do something against your wish, do it or I hit you on your head, what is your answer? You will be angry and say "I don't do it, big stick or no stick."

If the big stick is not there, we talk to each other, we influence each other, we hear each other's argument and we lead our lives without interference. Surely,

3. At the Bandung Conference in April 1955.

that is the only civilized way. Well, let us hope that the world will become gradually civilized.

The world will become civilized when people begin to realize that out of hatred and violence no good can ever come.

Some people imagine that the idea of peaceful coexistence is a new idea which was put out recently to the world. So far as we are concerned in India, that is a logical product of our thinking, not of today not even in the past generation. It is not I who put it forward—it does not matter who is the Prime Minister of India. It is the inevitable policy for India to follow, and if India follows any other policy, it will bring destruction and disruption.

It was Emperor Asoka 2300 years ago who inscribed on pillars and rocks this idea of coexistence. In the middle of a victorious war, Asoka strongly felt that war was bad and brought suffering to innumerable people. He then declared that in future he would fight only the war of righteousness. Asoka told the people that if they respected other people's opinion and faith, the others would respect theirs. Now, is that not a perfect way of putting and saying what toleration can do?

Nobody asks anyone to abandon his own opinion or faith, but everyone should respect the other's opinion.

I venture to say that this voice of Asoka is the true voice of India speaking through the ages. The voice which gives strength to India. Even though India fell many a time, that extraordinary something of the spirit kept her going. If we of the present generation forget that voice represented in our generation by Mahatma Gandhi, if we forget that voice for some more practical advantage and go some other way, then that day will be an evil day for India.

I hope that ultimately other countries will appreciate this policy also because it needs no compulsion on any country. Every country will go its own way and yet exercise its friendly influence on others by processes of friendly approaches. I have tried to put to you the reasons behind the basic urges of our policy because some people think that it is something which is produced out of a hat. That is not so.

In these critical times we have to adhere to some basic policies and principles. I do not believe that India or the world will prosper if it ignores completely ethical and modern approach to problems.

(iii) Myanmar

1. Power Blocs Not Good for Peace[1]

Question: Most of the countries are worried about the question of disarmament.

Jawaharlal Nehru: Disarmament concerns Big Powers, it is no good saying that small powers should disarm. There is nothing to disarm for them. It is for Big Powers to agree to have disarmament. It is not a thing which you can ask by majority of votes.

Q: Would the position change if small countries stopped accepting arms from Big Powers?

JN: That is something, I suppose, that would certainly help to some extent but the basic thing is the creation of these huge powerful blocs of nations afraid of each other. I do not think it is good to have military alliances and the like.

The approach of having huge power blocs and military alliances and the like is out of date now from the strictly practical point of view.

I do not think it is good to have military alliances and the like. I do not think it has practically any advantage to any country. All these approaches are out of date now from the strictly practical point of view.

Q: What is the strategic importance of Soviet earth satellite?

JN: I have already declared that it showed that the Soviets have scientifically advanced enough to be able to throw a missile probably anywhere on the earth's surface. More or less in the same way, the United States is certainly equally advanced scientifically for that purpose. So, they are both in a position to destroy each other, or destroy any other party.

Q: What is your message for Burma?

JN: You are celebrating your ten years of independence. That is a notable period and I know how difficult these years have been here and how step by step those difficulties have been overcome with courage and confidence. That itself is a very good augury for the future. So, we wish to send our good wishes to the Burmese Government and people on this occasion and for the future.

---

1. Talk with pressmen, Mingaladon airport, Yangon, 17 October 1957. From *The Hindu*, 18 October 1957.

Q: Have you got any assurance about economic assistance from Japan to implement India's Second Five Year Plan?

JN: I did not go to Japan to ask for assistance. We do not expect much assistance from Japan, some assistance would be there certainly but not much.

Q: Is there a way out of the troubled West Asia situation?

JN: You expect me to offer remedies to the world's ills? I have no comment to offer. I deal with my own problems. They are heavy enough.

Q: How was your tour, strenuous?

JN: I have got a cold but it is much better now. I had a very pleasant tour, rather exhausting two weeks.

III. BILATERAL RELATIONS
(i) Pakistan

1. Mangla Dam Project[1]

I have gone through these papers.[2] I think that it would be desirable for us to put in a note of protest in the Security Council about these proposals for Mangla Dam Project.[3] Such a note will have to be carefully drafted so as to ensure that it is factually correct. It need not be too long and details might be avoided. Perhaps the note itself may be relatively brief, but may have an annexure giving some details. Anyhow, something on these lines might be prepared for our consideration.

2. There is one aspect of this matter which has struck me. This is in relation to the Canal Waters dispute. It may well be said by engineers that one of the principal ways of providing water supply to West Pakistan and to replace what is being obtained from the Sutlej etc., now, might be through this Mangla Dam Project. That is, that from an overall engineering point of view of the problems of replacing the canal water supply to them from India and, of course, also of maintaining their own supply, Pakistan would require this project. This is for the engineers to say.

3. I mention this merely to keep this in mind although the question does not arise in this particular context. Even if it arises later, that will be a matter for

---

1. Note to M.J. Desai, Commonwealth Secretary, New Delhi, 10 August 1957. File No. 66-KU/57, p. 6/Note, MEA. Also available in JN Collection.
2. M.J. Desai said in a note on 7 August 1957 that the execution of the Mangla Dam project, which began in June 1957, was in violation of the UNCIP resolutions and of the assurance given to India that "the aggressor will not be allowed to consolidate his position in the J & K territory unlawfully occupied by him."
3. According to a report in the *Dawn* on 25 June 1957, this project involving an expenditure of Rs 1,000 million, was to cover an area of 100 square miles. About 122 villages in "Azad Kashmir" with a total area of about 42,000 acres were to be affected. Out of this, nearly 22,000 acres were under cultivation and the rest barren. The people affected by the Dam were assured to be compensated adequately with cash payment or canal-irrigated land.

some kind of mutual agreement between India and Pakistan in connection with the Canal Waters issue and only when the Canal Waters issue arrives in its final stage of agreement.

4. Even so, as far as I can see, this is really to maintain Pakistan supplies of water, not so much to replace the canal water they are getting now. Also this is a long-term project and not something that can have any effect for at least five years or probably many more years.

5. Therefore, our protest to the Security Council need not take this aspect into consideration. Nevertheless, we might ask our engineers what they think of this Mangla Dam proposal and if it has any bearing, in their opinion, on the Canal Water issue. In drafting our protest, we need not take this into consideration, and therefore, there need be no delay about this.[4]

---

4. On 21 August 1957, India's Permanent Representative at the UN, Arthur S. Lall protested to the President of the Security Council against Pakistan's plan to build a dam over the Jhelum river at Mangla (Mirpur district) in Pakistan-occupied Kashmir. Lall said that the Pakistan Government continued "the exploitation of the resources of the territory to the disadvantage of the people of Jammu and Kashmir." He referred to it as further violation by the Government of Pakistan of the Security Council resolutions and the categorical assurances given by the Prime Minister of Pakistan. Lall also enclosed an explanatory memorandum entitled "The Mangla Dam Project" which gave the background and cited reports from the *Pakistan Times* and *Dawn* on the details of the progress of the project.

2. Indians Employed in Pakistan[1]

Nawab Singh Chauhan:[2] Will the Prime Minister be pleased to refer to the reply given to Unstarred Question No. 18 in the Rajya Sabha on the 21st February, 1956 and state:

(a) whether it is a fact that the Pakistani authorities are still neither issuing temporary or permanent visas nor renewing such visas in favour of Indians employed in Pakistan; if so, how many employees are expected to be affected by these restrictions; and

---

1. Reply to a question in Rajya Sabha, 12 August 1957, *Rajya Sabha Debates*, Vol. XVIII, cols. 98-99.
2. Congress Member from UP.

(b) what steps Government have taken in this regard?

Jawaharlal Nehru: (a) and (b). It is not a fact that the Pakistani authorities are refusing to issue or renew 'F' visas in favour of Indians employed in Pakistan; though reports have been received that they have been following a very restrictive policy in the matter. The total number of Indians affected is not known.

We have taken up each case as it has come to our notice with the Pakistani authorities. We have also taken up with them the general question of granting and renewing 'F' visas to Indian Nationals employed in Pakistan.

3. Pakistan's Note to Security Council[1]

Radha Raman and four others: Will the Prime Minister be pleased to state:
(a) whether it is a fact that the representative of Pakistan Government in New York, has submitted a note to the President of Security Council making certain allegations against India regarding Kashmir issue;
(b) if so, the nature and contents of the note and whether the President of the Security Council has addressed any communication to the Government of India in this regard; and
(c) if so, what is the reaction of the Government and whether Government have sent any reply thereto?

Jawaharlal Nehru: (a) Yes, he has addressed a letter to the President of the Security Council.

(b) The Pakistan Permanent Representative's letter states that the Government of India have recently settled a large number of non-Muslims who are not residents of the State of Jammu and Kashmir, in certain districts of the Jammu Province. Further, that evacuee properties have been allotted to non-Muslim settlers of non-Kashmiri origin. Copy of Pakistan Permanent Representative's letter to the President, Security Council was received by our Permanent Representative in New York as a UN document in general circulation.

(c) The allegations contained in the Pakistani note are untrue and without any basis. According to the laws in force in the Jammu and Kashmir State no non-resident of Jammu and Kashmir can become a resident of that State and have

1. Reply to a question in Lok Sabha, 13 August 1957, *Lok Sabha Debates* (second series), Vol. V, cols. 8160-8163. Extracts.

the privileges appertaining to such residents. No evacuee property has been allotted to non-residents of Jammu and Kashmir. Evacuee properties have been allotted to refugees from the Pakistan-occupied areas of Jammu and Kashmir State who came over in large numbers and had to be resettled by the Jammu and Kashmir Government. These refugees were old residents of the State and were thus qualified as such.

Our Permanent Representative in New York has taken action to point out the false and baseless nature of these allegations to the President of the Security Council, and copy of his letter has been circulated as a UN document. A copy is placed on the Table of the House.

Radha Raman: May I know whether the Government of India is satisfied that these false allegations which are made by the Permanent Representative of Pakistan against the Government of India have not received any credence by the Members of the Security Council and whether the document which is circulated by the Security Council to its Members has received any cognizance by the Permanent Representative of Pakistan Government?

JN: How am I to enter into minds of the various Members of the Security Council of the UN? It is beyond me. All I can say is that the facts are straight, clear and simple and any person who takes the trouble to understand them is bound to be convinced that the Pakistan Government's allegation is utterly wrong.

D.C. Sharma:[2] May I know if the rules which governed the question of domicile of the inhabitants of Jammu and Kashmir when the Maharaja was there still hold and whether according to them no non-resident of Jammu and Kashmir can acquire any property there?

JN: Yes, Sir. They hold. There might have been minor modifications. But, it is really a continuation of those rules. For instance, if I may say so, if I wanted a piece of land in Jammu and Kashmir State, I cannot get it although I have some distant connection with Jammu and Kashmir....[3]

2. Congress Member from Gurdaspur, Punjab.
3. In this connection see also Nehru's statement in Lok Sabha on 2 September 1957, *ante*, pp. 532-533.

4. Visa Rules for Pakistani Visitors[1]

Reports have reached me that a good deal of unhappiness has been caused by a rather rigid and unthinking application of our new rules about people coming from Pakistan.[2] Thus, many people come to visit their relatives here. I am referring specially to the poor folk. They come sometimes when the wife who is here is ill to see her or they themselves fall ill, as many old people during the recent influenza epidemic.[3] In such and like cases a little relaxation about the period of stay by a few days would be desirable.

I am not suggesting that the rules framed should not be applied. But too rigid an application gives rise to too much suffering and has no advantage to us.

In cases of illness when an application has been made for extension of the visa, a demand is made by the office concerned for a certificate by the local Civil Surgeon. Apart from the difficulty of getting this even when the Civil Surgeon is found, he charges a fee usually of Rs 30/- or Rs 40/- which is quite beyond the means of the poor person concerned. I am told that this rule about a Civil Surgeon's certificate has caused much distress and people have gone about begging for money so that they can pay for the Civil Surgeon's certificate.

In the recent influenza epidemic large numbers of people were affected and among them were many from Pakistan.

I suggest that instructions might be sent to the State Governments concerned to be a little less rigid in dealing with individuals and to approach questions in a more human way, more especially, when poor people are concerned who have part of their families here. All I am suggesting is that short extensions might be given in case of illness or any other important happening.

My information has come chiefly from Uttar Pradesh. But I suppose this would apply to some other States also.[4]

1. Note to the Home Minister, New Delhi, 18 August 1957. JN Collection.
2. The President of India issued an Order in January 1957 to the effect that all Pakistani and South African nationals with valid passports would have to register themselves with the authorities and report their movements to the police while on a visit to India. If they overstayed, they could be deported like other foreigners by the Government. Some High Courts had held that the Government had no power to deport the large number of Pakistani nationals, who were stated to be staying in India on the expiry of their visas. This legal lacuna was removed by an Ordinance promulgated on 29 January 1957 and the Order issued under it, which amended the Foreigners Act, 1946 and the Registration of Foreigners Act, 1939.
3. See *Selected Works* (second series), Vol. 38, p. 809.
4. Nehru wrote a letter to Sampurnanand, the Chief Minister of UP, on similar lines.

5. India's Protest to the UN[1]

I have received two short notice questions as well as a notice under rule 197 in regard to the proposal of the Pakistan Government to build a dam over the Jhelum River in occupied Kashmir. These questions and notice are presumably based on the protest we have lodged with the United Nations. This protest was based on an item of news in the *Dawn* newspaper of Karachi about the proposal to build this dam. We have no other information about this project. It is clear from our protest that if there is such a proposal, it is opposed to the ceasefire agreement and to the resolutions of the United Nations Commission on Kashmir.[2]

If Mr Speaker so wishes, I can place a copy of our protest to the UN on the table of the House. There is no further information that I can give.

1. Note to Lok Sabha Secretariat, New Delhi, 23 August 1957. JN Collection.
2. See *ante*, pp. 634-635.

6. Assurance to SGPC[1]

I should like you to be present when I meet the representatives of the SGPC on the 27th August.[2] We should then make it clear to those representatives that we cannot ask the Pakistan Government to do something which is opposed to our own policy. But we are perfectly prepared to press for other requests. In any event, we should ask for an early meeting of the Joint Committee.

1. Note to Commonwealth Secretary, New Delhi, 25 August 1957. File No. 14/1/57-BL, p. 30/Note, MEA. Also available in JN Collection.
2. The SGPC deputation, led by Hukam Singh, gave an account of the difficulties of the Committee due to non-settlement of various questions connected with preservation and maintenance of religious shrines and holy places between India and Pakistan.

2. I do not know when the last meeting was held. Can we not immediately ask for a meeting of this Joint Committee without waiting for our interview with the SGPC people?[3]

3. You might send these papers to me a little before our interview with the SGPC representatives or preferably see me with them so that we can discuss the matter.

3. Nehru told the delegation also that the settlement of questions with Pakistan was always difficult but an early meeting of the Joint Committee would be arranged and the members of the Indian component would do their best to secure adequate maintenance of the principal shrines and also prepare the way for long term settlement on the lines proposed by the SGPC. This was noted on 28 August by M.J. Desai who was present at the meeting.

7. Violation of Air Space[1]

I agree that a formal protest should be made. In this protest it may be stated that as a matter of courtesy to the Prime Minister of Pakistan we allowed the aircraft to continue its flight, but it will be realized that this was a violation of our territory and it should not be repeated. We always are glad to give permission for flights of VIPs, but such permission should be taken before the flight.

1. Note to Commonwealth Secretary, New Delhi, 5 September 1957. JN Collection.

8. Refugees from East Pakistan[1]

I hope that our UN Delegation will have full material about the exodus from East Pakistan and the treatment of minorities there. Also the vast sums we have spent on these refugees from East Pakistan. I find that really very few in the world know about this. There is a lot of talk of refugees from various places, say, from Hungary and it would be very pertinent indeed to know about the refugees we have to deal with.

2. This question would also be coming up in the Committees dealing with the minorities question.

1. Note to Foreign Secretary, New Delhi, 6 September 1957. JN Collection.

9. To S.K. Patil[1]

New Delhi
September 8, 1957

My dear SK,

Yesterday I came across a draft letter which was supposed to be sent by us in regard to the Canal Waters issue.[2] I was surprised to read this draft because it seemed to say something which was contrary to what we had said before. On enquiry from the Commonwealth Secretary I discovered that my apprehension

1. JN Collection.
2. To hold consultations on Canal Waters issue W.A.B. Iliff, Vice-President of the World Bank, visited India and Pakistan with his team in June 1957. In a letter of 24 June, he asked for the views of the Governments of India and Pakistan on certain heads of agreement to form the basis of an approach to an international water treaty. These heads of agreement followed generally the Bank Proposal of 1954 but sought to provide some machinery for resolving points on which agreement could not be reached. India was willing to follow any practicable line of approach which held out promise of a satisfactory settlement on the basis of that proposal. However, Pakistan wrote to the Bank on 24 September seeking arbitration on the disputed questions. See also *Selected Works* (second series), Vol. 38, pp. 701-703.

641

was ill-founded. But the drafting in your Ministry had been so lacking in clarity that the impression I got was quite the reverse of what was apparently meant to be given.

I am afraid sometimes in our meticulous care to safeguard some position or other we drift into language which gives the impression that we are prevaricating. That is a bad impression to create.

I see that Pakistan has been protesting about some statements made by us regarding the Canal Waters on the ground that this was confidential matter and we had no business to disclose it. I do not know how far this accusation is justified. So far as I know, any statements made by us have been rather general and not specific. Anyhow, I feel the less we say about the Canal Waters the better.

Yours sincerely,
Jawaharlal Nehru

10. K.M. Cariappa's Visit to Pakistan[1]

General Cariappa came to see me this afternoon to report on his visit to Karachi. He had gone there at the special invitation of the President Iskander Mirza. Before going, he had asked me if he should accept the invitation. I had told him that he could certainly do so, as they were old comrades in the army. At that time, General Cariappa was full of his ideas about the settlement of the Kashmir issue and asked me if he could talk about it. I had told him that I did not particularly like the idea of his talking about it, but, naturally, if the question arose, he could not very well avoid it. I was afraid that he was likely to say the wrong things inspite of his earnest desire to be helpful.

2. As I expected, he did talk about Kashmir to President Mirza and hinted that the only feasible way of settling this matter was to accept more or less the status quo. President Mirza told him that it was impossible for him to do this or, indeed, to agree to anything except a plebiscite to which India was committed. Public

---

1. Note to Secretary General, Foreign Secretary and Commonwealth Secretary, MEA, New Delhi, 8 September 1957. JN Collection.

feeling was too strong on this subject. General Cariappa talked about this to Prime Minister Suhrawardy also, who was even more emphatic and rather aggressive. He said that if India agreed to a plebiscite, he would withdraw all the Pakistani forces leaving only the "Azad Kashmir" forces of 6,000 or so plus apparently some other odd people. He would be prepared, however, to limit the area of plebiscite to the valley of Srinagar and to the "Azad Kashmir" area. Gilgit and Chitral might be left out as they were obviously in favour of Pakistan. So also Jammu would be left out on the other side. About Ladakh, he seemed to think at first, that this might also be left out in favour of India, but subsequently was not clear on this subject.

3. I told General Cariappa that what I had feared had happened and his talk on this subject would naturally be interpreted that he was doing so at our instance. General Cariappa said that he made it perfectly clear that our Government had nothing to do with this. I pointed out to him that his saying this would not remove the impression from people's minds and it was very unfortunate that this talk had taken place on this subject.

4. General Cariappa also saw Feroz Khan Noon, who more or less took the same line.

5. All these people, according to General Cariappa, were under the impression that India was preparing to attack Pakistan and they said so to him. Why, they said, was this new purchase of Hunter aircraft and all the other arms that we were getting? Noon added that anyhow the Pakistan Government were getting their arms free, while we had to pay heavily for them.

6. President Mirza told Cariappa that there was a talk in Pakistan in diplomatic circles that he had been sent to Karachi to press President Mirza to get rid of Suhrawardy. Cariappa was much surprised at this and denied it indignantly.

7. Cariappa said that both the President and Suhrawardy complained bitterly about the behaviour of our Mission there and, more particularly, the High Commissioner, who, they said, was constantly intriguing against Pakistan and saying nasty things not only about Pakistan, but about the leading personalities there. He said these to foreign Diplomats there who immediately reported them to the President or the Prime Minister. President Mirza said that he was surprised that our High Commissioner did not realize that what he said to the Diplomats would be conveyed to them. Suhrawardy said that he would have declared the High Commissioner as well as perhaps some others *non grata*. But, for obvious reasons, he did not wish to take this step. However, he disapproved very much of the High Commissioner's activities.

8. Cariappa went to our own Mission twice. He said that the feeling there was as if they were in some no man's land and were unhappy about it.

9. Discussing the "Azad Kashmir" forces, President Mirza told him that they

were fine looking people. Cariappa expressed his surprise because Poonchis were not at all as some of the other Muslims in the army from the Punjab were. Cariappa thereupon said that if he saw fine looking people there, they must have been people from Camelpur and other areas in West Punjab who had been imported there and not real Poonchis. President Mirza apparently said that this might be so.

10. Cariappa was much impressed by the way the President's House in Karachi was run.

This is for your information and record.

11. To Mehr Chand Khanna[1]

New Delhi
September 28, 1957

My dear Mehr Chand,

Your letter of September 26th about displaced persons from Chitral. The case of Chitral is rather peculiar.[2] But, I do not see why we should go into the legalities of this matter. I do not suppose there are many people from Chitral here. I think that it is better to treat them on an ad hoc basis and, where it is considered necessary, to help them.

1. JN Collection.
2. For details on Chitral see *Selected Works* (second series), Vol. 33, p. 382.

12. The Case of Jamal Mian[1]

I understand that while the passport of Jamal Mian has been impounded, he has been informed that an emergency certificate will be issued to him for return to India or, more especially, to Lucknow. Should he, therefore, wish to raise the question of his passport after his return, he may do so. There is no particular point in returning his international passport to him.

I suggest that you might send for Maulana Mohammad Mian Faruqi,[2] MP, who is I think in Delhi and tell him that I have mentioned Jamal Mian's case to you (It was Mohd. Mian who spoke to me about him today). Tell him that we have been consistently receiving reports about the activities of Jamal Mian in Pakistan and elsewhere. These activities have been directed against India. We had hesitated in issuing a passport to him on the last occasion as the UP Government was opposed to this. Nevertheless, we decided to issue it. Our subsequent information has again been to the effect that Jamal Mian has taken an important part in anti-Indian activities and the UP Government has pressed upon us to impound his passport. In accordance with their wishes, orders were issued to this effect. Jamal Mian can, however, be given an emergency certificate to return to India, if he so wishes. The question of returning his passport to him at present does not arise. If he comes back to India under the emergency certificate, it is open to him to raise this question.

---

1. Note to Commonwealth Secretary, New Delhi, 30 September 1957. JN Collection.
2. (1904-1989); scholar, Al-Azhar University, Cairo; Congress Member, Rajya Sabha, 1952-60.

(ii) Nepal

1. Supply of Rice to Nepal[1]

Please see the letter from our Ambassador in Nepal.[2] I referred this to the Food Minister and he has put down his comments.

2. We are in a very difficult position in regard to rice, and the failure on the part of Burma has added to our difficulties. For us, to be generous at this time would be stretching generosity much too far. I am reluctant to do anything at all, but at the most, we might give as a gift ten thousand *maunds*. You may enquire from Finance about this. Meanwhile, you can write and explain to our Ambassador in Kathmandu that, in our existing position, it is beyond our capacity to indulge in these generous gestures.[3]

---

1. Note to Foreign Secretary, New Delhi, 3 August 1957. File No. 8 (36)-Nepal/57, p. 1/ Note, MEA.
2. Bhagwan Sahay, the Indian ambassador, referred to the Nepalese Prime Minister, K.I. Singh's request to release immediately 10,000 tons of rice at a concessional rate. Apart from "chronic shortage of funds" in Nepal, there was mismanagement in arrangement for supply and transmission of rice. He wrote that whatever certain politicians might say against India, the people of Nepal always looked to India for help and succour in their hour of need. He suggested that a free gift of 2000-3000 tons would be better than a concessional supply of 10,000 tons at Rs 10 per *maund*.
3. The Indian Government agreed to make a free gift of 10,000 *maunds* and the supply of 2,500 tons of rice on payment of full price of Rs 18 per *maund* at Calcutta.

2. To King Mahendra[1]

New Delhi
August 4, 1957

My dear friend,

Your letter of the 15th July reached me on the 23rd July. I appreciate your writing to me, and I thank you for it. I waited before sending a reply, as Your Majesty was busy with the formation of a new Cabinet.

Today, I have received your letter of July 29, in which you have been good enough to inform me that you have formed a new Government under the Prime Ministership of Dr K.I. Singh.[2] I earnestly trust that this Government will deal successfully with the difficult problems that Nepal has to face.

We, in India, have also our own problems which are troubling us greatly. There is food problem and the grave difficulty of foreign exchange. In addition, we have been threatened by large-scale strikes from some of our important services like the Posts & Telegraph. I still hope that these strikes will not take place. But, the grave risk is there, and we have to prepare for it.

In our efforts to advance the development of industrialization of India as rapidly as possible, we have added to our already heavy burdens. The taxes on our people were, as you know, even previously heavy. We have now added to these taxes and introduced new ones. This indicates our extreme desire to carry any burden so that India's development may not suffer. Your Majesty will thus see how we are trying to face our many difficulties and problems.

I understand that the food situation in Nepal at present is a difficult one. We will gladly help you in this matter, but our capacity to do so now is very limited because our own supplies of foodgrains are at a low level and prices have consequently risen. We were hoping to get a supply of rice from Burma, but this too has not come, and we do not know when we shall be able to obtain it. Our Ambassador must have informed you of our own position and our desire to help you to the best of our ability in this emergency.

Our Ambassador in Nepal, Shri Bhagwan Sahay, has my complete confidence and Your Majesty is always welcome to discuss matters generally with him. I

---

1. JN Collection.
2. Following resignation of Tanka Prasad Acharya on 7 July 1957, K.I. Singh of the United Democratic Party, formed a coalition Government on 26 July at the invitation of the King.

need not tell you that I am happy to hear from you whenever you wish to communicate with me.

With regards and good wishes,

Yours sincerely,
Jawaharlal Nehru

3. Air Services in Nepal[1]

Here is a letter from our Ambassador in Nepal about Patnaik.[2] I do not know if Patnaik has arrived at any arrangement with our Indian Airlines Corporation. All I know is that the Indian Airlines had no objection to his going there and working some internal system of airlines in Nepal. Possibly, the Indian Airlines may have agreed to lend him or hire out some of their planes. This can be found out from the Indian Airlines people here. Whatever it was, it could not have involved any direct responsibility by the Indian Airlines or the Government of India for anything to be done in Nepal. Ours is only a negative responsibility in this matter, that is, we did not object to Patnaik doing it, and we were prepared to give him some normal assistance on business lines. Anyhow, we can enquire from the Indian Airlines as to what the position is.

2. I do not quite see how we can give any assurance about the efficiency or the safety factor of air services that Patnaik might organize in Nepal. That will be his responsibility entirely. Patnaik is an adventurous person, both in the good sense of the word and the dubious sense; he is go-ahead and full of enterprise and has often pulled it off too. He has a fairly good business sense. I imagine that he takes safety precautions, because that is to his interest. He cannot afford

---

1. Note to Secretary General and Foreign Secretary, MEA, New Delhi, 8 August 1957. JN Collection.
2. Bhagwan Sahay wrote that Bijoyanand Patnaik had entered into some arrangement with the Indian Airlines Corporation under which a few planes would be leased to him for operating in Nepal. Sahay wrote that since the Nepal Government had given the right to operate to the Indian Airlines which was a Government of India Corporation, their consent had to be obtained before IAC began to operate through an agent or an associate. Besides, the Indian Government was responsible for good service and factors of safety.

to lose expensive aircraft. Anyhow, this can be impressed upon him. But, I do not see how the Government of India can be made responsible for the proper functioning of air services in Nepal. If we wanted that responsibility, we would have run the air services ourselves. It is because we are unable to do so that we agreed to someone else doing so.

3. After enquiry from the Indian Airlines, a reply might be sent to our Ambassador in Kathmandu.

4. To T.T. Krishnamachari[1]

New Delhi
August 20, 1957

My dear T.T.,

You will remember my reading out a telegram from our Ambassador in Kathmandu at the Cabinet Meeting today. This was a pathetic appeal from the Prime Minister of Nepal to me for mercy in the shape of rice. In accordance with the little discussion we had in Cabinet today, I drafted a telegram to our Ambassador offering to send another 20,000 *maunds* of rice. Before this telegram was dispatched, I got a letter from our Ambassador.[2] I stopped the telegram. I have sent another telegram to him tonight, a copy of which I enclose. In this telegram I have indicated that I shall follow it up tomorrow by more definite proposals.

I had a talk with Pantji and Morarji, who happened to come to my room in connection with the Congress Parliamentary Board meeting. I showed them the new letter from our Ambassador in Nepal (copy of which I enclose). They felt that in the circumstances we should try our best to help Nepal. The question was not so much of the price but of our ability to send rice.

---

1. JN Collection.
2. K.I. Singh had enquired from Sahay again about the position of the supply of rice from India. Singh also said that he was in very great difficulties and that Sahay should "beg Nehru on his behalf to have mercy on him..". In a letter on 14 August, Sahay explained the serious food situation in Kathmandu, Patan, Bhatgaon and Pokhra. He wrote that the surplus stock from Terai had already moved across the open border to the deficit districts of East UP and Bihar.

I sent for Ajit Prasad this evening and had a talk with him. He said that if there was absolute necessity, he could send three or four or even five thousand tons of rice in the near future, though of course he was not happy to do so. Ultimately he suggested that we might help the Nepal Government in the following way:-

1900 tons of rice are already going. Of these 1500 tons have been paid for in cash by the Nepal Government and 400 tons are a gift from us. Ajit is prepared to send, in addition to the above, 2000 tons immediately or as soon as the Nepal Government can lift them. Further he is prepared to send about a month later 1100 tons.

All this would amount to 5000 tons including the 1900 which is already on its way and of which 1500 tons have been purchased for cash by the Nepal Government.

I should like to have your advice about this before I commit myself. I should like to say that, apart from what we have sent or are in the process of sending, we are prepared to send 2000 tons immediately and 1100 tons in about a month's time. Further that we might be able to send some more rice in the future, subject to our procurement.

As for the payment for the additional rice that we send, that is, the 2000 tons plus 1100 tons, Ajit Prasad says that we should ask for payment in kind, though he is not very sure that we will get it. We may perhaps suggest, as an alternative, deferred payment in kind or cash. Our Ambassador in Nepal says something about selling this rice at Rs 10/- per *maund* and charging the balance of the price to the money we have allotted for the development schemes in Nepal which is, I believe, one crore. I do not particularly like this idea and I do not know if it is feasible or desirable.

Anyhow, I should like your advice in this matter.

I hope to see you in Parliament a few minutes before question hour tomorrow.

Yours sincerely,
Jawaharlal Nehru

5. Cable to Bhagwan Sahay[1]

Continuation of my last night's telegram. Food situation here now and at least till end of year even more difficult than I had thought. However, as we are anxious to help Nepal to our utmost ability, we propose following:

As explained in last telegram,1900 tons rice are being sent now. In addition, we are prepared to make available immediately 1600 tons. Within a month, we shall make available another 1500 tons.

All this will total up to 5,000 tons of which 1500 are part of Nepal's previous purchase and 400 tons are our gift. We suggest that payment for the remaining 3100 tons should be in kind in the course of the coming harvest.

This is most we can do at present. Position later will depend on success of procurement policies.

I think Nepal's real difficulty will be to transport in near future even the rice that we make available now.

I hope you will explain position fully to Prime Minister K.I. Singh and tell him that we are taking this step, which involves some risk to us, because of our extreme desire to help Nepal. We would not agree to do this with any other country.

1. New Delhi, 21 August 1957. JN Collection.

6. Trade and Travel Agreement Between China and Nepal[1]

I have read your note as well as the other notes in this file. I have also read again the agreement between China and Nepal.[2]

1. Note to Foreign Secretary, MEA, New Delhi, 23 August 1957. JN Collection.
2. The reference is to the Trade and Travel Agreement between China and Nepal, signed on 20 September 1956 at Kathmandu. See also *Selected Works* (second series), Vol. 35, p. 501.

2. As the Prime Minister of Nepal has definitely asked for our views and our advice in this matter, we cannot withhold them. It may be that our views leak out. We cannot help that. Not to give any advice, when we are asked for it, would be improper.

3. Two questions arise: (1) Whether the agreement or treaty between Nepal and China should be formally ratified or not, and (2) relating to the frontier between the two countries.

4. These two questions appear to me to be independent of each other. There is no reference to the frontier in the agreement. That subject is left open. Whether it was desirable to leave it open or not at the time the agreement was entered into, is a matter which does not arise now. The agreement was arrived at, signed and proclaimed. The Chinese Government has ratified it. The Nepalese Radio etc., have announced the agreement of the Nepal Government to it. The only formal step that remains is for the Nepalese Government to inform the Chinese Government of their ratification.

5. Normally speaking, an agreement which has gone through all these processes, has to be accepted by a successor Government, unless that successor Government comes in through some revolutionary process and is prepared to abrogate all previous treaties and understandings. There has been no such revolution in Nepal. The Head of the State still continues to be the King of Nepal who has entered into these treaties and engagements. Only the Government has changed. It would thus be a very extraordinary procedure for the present Government of Nepal to go back on this treaty or to refuse to ratify it. Such a procedure would inevitably be greatly resented by the Government of China. If any attempt is made, as is suggested, to make the ratification contingent on an agreement about the frontier, the Chinese Government might well say that they are not prepared to enter into any talks for a further treaty or agreement when the previous one was rejected at the last stage. If a new Government in Nepal has the right to do so, then the same contingency might have to be faced in the event of the present Government in Nepal changing. There can be no assurance about the future.

6. Thus, to imagine that this will be some kind of pressure tactics on the Chinese Government to induce them to agree to discuss the frontier question and further to agree to hand over a part of what is considered their territory now to Nepal, seems to me wholly unreasonable. The effect on the Chinese Government is likely to be the very opposite of this.

7. The actual agreement between the two countries, which now await formal ratification by the Government of Nepal, appears to have no objectionable clauses. It is a straightforward treaty between the two countries, chiefly relating to trade, pilgrims, the nationals of the two countries and the exchange of

diplomatic and consular missions. I do not see how the Government of Nepal can take exception to any part of this agreement. At the most, they may not like the establishment of Chinese consular missions in Nepal. But that appears to me inevitable. Nepal wants to have its missions in Tibet.

8. I do not know what talks took place in Nepal when this agreement was discussed between the representatives of the two countries. While these talks were taking place, we had several visits from the Ambassador of China in Delhi,[3] who kept us informed of the broad nature of these talks. He assured us that he was anxious to have the goodwill of India in this matter as they recognized India's interests in it. He further gave the impression that the initiative came from the then Prime Minister of Nepal, probably during his visit to China. He further said that they had no intention of opening a separate mission at Kathmandu at least in the foreseeable future.

9. Thus, the attitude of the Chinese Government appears to have been quite straightforward throughout. Apart from this agreement, they gave a large sum of money to the Nepal Government.

10. I really do not understand on what ground or pretext the present Nepal Government can go behind this agreement and refuse to ratify it. That would undoubtedly be an unfriendly act to China. It will bring no pressure on China and there might well be a good deal of pressure on the Nepalese residents in Tibet, who might be harassed in many ways. Thus, there is no advantage at all, even from the strictly practical point of view, in rejecting this agreement or refusing to ratify it at this stage.

11. My advice, therefore, would be to ratify this agreement in the normal course. So far as the second question is concerned, the one relating to frontier, this can certainly be raised as a separate issue. I do not think it should be related in any way with this agreement. Any such attempt to relate it will probably be disadvantageous to Nepal.

12. Whether on the merits this question of frontier should be raised at this stage or soon is another matter. I am unable to express any firm opinion about it, as I do not know the actual geography of the place and have seen no map. Nor do I know the historical background.

13. But from these papers it appears that the Chinese Government or the Tibetan Government have been in possession of these areas which appears to be about a thousand square miles, for a hundred years. Thus, long term possession is in favour of the Chinese Government. Everyone knows that it is never an easy matter to challenge old possession and few Governments accept the argument

3. Pan Tzu-hi.

that by giving up some territories they occupy, they will have what is called a scientific frontier. If scientific frontiers were sought between various countries in the world, the present map of the world would have to be changed greatly. I cannot personally conceive of the Chinese Government agreeing to this demand, even though it might be considered logical. I have no idea of the kind of population that lives in this territory which is claimed by Nepal. Is it predominantly Tibetan or Nepalese? But whatever it may be, the major fact remains that there is hardly any chance of the Chinese Government agreeing to give it up. As I have said above, delay in the ratification of the agreement will not bring any pressure for this purpose on the Chinese Government. So far as procrastinating tactics are concerned, probably no Government can beat the Chinese at this game.

14. If this question of a rectification of the frontier is raised, it should be raised in a friendly way. Anything in the nature of a demand backed by some action, which is in the nature of pressure, is not likely to be successful.

15. Thus, my view is that an approach about the rectification of the frontier can be made, if the Nepal Government so chooses, but there is very little hope of success. In any event, it should be treated separately from the ratification of the agreement.

16. It may be pointed out that we have some minor frontier disputes with China. The areas concerned are on the Tibetan border in the high mountains. They are very small and are of no great value to either country. Nevertheless, these matters have not been settled yet, although the Chinese Government has agreed to discuss them with us. This shows that even a small frontier dispute is not easy to settle, even though it may have no great significance. In Burma, there have been interminable arguments about their frontier disputes.

17. I suggest that a copy of this note of mine might be sent by airmail to our Ambassador in Kathmandu. He can give the substance of it to the Prime Minister of Nepal who should be told that we are sending him our views because he was good enough to ask for them.

18. There is no need at this stage to refer to the Historical Division. For our own information, however, we might ask the Historical Division to send us a note about this thousand square mile territory to the west of Mustang, which is now sought to be claimed by Nepal. We need not wait for this note before writing to our Ambassador in Kathmandu. If there is anything important in the Historical Division's note, we can communicate it to our Ambassador later.

7. To Bhagwan Sahay[1]

New Delhi
September 4, 1957

My dear Bhagwan Sahay,

About a week ago, I had a visit from Ram Narain Mishra of the Nepali Congress. I believe he comes from the Terai. He said that the Nepali Congress was much distressed at recent developments which were likely to give rise to a good deal of trouble, and they wanted my advice as to what they should do. The election date was the 22nd October, but there was no chance of elections being held then. Then, there was the question as to whether there should be a Constituent Assembly or a Parliament.[2]

There was also some sorrow expressed at the fact that we were supporting the present Prime Minister.

I told him that, as a Government, we would support any functioning Government or Prime Minister in Nepal. It was not proper for a Government to intrigue against another Government. So far as the Nepali Congress was concerned, we had supported it for a long time, and we still considered it as probably the biggest political organization in Nepal. But, we were not responsible for the mess made repeatedly. Nor were we responsible for any new Government formed there. That was for the King to decide, and we cannot impose our wishes on the King.

I told him that I had received a letter some days ago, which was purported to be signed by B.P. Koirala.[3] This letter was in very abusive language, and I did not believe that it could be from B.P. Koirala. It must be a fake letter. Ram Narain Mishra said that no such letter could have been sent by B.P. Koirala.

As Ram Narain had talked about the Nepali Congress considering a direct action move, I said that any such move would be unfortunate. They should work quietly for the election.

---

1. JN Collection.
2. On 3 August 1957, K.I. Singh announced that Nepal's first general elections would be held for a parliament with full powers to draft a constitution. On 9 August, Nepal's three major political parties—Praja Parishad, Nepali Congress, and Nepali National Congress—formed an alliance under the name of Prajatantric Morcha or the Democratic Front with the objective of consolidating and strengthening the democratic forces to meet "the present threat to democracy."
3. Nepali Congress leader.

As for the question of a Constituent Assembly or a Parliament, they could express their views in regard to it. But, this should not be made an issue to start direct action. That would be foolish. The ultimate decision of the King should be accepted. The King was after all the one stabilizing factor, and it would be unwise to try to weaken that factor or to have a struggle against him.

I am sending you this for your information.

Surya Prasad Upadhyaya has come to Delhi and wants an interview with me. I shall probably see him in two or three days' time. I am very busy during the next two days.

Yours sincerely,
Jawaharlal Nehru

(iii) Hungary

1. No Foreign Propaganda in India[1]

Will you kindly see these papers in regard to the applications for visas from some Hungarian student émigrés.

We have in the past followed a policy of not encouraging foreigners coming here for propaganda purposes in regard to problems affecting foreign countries. The propaganda might be for a worthy cause. But once we admitted people to carry on propaganda, we could not very well oppose this who wanted to indulge in counter-propaganda. We did not wish India to become a forum for this type of propaganda and counter-propaganda.

Even we grant asylum to any foreigner, as we have sometimes done, it is on the express understanding that he will not indulge in propaganda while he is in India. You can well understand that such propaganda may often be an embarrassment to us and create some international difficulties. In fact, to give permission for propaganda in regard to controversial issues is itself rather to

1. Note to Home Minister, New Delhi, 14 August 1957. JN Collection.

deviate from our broad policy of non-alignment. Naturally we sympathize with the people of many countries who have suffered either from foreign domination or other types of oppression. We have expressed repeatedly our sympathy for the people of Hungary. As a matter of fact, I have received many letters and messages of thanks from Hungarian emigres as well as people in Hungary for our expressions of sympathy.

There is another aspect to this question. The Hungarian question is coming up for discussion in the UN probably next month.[2] Just at that time to have Hungarian emigres carrying on propaganda here does not seem to me to be right.

I feel, therefore, that our decision not to grant visas to these persons was justified.

2. The report of the Special Committee on Hungary, established by a resolution passed on 10 January 1957 in the United Nations General Assembly to investigate and establish direct observations in Hungary, was to be discussed before the regular session began on 16 September 1957.

2. Meeting with the Hungarian Delegation[1]

I do not think there is any point in our delaying our reply till I have met the Hungarian delegation.[2] Therefore, the reply should be sent. I prefer the longer draft.[3]

2. I take it that the Foreign Secretary will be meeting the Hungarian delegation before I see them day after tomorrow. I should like him to send me a brief note

1. Note to Foreign Secretary and Joint Secretary, MEA, New Delhi, 15 August 1957. JN Collection.
2. Nehru met the Hungarian delegation on 17 August.
3. In response to the UN Secretary General's wish for reconvening the General Assembly to consider the UN report on Hungary, it was suggested that if the majority of the Members were in favour of the Assembly being reconvened on 10 September, India had no objection. However, the discussion of a controversial subject like this immediately before opening of the 12th session might not be entirely desirable. The report could be discussed concurrently with the 12th session without inconvenience. This would also ensure high level representation and avoid unnecessary expenditure.

about his talks with them. My own line of talk will be to lay greater stress on subsequent happenings which apparently continue even today, that is, arrests, detentions and executions. Further that, on general principles, we have been against the use of foreign troops in any country. It is difficult for us to object to this in one country and accept it as right in another. The continuance of large numbers of foreign troops gives rise to the impression that, without their help, the situation cannot be controlled.[4]

3. For our part, we would have preferred to avoid a discussion at this stage in the United Nations. But, in view of circumstances, this cannot be avoided. Even so, we would prefer it to be as far as possible without acrimony. We are not so much concerned with the past as with the present and the future.

4. I should like you to send me the UN report on Hungary,[5] so that I can glance through it before I meet the Hungarian delegation.

4. No record of this meeting is available.
5. The report condemned the Soviet Union for her intervention in crushing the Hungarian uprising in October 1956.

3. Soviet Approach to the UN Report[1]

The Soviet Charge d'Affaires came to see me today under instructions from his Government. He said that objective conditions in the world today were ripe for lessening tensions etc. The Soviet Government adhered to the Five Principles and was working for disarmament.

Then he referred to the coming 12th Session of the UN General Assembly and said that the Soviet Government would welcome the cooperation of the Indian Delegation with the Soviet Delegation in facing the major problems that came up there. But the Western Powers were bringing up the Hungarian question there in order to divert attention from the real problems. The Commission's report on Hungary contains slanderous accusations against the USSR and Hungary. Also it was an incitement to the reactionaries in Hungary. This approach

1. Note to Secretary General and Foreign Secretary, New Delhi, 21 August 1957. JN Collection. Also available in File No. 1(41)-UN-II/57, pp. 4-5/N, MEA.

was one of cold war. The Soviet Government hoped that the Indian Delegation in the UN would oppose this attempt of the Western Powers. Great importance was attached in Moscow to India's attitude in this matter.

I told him that, as the Soviet Government knew, India was devoted to peace and to working for the lessening of international tensions and disarmament. We did not want anything to be done which would add to tension. But as a Commission in Hungary had been appointed by the UN, and it had presented a report, this had to be considered some time or other by the General Assembly. It may well be that some Powers wanted to utilize this report for the purposes of the cold war and to criticize and condemn the Soviet Union and the Hungarian Government.

While we recognize that there was a good deal of incitement from outside last year and some reactionaries undoubtedly participated in the rising in Hungary, there also appeared to be little doubt that large numbers of students, workers and others had joined in this rising, because, as had been admitted by Mr Kadar[2] himself, many mistakes had been committed previously and also because of their desire to be free of any foreign control. India's policy has always been that there should be no foreign forces in any country and the people of the country should work out their own destiny.

The position in Hungary was no doubt a very difficult one, more especially because of developments in Egypt and the Israelite Anglo-French invasion there. Apart from what had happened last year, what troubled us greatly was the continuing repression there and the news of execution, arrests, deportations, etc. This was something which would undoubtedly be taken advantage of by the opponents of the Soviet Union.

The Charge d'Affaires then referred to the Presidentship of the next session of the United Nations. He said that there were two names proposed thus far. One was that of Munroe[3] of New Zealand and the other was that of Charles

---

2. Janos Kadar was the Prime Minister of Hungary.
3. Leslie (Knox) Munro (1901-1974); lawyer from New Zealand; taught at Auckland University college; President, Auckland District Law Society, 1936-38; Member, New Zealand Law Society Council, 1936-39; Editor, *New Zealand Herald*, 1942-51; New Zealand Ambassador to the US, 1952-58; New Zealand Permanent Representative to the UN, 1952-58; President, Trusteeship Council, 1953-54; New Zealand Delegate to Security Council, 1954-55; Chairman, First Political Committee, UN, 1957; President of the UNGA, 1957-58; UN Representative on Implementation of Hungarian Resolutions, 1958-62; Secretary-General, International Commission of Jurists, 1961-63; Member of Parliament, 1963-74; author of *United Nations: Hope for a Divided World*.

Malik[4] of Lebanon. Another name was now being considered and this was Dr Ali Sastroamidjojo.[5] This name was more acceptable to the Soviet and to some others provided it was acceptable to the Government of Indonesia and the Bandung countries.

I said I had not heard of Dr Ali's name in this connection. We considered it a good name, but obviously he could only stand if he was formally put forward by the Government of Indonesia and there was general support for him. Otherwise there would be no point in standing.

4. Charles Habib Malik (b. 1906); Lebanese philosopher, educationist and diplomatist; taught at American University, Beriut, 1927-45 and 1955-60; Chairman of various UN Committees between 1947-54; Minister of Foreign Affairs, Education and Fine Arts, 1956-57; President, UN General Assembly, 1958-59; Distinguished Professor of Philosophy, American University, Beirut, 1962-76; President, World Council of Christian Education, 1967-71; Jacques Maritian Distinguished Professor of Moral and Political Philosophy, Catholic University, Washington, 1981-82; author of *War and Peace, Problem of Asia, Problem of Coexistence, God and Man in Contemporary Christian Thought* and *God and Man in Contemporary Islamic Thought..*
5. Permanent Representative of Indonesia to UN.

4. Cable to Ali Yavar Jung[1]

Your telegram 412 August 24 to Foreign Secretary.[2]

2. It is difficult for us to indicate precisely what our attitude will be in regard to Hungarian discussion in General Assembly till we know what proposals are made. UN having appointed Commission on Hungary it follows that their report should be considered and we cannot oppose its consideration. We should have preferred this to take place somewhat later and in quieter atmosphere. Thus we

1. New Delhi, 25 August 1957. File No. 5 (31)-UN-II/56, Vol. II, pp. 192-93/C, MEA. Also available in JN Collection.
2. Jung, India's Ambassador in Egypt, wrote that Nasser would be grateful for precise indication of India's attitude and vote on proposal for discussion of Report on Hungary in the General Assembly. Jung presumed from the news messages that India was not opposing but would "abstain with explanation of vote." He informed that the Russians were pressing the Egyptians to vote for them.

cannot oppose proposal for discussion of report. What we dislike is exploitation of this situation for purposes of cold war and thus adding to international tensions.

3. I have often expressed my view publicly that Hungarian rising was essentially nationalist although there was no doubt incitement from outside as well as from reactionary groups inside. Suppression of this nationalist upheaval was tragic. Further we have made it clear that we do not approve of foreign troops in any country. This applies to Hungary as well as other countries of Western and Eastern Europe. We cannot, therefore, accept the explanation of the Soviet Government or the present Hungarian Government about events in Hungary last year. Nor can we accept the Western Powers' analysis of them. The UN Commission's report on Hungary, though impressive in many ways, is after all based on wholly one-sided testimony and cannot be called judicial document. It is true that Hungarian and Russian Governments are partly responsible as they refused to give facilities to UN Commission.

4. We would generally be against any condemnatory resolution. At the same time we cannot ignore what has happened and continues to happen in Hungary. What is peculiarly unfortunate is that repression, including executions, deportations, etc., have continued in Hungary.

5. A message from the Soviet Government came to us also pressing us to support them in regard to Hungary. We have tried to explain our position to them. We shall thus have to wait till we see resolutions put forward and then decide. It might perhaps be desirable for UN to suggest Hammarskjold[3] to visit Hungary. This would keep Hungarian question in view, as Western Powers desire, and at the same time not condemn Soviet or Hungarian Government. We sympathize greatly with Hungarian nationalist sentiment and would like to help it. But we feel that the only practical way of doing so is to avoid cold war condemnation and cold war tactics. During past year we have been bringing friendly pressures to bear on Soviet as well as Hungarian Governments so as to ease the situation of the Hungarian people and restore normal conditions.

6. You might explain this general attitude of ours to President Nasser.

3. Dag Hammarskjold, Secretary-General of the UN.

5. Message to U Nu[1]

Thank you for your message about the Hungarian question, which I received yesterday.[2] I agree with you that discussion of this at this stage will serve no useful purpose. But, since it has come up, we cannot avoid this discussion.

2. The UN report, however, carefully drafted, nevertheless, is based on one-sided evidence. That evidence is impressive. But refugees and émigrés are not always reliable witnesses and tend to exaggerate because of their own sufferings. However, I have no doubt that Hungarian rising was essentially nationalist, although it is true that there were persistent incitements from outside. Our attitude in regard to it has been from the very beginning that we do not approve of foreign troops in any country and, secondly, that the people should be given an opportunity to decide about their own future. This is a general principle which should be applied everywhere, including Hungary.

3. I entirely agree with you that it will be unfortunate if this discussion raises tensions and, in fact, does harm to the Hungarian people and their aspirations. I do not know what line the United States and the United Kingdom are likely to adopt. To some extent, though I am not sure, they do not appear to be anxious to take up an extreme line, but they will, no doubt, adopt the technique of cold war, which will be unfortunate. Any attempt at outright condemnation of the Soviet or Hungarian Governments appears to me undesirable.

4. All I can suggest is that we should endeavour to moderate tone of discussions and try to see that no extreme attitude is adopted. Perhaps, it might be helpful to say that the Secretary General, United Nations, might visit Hungary.

5. One important fact has to be remembered. The Hungarian rising coincided with the Anglo-French invasion of Egypt. This undoubtedly produced impression in Soviet Union that this was a joint move of Western Powers, which was likely to lead to world war. In this context, they felt that they dared not take any risks in Hungary. This is not a justification, but partly an explanation.

6. Our main concern, as you say, must necessarily be to take steps which promote peace and to avoid such steps as increase tensions.

1. New Delhi, 29 August 1957. JN Collection.
2. U Nu, Prime Minister of Myanmar, had written that it was difficult not to accept the basic conclusion of the UN Special Committee's report on Hungary. He was impressed by the fact that the report was unanimous and restraint was shown in drafting the report. He felt that besides looking into the rights and wrongs of the matter, it had to be considered in the larger background of promoting peace and helping the Hungarian people.

6. To Herbert V. Evatt[1]

New Delhi
August 29, 1957

Dear Mr Evatt,[2]

Thank you for your letter on the subject of Hungary.[3] I agree with you largely in your approach to this question. It has been our endeavour in the past to find some way to ease the situation in Hungary. This was the only way to help the Hungarian people. The approach of the cold war was bound to react unfavourably on the Hungarians. We shall certainly continue our effort.

I am very sorry to learn that your wife slipped and fell and fractured her wrist. I hope she has recovered.

All good wishes,

Yours very sincerely,
Jawaharlal Nehru

---

1. JN Collection.
2. Leader of the Federal Parliamentary Labour Party of Australia.
3. Evatt wrote that he made an appeal to the USSR Government seeking their intervention with a view to procure amnesty for the Hungarians following the armed revolt. To this he got the reply that it was exclusively a matter for the Government of Hungary. He wrote that Anna Kethley, Leader of the Hungarian Social Democratic Party in exile, would be most helpful in attempting to negotiate a just and democratic settlement of the Hungarian disputes. He appealed to Nehru to take immediate action in this matter.

7. Situation in Hungary[1]

I met the Soviet Charge d' Affaires this afternoon and spoke to him about Hungary. I referred to our last talk on this subject and reminded him that we are

---

1. Note, New Delhi, 6 September 1957. JN Collection. Also available in V.K. Krishna Menon Papers, NMML.

very much averse to any kind of mud-slinging in the United Nations or elsewhere on this subject. We do not think any condemnations will do any good to the people of Hungary or to anyone else.

2. I was worried, however, not so much about the past, but about reports of present happenings in Hungary. We were informed that large numbers of arrests and convictions were still taking place there and that the secret police which has ceased to function in the Soviet Union and Poland and other countries was still very much in evidence in Hungary. Our own Ambassador,[2] who had recently visited Budapest, also reported to us that while there had been some improvement in some ways in the situation, it was regrettable that so many political arrests were being made.

3. I said further that while it might be relatively easy to deal with past events, reports of present happenings of this kind would be much more difficult to deal with in the UN or elsewhere. It would strengthen the Hungarian Government's position much if there was an improvement in this matter in the present.

4. I mentioned to him also that I had received a telegram from some International Association of Jurists saying that trials in Hungary did not allow adequate facilities for defence.

5. I added that I hoped that the Soviet Government would exercise their influence in this matter in creating normal conditions in Hungary.

6. The Soviet Charge d'Affaires said that he would communicate what I said to his Government.

7. I think you might send a brief telegram to our Ambassador in Moscow informing him of what I have said to the Soviet Charge d'Affaires here.

---

2. K.P.S. Menon also represented India in Hungary.

8. India's Stand on the UN Resolution[1]

I do not think it will be desirable or feasible for our Representative to remain silent during the debate on any Hungarian resolution.[2] We do not yet know what final form this resolution may take, but, from such indications as we have had, it will be wholly unacceptable to us.[3]

2. When I said something about the UN Secretary General visiting Hungary, I merely repeated what had been suggested by someone in New York. I do not think we should make that suggestion.

3. On the whole, I am inclined to think that our Representative should say something when this matter comes up in the General Assembly. It is rather difficult to indicate precisely what he should say, when we do not know what the exact form of the resolution might be. I take it that Shri Arthur Lall has been informed of what I have said on the subject in the Lok Sabha.[4] That should be the broad line he should take up. If we know more about the resolution to be proposed there, we could indicate more precisely what might be said.

4. Only yesterday, I spoke to the Soviet Charge d'Affaires here, and laid stress on present conditions and the reports received by us about continuing arrests, prosecutions, etc., in Hungary. He said that he would inform his Government

---

1. Note to Defence Minister and Foreign Secretary, New Delhi, 7 September 1957. JN Collection.
2. Instructions had to be sent to Arthur Lall for the forthcoming debate in the UN General Assembly on Hungary. Krishna Menon's viewpoint was that it would be best not to participate in the debate and abstain on all resolutions that might be put forward as India's participation would have adverse repercussions on various problems before the UN. Besides, any resolution at the time would be based on the Special Committee's report, whose establishment and terms of reference India did not approve.
3. The US delegation to the UN had given a copy of the draft resolution on Hungary to Arthur Lall. Based on the Special Committee's report, the draft resolution held USSR responsible for violating the UN Charter, depriving Hungary of its liberty and political independence, and accused the Hungarian authorities of violating human rights and having been imposed by the Soviet intervention. The resolution condemned these acts and the continued defiance of the resolutions of the General Assembly, recognized the plight of the Hungarian people, called upon the USSR and the present Hungarian Government to desist from repressive measures and ensure the return of deported Hungarian citizens, and requested a special representative of the General Assembly to take such steps as he deemed appropriate in view of the Special Committee's findings.
4. See *ante*, pp. 519-520.

immediately. I think the Hungarian Minister or Charge here has also been spoken to by the Foreign Secretary.

5. I do not see what alternative resolution we can move. Probably, the best course would be for our Representative to speak explaining our attitude and then abstain from voting on the resolution.[5]

6. I should like the Defence Minister to see this and give us his own advice in the matter. This might, therefore, be sent to the Defence Minister first.

5. The resolution was passed on 14 September 1957 in the General Assembly by 60 votes to ten with ten abstentions including India.

9. To Bimal C. Ghose[1]

New Delhi
October 22, 1957

Dear Ghose,[2]

Thank you for your letter of the 21st October, with which you have sent me a report on Hungary and a report on your visit to Egypt. I have read both these with great interest.

About Hungary, as you say, two policies are suggested: one of broadly supporting the Kadar Government and the second, of condemning it and thereby condemning Russia.

It is, of course, a very difficult matter to decide what to do about Hungary. As you have said, it is generally admitted that no outsider can render much help to the Hungarian people and the only hope lies in a lowering of international tension. So far as our policy is concerned, it has been, if I may say so, something between the two you have mentioned above. We have not supported the Kadar

1. JN Collection.
2. Bimal Comar Ghose (1906-1961); taught Commerce in Calcutta University for several years; Editor, *Current Thought*, 1939-46; Member, Bengal/West Bengal Legislative Assembly, 1946-52; Member, Rajya Sabha, 1952-57; Member, Lok Sabha, 1957-62.

Government, but have on many occasions criticized its policy, more especially the continuing arrests and repression that have been going on in Hungary. We have done so in public, but more particularly in our diplomatic communications both to the Kadar Government and the Soviet Government. It is true, however, that we have not ceased to recognize the Kadar Government. We deal with it as a Government functioning there and because we feel that our not recognizing it would mean our cutting off all contacts with Hungary and withdrawing our Mission there. That would not help us in any way.

While we have expressed repeatedly our dissatisfaction at things as they are and as they were, and deplore them, we have avoided merely condemning, as we felt that that would not help in any way and would reduce such influence as we have with these Governments.

As regards Egypt, while what you say is largely true, I think, you are wrong in saying that no leading Egyptian has positively expressed himself in our favour in regard to Kashmir. Some of their most important newspapers, officially run, have written very strongly in our favour on the Kashmir issue.

Yours sincerely,
Jawaharlal Nehru

VI. Syria

1. Situation in Syria[1]

This is in continuation of my note dealing with my interview with the UK High Commissioner this afternoon. The first part of this note deals with our talks relating to the Kashmir issue.[2] I am now dealing with the further conversation

---

1. Note to Foreign Secretary and Commonwealth Secretary, MEA, New Delhi, 15 September 1957. JN Collection.
2. See *ante*, pp. 499-501.

with him in regard to Syria and the Middle East situation.[3]

2. I told the High Commissioner that I agreed that the present Government in Syria was what is called leftist. It may be that some of its leaders were Communist or pro-Communist. But I did not think that it would be right to say, as Mr Macmillan had said in his message to me, that Syria had "passed the point of no return" or that the situation was similar to that in Czechoslovakia before the Benes[4] and Jan Masaryk[5] affair.[6]

It was probably true that Syria was not an ideal democracy and much depended upon the army. As a matter of fact, none of the countries surrounding Syria could be called democracies. Probably, Syria was somewhat more democratic in its structure than these neighbouring countries.

3. Various developments in Syria and around led to increasing tensions in the area. Syria concluded a large-scale aid agreement with the USSR on 6 August 1957 in Moscow. On 13 August, the Syrian Government announced of uncovering a plot, backed by the US, to overthrow the Government and modify its independent foreign policy; and dismissed 10 army officers on 17 August. Shukri el Kuwatly, the President, held discussions with Nasser in Cairo for a federation between Syria and Egypt from 18 to 25 August. Statements from the Western and Soviet blocs added to the tensions. For example, Eisenhower said in a press conference on 21 August that the "old Soviet pattern" was emerging of offering economic and military aid and trying to penetrate the receiving country with agents and stooges. On 23 August, Radio Moscow accused the US of resorting to "Machiavellian methods" in an attempt to overthrow the Syrian Government. It was reported that the US Sixth Fleet had moved into the Mediterranean waters and two Soviet warships were speeding to reinforce the Soviet Fleet at its Albanian base. On 7 September, Dulles issued a statement reinforcing the US Middle Eastern policies. On 10 September, the Soviet Foreign Minister, Andrei Gromyko, talked about the threat of armed intervention in Syria and setting up certain Arab countries against it, e.g., Iraq, Jordan and Lebanon. Turkish troops were also reported to be concentrating on the Syrian borders. On 11 September, Syria sent notes to the Governments of Iraq, Jordan and Lebanon, whether they had expressed anxiety to the US over the build-up of Soviet arms in Syria.

4. Edvard Benes (1884-1948); Czechoslovakian statesman; worked in Paris with Tomas Masaryk for Czechoslovakian nationalism, 1915-19; Foreign Minister of the new state, 1918-35, also Premier, 1921-22 and President, 1935-38; resigned and left the country, 1938; set up a government in exile in England and its President, 1941-45; returned to his country in 1945 and re-elected as President, 1945-48; resigned after the Communist coup of 1948.

5. Jan Garrigue Masaryk (1886-1948); Czechoslovakian Ambassador in London, 1925-28; appointed as Foreign Minister in exile, 1941; returned to Prague with Benes in 1945 and remained in office till his suicide in 1948.

6. The Communists took over power in Czechoslovakia on 25 February 1948. Jan Masaryk, the Foreign Minister, a non-party member of the coalition government since 1940, committed suicide on 10 March 1948.

3. There could be little doubt that there was no Communist movement as such in any of these countries and not even in Syria. It was true, however, that Syria had relied and was relying on the Soviet Union. That was not because of Communism, but from a feeling of self-preservation. All the countries roundabout Syria were hostile to Syria and were being supported by some of the big Powers. Apparently, attempts had been made to bring about, through pressure, a change in the regime in Syria. These attempts failed, with their natural reaction in favour of the Soviet Union there. For many months past, the general impression was that Syria was being isolated, and these pressures were being exercised on her. The story of the US plot, which the Syrian Government had given out, was possibly considerably exaggerated. But, there could be little doubt about these pressures.

4. This question is, therefore, to be viewed not from the point of view of Communism, but of Syria being involved in these struggles of Great Powers for controlling the destinies of the Middle East countries. Also, the parallel with Czechoslovakia was wrong in many other ways. Syria was not contiguous to the Soviet Union. Syria, unlike Czechoslovakia, was a country far removed from communism, while in Czechoslovakia, there was a strong Communist Party. And then, there was Stalin in the old days, while now the situation was different.

5. It seemed to me that the attempts by the US to control the situation in Syria had not only failed, but boomeranged back and thrust Syria further away from them and into the arms of the Soviet Union. Any further attempt to exercise pressure of that kind would have the same result, and arms would be piled up on both sides, adding even more to the explosive nature of the situation.

6. It seemed to me quite clear from the geography of the situation that Syria could not possibly think of attacking any of the neighbouring Arab countries, or indeed any country. That was unthinkable. There was some chance of these Arab countries attacking her, because they were stronger. But the situation that had arisen now was that any military conflict might well bring in the Great Powers and thus lead to a much wider conflict. The message sent by Bulganin to the Turkish Prime Minister could not be ignored. I think it meant what it said.

7. Syria's relations with Egypt were very close, and my own impression was that Egypt had often counselled moderation to the Syrian Government and would no doubt continue to do so. We, in India, did not presume to have any such influence, but we had friendly relations with Syria and they attached some little value to our advice. In fact, we had been hearing from them lately in regard to the present situation. All these indicated that it was wrong to imagine that Syria was cut off from the rest of the world and was entirely dominated by the Soviet Union. The influence of the Soviet Union today indeed was considerable, and large-scale help had been given to Syria by them. But, it was not true that Syria

had become a Communist State or would be impervious to other factors. The danger was that military threats or operations by the Western Powers might push Syria more and more into the Soviet orbit in sheer self-defence. The so-called Eisenhower Doctrine[7] had not brought peace to the Middle East, and any action taken thereunder might well lead to a more serious crisis than the one we had to face now.

8. Thus, the position was that there was no real danger from Syria to any of the adjoining countries, and it would be extreme folly for Syria to take any aggressive step. If no further steps were taken which appeared to Syria to threaten her, the situation would quieten down. However, much the Soviet influence in Syria was disliked, there was no way to eliminate it by warlike measures, which indeed would increase that influence, apart from other dangerous consequences.

9. I mentioned to the High Commissioner that the Syrian Government wanted very much to have Mr Krishna Menon break his journey at Damascus on his way to New York. Unfortunately, this was not possible. Further, the Syrian Parliament had invited a Parliamentary Delegation from India. All this indicated how they were anxious to cultivate friendly and cooperative relations with other countries, and not to be tied up just to the Soviet Union.

10. The UK High Commissioner said that he would convey to Mr Macmillan what I had said to him.

11. As I have indicated in my other note of today, I should like copies of this note as well as of Mr Macmillan's messages to be sent to Mr Krishna Menon by air mail.

---

7. See *Selected Works* (second series), Vol. 37, p. 469.

2. Message to Harold Macmillan[1]

Thank you for your message about Syria,[2] which I received through your High Commissioner in Delhi. I agree with you that the situation there is a difficult and explosive one.

2. I have been watching developments in Syria for many months, and I paid a brief visit to Damascus in June last.[3] I found then a prevailing fear of being surrounded by hostile forces backed by some of the Great Powers. Economic pressures were being exercised against them. There was an intense nationalist feeling and a desire to do everything for self-preservation. Owing to certain military alliances, notably the Baghdad Pact, the countries surrounding Syria were becoming progressively more hostile to it, and the Syrians believed that these countries had the powerful support of the United States. They further believed that a deliberate attempt was being made to isolate their country and thus bring pressure to bear upon them so as to change the regime there.

3. It is true that recent changes there have brought a group of young army officers to the front, and some of these are pro-communist. But I am assured that communism as such has little strength or organization in Syria. I do not think the situation there can be compared to that in Czechoslovakia where there was a strong though minority Communist Party. Apart from this, the background of Syria is completely different. The Soviet Union has no common frontier with it, and the position even in the Soviet Union is different from what it was in Stalin's day. I am informed by competent observers that most of the leading officers in control in Syria now are young, intensely patriotic and nationalistic,

1. New Delhi, 17 September 1957. JN Collection.
2. Macmillan expressed his apprehensions regarding developments in Syria and commented that the effective control of the country was in the hands of the extreme left wing, although the Communist ideology had not been adopted and a façade of democracy was still preserved. He wrote that since the return of Khaled el-Azem, Defence Minister of Syria, from Moscow and the announcement of the 6 August agreement with the Soviet Union, the Syrian Chief of Staff, Major-General Nizamuddin, had been replaced by Colonel Bezri who was reliably reported to be a communist. This was followed by changes in the command of police and security forces, and dismissal and arrest of army officers Macmillan thought that these changes completed the consolidation of the position of the left wing elements of the army with considerable power for some time. He also wrote that the neighbouring States were disturbed at these developments and were sure that the democratic forces in Syria were "now completely immobilized."
3. For Nehru's visit to Syria in June 1957, see *Selected Works* (second series), Vol. 38, pp. 469-476.

and honest and idealistic. They are politically inexperienced and somewhat naïve. Their dominant urge appears to be a nationalist one and a desire to preserve the independence of their country from the hostile elements ranged against them. It is possible, of course, that they might take wrong steps. But I cannot imagine them to be foolish enough to adopt any aggressive measures against their neighbouring States. That would amount to suicide. If, however, they are driven to extreme courses by fear of any military or like action against them, then they may well rely even more on the Soviet.

4, President Kuwatly is certainly a moderating and stabilizing force, and he has great popularity. I know that the influence of Egypt has also been exercised in favour of moderation, and we have also advised the Syrian Government on these lines.

5. Reports of concentration of Turkish troops on the Syrian border would indicate that the danger comes from Syria's neighbouring countries rather than from Syria. Whatever the wishes of some people in Syria might be, the Syrian Government is in no position to exercise much pressure on its neighbours or to try to subvert their regimes. It is true that Syrian democracy is weak. It may be said that most of the other countries of Western Asia are also not very democratic, and there appears to be a cleavage there between governments and popular opinion.

6. I agree with you that the urgent need is to promote stability in the Middle Eastern area. I am convinced that this can only be achieved by removing the fear of armed intervention from either side or of attempts to change regimes by external pressure. Arab nationalism is a basic fact in all these countries, and communism is not even a distant prospect. But, if nationalism is driven to take help from communist, then the combination of the two might certainly be strong. The right course would appear to be to prevent such a combination from taking place and to allow nationalism to grow independently and to work out its destiny.

7. I agree with you about the importance to Europe of oil supplies from this region and of the necessity to help the tender plant of democracy to grow. But there is danger of democracy breaking down under fear or heavy pressures from outside.[4]

8. I have ventured to express my views frankly to you and give you my appraisal of the situation in Syria. We have fairly good contacts with Syria. The Syrian Government attaches some value to our advice. That itself indicates that they have not reached a point of no return.

4. Macmillan wrote that the Middle East was the obvious target for Soviet expansion, and the importance to Europe of oil supplies from this region gave it added value to the Soviet strategists. He expressed the desire of the West "to preserve the tender plant of democracy in the Middle East from the subversive tactics employed against it."

3. Cable to V.K. Krishna Menon[1]

Your telegram 574[2] and 575 October 17th.[3] My Japanese tour was very exhausting and I developed cold and slight temperature. After full rest here, I am much better and temperature is normal.

2. Banerjee's[4] reports from Syria have appeared to me to be objective and fully stating Syria's viewpoint.[5] When I was in Damascus last summer, President[6] and Prime Minister[7] there privately spoke to me highly about him.[8]

3. Our Ambassador in Ankara[9] reports that according to his information, reports of Syrian Government about Turkish troops on southern border are greatly exaggerated. These troops do not exceed thirty thousand and are totally inadequate for undertaking any offensive campaign. Also Turkish Government fully occupied with General Election scheduled October 27th. Many senior army officers have resigned from army as they are standing for election. Hence it appears most unlikely that any effective preparations are being made.

1. New Delhi, 18 October 1957. JN Collection.
2. Krishna Menon wrote from New York that the Syrian situation had been boiling up for some time. It was to prevent the matter from becoming internationalized like Kashmir, the Syrians postponed their original intention of going to the General Assembly. The reference to the Assembly could no longer be delayed as a coup d'etat in Syria was impending, according to Krishna Menon.
3. Not available.
4. Shisir Kumar Banerjee (b. 1913); civil servant and diplomat; First Secretary and Charge d'Affaires in Indian Embassy, Tehran, 1947-49; Deputy High Commissioner of India in Lahore, 1951-54; Consul General of India, San Francisco, 1954-56; Ambassador to Syria 1957-58; High Commissioner to Malaya, 1958-59; Ambassador to West Germany, 1964-67, to Japan, 1967-70.
5. On 16 October 1957, Syria formally requested the President of the UN General Assembly to hold a debate on "the threat to the peace and security of Syria." In the explanatory memorandum Syria charged Turkey with massing troops on Syrian frontier which "presaged an imminent attack."
6. Shukri el Kuwatly.
7. Sabri Asali.
8. Krishna Menon stated that Banerjee was unreliable both in regard to judgement and observations, and wanted his removal from such an extremely sensitive post to avoid any trouble for India.
9. V.H. Coelho was Indian Charge d'Affaires in Ankara.

4. India's Stand on Syria[1]

The Soviet Ambassador[2] came to see me at 9.45 tonight. He said that he had received two messages from Moscow to be conveyed to me. They were about Syria. He gave me an English version of them, reminding me, however, that this was unofficial. I enclose these two messages.[3]

2. I told him that we had been very much concerned about the Syrian situation and about the possibility of conflict. Our own impression was, however, that there was little chance of any aggression or military conflict now. There probably was some danger some time ago, but the matter had been so much publicized and world attention drawn to it in the UN and elsewhere, that it seemed to us very unlikely that any aggression or conflict would take place. Also, there were the Turkish elections and the resignations of a number of senior Turkish Generals to stand in these elections. I added that our own information received today about Syria was that the situation was calmer.

3. The Ambassador said that while there might be justification for our view, the danger persisted and we had to be very careful and not allow something to happen unawares. This was what happened in the case of Egypt last year. There was talk of peaceful settlement and all that, and suddenly there was aggression.

1. Note to Secretary General and Foreign Secretary, MEA, New Delhi, 25 October 1957. JN Collection.
2. Mikhail A. Menshikov.
3. The messages from the USSR referred to the possibility of a threat of armed aggression by Turkey on Syria. The first message mentioned the ceaseless military preparations of Turkey on border with Syria, where big armed forces of the Turkish army, known as the Hatay mobile grouping of forces, had concentrated. It was said to have been done in the interests of certain powers who were displeased with the fact that the Syrian Government, supported by the Parliament and the people, were pursuing a consistent policy of national independence and did not want to participate in aggressive blocs. An armed attack on Syria by Turkey, which was a NATO member, would spread the conflict to other countries as was evident from the statement of the US State Department. The message said that Syria would not be left alone in that case. The UN must not ignore the situation and should immediately interfere to prevent the war. The second message expressed the fear that the USA was trying to prevent discussion of the Syrian complaint in the UN. Their main purpose was not to allow the UN interference, to bring about split among the Arab nations supporting Syria, and to prevent the General Assembly from taking a decision on creation of a Commission on the spot. It also said that the idea of mediation between Syria and Turkey had no ground, since there was no controversy between the two. Under these circumstances, Indian delegation's active support to Syria in the General Assembly would be very helpful especially for creation of a UN Commission.

4. I agreed that we should remain alert and do everything in our power to prevent any conflict. So far as the Saudi mediation was concerned, this seemed to be off. At any rate, the latest reports indicated that. It was true that an attempt was made in the UN to postpone the debate there, but this had not wholly succeeded, and the postponement was only for three days. Of course, it might be possible that a further attempt might be made for postponement. So far as we were concerned, we were of opinion that the discussion should take place in the UK, and that it was desirable to have a commission of enquiry. Broadly speaking, we were supporting Syria in this matter.

5. I think that you might send a very brief telegram to Shri Krishna Menon informing him about the Soviet Government's messages to us, and adding that we had told them that we were not in favour of a postponement of the discussion in the UN. Further, that we thought that a commission of enquiry should be appointed as suggested by Syria.

(v) Malaya

1. Message on Malaya's Independence[1]

Ten years ago, almost to a day India attained Independence, this was no easy achievement and a 100 years of struggle preceeded it. After much violence in the early days, our great national movement, under Mahatma Gandhi's leadership turned to peaceful courses and thus built up the strength of the country on the right lines. As a result, when Independence came, it was by a friendly agreement between India and England and the memory of past struggles faded out and we continued on our free will to remain associated with the Commonwealth. Other countries like Burma, Ceylon and Pakistan also became independent. Recently Ghana joined the ranks of free nations and now comes the turn of Malaya. This is a great day not only for Malaya but for Asia, and we welcome it and send our

---

1. New Delhi, 13 August 1957. AIR tapes, NMML. Also available in JN Collection.

greetings to the people of Malaya on the achievement of independence. I look forward to close cooperation with them for our mutual advantage and in the cause of world peace and progress.

Even as countries of Asia shed their colonial status and attained independence, the face of Asia changes and the Commonwealth, with which some of us are associated, also is powerfully affected. I earnestly hope that this historic event will help the cause of peace and cooperation between nations. To Asia it is of a special importance. It is another forward step in the awakening and rejuvenation of this ancient Continent which has played such an important part in the world history. Today the world is in the grip of fear and the hydrogen bomb is the symbol of impending catastrophe. I hope that the countries of Asia will throw their weight on the side of peace, for without peace there can be no progress. *Merdeka!*

2. Message to Harold Macmillan[1]

I am grateful to you for your message which refers to Malaya which your High Commissioner conveyed to me on the 15th of August.[2] I thank you for letting me know about the various steps that have been and are being taken in Malaya for the completion of the constitutional processes.

The question of Malaya becoming an independent State soon and being welcomed to the Commonwealth was discussed by all of us last June when we met and we said in our communiqué that we "welcome an Independent Malaya as a member of the Commonwealth of Nations on the completion of the necessary constitutional processes."

These latter will, you have kindly informed me, be completed by the 21st of

1. New Delhi, 17 August 1957. JN Collection.
2. Macmillan wrote that the necessary constitutional processes for independence of Malaya were well on their way towards completion. In Malaya the agreement had been signed between the Queen and the rulers setting up the independent Federation and revoking the Federation of Malaya Agreement of 1948. Formal ratification of the Federal constitution by the Federal and the State Legislatures in Malaya would be completed by 21 August, the Order in Council in the UK would be made on 23 August, then Malaya would achieve independence on 31 August.

August. I am happy to hear this, although there was little doubt about it when we met.

We are ourselves sending a Minister of the Government of India and others to represent us at the Malayan Independence ceremonies on the 31st August in Kuala Lumpur.

I agree with the wording of the statement you propose to issue.[3] I join with you in wishing once again the New Malayan State success and prosperity.

3. Macmillan enclosed the following statement: "At their meeting in London in June and July of this year, the Commonwealth Prime Ministers extended to the Federation of Malaya their warm good wishes for its future on the eve of its achievement of independence and looked forward to being able to welcome the Federation as a member of the Commonwealth on the completion of the necessary constitutional processes.

The final stage in Malaya's progress towards independence has now been reached with the making of an Order by Her Majesty in Council giving the force of law so far as it is for Her Majesty to do so to the new constitution for the Federation and the constitutions of Penang and Malaka. H.M.G. in the United Kingdom are now happy to be able to announce after consultation with other Commonwealth Prime Ministers that they have all agreed that Malaya shall as from 31st August be recognized as a member of the Commonwealth."

3. To Tunku Abdul Rahman[1]

New Delhi
August 20, 1957

My dear Prime Minister,[2]
The attainment of independence by Malaya is a development of such significance to Asia and to the Commonwealth that I would have liked to participate personally in the Independence Day celebrations on the 31st August, 1957. It is, however, not possible for me to leave India during this month due to Parliament being in session and my other preoccupations. Two of my colleagues, Shri S.K. Patil, who is our Minister for Irrigation & Power and Shri Sadath Ali Khan, my Parliamentary Secretary for External Affairs, will be participating in the *Merdeka*

1. JN Collection.
2. Prime Minister of Federation of Malaya.

celebrations and rejoicing with you and the people of Malaya on this august occasion on our behalf.

The attainment of independence by Malaya is of special significance to Asia. It is yet another forward step in the awakening and rejuvenation of this ancient Continent, which has played such an important part in world history. I earnestly hope that this historic event will help the cause of peace and cooperation between nations.

Today the world is in the grip of fear and the hydrogen bomb is a symbol of impending catastrophe. I hope that the countries of Asia will throw their weight on the side of peace, for without peace there can be no progress.

Independence brings freedom but, as we all know, it also brings heavy responsibilities. Since India became independent, we have had to work harder than ever before in order to give economic and social content to our political freedom. You and your people will now be dedicating yourselves to this great task of raising the standards of the people so that they may have a free and full life. In this task you will have the fullest sympathy and support from the Government and people of India and our cooperation will always be at your disposal.

On behalf of the Government and the people of India, I offer to you, Mr Prime Minister, and the people of Malaya our heartiest good wishes for a bright and prosperous future.

With kind regards,

Yours sincerely,
Jawaharlal Nehru

4. Indian Doctors for Malaya[1]

M. Valiulla:[2] Will the Prime Minister be pleased to refer to the reply given to Starred Question No. 360 in the Rajya Sabha on the 22nd August 1956 and state:

(a) the number of Indian doctors who have agreed to serve in Malaya; and

1. Reply to a question in Rajya Sabha, 20 August 1957. *Rajya Sabha Debates*, Vol. XVIII. Col. 717.
2. Congress Member from Mysore.

678

(b) what are the terms and conditions of their service?

Jawaharlal Nehru: (a) The Government of Malaya have been permitted to recruit 100 doctors from India. A Malayan Selection Team that arrived in India some time ago has already interviewed the prospective candidates at various centres in India; but the number of doctors who have actually agreed to serve the Malayan Government is not yet known.

(b) The information regarding the terms and conditions of service is given in a statement which is placed on the Table of the House.

(vi) USA

1. Discussion on Current International Issues[1]

The US Ambassador saw me this afternoon and was with me for about an hour. He talked to me about his visit to Nepal first. He appeared to be favourably impressed by Dr K.I. Singh. He said that the US recognized India's special position in Nepal.

2. He then discussed with me his visit to the US and his efforts to put across India's case there and more especially the need of giving assistance to India for her developmental programmes. I made some notes on a paper which I attach. I need not say much about this because the Ambassador has been having long talks with the Finance Minister on this subject.

3. There was some brief talk about the present position in China and the difficulties the Chinese Government were facing because of drought, bad harvest, overenthusiasm, heavy machinery, etc.[2]

4. There was some talk about position in Syria. I told him that we were not very happy about this, but this was the inevitable result of driving Syria into a corner. If these pressure tactics were continued, the result will be to drive Syria

---

1. Note to Foreign Secretary, New Delhi, 26 August 1957. JN Collection.
2. For position in China, see *Selected Works* (second series), Vol. 38, pp. 785-791.

further still towards the Soviet. The only wise course would be to allow matters to settle down. I hinted also that President Nasser was a moderating influence.

5. The Ambassador asked me about Hungary. I told him what I have frequently said in public. That is that the Hungarian rising was, in our opinion, essentially a nationalist rising, though of course there had been other elements also involved. The rising took place because of dissatisfaction at many things that had been done there. The intervention of the Russian Armed Forces was probably brought about partly because of the new situation that had developed by Anglo-French intervention in Egypt and the expectation in Russia of a major war developing. It was unfortunate for Hungary that these developments had taken place in Egypt.

6. We felt that both in the interests of the people of Hungary and of peace generally, the tactics of cold war should not be pursued and condemnatory resolutions would not help. As the UN Commission on Hungary had presented a report, we agreed that this had to be considered. We would have preferred this consideration to take place in a better atmosphere. Anyhow we hoped that the main objective to be kept in view would be not to add to the tensions and thus worsening the present situation in Hungary so far as the people were concerned.

7. In the course of my reference to the Anglo-French intervention in Egypt, I pointed out that the Soviet Government undoubtedly thought that this intervention had taken place with the approval of the US Government. This was not in fact true, but they were justified in believing this and hence imagining that this was a prelude to a big war. The US Ambassador agreed and said that he could understand the Soviet Government believing that the United States had been consulted about this.

2. US Attitude on Syria and Hungary[1]

As I have already informed you I think, the US Ambassador spoke to me about Syria when he saw me. I had told him then that according to our information, Egypt was advising moderation to Syria. I had also told him that, whatever the facts might be, it was clear that Syria felt that she was being driven into a corner. An attempt was being made to isolate her. Because of this, she leaned much more to the Soviet side. If any further pressure was brought to bear upon her, the leaning would naturally increase. The best course, I thought, was to allow matters to settle down.

2. What the President said in Kerala obviously did not mean to imply any approval or disapproval of the Kerala Government.[2] The President is the Constitutional Head of the State and the Kerala Government is one of the State Governments. Before the present Government took office in Kerala, the President had made a programme to visit Kerala. After the assumption of office of the Kerala Government, the question arose whether the President should adhere to this programme or not. He decided that he should go there and we agreed with his decision. While there, he said something to the effect that we were a democratic Government and our tolerance and democratic character were evidenced by the fact that we accepted the result of the elections in Kerala even though we did not like them. These are not his words, but this was the general sense. It has been our policy to behave quite correctly to the Kerala Government from the constitutional point of view, even though it is well known that we disapprove many things that it has done and is doing. If we have to express our disapproval, we do so in confidential communications.

3. As for Hungary, the answer you gave to the Ambassador was quite correct.[3] We can come to no decision till we know what question is put there. I did say to the Ambassador that we were not in favour of condemnatory resolutions which could add to the tension.

1. Note to Foreign Secretary, MEA, New Delhi, 29 August 1957. JN Collection.
2. S. Dutt wrote on 29 August 1957 that the US Ambassador showed him a newspaper report of the President's speech in Kerala. The President was supposed to have approved of the experiment in Kerala and referred to coexistence while inaugurating All Kerala Hindi Prachar Conference on 13 August.
3. Dutt informed Nehru that the Ambassador enquired whether the Government of India had decided to abstain on a resolution on Hungary. To this, Dutt replied that there was no question of an advance decision either way at this stage and much would depend on what kind of resolutions were brought forward at the meeting of the General Assembly.

3. To John Foster Dulles[1]

New Delhi
2 September, 1957

Dear Mr Secretary of State,

Your Ambassador in Delhi has been good enough to hand over to me your kind message of greetings and good wishes on the occasion of the tenth anniversary of India's Independence.[2]

The occasion is for us one of special significance and also for reflection. We look back on a decade during which we have achieved some success in the tasks to which we addressed ourselves. Before us lie further heavy and onerous tasks and our determination to complete them is sustained and strengthened by the goodwill of friendly countries which has manifested itself in so many concrete ways.

I sincerely share your hope that the growing friendship between our two democracies will enable us to progress towards our common goal of world peace and prosperity.

Sincerely yours,
Jawaharlal Nehru

---

1. JN Collection.
2. Dulles, the US Secretary of State, wrote: " It gives me great pleasure to extend to you and to the people of India, on behalf of the Government and people of the United States, greetings and best wishes on the tenth anniversary of India's independence. Under your distinguished leadership, the achievements of India during the first decade of its independence have been an inspiration to freedom-loving people everywhere.

   It is my sincere hope that during the coming years the bonds of friendship between our two democracies will grow stronger and that we shall continue to make progress toward our common goal of world peace and prosperity."

4. US Military Experts in Pakistan[1]

Please see attached papers about the alleged visits of American Military Engineers etc., to Gilgit. In view of the latest information received from Intelligence to the affect that Colonel Roberts-E-Suetsar of the US Corps of Engineers in Pakistan was supposed to visit Gilgit on official duty from 12th September onwards and some of the other facts mentioned in this report, it might be desirable for you to see someone from the US Embassy. You can refer to the *Hindustan Times* report[2] and the contradiction issued by the US Embassy and tell them that according to our information Colonel Roberts-E-Suetsar was due to visit Gilgit. We should like to know if this fact is true or not. You might also mention that the Chief Engineer of the Central PWD of Pakistan visited Gilgit and Skardu, according to our information. Also that the contradiction issued by the US Embassy is not clear about Gilgit, Chitral, etc., and we shall be glad to have this matter clarified.

After seeing him, I think you might inform our Delegation in New York about the facts as we know them.

---

1. Note to Foreign Secretary and Commonwealth Secretary, MEA, New Delhi, 23 September 1957. JN Collection.
2. On 11 September 1957, *The Hindustan Times* published a report by a national of Pakistan occupied Kashmir, who served in Gilgit and Chitral as a civilian clerk and had crossed the ceasefire line recently. He spoke about the presence of US military engineers and experts in Gilgit, Chitral and other strategic areas, and military build up at fever pitch in POK; touring of US military experts in the North Western Frontier areas accompanied by high-ranking Pakistani officers; an all out drive to dragoon tribal irregulars; closing of the Khyber Pass at the behest of Americans with permission of transit only through a written authority signed and countersigned by various field commanders; building of an airfield at Chitral by American experts supposedly for civilian use; making Gilgit a military base with Pakistan Army and Air Force under US experts; stationing of Pakistani forces in the strategic Killick Pass between Hunza and Gilgit.

5. Cable to V.K. Krishna Menon[1]

Your most immediate telegram 543 of October 2 has only reached me here today. I am glad to have it. I have not yet received your en clair telegram to which you refer.

I know that various efforts have been made to appear to please US in regard to our foreign policy. I have made it clear on several occasions that our foreign policy remains and will remain unchanged. I may do so here also in public as I have already privately done to Japanese Ministers.

I had long talk today with Japanese Prime Minister and Foreign Minister and others, chiefly about disarmament and nuclear weapons explaining our attitude to them and necessity of not weakening in any way in regard to stoppage or suspension of nuclear test explosions. They appeared to agree. Talks will continue.

1. Tokyo, 5 October 1957. JN Collection.

(vii) UK

1. Message to Harold Macmillan[1]

I am grateful to you for the cordial personal message which your High Commissioner[2] delivered to me on the 13th August, 1957.[3]

I share with you the desire and hope that we can keep in touch and not merely rely on our occasional meetings or on official correspondence. I have always attached importance to personal exchanges of views and have derived much benefit from them in the past. We are looking forward to your visit in the New Year. Meanwhile I shall certainly write to you, should there be any important matter of mutual or world concern where I feel that an exchange of views will be useful.

Our economic problems, as you know, are somewhat disquieting, even though this is a temporary phase. We are making every effort to overcome them largely by imposing restrictions on ourselves. I thank you for your kind reference to the way we are dealing with them. I feel that our people will bear their present burdens, which we are obliged to impose on them, with fortitude in view of the objectives of our Five Year Plan.

As you know, I was not anxious to meet Suhrawardy personally, but I gladly acceded to your wishes in this matter. One has only to read Pakistani newspapers to realize that such meetings cannot be fruitful unless there is a change of attitude on the part of Pakistan.

1. New Delhi, 20 August 1957. JN Collection.
2. Malcolm MacDonald.
3. Macmillan referred to India's economic problems and wrote that he knew too well from their own experience how intractable and baffling these could be. He spoke about Nehru's talk with Suhrawardy and wished that some settlement of principle could be reached at on the question of the Indus Waters. Regarding disarmament talks he wrote that the Russians were very legalistic and would argue to the last point. Still these discussions tended to make war more and more unthinkable. He said that the trouble in Oman was on a very small scale and was played up into a big issue. He concluded by saying that although there were "a lot of problems today, we ought to count our blessings and not allow our troubles to weigh too heavily upon us. For really the world has grown to be a better place than, at any rate, at most periods in past history."

As regards the Canal Waters issue, I hope that there will be some agreement on principles. It is not clear to us yet whether Pakistan has accepted the principles laid down by the World Bank. In regard to the other problem, I hope that you agree with us on the principle that aggression must be vacated and that Pakistan should not be allowed to exploit her forcible occupation of our territory for making further demands and threatening our security. This is the basic issue in relation to Jammu and Kashmir.

I am glad to learn that despite your temporary economic difficulties, you are able to feel a sense of optimism in your country. For us both, the confidence of our people in regard to the future is as important as any tangible economic or other factor.

I am sorry that the talks on disarmament have not made much progress so far. I am glad, however, that these talks are continuing. Some time or other, agreement will have to be reached on a comprehensive scheme of disarmament. But, as I said at the Prime Ministers' Conference, even to achieve this and, a partial agreement to begin with would be helpful and would immediately create an atmosphere suitable for a larger settlement.[4] If major political issues, which underlie the cold war, are tied up with disarmament, then it will be difficult to achieve a solution even in a limited sphere.

You have referred to Oman.[5] We have already indicated to your Government our concern in this matter. There has been a good deal of public feeling on this subject and recently I had to answer short notice questions in our Parliament.[6] We have adopted an attitude of restraint and patience because of our close relations with you and our hope that you will soon have a settlement. I am glad to hear that you hope that the matter will be settled soon and I trust that this will bring satisfaction to the people of Oman.

I am grateful to you for your assistance in regard to the Hunter Aircraft. I hope that the negotiations that are being carried on in London will be concluded soon. Krishna Menon tells me that your Minister of Supply, Aubrey Jones,[7] has been very helpful and has been good enough to see our officers on several

4. See *Selected Works* (second series), Vol. 38, pp. 614-616.
5. British forces invaded Oman on 3 August 1957 on behalf of the Sultan of Muscat against the Imam of Oman. Macmillan wrote that it was on a very small scale and the "press works these things up into large affairs."
6. See *post,* pp. 710-711.
7. Aubrey Jones (b. 1911); British journalist and politician; served in *The Times,* 1937-39 and 1947-48; served in the Army, 1939-46; Minister for Economic Affairs and Materials, 1952-53; Minister for Fuel and Power, 1955-57; Minister of Supply, 1957-59; served as director of various companies, 1960-65; Chairman, National Board for Prices and Incomes, 1965-70.

occasions. I should like to express our thanks to him for the help he has given.

You are fortunate in being able to find time to do a great deal of reading, in spite of your heavy work and responsibilities. I feel a little envious of you because I have seldom found time for this ever since our Independence, and I feel a little unhappy at not being able to do something which I valued greatly in the past. Still I sometimes manage to steal a few hours for reading. The broad perspectives of history certainly help to lessen the burden of the present. And yet, the present is always with us and one cannot escape it. Sometimes, a feeling of distress comes over me, not so much because of any particular event as because what appears to be a deterioration of a sense of values and standards. I try to correct this and endeavour to develop a feeling of detachment. That was the teaching of the old philosophers both in my country and in other countries. But it is not an easy matter to be in the thick of events and yet be detached.

We have just celebrated ten years of Independence. In spite of the troubles we face today, I am filled with hope when I look back at this period and the progress we have made and are making. There is no doubt that, backward and undeveloped as this country still is in many ways, the lot of the common man not only in relation to the necessaries of life but also in self-respect and understanding of the world is much higher.

2. To Lord Home[1]

New Delhi
September 10, 1957

My dear Secretary of State,[2]

I am grateful to you for your letter of 16th July. I much regret not replying till now. I remember our discussion about the Economic Committee at the Prime Ministers' Conference. I am inclined to agree with you that a full-time Chairman is worth considering. I would, however, suggest that we try some arrangement for one year in the first instance and see how it works. I have no special views

---

1. JN Collection.
2. Alexander Frederick Douglas-Home was Secretary of State for Commonwealth Relations, UK.

about the selection of Vice-Chairman except that it is desirable to have the Vice-Chairman, if there is only one from a different geographical area and with different economic conditions from those of the Chairman. I would not like at this stage to make any suggestions myself which are much too specific in a matter of this kind.

I am, however, inclined to think that the Prime Minister of Canada,[3] who took much interest at the Conference on Commonwealth Economic Cooperation, may be requested to nominate for this post a person of suitable ability and position and one who is interested in the purpose of the Committee. I would like, however, to point out that whichever Government sends the officer, that Government should pay his salary and other expenses, since, as you know, we have no common fund or common Secretariat for the Commonwealth. The establishment of such fund would raise other problems on which there will be sharp differences of opinion. This matter, namely, a common Secretariat for the Commonwealth machinery, has been mentioned practically at each Conference and not found acceptance at any time. At the same time these expenses should not permanently be laid on the UK for the reason that the Committee meets there. In the meantime, the Colombo Plan could make a start for it or appoint the person.

I should be glad to have your reactions to these suggestions before I can come to a more final decision.

Yours sincerely,
Jawaharlal Nehru

3. Louis Stephen St. Laurent.

3. Cable to V.K. Krishna Menon[1]

Macdonald gave me two messages today from Macmillan. One of these was about Syria,[2] the other about Kashmir.[3] We are sending you by airmail copies of both messages and my notes of conversations with Macdonald.[4] Brief summaries given below.

2. Kashmir: Macmillan said that he had read our memorandum about Kashmir which I gave him on 5th July. He expressed his anxiety to avoid any public controversy in New York or elsewhere which might do harm or cause misunderstanding. While admitting our anxiety to make India's case plain about Pakistan's aggression, he was concerned lest we should not seek now to condemn Pakistan for aggression. He says that as we are all agreed to give effect to earlier parts of August 1948 Resolution, we should try to make some progress to that end.

3. I told Macdonald that while we had no desire to condemn or humiliate Pakistan, all our past experience had convinced us that any fruitful discussion or progress could only be made on the basis of accepting this aggression and Kashmir's accession to India. We were not bringing this matter now before the Security Council. It was Pakistan that had done so and which was not only carrying on its old campaign of threats and hatred, but there was new aggression in the shape of sabotage, etc.

4. Syria: Macmillan said that recent events there had led to conclusion that Syria had joined Communist bloc and had passed the point of no return. Situation similar to that of Czechoslovakia at time of Benes and Jan Masaryk. Consolidation of position of left wing elements of army in neighbouring states, etc. Middle East obvious target for Soviet expansion and importance to Europe of oil supplies etc. West cannot stand idle and allow this Soviet expansion. Therefore, he expressed his agreement with the statement of Foster Dulles of 7th September.[5]

---

1. New Delhi, 15 September 1957. JN Collection.
2. See *ante*, p. 671.
3. See *ante*, p. 502.
4. See *ante*, pp. 667-670.
5. In a statement on Syria on 7 September, John Foster Dulles said that President Eisenhower affirmed to carry out their Middle Eastern policies and authorized the accelerated delivery of economic and defence aid. The President expressed the hope that the international communists would not push Syria into any act of aggresion against her neighbour.

5. I told Macdonald that while it was true that some leftist elements friendly to Russia were in control in Syria, it was wrong to imagine that this meant communism in Syria. Policy of isolating Syria and bringing pressure to change regime there had driven Syria to rely on Soviet Union for sake of self-preservation. There was no question of Syria taking any aggressive steps against neighbouring countries. Danger was that aggressive steps taken by these neighbouring countries against Syria at instigation of Western Powers might bring about conflict. Bulganin's message to Turkish Prime Minister[6] could not be ignored. Any policy, therefore, to threaten Syria would have boomerang effect and create the very conditions which Western Powers wish to avoid. Only safe course was to allow matters to settle down.

6. Adnan Menderes.

(viii) USSR

1. To K.P.S. Menon[1]

New Delhi
September 2, 1957

My dear K.P.S.,

I have just received your letter of the 16th August.

I am glad that the Little Ballet Troupe and the Travancore Sisters[2] have both created good impressions in Moscow.

It is difficult for us to follow internal developments in the Soviet governmental apparatus. I will be sorry if Bulganin dropped out.

Today, I had a visit from the Soviet Charge d'Affaires with a message from his Government. This was about Middle East and Syria.[3] Evidently, they are rather alarmed at developments there. I spoke in the Lok Sabha today and said something about Syria and the Middle East.

1. JN Collection.
2. Padmini, Lalitha and Ragini, known as Travancore Sisters, were dancers and actors.
3. See *ante,* pp. 674-675.

Today, I received a photograph from Marshal Zhukov, which has been sent to me through your Embassy. I am glad to have this. Please inform Marshal Zhukov that I much appreciate this gift and am grateful for it.

Yours sincerely,
Jawaharlal Nehru

2. Soviet Aid to India[1]

The Soviet Ambassador[2] came to see me this morning. He began by saying that on the 31st July the Pakistan Ambassador to the USSR[3] had handed an aide-memoire to their Foreign Office about Kashmir. To this the Soviet Government had given a reply on the 11th October, that is, nearly ten weeks later.

2. The Soviet Ambassador gave me unofficial translations of these documents, making it clear that they should be treated as confidential and strictly non-official. I attach these two.

3. The Ambassador then spoke to me about some talk I had had on the 6th of September with the Soviet Charge d'Affaires about Hungary.[4] I had complained then about the arrests etc. still going on there. In this connection also the Ambassador gave me a note which I attach. This also was strictly non-official and confidential.

4. The Soviet Ambassador then spoke to me about the Bhilai Steel Plant. He said that the machines for this plant were now being got ready and would be ready before long and sent to India. The question of installing and working them would then arise. According to the agreement arrived at between the two Governments, about 515 Indian specialists were to be sent to the USSR for training to install and work these machines. Out of these only 55 had thus far been sent.

---

1. Note to Secretary General, Foreign Secretary, Commonwealth Secretary, MEA, New Delhi, 21 October 1957. JN Collection.
2. Mikhail A. Menshikov.
3. Akhtar Husain.
4. See *ante*, pp. 663-664.

5. This will delay matters greatly and unless people are trained with these particular machines they would not be able to install them or work them. At least 500 should be sent to the Soviet Union even for a short time to get to know something about these machines and to be in a position to install them when they reach India.

6. The stage has been reached when these trained specialists have become essential. If Indians are not trained to deal with these machines and install them, Russians will have to be sent for to do so. It is far better for the Indians to be trained for the purpose than for the Russians to be asked to come here to install them.

7. The Ambassador said that someone in his Embassy had discussed this matter with Shri Bhoothalingam[5] who had pointed out that the main difficulty was expenses. The Ambassador suggested that the Soviet Government would be prepared to consider this question favourably so as to lessen the expenditure involved.

8. He then asked me if he could see the Minister concerned, that is, Sardar Swaran Singh to discuss this matter more fully. I agreed and said that it would be desirable for him to meet Sardar Swaran Singh.

9. The Ambassador told me that he would be leaving Delhi at the end of his tenure soon after the celebration of the 40th year of the Soviet Revolution on the 7th November next, that is, he was likely to leave about the 10th or 11th of November. He expressed the hope that I might attend this celebration on the 7th November at the Embassy, partly because it was a very special one, being of forty years, and partly because this was his last year here. I did not promise anything, but, I think, I shall attend this celebration.

10. The Ambassador then said that he had been in Delhi for full four years. He came at the end of October 1953. These four years had been happy years for him and he had learned much. He was also happy that during this period greater understanding had developed between the two countries and their peoples. There was no doubt that India and Indians were exceedingly popular with the Soviet people.

11. I thanked the Ambassador and said that we had been happy to have him here during these years and we would be sorry at his departure.

---

5. Subramanya Bhoothalingam was Secretary, Ministry of Steel, Mines and Fuel.

(ix) Myanmar

1. To U Nu[1]

New Delhi
August 22, 1957

My dear U Nu,

I have received your letter of August 16.[2] Thank you for it.

I know something of your difficulties and can well sympathize with you, because our own position has been and continues to be an exceedingly difficult one both in regard to external finance and internal finance. So far as internal revenue is concerned, we have increased our taxes very greatly as also our excise duties. We are introducing now two completely new taxes—the Wealth Tax and the Expenditure Tax. The reaction to these taxes, as to any tax, is not a favourable one. But we have had no choice in the matter.

We can tax our people, even though that is no easy matter, and puts heavy burdens when the existing burdens are bad enough. But we cannot tax people in other countries and, therefore, the foreign exchange problem is one of peculiar difficulties. It can only be met by exports or by credits abroad. The very success of our developmental plans have involved large-scale expenditure and imports of machinery from abroad, both for the public sector and by private industrialists. In order to pay for this, we have drawn heavily on the sterling balances we had in London, which are gradually disappearing.

Because of this, it was a peculiarly difficult matter for us, just at this time, to make Rupees ten crores of foreign exchange available to you. But because of your difficulties and our promise, we have done so.

---

1. JN Collection.
2. U Nu referred to the withdrawal of Rs 10 crores out of Rs 20 crores loan from India and explained the financial difficulties Burma was facing at the time. His Government was exploring every conceivable avenue of raising additional revenue including some highly unpopular measures. U Nu wrote that they had been forced, most reluctantly, to raise the existing Foreigners Registration fees and also the fees charged for Stay Permits issued under the Immigration laws. He mentioned the cuts in expenditure involving large-scale retrenchment in the Government services, and abandonment of the Kalewa Coal Project.

The present economic situation in India is a very peculiar one. Essentially our economy is sound. The vast sums of money we have spent have been investments which will yield fruits later. But for the present and for the next two or three years at least we are going to have a very difficult struggle. It is essential that we should keep our prices down during this period, as any measure of inflation would upset our Five Year Plan and our economy completely.

But I need not worry you with all these problems and difficulties of ours.

Thank you for inviting me to break journey in Rangoon on my way to Japan. I shall be visiting Japan early in October, leaving Delhi on the 3rd October. On my way out, we shall not be stopping at Rangoon at all. Our first stop will be Bangkok and then Hong Kong. I am travelling by the Air India International which does not appear to stop at Rangoon. Even on my return journey, this Air India service flight does not appear to stop at Rangoon. I would, of course, very much like to have a chance of meeting you and having a talk with you. If it is at all possible, I shall break journey for a day or half a day.[3] But I am not quite sure yet if I shall be able to do it. I have to be back here by a certain time.

With regards and good wishes,

Yours sincerely,
Jawaharlal Nehru

3. Nehru reached Yangon on 16 October in the afternoon and left on 17 October.

2. Indians in Myanmar[1]

Shree Narayan Das:[2]
B.S. Murthy:[3]
Will the Prime Minister be pleased to state:
(a) whether any and if so, the extent to which difficulties of Indian nationals

1. Reply to a question in Lok Sabha, 2 September 1957. *Lok Sabha Debates* (second series), Vol. VI, col. 11300.
2. Congress Member from Darbhanga, Bihar.
3. Congress Member from Kakinada, Andhra Pradesh.

living in Burma regarding remittances to their dependants in India have been removed; and

(b) whether any and if so, the extent to which it has been possible to settle cases of claims of Indian ex-employees of the Burma Government for pension, gratuity, arrears of pay, leave, salary etc.?

Jawaharlal Nehru: (a) These difficulties have been removed only to the extent that recently the definition of the term 'dependants' to whom the remittances can be sent, has in the case of the employees of Government Departments, quasi-Government Departments and other autonomous Boards and Corporations, been enlarged to include aged parents minor brothers and sisters. In the case of the others, the term 'dependants' continues to mean wife and children only.

(b) There has not been much progress in this regard although there has of late been some improvement in the attention given to the individual cases which have been taken up with the Government of Burma by the Indian Embassy.

3. To U Nu[1]

New Delhi
September 4, 1957

My dear U Nu,

Thank you for your two letters of August 16 and 26, 1957.

I note what you say about reducing the limit of sales tax exemption from K ten lakhs to K one lakh. Previously you wrote to me about some kind of a poll-tax on foreigners. I quite appreciate your difficulties as we are ourselves facing great difficulties both in internal finance and foreign exchange. I hope, however, that the incidence of the tax will not fall on the poor.

You will have received my message I sent you on the 27th August, in which I stated that I hoped to spend some time in Rangoon on my way back from Tokyo.[2] I expect to reach there, if all goes well, at 1400 hrs on October 16th and to leave the next morning at 1015 hrs for India. The purpose of my visit is to meet you and your colleagues there and have talks about matters of common concern and

---

1. JN Collection.
2. It was a brief message (not printed) indicating Nehru's programme in Yangon.

the world situation. I hope that you will treat my visit as a private and informal one and will not have any special functions in connection with it, such as banquets and the like. Nor, indeed, is it necessary to have Guards of Honour. I am a little weary of these Guards of Honour.

With warm regards,

Yours sincerely,
Jawaharlal Nehru

4. Message to U Nu[1]

My attention has been drawn to Burmese press comments about reported violation of Burmese territory by Indian troops in the Naga areas.[2] I have been deeply distressed to read these comments. There can be no border dispute between India and Burma. If at any place there is some lack of clarity, this should obviously be settled in a friendly way by joint local inspection. For my part, I shall gladly accept your own decision in this matter without any further argument. If, however, you prefer it, we can have a joint team visiting this place whenever climatic conditions are favourable. Small patches of territory have no significance. What should normally be aimed at is some clear geographical boundary if that is available.

We have already issued directions to our armed forces on the border to withdraw immediately from the top of the ridge of Lungwa Tingva village to the western slope which, I am told, is admittedly Indian territory.[3]

I shall gladly take any other step in this matter which you advise me to take.

1. New Delhi, 14 September 1957. JN Collection.
2. This was regarding the border dispute relating to Lungwa Tingva village. It was stated in the Burmese newspapers that the Indian Army people removed Aung San's picture as well as the Burmese Flag. Nehru asked S. Dutt to enquire into this matter.
3. Nehru directed the Foreign Secretary to send a message for the Assam Rifles, clearly stating that "on no account must they take any step which raises controversy or conflict with the Burmese Government. If any question arises, it should be referred to us."

(x) China

1. Ill-treatment of Indian Traders in Yatung[1]

I have been reading a number of telegrams from Yatung about the ill-treatment of the Indian traders there. I think we should take up this matter very seriously. I do not see why we should put up with this kind of thing. We might even advise the Indian traders to come away from Yatung if they are not treated with courtesy and decency there. The Chinese Government should be addressed on this issue in clear and unequivocal language. The Foreign Bureau at Lhasa should also be addressed in this way.

2. I do not see why we should advise these traders not to have a hartal if they want to have one to show their displeasure.

3. Anyhow this matter must be cleared up one way or the other. We do not wish Indians to live on sufferance anywhere.

1. Note to Foreign Secretary, MEA, New Delhi, 24 August 1957. JN Collection.

2. Kalinga Airlines Services to Tibet[1]

You can certainly see these papers about the proposed Kalinga Airlines to Tibet.[2] When Patnaik came to see me about this matter some two or three months

1. Note to Defence Minister, 31 August 1957, V.K. Krishna Menon Papers, NMML. Also available in JN Collection.
2. Bijoyanand Patnaik spoke to Krishna Menon on 31 August about his project of a freighter-cum-passenger service to Tibet. Krishna Menon had already asked the Chinese Ambassador to convey this to Chou En-lai, who replied that the freighter or other service question might be discussed between the Governments. Krishna Menon enquired whether he could explore this possibility with Nehru's approval.

ago, I told him that I had no objection to his running a Service to Tibet from India, but, of course, the Chinese Government's permission would have to be taken. I asked him to see the Chinese Ambassador[3] here which, I believe, he did. About the same time, I think, we wrote to our Ambassador to sound the Chinese Government on this subject. The response of the Chinese Government, so far as I remember, was an evasive one and I got the impression that they did not wish to encourage any such service at this stage.

Patnaik talked about going to Peking to discuss this matter. I advised him to go there only if the Chinese Government expressed previously their willingness to see him. The last time I saw Patnaik, I told him to find out from the Chinese Ambassador about this matter.

Our position in this has been that we are agreeable to such a service, but we do not wish to sponsor it ourselves and this is a matter between Patnaik and the Chinese Government. We can, however, tell the Chinese Government that we have no objection to it and if they agree, we shall give the normal facilities at this end.

My impression is that the Chinese Government do not want any such service from India to Tibet at present at least. They are having continuing trouble in Tibet and they are not anxious to see many Indians going there. Recently, the Indian traders there have been badly treated and we have even protested both to the Chinese Government and the Dalai Lama.

In these circumstances I did not wish it to appear that we were overanxious to push this service to Lhasa.

3. Pan Tzu-Li.

3. Cable to S. Dutt[1]

I have received message from Premier Chou En-lai expressing his strong concern about Taiwan's inclusion in International Red Cross Conference.[2] Chinese Government have been protesting throughout on the issue of invitation to Taiwan. Apparently Rajkumari Amrit Kaur defends Taiwan's inclusion on ground this was mere acceptance of an independent Government and did not derogate from Peking's claim to represent China. It is said Taiwan is not even a member of International Red Cross. China is a member and there cannot be two Chinas. Rajkumari's contention accepts principle of two Chinas which we do not accept nor is it accepted by any other country. Premier Chou En-lai is greatly distressed at this approach and intends lodging telegraphic protest first to Standing Committee and then to Plenary Session. If Taiwan still attends, Chinese delegation will not attend Conference.

We have sometimes submitted to Taiwan being treated as China because some international organizations consider it so. But when India is active sponsor and Chairman of Preparatory Committee for us to do so is another matter. But on this occasion special difficulty arises because two Chinas being represented. It is obvious that our Government can be no party to this at any stage. Not only People's Government of China but Soviet Government and some other Governments will raise question of credentials and we must necessarily vote for one China only namely People's Government. We cannot associate our Government in any way with invitation to Taiwan and more especially in order to give direct or indirect support to two China theory.

Will you please explain this clearly to Rajkumari Amrit Kaur?

1. Hong Kong, 15 October 1957. File No. 28(31)/56-57-PMS. Also available in JN Collection.
2. Chou En-lai objected to Taiwan's inclusion in the International Red Cross Conference, to be held in India in October 1957 (See also *post,* pp. 743-746). He told I. J. Bahadur Singh, Counsellor and Charge d'Affaires, Indian Embassy in Beijing, that the attempt to include Taiwan was part of the general "US intrigue" to foster the "two China" idea. Chou's main concern was that Amrit Kaur, who was Chairman of Preparatory Committee for the Conference, was unwittingly playing into the hands of the protagonists of the "two China" theory.

4. Message to Chou En-lai[1]

Thank you for your message about International Red Cross Conference in Delhi. I am myself much concerned at developments about possibility of Taiwan's inclusion in this Conference which you have mentioned. I have been unaware of them and I am entirely opposed, as you know, to any recognition of Taiwan. Also we have never accepted the "two China" theory. This Conference is entirely a non-official affair and Government of India have nothing to do with it. Rajkumari Amrit Kaur was elected President in her personal capacity. She is no longer connected with our Government. I am immediately conveying your message to her and expressing my own strong opinion on this subject. But as organization is entirely independent international body, I cannot issue any direction. Even Indian Branch of Red Cross is non-official. I shall, however, do my best to dissociate our Government from any wrong action which might be taken.

1. Hong Kong, 15 October 1957. File No. 28(31)/56-57-PMS.

5. Message to Chou En-lai[1]

I have received your message of October 18 sent through your Ambassador in New Delhi about Red Cross invitation to Taiwan. I have had the past records examined. The Indian Red Cross Society issued invitations to various countries for the forthcoming Conference and were guided entirely by decisions taken from time to time by the Standing Commission of International Red Cross. This latter body alone can decide the form and procedure to be followed in issuing invitations to Red Cross Conferences. In September 1955, the Commission decided that the Government of Formosa should be invited as a member of the Conference and the Red Cross of Formosa as an Observer. When the Minutes of

1. File No. 28(31)/56-57-PMS. Also available in JN Collection.

700

September 1955 meeting were taken up in Geneva on 9th May, Prof. Pachkov (from USSR) drew attention to a contradiction in the text of these minutes, which said, "On the proposal of Lady Limerick[2] it was decided that the invitation to Chinese Nationalist Government would mention that it was extended solely on account of their Government's authority in Formosa", while the invitation list of 19th Conference mentioned "the Republic of China". Professor Pachkov thought that this title should be corrected in accordance with the proposal made at the earlier meeting. The Chairman agreed with the Soviet initiative and accordingly the title of Taiwan authorities was corrected and called "the Government of Formosa, Taiwan". This decision was acceptable to all members of the Commission except to Mr Nicholson (from USA) who made a reservation. I thought that this factual information would explain the circumstances in which the invitation to Taiwan was issued.

2. It will be seen from the above that the Indian Red Cross Society had no discretion at all about deciding which authorities should be invited to the Conference. It is possible that the Standing Commission felt that the authority in immediate control of Taiwan should be invited to a Conference which deals solely with humanitarian problems. However, according to our information, Taiwan is not participating in the Conference. As far as the Government of India are concerned, I need hardly assure you that we can never encourage, far less accept, the theory of "two Chinas" and left to ourselves, we would not have favoured invitation to Formosa at all.

2. Countess of Limerick (1897-1981); Poor Law Guardian, 1928-30; Chairman, Maternity and Child Welfare and Public Health Committees; Member for South Kensington on L.C.C., 1936-46; Privy Council representative on General Nursing Council for England and Wales, 1933-50; Member, Royal Commission on Equal Pay; Deputy Chairman of War Organization, B.R.C.S. and Order of St. John, 1941-47; Vice Chairman, British Red Cross Society.

(xi) Other Countries

1. Position Regarding Chitral[1]

As Dr Najibullah[2] is a friend of ours and is intelligent enough to understand our position in regard to Chitral, I suggest that a brief note on Chitral may be sent to our Ambassador in Washington[3] who can pass it on to Dr Najibullah. The note will state that the apprehension of the Afghan Government has no justification and is due entirely to the misunderstanding of a reply that was given to a question in Parliament here.[4] The reply was about the legal position vis-a- vis Pakistan. The question of Afghanistan did not arise at all. In the reply it was stated that legally Chitral was previously under the suzerainty of the Jammu and Kashmir State. That was practically all that was said and this was said in the context of Pakistan having taken possession of it.

Dr Najibullah will, no doubt, convey this to his Government.

---

1. Note to Foreign Secretary, 2 August 1957. JN Collection.
2. Najibullah Khan (b. 1914); Afghan diplomat; Assistant Director for Treaties Section, Afghan Foreign Office, 1934; Chief of League of Nations Department, 1935; General Director for Political Affairs, 1937; Minister of Education, 1946-49; Ambassador for Afghanistan in India, 1949-54; Ambassador in London, 1954-57; subsequently, Ambassador in Washington.
3. G.L. Mehta.
4. For Nehru's answer on Chitral see *Selected Works* (second series), Vol. 33, pp. 382-383.

2. To Pham Van Dong[1]

New Delhi
August 8, 1957

My dear Prime Minister,[2]

Thank you for your letter of 28th June.[3] The contents were telegraphed to me while I was in London and I took the opportunity to mention the matter to the UK and Canadian Prime Ministers and to show them your letter. My colleague, Shri Krishna Menon discussed the problems fully and in detail with Mr Selwyn Lloyd, the UK Co-Chairman, on 9th July.

2. Mr Selwyn Lloyd referred to the reply he had given to a question in Parliament in April last: "The policy of Her Majesty's Government continues to be based on the Geneva Agreements of 1954, including the Final Declaration, insofar as they remain applicable to existing conditions" and again on 10th July: "It is true that the Geneva Agreements, by which we stand, have not yet been fully carried out, but Honourable Gentlemen who seek to raise these matters should think whether they are not creating new tensions where things have been steadily quietening down" and stated that, while the United Kingdom stands by the Geneva Agreements of 1954, including the Final Declaration, existing realities have to be taken into account including the facts that it is two years since electoral consultations were to have been held, and that President Diem[4] adheres firmly to the view that the Government in the South of Vietnam cannot be held to be bound by agreements which it did not sign and in regard to which it made express reservations at the time. Mr Selwyn Lloyd, however, assured Shri Krishna Menon

---

1. JN Collection.
2. Prime Minister, North Vietnam.
3. Pham Van Dong wrote that the most valuable provisions of the Geneva Agreements were being seriously and systematically undermined by the American ruling circles and the South Vietnam authorities such as just and humanitarian treatment to the participants of the Resistance war and holding of consultative conference and free general elections to reunify Vietnam. The South Vietnam authorities' refusal to cooperate with the International Commission, introduction of war materials, weapons and hundreds of military personnel in South Vietnam by Americans, their plan to introduce atomic weapons into South Korea and instigate them to cancel the Korean Armistice Agreement had caused grave concern to the public in North Vietnam. Pham wanted Nehru, who was attending the Commonwealth Conference in London at that time, to pay attention to this while meeting other signatories of the Geneva Agreements.
4. Ngo Dinh-Diem was President of South Vietnam.

that the United Kingdom shall not cease to urge President Diem, by all means which they think are likely to be effective, to adopt a moderate and reasonable public attitude, and in particular to cooperate to the fullest possible extent with the International Commission.

Shri Kaul, the Chairman of the Commission in Vietnam,[5] who is here on short leave, has given me an account of the Commission's activities and I have impressed on him the necessity of the Commission carrying out its task effectively in the interest of peace in Vietnam.

With kind regards,

Yours sincerely,
Jawaharlal Nehru

5. T.N. Kaul was the Chairman of the International Commission for Supervision and Control in Vietnam.

3. To Norodom Sihanouk[1]

New Delhi
13 August, 1957

My dear friend,[2]

I am writing to you on the eve of India completing ten years of Independence. We are celebrating this occasion, which also happens to be a hundred years after the great struggle for Independence which took place in 1857-58. That was a violent struggle which was suppressed with great cruelty. Later other methods were adopted and, generation after generation, our people carried on this struggle for freedom till they attained it on the 15th August, 1947.

We achieved Independence and started on a new pilgrimage to a welfare state so as to raise the standards of our people and remove the curse of poverty. We have struggled hard during these years. While we have solved many problems, many more afflict us. Indeed the more we progress, the harder becomes the

1. JN Collection.
2. Norodom Sihanouk was former King and Prime Minister of Cambodia.

struggle and the greater the problems we have to face. We realize that a price has to be paid for everything good.

I am writing to Your Royal Highness and mentioning these struggles and difficulties of ours, because I know the great difficulties your country is facing. I know also that your country has a great leader in you who will not be deterred by these problems.

Cambodia is passing through a difficult period. That is inevitable for all nations who are trying to grow up and function as free and independent nations.[3] We have watched with great interest and concern the developments in Cambodia and our sympathies have gone out to you. May Your Royal Highness and your country triumph over all the problems and difficulties that you face and may Cambodia have the benefit of Your Royal Highness's leadership not only in maintaining her independence but also in carrying out the programmes for social and economic development for the benefit of the people of Cambodia.

I was distressed to learn that you were not keeping good health. I hope that you have recovered.

With all good wishes,

Yours very sincerely,
Jawaharlal Nehru

---

3. The Cambodian Government was facing difficulties in raising of capital, shortage of trained personnel, building infrastructure under their two-year development plan. They had also undertaken the construction of a port at Kompong-Som on the Gulf of Thailand, which would give Cambodia access to sea.

4. Algeria's Office in Delhi[1]

Please see the attached papers.[2] I do not see why we should object to the Algerian organization opening an office here unofficially. Government will in no way be concerned with it. The Congress might deal with them.

1. Note to Foreign Secretary, New Delhi, 15 August 1957. File No. 2 (7)-WANA/57, p. 2/ Note, MEA.
2. Foreign Relations Department of the AICC received a letter from Yazid, a member of the National Council of Algerian Revolution, who wanted to open an office in New Delhi. It was suggested that as Tunisia's office was being closed down, this accommodation could be given to the Algerians and "the whole thing would be kept a secret as was done in case of Tunisia."

5. Reducing the Number of Indians in South Africa[1]

The answer should be as follows:
   (a) Yes.
   (b) The General Assembly of the United Nations has been seized of the question of people of Indian descent in South Africa and it is hoped that a further debate will take place there during the next session when this matter should be raised. It is true, however, that thus far the South African Union Government have paid little or no attention to the directions issued by the UN General Assembly. There is at present no Indian Mission in South Africa.

The statement made by the South African Union Minister of the Interior[2] is not only against all cannons of international or domestic law but is opposed to the behaviour of civilized nations. It must be remembered that the people of Indian descent in South Africa are citizens of the South African Union. If the long range policy of the South African Union is to reduce this population, as the

1. Note, New Delhi, 15 August 1957. JN Collection.
2. T.E. Donges.

Minister of the Interior has said, it means a deliberate attempt to reduce the number of South African citizens. How a country can reduce a number of its own citizens without recourse to unconstitutional and uncivilized methods, is not clear. The only deliberate attempts of this kind that have happened in recent history, have been in authoritarian countries and world opinion has reacted strongly against such methods.

To be answered by Deputy Minister.[3]

3. This reply, to be given by Lakshmi Menon on the same day in Rajya Sabha, was in response to a question by Nawab Singh Chauhan—whether the statement by Donges, Minister for Interior in South Africa, on 21 May 1957 about their policy of reducing the number of Indians in South Africa had been received by the Indian Government and whether it proposed to take any action.

6. A Case Against Tashi Dorji[1]

I agree generally with what you have written above.

I do not think we should raise the question in this connection and at this stage, of the appointment of an Indian Agent in Bhutan. We should point out to the Bhutan Durbar, as you have suggested, what the correct status of the Bhutan agent is.

I agree that no warrant of arrest should be issued against Tashi Dorji.[2]

I am not quite clear about the withdrawal of the case. It may, of course, lapse because of the refusal of the Bhutan people to give evidence. Could we inform the Maharaja of Bhutan[3] about the correct position of the Bhutan Agent and the law governing such criminal offences in India. At the same time we might add that we have regretted the tone of the communications addressed by Tashi Dorji. In spite of this, however, because of our intimate relations with Bhutan, we do

1. Note to Foreign Secretary, New Delhi, 23 August 1957. JN Collection.
2. Tashi Dorji was the sister of the Queen of Bhutan, Kesang Aji.
3. Jigme Dorji Wangchuk.

not wish to embarrass the Maharaja and if he so wishes, we can withdraw this case.

I am suggesting this to you for consideration. I am not quite clear how to proceed about this, apart from what I have said, about a warrant not being issued against Tashi Dorji.

7. Developments in Oman[1]

Bhupesh Gupta:[2] Will the Prime Minister be pleased to state:
 (a) whether Government are aware of the developments in Oman;
 (b) whether Government have received any request from the Imam of Oman for help in defence of Oman's sovereignty and independence; and
 (c) if so, what action Government propose to take in the matter?

Jawaharlal Nehru: (a) Government have followed the developments in Oman chiefly from newspaper reports. There is an Indian Consul at Muscat[3] whose chief function is to look after the Indian population there. He has not been in a position to supply us with any detailed information about the developments in Oman.

 (b) We received, some time ago, indirectly a message purporting to come from some representatives of the Imam of Oman drawing our attention to British action in the territory of Oman.[4]

 (c) The Government of India have viewed with concern the news of the military action which has taken place in Oman. They have expressed to the United Kingdom Government their concern in regard to this action.

Bhupesh Gupta: The joint communiqué issued at the end of the Commonwealth Prime Ministers' Conference on July 5th declared: The primary objective of all Commonwealth Governments is world peace and security."

1. Reply to a question in Rajya Sabha, 23 August 1957. *Rajya Sabha Debates*, Vol. XVIII, cols. 1300-1303. Extracts.
2. CPI Member from West Bengal.
3. Mangaram Bavandas.
4. See *ante*, pp. 685-686.

Before this document was out, the British armed intervention took place. May I know whether the Prime Minister considers this action on the part of Britain—a signatory—as being in accord with the above-mentioned declaration? If not, in what light and how does he face this matter?

JN: I really do not know how it is my function to analyze a document issued and to see how much of it is in accord with anything. It requires very careful examination of the facts of the case, of the law and many other things. The mere fact that we view all this with grave concern shows that we do not think that it was in accord with the policies which normally should be pursued.

Bhupesh Gupta: The Prime Minister said in another place that he was not quite clear about the legal and constitutional position of Oman and the Sultan of Muscat. May I know what exactly caused this lack of clarity in an otherwise very clear mind?

JN: The lack of clarity is due to the lack of clarity of language in the various documents which relate to this matter. There is a certain treaty of Sib which, I believe, is dated 1920 or thereabout, which itself is not a model of clarity, and that is why I said the matter is not very clear. Broadly speaking, it has been thought that the Sultan of Muscat was a suzerain over these territories of Muscat and Oman and the Imam of Oman was a kind of a feudatory or autonomous ruler under that suzerain. That is the broad description and one does not know where to draw the line exactly.

Bhupesh Gupta: May I know if the Prime Minister is aware that in 1930, after a successful uprising, Oman became free and the Imam of Oman on behalf of the people of Oman became sovereign; that it was only in 1953, aided by the British, the Imam's regime was overthrown by the Sultan of Muscat and his rule was reimposed?

JN: I am grateful to the honourable Member for all this information which I would like to check....

H.D. Rajah:[5] May I know, Sir, from the honourable Prime Minister whether there were Indians in Oman and whether there were any casualties among the Indians?

JN: All that I know is that I do not think there was any Indian in Oman. Anyhow I have not heard of any casualty....

---

5. RPI Member from Madras.

8. To Eleanor Roosevelt[1]

New Delhi
August 25, 1957

My dear Mrs Roosevelt,[2]

I have received your letter of August 15th 1957 which you have been good enough to send me on behalf of the American Committee on Africa, Inc.[3] I thank you for it.

I need not tell you how very strongly all of us in India feel on this subject. We entirely agree with what you have written in your letter and what you have stated in the Declaration of Conscience. In fact, we have been repeating something like this for the last many years and have often taken the initiative in the United Nations on this subject.

I welcome the formation of your Committee under distinguished sponsorship. But, when you ask me to become a sponsor of this International Committee, I am placed in some difficulty. As Prime Minister of India, it will not be appropriate for me to join any such committee even though I might be completely in agreement with its objectives. It is for this reason that I have not joined other committees with which I sympathized.

Indeed, people of Indian descent in the Union of South Africa are among those who suffer from this policy of the Union Government. They are placed in the dock there and are undergoing not only terrible humiliations, but physical and material injury. They face a process not only of attrition, but almost something amounting to gradual extermination. The other day, a Minister of the South African Union Government said that it was their policy to reduce the number of the people of Indian descent in South Africa. It should be remembered that all these people of Indian origin there are South African nationals. The only connection they have with India is that, some time in the distant past, their

---

1. JN Collection.
2. International Chairman of the American Committee on Africa, New York.
3. She referred to the apartheid policy of South Africa and called upon Nehru and other world leaders to join them as sponsors of an International Committee in support of the enclosed Declaration of Conscience. She also urged these leaders to plan throughout the world public demonstrations on Human Rights Day, December 10, 1957 to protest against the apartheid policy of South Africa. However, Nehru asked U.N. Dhebar to join the organization.

families migrated to South Africa and settled down there. Most of these people have been born in South Africa and have never been to India. The only connection they have with India is some kind of a vague sentimental and cultural contact. Thus, the South African Minister wants to reduce the number of South African nationals who happen to be of Indian origin. How exactly this is to be done, is not clear to me. They cannot send them to India, because these people are not Indian nationals and we are not prepared to accept this or encourage it. Are they then going to adopt some horrible methods practiced by the Nazis in Germany?

All of us here feel very strongly about this. I am not distinguishing the case of the people of Indian origin in South Africa from that of the Africans there. The Africans, of course, must have first place in their own country. I am merely pointing out that it is not so much for us in India to join Committees of protest in regard to happenings in South Africa, as we are among the sufferers ourselves. It is right and desirable, however, that American citizens who live in a democratic society and whose Constitution guarantees them certain freedoms, should make the declaration such as you have suggested, with which we entirely agree.

Yours sincerely,
Jawaharlal Nehru

9. To T.T. Krishnamachari[1]

New Delhi
September 3, 1957

My dear T.T.,

N.R. Pillai has, I believe, referred to you the matter relating to Mohammad Ali Reza. It is evident that this is a matter of high international significance now and the King of Saudi Arabia[2] has great umbrage that we are not obliging him. We shall have to proceed very cautiously in this. It is not much good explaining to the King what our law is on the subject. I understand that according to the King he has sent Rs two and a half crores to Ali Reza through normal banking channels for jewellery for one of the Princesses. This can be easily verified.

The King threatens that if we do not wish Saudi Arabia to deal with us, then he is prepared to make his purchases elsewhere.

I understand that some revised instructions have been issued by your Ministry to the Customs people authorizing the release of such jewellery and such quantities of diamonds and other precious stones so seized, upto the extent such goods are established to have been purchased specifically on the King's account and out of the funds placed at his disposal for the purpose by the King. This may be all right. But I am afraid your Customs people are not noted for their courtesy. They may make it very difficult for Ali Reza to satisfy them on this account. Please instruct them to be very careful in this case. In fact it will be worthwhile for some officer of yours going from here for this purpose. I do not wish to get the hostility of a country apart from losing their Customs in India.

Yours sincerely,
Jawaharlal Nehru

1. JN Collection.
2. Abul Aziz Saud.

10. To Ahmed Soekarno[1]

New Delhi
September 18, 1957

My dear Soekarno,

I am greatly looking forward to your visit to India early in December. We have not met for a long time, and much has happened during this interval, which is of common concern to both our countries.

In world affairs, there has been crisis after crisis and, even now, the situation in the Middle Eastern region is grave. I think, it becomes more and more necessary that our two countries, together with others, should keep in close touch and cooperate, as we have done in the past.

In India, we have had grave difficulties, chiefly financial. The very pace of our progress in industrialization has created new problems for us. More particularly, the foreign exchange situation has given us much trouble, and we have had to cut down most rigorously our imports. We have raised our internal taxes also, till they are in some ways heavier than in any other country. We decided to do this to demonstrate our determination to face and overcome the external and internal financial troubles that we had to face.

In Indonesia, you have had your own troubles, and we have naturally been anxious that these should be resolved under your leadership.[2] I should like to tell you how happy I was to learn of the joint statement issued by you and Hatta after the conference you had earlier this month.[3] That joint statement has demonstrated your high statesmanship and that in spite of differences, the leaders

1. JN Collection.
2. Serious differences arose between Soekarno, President of Indonesia and Mohammad Hatta, the Vice-President, over Soekarno's policy of "guided democracy". See also *Selected Works* (second series), Vol. 37, pp. 520-522.
3. Under strong pressure from their colleagues and in response to an emotional national appeal, Soekarno and Hatta met to deal with the problems facing the country. At the end of their conference on 14 September they reaffirmed their pledge to cooperate with each other in fulfilling the objectives of the nation as stated in the Proclamation of 1945 and the *Panchsheel*. The declaration, issued by them, said that "the relations between the Central Government and the provinces have become normal again based on the provisions of the Constitution and the existing laws in a law-abiding State." Various decisions were taken to deal with the grievances of the regions—financial allocation, recruitment of "natives" of regions, grant of autonomous powers and redivision of territories, elimination of bureaucracy and quick action by the Centre etc.

of Indonesia can cooperate together for the fulfillment of the objectives of the nation. I have no doubt that this statement will create a new atmosphere in Indonesia and help in the solution of your problems.[4]

With all good wishes to you,

Yours sincerely,
Jawaharlal Nehru

4. However, Hatta met Nehru in Hong Kong on his way back from China. Nehru recorded in a note to M.J. Desai on 24 October (not printed): "...He also talked a little about conditions in Indonesia. He was not at all happy about them and criticized President Soekarno for his way of dealing with the situation. He did not agree with the President about his broad approach. He did not go into any details."

11. India and the Persian Gulf[1]

I agree. There is no reason whatever why we should get involved in the Persian Gulf.[2] The reasons that Shri Tyabji has given about India's interests in that area are really out of date and they can only be justified by saying that we inherit British policies. It is true that in this area the Indian Rupee has a definite place, but that is not enough to bring us in.[3]

Broadly speaking, I have been more and more inclined to an avoidance of entanglements in other places in the world. In addition to this fact, it would be the height of folly for us to function in regard to the Persian Gulf in such a way as to create ill will all round. The British would consider it an unfriendly act. What is more important is that Egypt and Saudi Arabia would dislike it greatly.

1. Note to Foreign Secretary, New Delhi, 18 September 1957. JN Collection.
2. B.F.H.B. Tyabji, India' Ambassador to Iran, wrote to S. Dutt on 10 August 1957 about his talks with Abbas Aram, the Iranian Secretary General for Foreign Affairs. He sought information about India's views in regard to Bahrain, to the future evolution of the other Persian Gulf Sheikhdoms, and whether India was prepared to discuss this further with the Iranian Government in order to evolve some kind of joint approach.
3. Tyabji told Aram that a large number of Indians were settled in the area, it was a vital sea route for India, and it might be called the "Indian Rupee area" as the Indian currency was more or less the official currency employed in most of the Sheikhdoms.

On the merits there is no particular reason why we should take any step about Bahrain or the Persian Gulf Sheikhdoms. We are not concerned and no question of freedom arises there. It is only a conflict surrounding oil.

Apart from all these reasons, it would be extraordinary if we stood out as champions of Iranian interests. Iran is not only a member of the Baghdad Pact but is also more or less a feudal country. Why should we get excited over this matter is more than I can see.

In the whole of the Middle East areas, (and this might be said to include Iran for this purpose) there is an internal conflict between the old feudal regimes and the new semi-democratic elements. By and large, the UK and USA have sided with the feudal regimes, which are destined to pass out in course of time, in spite of the help that they might get from abroad. That is why the US and British policy in the Middle Eastern countries is bound to fail, even though it might register temporary successes.

I read today an interesting article in the *New Republic* from H.A.R. Philby. Probably you must have seen it. Anyhow, I send it to you. This does not relate to Iran, but argument holds even for Iran.

12. Condition of Indians in Afghanistan[1]

Four or five Members of Parliament have just returned from a twelve-day visit to Afghanistan. They saw me this afternoon. Their general impression was that India and Indians were popular in Afghanistan. They were well treated.

There are apparently a large number of Indians working in Afghanistan now. Some of these are functioning on behalf of the UN or some UN Agencies. These Indians, that is, these working on behalf of the UN, mildly complained that they were rather ignored by the Indian Embassy.

One considerable lack in Kabul especially was that of a school for Indian children. There are many Indian children and they have no proper schooling. People there said that they were prepared even to find the money for it if the Government of India could help a little. I think that this matter deserves consideration. You might write to our Ambassador[2] there and ask him to submit

1. Note to Foreign Secretary, New Delhi, 29 September 1957. JN Collection.
2. S.N. Haksar.

his views. We can at least provide them with some teachers from India for this purpose.

The MPs told me that they were surprised at the official rate of exchange of the Indian Rupee, as fixed by the Government of India and our Embassy there. This was one Indian Rupee to four Kabuli Rupees. As a matter of fact, even the banks in Kabul give ten Kabuli Rupees for an Indian Rupee and probably in the blackmarket it is even more than that. Our employees there are apparently paid in Kabuli currency with the result that they really get half or even less than half of what they are supposed to get. In the other Embassies, payment is either made in their own national currency or at the rate of exchange which is more realistic.

If these facts are correct, I think, some action appears to be necessary.

13. East and South Asian Countries[1]

This is a brief note for record. My talks lasted for more than two hours and ranged over a wide variety of subjects. I am merely noting down a few points here.

2. The Vice-President of Yugoslavia[2] has been visiting a large number of countries in East and South Asia.[3] He has been to Japan, China, Mongolia, Indonesia, Burma and possibly one or two other countries. He talked mostly of his visit to China. I gathered the impression that the Chinese Government did not go out of their way for him. They were, no doubt, strictly polite, but there was no enthusiasm about it. He had no chance of meeting Chairman Mao Tse-tung, although he met Premier Chou En-lai.

1. Note to Foreign Secretary and Commonwealth Secretary on talks with the Vice-President of Yugoslavia, New Delhi, 2 October 1957. JN Collection.
2. Svetozar N. Vukmanovic (b. 1912); Yugoslav politician; Member, Communist Party, 1933 onwards; participated in the Active Resistance Movement, 1939-45; Deputy Minister, National Defence, 1945-48; Minister of Mining, 1948; Vice-President, Federal Executive Council; President, Central Council of the Confederation of Trade Unions of Yugoslavia, 1958-67; Publications include *Trade Unions in New Conditions*, *Socialist Construction and Economic System*, *Problems of Agriculture*.
3. He reached New Delhi on 1 October for a four day visit to India as part of his South East Asia and Far East tour.

716

3. His impression of Chinese economy was not very favourable to China. He acknowledged that he knew nothing about the agricultural side. But, so far as industry was concerned, the spurt of progress during the first few years is not likely to be kept up. This initial spurt was largely due to the industrial establishments in Manchuria, which had been broken up or despoiled during the World War, coming into action again. There was this very big base for industry in Manchuria, originally built by the Japanese, which was highly developed. The Chinese, with the help of the Russians, got this running and added to it. Hence the growth in industrial production.

4. But this pace was not likely to be kept up in other regions. Also, whatever the likely pace of industrial growth, the very great growth of population was continually balancing this, with the result that the net growth was likely to be little. The Vice-President, therefore, foresaw economic difficulties in China in the future. His observations were based more on general impressions than on precise data and, as I have said above, he knew nothing about the agricultural side which was important. He suspected, however, that all was not well with the collectives in agriculture.

5. He tried to discuss ideological matters with the Chinese Communist leaders, but he was not encouraged in doing so. He enquired from them how many full-time political workers (Communists) there were in the factories. He was told that in the Anshan factory,[4] which is very big, there were two thousand whole-time political workers. This appeared to him a very large number. It indicated that these political workers were spread out in large numbers all over the industrial and possibly the agricultural field.

6. He gathered the impression that Liu Shao-chi[5] was rather rigid in his approach to problems, though Chou En-lai was more flexible. There had been a return to rigidity and what was called anti-rightism. Altogether, the Vice-President was not happy with his experience of China.

7. In Mongolia, the Vice-President met Molotov[6] and apparently had a good talk with him. He found Molotov as rigid as ever in his opinions. He had not

4. Anshan Iron and Steel Works, a giant metallurgical complex of about forty plants, was built with the Soviet help.
5. (1898-1969); Chinese political leader; joined the Chinese Communist Party and became a party labour organizer in Shanghai; elected to the Politburo, 1934; Secretary General of the Party, 1943, Vice-Chairman, 1949, and Chairman of the People's Republic of China, 1958; during the Cultural Revolution (1966-69) he was denounced and banished to Hunan province; reportedly died in detention.
6. V.M. Molotov was former Foreign Minister of USSR but was expelled from the CPSU Presidium for Stalinist activities in 1957.

grown out of his Stalinism. When the Vice-President expressed his apprehension about the tremendous growth of Chinese population, Molotov said that there was no need for worry as the more communists with rifles, the better. The Vice-President pointed out that there could be no assurance that all these people would be necessarily communists. Molotov did not discuss the internal Russian politics.

8. Mongolia is a sparsely populated country, but they do not welcome their Chinese immigrants although China apparently would like to send some of their people there. Mongolia is much more under the Soviet influence than the Chinese. This was an indication to the Vice-President that the Soviet did not encourage Chinese expansion or colonization in these areas.

9. Speaking about Russia, the Vice-President said that Khrushchev's position in the Soviet Union was by no means unassailable. He was having a good deal of difficulty, chiefly from what he called the "apparatus" of the Communist Party. He meant by this the officialdom of the Communist Party, or the bosses, which was the steel-frame of the Party. Changes were taking place gradually even in this "apparatus", but it was not easy for them to grow out of their previous ways of thinking and habits of mind. In effect, this "apparatus" of the Communist Party inclined more towards the viewpoint of Molotov.

10. On the other hand, Khrushchev was definitely popular not only with broad masses of the people, but also with the rank and file of the Communist Party. Because of some opposition in the Party, however, Khrushchev had to go slow. But for this, he would have gone faster. The Vice-President was of opinion that Khrushchev should be supported in every way because he represented the progressive tendencies in the Soviet Union.

11. Zhukov, the Vice-President said, was probably the most popular man in the Soviet Union, even more popular than Khrushchev and he had, of course, the army behind him. There was no conflict between Zhukov and Khrushchev and both were pulling together. Malenkov[7] and Kaganovich[8] were of the old Stalinist brand.

12. In Hungary, the Vice-President said, the old Stalinists were coming back in control. A man, whose name I forget, who was the principal lieutenant of Rakosi,[9] has now come into prominence. The situation in Hungary was bad, but

---

7. G.M. Malenkov was former Minister of Electric Power Stations, USSR and at present Manager, USI-Kamenogorsk Hydro-Electric Station.
8. L. Kaganovich was former Deputy Chairman, Council of Ministers, but was expelled from CPSU Presidium in 1957.
9. Matyas Rakosi was General Secretary of the Hungarian Communist Party.

there was nothing to be done about it except to encourage Khrushchev in the Soviet Union.[10]

13. Our Vice-President, Dr Radhakrishnan, had frank and interesting talks with the Chinese leaders including Chairman Mao. As usual, Dr Radhakrishnan praised many things in China and noted their great discipline there. At the same time, he laid stress on humanism and individual freedom, etc. He asked Mao if he believed in coexistence. Mao said, yes. Then Dr Radhakrishnan asked: Does coexistence mean only with those with whom you agree or those with whom you disagree? If you disagree, you should try to convert the other person in a friendly way and not try to suppress him. Chairman Mao's answer was not wholly satisfactory.

14. About Formosa, Dr Radhakrishnan suggested that time was on the side of the Chinese now and he hoped that they would solve this problem by peaceful methods. There was no doubt that Formosa would come to them later. Mao replied that he was prepared to wait a hundred years.

15. Mao made another interesting remark. He said that they were not worried much about Korea or Vietnam. But they were definitely worried about the possibility of Japan building up her military might with the backing of the United States. In fact, the position of China vis-a-vis Japan was much the same as that of the Soviet Union vis-à-vis West Germany. Both were alarmed at the prospect of these two military minded and efficient nations building up their power.

16. Dr Radhakrishnan liked Dr Ho Chi Minh[11] who, in spite of his illness, came to receive him at the airport against the wishes of his doctors, and gave a banquet. That very night Ho developed double pneumonia.

17. He struck Dr Radhakrishnan as a sincere, earnest and simple man. Dr Ho told him that he was prepared to retire and efface himself if thereby he could bring about the solution of the Vietnam problem and the unity of the country.

18. Dr Radhakrishnan was not at all impressed by President Diem of South Vietnam, whom he considered as a man of little consequence. He told Diem that too much reliance on outside help did not build up a country.

10. Subsequent paragraphs deal with the impressions of S. Radhakrishnan, the Vice-President of India, of his tour of East Asian countries.
11. Former Prime Minister of the Democratic Republic of Vietnam.

14. Political Situation in France[1]

The French Ambassador[2] came to see me this morning. He had recently returned from France where, he said, he tried his best to expedite the ratification of the treaty of Pondicherry etc.[3] But owing to changes of government and like difficulties, this had been delayed. There were some people who were bent on delaying this even though they could not finally come in the way. However, the Committee on Foreign Affairs, which was an important body, had considered this matter and expressed itself in favour of ratification by, I think, 25 votes to 13.

2. The Ambassador said he was sorry for this delay but there was no help for it because of the difficult political situation in France.[4] Meanwhile, he had visited Pondicherry, since his return, and work was proceeding well there. The delay in ratification did not make much difference.

3. The Ambassador then said that he was speaking to me not on behalf of his Government but on a personal level. He spoke with some pain and emotion about the present state of affairs in France. He said things were bad there on the political level and it was not merely a political crisis but a crisis of the regime—crise de regime. This meant that democratic liberties and liberal ideas were all at stake. He was much troubled about this. Nobody appeared to be strong enough to form a government. Parliament there distrusted government and wanted to keep power in its own hands. This gave a greater sense of importance to each Deputy who hoped to be a Minister himself. This was most unfortunate and it hurt him to say all this about his own countrymen.

4. Anything that happened in France would have powerful reactions on Europe and the world. The French President[5] might have to send for General de Gaulle[6]

---

1. Note to Secretary General, Foreign Secretary, Commonwealth Secretary and Special Secretary, MEA, New Delhi, 30 October 1957. JN Collection.
2. Stanislas Ostrorog.
3. Pondicherry, Karaikal, Mahe and Yanam were formally ceded to India by a treaty signed with France on 28 May 1958.
4. The Government of Bourges-Maunoury lost the confidence vote in the French National Assembly on 30 September on the issue of certain constitutional changes in Algeria. Attempts by various leaders including Guy Mollet and A. Pinay etc. to form a Cabinet failed. Finally Felix Gaillard formed the Government with the support of other parties on 29 October 1957.
5. Rene Coty.

and ask him to form a government. That would seem a step towards authoritarianism and the French people do not like this.

5. I told the Ambassador that only yesterday I had been reading a report from Ambassador Panikkar in Paris. In this report he had more or less given the same analysis of the situation in France.

6. The Ambassador said that Shri Panikkar was getting on very well in Paris. He had wide contacts and was much appreciated in spite of the fact that he could not speak French. If he had known French, he would have dominated the scene there.

7. I asked the Ambassador why in view of these political difficulties an election could not be held. He seemed to think that an election would not solve these difficulties and the same trouble would recur.

8. I pointed out that it was very extraordinary that while this political crisis was threatening France, in other domains like industrial advance, science, literature, art, etc., France was doing very well. He said that this itself indicated that the French were not a decadent people but were full of life and vitality, but politically they appeared to be going to pieces.

9. The Ambassador then mentioned to me on behalf of his government this time that they were much distressed by the Japanese resolution in the UN about disarmament. I said that the only resolution I knew was about suspension of nuclear tests. We thought that this Japanese resolution did not go far enough and I saw no reason why there should be any alarm about it. We were strongly in favour of suspension, though we realized that we must aim at a full and comprehensive disarmament agreement. But we could not wait for the whole agreement to appear and some step forward had to be taken. Suspension of nuclear tests was not disadvantageous to anybody and meanwhile scientists and others could devise means of proper inspection and control and the general question of disarmament would also be considered.

6. Charles Andre Joseph Marie de Gaulle (1890-1970); French Army officer and politician; served as Captain, in First World War; General of Brigade and Commander, 4th Armoured Division, 1940; Under Secretary, National Defence, 1940; Chief of Free French, and President of French National Committee, London and Brazzaville, 1940-42; President of French Committee of National Liberation, Algiers, 1943; President of Provisional French Government of French Republic, Commander-in-Chief, French Armies, 1944-46; Prime Minister of France, 1958-59; President of France, 1959-69.

IV. GENERAL

1. Revision of UN Charter[1]

The Japanese Ambassador[2] came to see me today. He raised the question of the election to the Security Council and said that his Government hoped very much that India would support Japan's candidate for the Security Council. He referred to India's support in getting Japan into the UN.

2. I told him that I entirely agreed with him that Asia was not adequately represented in the Security Council. Important countries like Japan and India should be there as well as others. The present Constitution of the UN and the Security Council was not fair to Asia. There had been talks of a revision of the UN Charter and Constitution and normally this would have been desirable , but, in the peculiar circumstances of the world today, this would have led to another grave problem and conflict. So, India had proposed a resolution for the postponement of the Charter revision and this had been passed unanimously in the UN.

3. While, therefore, in theory we would like many things to be done, in practice we had to take the circumstances into consideration. So far as the Security Council was concerned, certain conventions and gentlemen's agreements had grown up. One of these was that East European countries should be represented, as Latin American countries, Commonwealth etc., are supposed to be represented. I do not think that the particular convention was a very good one and in fact, in practice, it has given rise to unfairness in representation. But the fact remained that there was that convention and we had tried to adhere to it. According to this, last year there should have been an East European representative elected to the Security Council. As a matter of fact, there was a long drawn out struggle in the election between Yugoslavia and the Phillipines. Ultimately, it was decided by a toss of the coin and Yugoslavia went there for a year and now the Phillipines came in.

1. Note to Secretary General and Foreign Secretary, MEA, New Delhi, 12 August 1957. JN Collection.
2. S. Yoshizawa.

4. We felt that if this convention about East European country was broken again, this would be unfortunate in many ways and would upset even the balance that was tried to be created in the Charter and by conventions.

5. The Ambassador said he knew about this convention, but Japan was not bound by it as she had just come in. Also he said that there was a possibility of Czechoslovakia contesting the Presidentship of the UN. In that case this difficulty would not arise.

6. I mentioned to him that Canada was probably standing as a Commonwealth representative for the Security Council. I also told him that the Prime Minister of Canada had actually said to me in London recently that in case India wished to stand for the Security Council, Canada would gladly withdraw. I had replied that we had no desire to push ourselves in this way and we were not standing this year.

7. Because of all these considerations, I told the Ambassador that it was difficult for us at this stage to say what the circumstances would be at the time of the election. We shall have to keep all these factors in mind and decide then.

8. I then told him that I was greatly looking forward to my visit to Japan and that I had decided to extend my stay there by two days beyond the original week. I said that I would leave the drawing up of my programme to the Japanese Government who could consult our Ambassador in Tokyo.[3] One thing I should like to do is to visit the elephant, Indira, in the Tokyo zoo. We had sent this some years ago there.[4]

9. In this connection the Ambassador said that the Tokyo zoo would very much like to have an Indian rhinoceros. In fact he had mentioned this to someone in our Ministry. If a rhinoceros could come when I was there, I could make the presentation. I told him that these rhinos are very limited in numbers and it is not easy to get them. In fact, the Delhi zoo has been waiting for them for some time. However, if it was possible for a rhino to be obtained for the Tokyo zoo, we shall gladly send it.

---

3. C.S. Jha.
4. Nehru went to Tokyo zoo to see the elephant 'Indira' which he had gifted to the Japanese children in 1949.

2. An Office in Dublin[1]

I confess that the question of opening a regular office in Dublin is not free from difficulty. There is no doubt that the Irish Government have felt, and continue to feel, that our not opening an office there is in the nature of a slight to them. When I went to Dublin last year, this matter was mentioned and, in fact, I told them that we hoped to open an office fairly soon. At that time, the building we had taken was found to be in a bad state. It is an old building, though a good one otherwise. Apparently, some kind of an inner rot had set in, and the wooden portions were in a bad way. I was told that this was not uncommon in some old buildings in Dublin, which were affected by the damp. Anyhow, the question of repairing it arose, and repairs were actually being carried out when I was there. I do not know what happened subsequently and whether the repairs have been completed or not.

2. The question of sub-letting this building, I think, does not arise, partly because of the terms of the lease and, more especially, because that would be a definite indication that we have given up the idea of having an office in Dublin. Any such indication would certainly be resented by the Irish Government.

3. It is true that an office in Dublin will not have any heavy work to do. Nevertheless, Dublin is a place with a fairly large diplomatic corps, and there has been a fairly intimate relationship between India and Ireland in the past. It would be a pity to injure this old relationship. When I went to Dublin last year with our High Commissioner in London, who is also our Ambassador in Dublin, the welcome given to us was extraordinarily friendly.[2]

4. From any normal point of view, it would seem essential that we should open an office in Dublin. We have been talking about this for two or three years at least, if not more. The only question that arises now, is as to whether owing to the financial stringency, we can postpone this. Of one thing, I am sure. We cannot give up the house, because that would have a definitely bad effect. Keeping the house unused is also, as the PAC pointed out, not proper.

5. In the balance, I feel that we should open an office there. It will not be right, I think, to send a Third Secretary. There is no point in sending a person of that type there. However small the staff might be, it should be headed by a First Secretary. As for the rest of the staff, I am inclined to think that it might possibly

---

1. Note to Commonwealth Secretary and Special Secretary, MEA, New Delhi, 13 August 1957. JN Collection.
2. Nehru was in Dublin on 6 and 7 July 1956.

be reduced even further than is suggested in the Summary. For instance, is it necessary to have an Assistant Registrar and a stenographer? Considering the work to be done there, I should imagine that one man is enough for that.

6. A chauffeur means a car. Presumably, we have to keep some kind of a car. What exactly is a cleaner meant for and what does he clean? Is that for the house or for the car? Perhaps, even one messenger would be enough. But, I am not sure.

7. I think that this matter should be referred to the Cabinet as there is a difference of opinion.

3. Delay in Granting Tourist Visa[1]

Even according to the time table laid down by the Home Ministry, three months have passed since this application was made.

Tourist visas are, I suppose, often taken, to begin with, because of the long delay in getting anything else. The procedure, even as laid down, appears to me much too long. But the time limit mentioned in it is often exceeded.

What I wrote about not allowing large numbers of foreigners to come here to settle down, surely does not apply to an odd individual. Apart from this, in the present case of Dr Staudt, even though she has applied for a temporary visa now, she has spent many years in India and actually owns property and, from all accounts, has done good work, for which she is needed. There is such tremendous lack of people interested in looking after children of leper parents that any such person is a valuable addition to our community.

I suppose a reference to the State Government means their referring the matter to the District Magistrate, who enquires from some policemen and finally we get the opinion of the policemen or, at the most, of the District Magistrate. Surely, the Government of India cannot function merely on the opinion of some junior District Officers. Here is a case of a person patently desirable, an old woman who has done excellent work in India during past years and who should be welcomed with open arms. We not only delay this greatly but create a bad impression abroad.

---

2. Note to Principal Private Secretary, New Delhi, 19 August 1957. JN Collection.

I should think that, even though an enquiry has to be made, two or three weeks, or at the most one month is the maximum period to be allowed. After that, we should not wait for any answer.

Please send a copy of this note to the Home Ministry and tell them that I am still waiting to know what is proposed to be done in her case. For my part, having given quite enough time to the UP Government, I would decide immediately in her favour.

4. To N.G. Ranga[1]

New Delhi
22 August 1957

My dear Ranga,[2]

I have only today seen some papers in the External Affairs Ministry in regard to the visit of the proposed delegation organized by the Indian Foreign Affairs Association to some countries abroad. It is said that this goodwill delegation will consist of eight persons and will make a tour of Ethiopia, Egypt, Sudan, Bulgaria, Hungary, Czechoslovakia and Mongolia. Possibly also Yugoslavia, Poland and Rumania.[3]

I understand that the idea of this delegation originated from the Foreign Affairs Association who then approached various foreign missions in Delhi and suggested to them that they should be invited as State guests. This was rather an odd way of proceeding because it puts the foreign mission or their government in a somewhat embarrassing position.

We can have no objection to individuals or small groups going abroad to any country except that just at this time we cannot agree to any expenditure in foreign exchange. But, apart from this, a private delegation going like this might well

---

1. JN Collection. Also available in File No. 17-39/57-AFR-I, pp. 10-11/Corr., MEA.
2. Member of Parliament and President of Indian Foreign Affairs Association.
3. In a note on 22 August, M.J. Desai wrote that the Indian Foreign Affairs Association proposed to send a delegation of eight persons on a goodwill tour of Ethiopia, Egypt, Sudan, Bulgaria, Hungary, Czechoslovakia and Mangolia. The delegation would spend about a week in each country as their guests and the members would pay for their own passage. Desai raised the question of conservation of foreign exchange and the imperative need of all-round economy.

be considered as an official or semi-official delegation and that might lead to embarrassing situations. For instance, people from that country might want to be invited by us here in return. Also some of the countries mentioned are involved in problems of international significance, such as Hungary to mention one of them. Normally, we would not have encouraged anyone to go to Hungary at present. Even in regard to other countries, great care has to be taken as to how to deal with the local or international situations affecting them. People there are very touchy and governments are still more touchy as to what is said or not said. Press conferences are held and questions are asked.

I do not quite understand how the proposed delegation goes from Europe suddenly to Mongolia. The distance, I suppose, between them must be about 10,000 miles. How is this covered? Does this involve a stay in the USSR or China?

I should like you to let me know what all this is about and how exactly this has arisen? You will appreciate that the practice of going to foreign embassies and asking for invitations is not a good one and should not be encouraged.

Yours sincerely,
Jawaharlal Nehru

5. Expenditure on Indian Delegation to the UN[1]

Mahabir Prasad:[2] Will the Prime Minister be pleased to state:

(a) the total annual expenditure incurred by Government on the Indian Delegation sent to the United Nations General Assembly;

(b) for how many members of this Delegation, the expenses are borne by the United Nations; and

(c) what is the usual strength of the delegation?

Jawaharlal Nehru: (a) The total expenditure for 1956 was Rs 4,30,000.

---

1. Reply to a question in the Rajya Sabha, 29 August 1957. *Rajya Sabha Debates*, Vol. XVIII, cols. 2339-40.
2. Congress Member from Uttar Pradesh.

(b) Only traveling expenses of 5 members of the Delegation of each Member State attending the session of the General Assembly are borne by the UN.

(c) It varies according to the number and nature of the items on the agenda; usually we name 20 to 25 persons for UN Assembly Delegations.

6. To Maurice Alhadeff[1]

New Delhi
September 13, 1957

Dear Mr Alhadeff,

Some time ago, I received through Air India International two paintings. They were rather lovely and I liked them very much. I was naturally interested to find out where they came from, but all the information I got was that they had been handed to the Captain of the Air India International aircraft to be brought to Delhi and delivered to me. I was greatly intrigued and naturally was anxious to find out who the generous donor of these lovely paintings was. I had a letter written to our representative at Accra,[2] but so far as I know, we have received no reply from him yet.

Today, I have received a letter from our High Commissioner in London who forwarded to me a letter from Mr Desmond Doig.[3] Mr Doig had met the High Commissioner also. It is only now from these letters that I have learnt that you were good enough to send these two fine paintings by African artists. I am indeed very grateful to you for them and for the generous thought that led you to send them.

Mr Doig has told us something of the great work you have done in the Belgian Congo to further the cause of the Africans there and, more particularly, how you have encouraged artists and sculptors and ivory carvers and other handicraftsmen there.

I am afraid my own acquaintance with Africa is limited and I have not had the opportunity of visiting Africa except Egypt and the Sudan. But I have long been deeply interested in Africa and the Africans. We have a considerable number of

1. JN Collection.
2. B.K. Kapur.
3. An artist and editor of *Junior Statesman*, Calcutta.

African students, both young men and young women, studying in various Indian Universities now. Most of them have come as Government of India scholars. It has given us great pleasure to give this opportunity to these young Africans to study in our Universities. I am sure that when they go back to their own countries they will be able to serve their own people well.

Please again accept my deep thanks for your generous gift.

With all good wishes,

Yours sincerely,
Jawaharlal Nehru

7. Urge for a Better Life[1]

I am grateful to you for inviting me today and giving me the opportunity of meeting you, seeing you in a group, I see you often enough flitting about at various functions. Some faces are very familiar indeed. I do not quite know what you expect me to say. Anyhow it is not going to be of any great importance, so far as news is concerned.

I am told that this Association has grown in the last few years considerably, it started with a very small membership of 7 and now it is 55, and in the Association you have representatives from many countries. I am very glad of this, for two reasons; one is that through you, we can get, to some extent the viewpoints of other countries and their reactions to events in India. That is, we profit by them and possibly other people in other countries profit by what you tell them about India. In this very complicated world today, changing, developing, it is, I think, of extreme importance, that as far as possible, we should get different viewpoints impinging on events, so that we can see from different viewpoints. Those of us who are engaged; engrossed in activities in our own country, and that this applies to people in other countries too, inevitably they look at it from their viewpoints, however much we may try to see it from a distance. I am afraid I do not have much time to read many newspapers. Sometimes, when I am very busy I actually miss them. I suppose the newspaperman naturally is following events from day

1. Speech at Foreign Correspondents' Lunch, New Delhi, 14 September 1957. PIB Files.

729

to day, with such intensity that to some extent he might well lose his perspective just as a person like me, functioning in those events tends to lose his perspective. There are two kinds of perspectives which I suppose are desirable . One is the wider perspective of the world in seeing your own country in that perspective. The other is the perspective of history, that is of the unrolling of events one after another, past and present, and seeing what is happening today, as a continuation of the past and thereby perhaps getting to understand it a little better. After all everything that happens does not come out of nothing. It is in continuation of something. Well, I do not know how far you succeed in getting the perspective.

Probably, I think, it is right to say that today we live in a greater age of change then ever before, and what is more, the pace of change becomes ever more rapid. What affects this change? Many factors, of course. I suppose, basically, it is the technological development of the world that has produced these tremendous changes which affect people's lives and people's thinking, and it is to the extent all these technological changes are affecting, let us say Asia, that you see all kinds of changes, and ways of thinking and people being uprooted from their old roots, taking place.

In these countries of Western Europe, including America—though America is somewhat different—you see a process in the last 200 years or so, of progressive changes, economic changes, technological changes, and life being governed by them, events producing changes, and all that, and that is ultimately derived from the advance of science and technology, and the world of Western Europe changed. In the United States, the same thing was happening, happening even more, but in the United States they have additional factors—vast areas—and other factors which governed the development of US. It was after the economic revolution had made considerable progress in these countries, that the political revolution in these countries took a more vital shape. Now, what is a political revolution? There are many kinds of it. There is the American Revolution, there is the French Revolution, and the Russian Revolution. I am not talking of some sudden thing happening, but rather certain basic changes which come gradually.

Now, the progress is reversed in a country where a political revolution comes without that economic background, the economic revolution is delayed. A political revolution releases energies, releases demands from the people who quite rightly want to better their condition, who want all kinds of good things of life, at least some of them, but the country is not strong enough or wealthy enough, or productive enough, to satisfy those demands, suddenly or quickly. So, a political revolution preceding an economic revolution is what you see in many countries of Asia. That is what you see, in India, and in other countries of Asia too. We became free, independent, politically conscious, everybody has a vote and everybody wants to better his own or her condition. We are trying hard through our Five Year Plans and the rest, but it is very difficult to catch up. Ultimately one might, but this creates social problems, problems of greater intensity than the social problems in countries where certain economic advance has already been made previously. That we have to face today. This is one of the major problems. If one goes too fast, one may well fail completely, the structure may break up, and if one goes too slow also the structure breaks up because the other things outrun the demands of other strong feelings and passions of the people. How to balance these things is the problem presumably of the statesman or the administrator, and it is in that connection then, that in trying to do that, well, you plan. That is, you approach this problem in an organized way. Your resources are limited. How best to use those resources, to give the highest results which cannot be high enough, but still the highest results feasible.

If you do not proceed in an organized way, then the result is that even the resources, or a part of them, may be frittered away without making any essential difference. That is, I suppose, the philosophy of the planned approach. A planned approach becomes necessary inevitably where you lack things. If you have things there is no question of planning, you have them, everybody has them or can have them.

There is one aspect I should like you to think over. You see in India today there are so many things that we want to do, obviously we cannot do them. Therefore, we have always to choose, to decide not to do good things that we want because there is something more important that has to be done. The other thing is very good too and desirable but we cannot do both; we have to choose the lesser evil of two courses, so as to avoid the greater evil.

Well, many of you wonder about India I suppose and see various aspects of this country, of great variety, and it is quite likely that you see many things which those of us who live here do not see, or do not take notice of because we are accustomed to it. Therefore, it becomes good for us to see ourselves as others see us, and thus learn something about ourselves which we might otherwise miss. I am quite convinced that any real understanding of a problem can only come from looking at it from a number of viewpoints, not only one's own but the viewpoints of critics and specially the viewpoints of people who can look at it without themselves being involved. I feel that all of you fulfill, not only some kind of function for newspapers or news agencies that you represent, but an important function in helping us to understand our own problems and difficulties, and even what is happening in the country which we might otherwise miss. I know, I have profited considerably by reading often, not so much news items, but an appraisal of the situation here, by people who have come from other countries.

Then, again while it is possible to see many sides of a picture, it does depend on the approach, the mental approach of the person, as to what he sees and what he does not. His mind may completely look at things objectively and yet even the objective approach may be diverted or even perverted by previous biases.

Or take another thing, whether your mind or my mind is receptive or not. If, my mind is a closed mind and is not receptive, I see my own reflection, wherever I go. I do not see the other thing, but rather my own reflection, my mind's reflection and I may miss many things, which I would see if I had been a little more receptive. Receptiveness does not mean changing one's mind, but being open to impressions. It is also difficult to judge oneself, but I believe, I am receptive to some extent, and I try to be so deliberately. Even in India, when I go to various parts, for the moment I belong to that part, my mind is open to the impressions and the feelings of that part. You may go to any place in India. You may go to Banaras. Many of you may have been there and you may be powerfully affected by the dirtiness and the smells of Banaras which are often painful to see or smell, and you may, therefore, come back with a strong aversion to Banaras, which would be completely justified in that limited sphere. I feel that way too, but if I go to Banaras, a long succession of pictures come to my mind, not so much of the present Banaras, partly of the present, but more so of Banaras, for what it has stood for in India's history for thousands of years. I see Banaras as something lasting for thousands of years, drawing people from all over India, teaching them, learning from them, and thereby, creating gradually something, which was representative of a continuing Indian culture for thousands of years. Banaras may be out-of-date. It may be, I do not know. To some extent they have to adapt themselves. My point is that whatever you may see depends on with what kind of eye you look at it. If you are not receptive, if you do not have a background of the knowledge of the past out of which the present has grown, you will see it in a limited way. I have given the example of Banaras. The example applies to every city or country in the world. Some tourist goes, say from India to some other place, totally unused to the surroundings, he does not understand, he dislikes or likes somethings, he comes back with good or bad impressions, as the case may be, without having tried to understand the other country—the background, historical, cultural, all powerful forces that have made that country what it is. Well, at any rate we can all try to understand. Whatever one's views may be, an effort to understand is helpful.

I have always found that inspite of tremendous political differences and rivalries between countries, it is quite extraordinary how people generally are not so different, and how they are friendly. All these strong hatred and other passions that one sees reflected sometimes in the columns of newspapers; and which are true in their limited context, and yet give a rather distorted view of the world where millions and millions of people are not possessed by this hatred, passions; they live peacefully, hospitably; they are decent; they misbehave sometimes, and they are like each other, whatever the country you go to. So, one gets a little friendlier outlook of the world, to the other people and realizes that there is still a good deal of hope for the world.

8. To Arthur Carl Matz[1]

New Delhi
September 26, 1957

Dear Arthur,

I have received your letter of September 15th, and was glad to read it.[2] I am glad that you are so much interested in peace in the world. We should all try to have a world in which people cooperate instead of quarrelling.

I send my love to you,

Yours sincerely,
Jawaharlal Nehru

1. JN Collection.
2. Arthur, a fourteen-year old ninth grade student from Maryland, wrote on 15 September 1957 that he had been studying about great peacemakers of the modern world and had been assigned with writing to some famous person. He wrote: "I decided on you, because of your great work in this field... I have been very interested in your views on Hungary and the Middle East.... But what really aroused my curiosity in you, was the way you have kept your country neutral in these troubled times. In my opinion, I think that you are one of the greatest men of peace of our time, and one who has done the most."

9. Cable to T.T. Krishnamachari[1]

Thank you for your telegram 807 September 26.[2]

2. Contribution to UN: I have seen previous papers in this connection and report of debates in UN Assembly. India's attitude was governed by papers sent to us by our Finance Ministry in which whole question was carefully considered.

3. UN Committee on contributions consists of ten members, each elected in individual capacity. They are, France, UK, Brazil, India (Chairman), USA, Czechoslovakia, Canada, Mexico, USSR and Pakistan. This Committee is governed by General Assembly's Directive Principles in this matter. The main principle is capacity to pay subject to no member-State contributing more than one-third of ordinary expenses in any single year.

4. According to capacity to pay, contribution of US comes to about forty-five per cent, but this was fixed at one-third. Ad hoc reduction of this to thirty per cent would conflict with principles laid down by General Assembly. Addition of new members to UN may result in some general reduction in contribution. Even so, according to principles laid down, US is not likely to benefit by this reduction because it is already supposed to pay much less than its capacity.

5. Thus far, not only Asian, African and Latin-American countries but also some European countries have opposed US proposal for reduction to thirty per cent. This might mean some addition to what they have to pay now. Indeed, I do not know of any single country which has supported US proposal. Lall,[3] as Chairman of Committee, took little part in the proceedings.

6. Another argument is advanced against proposal as money is very largely spent in US itself while dollar contributions affect other countries heavily. Our consistent attitude has been to urge lower contributions for underdeveloped countries and others with small capacity to pay. It would be strange if suddenly we changed our attitude which is based on Directive Principles of General Assembly as well as on opinion of great majority of countries. This would produce all manner of repercussions and would bring little credit to us. It would be said that we had changed our minds and our policy because of pressure from US and our hopes of getting aid from them. We would irritate most countries and our reputation would sink low.

1. New Delhi, 29 September 1957. JN Collection.
2. Krishnamachari reported about his discussions with various people in the US for securing financial assistance for India.
3. Arthur S. Lall, India's Permanent Representative in the UN, was the Chairman of the ten-member UN Committee on contributions.

7. So far as I know, at no previous time have US approached us on this subject, either here or in New York. India has in fact taken very little part in these discussions. It is the other countries that have taken the lead. It seems to me, therefore, that from every point of view our agreeing to US contribution being reduced to thirty per cent will not be justified.

8. The matter is complicated and has some history behind it. I suggest that when you go to New York you discuss this with Arthur Lall who will be able to tell you the facts, past and present.

10. Cable to Arthur S. Lall[1]

Your telegram 526 September 27.[2] Also Krishna Menon's telegram 528. Contributions to UN.[3] I have looked through papers in this connection. I do not think it is possible for us to go back on attitude that we have so far adopted. To agree to 30 per cent for US would be against Directive Principles of General Assembly, apart from creating other difficulties.

2. If there was general opinion that reduction brought about by addition of new members might be equitably spread out over all, including US, we need not oppose. Even this, however, would not be fully in keeping with principles laid down by Assembly. It can only be accepted as friendly settlement.

3. When Finance Minister comes to New York on October 1, you might explain situation to him fully. Meanwhile, if you think it desirable, you might discuss

1. New Delhi, 29 September 1957. JN Collection.
2. Lall wrote that at the last session the US member asked for reduction of US contribution from $33 \frac{1}{3}$ per cent to 30 per cent. He informed that Asian-African and Latin American countries were opposed to lowering of US ceiling as it would raise their share. Lall sought instructions on this issue and said that India had consistently supported and urged lower contributions for under-developed countries and others with small capacity to pay.
3. Since the beginning, the decision of the General Assembly was that the contributions of member-states were to be fixed on the basis of their capacity to pay. Accordingly, the US contribution would have been 50 per cent or more. This would have put one country in the UN in a position of financial dominance. The General Assembly decided on a ceiling of $33 \frac{1}{3}$ per cent as share of the highest contributor to the budget of the United Nations.

this question with US Representative in UN[4] and explain to him difficulties which most countries feel. We have no desire to take any lead in this matter or, in any sense, to crusade against US. But, in view of strong and widespread feeling among many countries, it would be desirable to have some agreed decision, if possible.

4. Please show this to Krishna Menon.

4. Henry Cabat Lodge.

11. A Case of Gold Smuggling[1]

As there was an informal meeting of the Cabinet today, I discussed this case of Dr Nardin with them.[2]

2. We are all concerned at the growth of gold smuggling in recent months, and we want this to be dealt with rigorously. I quite understand that the Finance Minister expressed a wish that Dr Nardin should be prosecuted. It is not normally a good thing for prosecutions to be waived or withdrawn in such cases. They become precedents for others. There have been recently some Americans who were arrested for smuggling.

3. At the same time, there are some special considerations in this particular case. From the Collector's account, it would appear that this is an individual case and probably the first case for the person concerned, though we cannot be quite sure of this. The fact that he tried to dispose of the gold in Chandni Chowk, Delhi, does indicate his certain naivety and lack of experience in such matters.

4. The gold worth about fifty thousand rupees or so has, of course, been confiscated. In addition, Dr Nardin has paid a penalty of Rupees ten thousand. Further, he has been in the police lock up for some weeks now.

5. There are all these considerations and, in addition, there is a request by the Italian Embassy and, I believe, the Archbishop of Delhi.

1. Note to Foreign Secretary, New Delhi, 30 September 1957. JN Collection. Also available in S. Dutt Papers, NMML.
2. Nardin, an employee of Montecatini, was in police custody on charges of gold smuggling and had paid a fine of Rs 10,000. In addition, his gold had been confiscated. Though the Collector of Customs, had decided against his prosecution, the Ministry of Finance started it on their own initiative.

6. When the Finance Minister wrote his brief note on this at the end of August, probably, all these facts were not before him.

7. After some discussion with my colleagues, we felt that, taking all the factors into consideration, we should adopt the second course suggested by Shri S. Sen,[3] that is to say, that we might inform the Italian Embassy that we are gravely concerned about this gold smuggling and it is not easy for us to withdraw cases which have gone to the courts. There are other like cases, and it raises difficulties if we begin to differentiate. We are criticized in public as well as in Parliament. However, as a special case, we are prepared to suspend proceedings against Dr Nardin if the Embassy undertakes to deport him to Italy and to arrange for his trial in an Italian court. We will supply the facts as we know them.[4]

8. You might inform the Finance Ministry of this decision.

3. Samar Sen, Joint Secretary, MEA.
4. In a note on 13 September 1957, Sen wrote that the punishment already given to him was adequate, particularly as he did not belong to any gang and this was his first offence. He was "a man of eminence and ability and had helped in India's fertilizer projects." Sen felt that "while he must pay the penalty for his misdeeds, we need not be too harsh on him or make him suffer the maximum punishment under the law."

12. External Publicity[1]

I have long been worried about our apparatus for external publicity. Whenever there has been a discussion in Parliament, there has been criticism of our publicity abroad. Members of Parliament and others who have gone abroad, have also criticized this. The criticism is not directed to individuals, who are often good, but, rather, to the methods adopted.

2. I think that we have not got into a rut, and we should try to get out of it. Negatively, we might restrict many of our activities which do not produce much results. Positively, we have to make a more direct and thought-out approach. In this matter, I think that we shall have to consider our relationship in regard to external publicity with the I&B Ministry. The I&B Ministry have good people in their own line, but it is doubtful if they have the political background which

1. Note to Foreign Secretary, Commonwealth Secretary and Special Secretary, New Delhi, 2 October 1957. JN Collection.

our Foreign Service people have. Also, the position of the publicity people in our foreign missions is sometimes rather invidious. They are a group apart.

3. Our publicity abroad is usually more or less the same for different countries. The same type of pamphlets, etc., are produced by the Publications Division. They are good pamphlets and publications. But, they do not pay any particular attention to the special needs of a country. I think, it is necessary that we should specialize a little in this matter. Obviously, the appeal to the United States will have to be different from the appeal to the Soviet Union or like countries. An appeal to Western Asia, again, will be still more different.

4. Then, again, there are thousands of Indian students as well as other Indian visitors going abroad. They can do a great deal for India if they are properly instructed and helped. We have often been told that Pakistani students abroad are very effective propagandists for Pakistan. Americans who come here under the Fullbright scheme or in any other way, are adequately briefed by the State Department before they come. Can we not do something to utilize this large number of our fellow countrymen? That would be a far greater gain than a few more publicity offices.

5. I am merely mentioning a few odd ideas that have struck me. What I want to be done is a reconsideration of our whole approach to external publicity. On my return from Japan, I should like to discuss this matter in the Ministry and, later, in the Foreign Affairs Committee. Meanwhile, I should like thought to be given to this in the Ministry.

13. Cable to V.K. Krishna Menon[1]

Your telegram 566, October 11, just received. I am replying as I am leaving Tokyo. I have not yet seen your three resolutions on disarmament.[2]

1. New Delhi, 13 October 1957. JN Collection.
2. The first Indian resolution on disarmament urged immediate suspension of all nuclear tests and called for the appointment of a scientific technical commission to recommend on adequate system of inspection. The second resolution asked for the establishment of another commission to make recommendations on a number of issues such as cut-off date for future production of fissionable material and control and inspection arrangements for conventional armaments. The third resolution advocated for enlargement of the Disarmament Commission and its sub-committee.

Japanese Government is obviously scared of saying anything which might offend Americans. Otherwise they are chiefly interested in economic development. Japanese Foreign Minister, Fujiyama, going to United Nations on 22nd October. He is rather friendly to India and perhaps more liberal in outlook. Would like you to meet him specially in New York?

14. Cable to V.K. Krishna Menon[1]

Krishna Menon telegraphs from New York that our delegation is getting no cooperation from Japanese Delegation on nuclear test resolution. Their draft is extremely weak asking for suspension of tests somewhat less than one year. Even the Western Powers have agreed to two years' suspension. As a matter of fact United States and UK have just completed their series of annual tests and will not normally have further tests till late next year. In these circumstances Japanese resolution does not mean anything.

Our resolution mentions no time limit for tests but automatically comes up before next General Assembly and thereafter whenever necessary. You might point this out to Kishi and specially that this has nothing to do with military and other alliances. It is a question of principle and present conditions are grave. In accordance with our joint communiqué we have to lay immediate emphasis on suspension of tests. We hope, therefore, that Japanese resolution will not be pressed to a vote and that the Japanese Delegation will support ours which in no way conflicts with it but is a little more positive. It would be unfortunate if Japanese resolution is pressed to a vote and we have to vote against it so soon after our Joint Declaration.

1. Hong Kong, 14 October 1957. JN Collection.

15. Cable to V.K. Krishna Menon[1]

Your three draft resolutions on disarmament have reached me. I have no particular comments to make as important consideration is what can best serve as possible basis for agreement and yet be an effective advance. More especially how we can stop nuclear tests.

There is one aspect, however, which I should like to mention. Our demand for enlargement of Disarmament Commission as well as of sub-committee, justified as it is, leads people to think that this is a measure to get India in. I do not like to create any impression that we are trying to push India. Indeed I am inclined to think that generally we can play a more effective role from outside and without embarrassing entanglements and jealousies.

This is just to let you know how my mind works. I am not suggesting any change in our attitude.

1. Yangon 16 October 1957. JN Collection.

16. Cable to C.S. Jha[1]

I have told you already about possibility of conflict between us and Japan over Nuclear resolutions in United Nations. Our instructions to our delegations to cooperate have no meaning when entirely different approaches have to be made even on an issue which should be treated as humanitarian and not political.

I have just seen that Japan is cosponsoring move to get South Korea and South Vietnam into United Nations. This is clearly a step in cold war and has to be resisted by us. It would completely undermine Geneva Agreements on Indo-China and put an end to any hope of unity of divided countries. We are particularly concerned as India is Chairman of Vietnam Commission and responsible for carrying out Geneva Agreement. As a matter of fact South Vietnam Government

1. New Delhi, 16 October 1957. File No. 5 (9)-UN-II/57, Vol. II, p. 457/C, MEA. Also available in JN Collection.

has consistently avoided accepting that agreement or acting according to its provisions. For South Vietnam to be put in UN is to encourage intransigence and intensify conflict in that area and indeed in whole of Indo-China.

17. Need to Give Up Cold War[1]

The root cause of trouble in the present day world, is cold war—each major power is afraid of the other and suspect the other.

Cold war is particularly out of date in the present day conditions even from the most practical point of view, apart from other reasons. The approach of cold war should be given up. The countries should be left, more or less, to develop themselves as they want, of course, with friendly help.

Question: Do you think the Soviet discovery of space missiles would intensify the cold war?

Jawaharlal Nehru: Yes, that is the opinion of some people. I do not think the so-called space missiles are likely to make any difference to warfare in the foreseeable future. They only indicate the capacity of a country to throw missiles at a long range. The solution to all this is not a question of finding clever words and phrases, but people making a different approach—a change of mental approach, a change of heart. Otherwise it is all playing about with words and phrases.

Q: Has the Disarmament Commission failed?

JN: The Disarmament Commission has not failed yet. It is bound to succeed some time or other, because there is no other way out.

Q: What will you do in the light of the British Prime Minister, Mr Macmillan's reported letter to Mr Kishi, Japanese Prime Minister, refusing to stop nuclear tests?

1. Talk with press correspondents on his return from his Asian tour on way to Delhi, Dum Dum airport, Kolkata, 17 October 1957. From *Amrita Bazar Patrika* and *National Herald*, 18 October 1957.

JN: I cannot stop them. India does not go in for test explosion. If others do not stop them they will be blown up. Unfortunately, we will be blown up, too.

Q: What are your comments on the resignation of Pakistan's Prime Minister, Mr H.S. Suhrawardy, last Friday?

JN: I have nothing to say on that. It is the business of the people there to set up a government of their own choice and it is not for us to meddle in that.

Q: The CPI has recently passed a resolution urging the resignation of T.T. Krishnamachari, Union Finance Minister.

JN: I do not normally take orders from the CPI. I am aware that certain remarks made by Krishnamachari have been torn out of context and attempts have been made to give an altogether different interpretation on them.

Q: What about the reported move for cutting down the Second Five Year Plan?

JN: To some extent it might have to be done. However, I have no idea in what way this would take place, if at all.

Q: Will the Government of India try to secure big loans from the USSR to meet the uncovered balance for the Second Five Year Plan?

JN: We have dealt with them on certain individual projects: we are considering the possibility of having Soviet aids on works other than those of the Second Five Year Plan too.

18. Delay in Issuing Passports[1]

Deputy Minister, Lakshmi Menon, told me that during her recent visit to Madras, she received many complaints about the delay in the issue of passports there.

1. Note to Foreign Secretary, New Delhi, 24 October 1957. JN Collection.

These passports were chiefly, I think, for Malaya. In fact, it was stated that there were four thousand pending cases of passports in Madras alone.

2. There must be something wrong about our system if there are such heavy arrears and consequent delays in dealing with these matters. I should like you to get figures from all our Regional Passport Offices to show the number of pending cases that they have got. Also how long it takes normally to issue a passport. Further, what is the greatest delay that has occurred in any particular case.

3. Does the normal procedure cause any delay or are rather special cases held up for some time?

19. Futility of Cold War[1]

Mr President,[2] Excellencies and Distinguished Delegates,[3]
Our President has already offered a cordial welcome to all of you on your visit to this country for this Conference. I should like to add to that welcome on behalf of the Government of India.

We welcome you here not only because yours is a great organization but, more particularly, if I may say so in all humility, because the type of work which you do is in tune with the spirit which we should like to encourage in ourselves. I do not say we would succeed in that in ourselves or anywhere else but, at any rate, we try to do so because, however much we may forget, somewhere at the back of our minds there lingers the voice of Gandhi, somewhere in the recesses of our minds in our racial memories there lingers the message of Asoka and others. We forget it often enough and we follow wrong paths, yet we do not quite forget it for it comes back to us from time to time, and because we feel that the essential basis of the activities of the Red Cross is in tune with that message, we bid you special welcome.

1. Speech at the 19th International Red Cross Conference, New Delhi, 28 October 1957. JN Papers, NMML.
2. Rajendra Prasad inaugurated the Conference.
3. Amrit Kaur, Chairman of the Indian Red Cross Society; Andre Francois-Poncet, Chairman of the Standing Commission of the International Red Cross; M. Leopold Boissier, President of the International Committee of the Red Cross; and Mr Justice Emil Sandstrom, Chairman of the Board of Governors of the League of Red Cross Societies, also participated in the Conference.

The Red Cross Organization saw light, I believe, nearly a hundred years ago in order to mitigate somewhat the horrors of war, to serve perhaps as some kind of a bridge between combatants and belligerents. Its work has grown since then, and I have no doubt that it has brought enormous relief and, more particularly, it has bridged these rival forces at a time when they were completely separated and isolated from each other. It has represented that aspect of human nature which may be said to be the more civilized aspect, in contradiction to the other which forgets civilization. But I suppose, whether as individuals or as groups, we are all rather a mixture of the civilized and the uncivilized, of the divine and the brute. And, I suppose that nobody can call war with its brutalities as the outcome of a high civilization. It may be something unavoidable or not, that is a matter for argument, but no one can call the deliberate infliction of suffering and destruction as a part of human civilization. But it represents as the human heritage, the heritage not of the civilized aspect of man but of some other aspect, and in order to balance that and to take up the divine or the civilized in man, it is always trying to make its efforts and the Red Cross, I suppose, represents one of those efforts.

Now, the Red Cross Organization came into existence almost as an outcome of war, as a child of war, to mitigate the horrors of war. What exactly is the position of the Red Cross in the present age to which reference has been made by some of the distinguished speakers before me. What is this child of war? How does it function in this age of cold war? Surely, its function is essentially the same even though it may not have to deal with people, hospitals and the life. It will have to deal with people whose minds are attuned to war and of the evils of war, even though they hate it, because of the compulsion of events perhaps. In other words, it is not, perhaps, quite enough to wait for war, its evils and its mutilations, for the Red Cross to come into action. Why not try to soothe and to heal the wounds of the spirit? Why not be a bridge between these various isolated hosts, separated hosts? I have no doubt that it is so to some extent even now, and as has been pointed out, it has endeavoured to bring some relief even in times of peace to those who suffer from disabilities or persecution and the like; and I welcome that. But I venture, in all humility, to put before this distinguished audience that the old approach of waiting ultimately for war to happen and then trying, seeking to mitigate it, is hardly adequate today when that possible war may well mean something that you cannot mitigate in anyway—the consequences of it—it may well mean destruction on a terrific scale.

How then do we meet this crisis? How does the Red Cross meet it? How do everyone of us meet it? It is not the special function of the Red Cross. It has become the function of every sensitive individual. But the Red Cross, being rather specialists in dealing with suffering humanity, and I suppose, thereby

AT A RECEPTION GIVEN BY THE INDIAN COMMUNITY, HONG KONG,
14 OCTOBER 1957

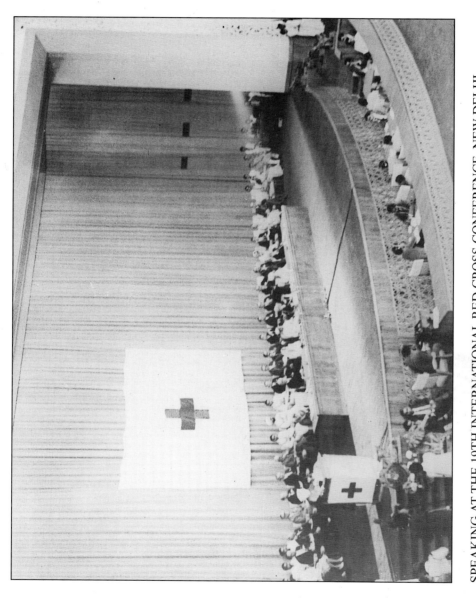

SPEAKING AT THE 19TH INTERNATIONAL RED CROSS CONFERENCE, NEW DELHI, 28 OCTOBER 1957

also gaining some knowledge in how to deal with the troubles of the spirit, how will they deal with the spiritual torment of today?

A distinguished speaker before me thought of the two systems, political and social, which apparently face each other. That is true. But may I suggest in all humility, for your consideration that there may be something else besides those two systems which seem to imagine that they have the world for conflict or sharing. There may, perhaps, be some other ways of achieving what we have in our minds without necessarily adopting one system or the other in its entirety. There may be many such ways. In any event, whether there are many or whether there are only two or three, how do we deal with this particular situation? Because, that situation brings war into the minds of people.

You will remember that in the Constitution of that great organization, the UNESCO, it is stated that wars begin in the minds of men. And, therefore, you should root them out from the minds of men. If we indulge in what is called cold war, that is indulging in war in our minds, and indulging is something worse than war; that is hatred which leads to war—hatred and fear.

How then is one to deal with this situation when there are conflicting policies, conflicting views? And we live on the verge of war and disaster. One may imagine perhaps that, well, one view is right and the other is wrong, and therefore, the right should put an end to the wrong. Some people may feel that way. But even so, it does not appear particularly easy to do that, whichever might be the right and whichever the wrong. And in the process of trying to do that, one does a great deal of wrong. Therefore, that approach does not lead anywhere, whatever approach is there, and if that approach does not lead anywhere, then the approach of what has been called cold war is a very inefficient approach leading nowhere. Some other approach has to be found, I do not know; it is for the great men of the world to think it out. But it is manifest, it seems to me, that the approach will have to be something very different from the approach of hatred and cold war which, it can be demonstrably shown, have not led to any reasonable result in the past, much less will it do so in the future.

It is not perhaps by laying stress on that aspect of human nature which so easily becomes brutish that we shall solve the question. I do not pretend to say that people in this country or any particular country are better than others. I believe that, broadly speaking, the people of India are rather gentle and yet I know very well that these so-called gentle people can and have misbehaved terribly on occasions. We, all of us, are these mixtures of the good and the bad and the question that arises is what policy we should pursue which might bring out the good rather than the bad; and surely, a policy of constant fear and hatred and cold war is not going to bring out the good in the individual or a nation, but rather bring out the bad.

Then, there is sometimes what is called 'coexistence'. Well, we of course do coexist, but not coexist in the sense that we have to put up with it, dislike it as we do, but rather shall I say, the more integrated variety of it, and ultimately, one comes to the conclusion that one cannot really proceed far if we always have the actuality or the prospect of violence that disturbs our mind and brings out what is worst in us—fears and hatreds. Our fears and hatred produce fears and hatred in the other. So, unless we get rid or try to get rid of this talk of violence itself, we cannot put an end to our problems. So, we come back to this grave problem, which is much deeper than these so-called differences in systems, political or economic. It is a problem of the tormented spirit of sensitive human beings today.

Perhaps those people for whom the world is just white or black, with no intermediate shades and therefore, who feel convinced of certain rightness of themselves and certain wrongness of all those who oppose them, perhaps they think it is in a sense well, because they are not troubled by doubts. But more sensitive people are troubled by doubts. Most sensitive men know that it is not a question of black or white and that anyhow it is not a good thing to pursue a wrong method even to gain a right object.

So, all these problems come to us. To all of us, whatever our vocation might be, and sometimes to those who are so firm in their opinions of their own rightness, I would like to say in the words of a famous Englishman who lived long ago—Oliver Cromwell[4]—who received a deputation, I think, from the City of London—I forgot what the deputation said, but it is immaterial—and he replied to that "Gentlemen, I beseech you to consider in the bowels of Christ whether it is possible that you might be wrong". It is always possible for any one of us to be wrong, and for us to imagine that we are always right, I venture to submit, is itself wrong. So, the only approach that we can make is an approach of tolerance and an approach of avoidance of violence and hatred. And I do think that if that approach were made, we would influence those who, for the present, may be opposed to us, far more than by the approach of fear or the threat of violence.

I venture to say this gathering because more than any other group of people this gathering represents the touch of healing, the soothing touch and what the world requires today, more than anything is this touch of healing not only to the body but to the tortured minds of humanity.

---

4. (1599-1658); English General and Politician; Puritan leader of the Parliamentary side in the Civil War; declared Britain a republic in 1649, following the execution of Charles I. As Lord Protector (ruler) from 1653, he established religious toleration and raised Britain's prestige in Europe on the basis of an alliance with France and Spain.

20. No Misuse of Diplomatic Bag[1]

Some time ago, Dr Krishnaswami, who is a member of some committee of the UN, saw me and gave me a report of his work. He mentioned then that he would like to send me some new books published in America. I told him that I would be glad to have them.

Two or three days ago some books sent by him were placed before me. He had evidently given these books to our Consulate General in New York to send them to me and they had been sent by diplomatic bag. I am told that the cost of sending these books in this way is a little over Rs 110.00. I think, it was improper to send these books by diplomatic bag. I have now to pay this sum of Rs 110.00. myself. The books could have been sent by sea mail. Even if they had been sent by normal airfreight, it would probably have been much cheaper. To use the diplomatic bag to send such things was not at all right, apart from its being an expensive way of doing things.

This kind of thing has happened previously also. I think that Special Secretary might write to our Missions abroad and tell them that they should not use the diplomatic bag to send packages etc., unless there is some special urgency. Also that they should not be used for private purposes. They might be told of this particular instance where I had to pay Rs 110.00 or more, which was quite unnecessary.[2]

---

1. Note to Secretary General, Foreign Secretary, Commonwealth Secretary, Special Secretary, New Delhi, 30 October 1957. JN Collection.
2. A letter to Arthur Lall was sent by M.O. Mathai indicating Nehru's viewpoint.

21. Cable to V.K. Krishna Menon[1]

Your telegram 591 October 27th.[2] It is difficult for me to advise you about the changing situation in regard to disarmament. You are the best person to judge.

2. I do not quite know to what precisely you refer in paragraph 4 of your telegram.[3]

3. I have no doubt about our policy being the right one. But it seems to me that real disarmament will not come because of some phrasing of a resolution which does not indicate any real change of heart, or some majority decision not accepted by those who count in this matter. These debates seem to me rather artificial, each important party trying to gain some advantage over the other without really intending to have disarmament. Disarmament can only come by a lessening of fear and tension. There appear to be no signs of this lessening and there is far too much hatred in the air for any real progress to be made.

---

1. New Delhi, 30 October 1957. JN Collection.
2. Krishna Menon discussed the general world situation. He wrote that he was consulting both Americans and Russians about disarmament and there was a slender chance about some good coming out of it.
3. He requested Nehru "to do what you can not to permit important people to blackguard me while disarmament and Kashmir issues are on."

V. PORTUGUESE POSSESSIONS

1. Conditions of Goa Prisoners[1]

Here is a letter about Goa prisoners and especially Mrs Sudha Joshi.[2] I am very worried about these people. Dr Gaitonde[3] was speaking to me today and telling me of the deepening frustration among the Goans in Goa and especially these prisoners. The Portuguese authorities are telling people that India has washed her hands more or less off Goa and are gloating at this fact.

What are we to do about this, that is, the prisoners? At any rate, we should not allow the impression to grow abroad that we have forgotten them and Goa.

Please have a brief and adequate reply sent to this letter saying that we are much concerned at this and we shall go on doing our utmost for the release of his wife and others.

1. Note to Foreign Secretary, New Delhi, 13 August 1957. JN Collection.
2. Letter, presumably from Sudha Joshi's husband, is not available in the files.
3. Dr P.D. Gaitonde was an eminent surgeon who was imprisoned in Lisbon in 1954-55.

2. To Sindhu Deshpande[1]

New Delhi
August 15, 1957

Dear Miss Deshpande,[2]

I have received your letter of 12th August about the Goan prisoners. I have read it with considerable distress and I can well appreciate how strongly you feel about this matter.

1. JN Collection.
2. A resident of Pune.

It is a matter of continuing sorrow and anxiety for us to realize that hundreds of Goans are suffering so much in prison and, what is more, losing heart. All I can say is that we are greatly concerned about them and we should like to do our utmost to get them out of prison. Indeed, this applies to the larger question of Goa also, with which their incarceration is so intimately connected.

I cannot discuss this complicated question in my letter. But you will no doubt realize the difficulties and complications that have arisen. The question of Goa is connected with international issues. One aspect of this is now before the International Court of Justice at The Hague.[3]

I quite agree with you that, in the past, the steps taken were not always wise. All I can say now is that we are giving constant thought to this question and whatever we think is feasible, will certainly be done.

Yours sincerely,
Jawaharlal Nehru

3. Portugal had filed a petition in The Hague Court that India had prevented her right of passage across Indian territory to the Portuguese enclaves of Dadra and Nagar Haveli, and asked the Court to declare this right.

3. Cable to Vijaya Lakshmi Pandit[1]

Your letter August 17th about fees for Frank Soskice[2] and others in connection with Portuguese case. agree with you that these fees are very heavy. Our Law Minister and Attorney General also think so. Unfortunately we did not try to fix these fees at earlier stage as we did in case of Professor Guggenheim[3] whose fee was fixed at one thousand pounds plus some daily expenses.

1. New Delhi, 22 August 1957. JN Collection.
2. British lawyer and Labour party MP.
3. Paul Guggenheim (b. 1899); Swiss international lawyer and Professor of International Public Law, Geneva University; Member of the Permanent Court of Arbitration, The Hague, 1951; Agent and Counsel for Switzerland and other countries in different cases before the International Court of Justice and European Court of Human Rights; Member, UN Committee for elaborating the Constitution of Erythrea, 1951-52; President, Swiss Society of International Law, 1964-69; Member of the Academy of Political and Economic Sciences of the Republic of Venezuela, 1964; Legal Adviser of the European Conference of Molecular Biology, 1967-68.

2. All these fees are governed by Soskice's fee. His junior automatically takes two-thirds and Waldock[4] has asked for the same sum as Soskice. While Soskice's fee, though very heavy, might be understandable, Waldock's fee is most unusual. Waldock's standing more or less the same as Guggenheim's.

3. We are, however, in a difficult position. It is not easy for Government to bargain about terms almost at last stage of the case. I had at first thought that it was not necessary for all these lawyers to go to The Hague for Preliminary hearing and Le Quesne and Waldock might be left out. But Attorney General says that Waldock has been most helpful of all in drafting preliminary objection and Soskice had made it clear previously that he must have Le Quesne.

4. There is no doubt that all these persons have done good work and have been very helpful. But fact remains that their fees are terribly heavy even from normal standards. Our Attorney General will be reaching London about end of first week September. It will be too late then for him to raise this question with Soskice and it will also be embarrassing for him to do so. Setalvad himself is charging us no special fee.

5. I think that the only feasible course to follow now is for you to see Frank Soskice informally and in a friendly way. Tell him that we very much appreciate work done by him and his colleagues in this case. But we have been put in some difficulty in regard to the fees and expenditure in this case. An all-out effort is being made in India at present for economy, more especially in regard to foreign exchange. Questions are asked in Parliament frequently about major items of expenditure including lawyers' fees paid by us. It is going to be embarrassing for us to justify fees that are prima facie very heavy.

6. In connection with Waldock's fee you might point out to Soskice that we had fixed a much smaller fee for Professor Guggenheim previously.

7. I do not wish you to argue with Soskice or to appear to haggle. Tell him that you want his advice. Whatever advice he gives finally will have to be accepted because we cannot change about now.

8. In the event of our preliminary objection against Portugal prevailing this case will end. In case, however, the case goes to full hearing then we shall have to consider afresh question of later fees.

---

4. Edgar A. Waldock was Professor of Public Administration and International Law in Oxford University.

4. Change the Firm of Solicitors[1]

I think that in view of what is said in Shri Mukhi's letter,[2] we might well revise our decision about the change of solicitors. In this letter it is stated that the new firm of solicitors, Bailey & Co. with whom our old firm has got merged, are demanding extraordinary fees in advance. Also, that they have sent threatening letters to the High Commission. Surely, in view of this, we can take some steps to change them and we need not wait for the Attorney General to be there. But it would, of course, be right for the Attorney General to be consulted before we sent any such direction. Please, therefore, consult him immediately. I think that Shri S. Sen should go to him and show him this letter and tell him that in view of what we now learn, we feel that it is desirable to change our solicitors immediately. There is no point in our holding on to a firm which sends threatening letters to us and demands excessive fees in advance, a practice which has not been followed in the past at any time.

If the Attorney General is agreeable to this course, then you should send a telegram to our High Commissioner. It might be on the following lines:

Refer to our last telegram about this matter in which we suggested that she might meet Sir Frank Soskice and have an informal talk with him and point out to him of our difficulties. Say that now we have received Mukhi's letter dated 22nd August in which he tells us about the High Commissioner meeting Mr Downs. In view of the threatening letters received from Bailey & Co. and their demanding 30,000/- in advance, against all previous practice, we agree that our firm of solicitors should be changed. The new firm of solicitors might then on their own account negotiate with Sir Frank Soskice about fees. Possibly, the High Commissioner has already seen Sir Frank Soskice. She will have to fit that in to the new course that is being adopted. Probably in any event, it would be desirable to see him informally. You might further mention that we have consulted our Attorney General about this matter and he agrees.

This is, of course, presuming that the Attorney General agrees.

---

1. Note to Foreign Secretary, New Delhi, 26 August 1957. JN Collection.
2. J.M. Mukhi had written from London on 22 August that Mr Downs, a partner in the new firm of solicitors, told Vijaya Lakshmi Pandit that Frank Soskice's bills were "fantastically excessive."

5. To Vijaya Lakshmi Pandit[1]

New Delhi
August 30, 1957

Nan Dear,

I received your letter from Oslo two or three days ago.[2] I am very glad you went there, rather than to some other place. I hope that the rest there, in those lovely surroundings, did you good.

I wonder if you met Prince Olaf,[3] the Regent. He has got a curious, rather hysterical laugh.

M.C. Setalvad, the Attorney-General, left Delhi today, and he is leaving for London in a day or two. I have discussed this question of the fees for the Portugal case as well as the solicitors and asked him to look into this matter himself and advise you. It is a delicate matter, more especially in so far as Sir Frank Soskice and others are concerned, and I do not want them to feel that we are backing out or doing something that is not quite proper. I have no doubt that the fees, as have been marked, are exorbitant. I do not know what normal fees are. Some of these people, like Hartley Shawcross, used to charge very fancy fees. I think, the whole thing has been rather mismanaged. I would like you, therefore, to abide by Setalvad's advice and let him deal with the matter directly or through somebody else. I should not like India Office people to bear the brunt of the responsibility for any decision.

We are up to our eyes in work and difficulties here. Tomorrow, the AICC is meeting. On top of all this, has come a terrible disaster in Jammu and Kashmir. The floods there have been terrific, in both places. I am told that the whole of the Valley is an enormous lake, except for some high ground sticking out, and all the villages have been swept away. Srinagar escaped submergence because of the night and day work of our Army, which is being praised there by everybody. The floods are very slowly receding now, but still continuing to do damage in the upper portion of the Valley. Most bridges have been swept away and, of course, all the crops have gone. Apart from future re-construction and all that,

---

1. JN Collection.
2. Vijaya Lakshmi had gone to Oslo for a week-long holiday.
3. Olaf V (1903-1991); King of Norway; married to Princess Martha of Sweden, 1929; Commander-in-Chief, Norwegian Forces, Second World War; succeeded his father, King Haakon VII on 21 September 1957.

the immediate problem is one of feeding these poor people there. As we ourselves are in great difficulty about food, this means a great burden.

You know that I have not been to Kashmir for four years. But, this disaster is compelling me to pay a brief visit, and I shall probably go there for a day early next week. I would have gone there even sooner, but for the AICC meeting and a debate on foreign affairs in the Lok Sabha on Monday, the 2nd September. I shall go there just for the day.

Your story about the Duke of Wellington is surprising, and rather distressing.[4] But, I do not understand what you mean by two pictures being sent to him. I thought only one was sent.

As a matter of fact, we have got another painting of the old Duke of Wellington, or rather the Marquis of Wellesly. Everybody says that this is far superior to the others. At one time, I thought of sending it to you for the Duke of Wellington, instead of the other picture. When, however, the other had been sent, I saw no reason to send another. But, there it is with us, or rather with Sri Prakasa in Bombay, and I am prepared to send it, if you think this necessary. Perhaps, you could get some other treasures out of the Duke, in exchange for this picture. Of course, having been bitten once, he will be rather shy to another venture. But, if he is really interested, he can have this examined.

Love,

Yours,
Jawahar

---

4. See *ante*, p. 184.

6. Violation of Indian Territory by the Portuguese Troops[1]

H.N. Mukerjee and seven others: Will the Prime Minister be pleased to state:
- (a) whether his attention has been drawn to press reports regarding Portuguese troops in Daman violating Indian territory and opening fire on the 27th and 28th August, 1957;
- (b) whether such action followed a recent encounter between Portuguese troops and underground nationalist forces;
- (c) whether it is a fact that an innocent villager was crushed to death by Portuguese jeeps as a reprisal; and
- (d) what steps have been taken in regard to the happenings?

Jawaharlal Nehru: (a) to (c). In so far as information is available to us about certain occurrences in the Portuguese territory of Daman, the facts appear to be as follows:

On the 26th August at about midnight, a Portuguese military patrol jeep was blown up in an explosion by a land mine about three quarters of a mile from the Daman Fort. The jeep was blown to pieces and the occupants numbering six were all killed. Portuguese soldiers following in another jeep searched the vicinity and arrested an innocent villager of Village Dhandas inside Daman. This villager, whose name is reported to be Kanji Homi Bari, was thrown on the road and a jeep ran over him, crushing him. Curfew was imposed in the locality.

Between midnight and 0330 hours on the 28th August, Portuguese border patrol fired continuously for over three hours in the direction of Tarak Pardi post which is inside Indian territory. Several bullets entered Indian territory. The fire was not returned and there were no casualties. Again at 0140 hours on the 29th August, Portuguese troops fired several rounds at Premavadi road post off Kunta in Indian territory. Some more rounds were fired at 0440 hours from Vad Chowkey which is in Portuguese territory. On all these occasions bullets entered Indian territory. The fire was not returned and there were no casualties.

On the 28th August at about 0130 hours Portuguese troops fired about ten to twelve rounds at our border patrol near Statosa post on the Savantvadi border. There were no casualties and the fire was not returned.

---

1. Reply to a question in the Lok Sabha, 5 September 1957. *Lok Sabha Debates* (second series), Vol. VI, cols. 12000-12003. Extracts.

(d) No action has yet been taken by Government. In fact, while we are determined to prevent the violation of our borders by foreign elements, no effective action is possible against incidents of this kind. We have found from experience that notes of protest to the Portuguese Government are quite useless.

H.N. Mukerjee: In view of the repeated and aggressive violations of international law and morality by Portugal, may I know if Government is seriously contemplating action other than registering protests and, if so, what roughly is such action likely to be?

JN: If the honourable Member refers to any possible action of the military kind, we are not contemplating any such action. Any other type of action that may be feasible will be taken.

H.N. Mukerjee: The Prime Minister told us the other day that the Government was rather surprised at certain Great Powers supporting Portuguese colonialism in India. May I know if he will take it up with such powers, particularly those in the British Commonwealth, at the diplomatic level, especially when he told us himself that several Indian nationals are involved in all these happenings and they are in Portuguese prisons?

JN: Yes, Sir.[2]

---

2. Later, a note was sent to the Commonwealth Governments. See *post*, p. 758.

7. To Nath Pai[1]

New Delhi
September 9, 1957

Dear Nath Pai,[2]

Thank you for your letter of the 9th September, with which you have sent me signatures of a number of people in regard to Goa.[3] You say that you had released these in January 1956. I do not remember seeing anything about them in the Press or, perhaps, I have forgotten it. It might be worthwhile giving publicity to them now again, if you agree.

It is not an easy matter for our Missions abroad to approach Opposition parties. They may meet them sometimes and discuss these matters, but they cannot ask them for statements. Our Missions are supposed to deal with the government of the day and to do anything behind the back of the government, would probably be resented.[4]

Yours sincerely,
Jawaharlal Nehru

1. Nath Pai Papers, NMML. Also available in JN Collection.
2. (1922-1971); was President, Socialist Youth International, Vienna; President, London Majlis; Vice-President, British Asian Socialist Fellowship (London); Vice-President, Congress of Peoples for Colonial Freedom (London); imprisoned during the Quit India Movement; PSP Member from Rajapur, Maharashtra, 1952-70.
3. Nath Pai had enclosed a statement on Goa signed by the leaders of the Social Democratic Parties of several European countries, whose signatures he had obtained in the autumn of 1955. Nath Pai released this statement to the Press in Rome in January 1956. He wrote that in pursuance of the same efforts, he approached some members of the British Parliament and a Goa Committee was formed with Anthony Wedgewood Ben as chairman. Its members tried to raise the Goa issue in the House of Commons on several occasions. Nath Pai reported this development to the Indian High Commission in London.
4. On 10 September 1957, Nehru met the Goa Committee of Parliament, consisting of Congress and Opposition members, about steps to counter Portuguese propaganda abroad in regard to Goa.

8. Communication to Commonwealth Governments[1]

I think it is necessary for us to address the Commonwealth Governments except Pakistan.[2] Indeed, I think, we should address other Governments too.

I agree with you that in our Aide Memoire, we should not expressly ask the Government concerned to try to influence the Government of Portugal. The part side-lined in this note should, therefore, be omitted. At the end of the note, however, some special reference to the repressive measures of the Portuguese authorities, and especially to the hundreds of Goans in jail, might be repeated.

1. Note to Foreign Secretary, New Delhi, 30 September 1957. File No. 11-21/57-GP p. 3, MHA (MEA). Also available in JN Collection.
2. S. Dutt had enclosed a draft note to be addressed to all Commonwealth Governments except Pakistan about the present conditions in Goa and in particular the condition of Goan prisoners. Dutt was not sure whether it should invoke the good offices of the Commonwealth Governments in securing alleviation in the conditions of the prisoners since these were Goan nationals. However, unless a specific request was made, these Governments might not take action.

VI. PONDICHERRY

1. Conditions in Pondicherry[1]

I saw a group of Communist MPs this afternoon about Pondicherry affairs. I had not seen your note at that time.

2. Among those who came, were Shri H.N. Mukerjee and two or three others. Subbiah,[2] the Communist from Pondicherry, was also with them. It was Subbiah who spoke. I made a brief note which I attach.

1. Note to Foreign Secretary, New Delhi, 7 September 1957. JN Collection.
2. V.K. Subbiah was Member of the Pondicherry Assembly at this time.

3. In effect, they said nothing definite to me. They complained of the lack of democratic functioning of the Assembly and of the Opposition not being represented in the Commissions. Further, that the Assembly sat only for two or three days in a month, and then goes into Committees where there is no opposition. Further, that the decisions are not implemented. And the Planning Board meets rarely. Also, that there is corruption.

4. No opportunity is given to discuss various issues in the Planning Board. The Police and Magistrates still function in the old bad way.

5. The Municipality in Pondicherry has a Communist majority. But, Government does not cooperate. Reference was made to the case of the Mayor last year, and it was suggested that his suspension just before the elections was intended to influence the elections.

6. As the de jure transfer is going to take place shortly, there should then be an election of a representative for the Lok Sabha and also general elections.

7. All this was very vague. I asked what had happened to the Mayor, and was informed that he had been convicted, but an appeal was pending. They complained that he was still suspended. I said that this was an extraordinary complaint when he had already been convicted.

8. In effect, nothing definite was said to me and only vague allegations were made.

10
PRESS CONFERENCE

1. National and International Issues[1]

Jawaharlal Nehru: I am meeting you after a long time at a press conference like this. The fault is partly mine but perhaps if you are a little more insistent, I could meet you a little oftener.

I think, the best way to begin is for you to put questions or note down some of the subjects you wish to talk about.

Subjects:
1. Syrian situation,
2. Finance Minister's impressions,
3. Impressions of your visit to Japan,
4. Journalists' Wage Board Award,
5. Law Commission's Interim Report,
6. Uttar Pradesh Municipal Elections,
7. My references about communism in India.

Question: You said in Japan that it is an odd thing that in India parties do not appear to hate each other so much.

JN: It is quite natural.

Q: 8. Yugoslavia consulted India before deciding on East Germany?[2] Is there any truth?

9. Food situation in India.
JN: There is no doubt that it has taken a bad turn because of drought. We had trouble in regard to floods etc., but trouble due to floods, though bad, is temporary and usually it is followed by a good harvest. But drought is much worse. And this time we expected a good harvest. With the smallest of showers in September or beginning of October, it would have been a good harvest but there is not a drop of rain in parts of Bihar, a good part of Bihar, part of UP, part of Madhya Pradesh, part of Orissa, and part of West Bengal—spread over larger areas, there is Maharashtra but a small area. But this is a block more or less. This has

---

1. Proceedings of a press conference, New Delhi, 21 October 1957. PIB files.
2. On 15 October 1957, the Yugoslav and East German Governments announced that they had agreed to establish diplomatic relations and exchange of representatives at the Ministerial levels.

created a difficult situation. We are trying to do something and the Food Minister has gone to Bihar (unless he has returned today, I do not know). There is no doubt as on other occasions, we will place the facts before the public. It is not a matter to be dealt with behind the purdah. This is a serious matter. Everybody has to understand and cooperate. It is not a party matter, a big thing for vast areas suddenly to come down to 50 per cent with regard to its production. It is, if I may say so, the most important thing which is in my mind at present.

Somebody asked about Yugoslavia, whether Yugoslavia consulted India or not. There is no question of consultation. I think, the day before it was announced in public, we received an intimation that this was going to be done and other countries also received intimation. So, there is no question of consultation and asking us what we thought or not.

Q: Is there any prospect of India similarly establishing diplomatic relations with East Germany?

JN: Not at present. We have trade relations, of course.

Much can be said about Syria and very little can also be said. At present, fortunately, so far as we can see, the situation has eased down considerably and the alarming prospects of a possibility of war are fading. But there is no doubt that, probably, the situation was a dangerous one, dangerous in the sense that small things lead to great things, a little war might lead to big war. You know how on both sides serious charges and counter charges have been made about Syria. Well, it is not for me to deal with the charges and counter charges. Normally, such charges have a tendency to be exaggerated. Even if there is some truth, the tendency is to exaggerate. But one important aspect of the Syrian situation had been that Arab nationalism had proved much too stronger than the Baghdad Pact. In all modern states, if I may say so, I would like to point out that nationalism in these areas, as indeed in Asia and elsewhere, is a force—the strongest force. Neither communism nor anti-communism comes up anywhere in this nationalism. Unless a force utilizes nationalism—well, it is communism or anti-communism, the real truth is nationalist sentiment. The Baghdad Pact has split up the countries and there is much danger. Of course, for Syria or for any other Arab country to be called communist is a very great exaggeration. Individuals, of course, there are individuals who may have communist sympathies, but the real thing is not communism but the play of great power politics there. That, of course, is much in evidence in all these countries. Anyhow, the present position is quite good, chiefly, I think, with reference to the United Nations. At present all parties are agreed on some kind of commission inquiring into it. I understand Syria has agreed and Turkey has agreed, something agreeable to the two.

Q: In connection with Syria, the matter is of common interest to the Asian-African countries. In regard to the second Bandung Conference, the Indonesian Foreign Minister[3] is reported to have said the other day in Cairo that imperialists were striving to prevent the convening of a second conference.

JN: The Indonesian Foreign Minister is supposed to have said that? It is not for me to criticize other Foreign Ministers. But when we discussed this matter, that is, with Colombo Powers as well as others, our feeling generally was that such a conference should be held in future sometime but the time has not yet come. That has been the general feeling.

Q: With regard to Syria, is the dispute between Syria and Turkey something of a local dispute or something connected with the Baghdad Pact.

JN: The dispute is that each accuses the other of going to attack, and, I believe, an attempt was made to hold together in this matter. But the Arab countries of the Baghdad Pact, well, did not agree to that and they felt that they should not go against time, nationalist feelings.

Q: Will India serve on the UN Commission?

JN: It is very difficult for me to answer. Of course, the question has not arisen at all.

Q: What is your attitude to Western Asia?

JN: I cannot say that. The normal attitude is to avoid undertaking any new burdens.

Q: Would you try for the stoppage of arms for the countries of Middle East including India?

JN: I think personally the time is coming rather rapidly when all these arms will be pretty useless.

Q: Could you say that the Russian satellite would affect politics?

JN: I do not think it affects directly the military aspect of the question. I can say that it shows that things can be thrown at any distance anywhere from one place

3. Dr Subandrio.

to another on the earth, weapons, missiles but the satellite indicates a tremendous jump in scientific advance. No doubt about that, although we have been expecting that something of this kind is bound to come whether it came from the Soviet Union or the United States of America. It is bound to come and it is rather in this matter a neck to neck affair, one power does it, the other also does it, leave aside the backward countries which cannot catch up with others. It is an advancement of science generally, no doubt. This can be done by other countries but the importance of this, which I have no doubt, will be gradually realized and that it does make our thinking, normal thinking, whether it is in defence or connected matters, rather out of date. In fact, if I may say so, the whole of our life, the world's life is changing and there are indications of how it is changing, but our minds have not kept pace with this changing rhythm which science is bringing about and hence the difficulties. In fact all these national frontiers and the rest become also rather out of date. When you think of going into inter planetary space, the world becomes small, much more so a national frontier. All this business of military alliances is similarly out of date.

Now, two or three matters relatively small matters. Somebody said about the UP municipal elections. They are not over yet. The first results were, I believe, rather unfavourable to the Congress. The second was more favourable. We shall see what the other results are. We can draw any conclusions from it which are justified. As far as I know, quite a large number of parties have been contesting and in many places the Congress has lost a large group of seats. There is nothing mystical about it. Congress has lost, it has lost. There is nothing to feel excited about it either way.

Then Wage Board Awards.[4] I am not an expert in this matter, except that I broadly know what the position was. Very soon results will be announced by the Ministry concerned. One thing I have rather regretted. I do not know how far it is true, but I have received complaints to the effect that some people among the working journalists, who have been taking part in what might be called the trade union activities, have been dealt with rather harshly by their proprietors. That, I think, is unfortunate—I cannot judge their case—but these complaints have been made to me. Quite apart from the merits of particular cases, it creates a bad atmosphere. You cannot settle these things in this way.

Q: What is the Government's attitude in view of the non-implementation by the majority of the proprietors?

JN: That I cannot say unless you give me to what extent they have not implemented that.

4. For details see *ante,* pp. 333-336.

Q: The Supreme Court has expressly said that from May last it should be implemented but they have not yet agreed even to that.

JN: If they offend laws, they will get into trouble.

Q: What is the Government doing? Now are they seeing, supervising the implementation. The Supreme Court specially said it should be from a retrospective date so that it may not cause undue hardship.

JN: There must be some excuse put forward, good or bad. They cannot ignore the Supreme Court surely.

Q: There is mass violation?

JN: It is always difficult to face mass violation of anything.

Q: Has your attention been drawn to the complaint of the Bombay Union of Journalists that Mr Shantilal Shah,[5] Labour Minister of Bombay, is also one of the proprietors, in fact the managing trustee of a paper and hence there is conflict?

JN: Yes, I have heard that. Well, I believe, I am receiving a deputation on the part of the newspaper proprietors.

Q: There is a strike going on in Delhi for the past three or four days in the *Pratap* and *Veer Arjun*; there is a regular strike and Government have not shown any interest. It is for the Labour Ministry, certainly they can take some action.

JN: Yes, but I do not think the Labour Ministry necessarily should jump into every strike that begins—I am not saying about this, I know nothing. I am merely saying that you do not expect the Labour Ministry suddenly to become a party in the sense.

5. Shantilal Harijivan Shah (b. 1898); participated in freedom movement and courted imprisonment, 1939-42; Member, Bombay Legislative Assembly; Minister for Labour and Public Health, Bombay Government till 1956; Minister for Education and Law, Bombay Government, 1956-1957; Minister for Labour and Law, Bombay State, 1957 and 1960; Minister for Law, Judiciary and Labour, Maharashtra, 1960-62; Minister for Education, 1962-63; Minister for Public Health, Law and Judiciary, 1963-1966.

Q: I am asking because Delhi is directly under the Centre.

JN: It may be.

Q: If Government does not take interest, who will take interest? There is no local government here.

JN: There is a local government here which functions under the Government of India; there is a local government surely.

Q: With reference to the Wage Board, the issue involved is this, namely that the Government appoints a Wage Board and it gives a decision, and nobody takes the responsibility of implementing it. This means that our faith in the whole institution of tribunals will be undermined. This is a very big issue.

JN: My impression was that the final decision about the Wage Board, I mean the Price Page Schedule, etc., has not yet been announced.

Q: When you were in Japan you had stated that the communists of India are working under the Constitution and for the implementation of the Five Year Plan. I wonder if your opinion has changed as far as the Five Year Plan is concerned, in view of their recent attack on Mr T.T. Krishnamachari and certain aspects of the financial situation in India?

JN: I do not quite know to what you are referring, to what I said in Japan. I hardly discussed the communists, in Japan. I mean the communists affirmed that they are working under the Constitution; I repeated what they said about it. Well, of course, as regards working within the Constitution, you can work within the letter of the law and yet perhaps not observe the spirit of it. There are many variations and gradations in regard to that.

Q: Do you find any difference between the communist attitude about working under the Constitution and the Congress attitude in 1937, when there was some gentleman's agreement and yet their saying they are going to break the Constitution?

JN: I do not think you are quite correct in saying that about the Congress attitude in 1937. Their aim was to gain further powers, not to break the Constitution.

Q: That was the wording of the resolution of AICC, that they were capturing power to break the Constitution. Do you think the communists are also doing something like that?

JN: I do not know; how am I to answer on behalf of the communists? I do not know if even they know quite what they want to do. There may be different viewpoints among them but obviously a Constitution like ours must come in the way, must inhibit some of their methods of activity. Obviously, also they must strive to build up their party strength in such ways as they can for any future election when it takes place. Any party does that. If it is done in a wrong way it is not justified, it is very difficult to say yes or no to these questions. One may do something within the letter of the Constitution and yet in a way which is perhaps not justifiable.

Q: There has been an apparent contradiction in high Congress thinking on the subject of the Communist Government in Kerala. While Shri Shriman Narayan Aggarwal thinks there is a rapid deterioration in the law and order situation, the Congress President says that the communists must be allowed to work the Government within the framework of the Constitution and not harassed by local Congressmen on every issue.

JN: Where is the contradiction between the two statements? I see none.

Q: That the communists are not within the pale of the law.

JN: You said that the Congress General Secretary said that the law and order situation is breaking down in a bad way. The Congress President said that they should be allowed to work within the law, of course, and they should not be needlessly harassed. There is no contradiction between the two. Both may be correct.

Q: Are you in agreement with the opinion of the Congress Secretary on the question of law and order in Kerala?

JN: Well, I do not think it is right for me as Prime Minister to express opinions about one of our constituent states in this way. But I think that there is undoubtedly a measure of apprehension, there is a great deal of apprehension in the minds of many people there about the functioning of law and order and about various pressures being exercised.

Q: What is Mr Krishna Menon's report about it. He was deputed by the AICC.

JN: You do not expect me to talk about a report made by some one to the Congress President. As a matter of fact, so far as I know there is no report in writing; at least, I am not aware of any written document about it.

Q: Reference was made in an earlier question regarding communists, to their vigorous attack on the Finance Minister and on some aspects of the Five Year Plan.

JN: So far as their attack on the general policy is concerned, whether it is the Five Year Plan or any thing, or their attack against the Finance Minister, it is the way they function. And in the best of circumstances, they cannot pull themselves out of certain stock expressions that they learnt by heart, slogans, expressions, and also attacking various people generally. It is quite easy for any one to discuss the Five Year Plan and point out what should have been done, what should not have been done. The Five Year Plan has come up against difficulties, and we all know it. Some were completely outside our control, we could not even think about it; some were such which might have been thought about. It is easy for the communists to make suggestions about the Five Year Plan. I have not got the whole picture as to what they say. I do not know, something of what they say may be correct. Broadly speaking, it is not a thought out thing at all, but only repeating some slogans. As for what they have said about the Finance Minister, as I said, I do not want to enter into an argument with the Communist Party about my colleagues, nor do I take their directions in such matters. My colleague, the Finance Minister, was reported to have said something about the communists, I think, before he went abroad. In the way it was reported, I was surprised, and I asked him about it, and he said that the report was not quite correct, context etc. That is what he said, I did not mean exactly what was reported. There is often talk in a particular strain and in a particular context. If it is pulled out of that context the same phrase may have some slightly different meaning.

Q: Did the Finance Minister say in which way the report of *The New York Times* was incorrect, because it was transcribed, and that was exactly what he had said. It is now six months since he made the statement, and several times I have asked the Government of India whether the Finance Minister had any comment, and whether he wished to say that the report was not true. Every time I have been told there was no comment from Mr Krishnamachari. Obviously, there cannot be any dispute about it.

J.N.: I have told you exactly what Mr Krishnamachari told me. He said that the context just gives a different complexion. There was a brief telegram. He said it was a casual talk. So, I cannot answer your question about it.

Q: Excuse me, this was not a casual conversation. It was an interview given to the paper, and it was reported. An interview between a Minister and a reporter is not quite casual. He has been in the United States for a number of days. If the report had been distorted, he could have corrected the impression.

JN: It is up to him to decide. He did not say it was distorted. He said that the thing was said in a particular context and if it is read in a different context, it might give a wrong impression. It is not that he denied having said anything.

Q: Is it possible that in any context it can make its meaning different? There is no possibility.

JN: It is obvious that Mr Krishnamachari is not, if I may put it mildly, favourably inclined towards communists.

Q: Surely that does not justify his saying that Russia and China will invade India?

JN: It has surprised me. Clearly, I think, he was making some philosophical remarks, rather casually, which may have a different significance in a different context. Because, obviously, there is no question of anything but the friendliest relations between us and China or Russia.

Q: How far do you agree with the reported remark of Mr Krishnamachari that India was really closer to the United States despite a superficial appearance to the reverse?

JN: Yes, not politically, but economically.

Q: He was not talking on the economic plane.

JN: On what plane does he talk, he being Finance Minister?

Q: In that report, first he is reported to have said that India has been forced to choose the policy of non-alignment out of economic necessity, that it is not a position of neutrality.

JN: If he has said that, I do not think he has made a correct statement. Our non-alignment, if you follow what I say, is an inevitable thing which any sensible Government in India must follow, or else it goes to the dogs. And it is a policy not of my Government, it is a policy to which we have been inevitably led by our previous thinking for the last two generations. Let me go a step further. It derives from Emperor Asoka, 2,300 years ago. It is nothing new. It is a basic thing, our whole lives and being and thinking are based on it. We do not get out of it because there is some incident or somebody gets excited here and there. It is a firm thing, we stick to it even if the Heavens fall, I make it clear.

Q: You just now said that in respect of economic matters, our policies are closer to America.

JN: Our economic contacts are far greater with England and America and other countries than they have been with others.

Q: In that context, the industrial delegation that has gone to America[6] is also reported to have said in Washington that there has been a rethinking in our Government circles about economic policies and that they are going back upon their nationalization and other spheres relating to the socialistic pattern of society. Have you any comments?

JN: It is not right for me to comment on what others have said, and from partial reports. All I can say is that I can positively state that so far as our broad economic thinking is concerned, it remains where it was. We are concerned, naturally with the Five Year Plan and the rest, and are constantly looking at it again. What part of it may be, because of stress of circumstances, to give up, what to postpone, what to carry on with. It is a different matter. If you are thinking in terms of nationalization, I do not know how many times I have stated in Parliament that we do not nationalize for the sake of nationalization. Only if something appears vital in connection with our programme, we take it up. We have said this in our last policy statement. We have no intention of any major active nationalization.

Q: In view of the divergence between the economic and foreign policy statements of Mr Krishnamachari, are you going to dismiss him?

JN: Mr Krishnamachari as Finance Minister has done a very fine job of work. He has carried a very heavy burden. In fact, in some matters there may be disagreement between me and my colleagues, it is a matter we discuss in Cabinet and come to a decision. We are all men, in our Cabinet, of a certain measure of intelligence, a certain measure of independent judgement which is brought

6. An industrial delegation led by G.D. Birla went to the US to mobilise resources.

together and then something results from it. That is a Cabinet decision. We do not function like school boys in a debate, or just criticizing each other in public meetings. We carry a heavy responsibility in the country particularly in matters economic. And taking into consideration the various aspects of the case which the Ministers in charge put forward and then follow the decision is a joint one. That is how the system of joint responsibility is carried on.

Q: In *The New York Times* Mr Krishnamachari is reported to have said that if foreign aid is not given the Five Year Plan will not go through. Is it so?

JN: I do not know what he said. It is patent that the Second Five Year Plan, even when it was drawn up, was not like the Laws of Medes and Persians, something unchangeable, invariable and all that. It was then said that we were making a flexible Plan which we would consider year after year. There is something, of course, you cannot change. You start a steel factory; you cannot decide halfway and give up. You cannot do that. So, there is an iron ore in the Plan which has to be gone through. There are other aspects of the Plan which would be undesirable to give up but which can be given up in a certain set of circumstances.

Q: But the real trouble is the capacity of foreign exchange. How the real trouble is to be overcome?

JN: India will go on if all the world is against India. There the matter ends. The thinking that India will go down because some countries do not help, is all wrong. Naturally, we have to change our way. We may die if necessary but we will go on. I have never heard this talk as if we are squirming and squirming, and will give up the ghost if we are not helped. We have seen bad days, we shall see bad days if necessary and see better days afterwards. We shall adjust ourselves to whatever changing conditions may indicate.

Q: Do you think that the vast gap in fulfilling the requirements of the hard core of the Plan, calls for not merely a rephrasing of the Plan what you have been talking about so far but a basic change of approach to the Plan itself and the hard core? The point is not purely fulfilling the whole plan or the hard core but fulfilling the hard core of the innermost or within the hard core.

JN: How can you change that basic approach I cannot understand. Nobody can change that basic approach to the hard core. What is the hard core? It means Iron and Steel plants, coal, transport, it means electrical power. How can you change these basic things?

773

Q: We are still thinking that the Plan was founded on the concept of physical planning.

JN: You are completely mistaken. There can be no real planning without physical planning. Financial planning is essential but secondary. I want to make that perfectly clear. You cannot plan without resources it is obvious, but there is no planning at all if it is all finances. Planning must deal with the physical things you want. If you don't deal with the things you want, it is a planning for profit or something else. We are not planning for profit. That will be for private enterprise. That is the difference. We stick to the physical always, limited and conditioned by the resources. You cannot do away with either. The moment you do away with physical planning, you have lost grip over the whole idea of planning. It does not fit in with the needs of a nation. What are the needs of a nation? The basic need, suppose you want power, electrical power, or some other power; you want coal in order to do something. You have to work that. Suppose we want to make machines—we have a plan today for machine making industry.

Q: When we have not got the resources to complete the projects in hand, would you recommend going ahead with the projects?

JN: We cannot take up anything for which we have no resources but we shall give up every secondary things for the primary thing we want to do. It is only conditioned by the resources. You cannot go beyond your resources for long. For a little while, you can but you are limited by the resources.

Q: What do you think of the achievements of the industrialists' mission?

JN: I cannot say. When they come back we will know.

Q: Mr Krishnamachari is reported to have said that if there was a communist revolution in India, China and Russia will come in to assist. Do you agree or disagree with that?

JN: If he said that, it was a slip, which I think, is untrue completely. There is going to be no communist revolution here. No other country is coming here. People who think in terms of communist revolutions are, if I may say so with all respect, out of date, including the communists. I do wish you to be a little more uptodate in your thinking in your questions. We are living in an age when something else is happening.

Q: There is an impression all over the country that we are not getting the same foreign aid as Yugoslavia?

JN: I do not think it is correct to say that we are not getting foreign aid. We have got foreign aid and we must realize that with all the goodwill of the world, there are difficulties in the way of other countries, legal and constitutional difficulties. It is not fair to criticize other countries because they don't throw money at you as much as you want. They have their own situations to face. They have helped us generously and we should be grateful to them and not be critical.

Q: There is a communist proposal for an all party conference to discuss the difficulties facing the Second Plan.

JN: So far as the Planning Commission is concerned it has got all kinds of advisory bodies which include members of other parties and they meet to discuss about the Plan but any other idea of people gathering together, more parties and discussing the Plan, I do not think it is a practical proposition.

Q: When you talked of communist revolutions, were you speaking particularly in case of India?

JN: Broadly about the world.

Q: Does the Sputnik make your problems less?

JN: No, it does not. But it does give one a perspective in thinking, in dealing with one's problems. We cannot guarantee that people will not behave foolishly in spite of all the cumulative wisdom of the ages.

Before I come to Japan, somebody asked about the Law Commission's interim report. Well, first of all it is a very serious matter the way newspapers have begun publishing secret documents and I may tell you that this is against the Official Secrets Act and I am afraid we shall have to take action in future. Whenever any secret document is published, we may have to take action and I speak after consulting lawyers. This has happened in connection with this report, my fortnightly letter to Chief Ministers is one of them. What has surprised me, if I may say so with all respect, is the lack of responsibility shown just for the sake of a scoop.

Q: Documents given to the press correspondents?

JN: Obviously, the persons who give it are more irresponsible but take this particular thing, the Law Commission. Here is something in a very elementary stage. Some enquiry is made, something is pointed out and enquiry is made, correspondence taking place and I have not a shadow of a doubt that the Law Commission after the results of this enquiry, will write something which will be very different from what they noted first.

Q: What are the things which are not confidential in the Government of India? Even the home going of a Deputy Minister is marked confidential.

JN: That is a different matter but have you any doubt that this paper was marked secret?

Q: Is it not true that even the tour of a Deputy Minister when he goes home is confidential?

JN: It would be a good thing if too much publicity was not given to all this touring.

Q: Is it not the duty of the press to expose those documents even if they are secret if this is in public interest?

JN: Obviously, any paper marked secret is not necessarily secret in the real sense of the word. It is true as somebody pointed out.

Q: This report, one day or the other is going to be published?

JN: Not at all. Temporary papers come and go. There are other papers coming in the Law Commission, there are replies.

Q: The subject is of public importance.

JN: I know that. It would have no particular value in publishing it or in dealing with it. Obviously, it is of public importance.

Q: What does the Official Secrets Act mean? Publication of secret documents involving the security of the State....

JN: That is for the courts to judge. Here is my fortnightly letter which has been published in extense. I consulted senior legal people. They said it is a clear infringement of the Official Secrets Act. It is a Letter to the Chief Ministers, a secret letter. Now, I do not know whether that letter of mine contained any secret endangering the security of the state. Nevertheless, that is the legal view by the highest legal authorities.

Q: I give you an instance. Government purchases certain aircraft from some British company. That British company published it from London. I was told the Defence Ministry could not give it even though it is published in London.

JN: That may be so. If there is a leakage in London what are we to do about that.

Q: Does it not mean that there should be rethinking in Government in indiscriminately marking all papers secret?

JN: That is true, perhaps, there is a tendency to make too many things confidential or secret.

Q: This Official Secrets Act was for a different purpose. Now we are a national government. What about the subject matter of the report?

JN: Which report?

Q: Law Commission's report.

JN: No report. There is no report yet. These are interim papers sent making some observations. When the report comes out it is obviously going to be published.

Somebody wanted to know about my impressions about Japan, I think, broadly speaking, I was very much impressed by Japan and the Japanese people. Of course, they are very vital people, hard working, disciplined and very artistic. They have a strong aesthetic sense. We can learn all these from them, including the artistic and aesthetic sense which we lack very much, I think. Then they have the sense of harmonizing colours. All these are little things by themselves but they give a colour to a person's life, to a people's life. They have an astonishing capacity to make small things go a long way, to make the best of small things. They gave me an extraordinarily friendly and warm welcome, and I am very grateful to them for that.

Naturally, on the political plane we did not agree about every matter, but we agreed about many matters also, and it is my effort whenever I meet people, more to find out the points of agreement and to lay stress on them rather than the points of disagreements. I have always found that there is much more to agree than to disagree, and that helps in our relations always.

Q: On the political plane one question in which both Japan and India have been strongly interested is test explosions of atomic weapons. Both have been devoting thought to this, but they have been confronted by the difficulty expressed by certain countries, particularly in the West, that they cannot agree to an unconditional suspension. In our own proposals, is it correct that we are now attempting to link up the plea for suspension with an overall framework of other guarantees which will make it more easy?

JN: I think, you will find in the Indian proposals the greatest stress on the immediate suspension of nuclear tests. In the joint communique, issued from Japan after our talks, you will find that there are three steps, if I may say so. One is the overall disarmament which, of course, should be the aim and we should work for it. The second was dealing with nuclear weapons, their production, control and all that. The third and the most immediate and vital is the suspension of nuclear tests. We agreed on that without any reservation and without any limitation or period of time, so that there is no doubt in my mind that any kind of disarmament is the most important and vital question today.

Disarmament ultimately has to be general. There cannot be disarmament in just a partial sense leaving the rest where it is. But one cannot suddenly bring about general disarmament all over, and it will have to be done step by step keeping the full picture in view. The first and immediate step should be, I think, a suspension of nuclear tests. That does not bring about any change to the disadvantage of any country. Even if it did, I think, they should be suspended. But practically, speaking, suspension does not bring about any disadvantage. Then you get a plain atmosphere to consider other parts of the problem and go ahead with dealing with nuclear weapons and general disarmament.

Q: Kindly comment on the change of attitude of the British labour leader, Mr Bevan, on this very question.

JN: I would not like to comment. As far as I know, his argument was that he wants to do this but he would like to get something in exchange for it. When one goes to bargain, one must have something to bargain with, that is his broad argument.

Q: Sometimes back there was a talk about the proposal which emanated from the Japanese Prime Minister for creation of a fund for the Asian countries to help one another. May I know what is the position?

JN: It will be discussed when definite proposals are put forward about them.

Q: Do you think India's interest will be served by confronting communists abroad and by fighting them at home?

JN: We try to comfort every suffering mortal. We try to be friendly with every country. We have no animus against communism. We do not understand this passionate crusading spirit of communism or anti-communism. It is not a question of our crusading against communism as in the nature of a religious crusade. We think that we deal with other countries as independent countries going their way, and it is none of our business to interfere with their internal matters. If they interfere with us then, naturally there is something like a conflict with anybody who interferes with us whatever the reason may be.

Internally we pursue certain policies and if anybody opposes those policies we argue with them and all that. But if the opposition is one of violence then it becomes a different stage.

As I said I do not agree with the communist theory. Part of it may be true, but parts of it, very essential parts, have been proved by experience to be wrong. But what has always disturbed me about communism is not the communist theory, the economic theory I mean with which I may or may not agree here or there, it is a matter of experience but the way it is tied up with violence and attempts at violent change, attempts at interference with violent change. That, I think, is some thing about the technique of communist action, which we in India have disputed very greatly right from the earlier days even though we have no animus against the pure theory. We thought our theory was better than the communist theory, that is a different matter and we thought we will win through, but where it comes to violence and violent interference, then it is on a different plane and we have to oppose.

Q: Would you like to say something on Kashmir?

JN: No.

Q: About the international character of communism, could you say something?

JN: Well, international character, I think, that the so called international communism does not really exist today in its real sense. Communist countries may form a bloc. That is a different matter. That is a power bloc. That is one of the reasons why we fail to understand the position today. By our bandying these terms, communism, anti-communism, when the conflict is between powers, who want to expand and who want to carry out their policies, they come into conflict. That has nothing to do with communism or anti-communism. There is no doubt about communist countries held together in that sense. But, if by international communism is meant a crusading gospel to spread communism, I think, there is no such thing now. Communism may be utilized for political purposes, but not with that semi-religious urge that existed previously.

Q: Have you not said several times in the past that the Communist Party in India has close ties with the communist parties of other countries at least that is the implication of what you said?

JN: I have said that.

Q: May I know whether that position is still there and whether the Communist Party here is tied up with the Communist Party of the Soviet Union, and whether that is the international character?

JN: No. It is true that the communist parties in various countries are probably keeping up contacts or the ties, with the Soviet Union. To what extent, I cannot say. But there is no doubt that mentally and spiritually, they look up there. And they may have physical ties too. But I do not call that international communism in the sense that I would have said there was such a thing about 20 years ago or in the earlier stages. It is a different thing. It is taking advantage, on the political plane, of communism elsewhere, but that is a different thing. That is like any major revolutionary movement which has affected humanity, it loses its driving power after a while. Even great religions, after a while, lost that and have lost it in history. In that sense, international communism is not that type of thing which it used to be previously.

Q: Three years ago, you spoke of sub rosa activities of some communist countries elsewhere. Will you say the same now?

JN: Sub rosa activities of some communist countries?

Q: Yes.

JN: Sub rosa activities of all kinds of countries, communist or non-communist?

Q: That time, you spoke specifically on this.

JN: The extent of that has been less than before. I do not know what you refer to what I said then.

Q: You were speaking in the Lok Sabha on the eve of your visit to China, your first visit. You said that what those countries were afraid of was not so much the communist party as such but of the sub rosa activities with reference to these parties.

JN: I do not understand altogether what I said and in what context. I do not remember.

Q: Some people in Kerala feel that they have got an apprehension that the Communist Party which is ruling them is just like a caged lion, because it is working under the Constitution and under the Central Government. They feel that if they come in full fledged power to the Centre, they will lose the democracy and the freedom they enjoy. What would you say?

JN: The communists come here?

Q: If they come in the Centre?

JN: To the Centre? Well, if that misfortune occurs, other misfortunes will follow.

Q: In a statement in Hong Kong you referred to the satellite and said that the satellite has brought in the fourth dimension or the ethical dimension.[6] If the implication from it is correct, you would welcome and approve some sort of a legislation and restraint on the progress and measure of scientific research.

JN: That is a strange corollary you draw from ethics. I do not think you can stop scientific research and I do not think you should stop it. If it leads you to the pit of hell, you should be prepared for it. But I do think that this advance in weapons has led humanity to the pass when you cannot fight one weapon with another. You go on in this way till you are crushed under the burden of arguments even if you do not have a war. Therefore, the ethical approach, which previously people probably thought rather impractical, has today become the essence of the practical approach. One has to consider these problems in some other way. One thing is

6. On 14 October while answering to a question on the general effect of the Russian earth satellite, Nehru said so and further elaborated it in a speech at a reception. See *ante,* pp. 628-631.

perfectly clear. The various approaches thus far made in the last generation or two including the war have failed to solve the world's problems, and if they are to be solved; if one problem has to be solved they have created half a dozen other and much more difficult problems. So, the failure of the normal way of thinking has been proved. I cannot say what other way of thinking is bound to lead to success, but anyhow, one should realize that going along in the old rut does not lead anywhere except possibly to disaster? Therefore, I suggest that some other dimension of thinking is necessary and that dimension may be the ethical dimension.

Q: What is part of the world which you have not seen?

JN: There are a vast number of places in India where I have not toured.

Q: In the world?

JN: I have not seen to the whole of South America, Latin America including Mexico. I have not been to Australia, a huge place. I have not been to Africa except for Egypt and Sudan.

Q: Would you like to go to the moon?

JN: The moon, no. I am not presently inclined that way.

Q: In the Ramanathapuram riots,[7] there was an incident of shooting five people. Each of them was tied, his hands behind his back, and taken out and murdered in cold blood. A member of the Board of Revenue was asked to make an enquiry and he has given his report. The position is most unsatisfactory, and the public reaction is that the procedure followed has been very arbitrary and unsatisfactory. As a result, there is a lot of agitation

---

7. In Ramanathapuram riots in September 1957 between Maravars and Harijans, the former considered themselves as a martial community and treated the Harijans badly. They imposed their decisions on the Harijans who were forced to vote the candidate whom the Maravars supported. But in the by-election of July 1957, the Harijans voted against the wishes of the Maravars. It became the cause for flare up that arose between them. Emanuel Shekhar, a Christian Harijan leader who advocated equality with the other communities, was murdered on 12th September. This worsened the situation. However, the riots broke out on 14 September when the Maravars forced the Harijans of a village named Arungulam to sing a song in favour of Maravars. A number of houses were burnt and several people from both the communities were killed.

in the South—that such a gruesome incident has gone without there being a proper enquiry. Would you kindly use your good offices with the Madras Government to institute a proper judicial enquiry?

Q: There is a report that in the last elections in the UN India voted for Japan, whereas according to convention you should have voted for Czechoslovakia.

JN: You are right about the convention. As for voting, it is a secret voting and I do not propose to inform you how we vote.

Q: Have you any Diwali message for our people?

JN: I told you in the beginning about this drought. It is a bad outlook. We shall have to face it with a great deal of courage and determination. We will do our best. So, while we enjoy our Diwali, we might give thought to this too.

11
LETTERS TO CHIEF MINISTERS

1[1]

New Delhi
August 1, 1957

My dear Chief Minister,

I shall not write to you today about foreign affairs. The internal and domestic situation fills my mind, as it must be yours, and I should like to refer here to some of the major problems before us.

2. I must confess that I have been feeling somewhat depressed and disturbed. This is not so much because of any particular matter or because of the difficulty of our problems. Difficulties have to be faced from day to day in the governance of a great country which is passing through a period of rapid transition. My distress is rather due to an inner disquiet at what I see happening in various parts of the country. A vague fear haunts me that we are succumbing to our old and corroding disease of lack of unity, disruptive tendencies and narrowness of outlook. The larger vision that inspired us and gave us strength seems to fade away and we are spending our energies in petty controversies and conflicts. Not even the internal and external crises, not even the atomic and hydrogen bombs about which so much is talked about, seem to shake us up and pull us out of this rather parochial outlook and complacency.

3. I wrote to you immediately after my return from my tour abroad and gave you some of my impressions of this changing world and its manifold problems.[2] Now, this outside world recedes into the background and I become enveloped in the atmosphere of India. It is not a clear atmosphere and the air is thick with petty controversies and little attention is paid to dangers that concern us and the great things that are happening in India and the world. Our Vice-President has, on several occasions, drawn attention to this weakening of the spirit and the crisis of character.[3] I cannot discuss these matters in this letter. Indeed my own

---

1. File No. 25(30)/57-PMS. These letters have also been printed in G. Parthasarathi (ed.), *Jawaharlal Nehru: Letters to Chief Ministers, 1947-1964*, Vol. 4 (New Delhi, 1988), pp. 518-553, 556-563 and 581-589.
2. For Nehru's letter dated 15 July 1957 see *Selected Works* (second series), Vol. 38, pp. 791-798.
3. For instance, S. Radhakrishnan in a speech at Mumbai on 15 June 1957 had said, "In our country moral life is shaken to its foundations. Love of wealth and power has gained wide acceptance...The present predicament is a challenge to us. It is a crisis of character. We have to subordinate our self-interest to public good, develop conscience about public funds, effect economies in our private life and public duty."

mind is not clear about them; but I wanted to tell you how troubled I feel and how I grope for some light.

4. It is possible that within nine or ten days, we shall have to face a number of strikes.[4] The major one appears to be that of the Posts &Telegraphs Employees. I met a large number of representatives of their Federation[5] and had a long talk with them. It was a friendly talk, and I came away with the definite impression that we understood and appreciated each other and that the strike was not likely to take place. To my surprise, I found the next morning that the decision for a strike had been confirmed. As you know, we had decided even previously to have a Commission[6] to examine thoroughly the pay structure of the Central services, keeping in view the economic situation in the country, the Five Year Plan, the salaries etc., given in the States and many other relevant factors. That was the basic and principal demand, not only of the P & T people, but of others. We went further and said that this Commission could consider the question of interim relief also. Further we could not go. Indeed, there was nowhere else to go to. The persistence in this particular strike as well as other proposed strikes, in spite of the friendly and cooperative attitude of the Government, leads one to the inevitable conclusion that forces other than economic are at play, that many of these people are led or misled by other urges and pressures. If that is so, then obviously, we cannot deal with them on the economic ground. The mere fact that a considerable number of employees' unions have simultaneously given notices of strike itself is significant. We are not dealing with different categories of people with different problems, but rather with something which does not necessarily relate itself to their economic demands.

5. I recognize, of course, that there is a common economic factor and that various circumstances, including the rise in prices of essential commodities, have had a considerable effect on the living conditions of our people. We have to pay every attention to this and do our utmost not only for our employees, but for others also. So far as Central Government employees are concerned, the decision to have a Commission on the pay structure as well as the possibility of this Commission recommending interim measures, is a major step to deal with

---

4. This refers to the call of strike given by the Posts and Telegraphs Employees Federation and the National Council of the Confederation of Central Government Employees Unions. See also *ante*, pp. 58-66 and 308-313.
5. On 26 July 1957.
6. On 17 July 1957, the Central Government had considered the appointment of a Second Pay Commission.

this problem.[7] In addition, we are trying to evolve procedures for a cooperative approach in all fields, both industrial and administrative, to deal with such problems from time to time and not allow them to grow till they become serious. We have had a measure of this cooperative approach in the past, but it has not gone far enough, more especially in the administrative field. There are Staff Committees and the like; but, broadly speaking, they have not been very effective. We should pursue this matter further so that there should be the closest contact and consultation at frequent intervals and a feeling should be created of partnership and common tasks in a joint undertaking. The successful working of that undertaking is essential not only for the larger good of the nation, but also for those who are employed in serving it. Good work can only be done when there is a feeling of contentment and we should endeavour to produce that feeling. It is true that we cannot do much that we want to, because of our lack of resources. But much can be done still and, above all, there can be a closer association, as among partners, which creates an atmosphere to the advantage of all concerned.

6. A recent conference dealing with industrial matters was, on the whole, a success and the resolutions passed should help in the maintenance of industrial peace and the solution of problems as they arise.[8] We have laid down that it is our objective to have the participation of workers in our industries and we are beginning in a small way. I am glad to note that a number of private industrialists have also accepted this proposal. Conditions in administration services are different and cannot be dealt with in the same way. But a friendly and cooperative approach in regard to conditions of work, amenities, etc., is equally important there.

7. Coming back to the possibility of a Posts & Telegraphs strike, it has become clear to us that the reasons for this and other proposed strikes are not wholly based on economic factors, though undoubtedly they play an important part. We were and are prepared to consider these factors to the best of our ability. But there appear to be other reasons also behind these threats of strike. In these circumstances, it is clear that the Government has no choice but to meet this situation firmly and to do everything in its power to carry on the services which are so essential for the life of the community and the nation. We shall do so and, in doing so, I hope that every attempt will be made not to worsen the situation

---

7. Appointed on 3 August 1957.
8. The Indian Labour Conference which met in New Delhi on 11 and 12 July 1957 recommended the setting up of a tripartite wageboards for fixation of minimum wages for the employees of certain industries including those in the public sector.

by threats and counter-threats or by violence of any kind. Our approach has to be firm, but it has also always to be friendly, because we deal with our own people whom we have to win over to what we consider, the right courses.[9] Threats have been held out not only to the Government, but to the people generally. Our answer is not that of counter-threat, but one of firmly carrying on our duties and meeting our obligations and serving the people. We can only do so with the goodwill and cooperation of the people generally, and we should seek always to obtain it.

8. The whole purpose of our Five Year Plans is to improve the lot of our people, to raise their standards of living and put an end to the curse of poverty. In our endeavour to do so, we have often to face the problem of giving relief today or strengthening our economy so as to be in a position to give them adequate relief tomorrow. We have to keep both in mind, for we cannot think only of today or only of tomorrow. If we forget today, then there is present unhappiness and frustration and social unrest. If we forget tomorrow, then there is no hope for us to improve the condition of our people to any considerable extent and we continue to remain undeveloped, static and living on the verge of poverty. It is not an easy matter to balance these two considerations, for there are many uncertain factors beyond our control. Yet our approach has been that while we should concentrate on laying the foundations of future advance by the development of industry and agriculture and by investing in them, we should also give present relief. How then has it happened that our Plans have gone away and we have to face all the difficulties that appear to overwhelm us? Why is our foreign exchange position so bad? Why have our calculations in the Second Plan been upset? Is all this due to our own failure in planning and in thinking ahead or is it due to something happening which was beyond our control and which we could not foresee?

9. I suppose both these reasons apply. It is true that many things have happened which we could not reasonably foresee. All our estimates have gone up greatly and chiefly because prices in foreign countries have gone up. The Suez Canal conflicts also hit us. Another new and unexpected burden has been in regard to Defence and we have had to import from abroad more foodgrains than we had expected.

10. Why has Defence suddenly come up before us in this way and forced our hands to spend more and more in foreign exchange, at a moment when we could ill-afford to do so, when indeed we wanted to save every bit of foreign exchange? Few things have pained me so much recently as to spend large sums of money on the apparatus for Defence. I wish we could avoid it and spend this

9. The Federation withdrew the call for strike on 8 August 1957.

money instead for our schemes of development and in bettering the lot of our people. But, in some matters, and most of all, where the safety and security of the country are concerned, there is no choice and no risks can be taken. All our efforts to live at peace with Pakistan have been frustrated and the leaders of Pakistan repeatedly declared India to be their enemy and, with the help of foreign countries, built up their military system. This build up has been very great indeed both in quantity and quality and it is patently aimed at India. There is little secrecy about it and we are told from public platforms that it may be used against us. It may not be used, to begin with, openly as in a war. But there are many other ways of starting trouble and some of these have been indicated with some frankness by ex-Major General Akbar Khan,[10] who has a reputation for ability and persistence.[11] If trouble starts, then it is difficult for us to say when and how it will stop. The information we get from many sources points to trouble and we are having foretaste of it already by many cases of sabotage in Kashmir itself.

11. This is the grave risk that faces us from external sources and we dare not be complacent about it. And so, in spite of our manifold difficulties, we have had to make this bitter choice and spend our precious foreign exchange for defence.

12. Then there is the question of food. We have had to get foodgrains from abroad at the cost of our foreign exchange. Whether we could have avoided this or not with better planning, it is a little difficult for me to say. It is becoming increasingly clear that all our planning, all our attempts at industrialization depend basically and ultimately on agricultural production and on the maintenance of adequate but moderate prices of foodgrains. I shall deal with this matter later in this letter.

13. Unexpected things have thus happened to upset our planning. Nevertheless, I feel that the fault is ours also. Perhaps we were too complacent, perhaps we did not look far enough ahead. Perhaps there was lack of coordination. After all, we have a Planning Commission and it is the business of the Planning Commission not merely to draw up our Five Year Plans but to look ahead and advise us from day to day, more especially in regard to any policy which might affect our Plan and our economy. Have we been wise in pursuing our past policies? I am by no means holding the Planning Commission responsible. In fact, I think

---

10. Had led the tribal invasion of Kashmir and Kalat in 1947 under the assumed name of General Tariq.

11. Some newspapers from Karachi reported on 21 July 1957 that Major General Akbar Khan had prepared a plan by which elements opposed to the Government in Kashmir would revolt and create disturbances which would compel the Government to order ruthless suppression.

that we have all to share the responsibility and I hope that we shall be wiser in the future. The fact is that there has been defective appreciation of what was likely to happen and this has got us into trouble. It is not much good having post mortems when we have so much work to do. But we must learn from this and not repeat the same mistakes in the future. If we plan, there must be coordination, there must be looking ahead. We cannot leave matters to the play of a market economy, of prices being pushed up and of odd things happening which we do not want to happen.

14. In this connection I should also like to point out that it has become essential for the Centre and the States to pull together and not to pull in different directions. I am not blaming the States for we have had a great deal of cooperation from them and I am grateful for it. But in the larger economy of the nation, we dare not follow any policies which contradict each other. Thus we have States which are surplus States in foodgrains and we have States which are deficit. The surplus States must realize that they have to think and act in terms of the country. If they do not, possibly they might make a little money by higher prices, but they will do so at a great cost not only to the country but ultimately to themselves. I would not even mind so much if the farmer got a better price, but I do mind the retailers and the wholesalers profiting at the cost not only of the community but ultimately of the future of the Plan.

15. I would repeat that the keystone of our planning is agricultural production. We can never have surpluses for industrial growth unless these come from agriculture. If, on the other hand, we have deficits in our food production, then instead of the surplus which would add to our strength, we have a process of corrosion of even the strength that we possess. I think that it is realized now how important this question is. But I have still a feeling that it is not realized adequately. It was with great difficulty that we raised our target of food production for the Second Five Year Plan to around thirty per cent or so. Our Planning Commission had originally asked for forty per cent and this was not a figure in the air for they had worked it out. When more production is asked for, immediately demands come for fertilizers etc. This is understandable, of course, but, nevertheless, a very great deal can be done by other kinds of manure, and not enough attention is paid to them, although they are far better in the long run. I know of cases where no fertilizer has been used and the land has been improved very considerably.

16. Food production means principally the production of wheat and rice now, although other grains count also. Even as between these two, rice is far the most important, because we require three times or more of rice than wheat in India. Therefore, it is rice production that has become of the utmost importance now. We heard a great deal, about two years ago, of Japanese methods and how

successful they were in increasing our rice yield. We were happy and grew complacent, a fatal thing to do at any time. Now it is rice that governs the situation and it is the prices of rice in the market that lead to most of our difficulties. The cost of living goes up, demands are made for higher wages and salaries, for pay commissions, and the like, people are unhappy and in difficulties, our estimates go up, our Plan suffers, and so on.

17. Next to food production, the question of the price of foodgrains is thus of vital importance. Indeed, the two are intimately connected. If the prices of foodgrains go up, then the whole fabric of our planning suffers irretrievably. That does not mean that we should make the poor farmer suffer. It means that we must give him a fair price, and no more, and that we should put an end to profiteering by middle men. How can we keep the price of foodgrains at reasonable levels? The only course appears to be to have a large stock of foodgrains available at every time, and even be prepared for natural calamities, floods, droughts, etc. That has been our objective for a long time. But, we have failed to achieve it. It is not possible to maintain large stocks of foodgrains if the Government has to buy them in the open market. It is well known that the moment Government goes into the open market, prices shoot up. The only other course, therefore, is for Government to purchase foodgrains compulsorily at fixed and reasonable prices. It was with this object in view that there was some Parliamentary legislation some two or three months ago.[12]

18. We have just had a debate in Parliament on food and agriculture.[13] In the course of this debate, a great deal was said against controls[14] and against compulsion in procurement of foodgrains. I do not like controls and I should like to avoid them, chiefly because they bring in their train a great deal of corruption. Apparently, we are not organised enough to deal with a widespread control system with any success. And yet, if circumstances compel us to do so, in order to save ourselves and the Plan, we shall inevitably have to go in for controls whether we like it or not. This fact must be kept in mind. For the present, there is no question of controls, and I have merely mentioned this so that we might think clearly about future possibilities. But, compulsory procurement of foodgrains at fixed prices is not controls in the larger sense, and I see no way out except this way.

19. At the present moment, we have to face this curious position that there is no real scarcity of foodgrains in India, possibly there is even a surplus. But, nevertheless, prices have gone up. We are told that there are substantial surpluses

12. See *ante*, p. 137.
13. In Lok Sabha, on 29 and 30 July 1957.
14. In fact, A.P. Jain stated that his Ministry was opposed to controls.

of rice in Andhra, Orissa and Madhya Pradesh, and that these surpluses have been hoarded by dealers, wholesale or retail. If that is so, then surely it is very odd that we should suffer these high prices.

20. Hard realities and the facts of life today compel us to think and not merely to rely on old ways and methods. Both the Centre and the States will have to look at these problems from the larger and coordinated point of view, if we have to save ourselves from drifting downhill and shattering the Plan. As a matter of fact, our critical foreign exchange situation, which has been made even more difficult because of food and defence purchases, is going to compel us to cut down many things that we have wanted to do and have even included in the Plan. That will be a very painful operation, and I am afraid no one is going to like it. It will affect many States as well as the Central Ministries. But, if circumstances compel us, then we shall have to swallow many a bitter pill. I want all the States to appreciate this position because so much depends upon their proper appreciation and cooperation. So much depends upon how we tackle the food situation and build up adequate stocks by getting foodgrains from those who are selfish and anti-social enough to hoard them today in order to profit at the expense of the community.

21. It seems to me that we should try to fix some definite prices for our foodgrains, especially rice and wheat, and adapt our policy so that these prices are maintained. We might even declare that we are going to do this and will not hesitate to take the necessary measures to that end. Such a declaration might well have a direct steadying effect as well as indirect consequences to our advantage.

22. Whether in food production or in many other matters, we have attached, as you know, the greatest importance to the Community Development Programme. That programme embodies something more than higher production. It is the outcome of a certain philosophy and it depends upon faith in our people and their capacity to make good, given the opportunity. If our people and that means ultimately our vast rural population, cannot make good, then all our planning is futile. Democracy means faith in the people plus, no doubt, many other things. The Community Development Programme is meant to develop self-reliance, self-respect and cooperation among the people. It has been criticized much, and the criticisms are often true. Nevertheless, it is, I believe, the biggest thing that we are doing in India and the biggest hope for our future. That hope lies not merely in some material advance, but rather in the building up of the people who, then, will be capable of advancing themselves.

23. It is the philosophy underlying cooperation that is behind the whole Community Development movement. This movement, as it grows, will include almost every activity in that area, affecting even the governmental structure. We

have always thought of the Community Development movement having its basis in the Village Panchayat and the Village Cooperative—the administrative and economic sides of village life.

24. I find, however, that there is some confusion about the kind of cooperative movement that we should have. My own idea has always been that a cooperative should be non-official. It must develop the people's capacity and teach them to rely on themselves. Also, that a cooperative must be some kind of a larger family, that is, there should be intimate relations among the members of the cooperative. If it is too large, then that intimacy is lost. If it is officialized, then the element of self-reliance and self-growth is lost. A cooperative is not just a credit-giving institution or a bank. It is, or should be, something with life and spirit in it, drawing its sustenance from its members and giving back something to them. This is the philosophical approach.

25. There has been some heated argument about agrarian cooperatives. Some people have urged them, others have vigorously opposed them. The chief argument of the opponents of this type of cooperative work has been that it is something akin to collective farming and, therefore, it is bad. That is not the argument. But, anyhow, cooperative farming is not collective farming and, in India, whatever we do has to be voluntary and based on the democratic method. There is no question of compulsion.

26. But, the question of cooperative farming really does not arise at this stage, except perhaps in new land or here and there where people may agree to it. The argument for cooperative farming is based on the very small holdings that farmers have. In countries where holdings may be twenty or thirty acres or more, this may not be necessary. But, where the holding is one or two acres, it is not possible to use many modern methods (I am not referring to tractors for the present) and our technique of farming will not improve. It is only when we employ better techniques that we can improve our yield.

27. However, cooperative farming, even if it is desired, cannot appear suddenly. We have to build up cooperatives for more limited purposes and get people accustomed to them. Later, if they so choose, they can take further steps forward.

28. There is also no particular reason why we should have one rigid pattern for the whole of India, which is so variegated and where conditions and climate vary so much. We can experiment in various ways. Whatever we do, we have to do it with the willing acceptance and cooperation of the peasantry. So far as our rural life is concerned, it will have to be coordinated more with the Community Development Programmes. The cooperative movement which is going to play such an important part in rural life, must also necessarily be so coordinated with it and should not be something apart. If it is apart, then both cooperation and community development will suffer.

29. You will forgive me, I hope, for writing rather discursively and at length about these questions. As a matter of fact, they have been dealt with fairly adequately in the Second Five year Plan Report. But, many people appear to have already forgotten what that Report contains and drift in different directions. Whatever the direction we go to it must be clear, and it is open to us to change it whenever we so feel. But, there should be no pulling in two directions at one time because that neutralizes all effort. I have written to you at length because I want you to think about these matters and for us perhaps to meet together to decide exactly what course we have to pursue.

30. In fact, I have in mind the possibility of a meeting of the National Development Council in the course of six weeks or two months to consider these important questions that I have discussed in this letter as well as others. The Central Government can do little good without the fullest understanding and cooperation of the States. But, the States also cannot do much without the understanding and cooperation of the Central Government. We have to pull together and to pull in one direction.

Yours sincerely,
Jawaharlal Nehru

II

New Delhi
August 15, 1957

My dear Chief Minister,

Today, in the tenth anniversary of our Independence, my mind naturally looks back to the achievements of these past ten years. Inevitably also, because of the centenary of the great struggle of 1857, we think of these hundred years of storm and stress, of ups and downs, of sacrifice and of ultimate success in so far as political freedom is concerned. All of us have heard and know something about the War of 1857. Till recently, most accounts of this War were from British sources and by British writers and were very partial to the British side of the story. It is true that even in the British histories, notably in Kaye[1] and

---

1. John William Kaye (1814-76); Secretary, India Office, 1858-74; author of *History of the Sepoy War* (3 Volumes, 1864-76).

Malleson's[2] massive volumes, there is much material for us to have some glimpses of the Indian side here and there. There was also a little volume by Edward Thompson,[3] which brought out more vividly the sacrifices and the sufferings of the Indians in this struggle and how ruthlessly the British forces had behaved. On the Indian side, so far as I know, the first book on the subject was Savarkar's.[4] As a history this was very inadequate and was tilted to the other side. It could not be considered an objective account and it was inaccurate in many parts. The chief virtue of it was that for the first time an Indian had presented the Indian side of this tragic story. Subsequently, other books have appeared by Indians, but hardly any of these could be called an objective history. Recently, more accurate and historical accounts have appeared, notably that of Dr S.N. Sen called *Eighteen Fifty-Seven*.

2. But whatever the written history might say, this war of Independence of 1857 still lives in the vivid memory of our people and many of the leaders of it are national heroes. I cannot speak for all parts of India, nor can I speak with any confidence of the younger generation today. But I remember very well that when I was a boy I used to hear innumerable tales of 1857. Later, when I wandered about the villages of what is now Uttar Pradesh, almost every village had a story to tell. We came across many people who had lost their relatives in this war, some of them had been blown off from the guns. It was said that along the long road from Kanpur to Allahabad there was not a tree which did not have a number of people hanging from its branches. My memories date back to the beginning of this century, when as a little boy I listened to these vivid stories which impressed me, as they must have impressed so many of my generation who lived in Delhi or Uttar Pradesh or Bihar or some other parts of the country where this war was fought fiercely and with valour. So, whatever the historians may write, the people's version of this great rising has coloured their thinking for a hundred years and still forms vivid pictures in their minds.

3. The War of 1857 was a major event, both from the point of view of the people and of the British Government. It ended a certain historical phase in India and began another. But, few people, perhaps, remember that even after 1857, there were a number of risings, though much smaller in character, which were ruthlessly suppressed. One interesting and significant one was, what is

---

2. George Bruce Malleson (1825-98); Author of *The History of the Indian Mutiny* (3 Volumes, 1878-80).
3. Eminent historian and writer on public affairs.
4. V.D. Savarkar's book *The Indian War of Independence, 1857* was published in 1909.

called, the Kuka rising in Southern Punjab.[5] The Kukas (now they are called Namdharis) were, and are, an agrarian sect of the Sikhs, rather closer to the Hindus than the other Sikhs. They were suppressed also with cruelty, and their chief and Guru was exiled to Rangoon, where, previously, Bahadur Shah had been sent. The interesting thing about these Kukas or Namdharis was that even after their suppression by military force, they continued quietly to follow a policy of non-cooperation in many matters. They were sturdy peasants, well-disciplined and they kept away from governmental schools or service and even avoided, I believe, using the post office. They used handspun and handwoven khadi. When Gandhiji's non-cooperation movement came, it was easy for them to fit into it.

4. But, these were sporadic outbursts. Indian nationalism took another turn and led, a little more than a quarter of a century after the struggle of 1857-58, to the formation of the Indian National Congress in 1885. It started with small beginnings and with what might be called a moderate objective. It was based on a new class, the British educated middle classes or rather the upper middle classes. They had been nurtured on British literature and British ideas, and spoke the language of British Liberals. How many of us remember that the Indian National Congress is seventy-two years old today? Broadly speaking, it might be said that the history of the Congress during this long period was the history of India, struggling for freedom and achieving it. Even as the Congress spread and affected more and more groups and classes of our people, so the strength of the nation grew. From the select English educated middle classes who started the Congress, it widened its appeal to the lower middle classes of India. This change-over brought a crisis in the Congress history, which used to be referred to as the Conflict between the moderates, led by the great Indian Gopal Krishna Gokhale,[6] and the extremists, led by Lokmanya Tilak. Even though the moderates appeared to have won, it was really Tilak who represented the new fighting spirit of India and the lower middle classes which were coming into the political field. Tilak won in the end, as he was bound to do, for he represented a new historic force that was coming into being. That was the second phase of the Congress.

5. The third phase came with Gandhiji, when the appeal of the Congress went to the peasantry and, to some extent, to the industrial workers. It was then that the Congress became broadbased on the masses of India and, even though a

5. The Kuka (Namdhari) movement for reestablishment of the Sikh power in North-West India, launched in 1857 by Guru Ram Singh (1816-85), was severely repressed by the Government and a number of his followers were executed and he himself was exiled to Yangon.

6. The most outstanding of the moderate leaders in the Indian National Congress.

fringe at the top left it, its strength and challenge to the British rule grew. This brings us to the Gandhi era in our history, which changed the face of India and, ultimately, brought Independence.

6. The Indian National Congress was, as its name implies, a national movement and not a class movement. Nevertheless, it is interesting to see how its class character changed gradually and it became more and more inclusive of the wider masses and, more especially of the peasantry. Even as this change took place, the purely political programme of the Congress underwent also a change, and it began to develop an economic outlook. That economic outlook was not very precise. But, broadly, it was governed by two features: one was its sympathy for the under-dog in India, and the second was its agrarian outlook. This demand for agrarian reform was inevitable because the vast number of peasants in the Congress made their influence felt, even though the leadership was largely middle class.

7. Thus, the national movement that developed in India, under Gandhiji's guidance and inspiration, had some peculiar features which were absent from the national movements of the other countries. It was something more than a political movement and, progressively, it had an economic content. Apart from this, it represented certain moral values which Gandhiji had impressed upon it repeatedly and persistently. Truth and non-violence, means and ends, were the foundations of Gandhiji's approach to politics. It would be an exaggeration to say that the people of India became wedded to truth and non-violence or that they attached importance to means more than ends. But there can be no doubt that they were very greatly influenced and inspired by Gandhiji's teachings and, because of that, their thinking and minds became progressively moulded by it. Thus, for the first time in the world's history we saw a great political and national mass movement wedded to these ideals and developing a technique of action which was wholly new and which undoubtedly has impressed the world greatly.

8. That brings us to recent times and to the achievement of Independence by that technique and those methods. Contemporaneously with Gandhiji's movement came the Soviet Revolution with its Marxist ideology and its stress on class struggle and violence. So far as ideals were concerned, there was perhaps no marked conflict in the ends to be reached between these two methods, although obviously there were many differences. But the basic difference was in the methods to be adopted and the psychology to be created. One was of peace and avoidance of hatred and violence, the other was full of class conflict and hatred and violence. Both ultimately wanted to do away with the domination of one class over another and thus do away with classes. It was obvious that in the existing social framework class conflict was inherent. But the way to deal with it and ultimately to put an end to it was vastly different.

9. Hardly any major struggle in history has ended without leaving a trail of extreme bitterness behind. More especially, this applies to national struggles against foreign rulers. The virtue of Gandhiji's method, even though large numbers of his followers fell very short of his teachings, was that the minimum of hatred was produced and when a solution and a settlement came, there was no marked trail of bitterness to pursue succeeding generations. It is strange to contrast this with the present day world full of fear and hatred and violence, dominated by the horrible spectre of nuclear warfare.

10. So, after ninety years of struggle since 1857, we have had ten years of Independence, and we have tried, with more or less success, to adapt some of the principles that we imbibed to the problems of national and international politics. I believe, we have succeeded in some ways to an extraordinary extent. I believe also that we have failed often enough. The measure of our failure is not so much what we may have done wrongly or what we might not have done which we should have done. That measure is the existence in a fairly marked degree today of provincialism, communalism, casteism and also the tendency to violence. In the course of the struggle against a common adversary, it was relatively easy to join forces and put up a structure of national unity. When that adversary left the scene, then the urge to unity become somewhat weaker and we begin to relapse into our separate groups and our parochial thinking. A not unfriendly foreign writer has described as our present-day bane this provincialism and separatism which takes various forms, the traditionalists who resent change, the massive inertia of the people, and the tolerance in India of the fourth rate. I do not think this is a correct description taken as a whole, but there are certainly elements of truth in it. There is plenty of so-called traditionalists in India who want to come in the way even of desirable change. But there are many others who are convinced that change is necessary if India is to progress and who work to that end. As for "massive inertia", I believe that India is dynamic today and progressively becomes more so. And yet it is true that there is this inertia of the people. Perhaps it is true that we are rather tolerant of the second rate or the third rate and this tolerance must necessarily come in the way of our becoming a first-rate nation. The fact is that below the surface of political and economic arguments and controversies, there is an inner conflict in India in regard to these matters and the future depends upon the result of this conflict. Of course, there can be no doubt about the results because there is no future in pure traditionalism, parochialism and intolerance of the third rate. But these failings come in the way of progress and delay it.

11. We often talk about communalism and casteism and condemn them. And yet, many of those who condemn them, are not wholly free from them. The boundaries are not clearly marked. This communalism is bad, because it

represents all those features which oppose real advance of India and which, in fact, create a psychology of separatism and narrowness of mind. In addition, it has a tendency to violence. Violence in India, whether it is based on religion or caste or economic doctrines, is even more dangerous than in other countries, for it leads immediately to disruptive tendencies. We have been too long in our history, victims of disruptive and fissiparous forces. No nation of the modern world can survive if the smaller loyalties are considered more important than the larger loyalty to the nation.

12. My last letter to you referred to the impending strikes of the Posts & Telegraphs workers and others. Fortunately, those strikes were called off. This whole incident has a lesson for all of us, both Government and workers as well as others, and unless all of us learn this lesson, we shall be faced with similar situations. We should not blame the workers, for they are often hard hit by economic circumstances. We must evolve ways of trying to solve problems as they arise, and not wait for a crisis. We must, above all, fashion our policy so that some relief comes to those who need it most. It is true that, at the present stage of our economic development, the measure of relief is bound to be limited, because if we give too much relief, there would be little or nothing left for future growth. It has always seemed to me that while economic questions are often not easy to solve in existing circumstances, an even greater difficulty comes from the manner of approach to these problems. If our approach is human, understanding and friendly, then much of the suspicion and distrust goes. Unfortunately, some people think of these strikes as political weapons. I do not deny the right of the workers to use the strike even as a political weapon. But, I am convinced that, in the existing circumstances in India, such strikes are harmful to workers and, of course, to the community generally. Strikes in essential services must necessarily create situations which are even more harmful.

13. As the strikes were called off, there was no necessity left for the Essential Services (Maintenance) Ordinance, and I am glad that the President has withdrawn it.[7] So far as the Bill which was passed by the Lok Sabha is concerned, it has no force unless it is passed by the Rajya Sabha also, and thus placed on the Statute Book. It is not our intention to take it to the Rajya Sabha.

14. As you know, we have two important taxation measures before Parliament—the Wealth Tax and the Expenditure Tax. Both are rather novel in India, and the Expenditure Tax is novel in other countries. It must be remembered that the Expenditure Tax really comes into effect a year later. It has to be passed this year, so that arrangements may be made meanwhile to give effect to it next year. I think, both these taxes are good in principle, and in the right direction.

7. On 12 August 1957.

Everything new, of course, is looked at askance, especially a new tax. We gradually get used to it and then the strangeness disappears. I think that these two taxes, with such variations in regard to details as might be made, will finally be less troublesome or burdensome than is imagined. I do not know what the final shape of things will be, as that depends upon the Select Committee and, subsequently, Parliament. But, I believe that the Select Committee and, indeed, all of us have examined them with great care, and made a number of minor changes, which cumulatively make a considerable difference. All kinds of reports appear in the newspapers about conflicts in the Cabinet or elsewhere. These are greatly exaggerated and, sometimes, quite untrue. It is obvious that in dealing with these problems, there are different approaches, and they have to be harmonized. That is what we have tried to do, and, I believe, we have succeeded in a large measure.

15. The fact that the country has to bear the burden of fairly heavy taxation if we are to proceed with our development, is obvious. If so, then the burden has to be spread out and must also fall on many who are not well-to-do. Otherwise, we cannot get the resources for our work. It becomes essential that a considerable part of the burden must fall on those who can really afford it. This does not mean that we are out deliberately to injure any group. We have always to remember that, in any step that we take, we do not affect adversely the productive apparatus of the country. A few crores in taxation are helpful, no doubt. But, what we want is production worth many hundreds of crores. It is this increased production that counts in the end, and that will help us to raise standards and gradually to fight the poverty of the country. If production lags behind, then we remain stuck up in the quick sands of poverty which sucks in an individual and the community alike. There can be no socialist pattern of society based on poverty.

16. In India there has been a long-standing controversy as to the relative virtues of heavy industry, light industry and cottage industries. This has often been argued on the basis of high principle, though lately it has been considered more from the practical point of view of our needs and resources. It is interesting to see the development of thought in China on these issues. China is different in its ideology from India. It is an authoritarian State broadly based on the Marxist theory. But it is clear that China does not follow the rigidity which characterized the growth in the Soviet Union. Also it is realized in China more and more that conditions in China and the Soviet Union differ greatly and no ideological pattern, which is divorced from practical considerations, can achieve success.

17. There is far greater similarity between India and China in regard to the problems that we have to face. Both countries have huge populations which are pre-dominantly agricultural. Both are industrially backward, though they are advancing with some speed in regard to industrial development. Nevertheless,

they have to go very far. There is a great deal of manpower in both as well as unemployment or under-employment. Heavy industry is essential to form the basis of industrial development. At the same time, heavy industry demands a great quantity of imports from abroad and foreign exchange for them. Also it does not go far in solving the question of unemployment.

18. To begin with in China, the greatest stress was laid on the development of heavy industry. Now it is being pointed out that the emphasis must change. A Director of the State Planning Commission in China stated in a report recently that 'modernized and mechanized construction demands heavy investment and a high technical level but only affords little employment; for a comparative long period, modernization and mechanization will not suit China". It is pointed out that some people were so concerned to get the most modern and most automatic equipment that they ignored the facts of China's present economy. It was necessary to build these heavy plants and they would continue to be built. But there should be not too much concentration on them. Modern plants were characterized by high efficiency, good quality, low costs and economy in the use of labour. These could only be produced by a highly developed industry and their construction required heavy investments and much time. China is still a backward country, but rich in manpower and short of funds and technical standards were only slowly rising. The question of foreign exchange also became important. The development of "automation" which was taking place in Europe and America thus had no place at present in China.

19. This new viewpoint in China, therefore, advocated the construction of medium sized and small plants even in the fields of metallurgy, coal mining and electric power. At present, it was pointed out that machines were not cheaper than manpower in China and this surplus manpower of the country was a prime factor when it came to deciding what sort of equipment to install. Industrial standards depended not on the equipment that was used in the factories but on the quantity and the quality of their products. Emphasis has also been laid in China that one great advantage of smaller plants was that they could be spread out throughout the country and could thus utilize local resources and give more employment and help the development of local economies.

20. This indicates a tendency in China to move away from the previous approach. The first approach was of laying excessive stress on heavy industry only. Then came a variation and it was stated that both heavy industry and medium and small enterprises were necessary and there was room for both. Now, the emphasis is rather more on the small industry and on employment. This does not mean, of course, that the leaders of China are now not in favour of heavy industry but rather that the emphasis should be changed and the heavy industry to be constructed should be such as to suit China and her excessive manpower.

The Chinese are thus taking a practical and pragmatic view of the problems that face them, more especially that of population and employment.

21. This Chinese viewpoint approaches much more the Indian viewpoint as laid down in our five year plans. We have refused to accept any rigid model or theory and our approach all along has been rather pragmatic. More particularly the question of employment has always been before us. We have built huge plants and river valley schemes and I think that this was necessary. The time may now has come for us to lay greater emphasis on smaller undertakings which are more spread out all over the country and which take advantage of local resources and develop local economies. This becomes necessary also because of the pressure on us of foreign exchange. Perhaps in some ways we are even now more industrially developed than China, although in other ways they have gone ahead of us.

22. Another interesting development in China is in regard to education. It is said that there are sixty-three million students in the primary schools. Then there is a big drop to 5,150,000 in the junior middle schools. The senior middle schools have 820,000 and the Universities and various institutes have 480,000. Great stress is laid that students coming out of the primary and middle schools must take part in agricultural production, and the value of manual labour is emphasized. While schools have developed rapidly in China, there is a tremendous lack of trained teaching staff. They are thus faced with the problem that students from the primary schools may not be able to go on to the junior middle schools and the junior middle schools may not be able to go on to the senior middle schools, and so on. Like us in India, China is having difficulty in finding enough money for proper equipment, buildings for their schools, etc. The quality of education appears to have gone down also partly because the quality of teachers has gone down.

23. I am convinced that there are enough resources in the country, though it is not always easy to get at them. We have to adopt a policy to encourage these resources being made available for productive effort either by the State or by the private sector. Both have to function in our present structure of society.

24. Having written so much about the past and present and about the larger matters that affect us today, I should like to refer to something which, I think, is rather important and which, perhaps, has not received much attention. We want both to exploit as well as to conserve our natural resources. Sometimes, the desire to exploit them outruns discretion, and we forget the part of conservation. In countries like the United States of America, exploitation of natural resources has gone on at a terrific pace, and now people there are worried about the future. The growth of science and technology, which has brought so much power to man, has sometimes made him ignore the fact that nature cannot be trifled with.

There is a certain interdependence between man and his environment, and any upsetting factor may bring about harmful consequences. We all know that if trees are cut down and forests removed, then this may affect the rainfall and might even convert a fertile area into a desert.

25. The highly industrialized countries of the world are now facing many problems both in the physical and psychological spheres of lack of adjustment of man to his environment. Too much bricks and mortar at the expense of green zones may produce consequences which are not good. Too much use of insecticides and herbicides may destroy some insect which might often play some useful role in the economy of nature. Too much destruction of birds has led to the growth of harmful insects which the birds used to eat. The construction of great hydroelectric dams or railway embankments may change the drainage of the countryside and lead to floods.

26. I have mentioned just a few of the possible harmful effects of even something good that is done. There is a certain economy in nature gradually established through the ages. We should certainly change this for man's benefit. But in so doing we should take every care that the change does not lead to some other evil consequences also, apart from the good that it is intended to do. Science today is producing any number of experts and specialists who are very good at their own particular piece of work, but who are apt to forget other aspects and consequences of what they may do. The expert knowledge of a person in his own field may not be enough. This has to be checked by experts in other fields and the expert has sometimes to be saved from himself.

27. The destruction of rabbits in some countries, though welcomed by the farmers, has led to some unforeseen results and now the farmers want the rabbits back. Science today is advanced enough to be able to give us insights into all these aspects and to the possible consequences of any step that might be taken. But this can only be done by a pooling of knowledge.

28. We have many large-scale river valley projects which are carefully worked out by our engineers. I wonder, however, how much thought is given before the project is launched, to having an ecological survey of the area and to find out what the effect would be to the drainage system or to the flora and fauna of that area. It would be desirable to have such an ecological survey of these areas before the project is launched and thus to avoid an imbalance of nature.

29. In regard to Himalayan rivers which misbehave so often and cause floods, it has been suggested that there should be a study of glacier recession in the Himalayas to enable a better understanding of nature and the behaviour of these rivers.

30. There is an International Union for Conservation of Nature and Natural Resources with its headquarters in Brussels. This Union devotes itself to the

805

encouragement of this larger outlook in regard to the conservation of flora and fauna and natural resources. I think, it would be a good thing if we in India developed this outlook also.

Yours sincerely,
Jawaharlal Nehru

III

New Delhi
September 3, 1957

My dear Chief Minister,

I am writing to you rather unexpectedly today. I ought to have been in Kashmir. Indeed I started early in the morning by air. When we reached near Pathankot, we were enveloped in clouds and visibility was almost nil. My pilot went high up to nearly 20,000 feet, but even this did not help him. As there were hills all round and in front, he did not think it wise to take a risk and turned back. We landed at Ambala and waited for the clouds to clear up. After an hour or two we made another attempt to go to Kashmir but were again frustrated. And so we came back to Delhi six hours after we had left.

2. I was going to Jammu and Kashmir at rather a short notice because of the terrible floods they have had there. From all accounts these floods have been on a much bigger scale than ever before. At one time the whole valley of Kashmir was practically one sheet of water. Large numbers of villages were swept away. Many bridges collapsed and the crops suffered great damage. Something of the same kind happened on the Jammu side also. The result is that both in Jammu and Kashmir, the Government and the people have to face a great disaster, and I wanted to go there as soon as possible to take a message of sympathy and help to the people there. Unfortunately, I could not go today, but I hope to make another and a more successful attempt a few days later.

3. Floods have become a common occurrence in many parts of India. Whether they are on a bigger scale than previously, I do not know. But one gets the impression that some basic climatic changes are taking place resulting in these frequent floods. In my last fortnightly letter to you I drew attention to the economy of nature being often disturbed by man's works. We have built railways in the

past without thinking of the effect of the embankments on the drainage system. Canal embankments also have interfered with the drainage and there are so many other things that we do without paying any attention to their effect on nature's economy and drainage. In future, I hope that whenever any such construction is made, the direct and indirect consequences will also be kept in mind and provided for.

4. The immediate reaction of the people to floods is to suggest that embankment and bunds should be built. These are undoubtedly necessary in many places, but every embankment or bund, while protecting one area, might lead to greater danger to another area. It is possible to protect selected areas or a city by bunds, but it appears too difficult to protect a whole countryside. Apart from these local protective works, it seems to me that attention should be paid to the rapid draining away of flood waters. We cannot stop these vast oceans of water which come down from the mountains, but we can so arrange that they are not allowed to collect too much and for too long.

5. There is another aspect of this question to which I drew attention on the last occasion and this is the possibility of a recession of the glaciers in the Himalayas, leading to the melting of the ice and an abundant quantity of water coming down from the mountains.

6. Our Parliament has been heavily engaged with the Finance Bill[1] and taxation measures. Both Houses have dealt with these subjects and while the burden has been heavy on every member of Parliament, the load on the Finance Minister can well be imagined. He has been continuously engaged day after day, and sometimes in two houses at the same time, in piloting these very difficult and exacting measures. The time actually taken in Parliament is only part of the labour involved. Select Committees and innumerable group meetings with MPs to explain to them the provisions of these measures and discuss amendments are much more exacting. It was inevitable that these rather novel measures should raise comment and criticism. No one likes taxation, much less novel forms of it. I believe that basically the approach now being made is a right one and the amendments accepted have improved the measures. We had to get out of the old ruts. Whatever the revenue producing capacity of these taxes might be in the near future, it is some advantage to get out of the static conditions of the past and to move in a new and more promising direction. The Finance Minister is entitled to a tribute from us for the great ability, courage and energy with which he has conducted these measures during the past many weeks. He will have little rest, as he will be going soon[2] to the USA, UK, Canada and perhaps some

1. The Bill was passed by Lok Sabha on 28 August 1957.
2. On 17 September 1957. He returned to India on 25 October 1957.

other country also. That too will be work of a most exacting kind. He will carry our good wishes with him.

7. We have recently had a meeting of the All India Congress Committee in Delhi.[3] In the main the discussions in this Committee related to the economic situation and more particularly the food problem.[4] Discussions in the Lok Sabha and the Rajya Sabha have also largely centred round these questions. It is right that this should be so, because we have to face these problems realistically and for that purpose there should be a wide understanding of them. I am convinced, as I have often said, that India's economy is basically sound, but it is also true at the same time that our potential wealth and resources may not be available to us when we want them and this creates great difficulties. We are facing these difficulties today.

8. The taxation policy pursued in a country is important. But, that is only a part of the many things that affect the economy of the country. We all talk about production, and without that no progress can be made. But, production itself depends not only on hard work, but on intelligent planning and a feeling of confidence. At the end of the First Five Year Plan, there was this feeling of confidence in our capacity to achieve what we had aimed at. Unfortunately, various factors have contributed lately to lessen this feeling of confidence. Many people and newspapers in foreign countries are constantly repeating that we have been too ambitious in our planning. Even in our own country, there are some who go on saying this, with the result that a feeling of doubt and depression is created. This lack of confidence in ourselves and in our resources is more harmful, perhaps, than anything else, and we have to combat it. I do not believe in a facile optimism, and we have to be realistic. But, realism does not mean a defeatist attitude, more especially when there is no reason for this.

9. More and more, it has come to be realized that agricultural production, and more particularly food production, is the vital foundation for our growth and even for the spread of industry. Prices, of course, are an essential factor, and they depend more on the quantity produced and its proper management than any other factor.

10. There was some discussion at the AICC meeting about cooperatives in general and especially cooperative farming.[5] Everybody agrees, I take it, that the cooperative approach is essential for us in agriculture, as in other matters.

3. Held from 31 August to 2 September 1957.
4. At the discussions, marked by strong criticism of food administration, the importance of implementing the Plan in full was also emphasized. Special stress was laid on the need to effect land reforms and develop cooperatives. See also *ante,* pp. 455-456.
5. See *ante,* pp. 455-456.

With the development of higher techniques, there is an inevitable tendency towards centralization. The small machine gives place to the big machine, and the big one to a bigger one still. Whether in the governmental apparatus or in industry or elsewhere, there is this drift towards ever greater centralization, which has certain evil consequences. The small shops give place to the great stores, and then to chain stores. Even newspapers develop in this way, and big chains of them are controlled by a single authority. That is the inevitable result of the growth of technology in a capitalist system. In a socialist system, the same trend occurs, with the major difference that the control is by the State. The evils of too much centralization are present, whether this takes place under private auspices or the State's, though, in the latter case, they might be mitigated to some extent. Undoubtedly, the centralization of power, whether political or economic, lessens the freedom of the individual.

11. We cannot do without centralization. And yet, we do not wish to be submerged by it. The only way out appears to be the spread of the cooperative method in industry and agriculture. In the governmental apparatus, it means also decentralizing many activities of the State although, inevitably, the Central Government in the modern State must be strong.

12 In the realm of industry, there will be State enterprizes and cooperative enterprizes. Even the State enterprizes, if they are to function with efficiency and success, cannot be tied up too much to departmental methods of working. They must be given a good deal of latitude and room for initiative.

13. In agriculture, cooperation becomes inevitable. There might be some excuse for individual farms working separately, provided these farms are big enough. But, where in India, a vast number of our peasants have not more than an acre or two, it is not possible for them to make any progress or to take advantage of modern techniques. I am not referring to what might be called mechanization of agriculture. Broadly speaking, too much mechanization is not the remedy in a country of abundant manpower and small holdings. But, there are numerous other techniques which can add to our production and which are quite beyond the resources of a small farmer. Under a cooperative system, where a number of peasants band together for common purposes, these techniques become available to them. It is admitted that in regard to numerous agricultural services, cooperative methods should be introduced. There is some argument, however, about cooperative farming.

14. This argument is rather premature in India at present, because we have not even fully taken the preliminary steps towards cooperative working. Our first concern must, therefore, be to build up multi-purpose cooperatives, apart from joint farming, and make them a success. It is only later that the question of joint farming arises. We cannot impose anything on our peasantry, and we can

only introduce these changes by their willing consent. That willing consent will only be forthcoming when they see the results of a particular method of working. If that method yields good results, then I have no doubt the farmer will adopt it.

15. Personally, I think that joint farming is desirable and necessary, in order to yield the best results. I am not thinking of vast farms, but rather of the people of a village joining together for this purpose. My conception of a cooperative is of an organization where people know each other and have a sense of kinship.

16. There are two cases, however, where it should be possible to have joint farming right at the beginning. This is where new land is reclaimed by the State, and it is open to the State to settle it in any manner it chooses. The second is in the case of Vinobaji's *Gramdan*. Cooperative farming could be tried there and results examined. If this succeeds there, then there will be no difficulty in spreading it elsewhere. In other areas, however, we must concentrate on the multi-purpose cooperative, which need not include joint farming.

17. Cooperation is not merely some kind of a business partnership or a means of obtaining credit. It is something much deeper than that, and involves a certain philosophy of life which we wish to encourage. It is only through this cooperative method that we shall raise the level of the peasantry even in cultural and like matters. The narrow parochial outlook, so much associated with the peasant, does not suit the new society that is growing up everywhere.

18. The situation in Western Asia, and more especially in Syria, is a serious one. It is not quite clear what is happening behind the surface of events. But, all kinds of pressures are apparently being exercised, and there is danger of trouble.

19. I have recently spoken in the Lok Sabha in a debate on Foreign Affairs.[6] I shall not repeat here what I said then. I would, however, like to draw your attention to what I said there, more especially in regard to Kashmir, Syria and Hungary. The Kashmir issue is likely to come up before the Security Council before long.[7]

20. We are having a number of Ministers from foreign countries visiting Delhi in the next few days. They are coming back from Malaya where they had gone to participate in the Independence celebrations.[8]

21. Perhaps, you know that in the United States of America, students often undertake some gainful work, manual or other, even while they are studying in colleges. A student who can earn money in this way for his fees and upkeep is admired there. In some other countries also students are encouraged to do this. In India, in spite of all that we have said, manual labour is still rather looked down upon, although this attitude is gradually changing. I think that our colleges

6. See *ante*, pp. 516-538.
7. The Jarring Report was debated in the Security Council on 25 September 1957.
8. Malaysia became independent on 31 August 1957.

and universities should offer every opportunity to the students to do some manual constructive work on payment. I am not suggesting any compulsion about it. But the opportunity should be given. This would result not only in a number of students earning some money, but also in buildings being put up by spare time work. It would be necessary, of course, in such cases to provide adequate expert guidance.

22. In the Roorkee Engineering University in the UP arrangements have been made for students to earn some money by part-time work in their spare time. I think, this is an excellent idea. Apart from other advantages, the mere fact of constructing something with their own hands and labour gives a feeling of psychological satisfaction.

23. Recently there has been some trouble in Rajasthan among the students. This was said to be in protest against the enhancement of fees. I know nothing about the merits of this question, but I was astonished and distressed at the manner some students behaved under the instigation of some outside elements. They tried to set fire to buildings, to destroy furniture, books, etc. If our political parties encourage this kind of behaviour among the students or indeed anywhere in order to gain some political advantage, then indeed the outlook is pretty dark. It is time that every decent person raised his voice against this degradation of our young people.

24. I should like to add that our Army worked magnificently during the floods in Jammu and Kashmir. It was largely because of their efforts that the city of Srinagar escaped disaster.

Yours sincerely,
Jawaharlal Nehru

IV

New Delhi
September 25, 1957

My dear Chief Minister,

Today, I met a Naga deputation which came to me to present a resolution passed by a Convention of the Naga Tribes, which was held about a month ago in Kohima.[1] I am glad to say that our meeting was a successful one, and I look forward to a cessation of the hostilities in the Naga areas which had distressed us so much during the past year and a half. A press statement about our interview will appear in tomorrow's papers and you will, no doubt, see it.

2. This Naga trouble has distressed me greatly, not because of its military significance, but because some of our countrymen were rebelling and we had to face this difficult situation. We could not deal with them as the British Government used to deal with rebellious people on the frontier or elsewhere, by bombing them. That is an easy but not a very human way of dealing with trouble, and we issued strict orders that there should be no bombing from the air of any kind. Our Army has had a difficult time because the terrain is wild forest land in the hills, with practically no communications. It is easy for any individual or group to carry on some kind of guerilla activities or to indulge in sniping or loot and then disappear into the forest. The Nagas, of course, are experts in forest lore and are tough people. I have always liked them, and those who have joined our Army make excellent soldiers. They have a fine sense of discipline.

3. During British times, there was some kind of an iron curtain round their areas, and people from the rest of India were not permitted to go there. Only some missionaries went, and they inculcated among the Nagas a hatred of the people of India. Some of the Nagas were converted to Christianity and were educated to some extent. Because of their education, they became the leaders of the Nagas. One of the last acts of the British officials before Independence was to encourage these Nagas to claim independence.

4. The Nagas are really not one tribe, but many tribes, and they have numerous dialects. In fact, the dialect changes every few miles and it is difficult sometimes for one Naga to understand another. Some kind of corrupted Assamese has become the lingua franca among these Nagas. Soon after Independence, Zapu Phizo emerged, and gradually he built up his position and began to be recognized as some kind of a leader. He had a curious career and is said to have been

---

1. For details see *ante,* pp. 207-208.

associated with Netaji Subhas Bose, though I do not know to what extent. During the past few years, I have met him twice, and he produced a very bad impression upon me. I told him then, and I have repeated it often, that the demand for independence was out of the question. But we were always prepared to consider anything else, even though this might involve some change in the Sixth Schedule of our Constitution. Our general policy was not to interfere with tribal people and to give them the largest measure of autonomy. For some years, the Naga movement was more or less peaceful. But, gradually, it drifted towards violence. Phizo achieved for the first time some measure of unity among these various Naga tribes. Some two years ago, a tribal Convention decided on a struggle for independence, and this led to organized violence of the guerilla type.[2]

5. We have been dealing with this situation for the last year and a half or more and, from a military point of view, have largely succeeded. But it was very difficult to deal with individual incidents. Meanwhile, the Naga people as a whole suffered very greatly. On the one hand, they were terrorized by the hostile groups and punished if they did not fall into their line. They had to give money and food and, on their refusal, their villages were burnt down and individuals were executed. On the other hand, the operations of our Army, inevitably, bore down heavily upon them. Our difficulty was to protect these people as we wanted to. It was not possible to protect every village from these depredations. Ultimately, it was decided to regroup the villages, so that we could give adequate protection to these new groups. This involved a good deal of inconvenience to the people, but it certainly gave them protection. This step led, to a large extent, to the isolation of the hostiles, and their morale began to suffer. Probably, it was mainly this step which induced most of the Nagas to decide to seek a settlement. Last month, a big Convention was held at Kohima in the Naga Hills District with the permission of the Assam Government. At this Convention every tribe sent its representatives, which totalled about 1,760 apart from about two thousand Naga visitors. For several days they argued heatedly. Ultimately, it was clear that the majority wanted to pass a certain type of resolution. There is a custom among the Nagas that, once the majority is known, then the particular resolution is passed unanimously and becomes binding on all the tribes. A good custom, which incidentally shows the discipline of these people.

6. The resolution was to the effect that the Naga Hills and the Tuensang Frontier Division of the NEFA should be constituted into a singly administrative unit under the Centre, that is, the Governor would act as an Agent of the President, and under the general directions of the External Affairs Ministry. It was also

2. See *Selected Works* (second series), Vol. 31, p. 142.

stated that this would be within the Union of India, that is, the demand for independence was clearly given up. It was this resolution that was presented to me by the delegation that saw me today. We had considered this matter carefully before I saw the delegation and we had consulted the Chief Minister of Assam also. The step we took, therefore, was with full consultation of all concerned. I told the delegation that I was glad that they had given up the demand for independence and had given us assurances to work earnestly to bring about peace and order in the disturbed areas. In the circumstances, therefore, I accepted the proposal on behalf of the Government of India and agreed to have the necessary amendment made in the Constitution during the next session of Parliament. I also agreed to an amnesty for all offences against the State and told them that the regrouping of villages would be stopped in future. Further that, as conditions improved in any area and were considered satisfactory by us, we would degroup the villages in that area. The delegation was happy at the outcome of our talks.

7. This is certainly a great step forward in this matter and brings peace in the disturbed Naga areas within our grasp. But there are still many hurdles on the way and it is possible that a small hard core element among the hostiles will continue to give trouble. Phizo himself, we are told, continues to be bitter and angry and curses the Nagas who went to the Convention or who approached us. I believe that Phizo is somewhat demented now. He is half paralyzed and has to be carried about. I do not think that his voice will carry much weight now and I am sure the great majority of the Nagas will stand by the decision of their convention. But some trouble may well still continue.

8. In my previous letters, I have referred to the critical situation in Syria and the Middle Eastern countries. The crisis appears to have been warded off and there is a little less of rattling of arms on both sides. American policy in regard to Syria has not met with success and it is said that it has met with a diplomatic reverse. This whole policy, based on the socalled Eisenhower doctrine, was unrealistic and has shown up the weakness of this doctrine. The whole purpose of this policy apparently was to keep out the Soviet Union from this Middle Eastern area. As a matter of fact, it has actually led to the Soviet Union pushing itself in a little more. It is quite absurd for anyone to say that Syria has become communist. All these Middle Eastern countries are far away from communism as anything can be. What has really happened is the play of Great Power conflicts in Syria and roundabout countries. In Jordan, some time ago, American arms and policies prevailed. In Syria, Soviet arms and policies prevailed. There is, however, a major difference between the two. American and British policies are largely based on supporting feudal regimes in these areas and have little popular backing there. The Soviet Union can take advantage of this fact and thus can influence the people

more and appear to be in favour of the nationalist elements there. Also, the Soviet Union happens to be next door, while the United States is far away.

9. The only obvious solution of these conflicts is for both these Great Powers as well as others to keep away from this area and to leave the countries concerned to work out their own destiny.

10. We have had more floods and there is, of course, the unhappiness caused by high prices, especially in regard to food. In Calcutta there have been big demonstrations and a Bank strike has also been going on for some days. Perhaps the strike will soon be over as the matter has been referred to a tribunal. It is interesting to note, however, that even in Calcutta, food prices have gone down, partly as a result of the West Bengal Government's action in seizing hoarded foodgrains.

11. In effect, there has been a general decline in prices of all food articles, including cereals, pulses, edible oils, sugar and gur, all over India. Last year, that is, between the first week of August and first week of September in 1956, there was a rise of 1.6 per cent in the prices of all commodities. This year, for the corresponding period, there has been a fall of 2.7 per cent. This is mainly due to the fall in the prices of agricultural produce by 3.7 per cent. This is a happy omen and it shows that the action taken by Government has borne result.

12. As you know, our Finance Minister is now in the United States. He will also visit Canada, England and West Germany. He is endeavouring to raise large loans or credits, which should be of great help to us in carrying through our Second Five Year Plan. Whether he will succeed or not I do not know. In either event we must realize that we have to depend chiefly on ourselves and any impression that we must finally depend upon others will be harmful.

13. I might mention here that a distorted account of what the Finance Minister is reported to have said rather casually to an American correspondent before he left India has given rise to a good deal of doubt and questioning.[3] There need be no doubt about our basic policies, whether political or economic. They remain and must remain as before. In the political domain, we shall continue to be unaligned to any group of powers; in the economic domain, we shall gladly accept help in the shape of credits or loans from abroad, but this cannot be allowed to affect our broad policy and our reliance on ourselves.

14. I have recently been to Mysore[4] to attend the *Gramdan* Conference

---

3. T.T. Krishnamachari was said to have told A.M. Rosenthal, *The New York Times* correspondent, that "the battle in India was a battle against communism too and that one of the reasons Kerala was lost to Communists was that enough money could not be spent on developmental activities of the State."

4. From 20 to 23 September 1957.

convened by the Sarva Seva Sangh at the instance of Acharya Vinoba Bhave. This was an unusual type of conference as various parties were represented there in addition to those who had been working especially for *Gramdan* under Vinobaji's leadership. You must have seen the statement issued after the conference.[5] I am convinced that Vinobaji's movement has great potentialities for good, both directly and indirectly in other spheres. It must be remembered that it is based essentially on a peaceful and non-violent approach to this and other problems. Even the agreement on this approach by all the parties represented there was all to the good. I hope that we shall all try to help and encourage in every way this *Gramdan* movement, keeping in mind always the basic approach behind it.

15. In the Ramnad District of Madras, conflicts between different castes created a serious situation for some days. These conflicts were described as communal. In effect they were due to the opposition of some higher castes to the claim of the Harijans for some measure of equality and more human treatment. Deplorable as this conflict was, it does bring out the changes that are taking place in the old order. It represents an attempt to find a new equilibrium in the social set-up. The Thevars who had been dominant in that region resented this change and hit out at the Harijans. The Harijans, however, were no longer prepared to submit to the domination of the higher castes and so the conflict. It was the duty of the State to prevent conflict but their sympathies were naturally with the Harijans in their demand for better treatment and equality.

16. The United Nations' General Assembly has started its session in New York. At the same time, the Security Council has been considering the Kashmir question, where, as usual, the Pakistan Foreign Minister[6] gave expression to an assortment of falsehoods.[7] No doubt these will be dealt with by our Representative when the time comes for his reply. At The Hague, in Holland, the case of Portugal versus India has also begun and our Attorney-General[8] placed India's case before

---

5. The statement issued on 22 September expressed its high appreciation of Vinoba's mission and his efforts to solve national and social problems by non-violent and cooperative methods. It appealed to all sections of the Indian people to support enthusiastically the *Gramdan* movement as land reforms initiated by the Government were not in conflict with *Gramdan* movement and the *Gramdan* and Community Development movements should complement each other.

6. Feroz Khan Noon.

7. Referring to Jarring's proposal, Noon said on 24 September that changes "if any, in occupied Kashmir are creations of India herself." And that "India surely cannot plead the length of her aggressive stay in Kashmir as an excuse for not honouring her international agreement."

8. M.C. Setalvad.

the International Court.[9] His speech, we are told, created a powerful impression.

17. I intend going to Japan on the 3rd October and to spend about nine days there. On my way back, I shall spend two days in Hong Kong and a day in Rangoon.

Yours sincerely,
Jawaharlal Nehru

9. On 24 September 1957, the Attorney-General of India explained to the Court India's objections to the Portuguese demand of a right of passage across the Indian territory for their officials including armed forces.

V

New Delhi
October 25, 1957

My dear Chief Minister,

Soon after my return to India from Japan, Hong Kong and Rangoon,[1] I sent you a note on my impressions of Japan.[2] These impressions dealt with the normal life of the Japanese people. I did not discuss political or economic matters. I have always tried, whenever I go abroad, to get in tune with the people of that country, to be receptive to them and more especially to understand their good points. Perhaps because I try to be receptive, they are also to some extent receptive to what I say. I do not try to put across something to them or to be vain enough to imagine that I have some special message to give them. But I do tell them of what we think and what are the springs which move us.

2. You know from newspaper reports and perhaps other sources, that I received a great welcome in Japan. And yet, it is difficult for you to realize the depth and warm-hearted character of this welcome. It was something unique even in my experience and, I was told that it was so also for the Japanese people. In fact, my visit turned out to be an intellectual and emotional experience to me as well as to the Japanese people. Why was this so?

1. On 17 October 1957.
2. See *ante*, pp. 550-633.

3. Partly, I suppose, because I arrived at a psychological moment insofar as the Japanese people were concerned. To some extent, they had lost their own moorings and were in search for some new anchorage. The old pre-War Japan, in which they had grown up, had been shattered by the defeat in War. It is not perhaps true to say that this was wholly shattered because there is a great deal of continuity. At the same time, I think, it is true that that old self-assurance had gone. Superficially, they had copied many Western, and especially American, ways. But at heart they remained, as ever, typical Japanese. No great race with long traditions can allow itself to be uprooted completely. But the shocks they had had, had been great, from the arrogance of victory to the depth of defeat and humiliation. Where had they gone wrong, they wondered, and were they following the right path now? It was true that Japan had made a remarkable industrial recovery. They had been helped in many ways in this and American Dollars had flowed in. The fact remained that it was the Japanese people, by their labour and perseverence, that had succeeded in making good. Their vitality and determination were evident.

4. But they searched for something deeper than industrial success and it was perhaps some glimpse of other avenues which led them to lionize me for the moment. That had little to do with my individual self, perhaps not even much with India. For the moment, however, India and India's policy seemed to offer some hope and escape to their tortured minds. Vaguely, this was connected with the Buddha, with Gandhi, and with our present policy of independence and non-alignment. They had not forgotten the bombs at Hiroshima and Nagasaki and the continuance of nuclear tests were a constant reminder of what might come in the future. I was told that the Japanese people were being haunted by an intolerable apprehension of a new war falling upon them and the world and of the immeasurable misery which this might bring forth. Was it possible that India's way might help somewhat in leading them or the world out of this impasse and drift to disaster?

5. It has been my good fortune to visit many countries of the East and the West, following varying and sometimes opposite policies. These countries sometimes were engaged in what is called "cold war". And yet, strangely enough, the welcome I had got from everyone of these countries was warm and popular. Surely that had nothing to do with me, nor perhaps even with India as an entity. I could only imagine that this welcome was due to the fact that we expounded a policy which was basically right and which found an echo in the hearts of people everywhere. It was not merely a negative policy of non-alignment, but something much more positive and dynamic, something which might perhaps help in solving the problems of the world and leading us to peace. There is a hunger for peace everywhere, and yet, so many countries constantly talk of war. It was this tragic

and terrible dilemma that possessed people's minds.

6. I spoke to the Japanese people, as I had spoken to others in Western countries, not merely of our present-day policy of non-alignment, but rather of the deep foundations dating back to the dawn of history, which had shaped India's thinking. I referred, of course, to Gandhiji, I spoke of the Buddha and of Asoka's Edicts. In Japan, I mentioned the Upanishads as one of the foundations of India's thought. From all this, I tried to derive a certain basic continuity which had not broken even in the days of our fall and decay.

7. Thus, the message I ventured to give in all humility, was not mine, nor was it merely of the present day. But, it was rather based on the wisdom of the ages of India as well as of other countries. It happened to be appropriate in today's setting of our tortured minds everywhere. Hence, the response of other minds, even though they might not have agreed to so much that I said.

8. I have referred to the "cold war" above. If I may say so, the approach I endeavoured to make, was the very opposite to this. The "cold war" is based not only on hatred and violence, but also on a continuous denunciation, on picking out the faults of others and assuming virtue in oneself. I tried to reverse this process even where I differed radically from those that I addressed. I spoke of their virtues and their good points, and made reference to our own failings. Thus, what I said found a warm spot in the minds of those who heard me. I did not convert them, and they did not convert me, in any basic way, but we influence each other greatly. It struck me how much more powerful was this approach, which was a feeble echo of what Gandhiji had taught us, how the approach of hatred led to an unceasing round of hatred, with no escape from it, how the opposite approach immediately led to relaxation and had a soothing influence.

9. I did not go to Japan, as I have not gone to any other country, to ask for anything except friendship and cooperation. I pointed out that, even though we differed in some matters, we agreed in many more, and if we cooperated in this larger field, the area of agreement would grow, and differences would gradually fade away. It would be foolish to imagine that the world's problems are solved merely by sweet platitudes. But, even these platitudes, if they are earnestly meant and appreciated as such, make the path easy for other approaches.

10. More and more, I have felt that the approach of conflict, whether it is of cold war or class war or any other involving hostility and a desire to destroy or humiliate the other party, is a bad approach which can never solve a problem. This does not mean that we should ignore the realities of today, political or economic. There are national conflicts and economic conflicts among classes, there is class war and, in India, there are all kinds of other conflicts based on province, language, caste, etc. We cannot deal with these by wishful thinking, nor can we surrender any vital principle which we value, for the sake of gaining

goodwill. A surrender of this kind does not gain goodwill or respect. We have to hold to our anchor and to our principles. But, doing so, our approach can be, and should be, as friendly and gentle as possible. Thus, we find entry into the minds of the others and, gradually, undermine opposition.

11. Unfortunately, we live in a world where the approach is totally different. We live in a country where a multitude of conflicts bear us down. Some people imagine that it is only through conflict that the right can triumph. It may be so. But the question is whether the conflict should be based on hatred and violence, or on an adherence to one's principles and, at the same time, always offering the hand of friendship.

12. We want a classless society, and we know that at present it is a class-ridden and caste-ridden society we have to deal with. We even carry about the signs and insignia of our castes, to distinguish ourselves from others. Many of us who talk about a classless society, are victims of the extreme spirit of caste which is something worse than a class; it is petrified class. These contradictions which face us at every turn, weaken our efforts because they indicate our own double-thinking on many of these subjects.

13. And so, I come to the conclusion that it is more important to adopt the right way, to pursue the right means, than even to have the right objectives, important as that is. No method and no way which is bound up with the creation of hatred and conflict and which bases itself on violence, can ever yield right results, however, good the motives and however good the objectives are. That, I think, should apply to our national and international policies as well as to our domestic, political and economic approaches. If it was once clear that our approach was going to be devoid of hatred and the spirit of conflict and discarded violence, then it does not matter very much what path we pursue. The errors we make, will be corrected.

14. When I think of the high mission that India is supposed to have, and then of what one finds in India today in the way of conflict over petty matters, caste and language, and the degeneration of our public life, I am a little disheartened. The gap between what we proclaim and what we do is terribly wide. But, yet, the old spark remains in us somewhere and illumines the darkness and gives us strength.

15. We have been facing great economic difficulties, questions of foreign exchange and internal resources. And the Second Five Year Plan, which had been for us a beacon of hope, is imperilled. We shall face these difficulties, of course, and I have no doubt we shall overcome them. The danger lies in the fact that, because of present day difficulty, we may forget those basic principles which have guided us and given us strength. All the industrial growth that we work for, will not be of much advantage, if we loose our soul. It becomes

necessary, therefore, in these present circumstances, to remember those basic qualities which we have valued in the past and which have been an anchor for us whenever storms have tossed our bark.

16. In addition to the difficulties which have absorbed our attention during the past many months, we have suddenly to face another play of an adverse fate. Even as we expected a good harvest and an abundant crop, drought descended upon large areas of Bihar, West Bengal, Orissa, Chhattisgarh, Eastern UP and some other areas, drought which shrivels up and kills and which is far worse than the floods that sometimes overwhelm and destroy. Our trials are many. Lately there has been some rain, welcome rain even though it was much belated. No doubt, it will do some good, but it cannot bring back what the drought destroyed and we have to face this difficult situation with a stout heart.

17. Our Finance Minister has just completed his lengthy tour of the United States, of Canada, of the United Kingdom and of West Germany. He has tried hard to obtain assistance for us in the shape of loan or long credits to enable us to meet the demands that will pour in. I do not yet know what measure of success will attend his efforts. Probably there will be some success, though not as much as we would have liked. Whatever this may be, we shall have to carry on, and indeed we will carry on. We shall learn again the basic lesson that a country has to rely essentially on itself even though it might welcome foreign aid.

18. During the past six weeks or more, ever since the last session of Parliament, there has been some kind of a lull in many of our activities. Partly this was due to our Finance Minister's visit abroad and our waiting for his return to know what the position was, partly this was due to my absence from India. Now, the time has come when we have to come to decisions about many important matters which await our consideration. These are not only individual matters, but they involve basic policies also. I earnestly trust that all of us, whether in the Central Government or the State Governments, will not only face these problems in a spirit of cooperation, but also with the firm desire to hold to our principles.

19. A new age and, indeed, a new world is gradually unrolling itself before our eyes. The tremendous advances of science and technology are far more revolutionary than so-called revolutions in the political and economic spheres. All our past thinking is out of date, even as all past methods of warfare are completely outmoded today. Yet, we think in the old way and try to solve the problems of tomorrow by the methods of the yesterday which are dead and gone. We shall have to think afresh not only in India, but in the rest of the world. Whether we shall do so or not, I do not know, for even these world shattering events in the domain of science have not produced an adequate impression on the minds of many people. We have the wretched language agitation in the Punjab, we have caste riots in the Ramanathapuram district in South India, we have threats

821

of strikes and we have innumerable petty wrangles which have no significance in the world of today.

20. In the United Nations, there is fierce controversy over the Syrian issue and the conflicts of Western Asia. I believe that the real danger of war is past. But we have been near it and we are not out of the woods. Logic and reason do not have much place left when fear and hatred obsess the minds of men. We have seen the full technique of cold war in action in Western Asia. It was out of the womb of the cold war that the present-day military alliances found birth; it was because of this that we had the tragedy of Hungary and the continuing horror of Algeria. Everything is governed by this background of cold war.

21. The Syrian development has shown, however, that the nationalism of the Arab countries is more powerful than the cold war or the Baghdad Pact. This pact failed when it met the challenge of nationalism and countries like Iraq and Jordan ignored their military alliance under the Baghdad Pact and sympathized with Syrian nationalism in peril.

22. In the United Nations, also, we are having the debate on Kashmir in the Security Council.[3] Our delegate, Shri Krishna Menon, has repeated our case with clarity and fullness.[4] But where minds are made up, and where the yardstick of judgement has nothing to do with the merits of the problem, these arguments do not convert. It is a matter of peculiar regret to me that the attitude taken up by the United Kingdom and the United States of America in regard to the Kashmir issue appears again to be totally unrelated to the facts of the case. I feel a little aggrieved because the promises often made to us privately are forgotten in public.

23. In Kashmir, trials[5] are going on in connection with the bomb explosions. These trials have already brought out how people in Pakistan have organized sabotage in Kashmir and have indulged in extensive bribery there.[6]

24. In Pakistan, as you know, a new Government has been formed.[7] We cannot

3. On 9 and 10 October 1957.
4. Krishna Menon reiterated that the Kashmir issue was not open to arbitration, and no resolution would make India shift her stand on Kashmir because on the basis of her complaint of aggression against Pakistan, the Security Council should first ask Pakistan to vacate aggression.
5. Trials were being held in Kashmir of 16 persons arrested in connection with 38 bomb explosions which took place from 18 June 1957 in which 6 people were reported killed and 17 injured.
6. The approver in the Kashmir sabotage case disclosed that a chain of bomb blasts in the Valley were planned by Pakistan with the approval and support of the Kashmir Political Conference and the Plebiscite Front.
7. A coalition Cabinet, formed on 18 October 1957, consisted of six members from the Republican Party, four (including the Prime Minister) from the Muslim League and three from the Krishak Shramik Party.

expect any marked change of policy in regard to India from this Government. It may be, however, that the language of the new Prime Minister[8] might be a little more courteous than that of his predecessor, Mr Suhrawardy.

25. In the International Court of Justice in The Hague, the case of Portugal versus India has been heard, or rather, India's preliminary objection has been stated with clarity by our Attorney-General and the other eminent counsel engaged. We cannot say what the decision on this preliminary issue will be even though we think that our case is a very good one.

26. Since I wrote to you last, one of our Governors Shri A.J. John of Madras, passed away suddenly.[9] His death has been a great sorrow to us, for he was an able and modest person and a fine gentleman who had served his country in many ways.

27. The International Red Cross is having its sessions in Delhi next week.[10] Many eminent persons from all over the world have gathered in our capital city for this purpose. I would wish that something of their healing influence might be applied to men and women all over the world, so that our humanity might emerge from the horror of the cold war in which we live.

Yours sincerely,
Jawaharlal Nehru

8. I.I. Chundrigar.
9. A. J. John died on 1 October 1957.
10. The 19th session of the Conference was held from 28 to 30 October 1957. And for Nehru's speech on the occasion see *ante*, pp. 743-746.

12
MISCELLANEOUS

(i) General

1. Message to Lakshmi Gandhi[1]

I am shocked and deeply grieved to learn of Devadas's[2] sudden death early this morning. He was like a younger brother to me. Ever since his boyhood nearly forty years ago, we have often worked together and been in prison together and his passing away is a great loss to us as it is to you and your children. May you have strength to bear this sorrow.

1. New Delhi, 3 August 1957. File No. 9/10/57-PMS. Also available in JN Collection. This message was sent through Chief Minister of Bombay. Lakshmi Gandhi, daughter of C. Rajagopalachari, was wife of Devadas Gandhi.
2. Devadas Gandhi, the youngest son of Mahatma Gandhi, died of heart-attack at Mumbai, where he was supposed to be staying for a week in connection with the work of Gandhi Smarak Nidhi. He was the Managing Editor of *The Hindustan Times*, New Delhi, from 1939 till his death.

2. To U.N. Dhebar[1]

New Delhi
August 7, 1957

My dear Dhebarbhai,
I enclose a letter about the Gandhi Smarak Nidhi. I do not know anything about the circumstances related in the letter. But, as you know, there is a general feeling that the Nidhi has not been working efficiently or satisfactorily.

1. JN Collection. Also available in AICC Papers, NMML.

I suppose something will have to be done. Apart from choosing a Chairman and Vice-Chairman,[2] I am inclined to think that a review of what has been done and what is being done and the methods of work etc., would be desirable.

Yours sincerely,
Jawaharlal Nehru

2. See also *post*, p. 835.

3. Reply to Durga Das[1]

Dear Shri Durga Das,

The Prime minister has received your letter of the 11th August and has asked me to reply to you.[2]

When you saw him recently, the Prime Minister told you that he did not interfere with the way a newspaper was carried on or who was appointed to it or not. Nor did he wish to come in your way in this matter, whatever his personal opinions might be. He is rather surprised that Shri Ghanshyamdas Birla should have brought him into this picture in the manner you have mentioned. No message of any kind was sent by him or on his behalf about you to Shri Birla. The question of "*Virodh*" or "withdrawal of "*Virodh*" does not arise. It is entirely for the proprietors of *The Hindustan Times* to deal with their paper in any way they like. The Prime Minister is no way responsible for it, nor does he wish to assume any responsibility.

1. Letter drafted by Nehru, New Delhi, 11 August 1957. JN Collection.
2. Durga Das of *The Hindustan Times*, New Delhi, wrote that Ghanshyamdas Birla told him that Nehru was not in favour of promoting him to the full editorship of *The Hindustan Times* and that he should get a letter from M.O. Mathai stating that Nehru had no objection to his appointment. He also wrote that Nehru assured him that he would not stand in the way of his professional advancement at a meeting that took place later. Since Ghanshyamdas did not receive any letter of approval from Nehru, he instructed his son K.K. Birla to appoint him as the Chief Editor, as soon as he received the necessary word from M.O. Mathai, Durga Das added.

4. Reply to Murari Sinha[1]

Please reply as follows to Shri Murari Sinha:

Dear Sir,

The Prime Minister has received your letter of August 14.

You have quoted from his *Autobiography*. That, as you will observe, was written in answer to Sir C.P. Ramaswami Aiyar. That context was quite different. As to whether he represents mass feeling or not would depend on the subject on which he is supposed to represent it. In some ways, he thinks he does represent mass surges very considerably. In other ways probably he does not.

People have a right to expect a better today and not to wait till tomorrow. But even today cannot be better unless tomorrow is provided for. A balance has to be sought between the two. A growing population always tends to lower standards. This can only be checked by growing production. Growing production means investment as well as other things.

Most people naturally do not think far ahead. That is why perhaps many of them do not like the decimal system. But the decimal system is quite essential for a country that wishes to advance in science, technology and industry. Every change creates some confusion, but the confusion passes and then the benefits of the change are appreciated.

In almost every country in the world there has been heavy inflation. India has, on the whole, had much less inflation than most other countries. It is realized, of course, that even the existing prices of foodgrains are an additional burden on large numbers of people. They have risen partly from domestic causes and partly international inflationary elements. It is certainly the policy of the Government to check these tendencies and to keep prices at a reasonable level. Apart from other actions the Government has taken, a Prime Committee has been formed under the Chairmanship of Shri Asoka Mehta.[2]

You refer to Prime Minister Nehru having been in absolute power for ten years. There is no such thing as absolute power almost anywhere and certainly not in any democratic country. There is some semblance of it in an authoritarian country. But even there it cannot go too far. In a conservative country like India, the choice has always to be made between some steps to be taken which bring about progress but for the moment are inconvenient, and taking practically no

---

1. Note to Private Secretary, New Delhi, 16 August 1957. JN Collection.
2. See also *ante*, pp. 141-142.

steps and thus fitting in with the conservatism of the people who do not want a change. Yet to accept the latter position is to invite progressive deterioration.

It is not possible for Prime Minister to indicate any reasonable income for a person, because in India standards are so terribly low that every reasonable income for the masses is outside our scope now. We can only aim at it for the future, the sooner the better and try to achieve it progressively."

5. To Ram Narain Chaudhary[1]

New Delhi
August 17, 1957

My dear Ram Narainji,[2]

Some days ago you sent me the proof sheets of an article you had written in *Bharat Sewak*.[3] I have now received the July number of this Magazine.

I read your article entitled "Are we Honest". I must tell you that I do not like it at all and I doubt if it will do any good. It might well do a good deal of harm. It is not a question of our not confessing our own weaknesses. This has to be done and should be done. But if it is done, it should be done properly. In any event, such an article should not have appeared without reference to Nandaji or me.

Yours sincerely,
Jawaharlal Nehru

1. File No. 2(188)/57-66-PMS.
2. Ram Narain Chaudhary was Information Secretary of Bharat Sewak Samaj.
3. In his article titled "Are We Honest", published in July 1957 number of *Bharat Sewak*, Ram Narain wrote that people questioned the apolitical character of the Bharat Sewak Samaj despite its claim to be a non-official, non-party and non-political organization. He also wrote that the complaint was because of the involvement of Nehru and Nanda in the administrative affairs of the organization. Chaudhary honestly answered complaints saying that the organization was funded by the Congress Party and some influential Party people had greater say in its administration.

6. Export of Monkeys[1]

Tajamul Husain:[2] Are Government aware that there is a world organization at The Hague, which is against vivisection of monkeys and that organization has sent a telegram to our Prime Minister requesting him not to export monkeys from this country and also that the whole civilized world is very much shocked at the fate of the Indian monkeys and it has aroused the indignation of the whole civilized world?

Jawaharlal Nehru: Government is not aware that there is a special organization for monkeys. There are organizations of course, but they deal with other animals too, apart from monkeys. I have received a number of telegrams, letters and memoranda both against the export of monkeys and a large number in favour of their export too. So, the civilized world appears to be divided on this point. Nobody, at least nobody here, wants to send monkeys just for the sake of sending them, certainly not for nuclear weapons, but they were sent because of certain very fatal diseases like polio and others were concerned and we had almost, if I may say so, received pittiest appeals saying: "Please don't stop this important work that we are doing for the eradication of these diseases." That was our difficulty. I might add for the information of the honourable Member who is concerned with monkeys being pests, of course they are pests in so far as agricultural commodities are concerned. But the monkeys sent are not the normal monkeys which worry our friend here. They are very special monkeys from Bengal.

---

1. Reply to a question in Rajya Sabha, 20 August 1957. *Rajya Sabha Debates*, Vol. XVIII, cols. 638-39.
2. Congress Member from Bihar.

7. To Morarji Desai[1]

New Delhi
August 24, 1957

My dear Morarji,

I am sorry to trouble you again about monkeys. I am sending you a letter I have received with some cuttings.

I was told that all the assurances given to us of good treatment of monkeys are forgotten and are not observed. Apparently, every morning at about 7.30 a.m. batches of these monkeys arrive at Delhi Station and they can be seen there in their misery. They have no food or water. Doctors are supposed to examine them, but nobody really takes the trouble to do so. I suggest that some of your officers might go to Delhi Station at 7.30 a.m. for two or three days.

The Society for the Prevention of Cruelty to Animals in London is keeping statistics of all the monkeys that pass through London from India. According to them, the number has increased and not gone down.

Yours sincerely,
Jawaharlal Nehru

1. File No. 44(19)/57-58-PMS. Also available in JN Collection.

8. To Zeenuth Fatehally[1]

New Delhi
August 29, 1957

Dear Zeenuth,

I am sorry for the delay in answering your letter of the 22nd August and, even more so, for the long time I have taken in dealing with the typescript you had sent me before I went to Europe. When I received your last letter, I tried to find

1. JN Collection.

out where your typescript was. I could not find it. There was a general hunt for it all over my office room and roundabout. Still, no trace of it. I felt rather unhappy.

I had taken your script with me to Europe, hoping to read it during the journey. The most I could do was to read a part of it.

Yesterday, we traced your script. This had gone with some other papers of mine, to the office of my Principal Private Secretary. So, I got it back and read through it rather rapidly today.

It is difficult for me to comment on what you have written as a whole, and I do not think you expect me to do so. I would like to say, however, that it seems to me rather overdone in praise and rather ornate.

Now, for specific comments in regard to facts.

Right at the beginning, you say that the Moghul Emperor, Farrukhsiyar, while holidaying in Kashmir, met Raj Kaul, an ancestor of the Nehrus. We have no evidence for this. All we know is that Raj Kaul came to Delhi and joined the Court here.

You have a note on page 5, enquiring as to the meaning of Jawaharlal. Presumably, Jawahar means diamond or jewel, and Lal means ruby.

"Kamla" should be spelt "Kamala".

At page 11, you say that I was sentenced nine times and spent fourteen years in prison. It is correct that I was sentenced nine times, but, I believe, I spent only about ten and a half years actually in prison.

At page 12, you refer to the Churchill story. As related it is not quite correct. It would not be correct to say that he made it a point to see me. I naturally used to see him on various occasions, at functions etc., when I went to London. He did not use the words to me which you have put down, and I might incidentally say that he would not address me as "Mr. Nehru". He said nothing about his being with me on my tour to America. What he did say to me and on some other occasions also, was something to the following effect:

"Nehru has conquered two of the greatest failings of human nature, fear and hatred."

This was, of course, a great compliment.

At page 13, you refer to the gathering of officials and others on August 14th at 11 a.m. in the Council Hall. You have mixed up two functions. My swearing-in as the Prime Minister of India, and a speech I delivered at a meeting of the Constituent Assembly. Independent India was supposed to come into existence at midnight on the 14th-15th August. Because of this timing, we held a special meeting of the Constituent Assembly just before midnight in the Constituent Assembly Hall (not in the Council Hall). It was at this meeting that I delivered a brief speech in which I said something about a tryst with destiny. We had timed this so that, immediately after the stroke of midnight, all the members present took a pledge. (This pledge is given in my speech).

I am sending you separately a volume containing some of my earlier speeches. This is called "Independence and After", and you will find this particular speech given in it right at the beginning. There are a number of other speeches also in it.

At page 14, you say that "Like Plato, they too had their minds fixed on an Ideal State. They wanted a democratic rule". The first sentence may, perhaps, be passed. But, it would not be correct to say that Plato wanted democratic rule. In fact, he thought in different terms.

Page 15: At the bottom, there is a story of my seeing a girl being molested by a group of persons. I do not remember any such incident of a girl. It is true that I saw many people looting and sometimes beating others, and I went for them.

Page 19: It is not quite correct to say that I walked behind Gandhiji's funeral cortege all the way to the cremation ground. I walked part of the way only and for part of the time, I was sitting or standing in that vehicle.

At the bottom of page 19, you mention that Lady Mountbatten led me back to where they all sat. I have no recollection of this particular incident.

Page 21: You say towards the bottom, that "Indira, now married to Phiroze Gandhi". "Now" is not appropriate, she married in 1942. Also, the right spelling of her husband's name is "Feroze Gandhi".

These are some hastily noted comments and corrections. I hope they are of some help to you.

I am returning the typescript to you.

Yours sincerely,
Jawaharlal Nehru

9. To R.R. Diwakar[1]

New Delhi
September 17, 1957

My dear Diwakar,

Thank you for your telegram which came some days ago. I am very glad you have been chosen the Chairman of the Gandhi Smarak Nidhi. This fund has been unfortunate in losing the eminent people connected with it. Although much good work has been done, it has never really got fully going. With you as Chairman and Sucheta Kripalani[2] as Vice-Chairman, I am sure that progress will be rapid now. You will, of course, have all our cooperation.

Yours sincerely,
Jawaharlal Nehru

1. JN Collection.
2. Also Congress Member of Lok Sabha from New Delhi constituency.

10. To Shyam Krishna Dar[1]

New Delhi
September 18, 1957

My dear Shyamji,[2]

Shyam Sunder Tankha[3] came to see me this afternoon and told me that an appeal had been filed in the High Court, Allahabad, against the decision on the election petition against me. In the course of our talk, he read out to me parts of a letter

1. JN Collection.
2. An ex-judge of Allahabad High Court and Chairman, Linguistic Provinces Commission, 1948.
3. Shyam Sunder Narayan Tankha (1898-1985); Congress Member from Uttar Pradesh; Member, Rajya Sabha, 1952-70; Chairman, House Committee, Rajya Sabha, 1962-63, Committee on Petitions, Rajya Sabha, 1966-68.

you had written to him about a month ago. I was much distressed to learn from this that you were in some doubt about my appreciation of the trouble you had taken on my behalf in this case. Perhaps I was at fault in this matter, as I had not written to you previously. I wrote a week or ten days ago and I hope you received my letter. I have been so overwhelmed with work that I delayed writing to you. I hope you will forgive me. I need not tell you how grateful I am for all the interest you took in this case and the work you put in for it.

Now there is this appeal in the High Court. I should like your advice as to what I should do about it. Naturally I would greatly like you to conduct it if it is convenient for you. But, as Shyam Sunder pointed out, normally a retired High Court Judge does not appear in that High Court unless there are some special reasons and some kind of permission has to be taken. That is entirely for you to judge, as you know these conventions and can best decide what should be done and what should not be done.

Unfortunately, Pathak[5] is away in our Delegation in New York and is not expected to return till the end of November or early in December. If it is at all possible for you to appear in this case without any impropriety, I shall be happy. If not, then please advise me what other steps I should take and indicate who might be approached for this purpose.

Yours sincerely,
Jawaharlal Nehru

5. G.S. Pathak, an ex-judge of Allahabad High Court, was Member, Indian Delegation to UN at this time.

11. Tibetan Edition of *Letters From a Father to His Daughter*[1]

I am glad that my little book, which I wrote nearly thirty years ago, is now appearing in a Tibetan translation. India is a country of many languages. A number of these are even mentioned in our Constitution and are officially recognized. But there are others, like Tibetan, which, though not mentioned in

1. Foreword to the Tibetan Edition of *Letters From a Father to His Daughter*, New Delhi, 19 September 1957. JN Collection. The book was first published by Allahabad Law Journal Press, in 1930.

our Constitution, are nevertheless known and spoken by many of our fellow-citizens and others in North East India.

I should like more of our books to be translated into Tibetan and I should like more of our young people to learn this language.

Long ago, there was a good deal of intercourse—religious, cultural and trade—between India and Tibet. Many of our books in Sanskrit or Pali were translated into the Tibetan language. While these books are to be treasured, it is necessary today to develop contacts through our modern languages so that there might be greater friendship and understanding.

This little book was meant for my daughter who was only ten years old when these letters were sent to her. I hope that children reading this book in the Tibetan language will like it.

12. To Y.B. Chavan[1]

New Delhi
September 19, 1957

My dear Chavan,

Some days ago, I received a letter from M.T. Vyas, Principal of the New Era School, Bombay.[2] I enclose a copy of it.

I was much interested to learn from this letter of the effect of some talks that Manuben Gandhi gave in Bombay to students. These simple and personal talks about Gandhiji are probably much more effective than the sermons many of us deliver. I think, Manuben should be encouraged to do this and facilities should be given to her to go to students of primary and secondary schools. Obviously, Bombay State will offer a better opportunity for this than other parts of India.

Yours sincerely,
Jawaharlal Nehru

1. JN Collection.
2. On 30 August 1955, M.T. Vyas wrote that he had invited Manu Gandhi, grand-niece of Mahatma Gandhi, to give talks on the life of Mahatma Gandhi. Her talks, full of anecdotes and incidents from the life of Gandhiji, were very appealing as they were from her personal experiences and served all the purposes of religious, moral and civic education. As a result of these talks, children had been demanding literature on Gandhiji written both by himself and by others, he added.

13. To Gulzarilal Nanda[1]

Lokaranjan Mahal,
Mysore,
September 19, 1957

My dear Gulzarilal,[2]

Some time ago, you sent me a copy of the report of the Committee appointed by the Administrative Committee of the Bharat Sewak Samaj. I am sorry for the delay in acknowledging it.

I have read this report. not being in intimate touch with the working of the office and the rest of the organization, it is difficult for me to make any helpful suggestions. But it is clear from this report as well as otherwise that there appears to be a lack of coordination in the working of the Central Office of the Bharat Sewak Samaj. It is equally clear that there should be coordination and harmony in the Central Office and, indeed, in the entire organization. If the Central Office itself sets a bad example, then the organization will gradually disintegrate.

Coordination is to some extent, a matter of rules and regulations as well as conventions. Also obviously, it involves the human factor and the capacity to cooperate among the people engaged in the work of the organization. If this capacity is lacking, then the best of rules cannot produce the desired result. It would be most unfortunate if in a voluntary organization devoted to the service of the people, this cooperation was lacking.

You will remember that when we discussed the formation of the Bharat Sewak Samaj, we talked about the difficulties that often arose in other organizations where rivalries occur and there is a quest for position and authority. We tried then to avoid this kind of rivalry and office-seeking. The only incentive we asked for was the desire to serve and, more especially, actual constructive work. We can offer no rewards. I did not want anyone to come with the inducement of bettering his status or position in the political or any other sphere.

Nevertheless, human nature being what it is, conflicts arise and there is a tendency for one person to boss over another. So far as the office is concerned, there has necessarily to be discipline and some organized method of working. It appears from the report you have sent me that difficulties have arisen because perhaps there are no adequate rules governing the working of the office and

---

1. JN Collection.
2. Chairman, Bharat Sewak Samaj, New Delhi.

there is no definition of the powers and functions of the difficult people in the office. The question of status as such should not arise, except in the sense that someone has greater authority or functions to perform. It is desirable, therefore, as suggested, that there should be a clearer definition of these powers and functions. If, even so, any difficult arises, it should be referred to the Committee. Minor matters should be decided by you as the Chairman. Indeed, the Chairman's authority should be clearly recognized.

Where questions of basic principle arise, the Central Board can consider them, but obviously it is not necessary or desirable for the Central Board to meet to consider petty matters. The Staff Committee may deal with many matters, but probably it will not be suitable for the consideration of any basic question.

I do not quite know who constitute the Staff Committee. Presumably the senior officers do so. It should be a matter of normal routine for these senior officers to meet and confer with each other frequently, not only to consider any particular matter that has arisen, but also to keep in touch with the various activities of the Samaj and help in coordinating them. It would not be a good thing for each Department to work independently of the other without much knowledge of what is happening elsewhere.

Although I have been honoured by being made the President of the Bharat Sewak Samaj, I am more or less an honorary President. The whole burden of the work has fallen upon you as Chairman. You are, in fact, the Working President of the organization. I do not myself see any necessity for changing your designation, but it should be quite clear that as Chairman you exercise all the authority of the working head of the organization.

There is some reference in the report to the termination of the service of Shri Chandra Bhan Sharma and the appointment of someone else in his place. I have heard something about this previously, though I am not fully acquainted with the facts. A matter of this kind should be dealt with by you in consultation with others concerned and with a view to promoting harmonious working. In the final analysis, your opinion should prevail.

I shall gladly be of any help that I can , but as things are, I am not in intimate touch with the working of the organization and this burden has to be carried by you.

Yours sincerely,
Jawaharlal Nehru

14. To Ajit S. Gopal[1]

New Delhi
19th September, 1957

Dear Ajit Gopal,

Your letter of the 15th August came to me some time ago. I did not quite know what answer to send you. I appreciate your sentiments and your desire to serve India. You are a lawyer practising in Uganda. I would hesitate to ask you to give up your present vocation and come to India and try some new vocation unless you felt a strong urge to do some particular thing. You can, of course, serve the cause of India even from where you are. Africa is a very important continent and it is going to change rapidly. We want friendly relations between Indians and Africans and Indians there should help the Africans.

If you like, you can come to India for some months and see things for yourself. That might enable you to decide for yourself.

Yours sincerely,
Jawaharlal Nehru

1. JN Collection.

15. To U.N. Dhebar[1]

New Delhi
October 22, 1957

My dear Dhebarbhai,

I enclose a letter from Kurur Nambuthiripad.[2] It makes interesting reading. At the end of it, he wants me to present to him a motorcycle which was given to me by Japanese students. As a matter of fact, these students had decided to present a car to me. I refused to take it. They insisted on the motorcycle. I suppose this will reach me some time or other. I have not got it yet.

You will agree that I cannot give a gift presented to me as Prime Minister, to a Congress organization. Normally, I pass these on to the Community Projects people to be given as prizes.

But, I think that Trichur deserves some sign of recognition. A motorcycle is too expensive a thing to give, but one or two bicycles might well be given. They should go from the AICC. I shall gladly pay for them, if you so wish.

Yours sincerely,
Jawaharlal Nehru

1. JN Collection. Also available in AICC Papers.
2. Nehru wrote to Kurur Nambuthiripad, a Congressman from Trichur in Kerala, on 20 October 1957 (not printed) that, "As for the presentation of a motorcycle to you, I am afraid it will not be proper for me to make a present of a gift given to me in Japan. Such gifts are considered by me national property. Most of them are sent to a museum, and one or two, like a motorcycle, have been presented by me to the Community Development Blocks as prizes for good work. I cannot pass these on to a Congress Committee."

16. To Jayaprakash Narayan[1]

New Delhi
October 30, 1957

My dear Jayaprakash,

I received your letter of the 27th October today. I was happy to receive it. I am sorry to know that you fell ill at Mysore.

There is no question of your apologizing to me for anything. All I want is your affection and you can hold any views you like. I am sorry that I appeared cold to you at the *Gramdan* Conference. We really had no occasion of meeting by ourselves. Sometimes, at public functions, one develops a certain exterior aspect which is perhaps a manner of self-protection lest one's feelings get the better of one.

You know that you will always be welcome, however much our views may differ about anything.

Yours affectionately,
Jawaharlal

---

1. JN Collection.

(ii) Rahat Ara's Case

1. To Govind Ballabh Pant[1]

New Delhi
August 28, 1957

My dear Pantji,

I enclose a copy of a letter from Rahat Ara, the daughter of Ch. Ghulam Abbas,[2] one of the leaders of "Azad" Kashmir. This lady was discovered by us after great trouble. Later she decided to go back to her parents in Pakistan. Her three children are at Swaraj Bhawan in Allahabad. We have to consider what we should do about them now.

Yours affectionately,
Jawaharlal

---

1. JN Collection.
2. Rahat Ara was abducted by Jagdish Chander in 1947, when he was serving with the Indian Army in Jammu. She could not be found till she and Jagdish Chander appeared before Bombay Police in December 1954. On the persuasion of her family, she had decided to go to Pakistan, leaving her three minor children with the abductor-father. The children were later admitted to the Children's Home in Allahabad at the father's request. Later Jagdish Chander managed to go over to Pakistan, converted to Islam, and was reunited with his wife. Rahat Ara and Jagdish Chander (now Khalid Mahmood) requested Nehru to restore their children to them in Lahore.

2. Rahat Ara's Request[1]

Some days ago, I received a letter from Rahat Ara, the daughter of Ch. Ghulam Abbas. This letter came to me, I think, through our Deputy High Commissioner in Lahore,[2] who had got it from Raja Ghazanfar Ali Khan.[3] I enclose a copy of this letter.

2. You will remember the case of Rahat Ara. For years we tried to trace her and it was after great difficulty that we found her. She had married meanwhile a young Hindu[4] and has some children from him. It appears from her letter that her husband went to Pakistan and apparently got converted to Islam and has got some work there.

3. Now the lady wants the return of three of their children who are now at an institution at Swaraj Bhawan, Allahabad. They are very fine children and have been well looked after. I would be rather sorry to send them away. But, I suppose, there is no help for it.

4. Before we decide anything, I should like you to write to our Deputy High Commissioner, sending him a copy of this letter from Rahat Ara. Ask him to make discreet enquiries about these people, that is, Rahat Ara and her husband, especially about the husband. Tell him we want to have as much information as possible so as to enable us to decide.

---

1. Note to Commonwealth Secretary, New Delhi, 5 September 1957. File No. 6-AP/57, p. 19/notes, MEA.
2. P.L. Bhandari.
3. Former Pakistan High Commissioner in India.
4. Jagdish Chander.

3. Details of the Case[1]

I have read through the various papers and letters in this file, including the letters from our High Commissioner in Karachi. I agree with Sardar Swaran Singh that we should look at this question from the human point of view. If both the father and mother want these children, I see no justification to keep them here. We May look after them well now, but how can we guarantee any future for them.

2. I have consulted some other colleagues of mine, and they agree that this is the only course open to us.

3. There is no particular hurry to return them, but at the same time there is no point in waiting to have a personal discussion with Shri C.C. Desai. The latter's viewpoint is very clearly expressed in his letters and I do not agree with it either in law or otherwise.

4. But we should certainly wait for the answer of our Deputy High Commissioner in Lahore. If that answer is satisfactory, that is, it makes it clear that both the father and mother want their children back, we shall have to send them.

5. The question then arises as to how we are to send them. For us to hand them over to the Pakistan High Commission here is out of the question. Someone will have to accompany them to Lahore. I think the best course would be for the father to come here to meet them and fetch them. There is some reference in these papers that the father being a deserter from the Indian Army will be afraid to come here as he might be arrested for his desertion. I have no clear recollection of what happened and how he deserted. My own vague recollection is that he was on the civil side in the Army when Rahat Ara delivered herself up to the Police, where was the father? Did he keep hidden and underground all this time or did he also appear before the Police or other people.

6. Even if the father is technically a deserter, I think that it is too late to take any action against him. If, therefore, we finally decide to send these children back, I would suggest that the father be invited here to see his children and then take them. We will have to give them an assurance to him that no action will be taken against him here. That would be the human way of sending the children, who are very young.

1. Note to Commonwealth Secretary, New Delhi, 6 September 1957. File No. 6-AP/57, pp. 23-24/notes, MEA.

7. It is not necessary to alert Swaraj Bhawan about the children. But I think that, after our final decision is taken, we should inform the lady in charge of Swaraj Bhawan about it. It would be improper for someone suddenly to turn up in Swaraj Bhawan to take custody of the children. It might even be better for the children to get to know gradually about this matter.

8. Meanwhile, however, we should wait for the reply of the Deputy High Commissioner in Lahore. When that comes, we can discuss this matter and finalize it.

9. Sardar Swaran Singh might see this note of mine and more particularly say what he thinks about the procedure I have suggested.

10. Our Deputy High Commissioner in Lahore should be asked to inform Rahat Ara that I have received her letter about her children and that we are giving consideration to this matter. Apparently her previous communications have not been acknowledged. I think, it is only right that some acknowledgement should go straightaway.

11. A copy of this note has been sent directly to Sardar Swaran Singh.

4. Final Steps to Solve the Case[1]

We have gone through all the preliminary enquiries and we can now agree to the return of these children. There is one thing, however, which has to be done and that is, to inform the children so that their minds may be prepared for this. There is no immediate need for fixing a precise date. I should like Indiraji to return here before we fix the date. The date may well be some time in the second half of November.

I suggest, therefore, that you might write to the authorities in charge of the Children's Home at Swaraj Bhawan, Allahabad, and give them a brief account of what has happened and of our decision to return the children to their parents. Ask them to inform the children in a friendly way, so that they might not in any sense, be upset by any sudden move. They can be told that they will go in about a month's time. When you get a reply from the Children's Home, we can then fix a date and take the other steps.

1. Note to Commonwealth Secretary, New Delhi, 17 October 1957. JN Collection.

Meanwhile, our Deputy High Commissioner in Lahore can be told that he can inform Jagdish Chander and Rahat Ara that we are agreeable to the children being returned. This will take some little time and we shall indicate the date some time later. This will be probably in the third or fourth week of November. He will have to come here for the purpose. He will of course be assured that he will not be arrested for the offence of desertion.

GLOSSARY

"Azad" Kashmir	the areas of Kashmir occupied by Pakistan
ahimsa	non-violence
bhagchasis	sharecroppers
bhoodan	literally gift of land, voluntary donation of land, a movement launched by Vinoba Bhave
dharti	earth, land, soil
gram sevaks	voluntary village workers
gramdan	voluntary donation of village
Hindu raj	Hindu rule, Hindu nation
Jai Hind	victory to India
Janmashtami	the eighth day of the first half of Bhadrapad, the sixth month of the Hindu lunar calendar, on which Lord Krishna was born
kala pani	transportation to distant lands for life imprisonment
kharif	monsoon crop, mainly paddy
kisan	a peasant, a farmer
kutchery	a court of justice in provincial towns
maida	refined wheat flour
maqbara	a large building enclosing a tomb
maund	a measure of weight around one hundred pounds
mazdoors	labourers
nazars	offerings
padyatra	travelling on foot with an objective
pahalwan	a wrestler

849

Paigah	one of the six categories of jagirs in Hyderabad during the Nizam's rule, highest in hierarchy after Sarf-e-khas
panchsheel	five basic principles of international conduct
pravesh nishedh	no entry
rabi	winter crop, mainly wheat and gram
rashtrapati	the Indian President
ritha	soap-nut, soapberry
riyasati	belonging to a princely state
sadbhavana	goodwill
samskriti	culture
santhals	a tribal community in the eastern and central India
Sarf-e-khas	Nizam's private lands whose revenues went to his privy purse and served to meet the expenses of his household and army
sarvodaya	a non-violent movement in India meant for the uplift of all men without distinction of caste, creed, sex or status
shramdan	voluntary contribution of labour for a public cause
Sikh raj	Sikh rule
suji	semolina
tamasha	spectacle, show
tehsil	a sub-division of a district
thanas	police stations
thumri	a style of classical Indian vocal music
tongawala	driver of a light horse-drawn two-wheeled vehicle
usar	sterile, barren land
zulum	oppression

INDEX

(Biographical footnotes in this volume and in volumes in the first series are italicized and those in the second series are given in block letters.)